DEVELOPMENTAL EVALUATION

Developmental Evaluation

 Applying Complexity Concepts
to Enhance Innovation and Use

Michael Quinn Patton

THE GUILFORD PRESS
New York   London

© 2011 The Guilford Press
A Division of Guilford Publications, Inc.
72 Spring Street, New York, NY 10012
www.guilford.com

Printed in the United States of America

This book is printed on acid-free paper.

Last digit is print number: 9 8 7 6 5 4 3

Library of Congress Cataloging-in-Publication Data
Patton, Michael Quinn.
   Developmental evaluation: applying complexity concepts to enhance innovation
and use / by Michael Quinn Patton.
      p. cm.
   Includes bibliographical references and index.
   ISBN 978-1-60623-872-1 (pbk.)—ISBN 978-1-60623-886-8 (hardcover)
   1. Project management—Evaluation.   2. Organizational effectiveness—
Measurement. I. Title.
   HD69.P75P3344 2011
   658.4′04—dc22
                                                          2010003096

To professional evaluators around the world

It is an honor and a privilege to be part of this complex, adaptive, dynamic, and still emergent profession and transdiscipline.

Many people worldwide have dedicated themselves to social innovation and making the world a better place.

Those who evaluate also serve.

Preface

I may not have gone where I intended to go,
but I think I have ended up where I intended to be.
   —DOUGLAS ADAMS (1952–2001), author of
    The Hitchhiker's Guide to the Galaxy

Douglas Adams captured perfectly how I feel as I come to the end of the journey that was writing this book. And in the words of another keen observer of and philosopher about things emergent and complex, Jerry Garcia of The Grateful Dead, it's been a long, strange trip.

I first wrote about developmental evaluation in 1994 for a special issue of *Evaluation Practice*, the predecessor to what is now the *American Journal of Evaluation*. Editor Midge Smith, who went on to found The Evaluators' Institute (TEI), invited 16 diverse evaluation professionals and scholars to write about the past and future of evaluation. Her invitation asked us to reflect on the major trends of the past decades and "more importantly, take a turn at the crystal ball to tell how you think the future of evaluation *will* and/or *should* go. . . . Speak to whatever aspect(s) of the profession that you feel passionately about" (Smith, 1994a, p. 213).

In her overview of the 16 contributions to the volume, one of the themes she identified was the belief and hope among several writers that program failures "could be lessened or even perhaps eliminated if evaluators become more involved in program development" (Smith, 1994b, p. 220). Expectations included the likelihood that evaluators' involvement in program development would increase as the profession became recognized as having contributions to make at the front-end design stage of new programs based on general knowledge about patterns of effectiveness. Smith quoted distinguished evaluation pioneer Eleanor Chelimsky as saying that "evaluation seems destined" to play a major role in the formulation of new programs and policies (p. 220). She went on:

Patton has taken the **boldest** moves in this direction with what he has defined as "developmental evaluation" where "The evaluator is part of a design team whose members collaborate to conceptualize, design, and test new approaches in a long-term, on-going process of development, adaptation, and intentional change. The evaluator's primary function in the team is to elucidate team discussions with evaluative data and logic, and to facilitate data-based decision making in the developmental process." (Smith, 1994b, p. 220; original emphasis)

Smith then pointed out that this potentially changed role for evaluators was already controversial and was likely to become more so in the future. Her prediction has proved prescient. Addressing those controversies is one of the purposes of this book.

I concluded my article on developmental evaluation in that volume, now over 15 years old, as follows:

The notion of developmental evaluation calls into question three traditional mainstays of evaluation: purpose, evaluand, and timeline. These three are intertwined in the classic definition of program evaluation as determining whether the program's goals have been met. This definition assumes a fixed program, a delimited time period, and a goal-attainment purpose. Developmental evaluation is a way of being useful in innovative settings where goals are emergent and changing rather than predetermined and fixed, time periods are fluid and forward-looking rather than artificially imposed by external deadlines, and the purposes are innovation, change, and learning rather than external accountability (summative evaluation) or getting ready for external accountability (formative evaluation).

Developmental evaluation has emerged as primary in my own practice because it affords unusual opportunities for me to be useful in working on issues I care about with imaginative and committed people whose values I respect. At this stage in my practice and life, after many years of project evaluation, developmental engagement on important issues matters a great deal to me. (Patton, 1994, p. 318)

That is as true today as it was when I first wrote those lines so many years ago. This book presents what I've learned since. Much of what I've learned has come from working with others and I want to acknowledge those contributions.

Acknowledgments

Frances Westley developed and directed the McGill–McConnell Fellows Program, which provided in-depth leadership development for 120 national voluntary-sector leaders across Canada. Frances had been searching for someone who could do evaluation training as part of the program and was pointed in my direction. My presentation was on utilization-focused evaluation but I mentioned developmental evaluation as an option for evaluating social innovations under conditions of complexity. Social innovation, I soon learned, was Frances's passion and she was deeply intrigued by the possibility that there could be an approach to evaluation that actually supported rather than impeded innovation. Thus began a collaboration and friendship that propelled me in the direction of this book as her questions and reactions pushed me to clarify the niche and processes of developmental evaluation. We designed an advanced week-long training module on developmental evaluation for graduates of the McGill–McConnell Fellows Program.

She also invited me to be part of a think tank on social innovation sponsored by Dupont Canada that she facilitated.

It was in that think tank, which met periodically over a 2-year period, that I came to know Brenda Zimmerman. Following the think tank and stimulated by it, Frances, Brenda, and I coauthored the book *Getting to Maybe: How the World Is Changed* (2006), which pulled together our understandings about social innovation and complexity. That book was to have included a substantial section on developmental evaluation but the editor seemed, like many people, to have an allergic reaction to the very word *evaluation*. She otherwise quite liked the book and was supportive, but remained convinced that no one would purchase, much less read, a book that included mutterings about evaluation. So what was to have been a substantial section, perhaps even a full chapter, on developmental evaluation was reduced to an occasional oblique mention and a lengthy, small-font footnote in the sixth chapter. That experience crystallized my resolve to do a full book on this topic that so many find distasteful, at least the *evaluation* part, not so much the *developmental* part, though that word is irksome to evaluators who define evaluation as judging merit and worth, and stop there. I don't have to worry about offending either group of folks for they won't come near the book. You, savvy reader that you are, mark yourself as different by even holding the book in your hands. But do be careful who you let see you reading it. Not altogether kind judgments and consequences can ensue from being associated with evaluation—even of the developmental variety. But good things happen too, often and in great quantity, once the door is opened. That, too, is the message you'll find in these pages.

The work with Frances and Brenda took another unexpected and emergent turn. Tim Brodhead, President of the J. W. McConnell Family Foundation in Montreal, which funded the McGill–McConnell Fellows Program, became intrigued by developmental evaluation. The McConnell Foundation adopted the adaptive cycle (featured in Chapter 7) as its theory of change for funding innovation initiatives across Canada (Pearson, 2007) and developmental evaluation as the approach most attuned to the adaptive cycle. That led the foundation to support a series of workshops in 2005–2006 in which I coached 10 evaluators from organizations across Canada on developmental evaluations they were undertaking. And that led one of the participants in those workshops, Jamie Gamble of New Brunswick, to write *A Developmental Evaluation Primer* (Gamble, 2008), which was published by the McConnell Foundation. These events, connections, and relationships have been central to the development of developmental evaluation and now to this book. I am deeply grateful.

Developmental Feedback

Jamie Gamble is one of four people who have read and provided important feedback about the book as I wrote it. Another was Mark Cabaj, also one of the participants in the McConnell-sponsored workshops. Mark and I collaborated in conducting a developmental evaluation. Through his community work he has tested out how developmental evaluation processes work with community-based innovators. Keiko Kuji-Shikatani and I worked together in planning the International Evaluation Conference in Toronto in 2005 supported jointly by the Canadian Evaluation Society and the American Evaluation Association (AEA). She works in the Ontario Ministry of Education and offered insights about the implications of developmental evaluation for government-based evaluators and evaluation users, as well as capacity development for evaluators. Ricardo Wilson-Grau and I crossed paths in workshops and at a meeting on complexity where he presented a paper on *Evaluating the Effects of International Advocacy Networks*. He has worked and lived throughout the world and is currently based in Brazil. He read through an international lens and consistently pushed me to write for international evaluators. You'll learn more about and from these experienced developmental evaluators because each responded to my invitation to provide advice to evaluators new to developmental evaluation. I've scattered their insights throughout the book to add spice along the way. Ricardo's advice is in Chapter 4, Mark's in Chapter 6, Jamie's in Chapter 7, and Keiko's in Chapter 10. That's their gift to you. Their invaluable but greatly valued gift to me has been to read and thoughtfully react as I wrote. They each contributed important corrections, new insights, probing questions, and much-appreciated encouragement. They played the role of developmental evaluators for my writing and that experience, as much as anything, has deepened my understanding of what a difference high-quality feedback can make. My thanks to each of you.

Contributions from Around the World

Others have provided valuable feedback on and contributions to particular chapters. Minnesota evaluator and long-time friend Gene Lyle read several chapters, and as an experienced internal, in-the-trenches evaluator, he's somewhat skeptical of hair-splitting distinctions evaluation theorists, including me, like to make. Gene's thoughtful cautions and encouragements about developmental evaluation are included in Chapter 2. Jean Gornick, now an evaluator after 20 years directing a community-based antipoverty organization in northern Minnesota, has generously allowed me to include the story of her efforts to adapt national models locally. Jean and I have been doing developmental evaluations together and I've learned from her keen sensitivity to how evaluation processes affect real people in the real world in real time and real ways (you see a pattern here), people struggling with the complexities of day-to-day community life. She helped keep me grounded in those realities even as she offered consistent support for my writing. Her story is featured in Chapter 6 with the full retrospective developmental evaluation of her antipoverty work in Chapter 9. Kate McKegg and Nan Wehipeihana are developmental evaluators working in New Zealand. Their experiences, insights, reflections, and advice are featured in Chapter 9. From Australia, Patricia Rogers has been working with complexity theory and its implications for evaluation for a long time, and she has become one of the leading thinkers in the world about these issues, as evidenced by her formidable globe-trotting schedule each year at which she makes presentations and consults on complexity-informed evaluation. She was writing a book on program theory (Funnell & Rogers, 2010) and evaluation as I was writing this book, so we exchanged e-mails of support as we experienced the ups and downs of writing and raced to the finish line nearly together. Her contributions are found throughout the book, but especially in Chapter 5.

Ehren Reed is a Senior Associate with Innovation Network who has been doing developmental evaluation on advocacy campaigns; his advice to novice evaluators is in Chapter 2 and a summary of his advocacy-focused developmental evaluation is in Chapter 10. Meg Hargreaves is a former doctoral student of mine who has gone on to become an accomplished developmental evaluation practitioner; examples of her work are highlighted in Chapter 9. Meg has teamed up with Beverly Parsons to offer professional development workshops on *Evaluating Complex Systems Interventions* before the annual conference of the AEA. Beverly's case study of a cross-scale and multifaceted evaluation of a family strengthening program is featured in Chapter 7. Hallie Preskill, a former AEA president, skillfully weaves developmental evaluations into the repertoire of ways she conducts learning-focused evaluations; she contributed an example to Chapter 6. Elliot Stern, distinguished founding editor of the international journal *Evaluation*, provided me with his reflections on the relationship between action research and developmental evaluation, which is included in Chapter 9. Bill Fear, writing from Wales, offered musings on evaluation methods, also included in Chapter 9. Mark M. Rogers is an experienced facilitator, trainer, mediator, program designer, and peacebuilder with vast international experience; he's also a clever cartoonist, who creatively turned some ambiguous complexity ideas I suggested into polished and pointed illustrations that you'll find here and there throughout the book. These diverse contributions from colleagues and friends, both singly and taken together, greatly strengthen the book. My thanks to one and all.

Colleagues

While I have learned from and am indebted to many more people than I can acknowledge, the contributions of a few additional noteworthy colleagues have been especially important as I've conceptualized developmental evaluation through the years, both its distinct niche and as a utilization-focused evaluation option: Marv Alkin, John Bare, Gale Berkowitz, Jane Maland Cady, Tina Christie, Julia Coffman, Mike Coplen, Brad Cousins, Stewart Donaldson, Glenda Eoyang, Malcolm Gray, Jackie Williams Kaye, Jean King, Karen Kirkhart, Kai N. Lee, Mel Mark, Donna Mertens, Marah Moore, Jonny Morell, Patricia Patrizi, Debra Rog, Andy Rowe, Kay Sherwood, Hazel Symonette, and Bill Trochim. This book has been heavily influenced by the opportunity to dialogue and work with international colleagues, especially Michael Bamberger, Fred Carden, Sarah Earl, Sulley Gariba, Alexey Kuzmin, Linda Morra Imas, Zenda Ofir, Donna Podems, Ray Rist, Jim Rugh, Steve Rothschild, and Bob Williams. TEI has provided the opportunity for me to teach developmental evaluation. Many of the exhibits in this book were developed for teaching in TEI and I've learned a great deal from the participants in those workshops. My thanks to Midge Smith, Ann Doucette, and Kathy Newcomer.

C. Deborah Laughton, Publisher, Methodology and Statistics, at The Guilford Press, has played a special role in the development of this book. For years I've been telling "C. Deb" about this book, discussing it over dinner at AEA and in e-mail exchanges between conferences. She has always offered just the right amount of encouragement to keep me moving forward. She understood and believed in this book from the first time we talked about it. She responded to draft chapters quickly with helpful editorial suggestions about where to fill gaps and reduce verbosity (though in this latter effort she was not altogether successful, through no fault of her own). She wasn't even surprised when the book turned out to be twice as long as I had predicted, both in time it took to write and number of pages needed to do the job. I promised it would be hers to publish when and if

I ever got it done. The pages that follow are a testament to her perseverance and support in helping me move from idea to reality, which is essentially what innovation development is all about.

Student Feedback

As I was writing, two doctoral students contacted me independent of each other seeking resources on developmental evaluation. I offered them draft chapters of the book if they'd provide feedback and ask questions about things that weren't clear. They did so diligently. My thanks to Karen L. Zannini Bull, Instructional Design, Development and Evaluation, School of Education, Syracuse University, and Lesli Hoey, Department of City and Regional Planning, Cornell University. When Chris Coryn, Director of the Interdisciplinary PhD in Evaluation, Western Michigan University, contacted me about coming to Kalamazoo to make a presentation, I was inspired by the experience with Karen and Lesli to propose that I would come if each of his students would read one chapter and provide rapid feedback about anything that wasn't clear. The deadline for the manuscript was approaching so I'd need responses in just 1 week if it was to be useful. The students drew chapters randomly and all present for my workshop met the time line except one, a remarkable rapid-response feedback performance. Adriana Bauer, Melisa Borgos-Colon, Jason Burkhardt, Julien Kouame, Lindsay Noakes, Diane Rogers, Michele Tarsilla, Gisele Tchamba, Carl Westine, and Kurt Wilson did due diligence pointing out opaque, unintelligible, and puzzling passages, for which I am grateful. Of course, with evaluation comes awesome responsibility, so if anything in the book remains the least unclear, it is entirely their fault. Daniela Schröter, Director of Research, Center for Evaluation, Western Michigan University, joined in the fun, providing helpful feedback and additional assistance with some graphics.

The Personal Factor

One gem of feedback from some of the student reviewers, echoed by a few others who read select chapters in draft, was that they became impatient with the stories about people with whom I've worked closely, people deeply involved in innovation and/or evaluation who have influenced my approach to developmental evaluation. One wrote:

> "The long story you told at the beginning of the chapter was kind of interesting but I didn't know why I was reading so much about this person. I was frustrated trying to figure out the point. I've never seen this kind of storytelling in an academic research book before. I'm not used to it. I think you should shorten the stories and get to the point. Students have to do a lot of reading. We need you to get to the point."

I appreciate the frankness of this feedback. And it gives me a chance to explain to students, and indeed, readers of all ilk, that *the stories are the point*. The people in the stories, what they do and how they think, are the point. If you skip the stories and the people, you will have missed the point. Here's why.

People matter. Relationships matter. Evaluation is not just about methods and data. Studies of evaluation use have consistently found that evaluation use is significantly increased when those in a position to make decisions understand the importance of reality testing and care about using data to inform their decision making. This is what has come to be called the *personal factor*.

> The personal factor is the presence of an identifiable individual or group of people who personally care about the evaluation and the findings it generates. Where such a person or group was present, evaluations were used; where the personal factor was absent, research on evaluation use consistently shows a correspondingly marked absence of evaluation impact. (Patton, 2008, chap. 3)

In each chapter, I feature the story of someone I've known well and worked closely with to highlight the importance of the personal factor. Some are clients. Some are colleagues. Some are both. Developmental evaluation, in particular, is *relationship-based*. No matter how rigorous, systematic, and elegant the methods, if the relationship between the evaluator and those developing an innovation doesn't work, the full potential of developmental evaluation won't be realized. By the way, you'll often find that point emphasized by the experienced developmental evaluators who contributed advice in sidebars featured throughout the book.

So you'll get to meet and spend more time with some of the people I've thanked in this preface: Mike Coplen, Jean Gornick, Tom Henderson, Kate McKegg, Steve Rothschild, Nan Wehipeihana, Frances Westley, and Brenda Zimmerman. It's a privilege for me to be able to tell their stories. Don't rush through them searching for the point. Linger a bit. Get to know them. They embody and epitomize the personal factor. Their stories are the point. And each developmental evaluation is a story.

MICHAEL QUINN PATTON
Saint Paul, Minnesota

Illustration by Mark M. Rogers.

Contents

List of Exhibits

1

Developmental Evaluation Defined and Positioned

Science has explored the microcosms and the macrocosms; we have a good sense of the lay of the land. The great unexplored frontier is complexity.
—HEINZ R. PAGELS, *The Dreams of Reason* (1988)

The evaluation version of this observation goes like this:

> Evaluation has explored merit and worth, processes and outcomes, formative and summative evaluation; we have a good sense of the lay of the land. The great unexplored frontier is evaluation under conditions of complexity. *Developmental evaluation* explores that frontier.

Developmental evaluation supports innovation *development* to guide adaptation to emergent and dynamic realities in complex environments. Innovations can take the form of new projects, programs, products, organizational changes, policy reforms, and system interventions. A complex system is characterized by a large number of interacting and interdependent elements in which there is no central control; self-organizing and emergent behaviors based on sophisticated information processing generate learning, evolution, and development

(Mitchell, 2009, p. 13). Complex environments for social interventions and innovations are those in which what to do to solve problems is uncertain and key stakeholders are in conflict about how to proceed. Informed by systems thinking and sensitive to complex nonlinear dynamics, developmental evaluation supports social innovation and adaptive management. Evaluation processes include asking evaluative questions, applying evaluation logic, and gathering real-time data to inform ongoing decision making and adaptations. The evaluator is often part of a development team whose members collaborate to conceptualize, design, and test new approaches in a long-term, ongoing process of continuous development, adaptation, and experimentation, keenly sensitive to unintended results and side effects. The evaluator's primary function in the team is to infuse team discussions with evaluative questions, thinking, and data, and to facilitate systematic data-based reflection and decision making in the developmental process.

The Distinction Emerges

Developmental evaluation as a distinct niche emerged in response to one of my client's questions and needs. It happened like this.

I had a standard 5-year contract with a community leadership program that specified 2½ years of formative evaluation for program improvement to be followed by 2½ years of summative evaluation that would lead to an overall decision about whether the program was effective, a common design and sequence. The leadership program served small, rural communities throughout Minnesota. During the formative evaluation, the program made major changes in many aspects of how it operated. Recruitment processes were expanded. Program activities were adjusted based on feedback from participants. New curriculum elements and small-group exercises were added and fine-tuned. Follow-up interviews with graduates led to new support initiatives after program completion. Formative evaluation focuses on improving a model. This program team was hungry for feedback and eager to make improvements, which they had done willingly and enthusiastically. Then it came time to close this highly creative phase of formative evaluation and move on to summative evaluation.

On a subzero February morning in northern Minnesota, I opened a program team meeting by announcing:

"We've had a great couple of years changing and adapting the program. I've been impressed by your openness and commitment to use evaluation feedback to make improvements. But now, in the next phase of the evaluation, called *summative evaluation*, the purpose is to make an overall judgment about the merit and worth of the program. Does it work? Should it be continued, perhaps even expanded? Have you come up with a model that others might want to adopt? This means that from now on you can't make any more improvements or changes because we need the program—the model—to stay stable in order to conduct the summative evaluation. Only with a fixed intervention, carefully implemented the same way for each new group of leaders in training, can we attribute the measured outcomes to your program intervention in a valid and credible way."

Mouths fell open. Staff was aghast. They protested:

"We don't want to implement a fixed model. In fact, what we've learned is that we need to keep adapting what we do to the particular needs of new groups. Communities vary. The backgrounds of our participants vary. The economic and political context keeps changing. New technologies like the Internet are coming into rural Minnesota and creating new leadership challenges. Small communities are becoming parts of regional networks. We need to get more young people into the program. Immigrants are moving into rural Minnesota in droves, creating more diverse communities. We need to reach out and adapt what we do to Native Americans. No! No! No! We can't fix the model. We can't stand still for 2 years. We don't want to do summative evaluation."

"But that's what my contract specifies," I replied, disconcerted by their resistance. "This is the way things work," I hastened to explain. "You do a couple of years of formative evaluation to stabilize the program model, then you do summative evaluation to determine if it works, if the targeted outcomes are achieved. That's how things work. That's standard practice."

"But that doesn't make sense for us. We'll just have to change the contract," the director offered. "Let's just keep doing formative evaluation. We want to keep improving the program."

"Then when do you want to do the summative evaluation?" I asked.

"Never," he responded without hesitation, "not if it means standardizing the program. We want to keep developing and changing."

"But the purpose of formative evaluation is to get ready for summative evaluation. At some point, you'll need to determine if the model works. At some point the board will need to decide whether to keep funding this program. People outside the program are interested and asking if it works. That means stabilizing the model to do a summative evaluation."

He looked at me sternly, challengingly. "Formative evaluation! Summative evaluation! *Is that all you evaluators have to offer?*"

Frustration, even hostility, was palpable in his tone. I found myself feeling defensive. In truth, those were the field's primary distinctions. That was, in fact, all we had to offer. "Well," I said, seeking inspiration in my coffee cup, "I suppose we could do, umm, we could, umm, well, we might do, you know . . . we could try *developmental evaluation*!"

"What's that?" asked the director.

"It's where you, ummm, keep developing."

"That's what we want to do," he said, obviously relieved. "We can make periodic reports on our developments to the board and to others interested in what we're doing and learning, but we want to keep developing. *Developmental evaluation.* I like it. Let's do that. So, how do we do it?"

"Well, it's kind of a new approach," I said, thinking to myself, like 1-minute new. "But it does seem to fit what you want to do, so I'm sure we can figure it out together." And thus began my foray into and education about developmental evaluation, a learn-by-doing process that has been, and continues to be, "developmental." This books reports what I've learned. But first let me finish the story.

My two evaluation colleagues and I became part of the leadership program's design team, which included a sociologist, a couple of psychologists, a communications specialist, some adult educators, a philanthropic funder, and program training and professional development staff. Our evaluation role was to bring evaluative thinking and data to bear as the team conceptualized, developed, and tried out new approaches for new groups, including immigrants, Native Americans, people from distressed rural communities, elected officials, and young people. The program developed new approaches in light of new federal and state policies affecting rural communities. The ongoing decline in many rural communities led to a more regional focus. As more than one cohort from a community went through the program, the issue of how to connect different cohorts arose. New funding opportunities opened up to support follow-up projects by program graduates. New staffing needs arose. The developmental relationship lasted over 6 years and involved different evaluation designs each year including participant observation, several different surveys, field observations, telephone interviews, face-to-face interviews, focus groups, case studies of individuals and communities, cost analyses, theory-of-change conceptualizations, futuring exercises, and training participants to do their own community-based evaluations. Each year the program changed in significant ways and new evaluation questions emerged. Program goals and strategies evolved. The evaluation evolved. No summative evaluation was ever conducted, no final report was ever written. The program continues to evolve—and continues to rely on developmental evaluation.

Periodic summative-type decisions were made along the way in that the foundation board had to budget to continue funding, sometimes approving major changes in strategic direction and augmenting funding accordingly. Developmental evaluation supported these summative decisions by the board by documenting the nature and results of program developments. What was judged to be working, however, was not a standardized and routinized model, but rather the ongoing development of leadership programming in response to changing conditions, lessons learned, and the emergent needs of different kinds of participants as the program expanded its outreach.

So, is the distinction between formative and developmental evaluation meaningful? Is it worth distinguishing *improvements* from *developments*? It has certainly proved meaningful and useful to those with whom I work. I think it's valuable to respect and maintain the original connection between formative and summative evaluation, that formative evaluation gets a program model ready for summative testing. I also think, as

my experience with the community leadership program illustrates, that developmental evaluation has a distinct purpose and niche beyond formative and summative evaluation. This book is about that niche.

I hasten to add that I am in no way denigrating of or hostile to formative and summative evaluation, nor am I suggesting that these approaches lack value. Quite the contrary. The point is that each approach, including developmental evaluation, fulfills a specific purpose and adds a particular kind of value. Indeed, in Chapter 7 we'll examine the niche of *preformative* use of developmental evaluation: development of an innovative idea or visionary intervention during a period of exploration to get the emerging model to the point where it is ready for traditional formative and summative evaluation with particular focus on determining if the innovation is a potential model that is scalable for broad impact. Let me elaborate.

Facing Complexity and Facing Reality: Or, Facing the Realities of Complexity

As I've discovered over the last decade, developmental evaluation as a distinct approach to evaluation has proven especially relevant and attractive to social innovators. These people are trying to bring about major social change by fighting poverty, homelessness, community and family violence, and by helping people with AIDS, severe disabilities, chronic diseases, and victims of natural disasters and war. Some of the daunting challenges social innovators face include skepticism, criticism, naysayers, disbelievers, and the ever-present very real possibility of failure, perhaps even the likelihood of failure. Canadian colleagues Frances Westley and Brenda Zimmerman and I studied successful social innovations and visionary social innovators. We reported what we found in a book entitled *Getting to Maybe: How the World Is Changed* (Westley, Zimmerman, & Patton, 2006). We found that fierce con-

---

⌒ Why Distinctions Matter

Language matters. Terminology matters. Distinctions matter. That great scholar and observer of all things human, Dr. Seuss (1953), illustrated the consequences of not making distinctions in his children's story "Too Many Daves." Mrs. McCave, it seems, had 23 sons and she named them all Dave. When she wanted one particular Dave and called out his name all 23 Daves came on the run.

Same thing happens if you don't distinguish types of evaluations. An entire volume of *New Directions for Evaluation* was devoted to *How and Why Language Matters in Evaluation* (Hopson, 2000).

This book is about developmental evaluation as a distinct type with its own name.

Edward Sapir (1884–1939), the great linguist and anthropologist, made the same point as Dr. Seuss, but with a bit more of an academic voice:

Human beings are very much at the mercy of the particular language which has become the medium of expression for their society. . . . We see and hear and otherwise experience very largely as we do because the language habits of our community predispose certain choices of interpretation. (quoted in Rheingold, 1988, p. 11)

viction is required to sustain innovation in the face of mounting internal and external obstacles. To be a change agent is to think boldly, to envision grandly. Complexity theory shows that great changes can emerge from small actions. Change involves a belief in the possible, even the "impossible." Moreover, social innovators don't follow a linear pathway of change; there are ups and downs, roller-coaster rides along cascades of dynamic interactions, unexpected and unanticipated divergences, tipping points and critical mass momentum shifts. Indeed, things often get worse before they get better as systems change creates resistance to and pushback against the new.

Traditional evaluation approaches are not well suited for such turbulence. Traditional evaluation aims to control and predict, to bring order to chaos. Developmental evaluation accepts such turbulence as the way the world of social innovation unfolds in the face of complexity. Developmental evaluation adapts to the realities of complex nonlinear dynamics rather than trying to impose order and certainty on a disorderly and uncertain world.

In general I've found that evaluation has a bad reputation among visionaries. This is for a variety of reasons, some fair, some not so fair. Leaders tend to attract and sur-

round themselves with believers: true believers, positive thinkers, and hope-springs-eternalists. This adds to the momentum and the flow of social innovation, which is particularly critical in the early stages. Criticism is well known to undermine creativity—which is why it's outlawed in brainstorming exercises. Visionaries, then, often eschew criticism, especially early in the process while creating a vision and recruiting allies and followers. Energy being always in short supply, those aiming to change the world focus their energy on what can be done, on strengths, not weaknesses.

In addition, many of those working in the domain of social innovation, including social entrepreneurs and inventors (Conger, 2009), have experienced evaluation methods that seem entirely unrelated to the nature of their enterprise. Identifying clear, specific, and measurable outcomes at the very start of an innovative project, for example, may be not only difficult but counterproductive. "Outcomes will emerge as we engage," say the social innovators.

"Not in my world," respond the funders and the evaluators. "Clear goals have to be established before you engage. And you need an explicit change model, a logic model to show how you'll attain your goals."

"Not in my world," respond the social innovators. "Time is of the essence and there's no time to lose. Every minute matters. We have to dive in and see what we can do." And thus is the battle between funders, evaluators commissioned by funders, and social innovators enjoined.

Unfortunately, resistance to evaluation can undermine social innovation if and when it becomes a resistance to reality testing. And evaluation is ultimately about reality testing, getting real about what's going on, what's being achieved—examining both what's working and what's not working. Jim Collins (2001), author of the best-selling management book *Good to Great*, studied with his research team how good companies become "great." Not many companies qualified for his study. Few made the transition

"No go. The evaluation committee said it doesn't meet utility specs. They want something linear, stable, controllable, and targeted to reach a pre-set destination. They couldn't see any use for this."

Illustrated by Mark M. Rogers.

⌒ Simple Reactions to Complexity: Context for Developmental Evaluation as an Approach to Complexity

Over the years I've reviewed a large number of evaluation guidebooks, position papers, terms of reference, and scopes of work that explain to evaluators how to deal with complexity. The common themes that have struck me are a two-pronged effort to first deny complexity (redefine the complex as simple) and then, failing that, to control it. Here are sample prescriptions I've collected that give you a sense of a prevailing worldview that gives rise to developmental evaluation as an alternative for dealing with complexity, to wit, actually acknowledging and dealing with it.

Conventional prescriptions for denying complexity

- Yes, the world is complex, but don't let that become an excuse. *Simplify and focus.* Things only appear complex because you haven't yet focused.
- What needs to be done only seems complex when you lack a framework for how to intervene. A clear framework simplifies the complex, makes it manageable, and tells you where to target your resources.
- Cut through the noise and find the essence. Don't be distracted by complexity. Get on with taking action and making a difference on key indicators. Move the needle of those indicators and complexity will take care of itself.

Conventional prescriptions for controlling complexity

- In the face of complexity, the first task is to identify clear, specific, and measurable goals. Clear direction and measurable goals cut right through complexity.
- Everything seems complex until you do a logic model. Sort out the complexities into a sequence of concrete actions that are clear, sequential, and logical.
- At its most effective and useful, evaluation makes the uncertain certain, the ambiguous unambiguous, the unknown known, the unpredictable predictable, and the complex simple.
- Accountability requires that programs manage and control complexity. Evaluation makes that possible.

Conventional quotations found in evaluation documents to justify avoiding complexity

- Nothing is more simple than greatness; indeed, to be simple is to be great.—Poet Ralph Waldo Emerson
- Nothing is particularly hard if you divide it into small jobs.—Industrialist Henry Ford
- Nothing is true, but that which is simple.—German literary luminary Johann Wolfgang von Goethe
- Life is really simple, but men insist on making it complicated.—Chinese philosopher Confucius
- Things should be made as simple as possible, but not any simpler.—Physicist Albert Einstein

And it is Einstein's wisdom that informs developmental evaluation and this book.

from good to great, but those that did all had leaders who lived the paradox between absolute dedication to a great vision and ruthless commitment to staring reality in the face. Collins called this the "Stockdale paradox" in honor of James Stockdale, the fabled U.S. Navy officer who survived years of torture in North Vietnamese prisons. Stockdale had an unwavering belief that he would survive and an equally unrelenting vigilance about his prisoner-of-war reality. He was constantly attuned to what was happening to him and his fellow prisoners, and adapted his survival strategies and tactics accordingly. When, after a short period of unusual good treatment, he realized that he was about to be used as propaganda to show how well prisoners were cared for, he brutalized his own face so that he could not be so used—or misused. Wondering how Stockdale managed to stay ever hopeful in the face of this day-to-day brutal reality, Collins asked him how he would characterize those who didn't make it, those who died in captivity. That's easy, Stockdale replied immediately: they were the optimists, those who said they'd be out by Christmas, and then by Easter, and then by summer's end, and then again by Christmas, always and only focusing on some future target of hope. They died, he said, of broken hearts.

The "good to great" companies Collins's team studied all shared an unrelenting belief in a future that seemed to those around them a delusion *and* an obsession with data about the reality they faced, monitoring the results of their initiatives and getting real-time feedback about what was working and not working, and how their environment was changing. They did not treat vision and reality testing, hope and data, as opposites. Rather, they immersed themselves paradoxically in vision-directed reality testing: no rose-colored glasses, no blind spots, no positive thinking. *Ruthless attention to reality was the common path to attaining their visions.*

The key to reconciling the tension between optimism and pessimism, dreaming and reality testing, is to tailor the methods of evaluation to the demands of innovation by tracking emergent and changing realities, illuminating perspectives about realities, and feeding back meaningful findings in real time so that reality testing facilitates and supports the dynamics of innovation. This is not simple to do, but it can be critical for adapting and sustaining social innovation. Developmental evaluation is designed to be congruent with and to nurture developmental, emergent, innovative, and transformative processes.

Developmental Evaluation and Complexity Theory

We have entered the *Age of Adapting Quickly.*
—MICHIKO KAKUTANI, Pulitzer Prize–
winning critic for the *New York Times*
(2009, p. C1)

Complexity as a construct is a broad tapestry that weaves together several threads relevant to innovation and evaluation. Exhibit 1.1 summarizes some complexity concepts that we'll be using throughout this book: nonlinearity, emergence, dynamical systems, adaptiveness, uncertainty, and coevolutionary processes. Innovation as something new, emergent, and adaptive exhibits characteristics and dynamics associated with complex adaptive systems. Developmental evaluation likewise centers on situational sensitivity, responsiveness, and adaptation, and is an approach to evaluation especially appropriate for situations of high uncertainty where what may and does emerge is relatively unpredictable and uncontrollable. Developmental evaluation tracks and attempts to make sense of what emerges under conditions of complexity, documenting and interpreting the dynamics, interactions, and interdependencies that occur as innovations unfold.

Positioning developmental evaluation as especially appropriate for complex situations requires a brief excursion into systems thinking and complexity theory. Chapters 4 and 5 examine these ideas and their implications in depth. As prologue, it's worth warning that this is treacherous terrain, easy to get lost in. Once, when hiking a rugged wilderness area of the Grand Canyon, I missed one switchback on the descent and started down the wrong drainage. Within 15 minutes I recognized my error, but I was on a steep slope run through with drainages, ravines, and ridges, converging, diverging, and crisscrossing. It took a couple of hours trying one direction and then another to find my way back to my companions. Hiking the Grand Canyon wilderness away from the main tourist trails, I learned, offered many

---

EXHIBIT 1.1 Characteristics of Complex Adaptive Systems

Nonlinearity. Sensitivity to initial conditions; small actions can stimulate large reactions, thus the *butterfly wings* (Gleick, 1987) and *black swans* (Taleb, 2007) metaphors, in which highly improbable, unpredictable, and unexpected events have huge impacts.

Emergence. Patterns emerge from self-organization among interacting agents. What emerges is beyond, outside of, and oblivious to any notion of shared intentionality. Each agent or elements pursues its own path but as paths intersect and the elements interact, patterns of interaction emerge and the whole of the interactions becomes greater than the separate parts.

Dynamical. Interactions within, between, and among subsystems and parts within systems are volatile, turbulent, cascading rapidly and unpredictably.

Adaptive. Interacting elements and agents respond and adapt to each other so that what emerges and evolves is a function of ongoing adaptation among both interacting elements and the responsive relationships interacting agents have with their environment.

Uncertainty. Under conditions of complexity, processes and outcomes are unpredictable, uncontrollable, and unknowable in advance. *Getting to Maybe* (Westley et al., 2006) captures the sense that interventions under conditions of complexity take place in a *Maybe World*.

Coevolutionary. As interacting and adaptive agents self-organize, ongoing connections emerge that become *coevolutionary* as the agents evolve together (coevolve) within and as part of the whole system, over time.

Note. Exhibit 5.6 in Chapter 5 presents the developmental evaluation implications of each of these dimensions of complexity.

---

opportunities to get sidetracked and lost, and we unwittingly and unexpectedly got lured into unplanned sidetrack adventures. Such uncertain and emergent adventures are reported by even the most expert Canyon hikers, like the renowned Harvey Butchart, who spent more than 1,000 days hiking the Canyon, covered some 12,000 miles, recorded 23 first ascents, and was often lost, sometimes with dire consequences, including the death of a young hiking companion (Butler & Myers, 2007; Patton, 1999).

Yes, sidetracks. Unexpected detours. Getting lost. Navigating tough terrain. Negotiating ravines and ridges. Steep ascents and terrifying descents. Diverging, converging, and crisscrossing. Watching for what emerges. Expecting the unexpected. Going with the flow. Riding cascades and waves of turbulence. These are the allusions and meta-phors of complexity. And of developmental evaluation. Complexity writings are filled with metaphors that try to make complex phenomena understandable to the human brain's hardwired need for order, meaning, patterns, sense making, and control, ever feeding our illusion that we know what's going on. We often don't. But the pretense that we do is comforting—and sometimes necessary for some effort at action.

So complexity theorists talk of flapping butterfly wings that change weather systems and spawn hurricanes, individual slime molds that remarkably self-organize into organic wholes, ant colonies whose frantic service to the queen mesmerize us with their collective intelligence, avalanches that reconfigure mountain ecologies, bacteria that *know* the systems of which they are a part without any capacity for self-knowledge, and

~ Framing Poverty as a Complex Issue

Mark Cabaj (2009a, 2009b) is a developmental evaluator working with Vibrant Communities, a comprehensive and innovative antipoverty program working across Canada. He and his colleagues recently synthesized 8 years of learning from the collaborations across Canada involved in Vibrant Communities. At the top of their list of important learnings is the importance of viewing poverty through the lens of complexity.

Unlike simple or complicated issues that can be effectively addressed by employing best practices or extensive research and planning, poverty is a complex issue. This means that it:

- Is difficult to define;
- Has tangled up root causes;
- Involves stakeholders with diverse values, interests, and positions;
- Varies from person to person and community to community;
- Is constantly evolving; and
- Has no obvious answers or measures of success

The developmental evaluation work with Vibrant Communities has meant using an adaptive approach to mobilizing stakeholders, crafting and evaluating strategies, and stewarding a long-term effort characterized by unavoidable tensions, fast-moving environments, and blunt and clumsy practices implemented by traditional organizations.

Alan Perlis, an award-winning computer scientist, once observed:

Fools ignore complexity. Pragmatists suffer it. Some can avoid it. Geniuses remove it. Simplicity does not precede complexity, but follows it. (quoted in Cabaj, 2009a)

black swans that appear suddenly and unpredictably to change the world. Complexity science offers insights into the billions of interactions in the global stock market, the spread of disease throughout the world, volatile weather systems, the evolution of species, large-scale ecological changes, and the flocking of migrating birds. Complexity theorists explain the rise and fall of civilizations, and the rise and fall of romantic infatuation. That's a lot of territory. I aim merely to add attention to the rise and fall of evaluations.

Utility

What brings me to complexity is its utility for understanding certain evaluation challenges. Complexity concepts can be used to identify and frame a set of intervention circumstances that are amenable to a particular situationally appropriate evaluation response, what I am calling here developmental evaluation. This makes dealing with complexity a defining characteristic of developmental evaluation's niche. Principles for operating in complex adaptive systems inform the practice of developmental evaluation. The controversies and challenges that come with complexity ideas will also and inevitably afflict developmental evaluation. The insights and understandings of complexity thinking that have attracted the attention of and garnered enthusiasm from social innovators will also envelope developmental evaluation—and be the source of its utility. Forewarned is forearmed. You are entering here the world of uncertain beginnings, muddled middles, and unpredictable endings that ripple on and on without end. This is the paradoxical comfort zone of people like photographer-provocateur Robert Frank who cursed "those god-damned stories with a beginning and an end" (quoted in Lane, 2009, p. 88). For those with a high tolerance for ambiguity and a grand sense of adventure, this is an exciting world. For those with big control needs who prize predictability and strive for certainty, not so much.

Dealing with the Unexpected

There is no such thing as a failed experiment,
only experiments with unexpected outcomes.
—R. BUCKMINSTER FULLER (1895–1983),
visionary and inventor

Developmental evaluation requires what distinguished and experienced evaluator Jon Morell has called "agile evaluators," those who learn to expect the unexpected and adapt with agility and flexibility, including changing the evaluation design, reconfiguring program theory, and responding to emergent stakeholder needs (Morell, 2010). There is a lot of lip service in evaluation about looking for unanticipated consequences and assessing side effects; in reality, these are typically token elements of evaluation designs, inadequately budgeted, and rarely given serious time and attention because of the overwhelming focus on measuring attainment of intended outcomes and tracking preconceived performance indicators. You have to go out into the real world, do fieldwork, engage in open inquiry, talk to participants in programs, and observe what

～ Global Complexity, Local Complexity

As this book was being written in 2008–2009, the news was saturated with evidence of global complexity: the global economic meltdown and financial crisis that began in October 2008 revealed the complex nonlinear dynamics of the interconnected and interdependent global economy, replete with uncertainties and tsunami-like ripple effects. The election of Barack Obama to the presidency of the United States changed the global political landscape, a fact highlighted when he was awarded the 2009 Nobel Peace Prize, not for anything in particular, but for everything in general. The long-term effects of technological innovation and the Internet are still unfolding, the implications just beginning to become evident. The threat of a worldwide flu pandemic has cascading effects on tourism, commerce, travel, and community life.

These global complexities spiral downward and become manifest in local uncertainties and unexpected developments. When the endowments of philanthropic foundations were hard hit, some programs and agencies that thought they had funding were suddenly without financing and had to close their doors. Local and state governments face huge and growing deficits, with uncertain consequences. The U.S. federal deficit is increasing at an unprecedented rate. Demographic trends, especially the unparalleled aging of the population, are creating new demands for services at every level of society. The effects of health care reform will not be known for years and are far from settled. Climate change looms. No one these days doubts the uncertain but very real dynamics of global change.

From a big-picture global systems perspective, these complex phenomena are interconnected: economic, political, demographic, environmental, social, cultural, technological, and health systems interlocked, interacting, and interdependent—with unknown and unpredictable consequences. All of this is sometimes labeled CONTEXT by evaluators creating fixed and static logic models that pretend and assume control and predictability: implement these activities and produce these outcomes. But global complexities and dynamics are not just context. They manifest themselves in local realities: changed conditions under which programs operate, new problems that participants bring to programs, and new challenges in meeting emergent needs. These well-documented and pervasive complexities have become part of public consciousness replete with local evidence of what theorists call *nonlinear dynamics* and common folk capture with the bumper sticker slogan "Shit Happens."

I don't find that it takes a lot of effort to convince people that the world is complex. The evidence is all about them. The question is *how to respond and adapt to that complexity*. That's no longer just a question for those trying to bring about change and those trying to survive change. It's a question for those evaluating change. *How do evaluators respond and adapt to the realities of complexity?* Developmental evaluation is one response.

is going on as innovations unfold to detect unanticipated consequences. In contrast to the casual and if-we-get-to-it-and-have-time-and-resources-after-everything-else-is-done way that evaluators typically approach the unexpected and unanticipated, the possibilities of unexpected impacts become likelihoods under conditions of complexity and developmental evaluators make expecting the unexpected fundamental to the work at hand. Organizational development researchers Weick and Sutcliffe (2001) found that high-performance organizations are always on the lookout for the unexpected. So are high-performing developmental evaluators.

Developmental Evaluation and Single-Loop versus Double-Loop Learning

Developmental evaluation supports learning to inform action that makes a difference. This often means changing systems, which involves getting beyond surface learning to deeper understandings of what's happening in a system. Social innovators and social entrepreneurs are typically trying to bring about fundamental changes in systems, to change the world (Bornstein, 2007). To do so, they have to understand how the system they want to change is operating and make changes that get beyond temporary and surface solutions to change the system itself. This involves *double-loop learning*.

For decades three stories have been endlessly repeated: one about the stream of ambulances at the bottom of the cliff instead of building fences at the top; one about the numerous dead bodies floating down the river while all we do is build more impressive services for fishing them out; and one about giving someone a fish versus the value of teaching that person how to fish. In reviewing these stories, distinguished Australian action research scholar and practitioner Yolande Wadsworth (2010) has commented that they are reminders about our repeated tendency to go for the short-term quick fix rather than to examine, come to understand, and take action to change how a system is functioning that creates the very problems being addressed. Double-loop learning involves systemic solutions and is supported by evaluation attuned to looking for system explanations and offering systemic insights. Chapter 5 explores in depth how systems thinking informs developmental evaluation.

Argyris and Schön (1978) distinguished single-loop from double-loop learning. In single-loop learning, people modify their actions as they evaluate the difference between desired and actual outcomes and make changes to increase attainment of desired outcomes. In essence, a problem-detection-and-correction process is *single-loop* learning. Single-loop learning is like a thermostat that knows when it is too hot or too cold and turns the heat off or on. The thermostat can perform this task because it can receive information (the temperature of the room) and take immediate corrective action.

In double-loop learning, those involved go beyond the single loop of identifying the problem and finding a solution to a second loop that involves questioning the assumptions, policies, practices, values, and system dynamics that led to the problem in the first place and intervening in ways that involve the modification of underlying system relationships and functioning. Making changes to improve immediate outcomes is single-loop learning; making changes to the system either to prevent the problem or to embed the solution in a changed system involves double-loop learning.

An Example of Double-Loop Learning

Harvard Medical School surgeon Atul Gawande (2007a) tells of visiting the Walter Reed military hospital early in the Iraq War. He participated in a session interpreting eye-injury statistics. The doctors were having considerable success saving some soldiers from blindness, a positive outcome. But digging deeper, the doctors asked why so many severe eye injuries were occurring. Interviewing their patients, they learned that the young soldiers weren't wearing their protective goggles because they considered them too ugly and uncool. They recommended that the military switch to "cooler-looking Wiley X ballistic eyewear. The soldiers wore their eyegear more consistently and the eye-injury rate dropped immediately" (p. A23). By asking these kinds of deeper questions about what's really going on and questioning basic assumptions about why things are happening, developmental evaluators help get at fundamental systems change implications and understandings. That's double-loop learning.

The Importance of Interpretive Frameworks

Management scholars Kathleen Sutcliffe and Klaus Weber (2003) examined the performance of business organizations in relation to the amount and accuracy of information used by senior executives as well as the "interpretive frameworks" they used to make sense of information. In a *Harvard Business Review* article they concluded that *the way senior executives interpret their business environment is more important for performance than the accuracy of data they have about their environment.* That is, they concluded that there was less value in spending a lot of money increasing the marginal accuracy of data available to senior executives compared to the value of enhancing *their capacity to interpret* whatever data they had. Executives were more limited by a lack of capacity to make sense of data than by inadequate or inaccurate data. In essence, they found that interpretive capacity, or "mindsets," distinguish high performance more than data quality and accuracy. After all, they concluded, the role of senior managers isn't just to make decisions; it's to set direction and motivate

～ Real-Time versus Developmental Evaluation

"Real time" refers generally to rapid feedback and response, linking data and action as close together in time as possible. The ultimate in real-time data analysis is reporting on stock market transitions in microseconds. In hospitals, real time means getting blood analyses or other diagnostic tests back to a doctor within a short time line that can range from minutes to an hour. In evaluation situations, real time typically means getting results to intended users in a day or two, or at most a couple of weeks, rather than in months or on a routine schedule of standard quarterly reports (a common information system reporting time frame).

Developmental evaluation aims for real-time feedback, but *not all real-time data use and evaluation is developmental.* Police departments use real-time data on increasing crime in a neighborhood to reallocate personnel from lower crime to higher crime areas. That is real-time evaluation and data use, but it is not developmental. This real-time use of data by police involves implementing a rapid response management approach, but the police are not developing that approach. In contrast, if crime data in a community indicated a national gang was moving into the community, the police could develop a task force to fight gang recruitment, infiltration, and crime and monitor emergent effects as the gang adapted to police attention so that police could adapt accordingly. That would be developmental evaluation because the intervention is emerging in real time and using evaluation data to adapt the intervention to what emerges in real time.

others in the face of ambiguities and conflicting demands. In the end, top executives must manage meaning as much as they must manage information.

Enhancing the quality and accuracy of our evaluation data through better methods and measures will add little value unless those using the data have the capacity to think evaluatively and critically, and be able to appropriately interpret findings to reach reasonable and supportable conclusions. Systems thinking, complexity theory, and developmental evaluation together offer an interpretive framework for engaging in sense making. As a complexity-sensitive, developmental evaluation unfolds, social innovators observe where they are at a moment in time and make adjustments based on dialogue about what's possible and what's desirable, though the criteria for what's "desirable" may be quite situational and always subject to change.

Developmental Evaluation and Accountability

Complexity-based developmental evaluation shifts the locus and focus of accountability. Traditionally accountability has focused on and been directed to external authorities and funders. Accountability-focused evaluators report independently to decision makers charged with making sure that resources are spent on what they're supposed to be spent on.

In contrast, for vision-and-values-driven social innovators the highest form of accountability is internal. Are we walking the talk? Are we being true to our vision? Are we dealing with reality? Are we connecting the dots between here-and-now reality and our vision? And how do we know? What are we observing that's different, that's emerging? These become internalized questions, asked ferociously, continuously, because they want to know. Those funding innovations join in the questioning and need to understand that the seriousness of inquiry

and resulting learning constitutes accountability.

That doesn't mean that asking such questions and engaging the answers, as uncertain as they may be, is easy. It takes courage to face the possibility that one is deluding oneself. Here the individual's sense of internal and personal accountability connects with a group's sense of collective responsibility and ultimately connects back to the macro, to engage the question of institutional and societal accountability. Throughout such discussions about accountability, the focus remains: What is getting developed? With what implications?

Developmental Evaluation as Utilization-Focused

Developmental evaluation is meant to communicate that there is an option in and approach to conducting evaluations that specifically supports *development*. This book will elucidate the niche, methods, and challenges of conducting developmental evaluations. In so doing, I place this approach within the larger context of *utilization-focused evaluation* (Patton, 2008c). Since utilization-focused evaluation is what I am best known for and most closely associated with, let me take a moment to make explicit how developmental evaluation flows from and can be positioned within the larger context and framework of utilization-focused evaluation.

Utilization-focused evaluation is evaluation done for and with specific primary intended users for specific, intended uses. Utilization-focused evaluation begins with the premise that evaluations should be judged by their utility and actual use; therefore, evaluators should facilitate the evaluation process and design any evaluation with careful consideration for how everything that is done, from beginning to end, will affect use. Use concerns how real people in the real world apply evaluation findings and experience the evaluation process. Therefore, the focus in utilization-focused evaluation is on achieving *intended use by intended users.* In developmental evaluation, the intended use is development, which I shall argue is a distinct and important evaluation purpose. The primary intended users are social innovators and others working to bring about major change.

In any evaluation there are many potential stakeholders and an array of possible uses. Utilization-focused evaluation requires moving from the general and abstract, that is, possible audiences and potential uses, to the real and specific: actual primary intended users and their explicit commitments to concrete, specific uses. The evaluator facilitates judgment, decision making, and action by intended users. Developmental evaluation, conducted from a utilization-focused perspective, facilitates ongoing innovation by helping those engaged in innovation examine the effects of their actions, shape and formulate hypotheses about what will result from their actions, and test their hypotheses about how to foment change in the face of uncertainty in situations characterized by complexity.

The utilization-focused approach is personal and situational. The evaluation facilitator develops a working relationship with intended users to help them determine what kind of evaluation they need. This requires negotiation in which the evaluator offers a menu of possibilities within the framework of established evaluation standards and principles. Thus, while concern about utility drives a utilization-focused evaluation, the evaluator must also attend to the evaluation's accuracy, feasibility, and propriety (Joint Committee on Standards, 1994). Moreover, as a professional, the evaluator has a responsibility to act in accordance with the profession's adopted principles of conducting systematic, data-based inquiries; performing competently; ensuring the honesty and integrity of the entire evaluation process; respecting the people involved in and affected by the evaluation; and being sensitive to the diversity of interests and val-

ues that may be related to the general and public welfare (American Evaluation Association [AEA], 1995).

Utilization-focused evaluation does not advocate any particular evaluation content, model, method, theory, or even use. Rather, it is a process for helping primary intended users select the most appropriate content, model, methods, theory, and uses for their particular situation. Situational responsiveness guides the interactive process between evaluator and primary intended users. This book presents and discusses developmental evaluation as one of the options now available in the feast that has become the field of evaluation. Utilization-focused evaluation can include any evaluative purpose (formative, summative, developmental), any kind of data (quantitative, qualitative, mixed), any kind of design (e.g., naturalistic, experimental), and any kind of focus (processes, outcomes, impacts, costs, and cost–benefit, among many possibilities). Utilization-focused evaluation is a process for making decisions about these issues in collaboration with an identified group of primary users focusing on their intended uses of evaluation.

A psychology of use undergirds and informs utilization-focused evaluation. In essence, research and my own experience indicate that intended users are more likely to use evaluations if they understand and feel ownership of the evaluation process and findings; they are more likely to understand and feel ownership if they've been actively involved; and by actively involving primary intended users, the evaluator is training users in use, preparing the groundwork for use, and reinforcing the intended utility of the evaluation every step along the way. Developmental evaluation carries this user involvement further than usual by creating a dynamic partnership between social innovators and the developmental evaluator. How that partnership gets built, and its potential pluses and minuses, will be one of the subjects I'll elucidate later. It is sufficient to say at this point that the language of "partnership" is not the norm in describing the relationship between an evaluator and those whose work is being evaluated. Thus, developmental evaluation invites both skepticism and controversy. We'll deal with both along the way.

Situation Recognition

Astute situation recognition is at the heart of utilization-focused evaluation. There is no one best way to conduct an evaluation. This insight is critical. The design of a particular evaluation depends on the people involved and their situation. The standards and principles of evaluation provide overall direction, a foundation of ethical guidance, and a commitment to professional competence and integrity, but there are no absolute rules an evaluator can follow to know exactly what to do with specific users in a particular situation. Recognizing this challenge, situation analysis is one of the "essential competencies for program evaluators" (Canadian Evaluation Society, 2010; Ghere, King, Stevahn, & Minnema, 2006; King, Stevahn, Ghere, & Minnema, 2001).

The idea—admittedly an ideal—is to match the type of evaluation to the situation and needs of the intended users to achieve their intended uses. This means—and I want to emphasize this point—*developmental evaluation is not appropriate for every situation.*

⁓ Situational Practice as an Evaluation Competency

The Canadian Evaluation Society has adopted five domains of competencies for Canadian evaluation practice, one of which is *situational practice*, defined as follows:

Situational Practice competencies focus on the application of evaluative thinking in analyzing and attending to the unique interests, issues, and contextual circumstances in which evaluation skills are being applied. (*www.evaluationcanada.ca/txt/20090531_competencies_companion.pdf*)

Not even close. Indeed, I shall argue that its niche is small and demanding. It will not work if the conditions and relationships are not right. I'll be specifying what those conditions and relationships are as we proceed. The point here is that every evaluation involves the challenge of matching the evaluation process and approach to the circumstances, resources, time lines, data demands, politics, intended users, and purposes of a particular situation. Matching requires astute situation recognition. This is not as easy as it may sound. Indeed, it is quite difficult and worth understanding why, so a brief excursion into breakthrough understandings in cognitive science and philosophy of science, heavy-going stuff, is worth mentioning as a context for understanding and framing developmental evaluation.

Substantial research has focused on human nonrationality, including the influential works of Nobel Prize in Economics recipient Daniel Kahneman, one of many who have established that how we decide what to do is far from rational.[1] Our rationality is "bounded" (Simon, 1957, 1978). This applies no less to well-educated professionals than to common folk. We all rely on deeply embedded heuristics, rules of thumb, standard operating procedures, practiced behaviors, and selective perceptions. We operate within and see the world through paradigms. A *paradigm* is a worldview built on implicit assumptions, accepted definitions, comfortable habits, values defended as truths, and beliefs projected as reality. As such, paradigms are deeply embedded in the socialization of adherents and practitioners. Our paradigms tell us what is important, legitimate, and reasonable. Paradigms are also normative, telling us what to do without the necessity of long existential

---

[1] For samples of a half-century of research on the nonrational nature of decision making, see Gigerenzer, Todd, and ABC Research Group (1999); Groopman (2007); Inbar (1979); Kahneman and Tversky (2000); Kuhn (1970); Simon (1957, 1978); Thaler and Sunstein (2009); Tversky and Fox (2000); and Tversky and Kahneman (2000).

or epistemological consideration. But it is this aspect of paradigms that constitutes both their strength and their weakness— their strength in that it makes action possible, their weakness in that the very reason for action is hidden in the unquestioned assumptions of the paradigm. This is now widely understood and generally accepted, but it is worth taking a moment to revisit the insights of Thomas Kuhn (1970) regarding how paradigms work. This excerpt is from his influential classic *The Structure of Scientific Revolutions*:

> Scientists work from models acquired through education and subsequent exposure to the literature, often without quite knowing or needing to know what characteristics have given these models the status of community paradigms. . . . That scientists do not usually ask or debate what makes a particular problem or solution legitimate tempts us to suppose that, at least intuitively, they know the answer. But it may only indicate that neither the question nor the answer is felt to be relevant to their research. Paradigms may be prior to, more binding, and more complete than any set of

rules for research that could be unequivocally abstracted from them. (p. 46)

That's what we're up against when we set forth the ideal of matching the evaluation to the nature of the situation. I repeat, then: *developmental evaluation is not appropriate for every situation.* This book will detail when it is appropriate. Chapter 7, for example, looks at when and how a developmental evaluation may generate a promising model that an innovator wants to take to scale, so the appropriate evaluation of that model becomes traditional formative and summative evaluation to assess its scalability and capacity for dissemination. It is also worth noting that developmental evaluation may appear alien to evaluators trained only in the traditional and dominant evaluation research paradigm, so it can evoke their hostility. The stakes can be high. Reactions to paradigm departures can be fierce. Evaluation distinctions matter because evaluation matters in this manic and politicized world of outcomes accountability. More on that later, too. So here's where we're headed.

"*Ladies and gentlemen, the chicken, and, in a related development, the egg.*"

Charting the Developmental Journey: Overview of the Book

Chapter 2, *Developmental Evaluation as a Distinct Purpose and Niche*, looks more deeply at the role and distinct contributions of developmental evaluation, including the implications of offering an option beyond formative and summative evaluation, the classic distinctions that have dominated evaluation for four decades. There are two distinct niches for developmental evaluation. The first is to support exploration and innovation *before* there is a program model to improve and summatively test. In that sense, developmental evaluation is preformative, but can lead to generation of a model that is subsequently evaluated formatively and summatively. The second niche is for those dynamic situations, like the one involving the leadership program example discussed earlier in this chapter, where program staff and funders expect to keep developing and adapting the program, so they never intend to conduct a final summative evaluation of a standardized and hypothesized best practice model. This niche is nonsummative in that it doesn't render an overall judgment of merit and worth about whether a model is effective and worthy of adoption by others, but rather supports ongoing real-time decisions about what to change, expand, close out, or further develop. The chapter will emphasize the differences between improvement versus development, and the implications of that distinction for evaluation practice. We'll also look at ongoing strategic thinking versus periodic strategic planning, positioning developmental evaluation as a form of thinking and acting strategically as an innovative intervention unfolds.

Chapter 3, *Thinking Outside Evaluation's Boxes*, introduces an extensive case example of program development and evaluation's role in supporting that development. The case illustrates and deepens our understanding of the implications of distinguishing program *improvement* from program *de-velopment*, while opening up discussion of developmental evaluation facilitated and conducted by both internal and external evaluators (it can be done by either or by both together). The case example illustrates some of the constraints that arise in complex development situations when traditional evaluation approaches are inappropriately imposed. In looking at situational responsiveness and matching an evaluation to the circumstances in which the program is operating and unfolding, we'll consider the pragmatic questions: *What is sensible evaluation? How do we decide what makes sense? What does it mean to be pragmatic?* This requires considering dominant notions of accountability and common barriers to evaluation utility and actual use, including cautions about misevaluation, misuse, and corruption of evaluation. The chapter closes with 10 key points about developmental evaluation illustrated by the case example. These include the importance of timely engagement and rapid feedback, and how evaluation can become the engine for program development such that ongoing program development and evaluation become mutually reinforcing, a way of doing business—indeed, a way of thinking. Project leadership and support for doing developmental evaluation are crucial, as are competent evaluators attuned to the challenges of developmental evaluation.

Chapter 4, *Situation Recognition and Responsiveness*, provides a framework for distinguishing simple, complicated, and complex situations, and the evaluation implications of these distinctions. *Complexity* is defined as those situations where uncertainty about what to do is high because both knowledge is insufficient and key stakeholders are in substantial conflict. The dynamics and uncertainties of complex adaptive systems make what to do to solve problems and change systems essentially *unknowable* in advance—thus the need for trying things out and quickly assessing what happens and what emerges, both intended and unintended, to inform the next steps in exploration, experimentation, innovation, and development.

The chapter closes with an evaluator's guide to decision making about design priorities matched to different contexts (simple, complicated, and complex).

Chapter 5, *Systems Thinking and Complexity Concepts for Developmental Evaluation*, opens with an excursion into systems thinking and its implications for evaluation, especially in contrast to the linear logic models that so completely dominate current evaluation thinking. Logic models have contributed tremendously to clarifying the IT question in evaluation: When we say IT works, or IT doesn't work, what is the IT? The program logic model describes the IT, which is why it has become the dominant and preferred tool in designing evaluations. But the very notion of an IT connotes a static, fixed, and mechanical cause–effect model where inputs lead to activities, which lead to outputs, which produce outcomes and impacts. That works well in simple situations of high certainty and high agreement about what to do. But such modeling has significant downsides and distorting effects in complex and dynamic situations where the IT is emergent, evolving, and adapting. Systems thinking and mapping offers an alternative to linear logic modeling. Having established that alternative framework, we'll examine the implications for developmental evaluation of the six characteristics of complex adaptive systems presented in Exhibit 1.1: nonlinearity, emergence, dynamic systems, adaptiveness, uncertainty, and coevolutionary processes.

Chapter 6, *How the World Is Changed: A Dialectic*, opens by considering the thesis that the world is changed top-down through widespread dissemination of best practices (a predominant theory of change). The antithesis or opposing proposition is that the world is changed bottom-up through grassroots adaptations of effective principles attuned to local contexts. I proceed to reject both the thesis and the antithesis and propose a complexity-sensitive, developmental evaluation synthesis position: *In the global village, change occurs in the middle where top-down and bottom-up forces collide, intersect, get entangled together, do battle, and otherwise encounter real-world complexities.* In considering this action-in-the-middle synthesis, we'll distinguish best practices from effective principles as a form of evaluation finding, and examine the implications of the distinction for both theories of change and evaluation results. We'll look at how this action-in-the-middle played out in an actual program example. The chapter concludes:

> When the primary source of change is bottom-up, the developmental evaluator helps local innovators take a broader systems perspective, including understanding and attending to larger cross-scale forces that can affect the success of local action, helping them draw on knowledge and principles from elsewhere. When the primary source of change is top-down, the developmental evaluator helps conceptualize and test local adaptations, as appropriate. When the sources for change are simultaneously top-down ("It's blowin' in the wind") and bottom-up ("All politics is local"), the developmental evaluator helps facilitate and navigate the interactive dynamics of the muddled middle.

Chapter 6 also looks at developmental evaluation of networks of change (in contrast to programs and discrete interventions). The chapter concludes with further elaboration of developmental evaluation questions for different situations.

Chapter 7, *The Adaptive Cycle and Developmental Evaluation*, looks at the concept of and research on ecosystem resilience and its implications for both social innovation and developmental evaluation. Ecologists studying the health and resilience of forests have found that these complex ecological systems adapt to fires, disease, and periods of drought through four phases that make up a recurring adaptive cycle: *release* (forest fire or other destruction); *reorganization/exploration* (new growth); *exploitation* (accelerated growth of some varieties over others in the competition for resources); and *conservation* (a mature forest dominated by one species).

This cycling through phases, with major transitions from one stage to another, can be observed not only in healthy ecosystems, but also in resilient social systems. However, if adaptation doesn't occur from one phase to another, the health of the system, or the organization, is threatened. The adaptive cycle has significant implications for evaluation with different approaches to and types of evaluation appropriate for different phases of the adaptive cycle. Developmental evaluation is especially well suited for the reorganization/exploration phase. This chapter aims to deepen our understanding of what it means to match evaluation to particular situations, and offers another framework for doing so. I'll also use the adaptive cycle to discuss and illustrate how developmental evaluation can generate an intervention model that leads to formative and then summative evaluation as an innovation moves through the phases of the cycle.

Chapter 8 examines *Developmental Evaluation Inquiry Frameworks*. Developmental evaluation focuses on developmental questions: What's being developed? How is what's being developed (what's emerging) to be judged? Given what's been developed so far (what has emerged), what's next? The developmental evaluator inquires into *developments*, tracks *developments*, facilitates interpretation of *developments* and their significance, and engages with innovators, change agents, program staff, participants in the process, and funders around making judgments about what is being developed, what has been developed, and the next stages of development. That's the broad panorama. But within that broad panorama, specific questions relevant to specific developmental process and impacts still have to be generated. And there are lots and lots of frameworks for generating and focusing questions. Since a dominant theme throughout the book is situational matching, this chapter offers guidance in how to decide which questions to use to frame a developmental evaluation inquiry. We'll look at 10 distinct inquiry frameworks as examples of alternative ways of focusing developmental evaluations based on the dynamics of the complex situation in which the evaluation is being undertaken and the predilections and worldviews of those engaged in social innovation.

Chapter 9, *Developmental Evaluation Bricolage*, is about the developmental evaluator as *bricoleur*, a kind of jack-of-all-trades do-it-yourself person who draws on eclectic traditions and integrates diverse approaches to get the job done usefully in a way that fits the situation at hand. The *bricolage* in the chapter will include reflective practice, action research, sensitizing concepts, abductive reasoning, systems change, methodological diversity, and retrospective developmental evaluation. We will look in depth at how reflective practice focused on an innovative sensitizing concept (like the idea of *innovation* itself, or systems change, or social justice) can be a powerful developmental evaluation approach for facilitating ongoing learning, engagement, and adaptation. We'll also take a brief look at pragmatism as one of the epistemological underpinnings for developmental evaluation.

Finally, Chapter 10 examines *Utilization-Focused Developmental Evaluation*, with a look at the implications of focusing on intended use by intended users for engagement practices, diverse designs, and adaptive methods. Developmental evaluation does not rely on any particular evaluation method, design, or tool. A developmental evaluation can include any kind of data (quantitative, qualitative, mixed), any kind of design (e.g., naturalistic, experimental), and any kind of focus (processes, outcomes, impacts, costs, and cost–benefit, among many possibilities), depending on the nature and stage of an innovation and the priority questions that will support development of and decision making about the innovation. This can include randomized controlled trials, surveys, focus groups, interviews, observations, performance data, community indicators, network analysis—whatever sheds light on key questions. Given the infinite possibilities, Chap-

⌒ *Developmental Evaluation versus Development Evaluation*

Developmental evaluation is easily confused with development evaluation. They are not the same, though developmental evaluation can be used in development evaluations. Confused? You are not alone. Read on.

Development evaluation is a generic term for evaluations conducted in developing countries, usually focused on the effectiveness of international aid programs and agencies (e.g., Carlsson, Eriksson-Baaz, Fallenius, & Lövgren, 1999; De Coninck, Chaturvedi, Haagsma, Griffioen, & van der Glas, 2008; Hanna & Picciotto, 2002; Independent Evaluation Group, 2009; Picciotto, 2002). *The Road to Results: Designing and Conducting Development Evaluations* (Imas & Rist, 2009) is an exemplar of this genre, a book based on the World Bank's highly successful International Program for Development Evaluation Training (IPDET), which the book's authors founded and direct, and on which their book is based. Full disclosure: I have been on the IPDET faculty since the program began.

Developmental evaluation, as defined and described in the *Encyclopedia of Evaluation* (Mathison, 2005, p. 116), has the purpose of helping develop an innovation, intervention, or program. In developmental evaluation the evaluator typically becomes part of the program or innovation design team, fully participating in decisions and facilitating discussion about how to evaluate whatever happens. All team members together interpret evaluation findings, analyze implications, and apply results to the next stage of development. The evaluator becomes involved in improving the intervention and uses evaluative approaches to facilitate ongoing program, project, product, staff, and/or organizational *development*. The evaluator's primary function in the team is to facilitate and elucidate team discussions by infusing evaluative questions, data, and logic, and to support data-based decision making in the developmental process. In this regard, developmental evaluation is analogous to research and development (R & D) units in which the evaluative perspective is internalized in and integrated into the operating unit. In playing the role of developmental evaluator, the evaluator helps make an intervention's development an R & D activity.

Part of the value of an experienced developmental evaluator to an innovation team is bringing a reservoir of knowledge (based on many years of practice and having read a great many evaluation reports) about what kinds of things tend to work and where to anticipate problems. Experienced evaluators have typically accumulated a great deal of knowledge and wisdom about what works and what doesn't work. More generally, as a profession, the field of evaluation has generated a great deal of knowledge about patterns of effectiveness. That knowledge makes evaluators valuable partners in designing as well as evaluating social innovations.

An evaluation focused on development assistance in developing countries could use a developmental evaluation approach, especially if such developmental assistance is viewed as occurring under conditions of complexity with a focus on adaptation to local context. Many of the examples in this book are of development evaluations, especially Chapter 3. But developmental evaluations are by no means limited to projects in developing countries. Developmental evaluation can be used anywhere that social innovators are engaged in bringing about systems change under conditions of complexity.

The *al* in *developmental* is easily missed, but it is critical in distinguishing development evaluation from developmental evaluation.

(cont.)

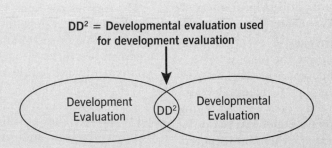

DD² = Developmental evaluation used for development evaluation

When I first labeled and wrote about *developmental evaluation* 15 years ago (Patton, 1994), development evaluation was not a distinct and visible category of evaluation practice and scholarship. Evaluations in developing countries were certainly being conducted, but an identifiable body of literature focused on evaluating development assistance had not attracted general professional attention. One of the most important trends of the last decade has been the rapid diffusion of evaluation throughout the world (Patton, 2008c, chap. 1), including especially the developing world, highlighted by formation of the International Development Evaluation Association (IDEAS, 2009), which launched in Beijing, China, in 2002.

Confusion about the distinct and sometimes overlapping niches of development evaluation and developmental evaluation is now, I'm afraid, part of the complex landscape of international evaluation. I hope this book helps sort out both the distinctions and the areas of overlap.

ter 10 presents 10 developmental evaluation engagement approaches and evaluation designs that are particularly appropriate for different complex systems challenges. The examples are meant to be generative and suggestive of the great variety of methods that can be used, not by any means prescriptive or exhaustive of design and methods possibilities. The specific developmental evaluation examples will be presented in a utilization-focused evaluation template so that for each example the following are specified: nature of the complex systems challenge; primary developmental purpose; primary intended users and developmental evaluation partners; key developmental evaluation questions; time line for feedback; and appropriate matching developmental evaluation engagement approach, design, and methods options. Examples presented will include rapid feedback interviews with program participants, bellwether surveys of influential policymakers, participatory action research, social network analysis, and randomized comparison trials of advocacy campaign messages.

Five Developmental Evaluation Purposes and Uses

As the book unfolds, I'll be making the case that developmental evaluation is particularly appropriate for but needs to be matched to five different complex situations and developmental purposes.

1. *Ongoing development* in adapting a project, program, strategy, policy, or other innovative initiative to new conditions in complex dynamic systems (the focus of Chapters 2, 3, 4, and 5).

2. *Adapting effective general principles to a new context* as ideas and innovations are taken from elsewhere and developed within a new setting, the work of developmental evaluation in the dynamic middle between top-down and bottom-up forces of change (the focus of Chapter 6).

3. *Developing a rapid response* in the face of a sudden major change or a crisis, like a natural disaster or financial meltdown, exploring real-time solutions and gen-

erating innovative and helpful interventions for those in need.

4. *Preformative development of a potentially scalable innovation* to the point where it is ready for traditional formative and summative evaluation; preformative developmental evaluation works with emerging ideas and visionary hopes in a period of exploration to shape them into a potential model that is a more fully conceptualized, potentially scalable intervention. (As models emerge out of exploratory and innovative initiatives, some may move into more traditional formative and summative evaluation to determine scalability and generalizability, while others remain in developmental mode, either undergoing further development or continuous experimentation in the search for new models.)

5. *Major systems change and cross-scale developmental evaluation*, providing feedback about how major systems change is unfolding, evidence of emergent tipping points, and/or how an innovation is or may need to be changed and adapted as it is taken to scale, that is, as its principles are shared and disseminated in an effort to have broader impact (discussed in Chapter 7). Horizontal scaling across systems or vertical scaling to broader systems may involve more than adaptation; these dissemination and scaling processes can evolve an essentially new development, the emergence of which can be documented and analyzed as part of a developmental evaluation.

Exhibit 10.1 at the beginning of Chapter 10 summarizes these five purposes including identifying particular complex systems challenges that give rise to each, primary specific developmental evaluation uses appropriate for each type, real-world examples of each with specific primary intended users for each type, and the implications of the different types for evaluation and social innovation.

Throughout the book I'll be positioning developmental evaluation as serving these five particular purposes and uses that, taken together, are different approaches for and windows into developing and evaluating social innovations. These five different uses of developmental evaluation match different situations. They provide different lenses through which to understand and engage in evaluating social innovations under conditions of complexity. Taken together they constitute a specific niche in the large and diverse field of evaluation.

Exhibit 1.2 provides an overview of the niche of developmental evaluation. I've contrasted developmental evaluation generally with some broad-brush traditional approaches to evaluation to help position developmental evaluation in the many-starred evaluation universe. These comparisons and contrasts are meant to be suggestive and illuminative, not definitive. Any one contrast is arguable, possibly overgeneralized, and oversimplified. Viewed as a whole, however, I hope the integration of these many elements provides a sense of what developmental evaluation offers.

But Exhibit 1.2 presents a lot of elements to keep track of and put together. So, bottom line: *How can you tell if an evaluation is truly developmental?* I'll offer a more sophisticated answer as the book unfolds, but let's start simply with purpose and outcomes: *Is the purpose and focus of the evaluation helping develop something? Is something getting developed? Did something get developed? If so, what? How? With what implications?* The focus of developmental evaluation is on (drum roll, please) *developing innovations*.

To borrow an old saying, the proof of the pudding is *in the eating.* Since the next chapter distinguishes *developments* from *improvements*, and will position developmental evaluation as different in important ways from formative and summative evaluation, let me offer this segue. Distinguished evaluation theorist and practitioner Bob Stake has explained, "When the cook tastes the soup, that's formative; when the guests taste the soup, that's summa-

EXHIBIT 1.2 Contrasts between Traditional Evaluations and Complexity-Sensitive Developmental Evaluation

Introduction and cautionary note: Evaluation is a diverse field with many models, approaches, methods, and purposes. Any generalizations about predominant tendencies in *traditional* evaluation (both formative and summative) are bound to be overgeneralizations. These contrasts are offered as a heuristic device to suggest thematic tendencies and general distinctions. The themes in the right column define developmental evaluation's niche. To focus that niche, I've contrasted developmental evaluation with some broad-brush traditional approaches to help position developmental evaluation in the many-starred evaluation universe. In doing so I emphasize that these comparisons and contrasts are meant to be suggestive and illuminative, not definitive. Any one contrast is arguable and oversimplified, and may not apply to a particular situation. Viewed as a whole, however, I hope the integration of these many elements provides a sense of what developmental evaluation offers in toto—and in tone.

	Traditional program evaluation tendencies	Complexity-sensitive developmental evaluation
1. Purpose and situation		
1.1. Evaluation purposes	Formative–summative distinction dominant: formative improves; summative tests, proves, and validates program models; accountability.	Supports *development* of innovations and adaptation of interventions in dynamic environments.
1.2. Situation where it is appropriate	Manageable and stable situation; root cause of the problem being addressed is known and bounded; intervention reasonably well conceptualized; goals known; the key variables expected to affect outcomes are controllable, measurable, and predictable.	Complex, dynamic environment; no known solution to priority problems; no certain way forward and multiple pathways possible; need for innovation, exploration, and social experimentation.
1.3. Dominant niche and mindset	Finding out if a program model works: focus on effectiveness, efficiency, impact, and scalability.	Exploring possibilities; generating ideas and trying them out; preformal model, so preformative; nonsummative in that ongoing innovation and development is expected, never arriving at a fixed intervention.
2. Focus and target of evaluation		
2.1. Target of change	Identified outcomes for intended program beneficiaries and participants; change in individual behaviors and performance indicators.	Systems change along a continuum from small local systems to disruptive social innovations aimed at major, cross-scale impacts on big problems.

(cont.)

	Traditional program evaluation tendencies	Complexity-sensitive developmental evaluation
2.2. Driving force of the intervention	Outcomes-driven; systems viewed as context.	Systems-change-driven; specific outcomes emergent, dynamic.
2.3. Evaluation results focus	*Formative*: improve and fine-tune the model; prepare for summative evaluation. *Summative*: Render overall judgments of merit and worth, success or failure.	*Development*: provide timely feedback for development; generate learnings and support action in the development process.
2.4. Evaluation locus	Evaluation is top-down (theory-driven) or bottom-up (participatory).	Evaluation helps innovators navigate *the muddled middle* where top-down and bottom-up forces intersect and often collide.
3. Modeling and methods		
3.1. Modeling approach	Design the evaluation based on a linear cause–effect logic model: specify inputs to activities/ processes, then outputs to outcomes to impacts. Causality is modeled, hypothesized, and predicted, then tested.	Design the evaluation using systems thinking to capture and map *complex systems dynamics* and interdependencies, and track emergent interconnections. Causality is based on pattern detection (inference to the best explanation), retrospectively constructed from observations.
3.2. Counterfactuals	Counterfactuals a dominant concern to deal with attribution.	Counterfactual formulations meaningless because of complexity: far too many variables and possibilities emerging and interacting dynamically to conceptualize simple counterfactuals.
3.3. Measurement approach	Measure performance and success against predetermined goals and SMART outcomes: specific, measurable, achievable, realistic, and time-bound.	Develops measures and tracking mechanisms quickly as outcomes emerge; measures can change during the evaluation as the process unfolds. Tracking the forks in the road and implications of key decisions as innovation evolves.
3.4. Attention to unexpected consequences	Typically token attention, if any at all, to unanticipated consequences and side effects.	Expect the unexpected. Serious attention to the unanticipated and emergent as a fundamental evaluation function.

(cont.)

	Traditional program evaluation tendencies	Complexity-sensitive developmental evaluation
3.5. Evaluation design responsibility	Evaluator determines the design based on the evaluator's perspective about what is rigorous. The evaluator has responsibility for and controls the evaluation even when and if stakeholder input is solicited.	Evaluator collaborates with those engaged in the change effort to *co-create* an evaluation that is useful and matches the innovation process philosophically and organizationally.
3.6. Methods approach and philosophy	*Rigorously methods-focused*: an evaluation is judged by validity and methodological criteria first and foremost; utility is viewed as methods-dependent. Traditional research and disciplinary standards of quality dominate.	*Utilization-focused*: methods are chosen in service to developmental use; methods derive from utility and pragmatic considerations; judgments about methodological quality are context-and-intended-use-dependent.
3.7. Interpretation and reasoning processes	Deduction first and foremost; some induction some of the time if qualitative methods used. Attribution analysis.	Abduction (inference to the best explanation) and pragmatism (discussed in Chapter 9). Contribution analysis.

4. Roles and relationships

4.1. Ideal evaluator stance	Evaluator is independent, whether located internally or externally. Credibility depends on independence.	Evaluator is part of the innovation team, a facilitator and learning coach, bringing evaluative thinking to the group, supportive of the innovators' values and vision. Credibility depends on a mutually respectful relationship.
4.2. Locus and focus of accountability	Accountability focused on and directed to external authorities and funders based on explicit preordinate criteria.	Accountability centered on the innovators' deep sense of fundamental values and commitment to make a difference; funders must buy into what gets developed and learned as the focus of accountability.
4.3. Organizational locus of evaluation	Evaluation often a compliance function delegated down in the organization and/or outside to an external evaluator.	Evaluation a leadership function: nurturing *reality-testing, results-focused, learning-oriented leadership*.

(cont.)

	Traditional program evaluation tendencies	Complexity-sensitive developmental evaluation
5. Evaluation results and impacts		
5.1. Desired and ideal evaluation findings	Validated best practices, generalizable across time and space.	Effective principles that can inform practice and minimum specifications (*min specs*) that can be adapted to local context.
5.2. Evaluation approach to a going-to-scale initiative or model dissemination	In evaluating dissemination of models and taking "best practices" to scale, the focus is on high-fidelity replication.	In evaluating dissemination and going to scale, the focus is on applying principles and adaptation to local context.
5.3. Reporting mode	Often ponderous, detailed formal reports; scholarly voice (third person, passive).	Rapid, real-time feedback. Engaged, present voice (first person, active).
5.4. Impact of evaluation on organizational culture	Evaluation often engenders *fear of failure*.	Evaluation aims to nurture *hunger for learning*.
5.5. Evaluation capacity built through the evaluation process	Usually not an objective; the focus is on getting credible evaluation results based on rigorous methods.	Building ongoing and long-term capacity to think and engage evaluatively is built into the process.
6. Approaches to complexity		
6.1. Approach to uncertainty	Aims for as much certainty and predictability as possible.	Expects uncertainty and unpredictability as givens in complex and dynamic situations.
6.2. Approach to control	Evaluator attempts to control design implementation and the evaluation process.	Learning to respond *to lack of control*; staying in touch with what's unfolding and responding accordingly—and agilely.
7. Professional qualities		
7.1. Key evaluator attributes	Methodological competence and commitment to rigor; independence; credibility with external authorities and funders; analytical and critical thinking.	Methodological flexibility, eclecticism, and adaptability; systems thinking: creative and critical thinking balanced; *high tolerance for ambiguity*; open and agile. Teamwork and people skills: able to facilitate rigorous evidence-based reflection to inform action.
7.2. Evaluation standards and ethics	Knowledgeable about and committed to evaluation's professional standards.	Knowledgeable about and committed to evaluation's professional standards.

tive" (quoted in Scriven, 1991, p. 169). More generally, anything done to the soup during preparation in the kitchen is improvement-oriented; when the soup is served, summative judgment is rendered by the guests who consume the soup. And what of developmental evaluation in this metaphor?

Developmental evaluation begins when, before cooking, the chef goes to the market to see what vegetables are freshest, what fish has just arrived, and meanders through the market considering possibilities, thinking about who the guests will be, what they were served last time, what the weather is like, and considers how adventurous and innovative to be with the meal. If the chef decides to follow a standard recipe, the situation remains appropriate for formative and summative evaluations based on fidelity to the prescribed recipe. If the chef decides to attempt a new creation, innovate, and develop a new dish especially well suited for these particular guests in the context of this particular evening, then the situation opens up the possibility for creativity and developmental evaluation. And when a guest and a cook create and concoct a soup together, that co-creation is developmental.

Bon appétit.

2

Developmental Evaluation as a Distinct Purpose and Niche

The business world, appropriately, emphasizes the bottom line. When Peter Drucker, the business management guru, turned his attention to the nonprofit sector, he was asked about their bottom line. He said it came down to two words: *Changed lives.*

Steve Rothschild had a vision. He wanted to reduce poverty by providing corporate employers with chronically underemployed or unemployed workers, especially men of color, helping them get and keep jobs paying a livable wage plus benefits.[1] Rothschild would bring to this vision considerable success in the business world. He is a former executive vice president of General Mills, and president of its yogurt subsidiary, where he led the campaign that made Yoplait the number-one yogurt brand in the United States. He wanted to apply his knowledge, experience, and success in the private sector to alleviating poverty.

Rothschild was referred to me by the McKnight Foundation, headquartered in

Minneapolis, because I had just completed a synthesis evaluation of 34 projects McKnight had funded in a major Aid to Families in Poverty initiative. He asked me to join an informal advisory group of diverse experts from government, not-for-profits, community organizing, consulting, corporations, universities, and political activists to help plan his initiative and develop an approach that could be taken to potential funders. The result was a major antipoverty training and employment program called Twin Cities Rise!

Rothschild brought to this effort a strong commitment to making a difference. In our first meeting, when I cautioned him that he was moving into an arena where many had tried and few had succeeded, he was undaunted and emphasized that the challenge appealed to him, much as the challenges of building the Yoplait business had almost 20 years earlier. He saw this new enterprise as a good fit with his intense desire to give some-

---

[1] "In 2009, the official US poverty threshold for a family of four was $22,050. In Minnesota, one fifth of families of color had incomes below this threshold" (*aspe.hhs.gov/poverty/09poverty.shtml*). For one approach to computing a livable wage, see *www.universallivingwage.org.*

thing of value and importance back to the community in return for his own good fortune. He was becoming what is called in the parlance of today a *social innovator.*

He brought to this initiative not only his corporate success and connections, but also experience with philanthropy and the not-for-profit sector. During his last 5 years at General Mills he had served on the board of the company's philanthropic foundation, one of the country's top corporate foundations, financed consistently with about 3% of pretax profits. He also served as a board member, and then chair, of Minnesota Public Radio (MPR), one of the most successful public radio enterprises in the country. In the sessions with the advisory committee he interwove vision, inspiration, and creativity with hard-core analysis, critical thinking, and thoughtful planning. He had reviewed and was openly critical of existing nonprofit and government-supported employment training programs. He was prepared to invest his own resources in this effort, put his credibility on the line, and visibly demonstrate a new way to do things.

The Twin Cities Rise! program that emerged focused on creating a self-supporting private–public partnership that would meet the needs of corporate employers seeking a skilled and diverse workforce. Coaches would work with chronically unemployed but motivated men of color to connect them with training, education, and counseling as needed, enhancing both hard skills (what they could do) and soft skills (positive attitudes and behaviors). The program would connect employers with potential employees and assure that the needs of both were met. Participants would undergo thorough assessment to determine their capabilities and needs.

The advisory group realized that the stakes were high and urged careful, detailed planning. The university professor in the group urged designing the demonstration as a randomized control trial with participants assigned to an experimental treatment group (those admitted to the program) and a control group (those put on a waiting list for later admission). The advisory group's advice reflected traditional wisdom and standard planning prescriptions. I offered different advice. I advised developing a set of principles that would guide program development but not to over-plan. "It won't make much difference what you plan," I insisted. "It won't be right. Just start working with a small group, learn what works, and make corrections as you go. And it's quite premature to even think about an experimental design. The program needs to get developed before it is subjected to such a formal, rigorous test. It will probably take years to get to that stage." Vigorous debate ensued.

Beyond Planning: Jumping into the Fire

No battle plan ever survives contact with the enemy.
—HELMUTH KARL BERNARD VON MOLTKE, chief of staff of the Prussian Army

Everyone has a plan . . . until he gets hit.
—MIKE TYSON, former world heavyweight boxing champion

In the early years of the program, Rothschild and staff were engaged in what management guru Tom Peters (1996) advocated in his book *Liberation Management* as READY. FIRE. AIM. The heavy planning mode, in contrast, is Ready. Aim. Aim. Aim. . . . "Ready, fire, aim" is the essence of what I was advising when I told Rothschild to open the program without more planning (he had already done quite a bit), experiment, pay attention to what happens, be ferocious about getting feedback, and learn by doing. Such advice runs counter to the conventional wisdom that extensive planning (aiming) should precede action. But detailed planning only works where you have a high degree of control and know what the critical factors are. Moreover, the costs of a detailed planning process in relation to its likely benefits need to be part of the calculation about how much planning to do. Costs include opportunity costs, the frustration of delays, and lost momentum when doors have opened, people are ready, and the innovators sense that the time to act is now. What might otherwise seem ill-advised and precipitous action can be undertaken with greater comfort (including easing the anxiety of funders) if the action is accompanied by a strong commitment to developmental evaluation to help in ascending the steep learning curve that successful innovators must be prepared to climb. Under conditions of high innovation, uncertainty rules the day. Control freaks perish. Paradoxically, one of the advantages of "Ready, fire, aim" can be a high and rapid failure rate that facilitates fast learning and speedily moving on (Shirky, 2007). Or as Irish author Samuel Beckett (1906–1989) poetically put it:

> Ever tried. Ever failed. No matter.
> Try again. Fail again. Fail better.

Evaluation Questions under Different Engagement Scenarios

When the complexity of the problem and the environment in which it prevails call for engagement based on "Ready, fire, aim," the evaluation questions are: What did you hit? How do you know? And what are the implications for what you do next? These are the questions the developmental evaluator keeps before social innovators as the process unfolds in a series of ready/fire/aim explorations.

Traditional goal-based evaluation is completely geared to *Ready, aim, fire*. The evaluator determines whether the preconceived target was hit. That's what evaluators have been trained to do and, on the whole, they do it well. What they aren't prepared for and typically don't know how to adjust to is social innovators whose entrepreneurial and creative mode of operating is *Ready, fire, aim*. The developmental evaluator still

figures out what was hit, if anything, and the systems implications of any hits, that is, watching for and documenting consequences for other things connected to the social innovation effort, but the analysis is not a simple measure of what was hit compared to a preconceived target. In providing feedback about what the innovator has "hit" (what immediate outcomes are *emerging*), the developmental evaluator engages the innovator by asking: What's your reaction to what you've hit so far? And what you've missed? What does this "hit" tell you? How does what you've done so far align with your values and vision? What does this "hit" (or "miss") tell you about what to do next? Why? This augments and intensifies the innovators' own intuitive processes with pointed questioning and systematic data to interpret progress (and setbacks), and formulate new hypotheses and next steps. Social innovators tend to be so busy engaging that they fail to systematically track what is developing and document the reasons they choose one path over another at critical forks along the innovation road. The developmental evaluation helps identify the dynamics and contextual factors that make the situation complex, then captures decisions made in the face of complexity, tracks their implications, feeds back data about what's emerging, and pushes for analysis and reflection to inform next steps, and then the cycle repeats.

Vision Encounters Reality: The Territory of Developmental Evaluation

My advice to Steve Rothschild to articulate guiding principles and get on with doing and learning, and cut short the planning phase, was not based on antiplanning screeds. What was the source of my unorthodox advice? When I met Rothschild the findings from my synthesis evaluation of 34 antipoverty projects were fresh in my mind. The McKnight Foundation had selected these projects through a competitive

"I'm neither a good cop nor a bad cop, Jerome. Like yourself, I'm a complex amalgam of positive and negative personality traits that emerge or not, depending on circumstances."

© Mick Stevens/Condé Nast Publications/*www.cartoonbank.com.*

proposal process. The combination of the foundation's prestige, the opportunity for well-funded, multiple-year grants, and the invitation to be innovative attracted proposals from many of the most experienced and knowledgeable people and organizations in Minnesota engaged in antipoverty work. The best thinkers about these issues took their best shot. They planned carefully and brought enormous in-the-trenches experience to these projects. And *not one of them unfolded as planned.* Not even close in most cases.

Even staff who had been working with people in poverty for a long time reported a steep learning curve in implementing new, innovative proposals. They had to adapt their plans to the realities of the people who entered their programs and the complex dynamics of the larger context within which they worked, for example, reforms in welfare policy, a revised federal definition of poverty, souring of the political climate, and the depressed state of the job market. Whether the focus was teenagers in poor families, underemployed people in low-wage jobs, mothers on welfare, divorced fathers

not paying child support, child care providers, or low-income parents with young children, the program staff had to be open to major adjustments and alter what they had planned to do to be effective. Those adjustments were grounded in extensive questioning of and careful listening to the people who came to their programs. Nor were such interactions a one-time event done only at intake. Assessment of a family situation typically unfolded over months. Core problems were often not evident at the initial screening. Trust had to be developed to get beyond surface appearances to fundamental issues. It took time to understand enough about a family's dynamics to put together a meaningful, workable change plan.

A major finding in the early implementation evaluations of the McKnight programs was the challenge of adapting to the unanticipated severity of participants' social and economic situations. Many families in poverty were in crisis when they applied to a program, but, having astutely figured out eligibility requirements, they hid the nature and extent of their crisis to qualify for admission and services. As participants revealed the crises that they had understated at intake but that preoccupied them, program staff learned it was essential to deal with participants' crises before moving on to longer-term goals, even though they aimed at and thought they were recruiting and admitting participants and families that were *not* in crisis. Making this kind of learning systematic and rigorous is a function of developmental evaluation. In the McKnight programs I regularly facilitated reflective practice sessions across the 34 programs to identify and extract lessons being learned and the implications of those lessons for ongoing development. (Chapter 9 discusses in some depth reflective practice as a developmental evaluation method.)

Poverty is complex. It is well documented that poverty in the United States is often associated with a plethora of problems including family violence, chemical dependency, physical and sexual abuse, inadequate nutrition, and personal feelings of anger, despair, and alienation. A program with a focus on job training, parenting, or schooling would find that it had to deal in some way with families' personal problems or living situation—for example, getting adequate food and housing—*before* progress could be made on the program's targeted outcomes. Different programs dealt with these challenges in different ways, as did Twin Cities Rise!, but they all had to learn a great deal about their participants to decide how best to respond—and whether to respond at all.

Rothschild's Twin Cities Rise! program would subsequently encounter this same steep learning curve and find that their initial assessments of participants had to be adjusted and readjusted as trust was built and new issues surfaced. They found that participants who entered the program had more difficulties making progress than had been expected, often because they came from more difficult situations than they had acknowledged when applying for entry to the program. In my role as developmental evaluator, I helped capture what was being learned and its implications for how the program was evolving, including implications for recruitment, assessment, and intake into the program; what kinds of staff were needed; what services were added to meet emergent needs; changing costs; and consequences for outcomes. Those familiar with lessons from effective antipoverty programs (e.g., Schorr, 1989, 1997) will note that this learning curve has been traveled before by others. But it is one thing to know from the research and evaluation literature that it takes time to build trust. It is another thing altogether to experience that challenge with real people in real time. Wisdom from those who have gone before can alert innovators to what to watch for, and can accelerate the climb up the learning curve, as I'll emphasize in Chapter 6, but some things just have to be relearned and adapted in the context of a new effort. This involves moving from abstract principles (*building trust takes time*) to action in context (building trust with OUR clients in OUR program takes this amount of time and involves these specific issues).

This point is worth reiterating because it is a source of contention and pushback from those who believe that better planning is the answer. Once the Twin Cities Rise! program got under way, staff did learn anew that participants had more problems, and more severe problems, than they had originally anticipated. Experienced social workers who know the story have insisted to me that the program's developers and staff *should have* anticipated that chronically unemployed men of color would come with multiple and severe problems, and planned for that eventuality. Point taken—and easy to assert in hindsight. But the advisory committee and staff believed that innovative approaches to screening, in-depth assessment, and individual coaching would make it different this time. Advance anticipation of what might happen is a tricky business at best and in general we're not very good at it (Morell, 2010), especially under conditions of complexity.

〜 *Advice from an Experienced Developmental Evaluator*

Throughout this book I'll be sharing advice from experienced developmental evaluators in response to the question "What would you tell someone new to developmental evaluation about doing it? Advice? Caveats? Potentials? Pitfalls? Lessons? Challenges?" Ehren Reed is a senior associate with Innovation Network and a specialist in evaluating advocacy and policy change efforts. His experience mirrors my own developmental evaluation work with Twin Cities Rise!, the program featured in this chapter.

BUILDING TRUST

One of the underlying premises of developmental evaluation involves a reconfiguration of the relationship between the evalua*tor* and the evalua*ted*. In developmental evaluation, the evaluator not only has a seat at the table but a voice in meetings to inform strategy and future direction. The term "embedded evaluator" has occasionally been employed to describe this role. In other words, the evaluation is no longer an external observation of the strategies being employed but rather *becomes* one of those strategies.

For many of the advocates I have worked with—who are often uncomfortable with the very concept of evaluation and have a propensity to view me as merely an extension of one or more of their funders—a great deal of work is required in the first months of an evaluation to calm their inevitable fears. On several occasions, early on in an engagement, I have been politely asked to momentarily step out of the room in the middle of a strategy meeting. I have always obliged, as a means of building that critical sense of trust. Until and unless that trust is established, a developmental evaluation will not prove successful. In my experience, there are a couple of important steps that can be taken to help establish trust.

First and foremost, as many evaluations come at the request of a funder, it is critical that that funder clearly articulate and demonstrate their support for developmental evaluation. Organizations that are accustomed to a certain reporting format, that are familiar with the old standbys of formative and summative evaluations, may be reluctant to believe that a funder will accept the results garnered from a developmental evaluation. Furthermore, I cannot overstate the need for the funder to reiterate that support time and time again. Once is rarely enough.

I have also found that, as an embedded evaluator, a revision of how I introduce myself and my role is required. The advocates with whom I have worked care passionately about their issues. And many face constant pressures from an equally passionate opposition. I have found that advocates' trust—and their willingness to provide me with the level of access and honesty required for a successful developmental evaluation—only comes when I share my own support for their issue and identify myself as an ally of their cause. So, rather than stressing the neutral objectivity that I will bring to the evaluation, I stress my expertise in evaluation and the facilitation of evaluative thinking. That's not to say that the evaluation design is not objective or sacrifices rigor. In fact, I have found that organizations involved in a developmental evaluation are more willing to ask difficult questions and identify their shortcomings and failures. The rationale behind the approach—to inform better strategies going forward—gives license to more honest introspection. I have found organizations participating in summative evaluations much more likely to make efforts to avoid or "spin" negative evaluation findings.

Bottom line advice: *Build trust*.

And as I said above, some lessons just have to be learned anew by new players, which can be a developmental evaluation function. Thus, the increasingly greater intensity and range of services provided by Twin Cities Rise! over time, much greater than originally anticipated, was partly a response to the severity of the problems encountered. And at every stage, the design team stayed focused on and guided by the principles we had identified at the outset: being purpose-driven, market-driven, learning-driven; valuing mutual accountability; and supporting personal empowerment (Rothschild, 2010).

Systems Issues: Boundary Management as a Developmental Evaluation Focus

Given the severity of problems people in poverty manifest, initiatives like the McKnight programs and subsequently Rothschild's employment program are often unable to respond effectively to everyone they'd like to help. As noted above, significant numbers of people in poverty come laden with severe mental and/or physical disabilities. Unable to provide needed services themselves, McKnight programs were often frustrated trying to make appropriate referrals for these people because no programs existed to serve such families. Costs were too high and successes too problematic. Thus, a willingness to learn in depth about participants' needs did not always result in the delivery of appropriate services when such services were beyond the program's capacity and unavailable elsewhere. A real person in real pain with real needs was standing in front of a staff intake worker. It's easy for an academic planning instructor or government policymaker to say, "Just tell them they're not eligible." But eligibility is not always so clear-cut. Judgments have to be made based on assessment criteria that are messy and, in the end, somewhat manipulable and even arbitrary. From a systems perspective, this is partly a boundary management problem.

Dealing with boundaries is a common and constant issue for antipoverty and community change programs, and, indeed, for all kinds of social innovations that start out with a narrow focus and find that changing what they've targeted morphs into changing other systems that affect what they've targeted. Boundary management is an ongoing challenge for staff. Helping people in poverty deal with boundary issues in their own lives adds another layer of complexity to program efforts. The McKnight programs were constantly pushing up against and having to figure out where to set boundaries: Who's eligible? What services are allowable for a particular family? When is a participant "out" of the program (dropped out, kicked out, drunk out, or hassled out)? Where does one program's responsibility end and another's begin? What can funds be spent for? What rules can be bent? The McKnight initiative's commitments to individualization, flexibility, and responsiveness exacerbated and multiplied boundary issues. Tracking boundary management decisions, the implications of changing boundaries, and how the boundaries of different systems interface are common developmental evaluation issues. Boundary decisions—*We'll do this and not do that*—aren't easy to establish and maintain. Boundaries develop and evolve. This will be one of our recurrent themes as we examine what developmental evaluation turns up in bringing systems thinking to innovative initiatives. Chapter 5 looks in depth at systems thinking and boundary issues in developmental evaluation.

In addition to program boundary issues, there are the challenges program staff face interpersonally in assisting participants who enter with their own boundary issues, including some who have been physically or sexually abused, highly dependent or codependent participants, or those with mental health problems. In many cases, participants look to staff for much more than program services; they hope for friendship, relationship counseling, and other very personal advice. Early in the life of the McKnight an-

∼ Elusive and Dynamic System Boundaries: A Focus of Developmental Evaluation

Lisbeth Schorr (1989) found in her groundbreaking work on successful antipoverty programs that effective programs aimed at helping the most disadvantaged typically offered "a broad spectrum of services" (p. 256) as well as emotional and social support. She reported on a Washington, DC, program that targeted a high-risk population in need of prenatal care but found that unless it dealt with more immediate needs like food and housing, the needs that the pregnant women themselves considered more urgent, "you just can't get them to pay attention to prenatal care" (p. 257). She cited Dr. David Rogers, then president of the Robert Wood Johnson Foundation, as having come to a similar conclusion. The foundation's accumulating experience had made him aware that

> "human misery is generally the result of, or accompanied by, a great untidy basketful of intertwined and interconnected circumstances and happenings" that often all need attention if a problem is to be overcome. Successful programs recognize that they cannot respond to these "untidy basketfuls" of needs without regularly crossing traditional professional and bureaucratic boundaries. (p. 257)

Untidy basketfuls of needs and permeable boundaries are characteristics of complexity—and prime territory for developmental evaluation.

Schorr found in her research on successful programs that most interventions "cannot be routinized or applied uniformly."

> [In successful programs] staff members and program structures are fundamentally flexible. Professionals are able to exercise discretion about meeting individual needs (which new mother needs three home visits every week and which needs only one during the first month), and families are able to decide what services to utilize (whether and when to enroll their child in the available day care program) and how they want to participate (whether to work in their child's school as a library volunteer, a paid aide, or a member of the parent advisory body). (p. 257)

What emerged in Schorr's research on effective interventions was not a recipe-like model, but rather a set of principles that had to be applied contextually, adapted situationally, and developed over time. This is the territory of developmental evaluation that helps systematically identify contextually sensitive applications, situational adaptations, and developments over time—and the implications of these developments for making a difference in the lives of the people targeted for help.

tipoverty programs, staff had to do a lot of learning about how to establish boundaries (both for the program and for themselves as professionals), decide how flexible to be about boundaries, and become educated about helping participants set limits. The way an organization deals with boundary issues (and helps participants deal with such issues) says a lot about its struggle, about what kind of an organization it has been and is becoming. These are development issues. Organizations and staff that are results-oriented, that is, *committed to doing whatever it takes to help people move out of poverty*, are particularly likely to push up against boundaries in the form of rules, other programs'

territory, rigid job descriptions, funding restrictions, and sometimes-ambiguous relationships with participants. New initiatives evolve and develop responses to these issues, often incrementally and informally, but in ways that fundamentally shape what the initiative becomes, which is virtually always different from what was imagined. Helping those involved track how such evolution occurs, providing feedback about developments, and facilitating reflection about implications for the innovation and its hoped-for outcomes are common developmental evaluation tasks. Those with the innovation vision and those involved in the day-to-day action of implementing the vision are often not very good at such tracking and making sense of what develops. They need help. They need some other eyes and ears to see and hear what is unfolding. They need developmental evaluation.

Developing Innovations versus Improving and Testing Models: Developmental Evaluation Distinguished from Formative and Summative Evaluation

Let me summarize what I hope is becoming clear: *developmental evaluation* guides action and adaptation in innovative initiatives facing high uncertainty. Where predictability and control are relatively low, goals, strategies, and what gets done can be emergent and changing rather than predetermined and fixed. Continuous development occurs in response to dynamic conditions and attention to rapid feedback about what's working and what's not working. *Developmental evaluation* supports innovation by bringing data to bear to inform and guide ongoing decision making as part of innovative processes.

This is especially true for *social innovations*, the focus of our book on *Getting to Maybe: How the World Is Changed* (Westley, Zimmerman, & Patton, 2006). Coauthor Frances Westley holds the J. W. McConnell Chair in Social Innovation at the University of Waterloo where she is pioneering uses of developmental evaluation in support of social innovation, which she defines as *an alteration of what is established by the introduction of new elements or forms (including new ideas, practices, or resource flows); in particular the alteration of social relationships to allow for transformation of intransigent and broadly based social problems.* Thus, social innovations may, or may not, take the form of formal programs. In the exploratory and developmental phase of social innovation, which we'll discuss at length in relation to the adaptive cycle in Chapter 7, the innovative activities can be preprogram-

matic, like working in a community to try out ways of engaging youth in environmental activism without the formal structure of a *program*. The shaping of that engagement can still benefit from the rapid feedback of developmental evaluation prior to the trappings that evaluators consider essential for *evaluability*, namely, clear, specific, and measurable outcomes and a formal logic model[2] specifying how those outcomes will be attained.

Developmental evaluation, in this regard, offers an alternative to the more typical approach to improving and testing models, namely, formative and summative evaluation, the classic distinctions that have dominated evaluation since the profession began. As I explained in Chapter 1, I am trying to expand the options available to evaluators, so by saying that *developmental evaluation* offers an alternative to formative and summative evaluation I am not suggesting replacing them. They serve important and distinct purposes, and I expect they will remain the dominant distinctions they now are. It is worth knowing what these traditional types of evaluation do and don't do, and that understanding is grounded in the origin of the distinction and jargon. The formative–summative distinction was first conceptualized for school curriculum evaluation by philosopher and *evaluator extraordinaire* Michael Scriven (1967). He called evaluating a curriculum to determine if it should be approved and disseminated for widespread adoption *summative evaluation*, evoking a summit-like decision or a summing up of effectiveness. The notion of summative evaluations quickly expanded to mean any evaluation conducted upon completion of a program or intervention to determine whether to continue, expand,

---

[2]Logic models have become a primary focus of evaluators in conceptualizing what is being evaluated; see Patton (2008c, chap. 10). We'll discuss the limitations of linear logic models in Chapter 5. For resources on logic modeling, see *www.uwex.edu/ces/pdande/evaluation/evallogicmodel.html* and *www.wkkf.org/Pubs/Tools/Evaluation/Pub3669.pdf.*

～ Growth versus Development: Insights from Systems Expert and Distinguished Management Consultant Russell Ackoff

Growth and development are *not* the same thing. Neither is necessary for the other. A rubbish heap can grow but it doesn't develop. Artists can develop without growing. Nevertheless, many managers take development to be the same as growth. Most efforts directed at corporate development are actually directed at corporate growth.

To grow is to increase in size or number. To develop is to increase one's ability and desire to satisfy one's own needs and legitimate desires and those of others. A legitimate desire is one that, when satisfied, does not impede the development of anyone else.

Development is an increase in capability and competence. Development of individuals and corporations is more a matter of learning than earning. It has less to do with how much one has than how much one can do with whatever one has. For this reason Robinson Crusoe is a better model of development than Jean Paul Getty. . . .

A lack of resources can limit growth but not development. The more developed individuals, organizations, or societies become the less they depend on resources and the more they can do with whatever resources they have. They also have the ability and the desire to create or acquire the resources they need.

An individual can grow too much. Some people and many societies believe that a corporation can too. But would anyone argue that individuals, corporations, or countries can develop too much?

Note. From Ackoff (1999, pp. 44–45).

or. disseminate it. A summative evaluation addresses the most fundamental question in evaluation: Did the program work? As I commented in Chapter 1, this requires clear specification of what the program intervention was in relation to intended outcomes, what is called the IT question in evaluation. When one says about a program that "it worked" (or didn't work), what is IT? What is the thing that worked or didn't work? To conduct a summative evaluation, the program must be identifiable, specifiable, stable, implementable, standardized, and replicable—otherwise, we don't know what's been evaluated. The IT is the model that is being evaluated. That's where formative evaluations come in.

Scriven argued wisely that before a curriculum is summatively evaluated, it should go through a period of revision and improvement, working out bugs and problems, filling in gaps, and getting student reaction, to assure that the curriculum is ready for rigorous summative testing. As happened with summative evaluation, the idea of formative evaluation quickly spread beyond curriculum evaluation to refer to any evaluation that improves a program and prepares it for summative evaluation by identifying and correcting implementation problems, making adjustments based on feedback, providing an early assessment of whether desired outcomes are being achieved (or likely to be achieved), and getting the program stabilized and standardized for summative assessment. It is not uncommon for a new program to go through 2 or 3 years of formative evaluation before conducting a summative evaluation.

Over time, formative evaluation has come to refer to any evaluation aimed at improving an intervention or model, but the implication has remained that such improvements are supposed to lead to a stable, fixed model that can be judged as worthy or unworthy of continued funding and, if found to have merit and worth, be disseminated and taken to scale. Moreover, both formative and summative evaluations operate within the assumption that the purpose of the evaluation is *to test a model*. This is critical to understand. Formative evaluations improve the model. Summative evaluations test the model to determine whether it produces the desired outcomes and assess whether observed outcomes can be attributed to the program. Through the dominance of the formative–summative distinction, the field of evaluation has reduced programs and innovations of all kinds to just two stages: first, the model improvement stage (formative evaluation) and then the model testing stage (summative evaluation). That's it. That's all evaluators have had to offer. That's how evaluators for 40 years have conceptualized their work. We've become fixated on models. And understandably so, because funders and policymakers are fixated on models. Best practice models. Silver bullet models. Quick fix models. Models. Models. Models.

But where does the model come from? What role is there for evaluation in the very development of a model, before it is even ready for formative evaluation?

Development versus Improvement

Consider an innovative idea like Rothschild's vision for Twin Cities Rise! that is being tried out in a highly dynamic environment where those involved are engaged in ongoing trial-and-error experimentation, figuring out what works, learning lessons, adapting to changed circumstances, working with new participants—*and creating a model*. They are interested in and committed to development. In arenas like poverty reduction, where knowledge about what works is scarce and highly contextual, the development stage may go on for years, as it has in Twin Cities Rise!

• The first pilot recruited 20 participants. Ninety percent dropped out.

• The pilot began with an extensive interview, testing, selection, and diagnosis process. The process was expensive and time-consuming. Potential participants were scared off. The original approach was abandoned and the whole recruitment and selection process had to be rethought and redesigned—more than once.

• The coaching approach assumed that the program would basically diagnose participants' needs and refer them to receive appropriate services in the community, supporting them in those outsourced services. But program staff quickly found that available training, education, and remedial services in the community were inappropriate and inadequate. Completely contrary to the original idea, the program morphed into creating and conducting in-house training.

• Finding good coaches proved a huge challenge. None of the first hires were up to the tough job of working effectively with the program's challenging population of chronically unemployed men. Staff lacked the necessary street smarts, savvy, and combination of empathy and toughness to help these men turn their lives around. Staff job descriptions, recruitment, selection processes, and support arrangements all had to be reconfigured—again more than once, a process still evolving as new categories of staffing and new divisions of labor have emerged in response to program growth.

• Everything took longer than expected. Participants in a succession of pilot cohorts made progress slower than expected. Dropout rates remained high for a long time. Staff turnover was a problem. These problems led to a series of experiments aimed at reducing dropouts, none of which solved the problem definitively, but included introducing a trial period of adjustment before full entry into the program.

• Individualized coaching gave way to standardized rules and procedures in a search for greater fairness and consistency, and as a way of handling larger numbers.

• The focus shifted from enhancing hard and soft skills to empowerment as the program's core strategy. This was a significant evolution in emphasis that led to reorganizing the entire sequence of participants' engagement in the program and had important implications for emergent outcomes related to the new emphasis on empowerment.

- Some original hopes proved unrealistic and were dropped, like working with large companies to make them more welcoming and supportive of minorities. Smaller companies in some cases turned out to be more receptive to minority placements.

These are examples of program developments not just improvements. Each made a significant change in what was being done and how participants were engaged. These changes affected outcomes, both attainment of outcomes and, equally important, the very conceptualization of outcomes, both short term and long term.

Improvement-oriented, formative evaluation focuses on making an intervention or model better. Developmental evaluation, in contrast, involves exploring the parameters of an innovation and, as it takes shape, changing the intervention as needed (and *if needed*), adapting it to changed circumstances, and altering tactics based on emergent conditions. During this fluid stage of exploration, what's being tried is more an approach than a model. Thus, developmental evaluation can support the exploration and conceptualization of an innovative idea and help innovators clarify, focus, and articulate what they are trying to do *as they do it*. Through this systematic feedback they reflect on and come to know what is unfolding and make sense of the extent and ways in which what is unfolding is what they hoped for, interpret what is not emerging in the desired directions, have data about the differences, if any, between what was hoped for and what's actually unfolding, make sense of those differences, and thereby become more focused and intentional in future adaptations.

Developmental evaluation is designed to be congruent with and nurture develop-

～ Improvement or Development?

Yoplait yogurt emerged in 1965 when two French dairy cooperatives, "Yola" and "Coplait," merged to become "Yoplait." In 1969, they licensed the brand, first in Switzerland and subsequently in countries around the world. For example, in Australia, National Foods has the license. General Mills obtained the license in the United States, which Steve Rothschild and his team successfully marketed.

As Yoplait became successful, People for the Ethical Treatment of Animals (PETA) protested that the discarded yogurt containers were a threat to wildlife, especially skunks. The tapered container design was just large enough that a *skunk* could get its head into the opening where it would become trapped by the thick hair on its head. The tapered container was a branding feature of Yoplait, so General Mills didn't want to change the tapered design, but in response to the PETA protests, the company designers added a rim on the bottom of the container that allowed the skunk to push the container off its head with its feet. A warning was also added that read: "Protect Wildlife: Crush Cup Before Disposal."

So we have several changes here:

1. The organizational merger that created the Yoplait brand;
2. Licensing the brand internationally; and
3. Modifying the container design.

Improvements or developments? What are the implicit data informing these changes? What else, if anything, do you need to know to distinguish whether these are improvements or developments?

These questions exemplify the boundary issues you may face in distinguishing formative from developmental evaluation.

mental, emergent, innovative, and transformative processes. Exhibit 2.1 contrasts improvements with developments to illustrate important qualitative differences.

Sometimes developmental evaluation leads to and lays the groundwork for formative evaluation, even summative evaluation. When and if the exploratory and developmental phase of innovation leads to a model that has potential for dissemination and being taken to scale, then the evaluation's purpose and focus may move into more traditional formative and summative evaluation. How this occurs, with examples, is the focus of Chapter 7.

After a decade of development, the Twin Cities Rise! model has stabilized, though it is far from static, and the program has conducted formative evaluations and commissioned summative evaluations. The groundwork for formative and summative evaluation came from the early work with developmental evaluation; new, innovative initiatives undertaken alongside the main model continue to use developmental evaluation. Later we'll examine in more detail some of the external forces that have shaped program development and the role of developmental evaluation in the program's evolution to its current model. First, as we scope out the territory of developmental evaluation, let's move from initial development of an innovation to ongoing development over a longer period of time. This was the situation that I faced in the example I described in Chapter 1 when the community leadership program I was evaluating decided to commit to ongoing development rather than undertaking a summative evaluation.

EXHIBIT 2.1 Improvements versus Developments: Examples

Program improvements	Program developments
1. Add a new topic to a training curriculum.	1. Change the entire scope, sequence, and delivery of the curriculum for a new target group.
2. Provide staff training to enhance the skills of current staff.	2. Change job descriptions and reconceptualize the priorities, qualifications, and needed competencies of staff.
3. Expand the recruitment effort to a wider target area.	3. Fundamentally change the recruitment strategy, for example, instead of direct advertising working through referral agencies.
4. Expand the staff to serve increasing numbers under the same basic model.	4. Add staff to significantly change the staff–participant ratio in order to provide more individualized and intensive attention to participants.
5. Fine-tune the program delivery based on participant feedback, for example, providing longer breaks and more small-group exercises to supplement lectures during training workshops.	5. Replace face-to-face workshop training with exclusively online training and support.
6. Add healthier food to children's preschool program lunches.	6. Make lunch an educational experience by engaging with children about food and nutrition, involving them in food preparation, and giving them homework assignments related to home nutrition.

Ongoing Development Informed by Developmental Evaluation

The only man who behaves sensibly is my tailor; he takes my measurements anew every time he sees me, while all the rest go on with their old measurements and expect me to fit them.
— George Bernard Shaw
(1856–1950), winner of the
1925 Nobel Prize in Literature

As noted above, summative evaluation renders a judgment of merit or worth about a stable and fixed program intervention based on explicit criteria like effectiveness, efficiency, relevance, and sustainability. Making such judgments has traditionally been evaluation's "gold standard" purpose. Summative evaluations judge a program's efficiency in goal attainment, replicability, clarity of causal specificity, and generalizability. But these summative criteria assume a targeted intervention in a fairly stable environment. Highly volatile environments, dynamic social innovations, and emergent interventions may demand *ongoing development* rather than striving to arrive at a fixed, stable model for replication.

I find that developmentally oriented social innovators don't aspire to reach the state of stability required for summative evaluation. They're constantly experimenting, adapting and developing what they do in response to program participants' feedback, changing conditions, new insights, and emerging challenges all around them. They don't yearn to arrive at a fixed model that can be generalized and disseminated. More often they aim to discover and articulate *principles of intervention and development*, but not a replicable model that says "Do A and you'll get B." They are committed to continuous progress, ongoing adaptation, and rapid responsiveness. No sooner do they articulate and clarify some aspect of the process than that very awareness becomes an intervention and acts to change what they do. They don't value traditional characteristics of summative excellence such as standardization of inputs, consistency of treatment, uniformity of out-

comes, fidelity of replication, and clarity of causal linkages. They assume a world of multiple causes, diversity of outcomes, inconsistency of interventions, interactive effects at every level—and they find such a world stimulating and challenging. They never expect to conduct a summative evaluation because they don't expect the change initiative—or world—to hold still long enough for summative judgment. They expect to be forever developing and changing—and they want an evaluation approach that supports development and change. That's why they resonate to developmental evaluation.

So do some funders—those that understand that funding innovation and systems change are different from making grants and funding projects with narrow, targeted outcomes.

Such funders and social innovators understand deeply the differences between improvement and development. Formative evaluation focuses on making something better—improvement—rather than making it different. "Development," as I'll be using the word throughout this book, means making something different at a level and in a way that actually changes the intervention to some significant degree. Such developments are driven by, in response to, and interact with the volatile environment and innovation dynamics that emerge in complex systems. Social innovators change what they're doing because they are attuned to and responsive as they experience new understandings. They are attentive to revelations from program participants as interactions deepen and trust builds. They watch for the effects of technology. They are quick to spot changes in the world around them that have implications for their own more narrow arena of action. They actually live by the clichéd mantra: *Expect the unexpected.* The commitment to adapt doesn't carry a judgment that what was done before was inadequate or less effective. Change is not necessarily improvement. Change is adaptation. Assessing the cold reality of change, social innovators can be heard to say:

At each stage we did the best we could with what we knew and the resources we had. Now we're at a different place in our development—doing and thinking different things. *That's development.* That's change. That's more than just making a few improvements. (Jean Gornick, former director of Damiano, a not-for-profit working on poverty alleviation in Duluth, Minnesota; quoted in Westley et al., 2006, p. 179; the Damiano development story is featured in Chapters 6 and 9)

Exhibit 2.2 (on pages 44–47) summarizes the differences between summative, formative, and developmental evaluation.

Strategic Thinking and Developmental Evaluation

The changes that the Twin Cities Rise! program went through, listed earlier, were *strategic developments*, not just program improvements. What's a strategic development? One that fundamentally alters how an organization does what it does.

I've suggested that detailed planning isn't very useful where knowledge is limited and the environment is turbulent. In further examining this premise, it's worth noting the important distinction between *strategic planning* and *strategic thinking*. The two are not the same. Indeed, the processes and paperwork of strategic planning often make it quite nonstrategic, a problem exacerbated when evaluators get involved and start prematurely demanding clear, specific, measurable, and time-delimited goals. The well-documented weaknesses and land mines of strategic planning that have contributed to its demise (Mintzberg, 2000), or at least to controversy about its utility, make *thinking strategically* all the more important. Thinking strategically requires understanding the nature and substance of an organization's knowledge assets (Boisot, 1998; Boisot, MacMillan, & Han, 2008) and deep engagement with systems thinking (Gharajedaghi, 2006) built on and congruent with adapting to the

dynamics of complexity, the focus of Chapters 4 and 5. Developmental evaluation supports knowledge assessment and strategic systems thinking and helps ensure that social innovators stay attuned and responsive to emerging realities. That's a mouthful. Let's see if I can make sense of its implications for practice.

Let's consider how businesses change. Management scholar Henry Mintzberg is an expert on business strategy. He defines *strategy* as consistent patterns of behavior over time. In his teaching and training, Mintzberg likes to ask, "Was Egg McMuffin, McDonald's breakfast in a bun, a strategic change for the company?" Some respond that it was a strategic change because the innovation constituted a new product aimed at a new market: breakfast eaters. Others say it was a product improvement but not a strategic change because it was still McDonald's fast food approach (strategy). He calls this "the Egg McMuffin syndrome," failing to distinguish different kinds of change—and evaluators manifest this syndrome every bit as much as business managers and strategic planners.

First, one must distinguish nonstrategic change (improvement within the existing strategy) from strategic change (development). Within strategic change, Mintzberg distinguishes changes in *position* from changes in *perspective*. Position focuses on what is done and the territory (landscape, space) in which it is done; for programs this is usually the target population and primary outcomes targeted. Perspective focuses on how something is done; for programs this means how staff work with participants and partners. Egg McMuffin was a strategic change in position (a new product aimed at a new market) but was not a change in perspective because it still involved producing standardized fast food. Changing a position within a perspective, Mintzberg says, is relatively easy because it just involves doing new things in an established way. Changing a position together with a perspective is more significant, for which he offers the imagined example of a gourmet "McDuckling à l'orange" served at your table instead of picked up at the counter. This kind of change is harder because "perspectives are deeply rooted in organizations, in their cultures" (Mintzberg, 2007, p. 8). But change still comes in response to different environments: after long hesitation, Euro Disney decided to serve wine in France because the French population demanded it. McDonald's has begun experimenting with variations based on location: including a crab sandwich on the menu in Maine, serving pastries in France, and offering gourmet coffee in upscale markets.

Changes in position and perspective can be *either* strategic or nonstrategic. Nonstrategic changes are improvements in implementing the existing strategy. A strategic change, in contrast, constitutes a development—a significant *strategic* departure from business as usual. Mintzberg considers offering a Big Mac on a whole-wheat bun to be a minor product improvement within the same strategic perspective (fast food). This would be considered an improvement by those who prefer whole-wheat to white bread, but it is not a significant strategic change in how McDonald's does business. However, targeting gourmet coffee drinkers represents a strategic change in position, not just an improvement in the way McDonald's has served coffee in the past.

Mintzberg's strategic distinctions emphasize that it is important to understand both the degree of change (strategic vs. nonstrategic) and the kind of strategic change occurring (position, perspective, or both). Nonstrategic changes are improvements that involve implementing the existing strategy better, for example, more efficiently. Strategic changes are developments in that they involve changes in the organization's focus or way of doing business. *Developmental evaluation is especially useful for tracking strategic changes.*

Let's apply these distinctions to Twin Cities Rise! Originally, Rothschild envisioned the model consisting of generalist coaches helping men of color locate appropriate training and education in the community (outsourcing all training). Improvements in this strategy involved getting better at selecting motivated men of color and supporting coaches to appropriately match participants to training and educational opportunities in the community. Strategic developments, beyond improvements, involved more fundamental changes. Changing the target population to include women and low-income whites occurred in part because new welfare-to-work legislation during the Clinton administration dramatically increased demand among women on welfare for employment training and the program responded to that increased need and demand. This did not involve a change in mission, which had always been on poverty, but did involve an important change in the program's participant composition. Using Mintzberg's distinctions, this constituted a change in strategic position—a change in target population and outcome (or a change in product, in business terms).

A major developmental change in strategic perspective involved the decision to bring most training in-house and create the program's own customized courses because outsourcing just wasn't working. The evaluation feedback from both participants placed in jobs and their employers concluded that available training and education in the community didn't meet the needs of the targeted participants. This led to adding to and changing the staff configuration, hiring trainers, placement specialists, and company recruiters, as well as redefining the role of coaches to specialize in what participants needed at different stages in the program. (That participants needed different kinds of coaching at different stages of the program was a developmental evaluation finding.) Other major strategic developments in perspective involved offering empowerment training for employees already employed in customer companies (not just program

EXHIBIT 2.2 Distinguishing Different Evaluation Purposes

Purpose	Key conditions	Priority questions	Common evaluation approaches	Key factors affecting use
Summative evaluation				
▪ *Judgment* of *overall* merit, worth, value, and significance of the program and model to inform and support major decision making. ▪ Determine the future of the program and model, including especially whether it should be disseminated as an exemplar and taken to scale.	▪ Well-defined intervention model supported by an explicit and testable theory of change. ▪ Stable, consistent, standardized, and high-quality implementation: *quality control.* ▪ Clear, specific, measurable, attainable, and time-bound outcomes. ▪ Sufficient control to permit attribution. ▪ Reliable monitoring and cost data. ▪ Funders and decision makers ready and willing to engage summative findings.	▪ Does the program work? ▪ Does it meet participants' needs and achieve desired outcomes? ▪ Should it be continued, terminated, expanded, disseminated, taken to scale? ▪ Does it add value for money? ▪ How do outcomes and costs compare to other options? ▪ To what extent can outcomes be attributed to the intervention? ▪ Is the program model and theory clear, stable, and well implemented? ▪ What, if any, unintended consequences are found? ▪ What contextual factors affect effectiveness? ▪ **Is this an especially effective practice that should be funded and disseminated as a model program, a *best practice*?**	▪ End-of-project (or end-of-funding period) external and independent evaluations. ▪ Outcomes and impact evaluation. ▪ Cost-benefit analysis. ▪ Theory-driven evaluation.	▪ Independence and credibility of the evaluator. ▪ Rigor of the design: validity and generalizability. ▪ Timeliness. ▪ Stability of the environment. ▪ Significance of the findings to decision makers. ▪ Funder and decision maker commitment to engaging with summative questions and making summative decisions.

Formative evaluation

- Improve the program.
- Fine-tune the model, clarifying key elements and linkages from inputs to activities and processes to outputs, outcomes, and impacts.
- Work out bugs in implementation; fix problems.
- Determine efficacy and effectiveness at a pilot level to establish readiness for summative evaluation.
- Stabilize and standardize the model to get it ready for summative evaluation.
- Test and validate instruments and procedures for summative evaluation.

- Draft program model to be fine-tuned.
- Establish criteria for quality implementation to guide and focus process improvements.
- Clear, specific, measurable, attainable, and time-bound outcomes to focus efforts at improvement.
- Processes and instruments for getting participant feedback.
- Management information system for monitoring.
- Staff ready and willing to identify and work on improving the program.

- What strengths and weaknesses show up as the model is implemented?
- What are participants' reactions and how can their satisfaction be increased?
- How can outcomes and impacts be increased?
- What works for whom in what ways under what conditions?
- How can costs be controlled and possibly reduced?
- How can quality be enhanced?
- Have all major elements of the model been identified and implemented in a consistent manner?
- Do the parts of the model fit together?
- What, if any, unintended consequences and contextual factors are found and what are the implications of these consequences and factors for the model's relevance as a potential exemplar for others?
- **Is the program model ready for summative evaluation?**

- Midterm evaluations.
- Logic model work and assessment.
- Participant feedback.
- Monitoring data on implementation and participation.
- Quality enhancement.
- Learning reviews.
- Process evaluation.
- Formative outcomes evaluation.

- Creating a learning climate, openness to feedback and change.
- Trust that evidence about weaknesses will not be used to punish staff or reduce funding before improvements can be made.
- Evaluator's skill in facilitating learning.
- Relevance of findings to staff; actionable recommendations for improvements.
- Clarity about what is required for the program to be deemed ready for summative evaluation.

(cont.)

Purpose	Key conditions	Priority questions	Common evaluation approaches	Key factors affecting use
Developmental evaluation				
▪ Help social innovators explore possibilities for addressing major problems and needs, and identify innovative approaches and solutions. ▪ Develop promising innovations. ▪ Support adaptation in complex, uncertain, and dynamic conditions. ▪ Document what actions innovators engage in, the short-term results and consequences of those actions, and their connections to the larger vision of the innovators. ▪ Identify *emergent* processes and outcomes that accompany innovation, and support making sense of their implications. ▪ Support ongoing development and adaption to changing conditions.	▪ Social innovators with a strong vision and commitment to making a difference. ▪ Willingness and capacity to act and innovate under conditions of uncertainty and turbulence. ▪ Commitment to use data and rapid feedback to make sense of what emerges during exploration and innovation, and use those emergent understandings to guide next steps. ▪ Funders willing to try out and trust the innovative process and developmental evaluation as a way of monitoring what emerges. ▪ Evaluators capable of operating without predetermined clear, specific, and measurable outcomes or a well-defined logic model.	▪ What is the baseline understanding of the situation? ▪ What are the vision and values that will guide innovation? ▪ What are the initial conditions and the nature of the environment within which action will occur? ▪ What is meant by innovation? ▪ What do rapid feedback and initial results reveal about progress in desired directions? ▪ What's considered "working" and "not working" as exploration unfolds and innovation is undertaken? ▪ What criteria emerge to tell the difference between "working" and "not working"? ▪ What processes and outcomes generate enthusiasm? Why?	▪ Developmental evaluation. ▪ Systems-and-complexity-based interactive design. ▪ Rapid assessment, rapid feedback. ▪ Emergent evaluation. ▪ Real-time evaluation. ▪ Ongoing environmental scanning and outcomes monitoring. ▪ Reflective practice. ▪ Participatory action research. ▪ Network analysis. ▪ Systems change mapping.	▪ Innovators and developmental evaluator(s) able to work together in partnership: mutua respect and trust. ▪ Getting busy and action-driven innovators to value and spend time in sense making, reflection, and data interpretation to inform ongoing innovation. ▪ Openness to what emerges. ▪ Adaptive capacity. ▪ Tolerance for ambiguity and uncertainty ("getting to maybe"). ▪ Balancing quality and speed of feedback. ▪ Nimble, agile. ▪ Integrate and synthesize multiple and conflicting data sources.

- Determine when and if an innovation is ready for formative evaluation as a pilot intervention.

- Sensitivity to initial conditions.

- What is unacceptable as things unfold?
- As exploration and innovation unfold, what's happening at the interface between what the social innovators are doing/accomplishing and what's going on in the larger world around it? How is the program as an intervention system connected to and affected by larger systems in its environment?
- What are the trends in those larger systems?
- What can be controlled and not controlled, predicted and not predicted, measured and not measured, and how do innovators respond and adapt to what cannot be controlled, predicted, or measured?
- How do evaluators and innovators together distinguish signal from noise to determine what to attend to?
- What factors affect and guide ongoing exploration and development?
- What innovations emerge that merit more formal implementation as pilot programs ready for formative evaluation?

participants) and creating a program for men in prison. Exhibit 2.3 distinguishes improvements from developments by applying Mintzberg's distinctions between position and perspective to changes made by Twin Cities Rise!

One other aspect of Mintzberg's work offers an important framework for understanding developmental evaluation in support of strategic development. Implementing strategy, he has found, is always a combination of deliberate and unplanned processes. In studying hundreds of companies over many years, he found that there is no such thing as a perfectly controlled, deliberate process in which intentions lead to formulation of plans, implementation, and the full realization of intended results. The real world doesn't unfold that way. As the graphic in Exhibit 2.4 shows, realized strategy (where you end up after some period of time) begins as intended strategy (planning), but not all of what is intended is realized. Some things get dropped or go un-

---

EXHIBIT 2.3 Changes in the Twin Cities Rise! Program: Position and Perspective Improvements versus Developments

Strategy distinctions	Improvements (nonstrategic)	Developments (strategic)
Original position: Who does the program serve? What is its niche?	*Position-focused improvements*	*Position-focused developments*
1. Targeted the chronically unemployed and underemployed, primarily men of color. 2. Thorough diagnosis of program applicants' needs and abilities. 3. Interim outcomes: enhanced hard and soft skills.	1. Got better at recruiting and selecting *motivated* men of color for whom the program was appropriate. 2. Developed better diagnostic instruments and processes. 3. Improved assessment and training in targeted skill areas.	1. Began targeting men *and* women, including whites in poverty driven by changes in welfare-to-work laws. 2. Stopped using diagnostic instruments and implemented a 2-month probation period to assess whether the program and participant match. 3. Made empowerment the focus of participant development.
Original perspective: How does the program work?	*Perspective-focused improvements*	*Perspective-focused developments*
4. Staff as generalist coaches who work with assigned participants throughout their time in the program. 5. Outsourced all training; no in-house training.	4. Got better at hiring coaches who could work with this challenging target population. 5a. Supported and trained coaches to find appropriate training placements outside the program. 5b. Created collaborations with suppliers of training and education to get them to customize their courses more to the program's needs.	4. Diversified staffing: coaches specialized for participants at different levels and stages in the program; trainers and instructional designers added; placement specialists and company recruiter positions added. 5a. Brought training in-house; the program created its own courses to meet its participants' needs. 5b. Started offering empowerment training for employees already employed in its targeted companies and prisons.

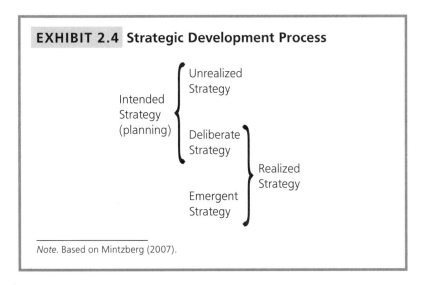

EXHIBIT 2.4 Strategic Development Process

Intended Strategy (planning) {
Unrealized Strategy

Deliberate Strategy }

Emergent Strategy } Realized Strategy

Note. Based on Mintzberg (2007).

done, becoming unrealized strategy. What remains, deliberate strategy, intersects with emergent strategy to become realized strategy. Emergent strategy comes from seizing new opportunities, which is a reason some things that were planned go undone as new and better opportunities arise (Mintzberg, 2007, chap. 1).

These insights about strategy implementation and realization in the real world contrast significantly with the classic accountability-oriented approach of evaluation in which program implementation and results are measured and judged based on what they planned to do and achieve (intended outcomes). Under such an accountability framework, an innovative and adaptive program that seizes new opportunities and adjusts to changing conditions will be evaluated negatively. Developmental evaluation, in contrast, expects that some of what is planned will go unrealized, some will be implemented roughly as expected, and some new things will emerge. Developmental evaluation tracks and documents these different aspects of strategic innovation—and their implications for further innovation and development.

Improvement versus Development: Does This Distinction Matter?

As a consultant I regularly get calls from people who need an evaluation conducted, often because that requirement is a string attached to their funding. Upon answering the phone, I'm asked, "Are you the Dr. Patton who does evaluations?"

"That is the rumor," I confess.

"We need one," the caller says in a voice mixed with relief, fear, and pleading.

"What kind do you need?" I ask.

"Kind?"

And thus begins the process of making distinctions. I proceed to pontificate that if you set out to buy a car, you have lots of choices and have to narrow the options to what kind you seek. Likewise if you're going out to eat: you'll have to decide what kind of food you want and what restaurant to honor with your culinary sophistication. Indeed, a purchase of any kind involves distinguishing among choices, as do decisions about entertainment, family activities, and self-improvement resolutions. The world is filled with options and menus. And so is evaluation. I have catalogued 80 different ways of focusing evaluations (Patton, 2008c, pp. 300–305), from accountability, accreditation, or appreciative inquiry to utilization-focused evaluation. There are purposes beyond formative and summative evaluation like knowledge-generating and accountability-focused evaluation (Patton, 2008c, chap. 4). There are goal-based versus goal-free evaluations; both process and outcomes evaluations; participatory versus connoisseurship approaches; real-world and theory-driven frameworks; internal versus external options; cost–benefit and transformative models; constructivist and realist evaluations. Engaging in evaluation requires distinguishing types, understanding options, and choosing among alternatives the type of evaluation that will serve the needs of those who will use the evaluation.

Michael Scriven, who gave us the original formative–summative distinction, is creator and keeper of evaluation's *Thesaurus* (Scriven, 1991). He has identified and named more evaluation concepts than anyone else in the profession. I once asked him how he came up with new terms and distinctions. He replied that he really didn't like "muddying up the field" with a lot of jargon, so he only created a term when he felt it was absolutely necessary. He said that as he noticed confusion about some issue or became sharply aware of some gap in the field, he would find it necessary to create some new terminology or to offer a new concept to help sort out the confusion and fill in the gap (Patton, 2000, p. 7).

∼ *Does the Formative versus Developmental Distinction Matter?*

Gene Lyle had a long and distinguished career as an internal evaluator in the Ramsey County Community Human Services Department in Minnesota. The AEA recognized Gene for his work by awarding him the Alva and Gunnar Myrdal Government Award in 2000. I asked Gene to review this chapter from the perspective of an internal, in-the-trenches evaluation practitioner. His perspective provides important balance to the argument I'm making in this chapter that the distinction between formative, summative, and developmental evaluation is important.

In our work we tried to do useful evaluation. We didn't worry about labeling a report formative or summative. The same report to the county board could include both recommendations for improving a program and recommendations for future funding. County commissioners didn't want to hear academic jargon like formative and summative. They wanted good evaluations that showed programs were being held accountable, were meeting goals, and were working to become more effective. So, what we did was evaluation, useful evaluation. I have always had a problem with the either–or distinction between formative and summative. A formative evaluation, in my experience, does not "prepare the program for summative evaluation." We did support doing ongoing formative evaluation. It was often the only type of evaluation that was ongoing, though it might contain, shall we say, "sort-of-summative" conclusions such as an annual report summarizing a year's activity based on aggregate data from the formative evaluation. Hardly anybody used the terms "formative," or "summative," let alone "developmental" (except in our little evaluation shop). It was just called "evaluation."

Policymakers and decision makers almost always want formative-type evaluation findings to provide assurance that things are working okay. Summative doesn't tell them that, at least not often enough. So for them, summative is not the gold standard. I think that's a definition we've stamped on ourselves as evaluators and it's not based on the reality I knew in my work. But then, I was an internal evaluator.

I would add that what is being described as developmental evaluation, more so than summative/formative, is *driven by the program*, not by the evaluator or by some evaluator/evaluation philosophy. If the program wants to identify what it's doing as development rather than improvement, then the program will want to do developmental evaluation.

That's precisely the circumstance that led me to distinguish *developmental evaluation*. I first identified developmental evaluation as an option in working with the community leadership program I described in Chapter 1. The original 5-year formative–summative evaluation morphed into an ongoing developmental evaluation when the foundation funders and program staff realized that they needed to keep adapting the program strategically as the economic, political, and technological environment changed and as the program reached out to new target participants, like immigrants, new businesses, and new generations of young people. Offering the program on Native American reservations represented a strategic change in position. Having participants design potential community change projects *during the program* constituted a strategic change in perspective in contrast to the original design that called for participants to wait until they returned to their communities to start work on specific projects. These weren't just improvements in the way the leadership program was conducted. They didn't just involve incremental changes in effectiveness and efficiency. They involved significant strategic developments.

While arguing that it's worth distinguishing developments from improvements, I also acknowledge that the distinction is neither absolute nor unambiguous. The distinction centers on different purposes and purpose involves matters of intention and perception. This is true in many distinctions of importance. Surgeons distinguish cosmetic surgery, which enhances one's appearance, from reconstructive surgery, which restores normality. In most cases the difference is straightforward, but because reconstructive surgery is typically eligible for insurance coverage while cosmetic surgery is not, gray areas emerge that involve judgment and perception. In home remodeling, repairs are treated differently from improvements for tax purposes. A new roof may be a repair in one circumstance (after a storm has blown off the old roof) but an improvement in another (when it has begun to leak after years of use). Purpose and intention matter. I don't think these distinctions are just academic nit-picking. Distinguishing developmental from formative evaluation is not, I hope, just an exercise in proliferating evaluation jargon. But for an alternative perspective from an experienced evaluation practitioner and colleague, see the sidebar on the previous page, *Does the Formative versus Developmental Distinction Matter?*

The Niche of Developmental Evaluation: Chapter Overview and Summary

Plans are useless but planning is indispensible.
—DWIGHT D. EISENHOWER, commander of Allied Forces in World War II and president of the United States from 1952 to 1960

This chapter began with my advice to social innovator Steve Rothschild that he and his design team stop doing detailed planning and *get on with learning by doing*. The chapter went on to distinguish strategic systems thinking from producing a strategic plan, and positioned developmental evaluation as supporting innovations and evaluating innovative strategies. Throughout this chapter I have distinguished developmental evaluation from more formal and traditional *model-focused* formative and summative evaluation (see especially Exhibit 2.2). I've emphasized especially, indeed emphatically, and perhaps ad nauseum, the importance of distinguishing improvements from developments. It's all about making meaningful distinctions.

It is important to consider these distinctions in light of Chapter 1's discussion of situation recognition. Different planning, program design, and evaluation approaches are appropriate for different situations. This is the recurring mantra of this book. Developmental evaluation fills one niche in the diverse evaluation universe. It is one source of light in an evaluation sky rich with glimmering objects—and vast expanses of darkness (a nod to those who inherently associate evaluation of any kind with the dark side). Developmental evaluation helps social innovators adapt to dynamic conditions, explore possibilities to see what works and what doesn't work, make sense of successes and learn from failures. And sometimes the data indicate that it's time to jump directly from ongoing development to a definitive summative conclusion, a recommendation expressed succinctly and powerfully by that great comedic evaluation genius W. C. Fields:

If at first you don't succeed, try, try again. Then quit. There's no point in being a damn fool about it.

3

Thinking Outside Evaluation's Boxes

Human beings, viewed as behaving systems, are quite simple. The apparent complexity of our behavior over time is largely a reflection of the complexity of the environment in which we find ourselves.
—HERBERT SIMON, recipient of the 1978 Nobel Prize in Economics for his pioneering research into the decision-making process in organizations

Creative Evaluation

A classic creativity exercise asks you to draw four straight lines through three lines of dots without taking the pencil off the paper. To solve the puzzle you have to draw lines outside the box made by the boundaries of the dots. (For the solution, see Infinite Innovations, 2009.)

This kind of creativity has come to be known as "thinking outside the box," short-hand for creative thinking. The last chapter looked at developmental evaluation as an option outside evaluation's traditional formative and summative boxes. It is well known that evaluation involves critical thinking. But developmental evaluation also requires creative thinking to engage in and support the creative processes of social innovation and to flow with the creative juices of social innovators. Creative evaluation (Patton, 1987) invites us to think outside the boxes of accountability mandates, evaluation as a compliance activity, fixed reporting deadlines, and narrow evaluator roles. This chapter offers an extended case example of how asking questions about what makes sense and connecting the evaluation process to ongoing program development leads outside evaluation's traditional boxes. The chapter concludes with 10 key points about developmental evaluation illustrated by the case.

This chapter aims to illustrate some of the thinking and questioning processes that undergird developmental evaluation, including how developmental evaluation sometimes intersects with and overlaps traditional formative and summative uses of evaluation. I also want to call attention to the interpersonal dynamics of developmental evaluation. It can all get quite messy. My experience with this innovative initiative over a 10-year period had significant influence on my thinking about evaluation use to support ongoing decision making and development. I have included this chapter to ground developmental evaluation in the messiness of real-world complexities. The next chapter addresses complexity concepts directly and links developmental evaluation to complexity theory. Those who are impatient with the inductive case method of learning may want to skip this chapter and move on now to complexity concepts. No problem—you know how you learn best. If you do move on, I would suggest that you return to this chapter at a later time to see if you can decipher how complexity concepts play out in this case. Developmental evaluation is not a linear process, nor is learning about it, and I considered putting this case example later in the book after delving into complexity theory. In the end, I decided to let the complexity theory applications emerge from this story of an actual adapted developmental evaluation—before we had introduced that term to identify what it is. We made it up as we went along, asking what made sense and what would be useful. For those who've decided to stay with the case, or at least begin it and see where it leads, let me introduce you to my mentor, Tom Henderson.

Of Plums and Prunes

Dr. Thomas H. Henderson was a Caribbean prune. In the sociopolitical cosmos where those close to people in power seek plum assignments, prunes merit distinct esteem. According to *New York Times* linguistic pundit William Safire, *prunes* are "plums seasoned by wisdom and experience, with a much thicker skin." Safire deconstructed the meaning of the term just after Barack Obama was elected president when prunes were much sought after to fill senior positions in the new administration. In 1980, while on the faculty of the University of Minnesota and living in deep snow-and-windchill territory, I got the plum assignment of codirecting the Caribbean Agricultural Extension Project (CAEP). The project aimed at improving agricultural extension systems in eight countries in the Leeward and Windward Islands, from Antigua to Grenada, plus Belize in Central America.[1] The project was based at the University of the West Indies in Trinidad where Tom Henderson was director of the department of agricultural extension. He was the seasoned prune to my fresh, unripened plum.

Why do I want to introduce you to Tom Henderson? Because he was the first person I worked with who *got it* about developmental evaluation. Tom lived and worked his entire life in a world of extremely scarce resources. He had to do a lot of things that he didn't like doing to grease the wheels of development: political things, administrative things, compliance things, nonsensical things. These going-through-the-motions things came with the territory of getting along in bureaucratic organizations, attracting resources, and carving out a little space to do the things he really cared about. He understood how the world worked and adapted accordingly, but these things were the source of many of the deep crevices on his pruned exterior. Where he lived inside, when he got a chance to do things he cared about and could to some extent control, he was ferocious about not wasting time and precious resources on things that didn't matter.

---

[1]The participating countries were Antigua, Belize, Dominica, Grenada, Montserrat, St. Kitts/Nevis, St. Lucia, and St. Vincent and the Grenadines.

Tom Henderson *got it* that evaluation could matter, but only if done right. In the Caribbean, that meant adapting it to the Caribbean way of doing things. That meant making it sensible—making it make sense, for *developmental evaluation is first and foremost about doing what makes sense.* It's grounded in pragmatism and situational adaptation. A lot of evaluation doesn't make sense. A lot of evaluation is design within tightly contained boundaries, narrowly prescribed parameters, and mandated templates imposed by people who want it done, and done their way, whether it makes sense or not. Developmental evaluation takes us outside evaluation's traditional formative and summative boxes; it questions the utility of mandated midterm reviews and external end-of-project evaluations. It asks whether these things make sense. That's the question Tom Henderson asked, so I want to tell you about Dr. and Professor Thomas Horatio Henderson and use his story to invite you to think about how to make evaluation make sense in your own setting.

I also tell Tom's story, as I tell the stories in other chapters of people engaged in developmental evaluation thinking and practice, to emphasize the importance of the *personal factor* in evaluation, as in all of life. People matter. Evaluation is not just about methods and data. Studies of evaluation use have consistently found that evaluation use is significantly increased when those in a position to make decisions understand the importance of reality testing and care about using data to inform their decision making. Tom Henderson was such a person.

History and Biography as Context: The Personal Factor

Born in Dominica in 1927, Tom Henderson came of age when Caribbean countries were still colonies. As a boy he worked in the Botanical Garden under British colonial supervisors. He credited his mother with instilling in him the attitude that racial epithets and derogatory comments about his African heritage revealed ignorance and colonial arrogance, but said nothing about him, so he learned to keep such derision from piercing beneath his increasingly tough black skin, letting the curses slide off him like the mud he worked in after a tropical rain. His intelligence and work ethic caught the attention of a recently arrived, younger supervisor. That led to an opportunity for training at the Imperial College of Tropical Agriculture in Trinidad. He next became one of the first students trained at the Eastern Caribbean Institute of Agriculture and Forestry in Trinidad. He returned to his home island and worked his way up through the ranks of agricultural extension in Dominica at a time when extension was still a colonial organization serving large plantation and estate owners. ("Extension" refers to the process of getting knowledge from universities to people who need and can use it in the real world, not just students in classrooms; agricultural extension involves "extension agents" who are trained to help farmers improve their farming. Historically, extension was either a government service or based in universities. In more modern times, all kinds of organizations engage in *extending knowledge* to people who need it.)

During a brief stint as a schoolteacher, Tom Henderson helped establish 4-H youth programs in Dominica. The 1960s brought new opportunities: He was awarded a graduate fellowship to the University of Wisconsin where he earned a PhD in agricultural education. For his dissertation he studied the development needs of extension systems and surveyed extension agents throughout the Caribbean to determine their training needs. The CAEP began as his vision, based on his needs assessment work. It took shape as a partnership between the Midwestern Universities Consortium for International Activities (MUCIA—the "Big Ten" American land grant universities) and the University of the West Indies, funded by the U.S. Agency for International Development (USAID).

∼ *The Personal Factor*

The personal factor is the presence of an identifiable individual or group of people who personally care about the evaluation and the findings it generates. Where such a person or group was present, evaluations were used; where the personal factor was absent, research on evaluation use consistently shows a correspondingly marked absence of evaluation impact (Patton, 2008c, chap. 3).

The personal factor represents the leadership, interest, enthusiasm, determination, commitment, assertiveness, and caring of specific, individual people. These are people who actively seek information to learn, make judgments, get better at what they do, and reduce decision uncertainties. They want to increase their ability to predict the outcomes of programmatic activity and thereby enhance their own discretion as decision makers, policymakers, consumers, program participants, funders, or whatever roles they play. These are the primary users of evaluation.

What we've learned harkens back to the influential insights of the Stanford Evaluation Consortium, one of the leading places of ferment and reform in evaluation during the late 1970s. Cronbach and associates in the Consortium identified major reforms needed in evaluation by publishing a provocative set of 95 theses, following the precedent of Martin Luther. Among them was this lustrous gem:

> Nothing makes a larger difference in the use of evaluations than the personal factor—the interest of officials in learning from the evaluation and the desire of the evaluator to get attention for what he knows. (Cronbach & Associates, 1980, p. 6)

Findings about the importance of the personal factor have been accumulating over more than a quarter century. Hofstetter and Alkin (2003) conducted a comprehensive review of research on evaluation use for the *International Handbook of Educational Evaluation*. They concluded:

> In sum, numerous factors influence use. The "personal factor" appears to be the most important determinant of what impact as well as the type of impact of a given evaluation. (p. 216)

And what does this mean in practice? They found:

> The evaluator could enhance use by engaging and involving intended users early in the evaluation, ensuring strong communications between the producers and users of evaluations, reporting evaluation findings effectively so users can understand and use them for their purposes, and maintaining credibility with the potential users. (p. 216)

Tom Henderson was tall, carried himself with easy distinction, and spoke softly but authoritatively. By the time I met him, his hair had turned white as the Minnesota snow, which he told me at our first meeting he had arranged to make me feel at home in the tropics. I was there to bring expertise in planning and evaluation. He was the expert and my mentor on everything Caribbean. I quickly learned that extension personnel and agricultural officials throughout the Caribbean held him in high esteem. He even knew all of the ministers of agriculture, chief extension officers, and leaders of farmers' groups. He even knew most of the extension agents throughout the Caribbean. His credibility and regular presence in the field established a foundation without which the project could never have even begun, much less succeed. He not only worked in agriculture, but advised on other development efforts.

Many international development prunes cover their seasoned wisdom, experience, and thick skin with a deep layer of cynicism. Not Tom Henderson. In 10 years working with him I never saw a hint of the pessimism and cynicism so often displayed by those who have worked for years on development problems. He was hard-nosed and realistic about the challenges of development, but he remained enthusiastic and visionary despite the difficulties of his work, the high risks of failure, and the many factors over which he had no control. He believed profoundly in the importance of education, especially extension education. And he never stopped learning. He took naturally to evaluation. After our first conversation about evaluation, he made it a part of every training course and applied his expertise about how things worked in the Caribbean to customize our approach to evaluating the overall project.

Formally, his work in preparing the original project proposal was called "needs assessment," but it would better be described as a "situation analysis." In 1996 he had headed a UNICEF team that conducted a situation analysis of children and families in Dominica and he told me afterwards that he much preferred that terminology. Tom Henderson understood the Caribbean situation. He not only knew all of the key players, he knew each and every small farming ecosystem in the islands. In graduate school he had studied the training and visit extension model (T & V) that was used in India to spread the Green Revolution. (The Green Revolution refers to the introduction of high-yielding varieties of seeds after 1965 and to the increased use of fertilizers and irrigation that led to dramatic increases in production that made India self-sufficient in food grains so that famine, once considered inevitable, was alleviated.) Under the T & V model, each week extension agents were taught one key practice that they then went out and taught to farmers. Hundreds of agricultural extension agents in a geographically large and similar agroecological area in India would be teaching the exact same thing that week: how to prepare the soil for the new, higher yielding varieties; then, in sequence, precisely how to plant, fertilize, cultivate, har-

vest, and store the precious grains. The T & V system required military discipline, detailed standardization, and precise adherence to specified protocols. T & V extension agents didn't need advanced degrees or a deep understanding of agriculture. They just needed to learn and communicate one thing at a time each week. Tom Henderson had visited India on a training mission and witnessed T & V firsthand. "It would never work in the Caribbean," he told me. "Never work. International agricultural experts come here, stay 2 days, know nothing about the local situation, and advise us to adopt T & V." Then he'd sit back and smile at the ignorance and arrogance. Familiar territory from his youth in the Botanical Garden.

Some things can be transported from one place to another, he would explain. He considered cricket a good example. Tom loved cricket. During the 1980s, the Caribbean cricket team set a then-record streak of 11 consecutive world match victories, called "Tests," and took special pride in twice trouncing their former colonial rival England. Cricket has well-established international rules. The pitch (playing field) has to be the same. The ball and bat have to be the same. The uniforms are regulated. It's all regimented, which makes it possible for the game to be international and fair wherever it is played.

Caribbean agriculture, in contrast, is highly diverse. Small farmers may grow citrus, bananas, cotton, yams, vegetables, or coconuts in varied combinations. They may have a few goats, sheep, chickens, a pig or cow, and sometimes a few rabbits. As we visited with farmers and toured their small fields, Tom would explain to me how the rainfall varied dramatically from one side of a small island to the other, often being heaviest in the middle; how soil types differed; and the effects of hills and volcanic outcroppings that contributed to distinct watersheds and microweather systems. He had studied pigeon pea production in Trinidad. His studies of banana production led to an in-depth and widely used study on "Constraints to the Adoption of Improved Practices in the Windward Islands Banana Industry." He knew how local markets varied, and how the ups and downs of international markets affected local farmers, especially the always fragile banana industry, which was heavily subsidized by England, but could not really compete with the large plantations of Central and South America.

And then there were cultural factors. Tom Henderson was fascinated by variations in culture. As we drove along rough back roads in an old Land Rover to reach remote fields, he would explain to me the local nuances in culture, politics, social norms, attitudes, language, sports, and music. Slight but important cultural and socioeconomic differences from island to island, and in different areas of the same island, affected how agricultural extension advice was delivered and received. The agricultural extension challenge in the Caribbean was matching advice, production advances, and new approaches to the situation of a particular small-farm family. A standardized T & V approach wouldn't work. Local context trumps everything else. Tom was also an enthusiastic bridge player, so when he insisted that "local context trumps everything else," he meant just that.

Here was where Tom Henderson and I found common ground. He saw the challenge of Caribbean extension as adapting advice and support to farmers so that it fit with and was relevant to the farmers' situation. I saw the challenge of evaluation the same way, as discovering situationally meaningful questions and bringing timely data to bear in usefully answering those questions. I had been an agricultural extension field worker as a Peace Corps volunteer in Burkina Faso (then Upper Volta) working among the Gourma people. My experiences in extension were the foundation for the utilization-focused approach I brought to evaluation. It will help you understand the perspective that informs this book and the partnership I formed with Tom Henderson if I tell you just a bit about my African extension experience.

More History and Biography as Context

It was 1967 and I went into the Peace Corps instead of going off to the Vietnam War, which was then raging. We were community development generalists working in very poor, rural villages where farmers engaged in subsistence agriculture, growing primarily millet and sorghum. I was assigned to the local agricultural extension service. In the region of Fada N'Gourma, soils were poor, water was scarce, infant mortality was high, infectious diseases were common and debilitating. Markets were underdeveloped, resources were few. We were young, idealistic, hopeful, and clueless.

We began by talking with villagers, listening to their stories, gathering their histories, learning about their experiences, and working to understand their perspectives. Gradually, as we learned the language, engaged with the people, and began to understand the local setting, project possibilities emerged: digging wells, building one-room schools, introducing cash crops, promoting new approaches to cultivation, and organizing cooperatives. But our role was always more one of facilitation than of actual doing. We figured out shared interests, helped organize groups for action, and helped them find resources. Our efforts were highly pragmatic, just trying to find something that would work, that might create a little leverage that could be used to gather insights into and start to address larger problems. In the grand scheme of things, our efforts were very modest.

I learned how to figure out what someone cared about, how to bring people together to identify shared interests, and how to match initiatives and resources to those shared interests. I learned to ground my change efforts in the perspectives, values, and interests of those with whom I worked, the indigenous people who were there before I came and would be there after I left. I learned to appreciate and honor local villagers and farmers as the primary stakeholders in change, and to see my role as facilitating their actions, not letting my interests and values drive the process, but rather deferring to and facilitating their interests and values.

As I have written elsewhere, my approach to evaluation grew out of those seminal community development experiences in Africa (Patton, 2004). From the very beginning, it was clear to me that I was not going to be the primary user of the evaluation findings. My niche would be facilitating use by others. I could apply what I had learned about how to figure out what someone cared about, how to bring people together to identify shared interests, and how to match evaluation designs and resources to those shared interests. I drew on what I had learned about how to ground my Peace Corps efforts in the perspectives, values, and interests of those with whom I worked, the indigenous program participants, staff, administrators, leaders, and other decision makers who were involved with the program before I came and would be there after I left. I learned to appreciate and honor these people as the primary stakeholders in using evaluation findings and to see my role as facilitating their actions, not letting my interests and values drive the process, but rather deferring to and facilitating their interests and values. In that way I tried to make myself useful to people struggling to survive in harsh, demanding, and volatile human services, education, social change, and public policy environments.

Fundamental Principles

Tom Henderson and I talked often about similarities between good extension work and useful evaluation. In the evenings after a day of planning, training, and working with small farmers, we'd sit *limin'*, the Trinidadian word for just hanging out, perhaps with a beer or rum and coke, talking about this and that. The conversation regularly turned to the fundamental principles that extension and evaluation share: targeting

information to the concrete needs of specific people (farmers in the case of extension, program staff and decision makers in the case of evaluation); being sure that information provided is relevant, timely, understandable, practical, accurate, and useful; following through to facilitate use of the information provided; and doing the work, whether extension or evaluation, in a way that supported ongoing learning, improvement, and development. (Based on these discussions with Tom, I have written about the similarities between extension and evaluation, shared principles, and the ways that effective practices in each field can inform practices in the other; see Patton, 1983, 2008b). Part of the reason I believe that Tom Henderson *got it* so quickly about the potential of evaluation was that he could relate to evaluation through his understanding of extension. Later in the life of the CAEP that we codirected, Tom and I began conducting training on evaluation throughout the islands as well as for a number of extension organizations in the United States, and we always began with an exercise comparing extension and evaluation challenges, trying to help extension staff and program participants connect with this alien and often fear-inducing notion of *evaluation*. Basically, this exercise established that extension educators work to get people to use information—*and so do evaluators*. Extension educators spend a lot of time considering how to overcome resistance to change. *So do evaluators*. Extension educators worry about communicating knowledge in a form people can understand and use. *So do evaluators*.

But I'm getting ahead of the story. It would be some years before Tom Henderson and I did evaluation training together. We first had to figure out how to approach evaluation in the project we were codirecting. That's the story I want to tell here. I recognize that few readers will have any interest in agricultural extension in the Caribbean in the 1980s. But that's not the focus or point. I invite you to engage with this story and example in search of principles of developmental evaluation. Look more deeply into the implications of the chapter title: *Thinking Outside Evaluation's Boxes*. Watch for principles that you might extract from this example. Indeed, practice extracting such principles, for extracting principles from reflective practice is one of the principal tools of developmental evaluation. See if you can understand enough about the Caribbean extension context to understand why we did what we did, and then, extracting the principles that undergirded why we did what we did, examine the relevance of those principles to your own situation.

Developmental Evaluation in Context

The CAEP provides an example of what a developmental evaluation can offer, how it can be implemented, and the difference it can make to program development. At the time this evaluation was conducted, in the 1980s, we didn't have the terminology or conceptual framework of developmental evaluation. We just wanted to do an evaluation that was useful and actually used. We stumbled into developmental evaluation as a result of being pragmatic and trying to do an evaluation that made sense for our situation and context. Looking back, key elements of developmental evaluation were present and this experience had a major impact on my subsequent identification and elaboration of developmental evaluation as a distinct approach. So, file this in the category of *oldie but goodie*, if you will, but it is central to understanding the journey of discovery that brought me to this book and it remains relevant as a concrete illustration of developmental evaluation, especially as distinct from formative and summative evaluation, as discussed in the previous chapter. Let me pursue that point.

CAEP aimed to improve national agricultural extension services in eight Caribbean countries. We began with a rapid reconnais-sance baseline study to identify the distinct farming systems in each participating island. An interdisciplinary team of agricultural researchers, social scientists, and extension staff did fieldwork and interviewed farmers for a period of 10 days to identify extension priorities for a specific agroecological zone. This process served as the basis for needs assessment and program development. It was also, quite explicitly and intentionally, an intervention in and of itself in that the process garnered attention from both farmers and agricultural officials, thereby beginning the extension mobilization process. In addition, the rapid reconnaissance survey served the critical evaluation function of establishing baseline data. Subsequent data on the effects of extension and agricultural development in the zone were compared against this baseline for evaluation purposes. Yet, it would have been much too expensive to undertake this kind of intensive team fieldwork simply for purposes of evaluation. Such data collection was practical and cost-effective because it served program development purposes, including building relationships with farmers, extensions officers, agricultural officials, and key people in the various ministries of agriculture. It also began the process of connecting agricultural researchers to extension workers and farmers, a project priority. By having extension staff and Caribbean agricultural researchers working side-by-side in the rapid reconnaissance teams, they came to know and understand each other as never before. Conflicts also emerged in those relationships. Documenting and understanding extension–research conflicts provided direction for early project initiatives aimed at establishing meaningful two-way communication between extension staff and researchers.

Emergent Understandings through Reflective Practice

Likewise, involving farmers and representatives of farmer organizations in the rapid reconnaissance teams began the process of bridging long-standing gaps in the region between agricultural researchers, extension staff, and farmers. During reflective practice sessions with the rapid reconnaissance teams following their work in the islands, the idea arose that CAEP should help establish some kind of ongoing connection between the various stakeholders in farming. This was an *emergent* idea. You'll hear a lot about *emergence* in developmental evaluation: watching for things to percolate up from interactions, capturing those ideas and new relationships, and placing them in front of project staff as options for further development. Let me emphasize this point—and expect me to return to it often, especially in the next chapter when we look at emergence as a central concept in complexity theory and in Chapter 9 when I'll detail how to use reflective practice as a developmental evaluation method. The reflective practice process of debriefing a project activity, in this case the interdisciplinary, cross-function, and multistakeholder rapid reconnaissance

teams' experience of assessing farmer needs in specific agroecological zones, had dual purposes. First, reflective practice aimed at capturing and learning lessons about how to conduct such assessments and improve the process when it would be repeated for evaluation purposes later in the life of the project, to document impact. Second, the reflective practice process had developmental purposes, to deepen the relationship among formerly disconnected farmers, extension staff, and agricultural researchers while also seeking creative ideas for future project initiatives and priorities. Reflective practice, as a developmental evaluation method, often includes formally facilitating sessions with those involved in and affected by an initiative to capture their experiences and perspectives. It is the formal data gathering, documentation, analysis of patterns, and feedback to project decision makers that makes this an evaluation activity. Often such debriefing sessions are done, if done at all, as informal, unfocused gripe sessions,

EMERGENCE

"OK, who pooped on the podium?"

Note: This cartoon caption was a winning submission in *The New Yorker* (2008) magazine cartoon caption contest. Michael Morris, one of the evaluation profession's deepest thinkers about ethics (Morris, 2008), submitted this clever winning entry. Hmmmm. Does this say something about your assessment of the state of ethics in evaluation, Mike? Illustration © Frank Cotham/Condé Nast Publications/*www.cartoonbank.com.*

without skilled facilitation, documentation, systematic data gathering, and analysis. Developmental evaluation can use regular debriefing sessions, whether called reflective practice or something else, both to capture important patterns that are emerging and, through the reflective process of interacting together, to facilitate creative synergies that allow new ideas and possibilities to emerge. We saw this in the reflective practice sessions of the Twin Cities Rise! program described in the last chapter, and we see it again here in the Caribbean.

The reflective practice debriefing sessions with rapid reconnaissance teams led to the idea—an emergent idea—of creating ongoing national agricultural development committees made up of the same diverse stakeholder groups that had participated in the agroecological needs assessments. As these were put in place and began working on local priorities, subsequent independent evaluation documented that they became an important and effective mechanism for private-sector and farmer influence on the setting of national agricultural policies and extension priorities. The roles and effectiveness of these committees varied from island to island. Some of the countries went beyond establishing a single committee and instituted extension, research, and marketing subcommittees. These subcommittees obtained farmer and private-sector input on priorities, objectives, and possible initiatives that might be undertaken in their particular policy area and passed their findings and recommendations up the chain of command to the ministers of agriculture. In some countries, after national committees were established, those who had been involved in the agrioecological needs assessment teams pushed for and helped organize district committees, which gathered input at the most basic level, that of the farmers themselves.

Randolph Mark had been an extension officer in Grenada, retired from extension, and turned to farming bananas and vegetables. He helped create and served on one of Grenada's district committees after partici-

pating in the rapid reconnaissance process. At a national meeting observed by an external evaluator (a process I'll describe shortly), he reported: "Our district committee has made suggestions for research and extension projects that matter greatly to farmers. Prior to formation of our committee, there was no direct link between the farmer and the ministry. Oh, there was supposed to be a link through the extension officer, but he didn't have much say or much authority. He wasn't in a position to take the farmers' problems to the right authorities. Now the problems of farmers can be taken from our district subcommittees to the national agricultural committee and we think that we'll finally see some things getting done."

Earlene Horne joined the committee in Saint Vincent. A widow with young children, she had a powerful persona, wasn't afraid to speak her mind, and had become a harsh critic of extension in her district. After participating in the rapid reconnaissance team as a farmer representative, she became energized by the possibility of change and became active in the National Farmers Union, soon elected as the leader of the group. She served on her country's national agricultural planning committee as well as its research subcommittee. She went on record at a regional conference saying, "When our subcommittee met with representatives from the institutions that deal with agriculture and agricultural research on St. Vincent—researchers from the University of the West Indies and the Caribbean Agricultural Research and Development Institute [CARDI], and the Ministry of Agriculture—we learned about and were able to understand for the first time what was going on in research in our country. We discovered that there was hardly any link or coordination between CARDI research and the ministry's research and work. There was a movement in our subcommittee to reorganize research so the ministry would know what CARDI was doing and CARDI would know what the ministry was doing, and extension and farmers would know what both were doing. We made that happen and we know that we have to be vigilant or they will backslide."

Inquiring Deeply into the Development Process: Questions and More Questions

Normally the kind of testimony to project effectiveness offered by Randolph Mark of Grenada or Earlene Horne of Saint Vincent, recorded by an external evaluator, might be reported in a self-congratulatory way in a project report or newsletter, and highlighted for a funder as evidence of project effectiveness. End of story. But a developmental evaluator hears more and pushes project staff to engage more deeply. Randolph Mark's quotation ends with the hope that something will get done, but no assertion that anything has happened other than better communications. Earlene Horne is pleased that extension staff, researchers, and farmers are communicating, but with what results? And what is the project's role in supporting vigilance and preventing backsliding? Indeed, the easy work in most any project is putting some structure in place to enhance communications. But then what? Does anything change? Can these new interactions and linkages be sustained? How? To what end? The developmental evaluator is vigilant in keeping these issues in front of project staff and decision makers by always asking: What's emerging? What does it mean? What's next? Why? What should we be watching for? What's being learned?

By persistently asking such questions, and asking them in a way that can be heard and valued by project staff, the developmental evaluator is not just supporting decision making about emergent issues. These questions, and staff's attention to them, build a culture of evaluative thinking into the project. That was my internal role in the project, to help build that culture of inquiry and development. I was able to play that role because Tom Henderson valued and affirmed it, and engaged fully with the evaluation,

modeling for younger staff how to integrate evaluation inquiry with ongoing program development. Developmental evaluation isn't sustainable if the only one observing what's going on and asking questions about what it means is the developmental evaluator. The developmental evaluator may be a coach, a technical assistance provider, a friendly critic, a burr in the program saddle, a living feedback mechanism, a light shining in the program's shadows, or a futurist looking ever ahead to what's next, and what's after that. The developmental evaluator may play all these roles and more. I did. But for the process to work, the staff must come to value this questioning, internalize it, get better at it, and ultimately do it themselves. The developmental evaluator facilitates developmental reflection, priority setting, and decision making, but the developmental evaluator doesn't do the actual developing. That's the staff role. The developmental evaluator's role and skill in bringing emergent observations and data before the staff may be ongoing, and in my experience can go on for years, but the ultimate test of the utility of developmental evaluation is that staff acts on the findings and values the process, becoming hungry for more and better data and feedback. Chapter 8 is devoted to inquiry frameworks for developmental evaluation, identifying different ways of deepening the developmental inquiry process.

The Rhythms of Developmental Evaluation

What I hope is emerging here is a picture of program development and developmental evaluation as mutually reinforcing processes, like dancers, separate but paying attention to each other's moves, both attuned to the surrounding music and rhythms of other dancers (the larger context), while themselves moving together and thereby moving forward. Sometimes the beat is hard and fast, like a Trinidadian Carnival street *soca*, as when a project is unfolding rapidly and observations of emergent realities are cascading in a crescendo of intense, focused development. Other times the dance is slow and easy-going, a light reggae beat that engages but does not exhaust, as when routinely collected data are examined as a check-in on the progress of planned and smoothly unfolding program implementation. And there are breaks in the dance, when the music stops and it's time to put evaluation aside, time to get refreshed. There are even times of collective orchestration involving a large number of diverse stakeholders together poring over findings, like a large steel drum orchestra, 100 strong, blending large bass drums with altos, tenors, and sopranos, to create a symphony.

Yes, I may have stretched this metaphor beyond recognition and any semblance of meaning, at least for those of you unfortunate souls who have not participated in Caribbean Carnival or heard in person one of the great Trinidadian steel drum orchestras (my condolences). But it would be irresponsible of me to discuss Caribbean agricultural development at such length without at least trying to evoke a bit of the ambiance and larger context. The point is this: There is, indeed, a rhythm and flow to the interactions between program development and developmental evaluation. As program development slows, developmental evaluation may slow; as program development intensifies, developmental evaluation may intensify. But the energy flow is not just one-way, program to evaluation. Developmental evaluation feedback can provide the energy that intensifies program development, or slows it down, encouraging program developers to stand still for a bit and take a look at what's going on and figure out what it means. Finding the interactive rhythm and flow between program development and developmental evaluation is part of the challenge—and reward—of engaging in developmental evaluation, in the developmental evaluation dance, if you will. More on that later, too. After all, this is only the third chapter. We're still just getting acquainted.

External Evaluators and Developmental Evaluation

Thus far I've been describing an entirely internal developmental evaluation process in which we used evaluation methods, processes, and findings to inform program development right from the beginning. We integrated program development and evaluation within the project. We had control over that integration. Tom Henderson and I, as codirectors of CAEP, shared a commitment to grounding project development in ongoing evaluation, systematic reflective practice, and attention to both anticipated data sources, like production data from farmers, and emergent observations, like the insights that emerged from the debriefings of the rapid reconnaissance teams. But *how could mandated external evaluation be made developmental?* Good question. You're already thinking like a developmental evaluator. *Or should external evaluation be made developmental? And could it?* Also good questions. Bring to the fore the skepticism of traditional evaluation, which would assert that external evaluation should stay focused on its independent accountability function. That's a fair concern. Good to surface it early on. So let's see how this played out.

When CAEP was funded by USAID, it included the typical mandate for an external midterm review to assess progress and identify weaknesses (mostly formative in purpose) and an external and independent end-of-project evaluation (expected to serve a summative purpose). Standard operating procedure. Now consider: Presumably, a summative end-of-project evaluation should inform the funder's decision about whether to continue, expand, reduce, or terminate the project. In this case, the 10-year project was funded in three phases. The first phase (1980–1982) was for startup and planning, with the subsequent implementation phase (1983–1986) requiring an independent end-of-phase evaluation before the third and final phase (1987–1990) could proceed.

⌒ *Who Can Do*
Developmental Evaluation?:
Internal versus External Evaluators

A long-standing issue in evaluation is the location of the evaluator inside or outside the program or initiative being evaluated, what has sometimes been called the "in-house" versus "outhouse" issue. External evaluators are presumed to have more independence and therefore more credibility when answering accountability questions or making summative judgments. Internal evaluators, in contrast, are expected to have more knowledge about what's going on with staff, more sensitivity to internal program dynamics, and a longer-term commitment to the program, all of which, it is hoped, increase trust, relevance, and use, especially for improvement-oriented (formative) evaluation.

Because of this long-standing differentiation between the roles of external versus internal evaluators, one of the first questions I get in presentations and training sessions is whether the developmental evaluator should be internal or external. I respond that developmental evaluation is a role not a location. The developmental evaluator supports development. I have conducted developmental evaluation as an internal evaluator and as an external evaluator, and know of both internal and external evaluators who have played the role of developmental evaluator. In either case, the evaluator becomes part of the development process, asking developmental evaluation questions, bringing evaluative thinking to the innovation team, and supporting ongoing decision making, adaptations, and development with real-time data and feedback. The first-order identity, then, is not that one is an internal or external evaluator, but that one is a *developmental evaluator*.

That sounds good in theory, but in the real world of funder decision making, the actual decision about whether to fund Phase 2 would have to be made long before the end of the phase. Here's where it gets interesting. The external midterm review of Phase 2 was scheduled by USAID to occur at the end of 1984, roughly 2 years into Phase 2 implementation, and the external end-of-phase evaluation would be due at the end of 1986. But given the USAID planning and budgeting process, the actual decision about whether to fund the third phase had to be made before the end of 1984, *even before the midterm review was scheduled to be completed.* A summative, end-of-phase evaluation submitted as scheduled at the end of 1986 could have no impact on Phase 3 funding, or even any impact on planning the next phase because those plans would have already been developed and approved prior to the end of Phase 2 if there was to be a Phase 3. Yet, the regional office of USAID in Barbados had to prepare and submit its budget recommendations for a possible third phase to USAID in Washington a full 2 years before the end of the second phase. This time line was necessitated by when the U.S. Agency for International Development had to submit its future budget priorities to the U.S. State Department for review, which would then be included in the president's budget to Congress, a process that itself takes a year or more.

Thus, working backward from the date when the regional office of USAID would have to make its Phase 3 decision (December 1984), and calculating when an evaluation would have to be submitted to inform that decision (November 1984), we had to consider when such an evaluation could actually be conducted and what it would focus on since actual Phase 2 implementation would have just begun when the summative decision about Phase 3 funding had to be made. Those were the realities (and still today quite typical of funding time lines worldwide). Hopefully, if I haven't completely lost you while trying to outline these funding realities (and, no, there will not be any dance allusions to lighten this bureaucratic saga), you may also have already surmised that the scheduled midterm review was not designed to ask questions and provide findings for informing a summative decision. That was to be the task of the external end-of-phase evaluation, which would be submitted 2 years after the actual funding decision had been made. Given these realities, *what kind of evaluation would make sense?*

Sensible Evaluation: Or, a Rant on Widespread Evaluation Nonsense

Let me pause here to allow you, gentle reader—yes, I have been schooled in *Miss Manners Guide to Excruciatingly Correct Behavior* when addressing readers (Martin, 2005)—to appreciate and ruminate on the excruciatingly incorrect, unsettling, impolite, and impolitic nature of the aforementioned query, to wit, *what kind of evaluation would make sense?* This is, of course, an outlandish question, one that would never occur to the legions of rule-making and proposal-format-enforcing contract administrators who require, demand, impose, audit, and rate proposals to assure that therein appearing are routine requirements for midterm and end-of-project evaluations. This is the most common evaluation template in the world, and has been for well over a quarter century, since organizations of all kinds—government agencies, international organizations, philanthropic foundations, and nonprofit doers of good—discovered ACCOUNTABILITY as their drug of choice and joined it with motherhood, replacing the traditional succor offered for public consumption on rare occasions when the public is actually paying attention. Its lack of nourishment and empty calories notwithstanding, ACCOUNTABILITY has proven wonderfully addictive, much more so than that previous pretender to the public throne of goodness, apple pie in the United States and *LogFrames* among international development funders. So we find mil-

lions of dollars spent each year assembling teams of so-called evaluators conducting these mandated reviews on a predetermined schedule. I refer to them as "so-called evaluators" because they are seldom in any way trained in or knowledgeable about evaluation, but have a few crucial traits valued above all, namely, being available to go forth on short notice with little understanding of the setting into which they are about to insert themselves and willing to pretend that what they are being asked to do makes sense. Not that they ask no questions. "How much flexibility is there in the evaluation design and in the daily honorarium?" they inquire, knowing that to commit themselves to conducting a midterm review of an unsuspecting program about which they know nothing in a setting where they have no experience, often in a language they don't speak, requires, well, flexibility in what they will do, how long it will take them to do it, and, given the challenges and even dangers that may be faced, naturally raises the question about what in the end they will be paid for their work. It is enough to drive a saint to drink.

And why you may ask, gentle and perceptive reader, is being available on short notice a distinguishing qualification for such undertakings? It seems that despite having predetermined the schedule for midterm and end-of-project reviews, and having inserted that schedule into various and assorted contract documents, the actual paperwork to create such teams seems to get neglected or delayed until the last minute. I regularly get requests, see many others, and hear of still more from colleagues, asking if the object of the solicitation would be available in 3 weeks to travel to Mali, or Chile, or Vietnam, or Omaha to undertake an evaluation assignment for several days, sometimes even weeks, conducting an external accountability review. Sometimes, but only occasionally, there's even a whole month's advance notice. Guess who's available for duty and service under such short time lines? Former saints long since driven to drink.

Thus do little-qualified and ill-prepared teams descend on programs and ask questions prepared at some distance from the program by a contract administrator who is following a standardized accountability and compliance protocol. This assures objectivity, which is important for credible accountability—objectivity in this case being synonymous with complete ignorance about what is going on and the questions asked being irrelevant to the local situation and context. What better ways to assure objectivity and independence than ignorance and irrelevance? Such designs are a wonder to behold. And watching such teams in action simply takes the breath away. They breeze in and breeze out, write a report that is filed dutifully under HAS BEEN EVALUATED, collect their honoraria and per diem, and await the next call, their qualifications for the next assignment having been nicely enhanced by having just completed yet another independent and objective evaluation. With such added experience, next time they may well get to lead the team.

You may think, gentle, perceptive, and hopefully tolerant reader, that I exaggerate, that I am too harsh. I assure you I'm being overly kind. I've included a sidebar in this chapter with examples of the stories I hear of such so-called evaluators engaging in corrupt, unethical, and harmful practices. But essentially, I'm ranting about basic incompetence and nonsense built into the system. Those interested in developmental evaluation, like all those interested in useful evaluation, will have to be prepared to face these barriers and challenges. I don't want to give the impression that this work is easy or without land mines.

~ *Reflections on and Cautions about Misevaluation, Misuse, and General Corruption, Concluding with a Note on the Desired Qualifications for Undertaking Developmental Evaluation*

The evaluation profession recognizes a critical distinction between *misevaluation*, in which an evaluator performs poorly or fails to adhere to standards and principles, and *misuse*, in which users manipulate the evaluation in ways that distort the findings or corrupt the inquiry. As in any profession, there are a few rotten apples who can spoil the harvest for everyone, leaving a long-lingering bad taste in the mouths of those who were hoping for something more succulent and nourishing. Because all evaluation, including developmental evaluation, takes place within this larger context of a few bad examples casting a pall over the whole, how people in programs engage with evaluators is affected by their conceptions about what evaluation is, their experience with how it is conducted, and their expectations about what constitutes sensible and *ethical* evaluation—as well as, not incidentally, what they've heard through the grapevine and the always-exquisitely-trustworthy-and-accurate rumor mill.

Sometimes, unfortunately, the evaluator is the problem. That's a fact and not just an unsubstantiated rumor. I worked with Alexey Kuzmin, a Russian evaluator, during his doctoral program. He has since coedited an excellent evaluation book published in Russian (Kuzmin, O'Sullivan, & Kosheleva, 2009). His dissertation included fieldwork on evaluation capacity building in Eastern Europe. He turned up a number of instances of unscrupulous evaluators engaged in unethical practices, which he reported at the International Evaluation Conference in Toronto in 2005. In one case, an American site visitor to a small program arrived late one day, left early the next, never visited the program, and refused to take the documents offered by the program. Some time later, the program director received an urgent demand from the funder for required documentation (the very documentation that the evaluator was supposed to have taken, analyzed, and presented to the funder) that took considerable expense to get to the funder; subsequently, the program was denied additional funding for lack of a completed evaluation.

(cont.)

In another instance in Russia, an external evaluator without any substantive expertise in the program's area of focus arrived. He spent a couple of days with the program, then disappeared, leaving an unpaid hotel bill and expenses that the program had to cover because it had made arrangements for his visit. A couple of months later, the program director received a draft evaluation report for her comments, but the deadline for sending comments had already passed. The evaluation contained numerous errors and biased conclusions based on the evaluator's own prejudices. The program director spent a considerable amount of time writing a response to the evaluation, but the evaluation, with its errors and negative judgments, had already been posted on a prominent website. The program had to resort to expensive legal action to have the evaluation removed.

The third example concerns a very affable evaluator of a program in Siberia undergoing an external midterm review. The American evaluation team leader was a charming man who gave a great deal of attention to the program director. In a private conversation with her, he talked in depth about an organizational development model he had recently implemented in another country in Central Europe. It gradually became clear that the evaluator would offer positive evaluation findings if the director hired him as a consultant to return and implement his model in her agency. He said, "I really want to say good things about your program. I want to support it, but I need to hear some things from you before I do that." The program director, feeling quite vulnerable, contacted a lawyer for advice about how to protect herself and her agency, advice she heeded, but found the whole experience traumatic (Kuzmin, 2009; Patton, 2008c, pp. 555–556).

Sometimes it's the funders and/or program staff who make doing useful evaluation difficult. Another of my former evaluation graduate students, Donna Podems, has written insightfully about the challenges of facilitating thoughtful discussions about and approaches to evaluation in an African context where both the funder and the programs being evaluated were resistant to meaningful evaluation—and largely ignorant about what meaningful evaluation would entail (Podems, 2007). The funder was insistent on by-the-book procedures whether appropriate or not, whether useful or not. The program staff was in understandable compliance mode: Just tell us what to do. Not an ideal situation, one might say. She has also written about the unnerving experience of having a funder insist on a standardized survey in an oral society where surveying was suspect and people were told what to say by those in power; where comparative statistics were demanded regardless of their validity, reliability, or meaningfulness—"Just give us numbers"; where the funder insisted on a report that validated their prior conclusions and painted only a positive picture; and in which the funder refused payment for evaluation services rendered until the report was written the way the funder wanted it written (Patton, 2008c, p. 551).

In short, nothing in this book is meant to suggest that conducting evaluations, especially developmental evaluations, is easy. The usefulness and meaningfulness of developmental evaluation depends on a dynamic, interdependent, mutually respectful, and mutually trusting relationship between the development evaluator and the innovation design team. Developmental evaluation is as much about that relationship as it is about evaluation processes and procedures. As a result, developmental evaluators need a strong grounding in evaluation ethics and standards of practice. And it doesn't hurt if the developmental evaluator is a skilled communicator, an excellent facilitator, culturally sensitive, methodologically competent and eclectic, manifesting a strong tolerance for ambiguity, flexible and responsive, and fundamentally *a good person*—that is, an all-around saintly type with exemplary character. In other words, *the usual evaluation qualifications*, only magnified tenfold under the challenges of engaging in the relationship-based, coevolutionary, and creative demands, not to mention the complex nonlinear dynamics, of developmental evaluation.

I am aware, gentle, perceptive, tolerant, and long-suffering reader, that I risk exhausting your patience with this rant. What does all this have to do with developmental evaluation? Two things. First, developmental evaluation takes place within this larger context. It is affected by people's preconceptions about what evaluation is, their experiences with how it is conducted, and their expectations about what constitutes sensible evaluation. So, when we ask the straightforward question, What kind of evaluation makes sense? it turns out not to be straightforward at all. What makes sense is a matter of perspective (another word for prejudice, literally, prejudgment). Prejudgments abound when it comes to what constitutes sensible evaluation. Those are the basis of evaluation's tradition boxes that developmental evaluation invites you to think outside of.

Second, I selfishly and self-servingly reviewed what constitutes typical evaluation practice so that you, ever-gentle and perceptive reader, would all the more apprehend what we had to overcome in order to turn CAEP's mandated midterm and end-of-project external reviews into developmental evaluation. I wanted to set the stage so you could more fully appreciate that seriously engaging the question—*What kind of evaluation makes sense?*—can take one in quite unforeseen directions with unexpected consequences, both delightful and dire. Stage set. On with the story, then.

Doing What Makes Sense

Doing what makes sense applies to any utilization-focused evaluation, not just to developmental evaluation. Some of what we did just followed good utilization-focused evaluation principles, but parts added a distinct developmental dimension. We'll sort out the distinctions as the story unfolds.

At the beginning of Phase 2, we convened an advisory group of agricultural officials, researchers, extension staff, and farmer representatives from the participating countries to consider the question of what kind of

external evaluation made sense. This group, officially the Regional Agricultural Extension Coordinating Committee, was popularly dubbed RAECC (pronounced Ray-Eck). With eight countries and regional agencies involved, RAECC's membership included some 50 stakeholders. Our deliberations in February 1983 were colored by a sudden change in context. We learned that a conference had just been held for directors of USAID missions in Latin America and the Caribbean. The dominant view at that meeting, we were told by the USAID program officer, was that funding extension projects in developing countries was not an effective use of aid—or USAID—funds. This represented more than a changed assessment of extension effectiveness. This change in how our project was viewed reflected a larger political change. CAEP had been originally designed in the late 1970s when President Carter had made helping the poor the centerpiece of American foreign assistance. Improving extension services to small farmers was consistent with that mission. Ronald Reagan, elected in 1980, made fighting the spread of communism the priority of foreign assistance. Extension programs fell into policy disfavor. The regional director of USAID was disinclined to fund Phase 3, his position in this regard emerging just weeks after the beginning of Phase 2.

Given this new political context of skepticism about both the political value and the cost-effectiveness of agricultural extension projects in developing countries, RAECC, acting as an advisory group, recommended that an evaluation begin immediately to inform USAID's funding decision for Phase 3 and that it provide data on the potential of agricultural extension to contribute to increased farmer productivity and income, including examining whether agricultural extension contributed to individual farmer entrepreneurialism, which could be considered an antidote to communism.

That was all well and good, for CAEP did aspire to increase farmer income through improved national extension services. Over the 4 years of Phase 2 (1983–1986), the project aimed to support major changes in the organization and delivery of agricultural extension. However, direct impacts on farmers early in Phase 2 (1983–1986) would be limited. Many of the extension staff would not return from advanced training courses until halfway through Phase 2 or later, and none of the hoped-for benefits of the project would be evident at the early stage of implementation during which the proposed new and urgent evaluation would have to be conducted. Because changes in extension organizations were timed to occur gradually throughout the life of the project in accordance with the absorptive capacity of poorly resourced extension services and with an eye toward making changes embedded and sustainable, it would take some time for measurable changes in extension organization and delivery systems to show up in changed farmer practices and increased income. How, then, could the question of long-term extension effectiveness in the Caribbean be addressed?

Over the course of a full day of intense deliberations RAECC participants examined the challenges, high stakes, and options for evaluation. We eventually landed on a creative approach that might not only inform the funding decision, but also contribute to program development, accelerate the implementation process, contribute to learning about critical dimensions of extension effectiveness, and inform staff priorities about where to focus limited resources. The idea for this evaluation grew out of the work that had been done by the rapid reconnaissance (recon) teams that had studied distinct agroecological zones in the various islands as part of the Phase 1 planning process. Those teams had documented great variability in farming systems and even greater variability in existing extension practices. While most extension agents lacked sufficient training, organizational support, or agricultural resources to be effective, a few old-timers were doing quite a bit of good work. Several of these veterans participated in the rapid recon teams. Recalling that, an idea emerged.

Understanding and Building on Excellence and Success

Here's what we proposed to USAID. We would work with USAID to assemble an independent team to conduct case studies of especially effective extension agents in all eight countries. This would involve what is called in qualitative methods a "purposeful" sampling strategy (Patton, 2002), seeking a small number of information-rich cases. We used a version of purposeful sampling called "extreme group case selection" or the success case method (Brinkerhoff, 2003, 2005). This involved identifying in each country an "outstanding agricultural extension agent," a person chosen through a nomination and selection process directed by each country's national planning committee for extension, which had been established in Phase 1. These committees included farmers, representatives of farmer organizations, ministry of agriculture officials, agricultural researchers, and others with interests in agricultural development. Following selection of outstanding agents, each would be asked to identify five farm families with which they had worked closely—farmers they believed they had helped in discernible, significant ways. The independent evaluators would then visit the farms, interview the farmers, family members, neighbors, knowledgeable others, and the extension agent who had worked with the family. These case studies would credibly establish the nature and extent of extension impact possible from well-trained, experienced agents.

Eight outstanding extension agents (one per country) each identifying five high-impact cases yielded 40 cases. This sample was designed to establish an empirical baseline for what effective agents could accomplish. It was assumed that the typical extension agent at that time had less impact than outstanding agents, often much less. However, by gathering data about the ideal that might be obtained, it would be possible to establish what might be achieved as an increasing number of well-trained agents began to operate more effectively with better support, appropriate supervision, and better equipment and transportation. Even the impact of experienced and effective extension staff could be expected to improve with better support and more resources. In effect, this evaluation would provide USAID, as the funder, with credible and concrete, field-based data about the potential long-term impact of agricultural extension programs on farm families in the Caribbean. These findings could then be used in policy discussions to decide if the level of possible impact was worth attempting to attain through continued funding of CAEP into Phase 3 when farm family impacts would become more evident in accordance with the original 10-year funding time line.

This strategy of sampling and studying successful cases is obviously unbalanced, and therefore biased. The purpose is not, however, to obtain a balanced picture of actual impact. The purpose is to generate data to consider possible impact. This purposeful and intentional sampling bias becomes a strength rather than a weakness because it provides important information for the policy process and funding decision that would otherwise be unavailable. Basically, the independent evaluation findings would allow the funders and implementation partners, who were also contributing real resources to the project, to answer this summative question: *Is it worth funding a Phase 3 to attain more of the kinds of impact demonstrated by current outstanding extension agents? Is the potential sufficient to merit further support?*

After extensive discussion, grounded in much initial skepticism and resistance, USAID agreed to reallocate the midterm and end-of-project evaluation budget to this accelerated evaluation design with the understanding that we would meet the typical requirements for midterm and end-of-project evaluation through an ongoing relationship with the external evaluation team.

The ongoing nature of the external evaluation was a major break with USAID tradition at that time. Indeed, the evaluators and project staff had some difficulty helping USAID personnel understand why we wanted the evaluators to be involved from the very beginning and then throughout the life of the project. But they agreed to try it out.

The external evaluators were chosen to have credibility with the major constituencies of the project, these being USAID, the University of the West Indies, and the Midwest Universities Consortium for International Activities (MUCIA), for which the University of Minnesota was the primary representative (which is how I came to be involved in the project). Each of these prime constituencies named one of the external evaluators. The fourth evaluator, Professor Marvin Alkin of UCLA, was chosen for his stature in the field of evaluation, because of his commitment to user-oriented evaluations, and because he was neutral from the point of view of the other three constituencies. He chaired the evaluation team.[2] Prior to finalizing the design, the evaluators met with representatives of each of these constituencies separately and facilitated an April meeting of the regional advisory group. Data collection took place in June and July. The evaluation report was ready in November 1984. The regional advisory group reconvened for 2 days in November to receive and discuss the findings. The USAID program officer participated in that meeting, which produced a resolution recommending Phase 3 funding. The evaluator who had been selected by USAID subsequently met with the USAID director in Barbados. He was able to directly address the director's questions and concerns with concrete data and high credibility. It was subsequently re-

---

[2]Evaluation team members were Jerry West, Agricultural Economics, University of Missouri, on behalf of USAID; Marlene Cuthbert, Communications, representing the University of the West Indies; and Kay Adams, Adult Education, The Ohio State University, on behalf of the Midwest Universities Consortium for International Activities (MUCIA).

ported to me independently by USAID staff members that this meeting was critical, because as noted earlier, the USAID director was not predisposed to continue funding for the project. The evaluation concluded that the project was effective and having an im-

pact, but that further funding and activities would be necessary and justifiable to institutionalize short-term successes and guarantee long-term success and long-term effectiveness. USAID did fund Phase 3. Using the Caribbean example, Exhibit 3.1 offers two

EXHIBIT 3.1   **Scenario Comparing Standard External Evaluation Contract Time Lines to Utilization-Focused Developmental Evaluation Time Line Adjustments That Match External Evaluation to Real-World Program Time Lines**

Imagined program time lines	Traditional, standard contract: Evaluation timing	Utilization-focused developmental evaluation time-line adjustments
January 2011: 5-year contract begins; contract through December 2015	Schedule external evaluation reviews: Midterm, formative evaluation, June–July 2013 End-of-contract evaluation fieldwork, June–July 2015 Final evaluation report due, December 2015	Figure out when decisions will be made: • What is the staff schedule for reviewing progress? • What is the timing of annual workflow planning? • What is the timing of major implementation steps? • When will the decision about the future of the program have to be made? Align evaluation with these time lines.
Annual staff planning retreats each November	No external evaluation activity in 2011 or 2012; external midterm review available for November 2013 retreat.	Developmental evaluation data gathered from the beginning and feedback provided in time to be reported and used for each annual staff retreat.
October 2013: International agency will make regional decision about whether to continue the program after 2015 in order to decide whether the program will be included in its 2016–2017 budget proposal to headquarters.	Midterm formative findings available about program progress to date. Funding continuation questions not addressed.	Work with funders to determine what information will be needed and can be gathered to inform the funding decision, including: What are the funder's developmental evaluation questions?
December 2015: Program funding for Phase 1 ends (2010–2015).	Summative, end-of-program evaluation report submitted 2 years after the future funding decision has been made. May (or may not) include attention to lessons learned since the main focus is on summative judgment about whether intended outcomes have been attained.	End-of-program developmental evaluation report submitted that documents developments to date and lessons learned, and is used to inform the next phase of program development (if the program is to be continued). It does not make a summative recommendation because the summative decision was made 2 years earlier.

evaluation reporting scenarios that contrast traditional evaluation time lines (standard midterm and end-of-project reviews) with a utilization-focused, developmental approach to evaluation timing in which data collection and feedback is matched to real-world program development and decision deadlines.

So far, so good. The evaluation provided relevant and timely data to inform the Phase 3 funding decision. Having evaluation findings available in time to inform the summative funding decision proved sensible. That sensible approach was a breakthrough in and of itself, but it is not developmental evaluation. It is a solid example of utilization-focused summative evaluation, but how did this evaluation approach contribute to program development? In what ways was it developmental evaluation? I'm glad you asked.

Developmental Evaluation Uses

The patterns of extension outcomes revealed across the 40 case studies showed locally situated effective practices that provided a framework for training. Indeed, the case studies describing the practices and methods of outstanding extension agents became the basis for developing the training curriculum for all extension staff. Those case studies became primary teaching tools and allowed us to use the case teaching method in training. Some of the outstanding agents became instructors in the training program. The process of identifying and selecting outstanding agents from each country drew attention to criteria of extension excellence among both farmers and agricultural officials, which had the effect of promoting increased professionalism and pride among veteran Caribbean extension personnel, which spilled over to new, much younger staff.

The eight extension officers of excellence, as they were called, attended the annual conference of the Minnesota Extension Service and participated in meetings of the Professional Extension Association. Several

returned to establish their own national extension agent associations, and subsequently a regional association, which had not been a project goal (and was thus an emergent outcome). This became an important new mechanism for increasing a sense of professionalism and dedication among extension agents.

The evaluators created an outcomes framework that captured the diverse outcomes within different agroecological zones. The project staff subsequently organized all required reporting around those outcomes. The annual work plan for project staff was based on that outcomes framework. Staff meetings routinely reviewed the elements of the evaluation as a way of directing implementation and focusing on those outcomes that were primary. The point here is that program implementation and evaluation became integrated and synchronized. As a result, the evaluation framework helped guide program implementation and constituted a framework for program planning and reporting that provided focus to staff activities, an example of what is called "process use" of evaluation in which the way the evaluation is conducted affects the program as much as the findings do (Patton, 2008c, chap. 5). This focus became more important as the project moved forward and staff encountered many opportunities to be diverted from those primary foci. Having organized the project work plan, staff meetings, and reporting around the key outcomes, the evaluation contributed substantially to keeping staff efforts from being diffused into other areas or activities that would have taken away from the primary purposes of the project.

In summary, the evaluation had a major impact on program development and project implementation. The evaluators and case studies brought visibility to the project throughout the islands and established extension excellence and impact on farmers as the focus of all subsequent program efforts. Finally, and not incidentally, the evaluation had a major impact on the decision to continue project funding. The evaluation's

⌒ *Highlights from an Outstanding Extension Officer Case Study Example (1983)*

Excellence in Extension Award recipient Clarence Thomas works in St. Vincent's southern district, where livestock production and fishing are important industries. The district has 3,000 full-time farmers, as well as many part-time farmers. Some farmers own land, some sharecrop, and some are landless, grazing sheep, goats, and cattle on public lands. "Very many of my young farmers are landless," Thomas said, "but some of them are among the best livestock producers in the district. The domestic and export markets for livestock are very reliable, and these young people have found raising livestock to be a way of making some money."

Thomas is working to change attitudes among young people about farming, "that it lacks dignity, economic opportunity, and social status." Thomas, called "Paddy" by almost everyone, worked with a primary school to pilot a basic course on agriculture. The ministry of education has now adopted the course as part of the curriculum in all primary schools. Thomas also lectures, gives demonstrations, and provides educational and other materials for agricultural classes at the local secondary school. Some are using what they've learned to improve the productivity of their parents' sheep and goats. Others have started flocks of their own.

"Even while they're in school, they're livestock producers," Thomas said. "I know of some who pay their school fees and buy their books from the profits of their sheep and goat production. A lot of the new techniques that farmers in my district are practicing were learned from the schoolchildren rather than directly from me. Some parents have been very grateful and have told me that their children had not been helping them on the farm before we started the agriculture program. I'd be very happy if some of these children would turn to full-time farming when they leave school."

Farmers learn the fundamentals of small stock health care at the livestock health clinics Thomas set up, where he teaches animal health care. He said, "When I initiated the livestock program in my district, there were six clinic locations. But the response has been so great that there are now 25 locations, half of which were set up by the farmers themselves. We run a series of clinics three times a year. On the average, 50 animals—mostly goats and sheep—are examined and treated at each location. We deworm, castrate, trim hooves, and treat for any sickness the animals might suffer given the limited equipment and drugs that we have."

Thomas also set up a program to work with young unwed mothers in cooperation with a social services program. He teaches the young women about backyard gardening and egg and rabbit production. He has raised money to buy rabbits; 11 of the women will receive a pair with the provision that they give some of the offspring to other unwed mothers. One young woman said she was able to save $60 in 3 months from the production of her garden. She reasoned that her family had consumed about $100 worth of vegetables and she also gave some to friends.

One of Thomas's major successes has been convincing farmers to upgrade their livestock. In-breeding was a major problem; few animals were castrated and stock was allowed to breed indiscriminately. Each Wednesday, Thomas castrates animals and talks to farmers about livestock improvement. He said, "Some farmers are castrating on their own now." The drive to upgrade livestock includes artificial insemination of cattle, which farmers are accepting after some initial skepticism, and the use of higher quality imported pure breeds.

Animal nutrition is another area of concern. Thomas said, "When I began working here, there was poor pasturage and overgrazing. Farmers didn't know how to feed even though there's much crop residue and good legume feeds. So, I identified some local legumes that are very nutritious. I am introducing *Leuucaena* and some good grasses, like Pangola, Bermuda, and African stargrass on farms."

direct costs were approximately $100,000 out of a total project budget of $5.4 million, under 2% of the project budget.

Elsewhere I have described CAEP and the evaluation in greater detail, including its multiple dimensions, methods, and uses (Alkin & Patton, 1987; Henderson & Patton, 1985; Patton, 1984, 1987, pp. 340–344). The purpose here has been to highlight the developmental aspects of the CAEP evaluation. Below are the central points this example illustrates.

Ten Key Points about Developmental Evaluation Illustrated by the Caribbean Example

Exhibit 3.2 summarizes developmental evaluation principles that are illustrated by the Caribbean example presented in this chapter. Each of these points is elaborated and discussed below.

1. *Thinking about what is useful and sensible for evaluation can open the door and establish the foundation for developmental evaluation.* "We have to make evaluation make sense," Tom Henderson would say. As in the case of the Caribbean project, this may require reconceptualizing a preconceived evaluation plan—for example, converting routine midterm and end-of-project external reviews into an evaluation process that begins at the beginning and continues throughout program implementation.

Developmental evaluation isn't some particular set of methods or recipe-like steps to follow. It doesn't offer a template of standardized questions. It's a mindset of inquiry into how to bring data to bear on what's unfolding so as to guide and develop that unfolding. What that means and the timing

---

EXHIBIT 3.2 Ten Key Points about Developmental Evaluation

1. Thinking about what is useful and sensible for evaluation can open the door and establish the foundation for developmental evaluation.

2. Developmental evaluation can include both internal and external approaches to evaluation.

3. Developmental evaluation can produce not just findings about progress but materials useful for program development (e.g., professional development processes, a template or focus for staff meetings and retreats, or a curriculum guide based on beneficiary involvement in evaluation inquiries).

4. Watching for and being open to what emerges is central to developmental evaluation.

5. Developmental evaluation requires timely engagement and rapid feedback.

6. Evaluation can become the engine for program development.

7. Ongoing program development and evaluation can become mutually reinforcing, a way of doing business, and a way of thinking.

8. Project leadership and support for doing developmental evaluation is a *sine qua non* (without which there is nothing).

9. Competent evaluators are essential for successful developmental evaluation.

10. Developmental evaluation produces more than improvements; it supports program development.

Note. See pages 75–79 for explanation, discussion, and elaboration of these summary points.

of the inquiry will depend on the situation, context, people involved, and the fundamental principle of doing what makes sense for program development.

The popular worldwide Nike slogan "Just Do It" is meant to celebrate finding and following one's passion. But in the evaluation world, "Just do it" means *compliance*. Just fill out the forms. Just follow the mandated reporting procedures. Just implement the predetermined evaluation template at the required, prespecified points in time. *Just do it!* Don't worry about whether it makes sense. Just do it. *Comply.*

Developmental evaluation embraces the *follow your passion* sense of "Just do it." The passion to be followed is what the innovators and doers care about, the vision they are pursuing, and the difference they want to make. Yes, innovators and social entrepreneurs are passionate, just as Tom Henderson was passionate about extension. His pruned exterior was always cool, calm, and collected, but I came to know his internal passion for developing extension and he came to see meaningful and sensible evaluation as support for furthering his vision.

Let me pause here to acknowledge the oxymoronic and paradoxical nature of this theme: sensible and pragmatic evaluation partnered with entrepreneurial and innovative passion. The connection comes in nurturing a passion for evaluative feedback and learning. A passion for evaluation? This, too, involves thinking outside evaluation's boxes. Evaluators are admonished above all to be dispassionate, unemotional, and analytical. Stay in your head. But I confess that I am passionate about evaluation, just as social innovators are passionate about changing the world. When we pursue our separate passions, and in the pursuit learn to make them mutually reinforcing, things develop.

2. *Developmental evaluation can include both internal and external approaches to evaluation.* It can be used by both internal and external evaluators, working either separately or together. The external developmental evaluation example in this chapter involved the external evaluators creatively designing the external evaluation to support program development as well as to serve accountability and the summative decision-making needs of the funder. The internal developmental evaluation involved the project staff using the external evaluation framework and findings to organize the project work plan and ongoing management of the project. When an organization has an internal monitoring and evaluation function operating as part of a regular program design, planning, and budgeting cycle, developmental evaluation can be aligned with that cycle.

3. *The evaluation produced not just findings but materials useful for program development.* The 40 case studies and insights about effective extension generated by the evaluation became the course curriculum and primary training materials for the course. Having those materials and insights generated by external, respected evaluators increased their credibility and value. This is an example of what is called *process use* (Patton, 2008c, chap. 5), in which an evaluation process proves useful in ways that go beyond just generating findings.

4. *Watching for and being open to what emerges is central to developmental evaluation.* The original rapid reconnaissance teams of Phase 1 unexpectedly offered a chance to learn about particularly effective experienced extension staff. That discovery gave rise to the idea from the regional advisory group of systematically identifying outstanding extension field staff and doing case studies of their impacts. That led, again unexpectedly, to using the case studies for the training curriculum, as well as using those outstanding extension staff as trainers. (The original design planned for permanent University of West Indies faculty to conduct the training.) Another unexpected development (and one that surely would have been opposed had it been deliberate) was the competition created among the eight countries to highlight their own

commitment to extension effectiveness. Island and regional newspapers and radio picked up the story of the search for outstanding extension staff and reported their stories once they had been identified. The next chapter examines emergence in depth as a central concept in complexity theory and the implications of emergence as a developmental evaluation focus.

5. *Developmental evaluation requires timely engagement and rapid feedback.* The rapid reconnaissance teams in Phase 1 that analyzed distinct agroecological zones set an early standard for gathering data intensely, analyzing it quickly while the multidisciplinary teams were still in the field, and immediately providing feedback to key stakeholders. Each team gathered data during the day and analyzed patterns and emerging issues at night. The next day's fieldwork built on previous findings and emergent patterns. After a week of fieldwork, the teams spent 2 days finalizing conclusions and writing preliminary conclusions about the state of agriculture and extension in the area studied. Those findings were shared with national extension staff and key government officials before the team left the island. At the time, such rapid feedback was unheard of—unprecedented. None of the researchers or others involved had ever participated in such a process. Those who received the findings had never experienced such rapid and pointed feedback.

For example, rules about grazing a horse or cow on public lands were confusing, applied haphazardly and arbitrarily, and believed to be highly political. Livestock extension agents had both regulatory and educational functions that were in conflict; regulatory actions undermined establishing educationally oriented relationships. The rapid reconnaissance feedback highlighted concrete case examples of how the current system of public grazing was operating and its negative implications for extension relationships with farmers, which led to both policy and procedural changes. A year later,

follow-up fieldwork included review of how the new procedures were being implemented by extension agents and interpreted by farmers, which led to still further clarifications and additional training: ongoing developmental evaluation of an evolving policy and its implementation and effects.

This same commitment to rapid analysis and feedback undergirded the external evaluation. The external team provided preliminary findings and draft case studies to project staff, national extension officials, and government leaders in each country before leaving for the next island. The evaluators worked fast and turned out results quickly. This was critical for transparency and credibility, which were essential for utility. The usual pace of life and work in the Caribbean is, shall we say, less than frantic. Indeed, one of the delights of living and working in the Caribbean was the laid-back approach to, well, everything. Thus, we had to develop a style of work that involved speed without speeding, hurrying up without appearing to hurry, slowing the process down in order to engage rapidly, communicating a sense of urgency without violating the larger cultural sense that all things come to those who wait, and wait, and wait, and wait. Paradoxical. In short, rapid reconnaissance and quick, timely feedback had to be adapted to the style and norms of the Caribbean. I was reminded of this watching the marvelous Jamaican sprinter Usain Bolt break world records at the 2008 Olympics. He ran faster than any human had ever run and did so with ease and grace, gliding leisurely to gold medals, lightly afloat in awesome speed, hardly appearing to expend any energy or work, but utterly determined to attain the finish line in record time. Developmental evaluation, though very process-oriented, must stay focused on and attuned to significant program decision points, both those that can be anticipated and those that arise unexpectedly. Mercury, with his winged shoes and headband, the archetype of speed, messenger of and to the gods of ancient Greece (birthplace of the Olympics), is the standard bearer of developmental evaluation—and emblematic of its dark side, appearing to be, or actually being, overly *mercurial*.

6. *The evaluation became the engine for program development*. At the time this was inadvertent and unexpected, but now it can be anticipated and made intentional. The whole process of selecting outstanding extension agents for case studies accelerated project implementation; dramatically increased project visibility among farmers, government officials, and media in the islands; and mobilized large and important segments of the population to engage in discussion about what constituted excellence in extension and who, locally, exemplified such excellence. This process and the early, accelerated evaluation time line increased pressure on the project to accelerate implementation of all aspects of the project. This generated, again unexpectedly, increased government resources and support to enhance project implementation. New international partners emerged as the project gained visibility and credibility.

7. *Ongoing program development and evaluation became mutually reinforcing, a way of doing business, and a way of thinking*. Because of project staff's exposure to the utility of evaluation early in project implementation, the staff bought into the evaluation and came to expect that gathering and using data and feedback would be the normal way the project would operate. This expectation brought rigor to the typical and inevitable sharing of anecdotes and war stories. The staff had seen what constituted a quality case study, one that included believable evidence and triangulated perspectives and data sources. When staff subsequently did internal evaluations that included case studies, the high standards set by the external evaluators guided those internally generated case studies later in the project.

8. *Project leadership and support for doing developmental evaluation is a* sine qua non (*without which there is nothing*). Tom Henderson *got it* about evaluation. He immediately embraced taking evaluation seriously, not just as a compliance activity for the funder, but as something we could learn from and use to set priorities and guide implementation. Never a word of resistance or defensiveness. As the widely esteemed and deeply respected "grand old man of Caribbean extension," he modeled engagement with evaluation for junior project staff, extension staff, and agricultural officials throughout the Caribbean, and the members of the regional advisory committee, none of whom had been engaged in anything but compliance evaluations before CAEP. As I said at the outset in introducing Tom Henderson, people matter. Leadership matters. The personal factor rules. Tom became an evaluation advocate and we cotaught an evaluation module in the regional extension course and subsequently did evaluation workshops together in all of the islands.

9. *Competent evaluators are essential*. I was still early in my professional career when I signed on as codirector of CAEP. I had administrative responsibilities on the project, not evaluation responsibilities, though I guided the internal evaluation process with Tom Henderson. But because of my background in evaluation, I had the advantage of knowing how to find a competent evaluator to undertake the challenging work involved in getting the 40 case studies done quickly and rigorously. The evaluation also involved conducting interviews with influential stakeholders and key knowledgeables, conducting site visits, dealing with international agency and national government officials, and directing an interdisciplinary and multinational evaluation team. The timeline was absolute. To influence the USAID funding decision, the evaluation report had to be in the hands of the USAID director in Barbados by November 1. But to have credibility with the broader advisory group, RAECC members, and to keep staff receptive, the evaluator would have to be able to deal sensitively, diplomatically, and respectfully with everyone from illiterate farmers in

poverty to distinguished senior members of national governments, many of whom would be suspicious about what was going on and how their governments would be portrayed in an independent, international evaluation report. And these are just hints of the political and cross-cultural challenges involved.

Marv Alkin was founder and director of the UCLA Center for the Study of Evaluation, where he made studies of the factors affecting evaluation use a primary focus. At the time he had cowritten one of the first major books on using evaluations (Alkin, Daillak, & White, 1979). He has subsequently gone on to publish extensively in evaluation (e.g., Alkin, 1985, 1990, 2004) and received the prestigious Paul F. Lazersfeld Award from the AEA for his many distinguished contributions to the profession. But that would come later. At the time he had never done anything like the evaluation proposed for CAEP, but he was intrigued by the possibilities, liked having an informed evaluation user on the inside (me), and agreed to take on the task. Later in the book I'll have much more to say about the competencies needed by evaluators to conduct developmental evaluations. Frankly, not many are up to the task. But if you want to engage in developmental evaluation, take the time to make sure you find someone with the combination of methodological competence, interpersonal skill, flexibility and openness, and integrity to do the job. (For a comprehensive review of general evaluator competencies that also apply to developmental evaluation, see Ghere et al., 2006; King et al., 2001.)

10. *Developmental evaluation produces more than improvements; it supports program development.* The uses of the evaluation did lead to improvements in the project, but the most important and lasting changes resulting from the evaluation were new, unanticipated developments that fundamentally changed the nature, approach, and impacts of the project. The case studies, case method of teaching, and deepened extension focus on farmer outcomes (not just providing services) were fundamental *developments*. The difference between improvement-oriented, formative evaluation and developmental evaluation was a central theme of the first and second chapters. The Caribbean case illustrates and reinforces this critical distinction.

4

Situation Recognition and Responsiveness

Distinguishing Simple, Complicated, and Complex

When patterns are broken, new worlds emerge.
—TULI KUPFERBERG, American
counterculture poet

Detecting Patterns

New York Times columnist David Brooks has devoted a highly successful journalistic career to observing successful people—and those not so successful—and detecting differences in their patterns. "Most successful people begin with two beliefs: the future can be better than the present, and I have the power to make it so" (Brooks, 2008, p. A37). This certainly describes the social innovators we studied in *Getting to Maybe: How the World Is Changed* (Westley et al., 2006). Evaluation helps focus and test these powerful beliefs, paradoxically supporting change by grounding change processes in reality testing.

One form of reality testing is situation recognition. "What is the situation you understand yourself to be in?" the evaluator asks the social innovator as part of establishing a baseline for documenting change. "How is

what you are doing a response to this situation?" Developments are grounded in and emerge from reactions to situations. One focus of developmental evaluation is documenting situation recognition, situational perceptions, situation-grounded understandings, and the consequences of situational responsiveness for what is developed as innovations unfold and are adapted in dynamic situations. This chapter presents a framework for situation recognition that distinguishes simple, complicated, and complex situations—and the implications of these distinctions for innovation and developmental evaluation. Another observation from David Brooks is germane as context here:

> Most successful people also have a phenomenal ability to consciously focus their attention. Control of attention is the ultimate individual power. People who can do that are not prisoners of the stimuli around them. They can

choose from the patterns in the world and lengthen their time horizons.

It leads to resilience, the ability to persevere with an idea even when all the influences in the world say it can't be done. A common story among entrepreneurs is that people told them they were too stupid to do something, and they set out to prove the jerks wrong.

It leads to creativity. Individuals who can focus attention have the ability to hold a subject or problem in their mind long enough to see it anew. (2008, p. A37)

Throughout this book I am featuring the stories of people who have demonstrated the ability to hold a subject or problem in their mind long enough to see it anew. These people illustrate the importance of the personal factor, that people make a difference. (The Preface discussed why this matters to the use of evaluation.) Brenda Zimmerman has been focusing on the problem of situation recognition and complexity for two decades. I want you to meet Brenda to provide a context for the framework of situation recognition that she has developed, a framework that defines complexity and, in so doing, defines the niche of developmental evaluation.

Detecting Complexity as a Distinct Pattern and Territory for Inquiry

Brenda Zimmerman has an unusually high tolerance for ambiguity and messiness. As an undergraduate majoring in zoology at the University of Toronto, she was fascinated by the complexity of living systems, including their messiness, and was openly skeptical of textbook portrayals of the natural world as orderly and predictable. She subsequently turned her attention from nature's systems to organizational systems, bringing that same skeptical inquiry to the neat textbook explanations she encountered during her doctoral studies (where she was the only female doctoral student in the strategy program at the Schulich School of Business at York University in Toronto, Canada). While

studying zoology she had developed sharp observational skills, going into the field and looking at how natural systems work in the real world. When she turned to observing organizations, she was struck by how what she saw with her own eyes contrasted sharply with the orderly descriptions and logical explanations in the academic organizational literature.

She proposed a dissertation observing how strategy unfolds in business organizations. Her doctoral committee of business school scholars wanted her to focus on a step-by-step description and analysis of the logic and sequence of strategic planning. She wanted to capture the messiness, ambiguities, and uncertainties of organizations' strategy processes, including manifestations of strategy outside of the formal planning process. She found herself at odds with her committee because she and they looked at and thought about organizations in fundamentally different ways.

She recalls being discouraged, a not altogether unusual state of mind for struggling graduate students, and wandered into a bookstore in search of diversion and relief from the cold Arctic air enveloping Toronto at that Christmastime. Not making much progress in her doctoral program at that moment, she thought perhaps she could at least get some holiday shopping done. As she wandered around the bookstore, a bold, large-letter title caught her attention: CHAOS. The title resonated, more as a feeling than as an intellectual perspective. It was James Gleick's book, subtitled *Making a New Science* (1987), which went on to become a bestseller, introducing general readers to developments in chaos theory. One of those readers was Brenda Zimmerman.

She started reading the book right there in the store, struck that the criticisms Gleick reported concerning traditional science were the same shortcomings she found in the organizational and academic business literature. While Gleick was describing what was being learned about the complexities of weather systems, physics, astronomy, and biological systems, she grasped immediately that these same concepts could illuminate organizational strategy and processes—something that had not yet been done. Just reading the table of contents and subtitles resonated deeply:

The Butterfly Effect. . . . Order masquerading as randomness. A world of non-linearity. "We completely missed the point."

Revolution. A revolution in seeing. . . .

Life's Ups and Downs. Modeling wildlife populations. Nonlinear science. . . .

A Geometry of Nature. . . . Transmission errors and jagged shores. New dimensions. The monsters of *fractal geometry.* . . . *The trash cans of science.*

Strange Attractors. . . . turbulence.

Universality. A new start. . . . Breakthroughs. . . . Clouds and paintings.

The Experimenter. . . . Flow and form in nature. . . . From one dimension to many.

Images of Chaos. The complex plane. . . . Art and commerce meet science. Fractal basin boundaries. The chaos game.

The Dynamical Systems Collective. . . . Measuring unpredictability. . . . microscale to macroscale. . . .

Inner Rhythms. A misunderstanding about models. The complex body. The dynamical heart. . . . Chaos as health.

Chaos and Beyond. . . . the snowflake puzzle. . . . Opportunity and necessity.

The book's back cover offered chaos as "a science of the everyday world, addressing questions every child has wondered about: how clouds form, how smoke rises, how water eddies in a stream." To which Brenda Zimmerman added: how organizational strategies unfold.

She submitted a new dissertation design to her doctoral committee proposing to study organizational strategy through the lens of chaos theory. The entire committee resigned. In search of support, she wrote a paper about the relevance of chaos theory to understanding organizational strategy and sent it to seven major organizational

theorists, none of whom she knew personally. Henry Mintzberg, a prominent management scholar at McGill University, called shortly after receiving the paper and invited her to come to Montreal for a conversation and sharing of ideas. He was already doing work distinguishing intended strategy from emergent strategy in analyzing *realized strategy* (what companies actually do vs. what they plan to do), which I discussed in Chapter 2. Her perspective, largely using ecological metaphors to describe organizational processes, paralleled Mintzberg's ideas.

Thus affirmed and encouraged, she returned to York University and hosted a meeting in which she invited some business and management faculty to hear her ideas. She used that meeting to find new doctoral committee members, faculty who shared an interest in her questions and approach. And it turned out there were some.

Her dissertation was an ethnographic study of a steel distribution company. She chose a steel distribution company rather than a high-tech company where grappling with rapid change and uncertainty might be more expected. She wanted to study a mundane business to show that her ideas were generalizable in many contexts. She presented her findings in two story formats, one using the equilibrium perspective dominant in the literature and the other using a chaos perspective. Just as she completed her dissertation, entitled "Strategy, Chaos and Equilibrium," two organizational theorists published books also using chaos theory ideas. Meg Wheatley's *Leadership and the New Science* (1992), written for a general readership, received widespread attention. Ralph Stacey's *Managing the Unknowable: Strategic Boundaries between Order and Chaos in Organizations* (1992) attracted a more academic following. Both authors went on to publish a number of works on complexity in organizational contexts. Those two pioneering authors were early influences and colleagues as Brenda Zimmerman turned her attention to complexity science applications in health care, working with both in the early 1990s.

During that decade, complexity became the broader conceptual umbrella for this arena of inquiry with chaos a narrower topic under that umbrella. Her research led to collaborating with Curt Lindberg and Paul Plsek to write *edgeware: insights from complexity science for health care leaders* (1998).

Brenda Zimmerman has now been looking at organizations through a complexity lens for more than 20 years. She recalls that when she first started writing about complexity and making presentations, North American audiences were either resistant or disinterested. She found much more receptivity in Europe; her first publications and conference papers on complexity were in Swedish, Italian, and Portuguese. In North America, she found practitioners more open and responsive than academics. She describes herself as a translator of complexity ideas, making them accessible to practitioners, nonprofit leaders, and policymakers. I asked her what kind of reception she gets these days.

"When I present to organizational leaders, there is often a huge sigh of relief, relief from the burden of having to be in control of everything. They find comfort in the complexity perspective, that you don't have to have everything figured out in advance. In fact, that you *can't* have everything figured out in advance. The leaders I work with tell me that they feel a kind of intuitive grasp of what I present to them as 'complexity,' but they haven't had a language to talk about that sense of things."

She recalls speaking to a group of arts and cultural executives, a group "feeling pretty beaten up these days by demands for accountability." One audience member came up afterwards to tell her that it took him forever to get through *Getting to Maybe* (Westley et al., 2006), the book we coauthored that includes stories of visionary leaders struggling with innovation and complexity. It took "forever," he told her, because each sentence reminded him of his own struggles, of his own vision, and brought him to tears to realize that he was not alone in what he experienced. Others struggled as he did, as he does.

For Brenda Zimmerman, complexity has come to be the lens through which she understands and engages as a scholar, but also as a teacher and a parent, and as a community volunteer, activist, and consultant. It shapes her perspective on everything she does. Today she is director of the Health Industry Management Program and associate professor of strategy/policy in the Schulich School of Business, York University, the largest and most diverse business school in Canada. She started a project there to get students involved in corporate responses to HIV/AIDS internationally, dealing with workplace policies and mobilizing corporate responses to deal with the epidemic. She's been invited to join the boards of nonprofit organizations to help them understand the implications of complexity as they set direction for their organizations. She's consulting with the ministries of health in Canadian provinces on using complexity principles for policymaking and interacting with the community.

In all this, she reports that the major struggle she encounters are simplistic and unrealistic demands for accountability under the widely accepted precept that people engaged in social change ought to know what's going to happen in advance of their engagement. The people making these demands, she says, seem to ignore what they know about the real world, about their own lives, or about biological and ecological systems, even at an elementary level.

"I'm simply stunned at the resilience of the mechanical metaphor. Policymakers and planners are still pushing the machine metaphor for health interventions. This mechanistic approach, that all we have to do is fix some faulty parts in the system, has deep roots and is hard to get past. The so-called evidence-based approach to medicine has become all-powerful, tied to and grounded in a mandate to make things predictable and controllable."

How, given this environment, I asked, does she engage people?

"I begin with distinctions between *simple, complicated,* and *complex.* I begin by honoring where people are and build on what they know. They know that some things are pretty simple and some things are complicated. And after we talk some, they get it that the complex is different from the complicated. I try to make it a challenge of matching: what works for what situations? That's the starting point.

"Different approaches are needed for different situations. So I begin by helping people differentiate situations. The rest flows from that."

Later in this chapter we'll examine in detail the implications for evaluation of Zimmerman's distinctions. Simple, complicated, and complex situations create different evaluation challenges. Developmental evaluation is especially appropriate for dealing with complexity. But before we go more deeply into complexity, let's take a closer look at the challenges of *situation recognition.* Her wisdom bears repeating: "I begin by helping people differentiate situations. The rest flows from that." And so it does. And so it will in this chapter.

The Challenges of Situation Recognition

Situation recognition involves matching an approach or intervention to the nature of the situation. Top-down dissemination of best practices works, but only for certain kinds of interventions in certain kinds of environments. The World Health Organization's campaign to eradicate polio depends upon careful, precise, and thorough replication of the same procedures every time a new case of polio is identified anywhere in the world. The logistics involved in planning a "mop-up" campaign for a polio outbreak include following a precise formula for the geographic area to be revaccinated, the amount of vaccine needed, the number of vaccinators, their training and supervision, the number of vehicles to cover the designated area in a specified amount of time, the temperature at which the vaccine must be stored and transported, and insistence that being vaccinated be voluntary.

Even in such a standardized, top-down campaign, however, situational variables come into play that can add elements of complexity. Atul Gawande accompanied an eradication revaccination campaign in India and reported visiting an area where Muslim mothers resisted the vaccination because they'd heard rumors of a Hindu plot to sterilize their boys (Gawande, 2004). Resistance to vaccination and an intervention to overcome that resistance still has to be customized to the local cultural and political situation, and the context that gives rise to the resistance. What may be appropriately understood as simple at one level can be understood as complex at another level and from a different perspective, a point we'll explore in some depth in this chapter with attention to the evaluation implications of different perspectives. The issue, in part, is the utility of distinguishing simple elements from complex ones because they involve different implications for action—*and* evaluation.

Developmental evaluation is particularly appropriate for a specific kind of situation: *complexity.* Understanding complexity and its implications for evaluation is critical to recognizing those situations for which developmental evaluation is well suited.

A Situation Recognition Heuristic: Distinguishing Simple, Complicated, and Complex

To facilitate situation recognition, it is useful to have a heuristic framework, some way of "cutting to the chase" by knowing what factors are important to consider when we encounter a new situation. Heuristics are shortcuts that tell us what's important to pay attention to. We can't look at everything. We never have perfect information. We can't consider all possibilities. We need some way of focusing. Heuristics do that. Research on decision making shows that heuristics "make us smart"—smart in the sense that we make intelligent decisions quickly. Heuristics direct us in making sense of things. They frame and inform decisions. Indeed, they make choices and action possible (Gigerenzer, Todd, & ABC Research Group, 1999; Kahneman & Tversky, 2000).

The National Stroke Association urges people to use a heuristic to determine if someone is having a stroke. Timely decision making is crucial. Speed saves lives. The heuristic urges: Act F.A.S.T. (see Exhibit 4.1).

Developmental evaluation informs fast action and quick reactions by social innovators. First, we have to decide if we're in a situation that is appropriate for developmental evaluation, that is, a complex situation, where the pace of actions, reactions, and interactions matter greatly. Zimmerman first applied the

distinctions between simple, complicated, and complex to health care (Zimmerman et al., 1998). In writing the book *Getting to Maybe: How the World Is Changed* (Westley et al., 2006) we looked at the implications of these distinctions for understanding social innovation. In this book I want to expand their application to illuminate evaluation situations and options.

Remember, the focus here is on utility. These distinctions help with situation recognition so that an evaluation approach can be selected that is appropriate to a particular situation and intervention, thereby increasing the likely utility—and actual use—of the evaluation. Using these distinctions involves mapping the territory and context within which an evaluation will take place to locate the evaluation within that territory. Moreover, these are relative and perspective-dependent distinctions, not absolute ones. A situation can be described as more or less simple, complicated, or complex. Utility resides in examining the implications and insights generated by asking to what extent a situation is usefully approached as simple, complicated, or complex, or some combination of the three.

EXHIBIT 4.1 Act F.A.S.T.

FACE	Ask the person to smile.	
	Does one side of the face droop?	
ARMS	Ask the person to raise both arms.	
	Does one arm drift downward?	
SPEECH	Ask the person to repeat a simple sentence.	
	Are the words slurred? Can he/she repeat the sentence correctly?	
TIME	If the person shows any of these symptoms, time is important.	
	Call 911 or get to the hospital fast. Brain cells are dying.	

Note. Based on National Stroke Association (2009).

The Degree of Uncertainty/ Degree of Conflict Matrix

The degree of uncertainty/degree of conflict matrix developed by Zimmerman (adapted from the ideas of Ralph Stacey as published in Zimmerman et al., 1998, pp. 136–143) is the basis for the heuristic that distinguishes simple, complicated, and complex situations. To make these distinctions, the matrix maps the situation along two dimensions. One dimension scales the degree of certainty about what should be done to solve a problem. We know how to eradicate polio: immunize all children. We don't know how to reduce global warming. Despite many competing ideas and plans, our knowledge is quite limited about both the causes of global warming and what interventions would work. Programs and interventions are close to certainty when the cause-and-effect relationship is highly predictable, as in the relationship between vaccination and preventing disease. At the other end of the certainty continuum are innovative programs where the outcomes are highly unpredictable. Comprehensive antipoverty initiatives involve considerable uncertainty. Extrapolating from past experience is problematic because each community is unique and there is no vaccine for poverty.

First heuristic dimension:
Degree of *certainty and predictability* about how to solve a problem

Close to   - - - - - - - - - - - - - - - - -   Far from
certainty   certainty

The second dimension depicts the degree of agreement among various stakeholders about an intervention's desirability, or alternatively, their degree of conflict. There is universal agreement that preventing polio is a good thing and that children should be vaccinated to eradicate polio worldwide. On the other hand, there is substantial political conflict about almost all aspects of global warming. To what extent is global warm-

ing occurring? To what extent is it caused by human activity (as opposed to being a natural earthly cycle)? What are the primary causes of climate change? How much urgency is there about intervening? What interventions, if any, will make a difference? Are the economic costs of intervening worth the likely results? On these and other matters, there is great disagreement.

Second heuristic dimension:
Degree of *agreement* or *conflict* about how to solve a problem

Close to   Far from
agreeing,   - - - - - - - - - - - - - -   agreeing,
little conflict   great conflict

Combining these two dimensions creates the borders of a territory that can be mapped, or a matrix, as shown in Exhibit 4.2. The horizontal axis captures the degree of certainty and predictability about how to solve a problem. The vertical axis displays the degree of agreement about what to do.

Simple Situations

High levels of certainty and agreement make situations fairly simple. *Simple*, as used here, is *a descriptive term*, not meant to be judgmental or pejorative. Simple is not simplistic or simple-minded. A simple situation is, simply, one in which knowledge and experience tell you what to do and there is widespread agreement about what to do. In such a situation, it is both possible and appropriate to intervene from the top down, as in the worldwide campaign to eradicate polio. The high degree of predictability and agreement permits detailed planning, controlled execution, and precise measurement of the degree to which predetermined targets are reached. A best practice model can be generated and subjected to a summative test.

A *simple* problem is how to bake a cake, a metaphor for capturing the characteristics of the simple originally offered by Zimmerman and Glouberman (2004). A

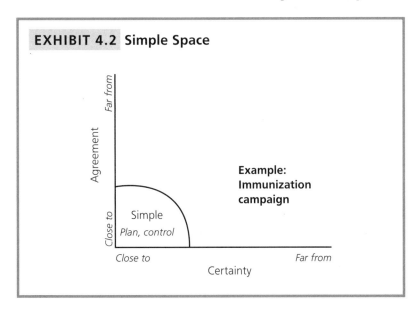

EXHIBIT 4.2 Simple Space

good recipe, like a best practice, provides detailed guidance about the steps to follow to achieve a desired outcome. A recipe has clear cause-and-effect relationships and can be mastered through repetition and by honing basic skills. Recipes present standard procedures and should provide sufficient detail that even someone who has never baked has a high probability of success. In simple situations, what needs to be done is *known*. Best practices for programs are like recipes in that they provide clear and high-fidelity directions. The standard procedures that have worked to produce desired outcomes in the past are highly likely to work again in the future. Assembly lines in factories have a "recipe" quality, as do standardized school curricula. Part of the attraction of the 12-step program of Alcoholics Anonymous is its simple formulation (which doesn't mean it's easy to do, even one day at a time).

Complicated Situations

As situations become less predictable and producing desired outcomes becomes less certain, we are moving into *complicated* territory. It is useful to distinguish *technical* complications from *social* complications. Sending

a rocket to the Moon is technically *complicated* because thousands of elements have to be coordinated for a successful launch (see Exhibit 4.3). Technical knowledge and expertise is needed to solve complicated problems. More than one area of expertise is needed and these must therefore be coordinated and integrated. In rocket science, formulae are used to predict the trajectory and path of the rocket. Calculations are required to ensure sufficient fuel based on current conditions. If all of the many technical calculations are done well, coordinated, and executed precisely, it is likely that the desired outcome—getting the rocket to the Moon—will be accomplished. Like integrating the many areas of expertise needed to get a rocket into space, coordinating large-scale programs with many local sites throughout a country or region is a complicated problem. When the degree of uncertainty and agreement are such that what needs to be done is challenging and difficult, but *knowable*, the situation is complicated. That is, how all the parts will fit together is initially unknown but can be figured out, and is therefore knowable, in complicated situations.

Socially complicated situations involve situations with many different stakeholders

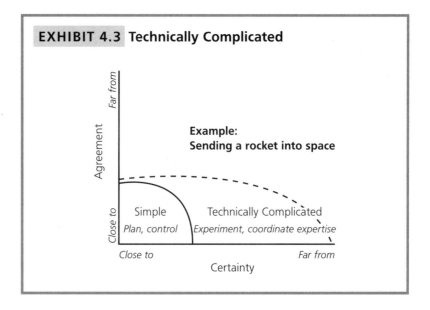

EXHIBIT 4.3 Technically Complicated

Agreement (Far from / Close to)

Certainty (Close to / Far from)

Example:
Sending a rocket into space

Simple
Plan, control

Technically Complicated
Experiment, coordinate expertise

offering different perspectives, articulating competing values, and posing conflicting solutions (see Exhibit 4.4). Whether resources should be spent to send rockets into space is more controversial than whether polio should be eradicated worldwide, thus rocket launches are more socially complicated than immunization campaigns (at least for purposes of illustrating the conceptual difference between simple and complicated). Abortion is an example of a socially complicated issue, as is what to do about the energy crisis. Everyone wants children to learn to read but there are intense disagreements about which reading approach produces the best result. Controversial issues like sex education are socially complicated. The more points of view there are and the greater the

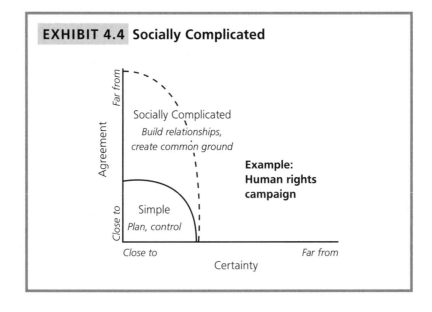

EXHIBIT 4.4 Socially Complicated

Agreement (Far from / Close to)

Certainty (Close to / Far from)

Socially Complicated
Build relationships, create common ground

Example:
Human rights
campaign

Simple
Plan, control

debate among different stakeholders, the more socially complicated the situation becomes. How diverse stakeholders will deal with their conflicts is initially unknown but knowable as the interactions unfold. Some of the disagreements may be about degree of technical complication (how much certainty there is about how to produce a desired outcome), but many disagreements are about fundamental value differences and how to even define the problem.

Mark Cabaj (2009b) of the Tamarack Institute in Canada has been conducting developmental evaluations in his work with Vibrant Communities (communities engaged in poverty reduction) and has found it useful to distinguish social complications from technical complications. It's not just that people in a setting disagree; it's the depth and source of disagreements. What makes socially complicated situations especially challenging is when those involved have fundamentally different perspectives and values, or operate from different paradigms about how the world works and what's important to do.

Cabaj pointed me to the work of a study of a child advocacy center by Russell Linden (2002) that he finds useful to illustrate socially complicated differences in perspective (see the table below). Linden identified a range of differences in culture and perspective between social workers and police officers when they are engaged in investigating suspected perpetrators of sexual abuse of children. These two important professional groups have different training, use different methods, manifest conflicting perspectives about each other as well as the people they're investigating, view themselves differently in the organizational pecking order, and come to the program's collaboration under different mechanisms. Such differences make for deep and enduring social complications in attempting to engage collaboratively.

Having distinguished the technically complicated from the socially complicated and given illustrations of each, we need to

⌒ Socially Complicated Example: Differences in Culture and Perspective between Social Workers and Police Officers When They Are Engaged in Investigating Suspected Perpetrators of Sexual Abuse of Children

Issues	Police perspective	Social worker perspective
1. Attitude toward perpetrators	Lock them up.	Rehabilitate them.
2. Training	Stay focused on facts; separate facts from feelings.	Develop and use interpersonal skills; tune in to feelings.
3. Approach	Don't trust; stay wary; be factual; get evidence; don't get taken in.	Form relationships; understand clients; empathize.
4. View of each other	Police view social workers as softies, too focused on victims' feelings.	Social workers view police as rigid, too black-and-white about people, not attuned to mitigating circumstances.
5. How they come to participate in a community innovation	Get assigned; part of the job.	Choose to get involved; want to make a difference.

Note. Based on Linden (2002, p. 23).

combine them to look at their interactions. A situation is *complicated* when there is either a high degree of uncertainty *or* a high degree of disagreement. If there is *both* high uncertainty and high disagreement (e.g., uncertainty is a primary source of disagreements and disagreements contribute to the uncertainty), we have moved into the arena of complexity.

Complex Situations

Complex situations are characterized by high uncertainty and high social conflict (see Exhibit 4.5). In studying social innovations, we were impressed by the uncertainty and unpredictability of the innovative process, even looking back from a mountaintop of success, which is why we called the book *Getting to Maybe* (Westley et al., 2006). Evaluating social innovations is a complex challenge, as opposed to evaluating simple and complicated problems. The outcomes of interventions aimed at solving problems under conditions of complexity are unpredictable. So many factors and variables are interacting, many of them not only unknown but *unknowable*, that there can be no recipe for success. And even if something that looks like a recipe emerges from one or two successful attempts to do something, the likelihood that the same result can be attained in other and different contexts is low. There are simply too many dynamic variables and unknowns to make recipe-like replication (or supposed best practices) predictable.

It's worth reiterating the interactions between high uncertainty and high disagreement. These interactions are volatile, uncontrollable, unpredictable, and unknowable in advance: *high uncertainty about how to produce a desired result fuels disagreement, and disagreements intensify and expand the parameters of uncertainty.*

Parenting is *complex.* Unlike the metaphor of a cooking recipe for a simple situation or the rocket-launching metaphor for a complicated situation, parenting involves huge uncertainties and no clear rules guaranteeing success to follow. Oh, to be sure, there are many parenting experts and many guides available to parents. But none can be treated like a cookbook for a cake, or a set of formulae to send a rocket to the Moon. In the case of the cake and the rocket, for the most part, we were intervening with inanimate objects. The flour does not suddenly decide to change its mind and gravity can be counted on to be consis-

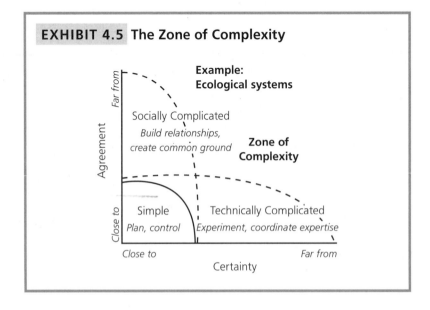

EXHIBIT 4.5 The Zone of Complexity

"I'm just a simple man preceded by an inordinately complex reputation."

Illustration by Mark M. Rogers. ©Victoria Roberts/Condé Nast Publications/
www.cartoonbank.com.

tent, too. On the other hand, children, as we all know, have minds of their own. Hence our interventions are always in relationship with them. There are very few stand-alone parenting tasks. Almost always, the parents and the child interact to create outcomes.

I have three quite different children, two boys and a girl, each with a different temperament and different interests. As a parent I tried to expose them to lots of possibilities—sports, music, art—and watched to see how they reacted. If one of them seemed to show interest in some activity, I'd try to provide more opportunities to engage in that activity. But I had to be careful. If I showed too much enthusiasm, I could create a backlash of disinterest. If I showed too little interest and failed to reinforce an activity, that could also undermine future interest. I was never sure how much to push, how much to lay back, how severe to be in disciplining, how permissive to be in supporting exploration, how intrusive to be in their budding friendships, and how engaged to be with school-work. Our goals for our children tend to be things like happiness, finding fulfillment, and realizing their full potential—hardly the clear, specific, and measurable goals demanded for summative evaluation and prescriptive best practices modeling.

Metaphoric Situational Comparisons

All perception of truth is the detection of an analogy.
—HENRY DAVID THOREAU (1817–1862),
   American author and naturalist

Exhibit 4.6 summarizes the distinctions between the three kinds of situations using the metaphors of a recipe to illustrate the simple, launching a rocket for the technically complicated, and raising a child for the complex. Brenda Zimmerman created these metaphoric distinctions and has used them with great effect in helping people understand complexity. It's worth recalling from early in this chapter how she says she works with people.

"I begin with distinctions between *simple, complicated,* and *complex.* I begin by honoring where people are and build on what they know. They know that some things are pretty simple and some things are complicated. And after we talk some, they get it that the complex is different from the complicated. I try to make it a challenge of matching: what works for what situations? That's the starting point. And that's how I came to use the metaphors of a recipe to illustrate the simple, send-

---

EXHIBIT 4.6 Simple, Complicated, and Complex Metaphors

Simple	Complicated	Complex
Following a recipe	*Sending a rocket into space*	*Raising a child*
The recipe is essential.	Detailed protocols or formulae are critical and necessary.	Highly prescriptive protocols have limited relevance or are counterproductive.
Recipes are tested to assure easy replication.	Sending one rocket to the Moon increases the likelihood that the next will also be a success, but success is never guaranteed.	Raising one child provides experience but is no guarantee of success with the next child.
No particular expertise is required, but cooking expertise increases the likelihood of success.	High levels of expertise and training in a variety of fields are necessary for success.	Expertise helps but only when balanced with responsiveness to the particular child.
A good recipe produces nearly the same cake every time.	Key elements of each rocket *must* be the same to succeed.	Every child is unique and must be understood as an individual.
The best recipes give good results every time.	Success depends on a blueprint that both directs the development of separate parts and specifies the exact relationship in which to assemble them.	Outcomes vary by child and remain uncertain over time.
A good recipe specifies the quantity and nature of the elements needed and the order in which to combine them, but there is room for experimentation.	There is a high degree of certainty of outcome if everything comes together in the right way, but also many places where things can go wrong.	Can't separate the parts from the whole; essence exists in the relationship between different people, different experiences, different moments in time.

Note. Based on Brenda Zimmerman in Westley, Zimmerman, and Patton (2006, p. 9), and Zimmerman and Glouberman (2004).

---

ing a rocket to the moon as complicated, and parenting as illustrating the complex [metaphors first used in Zimmerman & Glouberman, 2004].

"Different approaches are needed for different situations. So I begin by helping people differentiate situations. The rest flows from that" (Zimmerman, quoted in Westley et al., 2006, p. 9).

Cause-and-Effect Relationships

At the heart of the distinctions between simple, complicated, and complex is the extent to which cause and effect is or can be known. In simple situations cause and effect is known so interventions and their consequences are highly predictable and controllable. In complicated situations cause and effect is knowable as patterns are established through research and observations over time, but the many variables involved make prediction and control more precarious. In complex situations, cause and effect is unknown *and* unknowable until after the effect has emerged, at which point some retrospective tracing and patterning may be possible. These different degrees of *causal knowability* actually define the uncertainty dimension of the degree of uncertainty/degree of conflict matrix. Zimmerman has included causal knowability as a distinguishing characteristic of the complexity landscape from her earliest publications (Zimmerman et al., 1998, pp. 137–139). Management and organizational development consultant David Snowden has emphasized these different degrees of causal clarity to distinguish simple, complicated, and complex, with special attention to their implications for management planning and action (Snowden & Boone, 2007). We'll look at Snowden's contributions in more depth shortly.

A somewhat different use of the degree of uncertainty/degree of conflict matrix is found in the applications of Eoyang (2008b), Hargreaves and Parsons (2009), Parsons (2009a, 2009c), and Parsons and Hargreaves (2008). They use the matrix to distinguish organized (simple) systems from adaptive/self-organizing/organic (complex) systems. The organized to self-organizing conceptual framework uses the same matrix dimensions as Exhibit 4.5, but the terminology is different (organized vs. simple, self-organizing vs. complex). Their focus is the nature of the underlying organizing dynamics that characterize different systems (organized and predictable vs. self-organized and emergent). This framework is featured in the widely used guide *Designing Initiative Evaluation: A Systems-Oriented Framework for Evaluating Social Change Efforts* published by the W. K. Kellogg Foundation (2007, p. 8). They label the territory of highest uncertainty and greatest disagreement "unorganized (random)." The more common term is *chaos*. Let's take a look at chaos as distinct from complexity.

Chaos

On the far ends of the degree of uncertainty/degree of conflict matrix we enter the zone of chaos: intense conflict among key stakeholders and extreme uncertainty about what to do to achieve desired outcomes (see Exhibit 4.7). There is no clear dividing line between complexity and chaos. It is a matter of degree that has to do with how rapidly things are changing and the extent to which reverberations, ripple effects, and turbulent interactions are multiplying and cascading. Chaos is stressful, and feels like things are uncontrollable and unpredictable—because they are. Faced with chaos, we try to find some island of stability on which to hang out and weather the storm. Chaos is

---

～ Translating Simple, Complicated, and Complex into Three Realms of Medicine

The Innovator's Prescription (Christensen, Grossman, & Hwang, 2008) proposes a number of disruptive innovations for health care, one of which divides medicine into three realms that mirror the simple, complicated, and complex distinctions that are the focus of this chapter.

• *Precision medicine* (simple realm). Care for diseases that can be diagnosed precisely and for which treatments are predictably effective through well-established, evidence-based interventions. These are things like strep throat, urinary tract infections, and broken bones.

• *Empirical medicine* (complicated realm). Diseases for which treatment outcomes can be described in probabilistic terms, such as heart attacks and strokes, but for which there are multiple causes, many confounding factors, and uncertainty about whether interventions will work.

• *Intuitive medicine* (complex realm). Conditions that are diagnosed by symptoms and treated with therapies of uncertain efficacy, such as depression, multiple sclerosis, and many cancers. This is the realm of specialists working together in teams trying things out, monitoring responses, adapting to the specific needs of specific patients, and being especially attentive to how any given intervention can trigger side effects and complex adaptive reactions.

Precision medicine applying evidence-based practices could be done by nurse practitioners and physician assistants following formulas of care, with backup by generalist physicians when needed. But the overall system of physician training and practice would be shifted to the management of complex chronic diseases and wellness services, with medical personnel at every level practicing at the top rather than the bottom of their expertise.

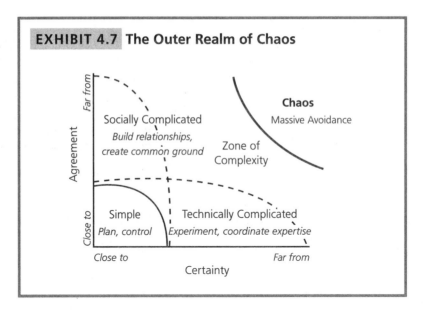

EXHIBIT 4.7 The Outer Realm of Chaos

largely to be avoided, though it is sometimes inflicted on us (think global economic meltdown). The function of chaos may simply be to make complexity look like a pretty good place to be. Complexity offers lots of uncertainty and turbulence, to be sure, but at least it's not chaos we reassure ourselves.

To get a sense of what chaos is like, read James Stewart's (2009) gripping and frightening account of "Eight Days" in mid-September 2008, the chaotic period when it was far from certain that the world economic system would avoid collapse. Things not only spun out of control beginning with the Lehman Brothers bankruptcy, but there was no way to even assess the magnitude of the damage—or either to predict, or control, much of, well, anything. What numbers there were (e.g., amount of worthless credit default swaps, or percentage of mortgages facing default)—and there were many such numbers—kept changing even as they were calculated. The problems not only couldn't be contained, they couldn't be defined. Economic policymakers talked about being on the edge of a precipice, experiencing "quantum shifts," and facing a situation "beyond anything we'd ever envisioned." They kept asking themselves and each other, "What's going on? and "How did this happen?" The

situation grew worse day by day, hour by hour, as the crisis of fear fed on itself and the system shut down. Panic precipitated more panic, a spiral of panic that fed on itself. Nothing was within a normal range. Rules were suspended. New policies were made up on the spot, then abandoned. It was chaos. Trying to figure out how and why it happened, and the long-term implications, will go on for decades and never be fully understood or resolved.

For a more up-close and personal account of being immersed in and trying just to survive chaos, read Tracy Kidder's (2009) account of a young man, Deogratias (Deo), caught in the Burundi genocide in 1994, or Canadian general Romeo Dallaire's account, entitled *Shake Hands with the Devil*, of trying to intervene in the Rwanda genocide as head of the miniscule United Nations peacekeeping force (Dallaire & Beardsley, 2004). Rampaging murderous gangs define chaos. Read those accounts and you'll never again use the word *chaos* to describe the mess in your office. In the midst of chaos there is only one concern and one all-encompassing criterion: survival. And you gather data on that minute by minute, second by second. So let's avoid chaos and limit our discussion here to simple, complicated, and complex.

Relative, Not Absolute, Distinctions

The distinctions between simple, complicated, and complex are not absolute. They are not right or wrong. They are matters of perception and judgment. There is not and cannot be a clear dividing line when the degree of uncertainty and the degree of disagreement, taken together, move a situation from complicated to complex. These are *sensitizing concepts* not operational measurements—and I know that drives some people crazy. I know because they tell me so. What are the dividing lines, they ask? How can I *be sure* to distinguish the simple from the complicated, and the complicated from the complex. You can't. These are heuristics. There is no complexity thermometer that gives degrees of uncertainty and disagreement on a standardized, all-purpose scale. The purpose of making such distinctions is driven by the utility of situation recognition and responsiveness. For evaluation, this means matching the evaluation to the nature of the situation. Before we look more closely at the implications of these distinctions for evaluation designs, I want to offer an additional caveat about using the distinctions and metaphors that illustrate them.

When working with a client or workshop group to make these distinctions about a specific intervention or program, participants within the group will often, indeed typically, disagree about what elements are simple, complicated, or complex. Their perceptions in applying the two dimensions of the matrix—how much is known about how to achieve the desired outcome (causal clarity) and how much agreement there is about what to do—can vary greatly. The conversations are quite revealing and important for generating dialogue among those involved about how they perceive the situation and the implications of those perceptions for all of what they do, including, but not limited to, evaluation. Let me illustrate this with an example.

I was working with a group of 20 experienced teachers to design an evaluation of an innovative reading program. They disagreed intensely about the state of knowledge concerning how children learn to read. Some expressed great certainty about how to teach reading to produce desired results and were equally certain that most people in the community agreed with them. They saw teaching reading as simple, felt certain of what constituted "best practices" (the reading recipe), and thought the challenge was to standardize use of the practices they believed in. Others felt that our knowledge of how the brain works is still quite primitive, that children develop in different ways, and that different children learn to read in different ways. For these teachers, the challenge was individualized reading instruction. They perceived reading as complex and resonated with the raising-a-child metaphor. The discussion was rich, respectful, and evocative, with huge implications for evaluation. Those who saw teaching reading as simple were comfortable evaluating outcomes with standardized tests. Those who saw teaching reading as complex preferred individualized assessments and a portfolio approach where each child's reading would be examined in the context of that child's development, interests, and progress in other areas of schooling. Different preferences for evaluation flowed from different definitions of the situation. We ultimately agreed on a mixed methods design that incorporated aspects of both sets of preferences.

Now let me also add a caveat about using metaphors to illustrate the distinctions. Ricardo Wilson-Grau, an international network development consultant and program evaluator, shared the following story with me. It is a cautionary tale about the cross-cultural interpretation of metaphors.

"A couple of weeks ago, I used the simple, complicated, complex metaphors in a workshop with a group of South Asian men and women (Bengali, Indian, Pakistani, Sri Lankan, and Bhutanese). In similar workshops with Latin Americans and Europeans, it worked marvelously well to explain the different cause–effect relationships. This time, however, it caused a totally unexpected uproar. Everyone except the Bhutanese Buddhist was terribly upset with the notion that raising a child was not simple and that baking a cake was not complex! The example worked so badly that I simply backtracked to the basic message that it is important to identify if there is low, medium, or high uncertainty about when cause-and-effect relationships are known, knowable, or unknown. The incident reminded me of a couple of conversations with Indian and Muslim men and women who argue very persuasively about the practical value of their parents arranging their marriages. Given these cultural differences, I stopped attempting to present *my* example. Now, I simply elicit from the group examples of simple, complicated, and complex situations."

Australian colleague Patricia Rogers, who has worked extensively with the simple, complicated, complex distinctions (2008, 2009a), has also cautioned that it is important to emphasize that these are ways of thinking about programs and other interventions. Making these distinctions can strengthen program theory (Funnell &

Rogers, 2010, chap. 3). It is not a matter of classifying interventions into categories that are *real*, but rather using the distinctions to generate insights that are useful and help us understand. Indeed, one way to use the distinctions is as questions rather than as categories. What aspects of the program or intervention are usefully viewed as simple? What aspects as complicated? And what aspects as complex? In the remainder of this chapter we'll be doing just that as we examine the evaluation implications of these distinctions.

When teaching students in her university classes, Brenda Zimmerman tells me, she asks them whether they consider their romantic relationships to be simple, complicated, or complex. In a similar vein, I have used romantic encounters as a metaphor for the complexities of developmental evaluation. When dating, each person is taking in information about the other, figuring out areas of shared interest and compatibility, watching for what's working and not working in the relationship, and making adjustments accordingly. Dating often includes surprises. Initial impressions may be confirmed or may be altered entirely with more interaction. There's ongoing assessment on both sides about whether to continue the

"You see our relationship as complex and developing. I see it as simple -- and over. So let's not make it complicated."

Illustration by Mark M. Rogers.

relationship, have another date, or take the next step. The language of uncertainty is often pervasive:

"Let's see where this goes."

"Let's try it out for awhile."

"What do you think about this?"

"How do you like that?"

"I'm not sure if this is going to work out."

You get the idea. Developmental evaluation of innovations involves ongoing observation, assessment, and feedback about how things are unfolding, what's working and what's not, and what's emerging, toward what outcomes. But, of course, in a culture with arranged marriages, the dating metaphor is both inappropriate and potentially even offensive. On the other hand, from what little I know about arranged marriages, the negotiations between those making the arrangement can be simple, complicated, or complex, or manifest elements of all three—depending on, well, you conjure up the number of potential factors and uncertainties involved.

Which reminds us that, at bottom, what makes things complex is that we're dealing with human beings, and our relationships with each other tend toward the complex, a point nicely made in an observation sent to me by Patricia Rogers. She forwarded the following quote from Hugh Mackay (2008), an excerpt from his presentation in the Australian Psychological Society's Annual Oration.

> Human relationships are inherently messy because they are driven more by emotional than rational factors—and thank goodness for that. . . . Because relationships are unpredictable and ultimately impossible to control, so are families, communities and organisations. . . . We need to shift our focus from control to participation and engagement; from resistance to adaptation; from an unhealthy utopianism to a more realistic acceptance of life's disorderliness, its irrationalities, its unpredictability, its disenchantments, as well as

its joys, its gratifications and even its occasional small triumphs.

With that observation as context, let's examine the evaluation implications of distinguishing simple, complicated, and complex situations and interventions.

Situational Evaluation: Implications for Practice

In a chapter on situational evaluation in *Utilization-Focused Evaluation* (Patton, 2008c), I emphasized that there is no one best way to conduct an evaluation. The design of a particular evaluation depends on the people involved and their situation. There are no absolute rules an evaluator can follow to know exactly what to do with specific users in a particular situation. As an evaluation unfolds, evaluators and primary intended users work together to identify the evaluation that best fits their information needs and the program's context and situation. This means *negotiating* the evaluation's intended and desired uses, and adapting the design to financial, political, timing, and methodological constraints and opportunities. Every evaluation situation is unique. A successful evaluation (i.e., one that is useful, practical, ethical, and accurate) emerges from the special characteristics and conditions of a particular situation—a mixture of people, politics, history, context, resources, constraints, values, needs, interests, and chance.

How difficult can it be to design an evaluation to fit the program's situation? Well, how difficult is it to play chess? There are some 85 billion ways of playing the first four moves in a game of chess (Pandolfini, 1998). Once the game starts, subsequent moves are contingent on and must be adapted to what one's opponent does and the unfolding situation.

To become more sophisticated and intentional about situational analysis in evaluation, one needs a framework to decide what to pay attention to because you can't track everything. This chapter has been suggesting that a beginning point is locating the situation on the degree of uncertainty/degree of conflict matrix (Exhibits 4.2 to 4.5). Research on evaluation use has identified other factors that come into play.

• *User characteristics*: How many stakeholders are affected by and involved in the evaluation? How do they perceive the "evaluation stakes" and how much agreement is there about what's at stake? How much do they know about evaluation: design, measurement, and methods options? What have been their past experiences with evaluation?

• *Contextual characteristics*: What else is going on in the organization engaged in the evaluation? Leadership stability or transition? Funding certainty or crisis? Cohesion or lots of conflict? Lots of history or a relatively new organization? And the larger political environment? Is there a shrill emphasis on accountability or more concern with innovation, risk taking, and learning? How turbulent is the environment? Degree of turbulence in an organization's environment has been a long-standing factor associated by organizational sociologists with complexity (e.g., Hage & Aiken, 1970). Brenda Zimmerman tells me she has been experimenting with using degree of environmental turbulence in place of degree of agreement in the matrix that maps simple, complicated, and complex. A three-dimensional matrix could include all three (and geometrically increase the degree of complexity in the situational analysis).

• *Evaluation characteristics*: What's the purpose of the evaluation? How is it expected to be used? How much time and funding are available? What existing data sources are available? How many different evaluation questions are there? What types and mix of methods will be needed to answer the evaluation questions? With what degree of confidence and certainty? How visible will the evaluation be? How politically sensitive?

• *Evaluator characteristics*: What's the evaluator's background, methodological exper-

tise, experience, and preferred approach—and how do these affect evaluation options? To what extent does the evaluator have the full range of "essential competencies" (King et al., 2001), including interpersonal, communication, conflict resolution, group facilitation, and political engagement skills?

These factors, and combinations thereof, affect how simple, complicated, or complex a particular evaluation will be. I noted earlier that Patricia Rogers (2008) has been working with the distinctions between simple, complicated, and complex in both her teaching and her evaluation consulting. Recipient of the AEA's Alva and Gunnar Myrdal Practice Award for substantial cumulative contributions to the field of evaluation, she has found it useful to focus on three key issues: governance, causal modeling, and outcome specification. Adapting her framework, we can generate the following questions and distinctions:

1. *Governance.* How will the intervention (innovation) and evaluation be governed and implemented? Working with a single program is relatively simple. Working with a number of well-organized, well-coordinated, and skilled-at-collaborating organizations is complicated. Working with a loosely connected network of different players and organizations that are self-organizing as the process unfolds is complex. (One might add that working with poorly organized, uncoordinated, and not-skilled-at-collaborating organizations can be chaotic.)

2. *Causal modeling.* This includes attention to causal strands, alternative causal mechanisms, and nature of the causal stream (linear vs. nonlinear).

a. *Causal strands.* A single causal pathway leading to a well-specified outcome is simple; cause–effects relations are known and predictable. Several causal paths leading to multiple outcomes, all needing to be coordinated, is complicated; cause–effect relationships are unknown but knowable with careful evaluation. Uncertain causal paths for achieving desired outcomes, especially where causal connections are intertwined, entangled, and overlapping, constitute complexity; cause–effect relationships are unknown and unknowable before effects have emerged, at which time it may be possible to track them backwards, or it may not be possible, as is likely the case, because of the number of dynamic interactions that have occurred.

b. *Alternative change mechanisms.* A single, controllable change mechanism, like giving hungry people food to eat, or an immunization, is simple. Different causal mechanisms operating within different contexts makes the situation, and the evaluation, complicated; comparisons across contexts with different activities are more challenging than comparing standardized mechanisms. Overlapping mechanisms, like adding education and health care to a food program, can make the intervention and evaluation complex.

c. *Nature of the causal stream, linear versus nonlinear.* Simple causal connections involve direct, linear cause–effect connections, as with an immunization; known and predictable nonlinear relationships are also simple, such as big jumps in basic needs during natural disasters, followed by declines when order is restored. Complicated causal connections involve several efforts aimed at the same outcome, where it is complicated to sort out the contribution of each effort to the eventual outcome; such complicated relationships can be nonlinear, but knowable with careful monitoring, and at least partially predictable. For example, exponential relationships and curvilinear ones, and relationships that have a threshold before there's an effect (e.g., rehabilitation programs where there's an effect once someone can walk unaided, or return to work), can be viewed as complicated because with some technical analysis the nature of the causal patterns can be worked out and become somewhat predictable. Complexity includes nonlinear interactions and flows in which small actions can lead to large effects (non-

linearity), or vice versa, and the nature and degree of nonlinearity cannot be controlled or known in advance, or even after the event in most cases, because there are too many interacting variables to sort out.

3. *Outcome specification.* Simple evaluations involve one or a small number of clear, specific, and measurable outcomes, not in conflict with each other, specified in advance. Complicated evaluations involve multiple, vague, and/or conflicting outcomes. Evaluation is complex when outcomes cannot be specified in advance because they are emergent; this makes pre–post comparisons and tracking changes against baselines especially challenging.

Nor are these static situations. The program you thought was simple at the first meeting with a single stakeholder turns out to be complicated when more stakeholders get involved with quite different conceptions of what's supposed to happen—and why. You thought everyone had agreed on the primary outcomes, making the situation fairly simple, then the program begins operating and unanticipated outcomes begin emerging, making the situation complex. Observing and tracking these changes so that innovators can more rapidly and effectively respond is often a crucial part of the work of developmental evaluation.

Making Evaluation Design Decisions

What happens when we're faced with complexity? The evidence from social and behavioral science is that when faced with complex choices and multiple situations, we fall back on a set of rules and standard operating procedures that predetermine what we will do and effectively short-circuit situational adaptability. The evidence is that we are running most of the time on preprogrammed tapes. That has always been the function of rules of thumb and scientific paradigms. Faced with a new situation, the evaluation researcher (unconsciously) turns to old and comfortable patterns. This may help explain why so many evaluators who have rhetorically embraced the philosophy of situational evaluation find that the approaches in which they are trained and with which they are most comfortable *just happen* to be particularly appropriate in each new evaluation situation they confront—time after time after time. Sociologists just happen to find doing a survey appropriate. Economists just happen to feel the situation needs cost–benefit analysis. A psychologist studies the situation and decides that—surprise!—pre–post testing with an experimental design would be appropriate. And evaluators of all kinds begin by looking for clear, specific, and measurable outcomes and requiring specification of a linear logic model that describes how those outcomes will be achieved. So it goes, over and over again. This is like a mouse "choosing" to eat cheese or a bear making a decision to "prefer" honey.

The point of this analysis is to raise a fundamental question: How can evaluators prepare themselves to deal with a lot of different people and a huge variety of situations? The research on decision making says we can't systematically consider every possible variable, or even 50 variables, or even 20 variables. What we need is a framework for making sense of situations, for telling us what factors deserve priority based on research and desired results. Such a framework, rather than providing narrow, specific prescriptions, should offer questions to force us to think about and analyze the situation.

Distinguishing simple, complicated, and complex situations is such a framework. Different evaluation questions flow from these distinctions. Those different questions have design, methods, and use implications. Indeed, the way we evaluate programs or interventions in each of these contexts is substantially different. Simple formulations invite linear logic models that link inputs to activities to outputs to outcomes like a formula or recipe. Complicated situations invite system diagrams and maps that depict the relationships among the parts (which we'll take up in the next chapter). Complex problems and situations are especially appropriate for

developmental evaluation in which the evaluation design is flexible, emergent, and dynamic, mirroring the emergent, dynamic, and uncertain nature of the intervention or innovation being evaluated. Chapter 8 looks in some depth at different inquiry frameworks for developmental evaluation and Chapter 9 considers methods implications and options. Before delving into those issues in depth later in the book, let me now illustrate the evaluation implications of these different ways of understanding a change initiative's situational context.

Applying Situational Distinctions to an Actual Evaluation: The Caribbean Agricultural Extension Project

Let's begin with sources and types of uncertainty. In Chapter 3, I cited Tom Henderson's observation that the standardized training and visit (T & V) agricultural extension that supported the Green Revolution in India would not work in the Caribbean because of its diversity and uncertainties. Farming in general is more uncertain than manufacturing processes because of weather and market fluctuations. These were magnified in the Caribbean. I want to use the Caribbean Agricultural Extension Project (CAEP) as an example of situational adaptation and developmental evaluation.

You may recall (or not) that when introducing this example in Chapter 3, I commented that there's a good chance that you're not interested in agricultural extension and that your primary interest in the Caribbean, if you have any at all, is as a tourist destination in winter. And you'd rather not have your time sunning on the beach and enjoying the waves intruded upon by knowledge that nearby are poor subsistence farmers struggling to get by. Besides, it's an old example. So let me reiterate why I think it's valuable.

I do a lot of training. Courses I teach at The Evaluators' Institute, in International Program Development Evaluation Training (IPDET), and for the AEA attract diverse participants. They come with specialized knowledge, which is the order of the day. They live inside the silo of their own organization with their own narrow knowledge base. Public health people initially have trouble with education examples. Criminal justice people have trouble with environmental protection examples. Social workers have trouble with economic development examples. To help people learn to transfer from one arena of expertise to another, to help them grasp and master the underlying concepts and principles, I find it helpful to have them work with examples outside everyone's expertise and time frames, which don't get sidetracked with contemporary events. So, while you may not have interest in Caribbean agricultural extension in the 1980s, that's not the point. The point is whether you can identify the underlying principles of complexity thinking and see how they apply to your own area of interest, expertise, and responsibility. That's why I introduced this example in Chapter 3 and that's why I'm building on it here. So, take a deep breath and come with me to the Caribbean isles. And be prepared. It's not all beautiful beaches and sunny skies.

In 1979, as the final planning for the CAEP was under way, Dominica was buffeted by Hurricane David, one of the strongest and deadliest Atlantic hurricanes on record. There was little local radio warning and no operational systems for disaster preparedness. With swirling 150 mile-an-hour winds, David pounded Dominica for 6 hours. Thirty-seven people were killed and an estimated 5,000 injured. Of the 75,000 population, 75% were left homeless, forced to sleep under rough shelter in the open or huddled in the homes of friends who still had roofs over their heads. Less than a year later, still recovering from David, Dominica was hit by Hurricane Allen, one of the strongest hurricanes in recorded history and one of the few hurricanes to reach Category 5 status. The combination of David and Allen devastated Dominican agriculture, destroying most coconut and banana trees. Indeed, the Dominican economy was almost totally destroyed, with ripple effects through the en-

tire social sector. Dominica's few roads and bridges were blocked or swept away. Electric power and piped water were cut off. Ironically, just before Hurricane David hit, Dominica had formulated and adopted a major 5-year development plan under the auspices of the World Bank. Tom Henderson told me that by the time the two hurricanes had done their damage, including ravaging government offices, no one could even find a copy of the 5-year plan, not that it was any longer relevant. Dominica suffered more damage from hurricanes in 1995 (Hurricane Luis) and 1999 (Hurricane Lenny). Hurricane Dean destroyed most of Dominica's banana crop again in August 2007. In November 2004 an earthquake occurred in the north of Dominica, causing millions of dollars of damage.

Then there is Montserrat, another island in the project, a beautiful green gem of volcanic hills and luscious valleys when I worked there throughout the 1980s. Known as the "Emerald Isle of the Caribbean" for both its Irish heritage and its resemblance to coastal Ireland, that all changed in 1995 when a sudden volcanic eruption buried the island's capital, Plymouth, in more than 40 feet of mud, destroyed its airport and docking facilities, and rendered the southern half of the island uninhabitable. More than half of the population left the island due to the economic disruption and lack of housing. Another eruption in 1997 killed 19 people.

Government instability is another source of uncertainty in the Caribbean. In Dominica, the interim government was barely 2 months old when Hurricane David hit. International aid efforts were hampered by charges of government corruption, including accusations of irregularities in distributing disaster relief supplies, hoarding rebuilding materials, and using aid for political purposes. A rift developed between USAID and Prime Minister Seraphin's government that interfered with disaster efforts.

But that rift was minor compared to the dissatisfaction of the United States with Grenada, which led to an invasion of that country in 1983. Following independence in 1974, Grenada experienced ongoing political strife leading to a coup in 1979 led by Maurice Bishop, who had close ties with and the support of Fidel Castro in Cuba. In 1983, a power struggle within Grenada, fed by international cold war politics, led to coups and countercoups, mass demonstrations, and eventually the murder of Bishop and several government officials loyal to him. The invasion of Grenada, led by the United States, was the first major operation conducted by the U.S. military since the Vietnam War. All Caribbean countries were affected by the international controversy that swirled around the invasion and its aftermath.

Now consider market uncertainties. Throughout the 1980s banana farmers worried about whether the Caribbean islands would be able to retain favorable access to the British market. Until 1992, the former British Caribbean colonies of the Windward Islands (Dominica, St. Lucia, St. Vincent, Grenada) and other former colonies had a contract that guaranteed a market in Britain. As a result, they exported exclusively to Britain. The banana industry dominated the economy of the Windward Islands, providing the main source of employment and earnings. On St. Lucia, 60,000 people, over one-third of the population, depended on the banana industry for their income. In Dominica, a third of the labor force and 70% of the population was dependent on bananas. On all the islands, bananas provided over half of all export earnings.

The emergence of the European Union and globalization of markets changed all that. The 1990s came to be known as the period of the Great Banana War, fomented in part by huge United States–based companies such as Dole and Chiquita. After years of hearings by and negotiations with the World Trade Organization, changing marketing agreements, protests and legal actions, in 2007 preferential access for Caribbean farmers to the European Union came to an end. For years, under the cloud of uncertainty about global markets and new trade agreements, Caribbean econo-

mists forecast devastating social, economical, and political consequences, including mass poverty, high levels of unemployment, and political instability. By 2006, banana prices had already dropped significantly, many farmers were leaving the land, and unemployment was on the rise. Then came the global economic crisis of 2008 and, as if all that was not uncertainty enough, a new strain of Panama disease is threatening bananas along with a variety of bacterial, viral, and fungal diseases, plus nematodes and other parasites (Dominique, n.d.).

The point of this Caribbean excursion is to illustrate the range of uncertainties in just one region and arena of action that can make a situation complex, including a high degree of uncertainty about what is known or knowable and a high degree of disagreement about what ought to be done.

- Economic uncertainties: global shifts in markets, trade agreements, exchange rates, inflation, and consumer preferences.

- Production uncertainties: diseases, pests, and conflicting advice about the cost-effectiveness of various practices, including fertilizers and pesticides.

- Farm management uncertainties about what mix of crops to grow and how to allocate scarce resources given market volatilities.

- Political instability nationally, regionally, and internationally with changes in governments, changes in foreign assistance priorities, and sometimes violent conflicts.

- Infrastructure uncertainties, where the condition of and access to roads, bridges, truck transport, commercial shipping of agricultural products, and communication links were all problematic.

- Organizational uncertainties with changes in food cooperatives, farmer groups, marketing boards, and extension staffs, as well as potential government corruption and competition among political parties.

- Social uncertainties with large-scale migration out of the islands to Europe, North America, and South America. Moreover, during times of economic hardship, *predial larceny* (agricultural theft from farmers' fields) increased.

- Dire weather uncertainties: hurricanes, volcanoes, and earthquakes.

Evaluation of the CAEP over 10 years had to take all these factors into account. It would have been inappropriate to focus narrowly on the technical training of extension agents and ignore the larger systems that affected how they operated and what they could do. It would have made the evaluation meaningless to gather data without sensitivity to the context that impinged on the performance and outcomes of extension. A developmental evaluation monitors these factors and takes them into account, facilitating adjustment and adaptation of training priorities—beyond improvements in training, though these may also occur, but the emphasis here is on developments and innovations versus improvements as discussed in Chapter 2. The developmental evaluation in the CAEP provided real-time information to support adapting service delivery to changed conditions, even working with funders and staff to change goals and outcome targets as the situation changed. For example, increased banana production could be the goal one year, while the very next year the priority would be shifting production away from bananas. The agricultural situation in the Caribbean was and is dynamic, volatile, uncertain, and emergent—in a word, *complex.*

That said, not everything was complex. There were aspects of the program that were comparatively simple, like teaching extension agents specific agricultural techniques, for example, how to propagate citrus trees, how to test soils, and how to harvest, pack, and transport bananas to market without bruising them. These parts of the training were aimed at increasing the technical knowledge of extension agents on topics about which agricultural scientists agreed and which small farmers wanted and need-ed help. These simple elements lend themselves to simple evaluation designs: pre- and posttests of knowledge, observations of behavior in the field, and feedback from farmers about what they've learned and used (evaluating adoption of effective practices).

Other aspects of the program were complicated. Many small farmers in the Caribbean diversify risk by diversifying their crops. On the same small plot of land, say 5 hectares, they may grow lime, coconut, and banana trees (each demanding different cultivation practices), yams, and others vegetables, both for consumption and for sale, and keep some animals—a couple of cows, some pigs, maybe rabbits, and certainly chickens. Many would also do some fishing. What constitutes the best mix of different crops and various animals, and allocating time, land, and farm inputs between subsistence and cash crops is complicated, requiring a farming systems approach that involves complicated trade-offs and comparative risk assessments matched to the farmer family's aspirations, labor availability, and resources. Evaluating farming system changes requires in-depth case studies of farm families as well as a sub-system of adjacent farmers within a specific ecological zone. Experts would disagree among themselves about the appropriate mix and farmers would disagree about how much risk to take on. Many factors have to be taken into consideration, weighed, and balanced—making decisions technically complicated.

The situation for extension agents, and therefore for the evaluation, were socially complicated by the fact that extension programs were not the only intervention going on. Extension priorities had to be negotiated with a variety of stakeholders including national governments; farmers' cooperatives and unions; marketing boards; international development agencies; world trade groups; and regional Caribbean associations like the Caribbean Agricultural Research and Development Institute (CARDI), the Caribbean Aquaculture Association, and the University of the West Indies. These stakeholders had conflicting agendas and priorities, often intensely so. Moreover, extension agents were often involved in collaborating with other programs like public health, conservation and environmental protection, water initiatives, microfinance, and education. Evaluation included surveys of the perceptions, knowledge, and priorities of key stakeholder groups and case studies of specific collaborative efforts.

The complex elements of the program included emerging interactions and networks among the outstanding extension agents identified by the project, tracking their new leadership roles (which were highly emergent, dynamic, and developmental). The project also created new connections and interactions between and among the various stakeholder groups under the auspices of a regional project advisory group (see Chapter 2 for details). This group helped design the evaluation and interpret findings, but bringing together these diverse players, each acting in their own self-interest and that of the entity they represented, led to unanticipated and unpredictable self-organized subgroups, which spawned new initiatives, political realignments, important interorga-

nizational dynamics that attracted resources, and networks sharing previously siloed information, some of which took action together. Evaluating these developments and their impacts required an emergent design that used well-placed key informants as listening posts, reporting what was emerging, and tracking new interactions, networks, and initiatives as they unfolded. None of these initiatives were anticipated in the project design. Each of these networks and initiatives developed their own goals, which themselves proved highly changeable, often so vague and fragile as to constitute moving targets. More like moving shadows across the ravines, valleys, hills, beaches, and waves of the Caribbean. Complex, indeed.

Exhibit 4.8 summarizes the elements of the program that were simple, complicated, and complex—and the evaluation implications of those different elements. This exhibit is also a template that can be used for any program or initiative to distinguish simple, complicated, and complex elements.

EXHIBIT 4.8 Simple, Complicated, and Complex Program and Evaluation Elements: Design Template Illustrated Using an Agricultural Extension Development Program

Program components	*Extension agent technical training:* Learning production knowledge and techniques. Learning specific extension training techniques.	1. Farming systems impacts: risk assessments affecting the mix of crops, animals, and allocation of inputs in relation to farm family situation. 2. Extension interaction and collaboration with diverse stakeholders and other programs.	*Networking and emergent initiatives among leaders and actors brought together under the auspices of the program:* spin-offs and ripple effects; self-organized subgroups exchanging information and taking action together.
Situation framing	Simple	*Complicated:* 1. Technically complicated 2. Socially complicated	Complex

(cont.)

Type of theory of change	*Linear logic model*: Program training increases knowledge and skills.	*Systems change*: 1. Farming systems are changed as production mix is altered. Farm family operations and ecosystems vary greatly. 2. Collaborations involve new arrangements and shared outcomes.	*Complex adaptive self-organizing networks*: Informal groups emerge and decide to collaborate around shared interests. Information exchanges affect individual and networked behaviors.
Degree of certainty about how to achieve desired outcomes (horizontal axis on the uncertainty/conflict matrix, Exhibits 4.2–4.5)	*High certainty*: There is scientifically valid knowledge about specific production techniques and training approaches. Highly experienced and knowledgeable instructors conduct the training; they have a track record of attaining results.	*Moderate to low certainty*: 1. Degree to which reallocations pay off depend on diverse and dynamic factors, many of which are outside the farmers' control. 2. Incentives and barriers to collaborate are inconsistent and variable.	*Very low certainty*: Outcomes are unclear and unspecified; not even possible to specify all the variables that come into play; high likelihood that chance encounters will play a part.
Degree of agreement about the desired outcomes (vertical axis on the uncertainty/conflict matrix)	High agreement that extension agents should be technically competent and knowledgeable about production and education techniques.	1. Diverse views about the best mix of production inputs and mix of products. Highly variable farmer views about appropriate and manageable risk. 2. Diverse views about the nature and degree of collaboration that is possible and desirable. History of operating in silos hard to overcome; much resistance. Uncertain about what is involved in collaborations.	Low agreement about how these leaders should engage together in the larger nonprofit sector; vague vision of engagement so what is done will be emergent and opportunistic.
Evaluation questions	Are the desired outcomes achieved? Can these outcomes be attributed to the program? Do the trained extension agents use their new skills effectively with farmers? To what extent do farmers adopt appropriate techniques?	How are farms and farming systems changed? How are relationships altered? How are extension's interactions with other development programs affected? How can efforts and impacts be aggregated and synthesized?	What informal groups of participants self-organize? What do these emergent subgroups do together? What impacts flow from their emergent activities? What developments occur over time?
Evaluation design	Pre–post assessment of changed knowledge, skills, and practices. Follow-up to assess application of new skills. Studies of farmers' adoption of new practices.	1. Case studies of farms and farming systems. 2. Case studies of collaborations focused on how organizations and organizational interactions are changed, and what they accomplish.	Developmental evaluation, tracking what emerges and develops over time. Also tracking how what emerges affects processes and outcomes in the simple and complicated arenas of the program, and interactions among program elements.

Variations on a Theme: The *Cynefin* Framework

Wise executives tailor their approach to fit the complexity of the circumstances they face.
— DAVID SNOWDEN AND MARY BOONE
(2007, p. 68)

This was the central message of "A Leader's Framework for Decision Making" by management consultants David Snowden and Mary Boone in their featured *Harvard Business Review* article. The article was designated as the Best Practitioner-Oriented Paper in Organizational Behavior in 2007 by the Organizational Behavior Division of the Academy of Management. As Brenda Zimmerman was refining the distinctions between simple, complicated, and complex in the degree of uncertainty/degree of conflict matrix, David Snowden and his colleagues in IBM's Institute of Knowledge Management were thinking in parallel terms that led to the *cynefin* framework, making the same distinctions, an impressive exemplar of independent discoveries by creative minds following the same path. Snowden, of Welsh lineage, chose the Welsh word *cynefin* (pronounced kun-ev'in) as the name of the framework distinguishing simple, complicated, complex, and chaotic. The Welsh dictionary translates *cynefin* as meaning haunt, habitat, acquainted, accustomed, or familiar, being both noun and adjective, and thus requiring context to understand its meaning in any given instance. Snowden resonated to this uncertainty that evokes the sense that our understandings depend on our interactions with each other and our environment, which includes cultural traditions, organizational norms, and the geographical/ecological setting within which interactions occur.

When Zimmerman distinguished simple, complicated, complex, and chaotic by the degree of agreement and uncertainty of a situation, she included distinctions between the known (simple), the knowable (complicated), and the unknowable (complex

⁓ *Advice from an Experienced Developmental Evaluator*

What would you tell someone new to developmental evaluation about doing it? Advice? Caveats? Lessons? Challenges?

Ricardo Wilson-Grau is an international social change network consultant and evaluator based in Rio de Janeiro, Brazil. He offers an "acid test" for developmental evaluation. An acid test referred originally to a procedure for determining whether a metal is real gold or not. It has since come to mean any test for the real thing.

THE ACID TEST

I suggest you apply the "simple–complex acid test" to the nature of the social change challenge your client faces. If she is confident she knows the relations of cause and effect between what she proposes to do and what the results will be, she faces a "simple" situation. She is challenged to do the right things right in order to bring about change, but developmental evaluation is not for her, although she would benefit from a formative evaluation midway through to make adjustments to keep her on track.

If, however, she cannot say with certainty what she will achieve, but is confident that by doing what she feels is right she will find the way forward to the change she wants to see, her challenge is "complex." She does not know the relations of cause and effect. This situation is ripe for a developmental evaluator to help her identify and understand, in real time, her results and how she contributed to them.

and chaotic). In making similar distinctions, Snowden's *cynefin* framework (Kurtz & Snowden, 2003; Snowden & Boone, 2007) emphasizes variations in the nature of causality and the corresponding implications for decision making and action.

Simple: linear, direct connection between cause and effect; easily observable, understandable, and verifiable. This is the arena where things are *known*, so best practices can be identified and applied. A leader's or manager's decision/action sequence is:

Sense → Categorize → Respond

Complicated: determining cause and effect requires analysis and expert investigation, so things are not yet known, but are knowable. Good, effective practices can be identified (but *not* "best"). The decision/action sequence is:

Sense → Analyze → Respond

Complex: cause and effect is contingent on contextual and dynamic conditions, and therefore unknowable; patterns are unpredictable in advance. Practice is emergent and contingent. A leader's or manager's decision/action sequence should be:

Probe → Sense → Respond

Chaotic: no observable or predictable relationship between cause and effect because of rapidly changing and highly unstable/turbulent systems dynamics, but some kind of action is required. The appropriate decision/action sequence is:

Act → Sense → Respond

Exhibit 4.9 summarizes and displays the *cynefin* framework.

New Zealand evaluator and leading systems thinker Bob Williams (see Williams & Iman, 2007) shared with me his experience using the *cynefin* framework.

EXHIBIT 4.9 Cynefin Framework

KNOWN—SIMPLE	KNOWABLE—COMPLICATED
▪ Cause-and-effect relationships are repeatable, perceivable, and predictable. ▪ Best practices and standard operating procedures are possible. ▪ Process reengineering. ▪ Sense making and action: Sense → Categorize → Respond	▪ Cause and effect are separated over time and space. ▪ Systems analysis and thinking. ▪ Scenario planning. ▪ Sense making and action: Sense → Analyze → Respond
UNKNOWABLE IN ADVANCE—COMPLEX	UNKNOWABLE EVER—CHAOS
▪ Cause and effect are only coherent in retrospect and do not repeat. ▪ Complex adaptive systems. ▪ Pattern management. ▪ Perspective filters. ▪ Sense making and action: Probe → Sense → Respond	▪ No cause-and-effect relationships are perceivable. ▪ Stability the focus of interventions. ▪ Crisis management. ▪ Sense making and action: Act → Sense → Respond

Note. Based on Snowden and Boone (2007).

"I was exploring a new method of handling patients within a health care situation. I got people to group those aspects of the situation into Snowden's four categories (simple/known, complicated/knowable, complex/unknowable, chaotic), acknowledging that a given situation has elements of all four states (each of which implies a different response—including strategies that might move an aspect of the situation from one 'state' to another and thus make it easier to manage). This then leads to some very interesting conversations about whether they were assuming that a problem was 'knowable' if only they worked hard enough, or that they were looking for 'best practice' when actually 'good practice' was what they should be considering.

"Some aspects of the situation were placed in more than one category. At this point all kinds of lightbulbs lit up. People realized that part of the problem they were experiencing was that different people were imagining that aspect from two different understandings of what is going on. They suddenly understood why they were having difficulty resolving or managing the situation: 'Oh, so you were managing it as if it were complicated and I was managing it as if it were complex—no wonder we were clashing over strategies.' "

Snowden's focus has been on teaching leaders and managers to make *cynefin* framework distinctions as a guide to decision making. Through his consulting business, Cognitive Edge (*www.cognitive-edge.com*) he has successfully transmitted the simple–complicated–complex–chaotic distinctions widely in the corporate world. My focus here is on its implications for evaluators. Exhibit 4.10 adapts his Leader's Guide to Decisions in Multiple Contexts and applies it to evaluation.

Situational Responsiveness and Developmental Evaluation

This entire chapter has been about how we figure out what situation we face so we can engage appropriately. In particular, I have been delineating and refining the niche of developmental evaluation as especially appropriate for interventions and innovations being undertaken under conditions of complexity. Applying Snowden and Boone's (2007) advice to leaders, the message of this chapter has been:

Wise evaluators tailor their approach to fit the complexity of the circumstances they face.

EXHIBIT 4.10 Decisions in Multiple Contexts: An Evaluator's Guide

Wise evaluators tailor their approach to fit the complexity of the circumstances they face.

The situation: Uncertainty/conflict matrix[a] and *cynefin* framework[b]	The leader's job	The evaluator's job	Evaluation challenges
SIMPLE High agreement about the problem and what to do; high certainty that the right action will produce the desired results; clear, direct, linear, predictable, and controllable cause–effect pattern. What needs to be done is known.	• Sense, categorize, respond. • Know what is known. • Manage based on facts. • Advocate for and implement best practices.	• Validate best practices (summative evaluation). • Monitor implementation of best practices to assure high fidelity, adherence, and quality. • Report departures from best practices and implications of those departures, especially implications for outcomes.	• Assuring that best practices fit new contexts (different from where the practices were originated and validated). • Detecting unanticipated consequences and context-specific implementation problems.
COMPLICATED Some disagreements about the problem and what to do. Expertise needed. The necessity of coordinating many areas of technical expertise and many actors introduces uncertainty about attaining desired outcomes. More than one effective way possible. Cause–effect linkages are context-contingent; discoverable with careful analysis, but neither obvious nor certain. Contingencies discernible (known unknowns).	• Sense, analyze, respond. • Find needed expertise to identify good practices. • Listen to and assess conflicting expert advice. • Use monitoring and evaluation to track what unfolds as good practices are tried.	• Validate effective practices and options with attention to context and system contingencies. • Convert expert advice into a testable theory of change. • Evaluate and report unfolding cause–effect complications and their implications. • Systems thinking.	• Designing a reasonable test of the theory of change (summative evaluation). • Understanding the system(s) and context(s) within which action unfolds. • Detecting and measuring both outcomes and contingencies. Facilitating interpretation of less-than-certain findings.

(cont.)

The situation: Uncertainty/conflict matrix[a] and *cynefin* framework[b]	The leader's job	The evaluator's job	Evaluation challenges
COMPLEX High uncertainty about how to produce desired results and great disagreement among diverse stakeholders about the nature of the problem and what, if anything, to do. Results highly dependent on initial conditions; nonlinear interactions within a dynamic system. No right answers; key variables and their interactions unknown in advance. Each situation is unique.	• Probe, sense, respond. • Foster dialogue, creativity, and innovation. • Watch for and interpret emerging patterns. • Be flexible and adaptive. • Make time for and engage in reflective practice to capture, understand, and interpret what is emerging.	• Identify and document initial conditions and monitor what emerges. • Provide ongoing, timely, and rapid feedback about what is emerging. • Track incremental actions and decisions that affect the paths taken (and not taken). • Facilitate regular reflective practice about what is *developing*. • Embed evaluative thinking in the innovative process.	• Keeping up with the rapid pace of change in turbulent and dynamic environments, and documenting developments. • Managing a flexible, emergent design. • High level of ongoing interaction and communication. • Combining creative and critical (evaluative) thinking in support of innovation. • Facilitating interpretation of emergent findings for action. Staying developmentally focused.
CHAOTIC High conflict among stakeholders; extreme uncertainty about what to do. Turbulence and volatility make pattern detection unreliable, even undecipherable. Dynamic interactions hard to follow, not even sure what to pay attention to. Unreliable information. What to focus on is unknown and a matter of great debate. Tense, stressful decision environment.	• Act, sense, respond. • Try things out and see what happens, watching for anything that works. • Manage what is manageable to establish some degree of order. • Don't yield to panic.	• Distinguish better and worse data; some information may be better than none, but interpret cautiously. • Find those parts of the action where evaluation can make an immediate contribution to help survive chaos.	• Acknowledging data inadequacies. • Being open and opportunistic about finding data. • Avoiding defaulting to the simple in an effort to exercise control and create the illusion of certainty where none exists. • Helping transition to stability in the face of chaos. • Don't be a burden.

[a]Based on Westley, Zimmerman, and Patton (2006); [b]Based on Snowden and Boone (2007).

5

Systems Thinking and Complexity Concepts for Developmental Evaluation

Eat when you're hungry.
Drink when you're thirsty.
Sleep when you're tired.
—Buddhist proverb

We'll skip eating and drinking and go right to sleep. How deep is your sleep deficit? Do you drive drowsy? Do you know your sleep inertia pattern? Do you experience daytime sleepiness? How about sleep apnea? Want to conduct your own evaluation and find out how your sleep deprivation compares to standards and norms? You could take the Multiple Sleep Latency Test (MSLT), or the Epworth Sleepiness Scale (ESS), or the Psychomotor Vigilance Test (PVT), or get assessed on the Karolinska Sleepiness Scale (KSS).

From an evaluation modeling perspective, sleep is an input. Performance is an outcome. Sleep deficit is "a performance killer" according to Dr. Charles A. Czeisler of the Harvard Work Hours, Health, and Safety Group in the Division of Sleep Medicine, Harvard Medical School.

It amazes me that contemporary work and social culture glorifies sleeplessness in the way we once glorified people who could hold their

liquor. We now know that 24 hours without sleep or a week of sleeping four or five hours a night induces an impairment equivalent to a blood alcohol level of .1%.

We would never say, "This person is a great worker! He's drunk all the time!," yet we continue to celebrate people who sacrifice sleep. The analogy to drunkenness is real because, like a drunk, a person who is sleep-deprived has no idea how functionally impaired he or she truly is. Moreover, their efficiency at work will suffer substantially, contributing to the phenomenon of "presenteeism" [At work—but out of it], which exacts a large economic toll on business. (Czeisler, 2006, pp. 55–56)

Dr. Czeisler goes on to explain that sleep deprivation is not just an individual health hazard; it's a public one, significantly increasing the risk of occupational injury and driver fatigue. In a series of studies, his team assessed the effects of extended work hours on hospital residents' sleep and health, as well as patient safety. They found that residents who had worked 24 hours or longer, which was not unusual, were 2.3 times more likely to have a motor vehicle accident following such a long shift compared to working less than 24 hours. They further found that the monthly risk of an accident increased by 16.2% after each extended duration shift. In a randomized trial they found that hospital interns who worked a traditional on-call schedule slept 5.8 hours less per week, had twice as many attentional failures on duty overnight, and made 36% more serious medical errors and nearly six times more serious diagnostic errors than when working on a schedule that limited continuous duty to 16 hours (Lockley, Landrigan, Barger, & Czeisler, 2006).

The National Sleep Foundation (2009) estimates that 70 million people in the United States experience sleep problems, with about 40 million suffering from a chronic sleep disorder, though most remain undiagnosed and untreated. They estimate that sleep deprivation and disorders cost over $100 billion annually in lost productivity, medical expenses, sick leave, and property and environmental damage. Czeisler's (2009) research estimates that 250,000 Americans, mostly young drivers, fall asleep while driving every day; as many as 8,000 Americans may be killed annually in drowsy-driving crashes.

So what does all this have to do with developmental evaluation, other than the likelihood that a lot of social innovators, program directors, policymakers, and evaluators are seriously sleep-deprived, thereby risking bad decisions, not to mention accidents and health problems? Well, that itself is no small thing. In March 2009 I led an evaluation team participating in the International Conference on Fatigue Management in Transportation Operations. For 3 days we heard research findings on how sleep deprivation and fatigue increase accidents and fatalities among truck drivers, railroad engineers, airline workers, police officers, and emergency medical personnel. We were immersed in analyses of sleep deficit effects, sleep inertia, sleep apnea, narcolepsy, drowsy driving, and falling asleep at the wheel. So, as a general method for increasing the validity, reliability, accuracy, and utility of evaluations, the first recommendation has to be, *get some sleep.* Stop writing evaluation reports in the middle of the night when you're likely *sleepless-drunk.* And those of you receiving evaluation reports, stop pulling them out of your big to-do stack at the end of the day when you're exhausted. Getting people to read, understand, and use evaluation reports face enough barriers without adding the confusion, apprehension, and misconceptions that arise from reading when sleep-deprived. So that's my public service announcement and fulfills my conference commitment to do something in my own arena of action about fatigue management. Excuse me, now, while I go take a nap. . . .

Okay, I'm back. And you may still be wondering, what does all this have to do with developmental evaluation? Just this: fatigue management interventions offer rich examples of how applying systems thinking and a complexity lens can inform developmental evaluation designs and enhance the utility of findings. As always with utilization-focused developmental evaluation, we begin with the *personal factor,* which in this case means locating and working with someone who cares about using evaluation to develop effective fatigue management interventions. Let me introduce you to Mike Coplen.

From Train Brakeman to Locomotive Engineer to Evaluation Champion

Mike Coplen received the 2009 Alva and Gunnar Myrdal Government Award from the American Evaluation Association (AEA). He was recognized for his role in championing evaluation in the U.S. Department of Transportation, specifically for "his efforts as an internal evaluator embracing statistical analysis, safety communication, behavioral analysis, and utilization-focused evaluation" (AEA, 2009). At the time of this writing, he was senior evaluator and director, Culture and Safety Performance Studies, Human Factors Program, Office of Research and Development in the Federal Railroad Administration. He specializes in *human factors research and development*, which involves understanding the relationship between human behavior and transportation safety and productivity. Human factors make transportation safety complex. No matter how mechanically safe a vehicle is, as long as a human being is needed to operate it, human factors will trump mechanical factors in efforts to reduce safety. Coplen knows this from personal experience. He began his railroad career as a brakeman in 1978 and then worked as a locomotive engineer from 1979 until 1985. During that time he became increasingly concerned about the dangers brought on by fatigue resulting from long hours, irregular scheduling, and interrupted sleep. Being naturally inclined toward evaluation, long before he even knew the field existed, he began recording what he was experiencing.

"I have records documenting having worked more than 170 hours in a 2-week period. For several months I kept a log of my work–rest schedule, revealing from as little as 0 hours to as many as 17 hours of sleep in a 24-hour period. Sometimes in one 24-hour time frame, I'd have up to seven distinct sleep periods as I tried to catch naps. I've been called to work a 12-hour shift after having *no* sleep the prior 24 hours. On one trip like that I nearly crashed a loaded coal train into a caboose of the standing train ahead of me. The rear brakeman and conductor jumped from the train, as well as the head brakeman and fireman on my train. As the last person out the door I was the only one to remain standing as our train slowly crawled to a stop less than a ½ car length away from the caboose as it was beginning to pull away."

Human factors include organizational dynamics. Coplen has experienced firsthand

how animosity between management and labor affected safety. He cites as examples the catastrophic collisions that occurred early in his career, in 1984 in Wiggins, Colorado, and Newcastle, Wyoming.

"They occurred on the same railroad only weeks apart. In both instances several people were killed, some of whom were personal friends of mine. Both crashes happened between 3 and 5 o'clock in the morning. After the railroad preemptively sued the surviving employees of those accidents for negligence in falling asleep on the job I decided to offer to the NTSB [National Transportation Safety Board] the data I had been collecting for the past several months on the sleeping patterns of train crews. Subsequently, I was asked to testify in public hearings on those accidents. Shortly thereafter I was *required* to provide a urine sample as part of a *routine* physical. While I was never fired or disciplined, after that I certainly felt as if I were being watched closely.

"Another friend of mine left railroading after having suffered a severe back injury. He was riding the side of a rail car in the middle of the night, and was clipped by an unmarked close clearance hazard he did not see. Management hounded him on the way to the hospital, and even in his hospital bed, for any evidence of personal guilt so that they might mitigate any potential liability claim."

These experiences led Coplen from working on railroads to studying railroad safety. He recalls that when he began his career as a researcher with the Department of Transportation, "I had high hopes for making a difference in safety with the railroad industry." He found that the challenge was not so much doing the research as getting it used— another human factors problem.

"One of my first projects was to understand how and why some people don't comply with railroad operating rules. I conducted a focus group with members of the Operating Rules Association, mostly midlevel managers responsible for monitoring and disciplining employees who violate the rules. I produced a report called *Compliance with Railroad Operating Rules*, which highlights the pressures senior managers place on midlevel managers to expedite trains, who then encourage employees to overlook safety and operating rules so they can keep trains moving.

"While this was not a highly technical document, nevertheless I was excited. Here was evidence, directly supported by numerous quotations from various midlevel managers from around the country, which suggested senior managers indirectly pressured lower level managers to encourage employees not to comply with safety and operating rules. But after the report was published I was left with a lingering question. . . . *So what? Now what?*

"Some people told me they thought it was a really good report, but I have no way of knowing how many people actually read it, let alone used it to improve safety. And if they did, what kinds of changes did they make as a result? What impact did it have? It's quite possible it had the *opposite* effect of what I intended. Some savvy lawyer may have gotten hold of it to help justify an employee's liability claim against a carrier. Wouldn't that be wonderful! That would help explain why it is so difficult sometimes to get railroads to cooperate in our research projects, projects that could potentially make significant improvements in safety across the entire industry."

Mike Coplen wants to conduct human factors research and evaluations that have an impact on safety. But getting findings used is complex. "If I've learned anything from my experience as a program manager over the past 10 years it's that all too often our research reports do little more than gather dust in the hallowed halls of federal science. I've come to realize that there is an art, a

craft, and a science to increasing the use and impact of R&D projects and evaluation." He is especially concerned about fatigue, which has been a problem since the earliest days of railroading, and, he asserts, "continues to be one of the most important and controversial safety issues today." Progress is hampered, he believes, by "the culture of mistrust between labor and management, and between the industry and the FRA [Federal Railroad Administration]. This culture of distrust is legendary. While important inroads are being made with regard to research and demonstration projects to improve critical safety issues and safety culture, we still have a long, long way to go. Evaluation is needed to support progress, especially evaluation that pays attention to human factors complexities."

Coplen's experiences of the dysfunctional organizational dynamics of railroads parallels what Congress found in its investigations of the two space shuttle disasters: the dysfunctional, conflict-laden, and politicized decision-making culture of NASA contributed significantly to both accidents. Mechanically, the failure of the O-rings in the first disaster and the loss of a foam shield in the second were the direct mechanical causes of the accidents. (These are elements of the technically complicated nature of launching a rocket discussed in Chapter 4.) But deeper, more complex organizational issues allowed those mechanical failures to go uncorrected. A comprehensive independent investigation of the 2002 *Columbia* tragedy concluded that NASA's culture of complacency, nurtured by a string of successes since the 1986 *Challenger* disaster, led to a habit of relaxing safety standards to meet financial and time constraints, for example, defining a problem as insignificant so as not to require a fix that would cause delay. The investigation concluded that NASA mission managers fell into the habit of accepting as normal some flaws in the shuttle system and tended to ignore, not recognize, or *not want to hear about* such problems even though they might foreshadow catastrophe. Such repeating patterns meant that flawed practices embedded in NASA's organizational system continued for years and made substantial contributions to both accidents (Columbia Accident Investigation Board, 2003).

Mike Coplen brings to evaluation inquiries an unusual affinity for seeing complex system relationships and taking them into account when designing evaluations and interpreting findings. He understands the interconnections between individual actions, organizational dynamics, and interactions with the larger cultural and societal context that affects safety and the success of interventions, like those aimed at more effective fatigue management. His background in human factors research makes him suspicious of standardized, rule-based interventions that fail to be sensitive to dynamic contexts and changing conditions. Yet federal transportation has been dominated by a rule-making mentality. Find a problem. Solve it with a new rule. Rules, like recipes, work in simple space. Situational awareness and adaptation are needed in complex space. There are problems for which rules are the solution, but, Mike Coplen believes, the railroad safety problems amenable to rules-based solutions, like low-hanging fruit, have all been picked clean over the last 75 years. The next generation of solutions will have to deal with complexity.

Coplen was responsible for featuring evaluation at the 2009 International Conference on Fatigue Management in Transportation Operations. Our evaluation team found little systematic evaluation of fatigue management interventions and a gap between research on fatigue and development of interventions based on research findings. The opportunity to interact with fatigue researchers provided insights into what a developmental evaluation approach can offer. An example is an occupational screening and treatment program for obstructive sleep apnea implemented in a city police department, which I want to use to illustrate how developmental evaluation can use systems thinking and complexity ideas.

Project SleepBetter

Project SleepBetter is a composite I've created based on actual interventions and research still under way. Police officers are a prime target for fatigue management because of their demanding schedules. Round-the-clock policing often leads to overnight shifts and long hours, which results in severe sleep deprivation and misalignment of circadian rhythms. Moreover, police officers are predominantly male and often overweight, factors associated with high risk for obstructive sleep apnea. An example of an intervention that has been evaluated involved showing police officers a 30-minute educational video on sleep hygiene, caffeine use, and obstructive sleep apnea. Following the presentation, officers could volunteer to complete a survey that assessed their apnea risk. Those with high risk were offered an examination by a sleep medicine physician and, if warranted, were further assessed using a portable device for two nights at home. Treatment was offered to officers if their Apnea–Hypopnea Index indicated they could benefit.

The research used a randomized controlled design in which half of the city's police districts were provided the program and half were not. Districts were paired by size and officer workload prior to randomization. In accordance with traditional research norms, the intervention was conceptualized and implemented with attention to assuring high fidelity of the intervention. But viewing the intervention as a social innovation in a complex environment, a number of developmental evaluation issues surface, so this example provides an opportunity to examine how a developmental evaluator would approach such an intervention. The environment is complex because various stakeholders will have conflicting views of what constitutes fatigue, how widespread it is among police officers, and thus whether an intervention is needed. Different interventions may well be needed for different situations, for example, with rookies versus veteran officers, or with teams versus individuals, or with men versus women, or with officers in varying physical health conditions. Moreover, the proposed intervention and its potential variations still needs further development before it can be either formatively evaluated or summatively tested to permit confident prediction of what results will be attained. Defining the situation as complex opens the possibility of engaging in a developmental process with developmental evaluation *before* moving to a summative evaluation, which could include conducting a randomized controlled trial. Let's look at what needs to be developed and potential developmental evaluation questions. Exhibit 5.1 offers a developmental evaluation framework for Project SleepBetter.

EXHIBIT 5.1 **A Developmental Evaluation Framework for Project SleepBetter**

What has to be developed?	Developmental evaluation questions
1. The recruiting educational video about sleep issues has to be developed.	What's the core content? What's the central message? How do officers react? When and how do officers view it? How is the invitation to view the video framed?
2. Trust with police officers has to be developed.	What affects officers' decisions to join the study or refuse to join? How do they perceive the study and the researchers? (Researchers have learned that there are often suspicions about the *real agenda* of studies and rumors abound about how study findings might be used by management to impose new rules. Overweight officers can be especially worried about negative repercussions.) What breach-of-privacy concerns arise for officers?
3. A relationship with the police department has to be developed.	How does the department perceive its role in the study? How would police department concerns about potential negative public perceptions regarding the intervention be handled? How, if at all, could departmental records on officers' performance be collected, including accident rates, work days missed, health problems, and height and weight measurements from annual physicals? How can such data be used?
4. A relationship with the police officers' union has to be developed.	How do union leaders perceive the study benefiting police officers? What are their concerns, both initially and as the study unfolds? How do issues of fatigue relate to other union priorities?
5. The process of moving from assessment to treatment has to be developed.	Where will examinations by the sleep medicine physician take place? (A solution in some such initiatives is to conduct the examinations in the union hall.) To whom will examination results be made available? What if a severe problem is identified, but the officer refuses treatment? How will the costs of treatment be managed? Who will pay? For how long?
6. A process for dealing with contingencies has to be developed.	Once the study is under way, how will rumors and perceptions about what is going on be tracked and responded to? How will unexpected critical incidents be handled?
7. Data collection procedures have to be developed taking into account the issues raised by the potentially high-stakes nature of the intervention.	What observational data, if any, can be collected, for example, using in-vehicle alertness-monitoring cameras mounted on the dashboards of police cruisers? (Police rejected this data collection option in some study proposals.)

In actual studies, all of the developmental issues identified in Exhibit 5.1 have arisen and had to be managed. How researchers discovered and resolved these issues affected the intervention, implementation of the study, and, ultimately, the findings. For example, the researchers originally asked station commanders to contact officers on shift to notify them about the recruitment sessions and a scheduled educational presentation. But they received feedback from the union that officers in some stations were reluctant to participate in the program because they had the impression that management was involved in the data collection effort and worried that it might be used inappropriately for personnel decisions. After consultations with both management and union officials, the researchers revamped recruitment to minimize the involvement of station commanders, instead enlisting lower-down-in-the-station "detail" police officers for assistance in scheduling and recruitment. This is a developmental adaptation. In traditional research, such an adjustment is typically viewed as just solving an implementation problem and moving on. Thinking of such an adjustment as a development (not just a problem solved) opens up the opportunity to learn more about the principle of getting "buy-in" and thereby making buy-in a principle of the intervention. Thought of in this way, the intervention being developed was not just the treatment of obstructive sleep apnea for individual police officers but rather a systems change intervention that included incorporating a fatigue management program in a police department.

Nor can responses to these matters be standardized. Different police departments, different police unions, and different cities will present different challenges and require different adaptations. The researchers learned that buy-in was critical and that they had to work hard to engage and build trust with both the police union and administration, and to communicate clearly to everyone that the study group was independent of both entities. The difficulty of getting buy-in was illustrated by negotiations with a local large metropolitan police department that had expressed strong interest in the intervention, even signing a letter of intent. But after more than a dozen meetings with this group, they were unable to secure final approval for the project with that department, although those responsible never officially declined to participate. (A retrospective developmental evaluation of that case could shed light on what actually happened. I'll discuss *retrospective developmental evaluation* in Chapter 8 and provide an in-depth example at the end of that chapter.)

Systems Thinking

Thinking about the intervention as a systems change intervention rather than just an individual treatment intervention has implications for how even the individual treatment is conceptualized and evaluated. Exhibit 5.2 depicts Project SleepBetter as a classic linear logic model. The program recruits police participants through an educational presentation. As a result of the video, police officers learn about the dangers of obstructive sleep apnea (OSA), which constitutes increased knowledge (an initial outcome). Based on this new knowledge, officers agree to be screened and examined for OSA. Police officers with OSA then agree to treatment, which constitutes an attitude change, another initial outcome. That attitude change supports the desired behavior change, which is that those officers with severe OSA follow the sleep treatments prescribed by the sleep medicine physician. If treatment is successful, compliant police officers experience healthier sleep (an intermediate outcome), and feel more rested and less fatigued. As a result, these officers have higher performance, fewer absences, and reduced accidents.

This model constitutes a classic educational intervention in which knowledge and attitude change are hypothesized to lead

---

EXHIBIT 5.2 **Linear Program Logic Model for Sleep Intervention with Police Officers**

Program recruits police participants through an educational presentation.

Police officers learn about the dangers of obstructive sleep apnea (OSA) (increased knowledge).

Officers agree to be screened and examined for OSA.

Police officers with OSA agree to treatment (attitude change).

Those with severe OSA follow the sleep treatments prescribed by the sleep medicine physician (behavior change).

Compliant police officers have healthier sleep (intermediate outcome).

More rested, less fatigued officers have higher performance, fewer absences and accidents (desired outcome).

---

to behavior change and desired outcomes. The model treats the individual police officer as an autonomous, self-reliant, self-determining individual making rational, knowledge-based decisions about what to do in his or her own best interest. It is a simple framing of how change occurs. But everything we know about how human beings really make decisions tells us that this model is far out of touch with reality. Human beings are not rational information processors. We are highly emotional, social beings. We don't make decisions as autonomous individuals. Our decisions are influenced by those we have relationships with, seek advice from, and care about, and who care about us. We are entangled in networks

of relationships. Our emotions come into play, what distinguished economists Akerlof and Shiller (2009) call our "animal spirits." Taking a behavioral economics approach, they show "how human psychology drives the economy, and why it matters for global capitalism." It also matters for fatigue management programs—and all other interventions that involve human beings, harkening back to Mike Coplen's human factors perspective. Exhibit 5.3 depicts one possible map of the web of relationships that could affect an officer's decision to undergo OSA screening, participate in treatment, and, critically important, maintain the treatment, probably for the rest of his or her life, which is no small thing. People who are likely to influence a police officer's decision about OSA screening and treatment include the officer's spouse or significant other, various family members, the officer's partner, the peer group of which he or she is a part, and the officer's supervisors, personal doctor, and other influential relationships. An intervention with an individual officer is an intervention into that network of interdependent relationships.

This kind of mapping and systems thinking offers windows through which one can watch for complex effects. A developmental evaluation is attuned to both linear and nonlinear relationships, both intended and unintended interactions and outcomes, and both hypothesized and unpredicted results. Oh, yes, much research and evaluation claims to look for both the expected and the unexpected, but, in reality, narrowly goal-focused evaluations based on linear logic models seldom do so seriously (Patton, 2008c, pp. 273–277). The sources of nonlinearity, emergence,

and unpredictability are deeply enmeshed in the complex web of relationships that we all experience. Scuttlebutt about a study like Project SleepBetter will emerge quickly and get passed through the police grapevine like champagne rippling down a tall pyramid of glasses at a wedding reception. A developmental evaluation would tap into that scuttlebutt in a systematic way through a network of well-placed key knowledgeables who understand and support the project's purposes. The developmental evaluator may have to do detective work on how the police are reacting to elevated attention to and a proposed intervention for fatigue. All kinds of ripple effects may occur because fatigue is not an isolated factor. It goes to the heart of one's well-being, way of life, priorities, and habits of daily living. Not only does sleep, or lack thereof, affect one's own internal neural networks, but the effects of fatigue can ripple through one's social and professional networks. That's why the systems-thinking

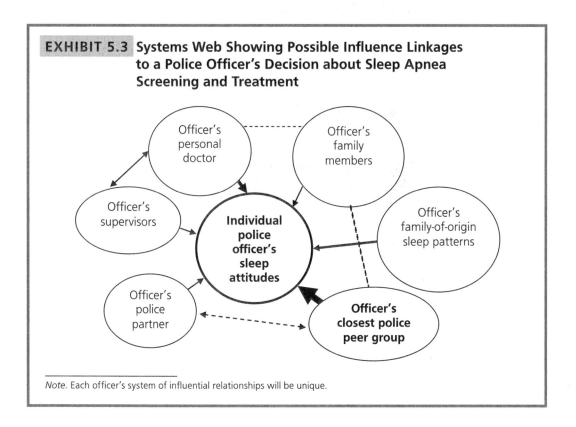

EXHIBIT 5.3 Systems Web Showing Possible Influence Linkages to a Police Officer's Decision about Sleep Apnea Screening and Treatment

Note. Each officer's system of influential relationships will be unique.

developmental evaluator needs a map not only of the individual police officer's network of influences and relationships, but also of ways to gauge the effects of and provide feedback about the contextual factors that may affect the intervention as manifest in organizational norms and larger societal values depicted in Exhibit 5.4. To make such a map manageable, begin with only the most basic and critical influences and their relationships.

The Power of Context

This kind of systems-oriented conceptualization of an intervention-and-change process makes sensitivity to context critical in a developmental evaluation. As best-selling author Malcolm Gladwell (2002) observed in *The Tipping Point*, "The Power of Context says that human beings are a lot more sensitive to their environment than they may seem" (p. 29). Resistance to an intervention,

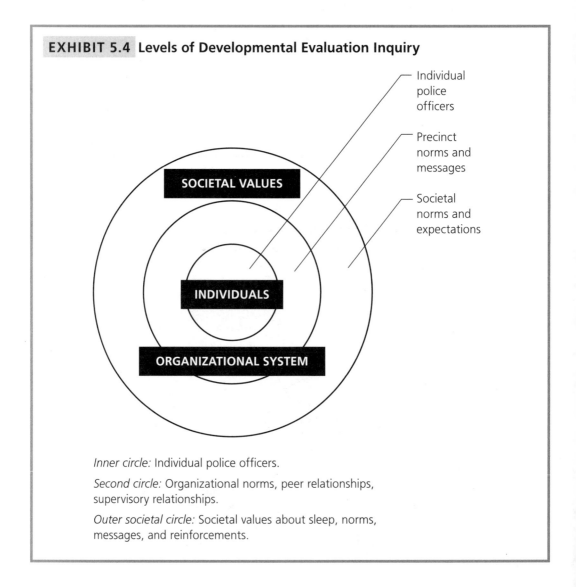

EXHIBIT 5.4 Levels of Developmental Evaluation Inquiry

Individual police officers

Precinct norms and messages

Societal norms and expectations

SOCIETAL VALUES

INDIVIDUALS

ORGANIZATIONAL SYSTEM

Inner circle: Individual police officers.

Second circle: Organizational norms, peer relationships, supervisory relationships.

Outer societal circle: Societal values about sleep, norms, messages, and reinforcements.

"For all his brilliance, we're going to have to replace Trewell. He never quite seems able to reduce his ideas to football analogies."

like treatment for OSA, is likely to be more than individual recalcitrance. Going without sleep in a commitment to get the job done is viewed by society as heroic, whether the heroes are police officers working double shifts, medical residents working 24 hours in the emergency room, or students studying all night for an exam. When I was growing up, drunkenness was considered funny (look at old Dean Martin comedy routines), smoking was cool (peruse movies from the 1950s), and sexual harassment was just "boys being boys." These societal attitudes and the behaviors they reinforced had to be changed in order to get serious about enforcing drunk-driving laws, outlawing smoking in public places, and punishing sexual harassment. If society views going without sleep as heroic, then police supervisors are free to, even expected to, demand such heroic behavior from police officers whose romantic ideal is already infused with heroism. Treat-

ing the individual officer as the sole and isolated target of an educational intervention is to ignore the larger societal and systems influences that affect individual decisions and behaviors. Thus, the developmental evaluator asks questions about and looks for data that illuminates how organizational and societal norms and messages affect individual decisions and outcomes, thereby providing feedback to those engaging in innovative systems change initiatives about how their efforts are being received, understood, and reacted to at multiple levels. On a broader systems change level, the developmental evaluator would also help track and document changes and developments in societal norms and how policymakers and the general public are coming to understand and react to emergent sleep- and fatigue-related issues, and how those societal developments interact with and affect local interventions and innovations.

The Complexity of Systems Thinking

In the large and growing universe of evaluation approaches, systems thinking is by no means unique to developmental evaluation, but it is central to it. Bob Williams, a leader in applying systems thinking to evaluation, monitors systems approaches from his global sensing station in New Zealand. He coedited the first expert anthology on *Systems Concepts in Evaluation* (Williams & Iman, 2007). He estimates that as many as a thousand separate frameworks and methods "fall under the systems banner." Why? "Because there is no single agreed-upon definition of a 'system.' " Nor is there ever likely to be. Indeed, Bob argues, at the core of systems thinking is attention to the inevitable arbitrariness of boundaries, a variety of perspectives, and dynamic, entangled interrelationships, all of which apply as much to the complex world of systems theories, frameworks, and approaches as to other phenomena. (For comprehensive reviews of different approaches to systems thinking, see Midgley, 2003, and Williams & Iman, 2007.)

So amid all this definitional confusion and competing perspectives, what is the allure of systems thinking? Systems thinking takes on and provides new insights into the enduring issues of human experience, interaction, and efforts at development. What are these issues? A short list, in no particular order of importance, includes "power, control, unanticipated consequences, unacknowledged interests, differing motivations, and rapidly changing circumstances" (Williams, 2008, p. 16). Astute social innovators *and* developmental evaluators are attuned to these issues. In Chapter 8 I'll present a systems-based inquiry framework. Developmental evaluators need competence in systems thinking and systems-based inquiry to effectively incorporate systems ideas into an evaluation and facilitate appropriate and relevant systems-sensitive interpretations of findings.

Complexities of Complexity

Most of all, we need to preserve the absolute unpredictability and total improbability of our connected minds. That way we keep open all the options. . . .
—LEWIS THOMAS, biologist
(quoted in Johnson, 2001, p. 9)

Having distinguished simple and complicated situations from complex ones in Chapter 4, and having examined more closely how systems thinking undergirds developmental evaluation, let us now look more specifically at complexity as a lens and framework for developmental evaluation. The basic premise here is that evaluation in complex adaptive systems is more likely to be useful if the evaluation is informed by complexity con-

～ How Can Complexity Theory Contribute to More Effective Development and Aid Evaluation?

The dialogue on this question in London, at the Diana, Princess of Wales Memorial Fund, on July 3, 2009, is an example of the attention being given to using complexity concepts to inform evaluation. It was the sixth in a rolling series about how complexity is useful in the aid and development sector.

During the dialogue, distinguished development scholar Robert Chambers of the Institute of Development Studies suggested that the developing world may be on the verge of a methodological breakthrough by taking complexity ideas seriously. Poor people's lives and realities are emergent, very local, diverse, nonlinear, and unpredictable, he emphasized. They are adaptive agents. All these concepts from complexity theory are the realities of poor people around the world. In that context, he asked: "Whose complexity counts and who counts complexity?" (quoted in Panos London, 2009, pp. 5–6).

For the full report on the dialogue, see *www.panos.org.uk/?lid=29888*.

cepts and understandings. This is a pretty straightforward premise—derived from the importance of matching the evaluation to the nature of the situation. Those applying complexity concepts to evaluation have long documented and emphasized the difference a complexity lens can make to the relevance and usefulness of both evaluation processes and findings (Eoyang, 2008b; Eoyang & Berkas, 1998; Hargreaves & Parsons, 2009; Panos London, 2009; Parsons, 2009a, 2009b, 2009c; Patton, 2008c, chap. 10; Ramalingam & Jones, 2008). But a word of caution is in order, which I now offer.

Controversy and Ambiguity

John Paley of the University of Stirling, whose influential work on nursing as a complex adaptive system is an exemplar of the practical application of complexity understandings, worries that "the over-hasty adoption of complexity ideas is essentially just one more intellectual fad" (2007, p. 234). Among the myriad systems approaches is a subset of ideas focused on complex adaptive systems, a distinct *myriapod* (subfield) within the larger *systems genus.* Complexity concepts, like systems ideas more generally, include an assortment of interconnected, overlapping, sometimes obtuse, but always interdependent ideas. *Complexity science* may not be a science. *Complexity theory* may not be a coherent theory. These things are matters of perspective and academic argument. For example, Robin Nunn of the Institute for the History and Philosophy of Science and Technology, University of Toronto, has used complexity concepts to study complexity science and theory, a through-the-looking-glass exercise that turned complexity on itself, concluding:

> There is no general agreement that there is a separate science of complexity or even that it is science. . . . The subject called complexity science shifts, like a pseudo-science that refuses to be refuted, as the subjects studied under the complexity view change. . . .
> Defining complexity theory is elusive. . . . A

single physics-like equation is insufficient to cover all of complexity theory. But a large part of complexity theory can be stated in only four words: sensitivity to initial conditions. This is a compact way of saying that complex systems are nonlinear, inherently unpredictable, and dependent on history. (2007, pp. 95, 99)

While complexity ideas raise doubts about linear, formulaic, and mechanical models of the world, controversies surround complexity constructs, raising doubts about whether agreement can ever be reached on core constructs. What is not in doubt is that complexity ideas are in vogue, have a lot of currency these days, and thereby have attracted ardent adherents and fervent critics. Such a development is not a surprise, especially in the academy, which is ever sensitive and insensitive to initial conditions, both at the same time. *Plus ça change, plus c'est la même chose* (The more things change, the more they're the same thing). Paradoxical.

But that's all by way of context, to prepare you to deal with controversy and ambiguity, which come with the territory. To navigate the labyrinth of complexity concepts and applications, including controversial and ambiguous dead ends, I find it useful to be pragmatic and stay focused on evaluation use. So, I offer one final reminder along those lines and then move on to examining complexity concepts.

Pragmatism about Complexity Ideas: Staying Focused on Utility

All models are wrong, but some are useful.
Essentially, all models are wrong, but some are useful.
Remember that all models are wrong; the practical question is how wrong do they have to be to not be useful.
All models are false but some models are useful.
Most models are wrong, but some are *useful.*

—Variations on an observation by
GEORGE BOX, professor of statistics,
University of Wisconsin

As I said in the opening chapter, *what brings me to complexity is its utility*. It identifies a set of intervention circumstances that are amenable to a particular situationally appropriate evaluation response, what I am calling here developmental evaluation. *Complexity is a defining characteristic of developmental evaluation's niche.* Principles for operating in complex adaptive systems inform the practice of developmental evaluation. The controversies and challenges that come with complexity ideas will also and inevitably afflict developmental evaluation. The insights and understandings of complexity thinking that have garnered enthusiasm from social innovators will also envelope developmental evaluation and open pathways for increasing the credibility, relevance, and utility of evaluation undertaken from a specifically developmental perspective.

Ramalingam and Jones (2008), in a comprehensive review of the application of complexity theory to international humanitarian aid, distinguish three points of view about complexity theory: champions, critics, and pragmatists. Their description of pragmatists nicely summarizes my own perspective, so I cite it here:

> The pragmatists, for whom complexity provides interesting and potentially useful parallels, are exploring the relevance of complexity science to social systems and organisations, and working to assess the practical benefits that arise from its application outside the natural sciences. . . . This work suggests that complexity is a lens that helps us look at our world and shape our action but, importantly, that it is a set of concepts and tools that should not be treated as the "only way" to look at and do things. The pragmatists tend to accept the work-in-progress nature of complexity sciences, and the challenges that arise from drawing on diverse and varied bodies of knowledge. These challenges create issues around definition, measurement, analysis and coherence, and lead to a general acknowledgement that there is a need for a deeper theoretical understanding and further practical applications. (2008, p. 6)

So, from a pragmatic perspective, what are some of the compelling complexity constructs that inform developmental evaluation?

Useful Complexity Constructs for Developmental Evaluation

The remainder of this chapter is devoted to elucidating and applying to evaluation six central complexity ideas: nonlinearity, emergence, adaptation, uncertainty, dynamical systems change, and coevolution. Exhibit 5.6 near the end of the chapter summarizes these complexity concepts and their implications for developmental evaluation.

Nonlinearity

This is not a question of too little data or too little computer power: methods developed for linear systems give the wrong answer when applied to nonlinear questions.
—LEONARD SMITH, *Chaos* (2007, p. 115)

Nonlinearity as a complexity construct captures sensitivity to initial conditions in which small actions can stimulate large reactions, thus the *butterfly wings metaphor* (Gleick, 1987). Nassim Nicholas Taleb (2007) has added to popular culture the metaphor of *black swans* in which highly improbable, unpredictable, and unexpected events have huge impacts—the global financial meltdown in late 2008 is a primary example. Malcolm Gladwell (2002) popularized the idea of tipping points, when major shifts occur to change the whole landscape of action. Let's look at how these metaphors would inform a developmental evaluation of a fatigue management program in a police department.

Support for the program (or vocal opposition) by one highly respected and experienced senior officer could dramatically affect how junior officers perceive the program. Inference of support (or opposition) might take the form of a chance remark overheard and passed on quickly through the grapevine. Suddenly, the program has widespread legitimacy (or lack of credibility) because one influential person at a chance moment made a casual remark. That's a version of the butterfly wings effect, only instead of wings flapping it's the effects of an undulating tongue. The developmental evaluator needs to be plugged into the rumor mill to capture such effects as they reverberate and start to affect receptivity to the innovation.

A black swan effect could take the form of an unexpected critical incident, say, for example, that same senior officer, but this time in a fatal car accident in which there are hints that he fell asleep at the wheel after a double shift. Suddenly, the entire environment is galvanized. The whole context has changed. The environment in which the fatigue management intervention had been introduced has fundamentally altered. Social innovators recognize such critical incidents as windows of opportunity that must be taken advantage of quickly, for they can open and close rapidly. The developmental evaluator needs to be able to find out about such critical incidents in real time (or at least ASAP, as soon as possible) and be able to monitor their effects and provide feedback about their implications as they ripple through the system in which the intervention is unfolding.

Over the years I've interviewed hundreds of program participants asking them to identify those aspects of a program that had the greatest effect on them. They can identify the extent to which they've attained hoped-for outcomes, but I regularly find that the most effective programs have impacts well beyond targeted results. A leadership program not only provides new knowledge and skills, but leads to life-transforming decisions about career and relationships. A job training program increases both hard and soft skills, but also leads to a new identity and lifestyle, one that persists and leads the participant to say, "Everything has changed." An antipoverty program not only gets much-needed basic resources to a family, but changes the family system from chaotic to stable, affecting all those in the network of that family. An environmental innovation increases an organization's recycling commitment and actions, but also ripples into larger and longer term

commitments focused on how the organization thinks about its relationship to the community in which it operates, and this affects decisions in multiple arenas beyond the environmental emphasis of the intervention. A fatigue intervention not only helps a police officer get much needed rest but by controlling his sleep apnea gets him back in the same bed with his wife and he says of the program: "It saved my marriage and my life." That is a nonlinear outcome.

Nonlinear effects can be negative as well as positive, throwing participants into a downward spiral. A participant seeking job skills encounters hard-core drug users and becomes an addict. A young woman in a welfare-to-work program is raped by a male staff member, is devastated emotionally, and becomes a single parent mired in poverty. A young father in an early childhood parenting program is so embarrassed and intimidated by his lack of knowledge that he abandons his pregnant girlfriend, certain that he'd be a horrible father when his initial openness to learning suggested otherwise. An organization that goes "green" attracts attention in the community, leading to angry demands for other community-based support, overwhelming the organization, and leading it to retreat from community involvement of any kind.

Impacts can extend well beyond planned outcomes. Small initial endeavors can have big impacts. Big initiatives can manifest little or no impact. These are nonlinear effects and evaluators need to expect them, watch for them, document them, and help innovators interpret their significance and implications.

Tipping points are nonlinear. The notion of a tipping point involves asking the question of when the momentum of an innovation or intervention shifts from slow, gradual, and incremental acceptance to rapid, fast, and widespread acceptance. There is no formula to predict tipping points, but the qualitative pattern involves early adopters being watched by others who, if they see or hear about positive results for those early adopters, try the innovation themselves. Soon, everyone wants in on the action. (A negative tipping point involves cumulative resistance.) Because tipping points can't be predicted in advance, but their consequences are huge, developmental evaluators create ways of tracking the adoption (or resistance) patterns, which includes understanding who is adopting (or resisting), to whom they are connected, and their reasons for adoption (or resistance)—all in real time, not just retrospectively at the end of the project. Nor are the patterns of resistance and adoption static. I've evaluated innovations where early resisters subsequently became adopters once the benefits were clear to them as they observed early adopters. I've also seen early benefits that were not sustained as unexpected costs and problems emerged. These are examples of the nonlinearity of innovation adoption and a prime reason that a precise tipping point cannot be known in advance. A role for developmental evaluation is to watch for and find out when a tipping point appears to be emerging, or has emerged, and to help social innovators identify and anticipate what indicators might suggest a tipping point has been achieved, or is close.

Emergence

Even the most optimistic champions of self-organization feel a little wary about the lack of control in such a process. But understanding emergence has always been about giving up control, letting the system govern itself as much as possible, letting it learn from the footprints. We have come far enough in that understanding to build small-scale systems for our entertainment and edification, and to appreciate more thoroughly the emergent behavior that already exists at every scale of our lived experience. Are there new scales to conquer, new revolutions that will make the top-down revolutions of the industrial age look minor by comparison? On the hundred-year scale, or the scale of millennia, there may be no question more interesting, and no question harder to answer.

—STEVEN JOHNSON, *Emergence*
(2001, p. 234)

Emergence as a core complexity construct tells us that innovators can't determine in ad-

vance what will happen, so evaluators can't determine in advance what to measure. We have to be watching for whatever emerges. We have to expect the unexpected. We have to be prepared. In a lecture on scientific discovery given at the University of Lille in 1854, Louis Pasteur asserted: *"Dans les champs de l'observation le hasard ne favorise que les esprits préparés"* (In the fields of observation chance favors only the prepared mind).

The idea of emergence in complex adaptive systems alerts the observer/evaluator to watch for patterns of self-organization among interacting agents. What emerges is beyond, outside of, and oblivious to any notion of shared intentionality. Each agent or element pursues its own path but as that path intersects with others, and the agent interacts with others, also pursuing their own paths, patterns of interaction emerge and the whole of the interactions become greater than the separate parts. When the screening program for OSA is introduced into a police department, each individual officer considers whether to participate based on his or her own motivations and understandings. The traditional linear logic model focuses on affecting each individual's knowledge, attitudes, and behaviors. But the systems map we constructed portrayed and forecast a set of interactions, first among police officers, but then among police officers and their

"She's the most effective of our emerging new pathogens."

© Edward Koren/Condé Nast Publications/*www. cartoonbank.com.*

family members, friends, and other people of influence in their lives. Certain subgroups of police officers are likely to emerge, both those who are inclined to participate in the program and those resistant to participation. People inclined toward each perspective (participation or resistance) will find each other and reinforce each other's inclinations (a manifestation of self-organizing emergence in complex dynamic systems). The nature, size, cohesion, and endurance of such subgroups will likely be a prime determinant of the program's success.

Other interactions that might be important in Project SleepBetter include how discussions of sleep patterns intersect with discussions of and concerns about diet, exercise, job stress, aging, career aspirations, and family responsibilities/relationships— all of which we know are interconnected. But the precise nature of those interconnections among a particular subgroup of police officers in a particular city during a particular fatigue management intervention are inherently unknown. So we have to watch for what emerges, for example, by regularly interviewing some well-placed police officers to find out what the scuttlebutt is (a methodologically advanced social science research technique we'll dub the *scuttlebutt tracking technique*). Or we can have periodic reflective practice sessions with groups of officers to have them talk together about what they're hearing and observing (see Chapter 9 for how to conduct reflective practice sessions in a developmental evaluation). Or, like volunteer weather or news reporters networked throughout a region, we solicit police officers to serve as *listening posts* who contact us whenever they hear something of interest about the intervention, whatever that may be. Or we send out periodic e-mails to key informants in the department, asking highly sophisticated and deeply probing questions like: What are you hearing about the sleep screening program? What's going on?

Of course, the developmental evaluator is still monitoring intended outcomes and any predetermined program goals, both progress toward goals and any changes in those goals, either explicit or implicit. The evaluation will include how the program identifies police officers with OSA, recruits them into treatment, and treats their OSA; whether treatment increases the quality and quantity of their sleep; and thereby the extent to which, if at all, job performance is affected. These intended and predictable elements of the intervention will be central to the evaluation design. At the same time, understanding a situation as complex invites evaluators to go beyond the usual token nod toward unanticipated consequences, for example, the routine practice of adding one question at the end of a goals-focused questionnaire that asks, "Were there any other effects of the program?" Taking emergence seriously means engaging in real fieldwork that probes for what's emerging and its significance, meaning, and implications. Taking emergence seriously in the face of uncertainty means "anticipating surprise and responding to the inevitable" unintended consequences of both innovations and evaluations (Morell, 2010). This begins by freeing one's mind from the constraints and blinders of narrow goals-focused evaluation to be open to and look for unanticipated impacts and surprises. Renowned U.S. Civil War general Robert E. Lee is reputed to have said, "I am often surprised, but I am never taken by surprise." His mindset was to be prepared for the unexpected—ever watchful, ever observing, ever open to dealing with whatever emerged. Not a bad mindset for a developmental evaluator.

I once evaluated a leadership program for higher education administrators that involved Outward Bound–type wilderness experiences. I went along as a participant observer/evaluator. By the end of the second day of a 10-day hike, most of the participants had subdivided into two groups, dubbed by participants the "truckers" and the "turtles." The truckers arose in the morning, found out what the day's destination was, and set off to get there as quickly as possible. The turtles, in contrast, meandered along having deep conversations, taking lots of rest breaks to admire the views, and stopping often to revel in the cacti that dotted the desert environment. The emergence of these two groups was neither planned nor anticipated (though, in retrospect, they may appear obvious). Had I not been along, for example, if the evaluation had only involved a follow-up survey about intended experiences and outcomes, I might not have known about the emergence of these self-organized subgroups. But in fact the two groups had markedly different ways of engaging the wilderness, had substantially different program experiences, and reported significantly different outcomes both personally and professionally. For example, the truckers were more likely to report increased self-esteem and self-confidence, while the turtles were more likely to report a greater sense of community and feelings of being supported.

Let me pause and add emphasis here: *In 40 years of evaluating programs, I can't remember ever evaluating a program in which self-organizing subgroups did not emerge. And those subgroups always have different experiences and manifest different outcomes that are, in part, a function of being in the subgroup.* We're a highly social species. People don't go through programs as individuals. They find others to whom they're attracted, for whatever reasons and in whatever ways, and they experience the program together. Even a confidential fatigue intervention targeted discretely at individual police officers will become a subgroup experience as officers getting help find each other and share experiences.

Moreover, the more open, participatory, individualized, and innovative the intervention, the greater the importance such subgroup self-organizing is for understanding program experiences and outcomes. Highly individualized and participatory programs, in which participants play a substantive role in determining program processes and priority outcomes, will heighten elements of complexity. The outcomes will vary for different participants based on their differing needs, experiences, situations, and desires—

and the emergent subgroups within which they engage in the program.

So, while attending to unanticipated consequences should be part of any evaluation, for developmental evaluations it is central. Developmental evaluators must anticipate emergence, track emergent interactions among key players, both formal and informal, both planned and unplanned. Map networks, system relationships, and self-organizing subgroups. Track information flows, communications, and emergent issues. Emergence applies to both processes and outcomes. Watch for and assess not only what emerges, but what declines or even disappears. Disappearance is the other side of the phenomenon of emergence. For example, the wilderness program planned to devote every evening to group debriefs and facilitated discussions, but people were too tired after a day of hiking to bring energy to such a process; it disappeared. On the other hand, afternoon breaks in small groups as a check-in/how-are-things-going formal process emerged and became an important formal vehicle for reflection among participants. The unplanned emerges; the planned disappears. Both are important, as is what unfolds as planned.

And some things simply remain uncertain, a complexity theme we turn to shortly. The program staff and funders had hoped to figure out what aspects or components of the wilderness experience emerged as having greatest impact on participants. But the experience couldn't be reduced to discrete, analyzable elements that manifested concrete cause–effect mechanisms. The impact, participants reported, came from *the whole experience*, everything taken together, including interactions with each other over time. In one way, *the whole experience* as the source of impact is an answer, an important answer—and one consistent with systems thinking and insights. *It's not the parts, it's the whole.* But what is the whole? "The whole is the whole," participants insisted. The parts had emerged and then merged together, morphing from once-distinct elements into a whole, a gestalt, a totality. The group even adopted this perspective as their shared explanation of what had happened to them. But this was also a way of refusing to further analyze what had happened to them. It gave the experience an air of mystery and an emotional feel of completeness and closure. The tautological explanation "The whole is the whole" was a way of saying to those who asked them about what had happened (including this evaluator), "I can't explain it. It was a whole. The whole is the whole. You had to be there." In today's world such conclusions take the deeply insightful and helpful form of proclaiming about everything and nothing in particular: "It was what it was. It is what it is. What it is, it is. What it's not, it's not. That's the way things are." Get it?

What does the developmental evaluator do with such quotations? Report them. Document how such explanations are different, if they are, from what people said at earlier points along the way. Track developments in both participants' outcomes and their explanations of outcomes. See what emerges. Report what develops. Think about what it means. *The whole is the whole* actually says a lot, including implicit advice to funders and those interested in potentially adopting or adapting the program: Don't just focus on

---

⌒ Food and Eating as Complex

Like sleep, food can be seen as simple, complicated, or complex. Michael Pollan, in his best-selling book, *In Defense of Food: An Eater's Manifesto* (2009), looks at food holistically as part of a complex system that includes culture-influenced eating norms, family interaction patterns around dining, lifestyle choices, ethnicity, variations in individual physiology, agricultural production systems, market systems, public policy, nutrition science, and historical food consumption patterns and preferences. His comments about food and how it is studied can be applied to any program or social innovation and has important implications for using systems thinking in developmental evaluation.

SIMPLE SCIENCE FOR A COMPLEX PHENOMENON

Pollan notes that nutritional science typically involves studying one nutrient at a time, an approach that is "deeply flawed":

> "The problem with nutrient-by-nutrient nutrition science," points out Marion Nestle, a New York University nutritionist, "is that it takes the nutrient out of the context of the food, the food out of the context of the diet, and the diet out of the context of the lifestyle." (p. 62)

He wonders, then, why nutrition is studied as and reduced to a simple phenomenon when it is clearly complex. The bias toward randomized controlled trials means that the methods most esteemed by peer reviewers in academic journals determine what questions get asked and how they get answered.

> Scientists study variables they can isolate; if they can't isolate a variable, they won't be able to tell whether its presence or absence is meaningful. Yet even the simplest food is a hopelessly complicated thing to analyze, a virtual wilderness of chemical compounds, many of which exist in intricate and dynamic relation to one another, and all of which together are in the process of changing from one state to another. So if you're a nutrition scientist you do the only thing you can do, given the tools at your disposal: Break the thing down into its component parts and study those one by one, even if that means ignoring subtle interactions and contexts and the fact that the whole may well be more than, or maybe just different from, the sum of its parts. This is what we mean by reductionist science. (p. 62)

(cont.)

Pollan acknowledges that scientific reductionism has generated important knowledge, but goes on to emphasize that "it can mislead us too, especially when applied to something as complex, on the one side, as a food and on the other a human eater. It encourages us to take a simple mechanistic view of that transaction: Put in this nutrient, get out that physiological result" (p. 63).

Because people differ in important ways, individual physiological, lifestyle, genetic, gender, ethnic, social, cultural, and economic factors come into play, affecting even basic nutritional chemistry, which unfolds in importantly different ways in different people.

We all know that lucky soul who can eat prodigious quantities of fattening food without ever gaining weight. Some populations can metabolize sugars better than others. Depending on your evolutionary heritage, you may or may not be able to digest the lactose in milk. Depending on your genetic makeup, reducing the saturated fat in your diet may or may not move your cholesterol numbers. The specific ecology of your intestines helps determine how efficiently you digest what you eat, so that the same 100 calories of food may yield more or less food energy depending on the proportion of Firmicutes and Bacteroides resident in your gut. In turn, that balance of bacterial species could owe to your genes or to something in your environment. So there is nothing very machinelike about the human eater, and to think of food as simply fuel is to completely misconstrue it. (p. 63)

Food, like sleep, is basic. But neither is simple. It is precisely because food and sleep are basic that they interact with and must be understood in the context of all of our interrelated and complex biological, social, cultural, economic, political, and psychological systems. I've found explaining food and sleep from the perspective of complexity to be a good way to introduce complexity to people new to systems thinking and its implications, including its implications for social innovation and developmental evaluation.

"You're a very complex carbohydrate."

© Arnie Levin/Condé Nast Publications/*www.cartoonbank.com.*

the parts. Don't start picking and choosing elements. Don't try to save money by cutting some things out. Do the whole thing or don't do it at all. Think holistically. Even as you adapt. *The whole is the whole, even as it changes and evolves.*

I mentioned earlier that over the years I've

interviewed hundreds of program participants asking them to identify those aspects of a program that had the greatest effect on them. Often they talk about some unplanned program element like an unexpected critical incident, or people they met, conversations with other participants, or a passing remark by a staff person that came at just the right moment and was delivered in just the right tone to be heard and leave a lasting impression. I've been involved for years studying powerful personal learning by gathering stories from people about times when they've had a *powerful personal learning experience*, positive or negative, recently or a long time ago, in any setting under any circumstances—they chose the story to tell without constraint or predefinition. The common pattern in such stories is of initially small, incidental, and surprise encounters that blossomed into life-changing, transformational events. Think about a powerful learning experience in your own life. If your life is like that of the many people I've talked to, you'll recall something that started out small but gathered momentum and became, in the end, huge in significance. That's a nonlinear, emergent pattern. It happens all the time in programs and innovations. It's worth watching for and capturing because it gives us a deeper understanding of how change actually occurs and lets us interpret observed outcomes in terms of the intersection of planned and unplanned occurrences. Creating windows and doors for nonlinear, emergent effects is the job of the social innovator. Anticipating, watching for, and capturing the unexpected so that it can be recognized, tracked, and interpreted is part of the job of an observant developmental evaluator.

Adaptation

Dynamic complexity arises because systems are . . . adaptive. The capabilities and decision rules of the agents in complex systems change over time. Evolution leads to selection and proliferation of some agents while others become extinct. Adaptation also occurs as people learn from experience, especially as they learn new ways to achieve their goals in the face of obstacles. Learning is not always beneficial, however.
—JOHN D. STERMAN, *Business Dynamics* (2000, p. 22)

Adaptation is at the center of complex adaptive systems. Interacting elements and agents

respond and adapt to each other, and to their environment, so that what emerges is a function of ongoing adaptation both among interacting elements and the responsive relationships interacting agents have with their environment. Innovators adapt. Evaluators of innovative programs will have to follow those adaptations and adapt the evaluation design accordingly. Thus, developmental evaluations must also be *adaptive*.

Every evaluation situation is unique. A successful evaluation (i.e., one that is useful, practical, ethical, and accurate) emerges from the special characteristics and conditions of a particular situation—a mixture of people, politics, history, context, resources, constraints, values, needs, interests, and chance. Versatility, flexibility, creativity, and responsiveness underpin all utilization-focused evaluations. I've described the consultative interactions that go on between evaluators and intended users in utilization-focused evaluations as "active–reactive–interactive–adaptive" (Patton, 2008c, chap. 6). The phrase is meant to be both descriptive and prescriptive. It describes how real-world decision making actually unfolds: act, react, interact, and adapt. Yet it is prescriptive in alerting evaluators to consciously and deliberately act, react, and adapt in order to increase their effectiveness in working with intended users. In developmental evaluations, the necessity of adaptation gets taken to the next level. Like innovation itself, adaptation becomes an ongoing way of engaging.

The implications of an adaptive stance have been most fully developed in work on adaptive management, which originated in the adaptive environmental assessment and management work developed by the ecologists C. S. Holling (1978) and Carl J. Walters (1986), and elaborated through case examples in edited volumes by Gunderson and Holling (2002), Westley and Miller (2003), and Williams, Szaro, and Shapiro (2007). *Adaptive management* is a systematic, iterative process for making decisions in the face of uncertainty, reduced control, and low predictability, through ongoing system monitoring. The process essentially involves learning by doing and observing. This parallels the process stipulated by knowledge management consultants David Snowden and Mary Boone (2007), who advise that when facing complexity, probe first, then sense, then respond. Probing is the doing. Sensing is the observing (where chance ever favors the prepared mind). And responding is the adaptation. This sequence of engagement is significantly different from the classic management approach of plan, then plan some more, then implement. And don't respond or adapt. Just keep implementing the plan.

Project SleepBetter illustrates how seemingly minor implementation adaptations can benefit from evaluation tracking and evaluation adaptations. As noted earlier, before beginning the educational visits to police stations, the project team conducted an outreach program to raise awareness within the police community about the project's potential benefits. The team developed marketing materials to publicize the program including print advertisements, flyers, study-specific brochures, and a frequently asked questions document. They then conducted outreach at three levels: (1) directly contacting station commanders; (2) sending packets of marketing materials to each station for distribution to officers on an individual level; and (3) posting advertisements in issues of the local union newsletter and an online bulletin to inform all union members about the project. Station commanders were asked to contact officers on shift to notify them of scheduled presentations, but, as noted earlier, union contacts reported that officers in some stations were reluctant to participate in the program due to concerns about management involvement and possible access to, and potential misuse of, the data. In response, the team adapted the recruiting process to minimize the involvement of station commanders, instead working with detail police officers.

The evaluation's sample composition and size then had to be adapted as the re-

cruitment process changed. The original evaluation design, based on the original implementation plan, would have targeted station commanders for interviews. Given the changes in recruitment process, detail police officers have to be added to the sample. Questions asked of both station commanders and detail police officers will need to probe how recruitment is perceived and implemented, and the consequences thereof. Moreover, the evaluation will have to monitor and adapt the design as the results of recruitment emerge. The project team will have set minimum participation targets, but if the program creates momentum and reaches a tipping point where participation dramatically increases, sampling changes and questions asked will have to be adapted accordingly. Likewise, if major resistance emerges and participation targets aren't met, that will change the evaluation sample and questions asked.

Evaluation feedback also supports adaptation. Regularly capturing the perspectives of key actors at different levels and in different subgroups helps the intervention team to understand what's emerging and adapt appropriately. A developmental evaluator may organize findings to present different perspectives, putting them in dialogue with each other to identify emergent issues; this can even be done face to face by bringing those with different perspectives together for reflective practice (a process presented in Chapter 9 on methods). Moreover, by capturing and tracking innovation adaptations and their significance, the evaluation deepens awareness of and sensitivity to the adaptive process, which may otherwise be so incremental and emergent that the innovators themselves aren't fully aware of the adaptations they're making—and why they're making them. The developmental evaluator pushes for clarity about the thinking processes and innovator experiences that undergird adaptations. That heightens learning without which there is lots of doing, but no learning by doing.

I was once covering this material in a workshop when a participant raised his hand, identified himself as a former Marine officer, and said, "The mantra of the U.S. Marines when the lights went dim was *adapt, improvise, and overcome*." Not bad advice for developmental evaluators. But overcome what? In part, the tendency to want to control and impose design structure in the face of uncertainty.

Uncertainty

We can't figure this out. I've been in the forecasting business for 50 years, and I'm no better than I ever was, and nobody else is either.

> —ALAN GREENSPAN, former chair, U.S. Federal Reserve Bank, in an October 8, 2007, television interview explaining why economic forecasters missed the housing bubble that contributed to the subsequent global financial crisis

Under conditions of complexity, processes and outcomes are unpredictable, uncontrollable, and unknowable in advance. Uncertainties flow from turbulence in the environment, both evolutionary and transformational changes in systems, and the limits of knowledge. The predictability of program outcomes is heavily dependent on the state of research knowledge about how to produce desired outcomes. Correspondingly, the evaluation of the extent to which outcomes are attained is likewise dependent on the state of research knowledge. A polio vaccine will prevent polio. The outcome is certain and predictable. Thus, evaluation can stop with implementation and coverage: Was the vaccine properly administered to the entire targeted population? No long-term follow-up is needed to determine whether vaccinated children will get polio. Research has answered that question. This is simple. There is a direct, immediate, known, predictable, and therefore certain relationship between vaccination and polio prevention. And once vaccinated, the outcome endures.

In contrast, both quantity and quality of sleep is dependent on a large number of individual and environmental factors, is subject to both short-term and long-term variation, and sleep problems stem from a variety of underlying factors (and interactions among those factors), and lead to a range of consequences, including but not limited to fatigue. Sleep patterns are a function of individual physiology, age, gender, mental health, work patterns and demands, family dynamics, culture, geography, and, if you believe the mattress advertisers, your *sleep number*. A fatigue management intervention can be further affected by organizational culture and politics, competing organizational priorities, performance norms, the timing of the intervention in relation to the business cycle, relationships with co-workers, and a variety of factors related to the work environment (stress, degree to which work is routine or variable, flexibility of work hours, scheduling patterns, etc.). The situation is complex and the results of the intervention are uncertain, as is the case with Project SleepBetter.

Uncertain interventions and unpredictable outcomes can intersect with and be affected by larger societal uncertainties. A global financial crisis of the kind that began in late 2008 or the swine flu pandemic that emerged in early 2009 will reverberate through every program and organization. The dynamics of uncertainties in the larger environment will affect the dynamics of uncertainties in a local program; that's the nature of cross-system interdependencies. What affects program delivery and outcome uncertainties affects evaluation. Ironically, the typical evaluator response to program uncertainty is to insist on greater clarity, require more detailed work on the logic model, and demand more specificity about expected outcomes. Evaluators believe that such demands are helpful because evaluators are trained to value clarity, specificity, and measurability. As a result, most evaluation designs are rigid, fixed, and inflexible, as if occurring in a sheltered cocoon, impervious to what's going on around them. In contrast, developmental evaluation assumes uncertainty in complex situations, and therefore builds flexibility and adaptability into the design, including the possibility that both program processes and outcomes can change, so evaluation measures of program processes and outcomes will have to change too.

In considering uncertainty as a dimension of complexity, it is important to distinguish risk versus uncertainty, a distinction highlighted in the classic work of economist Frank Knight (1921). Risk applies in a situation where you have a sense of the range and likelihood of desired outcomes. Risk can be calculated in simple and complicated situations. Uncertainty describes the situation where it's not at all clear what might happen, let alone how likely the possible outcomes are, as was the case with both the global financial crisis and the swine flu pandemic. No one knew how deep or long lasting the financial crisis would be. No one knew initially how the flu virus might mutate and spread. Knight emphasized that risk involves a two-part probability calculation: first, the likelihood of an occurrence or result and, second, the nature and extent of the probable consequences (good or bad). However, when too little is known either to calculate the likelihood of occurrence or to assess consequences, that is, where degree of risk is essentially immeasurable, that is full-scale uncertainty. Prior to the global financial meltdown in 2008, financial managers thought they had good estimates of risk, but the actual events that unfolded were extreme outliers, outside their range of probabilities or imagined consequences. "What happened was unimaginable" said many financial experts and money managers after the meltdown. Financial managers and policy economists faced unparalleled uncertainty: a mammoth black swan (Taleb, 2005, 2007; Triana & Taleb, 2009).

Uncertainty in the physical world is often a consequence of the absence of sufficient research knowledge. The assumption is that, over the long term, science will fill in the knowledge gaps. In quantum physics, however, uncertainty may be considered a fundamental and unavoidable property of the universe. The Heisenberg uncertainty principle posits that an observer can never know precisely both the position and the velocity of a particle. The uncertainty principle has been adopted and applied in the social world, more appropriately as a metaphor than a description of fundamental social reality, to assert that in complex systems, we can never completely disentangle all the interacting variables, including the effects of our efforts to observe what is going on. The very act of observation can affect what is observed. This is especially the case in evaluation, where, for example, what gets measured gets done. More generally, evaluation itself can be an intervention, either intentionally or in unintended ways, as the evaluation process affects both the program and those experiencing it (Patton, 2008c, chap. 5). In this regard, evaluation can actually increase both complexity and uncertainty, being yet another thing that interacts in the system.

Developmental evaluation acknowledges uncertainty, expects it, and accepts that evaluation can increase complexity even while attempting to understand it, by being one more factor among the many already operating and interacting. A primary strategy for coping with uncertainty applies to both programs and evaluations and the interactions between the two: shorten and speed up feedback. The longer the time horizon, the greater the uncertainty. Long-term outcomes and impacts are especially uncertain.

It is worth recalling here the findings about "good to great" companies reported in Chapter 1. Jim Collins's (2001) team found that great companies shared an unrelenting belief in a long-term vision *and* an obsession with data about the day-to-day realities they faced. They constantly monitored the results of their initiatives to get real-time feedback about what was working and not working, and how their environment was changing. They did not treat vision and reality testing, hope and data, as opposites. Rather, they immersed themselves in vision-directed reality testing. Ruthless attention to emerging reality, day by day, week by week, month by month, was the common path to attaining their long-term visions. They faced uncertainties by monitoring both effectiveness and emergence, and adapting accordingly.

Dealing with uncertainty becomes something like playing the child's game Chutes and Ladders. With the toss of the dice (luck, uncertainty), a player's progress along the game board can be accelerated toward the desired destination (ascending a ladder) or impeded (descending a chute). Developmental evaluation tracks the progress of an innovation, provides feedback to help innovators track their progress, including distinguishing chutes from ladders, and then monitors the next roll of the dice (see what's unfolding as it unfolds). Two calculations by innovators are ever in tension along the way as they ask, How do we find the ladders that take us to the next level and how do we avoid the chutes that set us back? These are equivalent to the ongoing risk calculations that businesses and financial investors have to make, calculations that are especially uncertain in times of economic and/or political turbulence. They have to worry simultaneously about sinking the boat (failure) or missing the boat (missing an opportunity). Developmental evaluation provides data about the direction the boat is sailing, how far it has come, and how much water, if any, the boat is taking on. And any changes in destination due to changed conditions. Emergent understandings and calculations of risk in complex dynamic situations provide some sense of the factors at play, and how to monitor those dynamic factors, but humility about control and prediction is the fundamental mindset, allowing the innovator to be vigilant without becoming conservatively risk-averse.

Daniel Gilbert (2009), professor of psychology at Harvard University, in discussing the human aversion to uncertainty, points to an experiment at Maastricht University in the Netherlands. Subjects were given a series of 20 electric shocks. Some knew they would receive an intense shock on every trial. Others knew they would receive 17 mild shocks

and three intense shocks, but they didn't know on which of the 20 trials the intense shocks would come. Fear reactions were measured by heart rate and galvanic skin response. The findings revealed that those who were uncertain about what each shock would bring were more anxious than those who knew for sure that they'd receive an intense shock. In a similar vein, Gilbert reviewed a number of different studies about reactions to known negative health conditions versus uncertain risks. He interprets the cumulative results as showing that

> [p]eople feel worse when something bad *might* occur than when something bad *will* occur. Most of us aren't losing sleep and sucking down Marlboros because the Dow is going to fall another thousand points, but because we don't know whether it will fall or not—and human beings find uncertainty more painful than the things they're uncertain about. . . .
>
> Why would we prefer to know the worst than to suspect it? Because when we get bad news we weep for a while, and then get busy making the best of it. We change our behavior, we change our attitudes. We raise our consciousness and lower our standards. We find our bootstraps and tug. But we can't come to terms with circumstances whose terms we don't yet know. An uncertain future leaves us stranded in an unhappy present with nothing to do but wait. Our national gloom . . . [is] a matter of insufficient certainty. (p. 1)

Developmental evaluation offers a strategy to help social innovators cope with uncertainty by tracking developments in real time, facilitating assessments of what those developments mean, and supporting evaluation of alternatives going forward. This process is inherently dynamic—and even more often *dynamical*. Is that really a word? (This was the first question I was asked after a presentation on "dynamical complex contexts" at the AEA annual conference; see Patton, 2009.) Yes, it really is a word. Get to know it and start to use it, for it describes a pervasive pattern of turbulent and uncertain change in complex systems.

Dynamical Systems Change

How many different ways can we say that the future will be different from the past? What exaggerated phrases of shock and awe have we heard over the past weeks? Each day brings new surprises and more uncertainty about how the future will unfold. How can we as individuals, families, communities, and nations cope with such instability?

First, we need to realize that these big patterns are not different in kind from the patterns of change we face every day. When changes are smaller or more local, we can convince ourselves that we know what is happening. We take change for granted. We help ourselves believe that we have been there before, that the future isn't all that different from the past, that we can continue "business as usual." But even the changes we can comprehend and cope with carry the seeds of a radically new kind of change.

In human systems dynamics, we call this new kind of change *dynamical. . . .*

Dynamical change relates to the behavior of complex systems, where patterns of change are completely unpredictable. Dynamical change is marked by:

- Fractal patterns when change at one level instigates or prevents change at another level. . . .
- Intermittent jumps and cascades when the system seems stuck as tension accumulates then breaks loose with abandon
- Networks of connections that can either hold a system stable or move it quickly into new patterns
- Self-organizing patterns when interacting parts generate coherent system-wide patterns

Dynamical change influences objects that are already in motion. It does not follow smooth dynamic paths because the number of variables is large and/or unknown, the system is open to outside influences, and the forces have the potential to amplify each other.

—GLENDA EOYANG, founding executive director of the Human Systems Dynamics Institute (2008a)

Dynamical systems are characterized by continuous interaction and change. They are fluid, which evokes the science and study of fluid dynamics. Aerodynamics is the study of gases in motion while hydrodynamics is the study of liquids in motion. Molecular dynamics examines motion on the molecular level, while thermodynamics includes relationships between heat and mechanical energy at the cosmic level. In the social sciences we have specializations in the dynamics of various units of analysis, for example, group dynamics (the study of social group interactions and processes), family dynamics, organizational dynamics, and community dynamics. Power dynamics in sociology examines influence relationships. Economists focus on market dynamics. Psychodynamics scholars study the interrelationships of mental, emotional, attitudinal, motivational, and personality forces and interactions, both conscious and unconscious. Neurodynamics focuses on the spatiotemporal relationships and interactions of neural activity and brain functioning.

What these diverse fields have in common is attention to change: interacting forces, interrelationships, variation, rhythms, motion, and movement. The opposite of *dynamic* is *static*: inert, motionless, inactive, fixed, and unchanging.

Evaluation focuses on whether change has occurred, the nature and degree of change, and the factors that lead to change. Assessing, understanding, and explaining change is at the center of evaluation. It is ironic, then, that static thinking dominates evaluation, especially summative and impact evaluations. The central evaluation questions traditionally given highest priority are: Did IT work? And can we attribute the results to the intervention? These questions imply and assume a static and fixed relationship between cause and effect, between program and outcome, between intervention and impact. The idée fixe in evaluation is of a standardized, controlled, replicable, high-fidelity intervention that can predictably produce standardized outcomes. The usual evaluation conceptualization of what constitutes a program is static. The relationship between program processes and outcomes is modeled as static. The most esteemed evaluation design by those who call it the "gold standard," a randomized controlled trial, is static. The rigor of experimental designs depends on controlled, standardized, and fixed interventions. Such designs typically involve gathering data at two points in time, pretest and posttest, then comparing the treatment group to the control group statistically. Ideally, participants are assigned to treatment and control groups randomly. Such designs assume an identifiable, coherent, standardized, fixed, and consistent treatment. During the experiment, the treatment must be implemented as relatively constant and unchanging. Indeed, evaluators often impose rigorous monitoring procedures to assure standardized, high-fidelity treatments. Programs must agree not to introduce changes during the evaluation. The purpose of these designs is to determine the extent to which the program (treatment) accounts for measurable changes in participants in order to make a summative decision about the value and effectiveness of the program in producing desired change. While aimed at assessing and attributing change, these designs are fundamentally static. They assume that change efforts can be boxed off from the larger world, with participants put in discrete, contained boxes called "treatment" and "control," and isolated from outside influences. What actually happens in those

boxes is largely unknown, which is why they are called "black box" designs. Such evaluations are based on a mechanical, controlled, and simple view of social change. (For a current example of such static and rigid evaluation design thinking involving US $650 million in evaluation funds for education grants, see Viadero, 2009; for an extended discussion of the gold standard debate in evaluation and alternatives to randomized controlled trials for establishing causality, see Patton, 2008c, chap. 12; and for a government accountability report concluding that a "variety of rigorous methods can help identify effective interventions" in program evaluations, see Government Accountability Office, 2009.)

Evaluators' typical use of surveys is also static. Program participants are asked a predetermined, standardized, and fixed set of questions at a moment in time, or two moments: pretest and posttest. The results are like a photograph, void of surrounding context, capturing only what the camera focuses on at that moment. Contrast such a photograph to a panoramic video of the same scene and you immediately have a sense of the difference between static and dynamic.

Which brings us to system dynamics as an alternative perspective, one grounded in complexity understandings and attuned to the ongoing adaptations that emerge in complex dynamic systems. System dynamics as a framework assumes and therefore watches for interactions and interconnections, circular and interlocking relationships, that create internal feedback loops affecting how the entire system behaves. External feedback loops that emerge from interactions with the larger environment can also come into play. An example of a common feedback loop in the Internet age is the popularity and impact of top-ten lists, like the most viewed or most forwarded articles in the *New York Times*. These online rankings, being public, constantly updated, and easily accessible, create a positive feedback loop. This means that the more popular something appears to be, the more popu-

---

⌒ **Cognitive Dissonance about Social Change and Complexity**

Most development professionals and organizations that I have exchanged ideas with about social change, agree that social change is a non-linear, long-term, and often unpredictable process requiring efforts at multiple levels. However, most organizations continue to frame their strategies in measurable, cause–effect terms as if their programs can be evaluated in isolation from other efforts, and can demonstrate effectiveness in the short term.

Note. Virginia Lacayo in Lacayo, Obregon, and Singhal (2008, p. 138).

lar it will become. As more people pay attention to something, and call the attention of others to what they're paying attention to, a rapidly ascending spiral of interest is generated that has its own self-perpetuating momentum, until the ascending momentum reverses direction, which can happen suddenly and without warning. Advertisers are learning how to create and manipulate such momentum (Bialik, 2009). As people become more aware of these manipulations, resistance and negative feedback loops can ensue, as has happened with the increasingly negative reaction to telephone solicitations, with carryover effects on research-oriented telephone polling.

Time delays in the effects of feedback loops are of special interest in system dynamics. A classic labor market example is how perceptions of job opportunities in various fields flow and ebb. When the popular perception is that teaching jobs are plentiful, young people will be encouraged to go into teaching. This leads to oversupply until young people are discouraged from going into teaching. Such oscillating cycles of demand and supply are the basis of market booms and busts. When I was working in agricultural extension in Burkina Faso in the 1960s, we were told to encourage African farmers to grow cotton because the world price was high. What we didn't know was that agricultural development workers throughout Africa were saying the same thing. Cotton production shot up and the world price plummeted, but the delay in pricing information meant that large numbers of farmers were still committed to cotton production before they learned that the market had collapsed.

Such cycles occur in organizations. People are encouraged to copy others on e-mails to keep everyone in the loop until the volume becomes overwhelming and the new norm becomes copying only on a need-to-know basis. That leads to too little sharing until more *cc-ing* is encouraged, then accelerates, and the cycle repeats. Likewise with cycles of face-to-face meetings versus e-mail commu-

nications, or producing full reports versus short memos. These patterns run in cycles. System dynamics captures and diagrams these cycles and their consequences.

The formal field of system dynamics, now heavily based in computer modeling and simulations, had its origins during the mid-1950s with the work of Professor Jay Forrester, an engineer turned management scholar and consultant at the Massachusetts Institute of Technology. System dynamics is one of the more prominent approaches to organizational development and systems-oriented evaluation (e.g., Burke, 2007; Sterman, 2000), but is not the only one. Human systems dynamics is another (Eoyang, 2003, 2007), with special emphasis on and sensitivity to the human dimensions of system dynamics, that is, the ways in which consciousness, reflection, intentionality, and social interaction introduce dynamic elements that can be different from ecosystem dynamics.

For our purposes here, what these approaches share is what is important. They share a view of systems as *dynamic*. In developmental evaluation applications, this focuses our attention on how interventions and treatments (to use experimental terminology) change in subtle but important ways as staff members learn, as clients move in and out, and as conditions of delivery are altered. Where the experimental evaluator is oriented to control and fixed, standardized interventions, the developmental evaluator expects adaptation, which means being ever alert for interactions that create emergent feedback loops that reverberate through the system and affect behaviors within that system. I expect people in a program (including those in a treatment group) to talk to each other, interact about what's going on, get feedback from each other about what they see is happening, and adjust their participation accordingly. They are not automatons responding mechanically to manipulation. They are human beings responding as social beings, creating meaning together, adapting behavior in subtle but consequential ways, and acting on their environment even as it acts on them. Their experience of the program develops over time. It is not static. It is dynamic. Developmental evaluation aims to capture, understand, and interpret those dynamics.

To expand our awareness of dynamic variations, it is worth distinguishing *dynamical change* from both the dynamic and the static.

> Physical scientists distinguish among three ways to describe change over time—static, dynamic, and dynamical. Each kind of change requires different systemic evaluation approaches. A *static* description presents a system at rest. Change, when it comes, is the result of specific interventions that shift the system from one stable point to another. A *dynamic* description acknowledges change over time, but it assumes a smooth trajectory. Physical examples include the parabolic path of a moving projectile—direction and speed change continually in response to the momentum of the object and the pull of gravity. *Dynamical* change is influenced continually by variables that are interdependent (rather than independent or dependent). When change in a system is dynamical, the system may shift from rest to rhythmic oscillation to random thrashing. These changes seem to be spontaneous, but they are driven by the internal dynamics of the system itself as the constraining conditions interact with each other to influence the behaviors of agents in the system. (Eoyang, 2007, p. 127)

System dynamics approaches focus on cycles and feedback loops as sources of change. *Dynamical* phenomena call our attention to evolving systems that manifest unpredictable iterating, up-and-down, back-and-forth, and bifurcating patterns. This means that as various elements of a system interact, they affect each other by sometimes bouncing off each other, sometimes merging, and sometimes merging briefly then separating into new entities. Pretty abstract, I know. Exhibit 5.5 discusses, illustrates, and provides visual graphics of the distinctions.

EXHIBIT 5.5 Static, Dynamic, and Dynamical Contextual Cohort Analysis

To illustrate a practical evaluation application of the distinctions between static, dynamic, and dynamical, consider using those distinctions to characterize different participants based on the degree of stability in their lives. In his important book *Personalizing Evaluation*, Saville Kushner (2000) called attention to the change in perspective involved when we look at program participants as people with lives beyond the confines of a program and understand their patterns of participation and outcomes *in the context of their lives*. For example, program staff working with people in poverty have long observed that participants with chaotic lives (chronically sick children, mental illness, in-and-out-of housing, episodes of family violence, unstable employment) find it quite impossible to focus on narrow program outcomes like increasing their job skills or greater literacy. Evaluators also know that *intervention dosage*—how much of the program participants actually experience—is related to variations in outcomes. On the whole, people who experience the full program (full dose) are expected to attain higher outcomes than those who miss a lot of the program (low dose). Dosage is usually thought of and measured along a single dimension from more to less. The notion of *dynamical dosage* adds a pattern of variable or volatile dosage, sometimes high and intense, sometimes low, even miniscule. So, two people could participate in 50% of the sessions, but one pattern was static (came every other time) while the other was dynamical (came a few times, missed a few times, then came a few times, missed a few times, and stayed different amounts of time even when participating, often arriving late or leaving early, or both).

(cont.)

Consider then further distinguishing participants whose lives are (1) stable (static), from those whose lives are (2) *dynamic* (e.g., progressing in a desired direction, like becoming more active in the community, or getting physically healthier by eating better and exercising more), versus (3) those whose lives are *dynamical* (pattern of ups and downs due to sudden and unexpected changes like loss of job, a sick child, a strained back, intermittent drug use, or on-and-off relationship with an abusive partner). Dynamical lives are chaotic lives.

At the 2009 annual conference of the AEA, where President Debra Rog focused evaluators' attention on the theme of *Context and Evaluation*, I applied these distinctions to distinguish different patterns of participation in a professional association.

Pattern	Pattern definition	Pattern observed in an individual's participation in a professional association annual conference (like AEA)
Static	Stable, predictable, and known.	The same degree and nature of participation year after year.
Dynamic	Changing in an evolutionary and fairly manageable direction, either up or down (increasing or decreasing), constituting a relatively smooth trajectory.	Begin participation as a novice or newcomer, then gradually and consistently increase involvement and participation over the years, an upward trajectory of increasing engagement.
Dynamical	Change pattern is volatile, up-and-down, unpredictable, turbulent, nonlinear, and complex. Bifurcations (splits in direction) can occur.	Participants who come one year, miss a couple of years, show up again for a few years, then miss a few years, their participation up and down. Might go to another association conference as a priority for a while (bifurcation).

Note. Based on Patton (2009).

These same distinctions can be applied to a program or innovation to distinguish the context within which different programs or innovations are implemented.

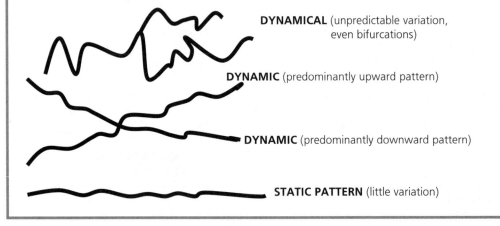

DYNAMICAL (unpredictable variation, even bifurcations)

DYNAMIC (predominantly upward pattern)

DYNAMIC (predominantly downward pattern)

STATIC PATTERN (little variation)

Think about the global financial meltdown and policy responses in late 2008 through 2009. The interactions were dynamical. Some companies went bankrupt. Others merged. Some mergers led to new spinoffs. The government, through the Federal Reserve, became primary stockholder (and therefore the owner) of certain companies to allow them to avoid bankruptcy. Some companies were "allowed to fail" while others were deemed "too large to fail," but not only was what distinguished one from the other hard to tell, but the rules and categories themselves changed as the crisis deepened. The situation was *dynamical*. A crisis that began in the housing and mortgage industries morphed into a banking industry crisis, then into an insurance industry crisis, then again into an auto industry crisis, the consequences of which reverberated back to deepen the banking and mortgage crises, and along the way precipitated a worldwide plunge in the stock and bond markets, with cascading effects into the huge money market fund system. The effects and consequences rippled out into the philanthropic sector as endowments saw losses of a third to a half of assets, which led to huge reductions in funding to the not-for-profit sector. Unemployment soared, which deepened the housing crisis as more mortgages were foreclosed, which led to more government intervention. And I'm barely sketching the outlines of the crisis (for details, see Stewart, 2009).

The evolutionary rule of dynamical systems tells us that we can only know how a system is functioning a short time into the future. What emerges during one time frame will become a new starting point for what emerges during the subsequent time frame. These aren't the dynamics of a cycle, but rather the dynamics of evolutionary, even transformative, development. Each system iteration involves some change in the system itself, great or small, but different— and those differences aggregate and accumulate, not just quantitatively but qualitatively, potentially reaching tipping points.

Small changes may have large effects (butterfly effects).

Developmental evaluation tracks these innovation and system dynamics by documenting the forks in the road, the interactions among elements, and the consequences for both desired results and unanticipated consequences. Sometimes this simply involves regular interviews with key actors to capture what they're seeing and deciding. Sometimes it involves facilitating formal reflective practice sessions with those involved. Chapters 8 and 9 will discuss inquiry frameworks and methods in depth. The point here is to give a sense of what the developmental evaluator is looking for and how sensitivity to potentially dynamical cascades is part of the charge.

Bifurcations can occur. A bifurcation occurs when a small, incremental change in a system accelerates suddenly or shifts dramatically such that a qualitative or systemic change becomes manifest. At the bifurcation point the system may change its interconnections, split into new structures, or merge with other system elements. Bifurcations of two kinds are useful to distinguish. *Local bifurcations* occur within the boundaries of the system of interest. For example, as I emphasized earlier in this chapter, it is common in programs for subgroups to emerge. In a sleep program this could be people with severe sleep apnea who are married versus those who are single. Their lives and lifestyles, motivations, and concerns can be quite different, and as they find each other and interact, they may have substantially different program and treatment experiences (and outcomes), even as the turtles and truckers did in my earlier wilderness program example. *Global bifurcations* occur when different systems collide, or when a system is dramatically affected by interactions with and turbulence in its environment. Severe cutbacks in programs due to the economic crisis are an example, especially where those cutbacks lead to different levels of service for different people. So, for example, if a fatigue management program has begun implementation when staff cutbacks occur due to a budget crisis, remaining staff may be required to work longer hours and take on more responsibilities, thereby experiencing both greater stress and increased fatigue. Or the sudden threat of a pandemic, like swine flu in early 2009, can affect how, when, where, and how frequently people come together, creating dramatically different participation and dropout rates in programs.

In tracking such dynamical developments, the developmental evaluator not only reports findings but participates in discussions about options for responding and adapting. The developmental evaluator can be part of the innovation team, playing the role of bringing data to bear, providing feedback, and generating options based on what is emerging. In such a role, the evaluator is manifesting another important complexity theme: coevolution.

Coevolution

An important property of complex systems is the way they exhibit self-organizing behavior driven by co-evolutionary interactions. This adaptive capacity enables them to rearrange their internal structure spontaneously.
—ELIZABETH GARNSEY AND
JAMES MCGLADE, *Complexity and Co-Evolution* (2006, pp. 3–4)

In the final section of this chapter, we'll examine the relevance for developmental evaluation of the complexity idea of *coevolution*. In particular, this will help elucidate the role of developmental evaluators as we interact with social innovators in ways that influence both the innovation and the evaluation as each emerges and unfolds. In the working relationship between the social innovator and the developmental evaluator, both the innovation and evaluation are cocreated and coevolve. This section is about the theory and practice of coevolution. We begin with theory and the important contributions of Ralph Stacey.

Ralph Stacey (1992, 1996, 2001, 2007) is one of the leading thinkers about the implications of complexity for organizational development. His insights about organizational change, and his extensive experience as an organizational management consultant and scholar, have implications for developmental evaluation. In describing complexity, he prefers the imagery of "complex responsive processes" instead of the more widely used "complex adaptive systems." The language of complex adaptive systems comes from ecology. The language of complex responsive processes emphasizes *human factors* (remember, we began this chapter with Mike Coplen and his work on human factors in transportation safety) and is grounded in social psychology, especially the work of George Herbert Mead. Human action is enmeshed in social interaction and communication, which involve a set of distinct but inseparable actions: gesture and response to gesture; generalizing and particularizing; and human consciousness ("I") and self-consciousness ("me") as distinguishable but inseparable selves. Stacey looks at the patterns that get established during these social interactions as the basis of habits but, because such interactions are dynamic, and often dynamical, they include the potential for transformation.

> We have the capacity to reflect imaginatively on these patterns, both local and population-wide, articulating both the habitual and the just emerging transformations and in doing so either sustain the habitual or reinforce the transformation of habit. (2007, p. 314)

Stacey emphasizes that the significance of his distinction between complex adaptive systems versus complex responsive processes is derived from the uniquely human capacity to interpret and apply generalizations in the face of a particular interaction.

> In complex adaptive systems, the agents follow rules, in effect, they directly enact generalisations. If humans simply applied generalisations in their interactions with each other

then there would be no possibility of individual imagination and spontaneity and hence no possibility of creativity. We would simply be determined by the generalisations. It is in the essentially conflictual particularising of the generalisations, which have emerged over long periods of human interaction, that socially constructed, interdependent persons display spontaneity, reflection, reflexivity, imagination and creativity as well as conflict. (2007, pp. 314–315)

"Conflictual particularizing of generalizations" is a dense construct, a lot to penetrate the meaning of. Stacey is basically describing how we are constantly negotiating between what we know (or think we know) about the world in general and what we face in any specific moment or situation. He views human spontaneity as emerging from this interplay of general and particular, making this tension closely associated with the possibility of transformation and novelty in human interaction, which are essential sources of innovation. One form this can take is working out particular applications of general understandings. In organizations this is often a conflict-laden process as competing suggestions for particularizing are debated. Stacey traces his view of complexity to Mead, including how to think about causality in complex responsive processes:

What Mead presents is a complex, nonlinear, iterative process of communicative interaction between people in which mind, self and society all emerge simultaneously as the living present. Mead is concerned with local interaction as the present in which population-wide patterns emerge as social and personality structures. If one takes the complex responsive processes view then one thinks of the emergence of long-term, widespread, coherent patterns of relating across a population emerging in the local processes of relating. It follows that there is no need to look for the causes of coherent human action in concepts such as deep structures, archetypes, the collective unconscious, transcendental wholes, common pools of meaning, group minds, the group-as-a-whole, transpersonal processes,

foundation matrix, the personal dynamic unconscious, internal worlds, mental models and so on. Instead, one understands human relating to be inherently pattern forming—it is its own cause. (2007, pp. 315–316)

This constitutes the basis for Stacey's view of an organization as "a social object," meaning it is a social construction of reality, which means "the organization is nothing more or less than the iterated ongoing processes in which people are together particularizing the generalizations in terms of which they perceive their organization" (2007, p. 316). Emergence and innovation can be observed in, and are an inherent part of, people's social interactions and meaning making. I realize that Stacey's formulation may read as gobbledygook to those who have somehow escaped socialization and indoctrination into the arcane worlds of sociological and social psychological theory, but having not escaped that Arcanum, indeed, having spent some years mired therein, I wanted to share with you, gentle reader, the brain pain. Seriously, Ralph Stacey has thought about these issues for a long time and his many writings have been and continue to be influential (1996, 2001, 2007). He calls our attention to the importance of understanding and tracking how people in organizations are making sense of what is going on as they interact, share views, argue, and in many different ways, both overt and subtle, influence each other and the whole organization toward a social construction of their shared reality. These are the *complex responsive processes* that he highlights.

What are the implications for developmental evaluation of Stacey's emphasis on *complex responsive processes*? His focus is on relationships and interactions. Evaluators are trained to focus on methods, measures, and findings, and, in the tradition of positivist science, compartmentalize relationships and interactions, working to keep the findings uncontaminated by social engagement. But interpretation of data requires social interaction to make meaning. We interact not only with the data, but with each other. Thus is knowledge *socially constructed*. It has ever been so and is so now. This does not mean there is no possibility of reality testing, or even of truth, though Simon Blackburn's comprehensive guide to *Truth* (2005) makes it clear that the journey to that rare place can be treacherous and is always disputatious. Reality testing and shared truth in an evaluation emerge from dialogue and deliberation (House & Howe, 1999, 2000). What emerges from the interactions between developmental evaluators and social innovators is a narrative about what's going on and what it means. In Stacey's terms, "knowledge arises in complex responsive processes of relating between human bodies, that knowledge itself is continuously reproduced and potentially transformed. Knowledge is not a 'thing,' or a system, but an ephemeral, active process of relating" (2001, p. 4).

Using Project SleepBetter as an example, the narrative on which the intervention was originally based focused on helping individual veteran police officers deal with sleep apnea and its debilitating and fatigue-inducing effects. However, as a developmental evaluator asks systems questions and calls attention to the social interactions and police station organizational context within which the project is occurring, the narrative expands to include changes in families, relationships among police partners, even the culture of the police station, and, if successful in changing understandings and norms about sleep, becomes a narrative about police work and the police force. The sustainability of the sleep intervention ultimately depends on this shift in narrative, moving beyond helping individual officers to changing the institution of policing with regard to how sleep is understood and healthy patterns of sleep are supported, rewarded, and reinforced. If and when that larger narrative takes hold, it will be a result of complex responsive processes of interaction at various levels of the police force not the linear implementation of a sleep apnea screening and treatment program for individual officers.

The sense-making interactions between developmental evaluators and social innovators around data lead to both insights about next steps and questions for further inquiry, both clarity and confusion, greater certainty and greater uncertainty. This is the essence of the paradox that the more I know, the less I'm sure about; the deeper my insights, the more I realize how much I don't yet know. In the face of uncertainty, we can gain greater certainty about the nature of uncertainty, and its implications for action. Robert Burton, a physician who has studied and written about the "juggling act" of dealing with certainty and uncertainty, has concluded:

> Certainty is not biologically possible. We must learn (and teach our children) to tolerate the unpleasantness of uncertainty. Science has given us the language and tools of probabilities. We have methods for analyzing and ranking opinion according to their likelihood of correctness. That is enough. We do not need and cannot afford the catastrophes born out of a belief in certainty. As David Gross, Ph.D., and the 2004 recipient of the Nobel Prize in physics, said: "The most important product of knowledge is ignorance." (2008, pp. 223–224)

Coevolution, then, is about dealing with the uncertainties of complexity together: looking at the data together and making sense together. Out of these interactions about what is known and unknown, more and less certain, interpretable and uninterpretable, a somewhat coherent narrative emerges. Developmental evaluation captures that narrative, with all its twists and turns. We are tracking and recording the unfolding story of social innovation, sharing the story for reflection, reactions, revisions, and interpretation, and, through the interactive process, facilitating and co-creating the emergence of a coherent narrative. This is a narrative that includes not just the social innovators and the developmental evaluator, but also others with a stake in what has emerged and how it is interpreted, as developmental evaluation plays a bridging role between funders and social innovators, especially in high-trust, high-experimentation grants. This too is a kind of coevolution.

What emerges through coevolution is coherent in the sense that one can follow what has developed, not necessarily that those developments all make sense. More paradox. Sense making doesn't happen all at once. It is ongoing, subject to revision and reconstruction in light of further emergence. By facilitating shared social construction, meaning making, and reality testing, thereby energizing and catalyzing complex responsive processes, the developmental evaluator is engaged with and im-

mersed in the coevolution of what is being developed.

Finally, the effects on an innovation, program, or initiative of developmental evaluation co-creation is an example of what the field of evaluation has recognized as *process use* in which an evaluation affects what is done not just through findings, but through the very inquiry processes of evaluation. For example, asking questions can affect what innovators do by focusing their attention in a different way and that effect occurs before any data have been collected. Attention to process use is an important new direction

⌒ Coevolution and Evaluation Process Use

Process use occurs when those involved in the evaluation learn from the evaluation process itself or make changes based on the evaluation process, for example, the questions asked, rather than just the evaluation's findings. Indeed, process use typically occurs before there are findings as interaction around formulating evaluation questions starts to affect how those involved are thinking about what they're doing. That changed thinking is a form of process use.

The coevolution of an innovation that occurs as a developmental evaluator works with an innovation or program design team will typically manifest many types and levels of process use. Process use includes cognitive, attitudinal, and behavior changes in individuals, and program or organizational changes resulting, either directly or indirectly, from engagement in the evaluation process and learning to think evaluatively (e.g., conceptualizing the dimensions of the innovation, setting inquiring priorities, paying attention to what is emerging). An example of or evidence for process use is when those involved in the evaluation later say something like this: "The impact on our initiative came not just from the findings but also from going through the thinking process that the evaluation required." As always, the most convincing evidence that learning has occurred is subsequent translation into action. Process use includes the effects of evaluation procedures and operations, for example, the premise that "what gets measured gets done," so establishing measurements and setting targets affects program operations and management focus. Looking for what is emerging is a form of process use because it changes what people are paying attention to. These are uses of evaluation processes that affect programs and innovations different from use of specific findings generated by an evaluation (Cousins, 2007; Patton, 2008c, chap. 5).

PROCESS USE AS A USEFULISM: A SENSITIZING CONCEPT

Process use is best understood and used as a sensitizing concept, or "usefulism" (Safire, 2007). A *usefulism* is an idea or concept that calls our attention to something, but that something takes its meaning from and must be defined within a particular context, like being "middle-aged" or manifesting "wisdom." A *sensitizing concept* raises consciousness about a possibility and alerts us to watch out for it within a specific context. That's what the concept of "process use" does. The concept *process use* says things are happening to people and changes are taking place in programs and organizations as evaluation takes place, especially when stakeholders are involved in the process. Watch out for those things. Pay attention. Something important may be happening. The process may be producing outcomes quite apart from findings. Think about what's going on. Help the people in the situation pay attention to what's going on (Patton, 2007).

in evaluation over the past decade (Cousins, 2007; Patton, 2008c, chap. 5), one that calls out attention to and is grounded in the complex responsive processes highlighted by Stacey. (See the sidebar on process use.)

As a developmental evaluator captures, organizes, feeds back, and reports to others the narrative that emerges from social innovation, the evaluator is contributing to change. We are not just bystanders and sightseers. Co-creation and coevolution involve engagement. We engage and contribute by embedding evaluative thinking and inquiry at the heart of innovative and change-making processes. How we handle that engagement makes a difference to what happens. David Bornstein has studied successful, change-making social entrepreneurs. His description of and summary conclusion about effective innovators is fundamentally emergent and developmental. A learning process is involved. Developmental evaluators can facilitate and support that learning process. He concludes his book *How to Change the World* (2007) thusly:

> If I have learned one thing from writing this book, it is that people who solve problems must somehow first arrive at the belief that they *can* solve problems. The belief does not emerge suddenly. The capacity to cause change grows in an individual over time as small-scale efforts lead gradually to larger ones. But the process needs a beginning—a story, an example, an early taste of success—something along the way that helps a person form the belief that it is possible to make the world a better place. Those who act on that belief spread it to others. They are highly contagious. Their stories must be told. (pp. 290–291)

Developmental evaluators can be the storytellers, and that is one important role. But we also contribute by helping those who believe they can make a difference test that belief. Success breeds success. And the ineffective may learn to become effective. But those who do not learn to be effective need the hard-to-hear feedback that they are not effective. Indeed, in some cases they do

harm, if in no other way than by diverting resources from more effective alternatives. Bornstein tells the stories of successful social entrepreneurs. Developmental evaluators do that as well, but we also have an obligation to capture and tell the stories of failure. Harder still can be capturing and telling the stories of uncertainty, where the outcomes remain in doubt. That is the essence of what we've called the challenge of *getting to maybe*.

Social innovators aim to serve by changing the world. Those who evaluate also serve.

Complexity-Sensitizing Concepts

This chapter has reviewed a set of six interdependent complexity concepts that undergird developmental evaluation: nonlinearity, emergence, adaptation, uncertainty, dynamic and dynamical interactions, and coevolution. These are sensitizing concepts. Qualitative sociologist Herbert Blumer (1954) is credited with originating the idea of the "sensitizing concept" to orient fieldwork. Sensitizing concepts in the social sciences include nominally defined notions like victim, stress, stigma, and learning organization that can provide some initial direction to a study as one inquires into how the concept is given meaning in a particular place or set of circumstances (Patton, 2002; Schwandt, 2001). The observer moves between the sensitizing concept and the real world of social experience giving shape and substance to the concept and elaborating the conceptual framework with varied manifestations of the concept. Such an approach recognizes that while the specific manifestations of social phenomena vary by time, space, and circumstance, the sensitizing concept is a container for capturing, holding, and examining these manifestations to better understand patterns and implications.

Evaluators commonly use sensitizing concepts to inform their understanding of situations. Consider the notion of *context*. Any particular evaluation is designed within some *context* and we are admonished to take *context* into account, be sensitive to *context*, and watch out for changes in *context*. But what is *context*? The 2009 annual meeting of the AEA had as its theme, chosen by President Debra Rog, CONTEXT and EVALUATION. Evaluators made presentations and had animated discussions about context. Systems thinkers posited that system boundaries are inherently arbitrary, so defining what is within the immediate scope of an evaluation versus what is within its surrounding context will inevitably be arbitrary, but the distinction is

still useful. Indeed, being intentional about deciding what is in the immediate realm of action of an evaluation and what is in the enveloping context can be an illuminating exercise—and different stakeholders might well provide different perspectives. In that sense, the idea of *context* is a sensitizing concept. Others, seeking an operational definition of context, ranted in some frustration about the ambiguity, vagueness, and diverse meanings of what they, ultimately, decided is a useless and vacuous concept. Why? Because it has not been (and cannot be) opera-

∽ Defining and Measuring Complexity

Melanie Mitchell (2009) has been studying and working with complexity ideas for more than two decades, including working with leading-edge complexity thinkers at the prestigious Santa Fe Institute, the citadel of complexity ideas. She tells of organizing a panel there of distinguished complexity scholars from diverse fields like physics, computer science, biology, economics, and decision theory. Sadly, no evaluators appear to have been invited, but otherwise the group represented the wide panorama of scientists working with complexity. Once the panelists had presented their latest thinking, she says that the first question from students was: "How do you define complexity?"

She reports that everyone on the panel laughed because "the question was at once so straightforward, so expected, and yet so difficult to answer. Each panel member then proceeded to give a different definition of the term. A few arguments even broke out between members of the faculty over their respective definitions. The students were a bit shocked and frustrated. If the faculty of the Santa Fe Institute—the most famous institution in the world devoted to research on complex systems—could not agree on what was meant by complexity, then how can there even begin to be a science of complexity?" (p. 94). Her answer is important.

She explains that "there is not yet a single science of complexity but rather several different sciences of complexity with different notions of what complexity means. Some of these notions are quite formal, and some are still very informal" (p. 95). Figuring out how diverse notions relate to one another in the "overly complex notion of complexity" lies in the future and "is work that largely remains to be done, perhaps by those shocked and frustrated students as they take over from the older generation of scientists" (p. 95).

She goes on to review the history of many scientific concepts from different fields and notes that disciplines develop around debates over definitions and measures. That such fervent debate goes on is itself an indicator of the significance of the ideas that arouse such passion. We are a long way from operationalizing complexity. Mitchell reviews the efforts to date. The last chapter (Chapter 4) positioned social complexity in the territory defined by the degree of certainty/degree of agreement matrix (see Exhibit 4.5) where we are highly uncertain about how to attain a desired outcome because of the dynamic interactions among many variables and there is significant disagreement among stakeholders about what to do. But there are not precise operational measures for these two dimensions. They are highly context-dependent.

That's why *the idea of complexity* remains *a sensitizing concept*. It calls our attention to situations where uncertainty, disagreement, emergence, dynamical interactions, nonlinearity, and coevolution require evaluation adaption and responsiveness to track, understand, and provide feedback about innovations in rapidly changing contexts.

tionally defined—and they displayed a low tolerance for the ambiguity that is inherent in such sensitizing concepts (Patton, 2009).

A sensitizing concept raises consciousness about something and alerts us to watch out for it within a specific context. That's what the complexity concepts do. They tell us, things are happening to people and changes are taking place in programs and organizations as innovations and interventions unfold. Watch out for what's emerging under conditions of uncertainty. Pay attention to nonlinearities and dynamic interactions. Watch for and facilitate adaptation as part of a coevolutionary process. The innovative process may be producing outcomes quite different from what was expected. Observe and think about what's going on. Help social innovators pay attention to what's going on. Observe what is developing and facilitate further development. Chapter 9 discusses how sensitizing concepts can be central to and provide focus

for developmental evaluation inquiry, and provides an extended example.

Sensitizing concepts are not judged by whether they have "achieved" a standardized and universally accepted operational definition. Complexity concepts have not been operationalized, will not be operationalized, and do not lend themselves to operationalization. Judge these concepts instead by their utility in sensitizing us to how to evaluate developments under conditions of complexity. (For an extended discussion of operational constructs vs. sensitizing concepts, see Patton, 2007.)

Exhibit 5.6 depicts the dynamical interconnectedness of these six sensitizing concepts. Their meanings overlap and intersect. There is no order to how they enter into a developmental evaluation. Linearity ought not be imposed on them. The concepts themselves provide broad direction rather than narrow focus, and can be used and adapted,

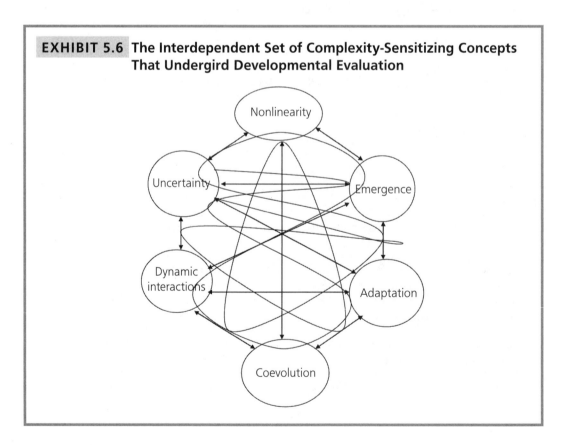

EXHIBIT 5.6 The Interdependent Set of Complexity-Sensitizing Concepts That Undergird Developmental Evaluation

separately and together, as evaluation issues emerge in the face of uncertainty and complexity. Taken together they are integral dimensions of the dynamical, coevolutionary process of developmental evaluation.

Exhibit 5.7 (on pages 150–151) summarizes the evaluation implications of these six sensitizing concepts.

Human Beings and Their Interactions as the Source of Complexity

Developmental evaluation, because it occurs in human systems with real, live, interacting human beings, is particularly attuned to human factors as the source of complexity. Mike Coplen, introduced early in this chapter, offers expertise in how human factors affect transportation safety. Glenda Eoyang has made human factors the centerpiece of her consulting work in Human Systems Dynamics. Ralph Stacey makes the social interactions of interacting and meaning-making human beings the core of his insights into complex responsive processes. Brenda Zimmerman and David Snowden emphasize that human thinking processes and engagement need to be adapted to the nature and degree of complexity they face. What runs through the work of these complexity thinkers and scholars, working from quite diverse traditions with varied backgrounds in different settings, is that interacting human beings are the primary source of complexity.

Evaluators have traditionally entered programs and innovations first and foremost as methodologists (as opposed to human beings), purportedly independent of the systems they study. Complexity theory exposes the self-delusion of thinking about evaluation in this way. Evaluators are also human. Evaluators inevitably interact with other human beings in the settings being evaluated, gathering data from program participants, interviewing staff, and negotiating with administrators and funders. In so doing, evaluators add another layer of complexity to program processes and innovations, even when (perhaps *particularly when*)

they attempt to make simple that which is complex, which is what evaluators have been most trained to do. Developmental evaluation acknowledges that as evaluators we become part of the complex adaptive systems we evaluate and takes into account the ways in which evaluation processes become part of the development process. Our individual human proclivities and patterns also become part of those system dynamics.

Which brings us full circle back to the question I posed at the beginning of this chapter: How deep is your sleep deficit? Throughout I have used Project SleepBetter as an example to illustrate how complexity concepts could inform developmental evaluation. Complexity concepts sensitize us to and raise our consciousness about the realities of real-world uncertainties. *Raising consciousness* is a sensitizing concept I recall fondly from the social activism of the 1960s. Consciousness, it has been said by some forgotten village wit, is that annoying time between naps. In that between-time, we reflect on many things, including sleep. Since, as I write, the global financial crisis still has the world in its uncertain and unpredictable grasp, it may be appropriate to close this long day's journey into complexity by citing Arthur Schopenhauer's analysis of sleep using financial metaphors:

> Sleep is the interest we have to pay on the capital which is called in at death; and the higher the rate of interest and the more regularly it is paid, the further the date of redemption is postponed.

Insightful, but hardly poetic. For that we need Shakespeare:

> Sleep that knits up the ravell'd sleave of care,
> The death of each day's life, sore labour's bath,
> Balm of hurt minds, great nature's second course,
> Chief nourisher in life's feast. (Macbeth, Act II, Scene 1)

And so I put this chapter to bed.

EXHIBIT 5.7 Characteristics of Complex Systems and Implications for Developmental Evaluation

Characteristics of complex systems	Implications for developmental evaluation
1. *Nonlinear*: Sensitivity to initial conditions; small actions can stimulate large reactions, thus the *butterfly wings metaphor* (Gleick, 1987); *black swans* (Taleb, 2007), in which highly improbable, unpredictable, and unexpected events have huge impacts; and tipping points (Gladwell, 2002) when major shifts occur changing the whole landscape of action.	Watch for, sample, and study critical incidences. Assess and map tipping points and other changes in the intervention landscape. Use mixed methods to capture when cumulative quantitative changes in key indicators become substantively significant qualitative shifts. Don't confuse linear logic models and strategic plans with what actually goes on in programs. Look for contextual changes that shift program patterns, forks in the road that move the program in new directions, and sudden (or gradual) responses to unexpected developments.
2. *Emergence:* Patterns emerge from self-organization among interacting agents. Each agent or element pursues its own path but as that path intersects with other paths, and the agent interacts with other agents, also pursuing their own paths, patterns of interaction emerge and the whole of the interactions cohere, becoming greater than the separate parts. What emerges can be beyond, outside of, and oblivious to any notion of shared intentionality (Johnson, 2001).	Be especially alert to formation of self-organizing subgroups who have different experiences of the program and, correspondingly, different outcomes. Anticipate and expect emergent issues and take seriously the search for unanticipated consequences, tracking interactions among key players, both formal and informal, planned and unplanned. Map networks, system relationships, and subgroups. Track information flows, communications, and emergent issues. Emergence applies to both processes and outcomes. Watch for and assess not only what emerges, but what declines or even disappears. Disappearance is the other side of the phenomenon of emergence. The unplanned emerges; the planned disappears. Both are important, as is what unfolds as planned. The evaluation design is also emergent.
3. *Adaptive*: Interacting elements and agents respond and adapt to each other, and to their environment, so that what emerges is a function of ongoing adaptation both among interacting elements and in the responsive relationships interacting agents have with their environment. Adaptive management is a systematic, iterative process for making decisions in the face of uncertainty, reduced control, and low predictability, through ongoing system monitoring and response to changes in context. The process essentially involves learning by doing and observing, then making adjustments based on what has been learned, and repeating this cycle of sensing, learning, and adapting over and over.	Regularly capture perspectives from key actors in different but interacting systems about what's going on. Put these perspectives in dialogue with each other to capture and track adaptations and their significance. Both new processes and new outcomes may emerge, requiring new evaluation design elements and measures. *The evaluation itself must be adaptive.* An adaptive mindset essentially involves learning by doing and observing. This parallels the process recommended by knowledge management consultant David Snowden when facing complexity: probe, sense, respond (Snowden & Boone, 2007). Probing is the doing. Sensing is the observing (where chance ever favors the prepared mind). And responding is the adaptation. The feedback provided by the developmental evaluator informs the innovators' adaptive process, including heightening awareness of what incremental adaptations are occurring so that learnings can be identified and captured. The evaluator may also point out when innovators are not being adaptive despite what is emerging; or when there is increasing uncertainty within a system but the innovators are behaving as if they've figured things out and know what is happening.

(cont.)

Characteristics of complex systems	Implications for developmental evaluation
4. *Uncertainty:* Under conditions of complexity, processes and outcomes are unpredictable, uncontrollable, and unknowable in advance. Emergent and adaptive self-organization can create idiosyncratic bumps in patterns that become mounds that sometimes go on to become idiosyncratic mountains, or at other times erode into nothingness, and it's impossible to know ahead of time which pattern, if either, will prevail. Not acknowledging and dealing with uncertainty and unexpected events can lead to a spiral of disruption with things getting worse (Weick & Sutcliffe, 2001, p. 2). Uncertainty is a defining characteristic of complexity (Westley et al.,2006). Evaluators face uncertainties no less than innovators, so evaluators need to learn to "anticipate surprise" (Morell, 2010).	Identify and acknowledge sources of uncertainty, including inadequate knowledge about how to produce desired outcomes; disagreements among key actors about what to do, including value conflicts; and turbulence in the larger environment. Work with key stakeholders and primary intended users on an ongoing basis to understand the implications of uncertainty. Nurture tolerance for ambiguity and messiness. This means resisting the temptation to address uncertainty by imposing order and control through evaluation by forcing the complex into a simple linear evaluation logic model with predetermined clear, specific, and measurable outcomes. Provide rapid feedback about unexpected events and their implications. Early detection of and feedback about emergent patterns can be critical. In early stages of trouble or opportunity, the unexpected may give off *weak signals.* "The overwhelming tendency is to respond to weak signals with a weak response." Understanding the potential significance of weak signals and responding strongly "holds the key to managing the unexpected" (Weick & Sutcliffe, 2001, p. 4).
5. *Dynamical*: Interactions within, between, and among subsystems and parts within systems can be volatile, changing rapidly and unpredictably due to the interdependence of key factors and variables. "The system may shift from rest to rhythmic oscillation to random thrashing. These changes seem to be spontaneous, but they are driven by the internal dynamics of the system itself as the constraining conditions interact with each other to influence the behaviors of agents in the system" (Eoyang, 2007, p. 127). See Exhibit 5.5.	Track and document not only whether change occurs, but how and why it occurs. Processes and outcomes can be both dynamic and dynamical; pay attention to both and their interrelationship. Create a flexible and responsive data collection system that can mirror adaptive, emergent, and dynamic/dynamical developments, so that fieldwork can speed up and slow down in sync with the intervention's rhythms of change. Engage in ongoing monitoring of shifts in levels of activity to capture dynamic/dynamical transitions. Analyze and distinguish contextual factors and participation patterns that are static, dynamic, and dynamical, and the implications of these different patterns (see Exhibit 5.5).
6. *Coevolutionary*: As interacting and adaptive agents self-organize, ongoing connections emerge that become *coevolutionary* as the agents evolve together (coevolve) within and as part of the whole system, over time.	Developmental evaluation will coevolve with the innovation and intervention, both affecting innovation and being affected by it. This is a process of co-creation. The evaluation will not be independent and separate from the innovation but will be interdependent with it, and with those involved in it (as part of a team), as the evaluator provides feedback, facilitates conceptualization of the change process, and both captures and generates perspectives about what is happening, and why. *Process use,* in which evaluative thinking affects the intervention, will be as important as findings use.

6

How the World Is Changed

A Dialectic with Thesis and Antithesis and Developmental Evaluation as the Synthesis

Change is inevitable—except from
a vending machine.
—ROBERT C. GALLAGHER, author

Thesis: The world is changed top-down through widespread dissemination and replication of validated best practices.

Antithesis: The world is changed bottom-up through grassroots innovation grounded in indigenous knowledge and local context.

Synthesis: In the global village, change occurs in the middle where top-down and bottom-up knowledge and interests collide, intersect, get entangled together, do battle, find common ground, and otherwise encounter real-world complexities as effective general principles are adapted to local context.

Developmental evaluation operates at this historic middle intersection. This chapter positions developmental evaluation as an approach to navigating through the dynamic middle labyrinth where top-down and bottom-up forces interact.

How change occurs is the central development issue of our times. This chapter takes on that issue and explains the role of developmental evaluation as part of the change process. To do so requires positioning developmental evaluation in relation to—and in contrast to—the dominant alternatives: top-down versus bottom-up approaches. The positioning of developmental evaluation flows from and is grounded in the premise that complex adaptive systems require an evaluation approach appropriate to the dynamics of change under conditions of complexity. Previous chapters, especially Chapters 4 and 5, have established the niche of developmental evaluation as attuned to complexity. The relevance and appropriateness of developmental evaluation depends on how one views the nature and dynamics of systems change and the challenges facing the world going forward. In this regard, innovation scholar Thomas Homer-Dixon (2006) has summarized the future succinctly:

In coming decades our resource and environmental problems will become progressively harder to solve; our companies, organizations, and societies will therefore have to become steadily more complex to produce good solutions; and the solutions they produce—whether technological or institutional—will have to be more complex too. (p. 251)

Developmental evaluation operates in that complex space.

Top-down dissemination of best practices is appropriate for simple space (high certainty about what to do and high agreement that it should be done) and is accompanied by fidelity-monitoring evaluation that judges the extent to which replications are fully implemented and true to a validated best practice model. Bottom-up change processes are supported by participatory evaluation approaches that support grassroots engagement, often assuming that local people know best what to do—a simple formulation, though things quickly become complicated where subgroups of local people are in conflict about what to do. Developmental evaluation offers a middle path: navigating, sorting out, making sense of, and adapting effective principles to local context under conditions of complexity, when it's not clear what should be done because of inadequate knowledge, the large number of interdependent factors that have to be taken into account, the complex adaptive nature of the system where innovation is occurring, and disagreements among various stakeholders about how to proceed and where to place priorities. Developmental evaluation acknowledges, tracks, and takes into account knowledge, theories, principles, and effective practices that are being disseminated and taken to scale. Developmental evaluation also acknowledges, tracks, and takes into account grassroots knowledge, indigenous theories about how the world is changed, local values and principles, and traditional practices that are part of any particular context where change is being undertaken. As these top-down and bottom-up forces inter-

sect, developmental evaluation helps find a way through the labyrinth of adaptation.

This chapter begins by examining the major competing perspectives on how the world is changed and then offers an in-depth example of how adaptation based on effective principles (rather than replication of best practices) unfolds in a local context. Distinguishing between adaptation of effective principles versus replication of best practices will be a central theme of this chapter.

Competing Perspectives on How the World Is Changed

In Chapter 3 I introduced Tom Henderson, a man in the middle who witnessed and experienced a lot of changes in his beloved Caribbean. He was deeply interested in how change occurs, from changing the attitudes and practices of individual farmers to changing national extension organizations and international markets. He served on World Bank, United Nations, and Food and Agriculture Organization (FAO) international teams doing agricultural extension assessments in various parts of the world. He studied competing approaches to change during his doctoral studies at the University of Wisconsin. To him these weren't just academic theories. He lived their implications when faced with the preferred models of international aid agencies and the demands they imposed on funding for agriculture programs in the Caribbean.

Tom ruminated that a worldwide battle was going on over how the world is changed, whether top-down or bottom-up. That battle has intensified today. It is at once a battle of ideas and a battle for territory in the landscape of change. Control and expenditure of billions of dollars is at stake, money from international agencies, philanthropic foundations, multinational corporations, and global initiatives involving both governments and nongovernmental organizations, often in partnership. Also at stake, and no less important, is the time, energy, and commitment of people engaged in social change.

This isn't a battle between good and evil, the world's oldest and most enduring dualism alongside us versus them. This is a battle between competing "goods," well-intentioned and deeply committed people on both sides who share the value of making the world a better place for millions who suffer from hunger, disease, violence, and poverty. Thus, the two sides are not distinguished by their goals, but by their means. They pursue opposing strategies for bringing about change. Those strategies sometimes coexist in parallel silos. And sometimes they slide past each other, or encircle and intertwine. And often they meet head-on, with a crash that leaves damage and victims.

Evaluation enters this fray as arbiter of what works. It's a needed, even a critical role. The competing claims must be carefully examined, subjected to empirical test, and judged as worthy or unworthy based on the preponderance of evidence. Evaluation is meant to play this role and aims to do so. But there's a small problem. Behind evaluation's ideal role as empirical arbiter is intense debate among evaluators about what constitutes credible evidence and *evaluation best practices*. Evaluators enter the fray mired in pervasive and long-standing biases about how to conceptualize and assess change, biases that originate in methods training, and can inadvertently but decidedly make evaluation the handmaiden of one side in the battle. Nor is the problem easily solved because most evaluators are unwitting pawns in the game of change, oblivious to serving one side of the engagement while undermining the other. Top-down evaluators who favor randomized control trials as the ideal dismiss bottom-up, participatory evaluations as soft and unscientific, not even worthy of being called evaluation research. Evaluators operating at the grassroots level and using participatory approaches wonder what universe "randomistas" live in where they think they can exercise control over the messiness of the real world and transplant their supposedly scientific findings without regard to local context. The gap in perspectives is huge and, as near as I can tell, growing.

This is old territory to some, often characterized as the "paradigms debate" in which researchers and evaluators operate from fundamentally different epistemological and ontological assumptions (Patton, 2008c, chap. 12). It can seem pretty academic. Boringly so. Stifle a yawn. But, alas, these differences matter. They affect how billions of

---

ᔕ Complementary Pairs

Top-down and bottom-up can be thought of as one of many complementary pairs such as integration–segregation, convergence–divergence, competition–cooperation, formal–informal, part–whole, and individual–collective that constitute coexisting tendencies in dynamic systems. Instead of viewing such oppositions as dichotomous and conflicting forces or choices, the notion of complementary pairs emphasizes their relationship to each other and the way in which each is necessary to understanding and making sense of the other. Top-down can't be fully understood or even inquired into without some notion of bottom-up, and vice versa. Looking at the conceptual and actual interrelationship of these contrasting dynamics instead of focusing only on their differences opens up the idea that these coexisting dynamics interact in some coordinated manner, what is called coordination dynamics. Linking two seemingly opposite ideas together invites inquiry into the "complementary pairs of coordination dynamics" and the "coordination dynamics of complementary pairs." Developmental evaluation explicitly acknowledges and negotiates the interactions between top-down and bottom-up dynamics as *complementary pairs*.

Note. See *The Complementary Nature* (Kelso & Engstrøm, 2008) and *Coordination Dynamics: Issues and Trends* (Jirsa & Kelso, 2004).

"I don't know, Zeus. Athena suggested we watch it for a few eons instead of breaking up this mess now. The increasing complexity might be entertaining to track."

Illustration by Mark M. Rogers.

dollars are spent on social change initiatives and evaluation of those initiatives. And one can't understand the niche and contribution of developmental evaluation without some appreciation of this debate, a debate about both how change occurs and how evaluation should be conducted, for the two are deeply intertwined. Old-timers, tired of the debate, may want to skip this chapter. Those of you who may wonder what all the fuss is about are invited to read on.

The Top-Down Approach

The top-down approach is epitomized by the dissemination of *best practices*, also known as *evidence-based practices*. These are standardized procedures sometimes but not always validated through randomized controlled experiments or, as second choice, quasi-experimental designs. These designs, imitating pharmaceutical and agricultural research, aim to produce the best results in addressing a particular problem, like increasing children's reading scores or growing corn in Iowa. As explained in Chapter 4, however, best practices only work in simple situations on simple problems where key causal variables can be identified, manipu-

lated, and controlled, like using mosquito nets to reduce mosquito bites and thereby reduce the spread of malaria. Best practices are recipes that prescribe exactly what to do *regardless of context*. The very designation as "best" makes them context-free. Meanwhile, the language of "best practices" has become so pervasive and the desire to be engaged in something that qualifies as a "best practice" is so politically attractive that some so-called best practices are no more than a successful local approach to a widespread problem whose enthusiasts believe that what worked in their own little pond would certainly work in other ponds, even in the ocean.

Knowledge disseminated in the form of best practices has swept like flu throughout the globe, infecting all sectors of society. Government agencies publish best practices for education, health, highways, and welfare reform. Philanthropic foundations aspire to discover, fund, and disseminate best practices. Corporations advertise that they benchmark and follow best practices. Management consultants teach best practices. Finding, validating, and promulgating best practices has become a lucrative line of business. For example, Best Practices®, LLC offers a range of services related to benchmarking and adopting best practices including a "Best Practice Database" to support *best-in-class performance*:

- Link Best Practices to Strategy Fulfillment
- Best Practice Identification Systems
- Best Practice Recognition Systems
- Communicating Best Practices
- Best Practice Knowledge Sharing Systems
- Ongoing Nurturing of Best Practices (Best Practices, 2009)

The U.S. government version of this is the What Works Clearinghouse (WWC) established in 2002 by the U.S. Department of Education's Institute of Education Sciences to provide educators, policymakers, researchers, and the public with "a central and trusted source of scientific evidence of what works in education." Evidence for what works is limited to randomized controlled trials or quasi-experimental designs. An example of a model examined by WWC is Literacy Express, a preschool curriculum for 3- to 5-year-old children. The model curriculum provides standardized units on oral language, beginning reading and math, and socioemotional development. The model includes directions for arranging the classroom, scheduling activities, managing students, teaching materials, and training staff. WWC analyzed two evaluations that met evidence standards and concluded that Literacy Express had "positive effects on print knowledge and phonological processing, [and] potentially positive effects on oral language and math" (What Works Clearinghouse, 2007).

Once validated through summative evaluation, a model is ready for dissemination and the primary issue becomes assuring *fidelity* to the model as it is adopted—and evaluating that fidelity. JUMP Math offers an example. This standardized teaching model was developed by mathematician John Mighton in 1998. By 2003 JUMP programs ran in 12 Toronto inner-city elementary schools involving more than 1,600 students. It has evolved into a classroom curriculum with a complete package of materials intended to cover all elementary school grades. The program has since been adopted in schools throughout North America and other regions of the world. For teachers and students to realize the full benefits of the approach, those who are supporting dissemination of the program want *high-fidelity implementation*. This is true for any model that gets identified as a "best practice" or an "evidence-based model" or a model validated by a review process like the What Works Clearinghouse. To evaluate fidelity is to assess adherence to the core blueprint specifications of how a model program is supposed to be implemented.

Disseminating a model is often referred to as *going-to-scale*. (The comparable research terms are "external validity" or "generalizability.") Going-to-scale means moving the model beyond its original, local setting, where it was validated, into national and international adoption. The evaluation focus in such top-down, going-to-scale dissemination of best practices is assessing adherence to the core specifications of how the model program is supposed to be implemented. Models that aim at widespread dissemination strive for careful replication; the degree to which that replication is attained is the primary implementation evaluation question. The presumption is that rigorous adherence to a validated model will produce the same outcomes as those attained when the model was evaluated and validated summatively. That presumption must be evaluated by measuring outcomes in new settings where the model has been adopted. This approach continues to be championed by the U.S. Department of Education Institute of Education Sciences, which, once again in 2009, when final rules for the department's $650 million Investing in Innovation Fund were announced, advocated limiting grants to interventions validated with randomized control trials and then using further randomized controlled trials to evaluate validated models as they are replicated throughout the country.

Top-down approaches derive in part from the experimental research paradigm just reviewed and in part from the appeal of models of successful global franchises in the private sector. I've talked with many philanthropic funders, policymakers, and social entrepreneurs who clearly have something like a McDonald's restaurants franchise model in mind, consciously or unconsciously, when they dream of creating a widely admired school curriculum and taking it to scale, or replicating a successful antipoverty intervention worldwide. They are sometimes aware of the shadow side of the McDonald's story, that Ray Kroc used predatory business practices to force the McDonald brothers out of the fast-food business, that he was accused of being unscrupulous, and that for many McDonald's has come to symbolize Americanization and homogenization worldwide, and is a target of derision in debates about obesity and corporate ethics. Still, for social innovators there's a glimmer in the eye in imagining such success, not in service of profit, but for bettering the human condition. And rather than dreaming of becoming the antipoverty program version of McDonald's worldwide, or replicating Sam Walton's success with Wal-Mart by creating and disseminating an efficient, effective, and low-cost health clinic model around the globe, they may call forth the success of Nobel Peace Prize–winner Muhammad Yunus, who founded Grameen Bank and has made microfinance a worldwide model for distributing small loans to people in poverty. So what factors make for successful dissemination of best practices?

Best Practices for Replicating Best Practices

Szulanski and Winter (2002), in an influential *Harvard Business Review* article, compared successful and unsuccessful initiatives to replicate best practices in major businesses. They called replication "getting it right the second time," or third time, or fourth time, the first time having been when the best practice was validated. They identified five best practices for successful replication of best practices.

1. Be sure that the practice to be replicated has been carefully validated and is worth copying (in evaluation terms, it has received a positive summative evaluation).

2. Procure a detailed template that includes all elements of the best practice being replicated (the recipe for success).

3. Copy the best practice *exactly*. EXACTLY!

4. Never make changes, even minor ones, until after you have had success with the replicated practice and know precisely how it works.

5. Retain the original template so that you can return to it if any changes you make

---

∽ *Going to Scale McDonald's Style*

The corporate exemplar of going-to-scale is McDonald's restaurants. McDonald's began in 1940 as a single restaurant run by brothers Dick and Mac McDonald in San Bernardino, California. They created what they called the "Speedee Service System." Their success led them to franchise their model. Ray Kroc opened the ninth McDonald's franchise in Des Plaines, Illinois, in 1955. He subsequently bought out the McDonald brothers and began going to scale worldwide, making sure that any McDonald's anywhere in the United States, and subsequently anywhere in the world, followed the same standardized practices to produce the same tasting hamburgers. McDonald's expanded to 31,000 restaurants in 120 countries and territories around the world, serving an estimated 50 million customers daily and employing more than 1.5 million people. The site of the McDonald brothers' original restaurant is now a monument.

diminish results (which they consider likely if you are presumptuous and unwise enough to mess with the original recipe).

In reporting their findings and providing this guidance, they emphasized that most best practice replication attempts fail because those implementing the replication start tinkering. They admonish: *Copy best practices exactly.* One purpose of high-fidelity evaluation is to catch tinkerers early and get them back on the primrose path of exact replication, hopefully before they've completely screwed up the best practice model. *Copy best practices exactly.* This is the perspective that has permeated government, philanthropic, and nonprofit efforts at spreading best practices. This is also the basis of opposition to developmental evaluation. It's important to understand the logic and pervasiveness of the top-down best practices approach because the dominance of this kind of thinking is a central feature of the context for developmental evaluation.

The Center for What Works focuses on benchmarking and best practices for nonprofits generally. The Cochrane Collaboration, based in England, focuses on evidence-based health care globally and bills itself as "the reliable source of evidence in health care." The Campbell Collaboration, headquartered in Oslo, conducts systematic reviews on the evidence supporting social interventions in education, crime and justice, and social welfare. The Canadian Health Services Research Foundation supports the evidence-informed management of Canada's health care system by facilitating dissemination of knowledge about research-validated practices. The prestigious and influential organization Public/Private Ventures promotes "Strategies for Effective Program Replication" (Summerville & Raley, 2009). The U.S. Department of Health and Human Services supports Evidence-Based Practice Centers that synthesize and disseminate scientific evidence about effective health

care. The private, nonprofit Coalition for Evidence-Based Policy has undertaken the Top Tier Evidence Initiative to identify and certify federal programs and interventions that meet the standard of using randomized experiments to show sizable, sustained benefits (Government Accountability Office, 2009). The What Works Clearinghouse focuses on validating evidence-based educational programs. The International Initiative for Impact Evaluation (2009) brings together an extensive network of partners to support "the production and use of evidence from rigorous impact evaluations for policy decisions that improve social and economic development programs in low- and middle-income countries." Funders of the International Initiative for Impact Evaluation include the Bill and Melinda Gates Foundation, the Hewlett Foundation, the UN Foundation, the African Development Bank, CARE, and Save the Children (USA), among many others. The What Works Working Group, operating under the auspices of the Center for Global Development's Global Health Policy Research Network, seeks "proven successes in global health," and is also funded by the Bill and Melinda Gates Foundation.

The examples above are a mere sampling of the prestigious and powerful organizations devoting huge resources to the search for and dissemination of best practices. They share the top-down, going-to-scale theory of how the world is changed summarized in Exhibit 6.1. Evaluation is front and center in the campaign to discover and spread best practices because evaluation is the source of evidence that such practices work and deserve to be crowned as *best.* (Later in this chapter, Exhibit 6.4 presents a graphic of bottom-up change and Exhibit 6.5 presents a graphic of developmental evaluation facilitating action in the middle where top-down and bottom-up forces intersect and sometimes collide.)

The strengths of the top-down model are also the sources of its weaknesses. High fi-

EXHIBIT 6.1 **Top-Down, Going-to-Scale Theory of How the World Is Changed**

1. Identify a promising intervention (e.g., theory-based model).

2. Standardize and stabilize the intervention (formative evaluation).

3. Rigorously test the intervention: one or more summative evaluations using randomized controlled trials and quasi-experimental methods; meta-analysis of multiple such evaluations (summative evaluation; meta-analysis).

4. Summative evaluation and meta-analysis results are peer-reviewed by qualified researchers for validation as an evidence-based best practice model (scholarly, credible peer review evaluation).

5. Publish and disseminate the findings about the model (consensual validation as findings spread).

6. Policymakers and funders support replication of the model throughout the country or world, advocating and financing taking it to scale.

7. Practitioners and adopters in many organizations and communities implement the model *exactly as tested and validated* (monitoring and evaluation of adoption).

8. Evaluators independently monitor fidelity of implementation (fidelity of implementation evaluation).

9. Participants in the intervention receive and benefit from the model, attaining and manifesting intended outcomes (outcomes evaluation).

10. People are helped. Indicators of social, health, educational, and/or economic well-being improve (impact evaluation).

delity can become rigidity. The focus on replication reduces sensitivity to context. Things that work quite well at one scale may not work well at a larger scale, just as successfully crossing a large lake in a sailboat doesn't mean you are ready to cross the Pacific Ocean. Indeed, one of the central issues addressed by developmental evaluation in the muddled middle where top-down and bottom-up approaches to change meet is how scale adds layers and levels of complexity to the processes of social innovation. Top-down models of change require a high degree of knowledge about the variables and factors that lead to change and a high degree of control over those variables and factors (the simple situation in the degree of uncertainty/degree of conflict matrix of Chapter 4, Exhibit 4.3). Going to scale can increase logarithmically the factors that affect success while simultaneously reducing control over those factors.

With the power, dominance, and simple seductiveness of the top-down best practices approach as context—and a formidable context it is—let's turn to alternative wisdom about how the world is changed, the view that major change requires adaptation of effective principles not replication of prescriptive models.

Adaptation versus Replication: Principles for Developmental Evaluation

Lisbeth Schorr (1997), as director of Harvard's Project on Effective Interventions, has made what may be the most important, comprehensive, and insightful analysis of the idea of "Spreading What Works beyond the Hothouse." She found that innovative demonstration projects, even those aimed at major systems change, often innovate only at the margins and thus may serve as no more than a safety valve by releasing pressure for change without threatening the status quo. In some cases, an effective demonstration of a new way of doing something has the un-intended consequence of alerting the status quo to a potential innovation, allowing resisters to figure out how to undermine any effort to expand the innovation, with such an increase in organized resistance amounting to a change in context. Of particular importance to developmental evaluation when involved with efforts to go to scale, she found that "the techniques that work to beat the system [make the innovation successful] when the model program is small and marginal can no longer help when it is time to expand and break through the Ceiling on Scale. . . . Efforts to reach greater numbers bring greater visibility, and greater visibility creates new demands to comply with old rules. That is why innovative programs

---

～ A Plea for Methodological Diversity and Appropriateness

Lisbeth B. Schorr is a senior fellow at the Center for the Study of Social Policy, a lecturer in social medicine at Harvard University, and the author of two important books on social innovation and change (1989, 1997). She offered this assessment of the current state of evaluation in The Chronicle of Philanthropy.

How evidence is defined will determine whether the demands for evidence will strengthen or undermine the nation's capacity to respond effectively to social needs.

The definition most aggressively promoted today holds that approaches to solving social problems should be considered evidence-based only when they have been found effective by research methods involving random assignment of participants to experimental and control groups. . . .

The prevailing definition of evidence is so narrow that its continued ascendancy will inevitably reduce the chances of expanding promising strategies and developing effective new responses to urgent social needs.

Unless we stop ranking possible solutions to problems by their evaluation methodology and find ways to judge how well they accomplish important goals, we will be left with a seriously impoverished tool kit. If government agencies and private grant makers, afraid of being considered not rigorous, unscientific, or wasteful, choose to support only those efforts that meet the randomized-trial test, we will be robbed of:

- Good programs that do not lend themselves to random-assignment evaluations.
- Reforms that are deeper and wider than individual programs.
- Innovations of all kinds.

We risk losing programs that do not lend themselves to random-assignment evaluations because such programs feature multiple interactive components and significant front-line flexibility. And they work best when they can be tailored to unique and changing local conditions and can emphasize hard-to-measure ingredients like respectful trusting relationships.

Note. From Schorr (2009, pp. 33, 37).

cannot grow and thrive in an unchanged system" (p. 27).

Schorr has identified several critical mistakes commonly made in efforts to take innovations to scale. A decade after her provocative analysis these classic mistakes are as widespread as ever. The problem begins, she found, with the mental models people have about replication: "franchising, mass production, and biomedical science turn out to be misleading analogs; we underestimated the importance of local variation, local ownership, and the subtleties of effective interventions; and we ignored the critical role of the external environment" (1997, pp. 27–28). She concluded:

• We didn't realize that people-centered interventions can't be turned out like widgets. Most front-line staff in successful programs can testify that while they operate on a body of shared knowledge and skills, a significant portion of what they do cannot be standardized. The good ones are forever responding to contingencies. . . . The most promising interventions rely on at least some components that change from one site to the next, and that evolve with considerable variations over time.

• We didn't realize that local people may have to reinvent parts of the wheel. Even when local people set out to replicate someone else's intervention, they find they have to adapt it to local conditions to make it work. Veterans of successful community-based programs agree that people implementing programs in new settings must be able in fundamental ways to make them their own.

• We underestimated the subtleties of effective interventions. Even the best practitioners often can't give usable descriptions of what they do. . . .

• We failed to see that you can't grow roses in concrete. Human service reformers and educators alike thought the challenge was to develop new ideas, not to change institutions. They assumed an innovation or a "good product" would become part of a mainstream system because of its merit, unconstrained by the system's funding, rule making, standard setting, and accountability requirements—all of which are likely to be inconsistent with the innovation. (pp. 28–29)

Schorr (1997) suggests that the failure to appreciate the importance of context, which is the unifying theme in these failures to achieve scale, derives from oversimplistic ideas about how replication works based upon dissemination of new agricultural products to farmers and naive efforts to follow private-sector franchising models

> where context is simpler. In the private sector, the context is the market, and profit is the measure of success. Rules and regulations may intrude, but they stop short of prescribing the very essence of what the enterprise does and how it does it. By contrast, human services, education, and community building are shaped by highly complex systems that specify what you may or may not do. (pp. 29–30)

So, Schorr's astute analysis highlights once again that complexity emerges as a difference maker. I find that the mental model common among those who use the language of replication and generalization is that of empirically generalizing from a sample to a population, a mechanistic procedure that involves adhering to statistical rules and at least has the good sense to suggest confidence intervals and error calculations that make explicit the reality that even statistical generalizations are governed by laws of probability and making the transition from sample to population is less than certain. Indeed, a long-standing concern about generalizing from experimental findings (the issue of external validity) is that the greater the controls introduced in the experiment to achieve internal validity (to validate that the intervention caused the measured outcome), the greater the threat to external validity (generalization and replication) because the experimental controls create artificial conditions that will not pertain in the real world. The debate about the conditions under which research findings can be generalized is relevant and instructive because it is the larger context for considering the extent to which evaluation findings about effective program models can be generalized. The adaptive focus of develop-

～ Advice from an Experienced Developmental Evaluator

Mark Cabaj is executive director of Vibrant Communities, which assists people to build strong communities through local action. He is a founding Principal of Tamarack—An Institute for Community Engagement, based in Waterloo, Ontario. He lives in Edmonton, Alberta, and has written extensively about community development issues (Cabaj, 2007, 2009a, 2009b). Mark participated in a series of developmental evaluation workshops we did together in 2005–2006 and we collaborated on a developmental evaluation of a social innovation collaboration initiative. Here are Mark's latest thoughts and advice.

1. *Developmental evaluation is a specific niche.* The number of situations in which developmental evaluation is appropriate is less than I had originally understood, but its value is much greater than I ever anticipated. I can only imagine how much better our evaluation work could have been in the past had we not used "formative" and "summative" approaches to what were clearly "developmental" situations: situations of high turbulence, adaptations of models from elsewhere, in the exploration phase of an intervention, or in environments of high uncertainty and multiple stakeholders with diverse values, interests, and positions.

2. *Developmental evaluation involves facilitating group engagement.* At the heart of developmental evaluation is group engagement, that is, framing *what* a group is trying to change and *how*, quickly surfacing and rigorously *making sense* of sometimes very ambiguous data, and doing so in *real time* to help people make day-to-day decisions.

3. *Developmental evaluation is situational, responsive, and emergent.* If you crave evaluation templates, formulas, and frameworks, you will be frustrated with developmental evaluation. Developmental evaluation work is unavoidably situational, focused on asking the right questions at the right time, developing practical evaluative methods that take into account who needs what information, when, and for what purpose. Moreover, given the emergent nature of most developmental situations, with changing contexts, new players, and new learnings, the questions and evaluative processes are apt to evolve as well. I suspect that people who are comfortable with modern jazz are more likely to feel comfortable with this reality than those who prefer meticulously interpreted and orchestrated sounds of a symphony by Mozart.

4. *Developmental evaluation is not for everyone. It requires ongoing professional development.* I am not sure that just anyone can become a good developmental evaluator. I have met very experienced evaluators who struggle to redefine their role from "external expert" to a participant in a developmental enterprise. Many can't seem to shake methodological preferences that meet the gold standard of academia or policymaking, but are unrealistic in real-life settings. Their instinct is to press social innovators for clarity about goals and models before proceeding when *reduced fuzziness* can be achieved only through action and experimentation. Alternatively, I have encountered people with a developmental mindset and spirit, but who lack the domain knowledge of the issue at hand, or lack research skills, and have no desire to build up their capacity in these areas. I know that I feel someone serious about developmental evaluation—and I am beginning to count myself in that category—should treat it like a craft and commit themselves to improving their capacity as a developmental evaluator over the long term.

5. *Make sure that the evaluative situation is developmental.* This is a big lesson. Making sure that the evaluative situation is developmental—and not formative or summative—is a necessary but insufficient condition for a good developmental evaluation assignment. The participants in a developmental enterprise have to be committed to making decisions guided by data (i.e., testing out how their beliefs, ideas, and hunches play out in reality), capable of investing time and energy to get involved in *sense making* of data when it comes, comfortable with ambiguity, and okay with being periodically challenged by the developmental evaluator. It's important to assess whether these conditions exist before an assignment, to strengthen them throughout the process, and to *part ways* when they don't.

(cont.)

6. *The trickiest parts of developmental evaluation for me?* Let me give you three:

- First, constantly staying on top of the evolving developments—which are often happening all over the place and in unpredictable ways—and adjusting the evaluation processes used to make sure they are still relevant. There is no cruise control on a developmental evaluation assignment. The road changes all the time.

- Next, managing boundaries. I love being part of the team developing a new model, program, or strategy but have to be on guard to make sure that I focus on my job of making sure people are being *evaluative* when making decisions. I find myself periodically getting involved in the actual development work itself (e.g., making recommendations on options, stating preferences) rather than assisting the social innovators to carry out this work. Managing the boundaries between these roles is important and difficult.

- Third, being diligent about recognizing what is—and what is not—a developmental evaluation situation. Not every situation is a developmental one. Some situations are formative and summative as well. Some situations have aspects of all three. Some morph into each other over time, for example, a developmental situation evolving into a formative one. I need to constantly pay attention to whether the subject of the evaluation is being crafted (developmental), refined (formative), or judged worthy of sustaining or scaling up (summative).

mental evaluation and the credibility of developmental evaluation processes and findings depend in part on an understanding of these issues, so let's take a moment to look at how some evaluation pioneers have sorted out and dealt with the challenges of generalizing. I review these classic reframings of the issue both because I find them still relevant and to acknowledge that they have shaped deeply my approach to developmental evaluation. In connecting theory, methodology, and practice, it helps to know the theory and methodology, which is what we now peruse. Then we'll take on practice.

Reframing What It Means to Generalize: Conceptual and Methodological Adaptations to Inform Use of Developmental Evaluation Findings

Generalizations decay. At one time a conclusion describes the existing situation well, at a later time it accounts for rather little variance, and ultimately is valid only as history.
—LEE J. CRONBACH (1975, p. 122)

Lee J. Cronbach (1975, 1982, 1988) was one of the major figures in psychometrics and research methodology, and a pioneer in adapting research methods to serve the realities of decision makers. He recognized that the purposes of research and evaluation are different in important ways, especially since real-world decision makers don't have the luxury of waiting for definitive research findings before taking action. He devoted considerable attention to the issue of generalizations. He was a central figure in debates about the virtues and limitations of experimental designs for generating practical results that could be widely disseminated and taken to scale. He concluded that social phenomena are too variable and context-bound to permit straightforward empirical generalizations. He offered this advice:

Instead of making generalization the ruling consideration in our research, I suggest that we reverse our priorities. An observer collecting data in a particular situation is in a position to appraise a practice or proposition in that setting, observing effects in context. In trying to describe and account for what happened, he will give attention to whatever variables were controlled, but he will give equally careful attention to uncontrolled conditions, to personal characteristics, and to events that occurred during treatment and measurement. As he goes from situation to situation, his first task is to describe and interpret the effect anew in each locale, perhaps taking into account factors unique to that locale or series of events. . . . When we give proper weight to local conditions, any generalization is a working hypothesis, not a conclusion. (1975, pp. 124–125)

I think this advice captures well the task for the developmental evaluator when supporting efforts aimed at taking an innovation to scale. Pay particular attention to how an innovation unfolds within a particular context. In trying to describe and account for what emerges, give attention to whatever factors were controlled as well as to uncontrolled conditions, important personal characteristics of those involved, and significant events that occur during the innovation and scaling-up processes. As the developmental evaluator goes from situation to situation, his or her first task is to describe and interpret the innovation anew in each locale, perhaps taking into account factors unique to that locale or series of events. Give proper weight to local conditions and treat any generalization as a working hypothesis, not a conclusion. Excellent advice from one of the best.

Another evaluation pioneer whose insights and advice deserve the attention of developmental evaluators is Robert Stake (1978, 1995, 2000, 2010). This master of case study methods worries that researchers and evaluators are too preoccupied with making generalizations, indeed, so focused on generalizing that they fail to do justice to the specific cases before them. He admonishes evaluators to do a good job of "particularization" before looking for patterns across cases. He quotes William Blake on the subject: "To generalize is to be an idiot. To particularize is the lone distinction of merit. General knowledges are those that idiots possess." Tell us what you really think, Bob. Stake continued:

Generalization may not be all that despicable, but particularization does deserve praise. To know particulars fleetingly, of course, is to

know next to nothing. What becomes useful understanding is a full and thorough knowledge of the particular, recognizing it also in new and foreign contexts. That knowledge is a form of generalization too, not scientific induction but naturalistic generalization, arrived at by recognizing the similarities of objects and issues in and out of context and by sensing the natural covariations of happenings. To generalize this way is to be both intuitive and empirical, and not idiotic. (1978, p. 6)

Stake calls case-based pattern detection *naturalistic generalization* in contrast to the more mechanical generalizations derived from tightly controlled experiments. To arrive at naturalistic generalizations requires both data and *reasoning*. The interpretation and meaning of observed patterns come from multiple encounters, and are modified and reinforced by repeated encounters. Moreover, interpretation and meaning emerge from social interactions between people looking together at observed patterns. Stake's approach in this regard recalls and is consistent with the social adaptive processes of coevolution and co-creation between the social innovator and the developmental evaluator discussed in Chapter 5. Stake explains:

In life itself, this [naturalistic generalization] occurs seldom to the individual alone but in the presence of others. In a social process, together they bend, spin, consolidate, and enrich their understandings. We come to know what has happened partly in terms of what others reveal as their experience. The case researcher emerges from one social experience, the observation, to choreograph another, the report. Knowledge is socially constructed, so we constructivists believe, and, in their experiential and contextual accounts, case study researchers assist in the construction of knowledge. (2000, p. 442)

This view of how we understand and act in the world is at sharp odds with the top-down view of knowledge creation and dissemination in which the results of tightly controlled experiments are spread through high-fidelity replication. Stake's naturalistic generalization approach evokes an image of the developmental evaluator and the social innovator looking at patterns together, making sense of them, deciding what they mean, and using those understandings to adapt what is done to new settings and contexts, the very process that Lisbeth Schorr identified as most effective in spreading innovations.

The voice and insights of a third evaluation pioneer deserve to be included in this walk down memory lane through the wisdom of great evaluation thinkers, those who have pondered at length and in great depth about the challenges of creating general knowledge and taking effective interventions to scale. Egon Guba (1978) emphasized the importance of staying open and observant in moving from one situation to another:

> In the spirit of naturalistic inquiry [evaluators] should regard each possible generalization only as a working hypothesis, to be tested again in the next encounter and again in the encounter after that. For the naturalistic inquiry evaluator, premature closure is a cardinal sin, and tolerance of ambiguity a virtue. (p. 70)

Egon Guba and his intellectual partner and wife, Yvonna Lincoln, emphasized appreciation of and attention to context as a natural limit to naturalistic generalizations. They asked, "What can a generalization be except an assertion that is context free? [Yet] *it is virtually impossible to imagine any human behavior that is not heavily mediated by the context in which it occurs*" (Guba & Lincoln, 1981, p. 62, emphasis in the original). They wrote: "The trouble with generalizations is that they don't apply to particulars" (p. 110). To deal with this "trouble," they proposed substituting the concepts "transferability" and "fittingness" for generalization, especially when dealing with qualitative findings, but the concepts they offer have wider applicability.

The degree of *transferability* is a direct function of the *similarity* between the two contexts, what we shall call "*fittingness*." Fittingness is defined as degree of congruence between sending and receiving contexts. If context A and context B are "sufficiently" congruent, then working hypotheses from the sending originating context may be applicable in the receiving context. (Lincoln & Guba, 1985, p. 124; original emphasis)

Extrapolation

These evaluation pioneers shared a skepticism about mechanical generalizations from experimental designs and emphasized instead the importance of thinking about, contextualizing, and making reason-informed judgments about the relevance of extrapolating discoveries from one time and place to another. *Extrapolation* is the key idea here. Extrapolation implies reasoning about findings. Cronbach founded and directed the Stanford Evaluation Consortium in 1974, a group of scholars and students who thought about evaluation as a "novel political institution" (Cronbach & Associates, 1980, p. x). On the one hand, they found little value in experimental designs that were so focused on carefully controlling cause and effect (high internal validity) that the findings were largely irrelevant beyond that highly controlled experimental situation (low external validity). On the other hand, they were equally concerned about entirely idiosyncratic case studies that yield little of use beyond the case study setting. They were also skeptical that highly specific empirical findings would be meaningful under new conditions. They suggested instead that designs balance depth and breadth, realism and control, so as to permit reasonable "extrapolation" (pp. 231–235).

Unlike the usual meaning of the term "generalization," an *extrapolation* clearly connotes that one has gone beyond the narrow confines of the data to *think about other applications of the findings*. Extrapolations are modest speculations on the likely applicability of findings to other situations under similar, but not identical, conditions. Extrapolations are logical, thoughtful, case-derived, and problem-oriented rather than only statistical and probabilistic. Extrapolations can be particularly useful when based on information-rich samples and designs, that is, studies that produce relevant information carefully targeted to specific concerns about both the present and the future. Users of evaluation, for example, will usually expect evaluators to thoughtfully extrapolate from their findings in the sense of pointing out *lessons learned* and potential applications to future efforts.

Interocular Significance

Let's bring one final evaluation pioneer in to shed light on how to think about replications. In his classic reflections on *Hard-Won Lessons in Program Evaluation*, Michael Scriven (1993), who gave us the formative–summative distinction, took on the misinterpretation and misuse of statistical significance as a basis for deciding to replicate an innovation. He used the evaluation of the popular children's educational television show *Sesame Street* as his example, but his point was more generic. I quote him at length because of the significance, not statistical but substantive, of where he ends up.

> Establishing statistical significance is the easy part of establishing significance. . . .
>
> [T]he "Sesame Street" evaluation, even though biased in the direction of positive results, only established a trivial difference between the experimental and control groups; but the size of these groups was so large—thousands of pupils—that this tiny difference was statistically significant, and in favor of the group viewing the program. It was a real difference, but for $7 million it was truly insignificant. Yet, the evaluation report did not mention the absolute size of the difference; it only gave the extent of the statistical significance. In those days, and perhaps even now among many people, that was the only cachet that counted.

Size is one way to statistical significance, but it often gets in the way of good evaluation and good development. . . . [A] set of well-planned, well-developed, and well-followed-up small evaluations is almost certainly better than a large-scale evaluation of a multisite project.

If we are interested in real significance, we ignore little differences such as in the "Sesame Street" case for another reason besides their negligible cost-effectiveness. We ignore them because, although they are very likely real, *they are very unlikely to hold up in replications.* Fred Mosteller, the great applied statistician, was fond of saying that he did not care much for statistically significant differences, he was more interested in *interocular differences*, the differences that hit us between the eyes. He thought that the function of statistical significance was to help identify the effects that might be refined to the point where they showed really significant, that is, interocular differences. (pp. 70–71; emphasis added)

Seeking interocular significance. Extrapolating. Particularizing and contextualizing. Making naturalistic generalizations. Adapting innovations. These are methodological principles that we can use to inform effective, useful, credible, and meaningful developmental practice. I have brought forward these insights from evaluation pioneers because their work is too little appreciated and honored today when only the latest hot idea and research assertion garners attention. These classics, these golden oldies, remain relevant, I believe. The insights of Cronbach, Guba, Schorr, Scriven, Stake, and Lincoln about how evaluation findings in one place can inform innovations in another place can be extrapolated to inform developmental evaluations conducted in the muddled middle of social change. Evaluation history is the context for current practice, and I want to acknowledge and honor that context in the form of the ideas from these pioneers. What they point to, I believe, is the importance of distinguishing *best practices versus effective principles.*

Best Practices versus Effective Principles

A model is not something to be replicated but rather it is a demonstration of the feasibility of a principle.
—JOHN DEWEY (1859–1952), American philosopher

The metaphor for best practices in simple situations is the recipe. The metaphor for dealing with complexity is parenting. (See Exhibit 4.6 in Chapter 4 for elaboration of these distinctions and metaphors.) Parenting is highly variable and situational. There can be no recipe or set of specific rules. But there can be and are effective principles, like "nurture each child's uniqueness." Notice the language: *effective* principles, not *best* principles, because there is no way of establishing "best." Best practices are specific and highly prescriptive. *Add one-quarter teaspoon of salt.* Principles provide guidance. *Season to taste.* Some self-appointed authorities offer best practices about parenting. *Limit children's television viewing to no more than 1 hour each night.* The corresponding principle would be: *Monitor and set limits on children's television viewing so that children are involved in a range of development-enhancing activities.* The precise nature of these limits will depend on the child, the family, the day of the week (school days vs. weekends), the season (holiday season vs. school season), and what shows the child (and family) watch. The absurdity of a *best practice* for television-related parenting is the fact that most of the world's children don't have televisions. So right away, a contextual limitation is required: yet even families that have televisions and consider the amount and content of television viewing an issue will be different enough that no single prescription can be reasonably formulated and applied to all.

Effective principles have to be interpreted and adapted to context. Best-selling management books like *In Search of Excellence* (Peters & Waterman, 1982), *Good to Great* (Collins, 2001), *The Seven Habits of Highly Effective People* (Covey, 2004), *Lessons in Leadership* (Drucker, 1998), and *The Five Most Important Questions* (Drucker, 2008) offer effective principles, not best practices. Not incidentally, these works are based on qualitative case studies (Patton, 2002), not randomized control experiments.

Principles provide guidance for action in the face of complexity. Exhibit 6.2 (on page 168) contrasts examples of best practice statements with effective principle statements. Developmental evaluation can assist innovators in identifying, applying, and adapting effective principles. To see how that occurs, let's turn the kaleidoscope away from top-down change based on best practices and look at change from the other end.

From the Grassroots to the Adaptive Middle

Bottom-up change begins at the grassroots, building on local knowledge and adapting to local conditions. The story of Steve Rothschild's creation of Twin Cities Rise! that opened Chapter 2 is an example of a bottom-up social innovation, one that Rothschild would eventually like to take to scale. But the program was designed and based on principles not best practices, principles like being purpose-driven, market-driven, results-driven, and accountability-driven (Rothschild, 2010). In the next section we're going to look at a different bottom-up change process, the experience of adapting a national model locally based on principles rather than pursuing high-fidelity replication. Bottom-up adaptation emphasizes the importance of buy-in among those who must identify and implement changes as well as those who are the targets of change. Buy-in comes from understanding, involvement, and a sense of ownership of the processes of change within a local context but informed by more general principles, what Stake called naturalistic generalizations and

EXHIBIT 6.2 Best Practices versus Effective Principles

Best practices are specific prescriptions (recipes) about what to do. In contrast, principles provide guidance that must be interpreted, applied, and adapted situationally in context. Evaluation of the dissemination of best practices focuses on validating high-fidelity adherence to the best practices model. Evaluation of dissemination of effective principles focuses on capturing contextual interpretations and adaptations, assessing their effects and consequences, and feeding back the findings to inform ongoing principles-based adaptation—the niche of developmental evaluation.

Focus of action	Best practice prescription	Effective principle guidance
Cooking	Add ¼ teaspoon of salt.	Season to taste.
Time management	Set aside the last hour of the workday to respond to nonurgent e-mails.	Distinguish urgent from nonurgent e-mails and manage e-mail time accordingly.
Investing	For individual small investors, own only three diversified mutual funds and no more than 10 individual stocks, which is all a small investor needs and can manage.	For individual small investors, own as few or as many mutual funds and stocks as you can understand, regularly monitor, and reasonably manage.
Staff meetings	Start each week with a staff meeting of no more than 1 hour.	Hold staff meetings at regular intervals and as needed based on the nature of the staff and the purpose of staff meetings.
Education	Every primary school-age child should read at least 15 minutes a day.	Children should read regularly and consistently based on their interests and ability.
Exercise	Engage in 30 minutes of aerobic exercise every day.	Create a regular exercise regimen that is sustainable to meet your fitness and health goals given your age and lifestyle.
Evaluation	Deliver the final report by the date specified in the contract or terms of reference.	Target delivery of the findings to be useful for informing important decisions and actions. Monitor emergent issues that may influence and change the timing of when findings will be most useful to primary intended users.

Cronbach called extrapolations. These are the adaptive principles that Lisbeth Schorr (1997) documented as effective for spreading innovations.

For those with lots of grassroots experience, the story and example that follow will be quite familiar, perhaps painfully so. But I regularly encounter students, funders, and policymakers who have only the vaguest notion of what grassroots change actually involves. In the interests of full disclosure,

some who read and provided feedback on this chapter responded that the example went on too long, offered too much detail, and was too contextually specific. Just *get to the point*, they said. From my perspective, the story is the point. This is the show-don't-tell part of the book, though at the urging of reviewers I still do more telling than I'd like. Still, people respond differently to stories. I understand that. You may get lost in the details, or decide that the context of this story isn't relevant to your world, or perhaps you just get bored. That's fine. That's important to know. It may mean that you're not well suited for developmental evaluation, because the work involves lots of contextual details and sense making. But that's your call. Mine is to share what I consider an important and illuminative story. Work with me here, people. Let's go to the grassroots.

Damiano: A Story of Evolution and Adaptation Where Local Needs and Initiatives Intersect with National Trends

For 20 years, Jean Gornick worked with people in poverty in northeastern Minnesota. She directed the Damiano Center in the Central Hillside neighborhood of Duluth. Damiano began operation as a soup kitchen in March, 1982. The 85,000 residents of Duluth faced tough times. Taconite mining, critical to the economy, was in steep decline. The regional farm economy was in crisis with four- and five-generation family farms going under. The local Air Force base, a major employer, was closed, as was a regional pizza headquarters and a production plant. The unemployment rate hit 15%. Local churches responded to what religious leaders perceived as an emergency situation by opening a *temporary soup kitchen*, promising "It will be closed as soon as it is no longer needed."

More than a quarter-century later, that time has not yet come. A crisis response to temporary needs emerged to become a permanent program in an ongoing, much-valued community-based organization. In 2008, the soup kitchen served over 91,000 meals. The soup kitchen became the core of the Damiano Center, a name derived from the Church of San Damiano in Assisi, Italy, birthplace of Saint Francis, who was renowned for his dedication to helping the poor. The story of the Damiano Center is one of emergence, ongoing adaptation, and responding to new situations, needs, and opportunities. It is a story of develop-

ment from the bottom up in response to local needs while reacting to and riding national trends. Understanding the view from the trenches, with Jean Gornick as our guide, will help us understand how national models are sometimes adapted as they are implemented locally. Gornick didn't think of herself as a social innovator trying to create something new. Quite the contrary—she was usually struggling just to keep programs operating. But that necessity included a lot of invention, which took the form of local adaptation of others' models. I am including parts of the Damiano story here to provide a real example of bottom-up adaptive development. There is even some developmental evaluation along the way.

Admittedly, Damiano's developmental adaptations occurred without an official developmental evaluator. Yes, it's painful to acknowledge, but sometimes (and *only* sometimes) good things happen without (or even in spite of) formal evaluation consultation. But, though she didn't call what she was doing developmental evaluation, she was doing it. And that's another reason I'm telling this tale, because it's an example of internal staff systematically experimenting and examining the results of what they tried, and making adjustments accordingly. You don't need a developmental evaluator to do developmental evaluation. Indeed, one of the most common reactions I get to my presentations and workshops on developmental evaluation is, "That's what I've been doing, but didn't have a name for it. Thanks for giving it a name and rationale." So, on with the story.

By the mid-1990s, Damiano had been serving meals for over a decade, but the environment and context were changing, as were the needs of those in poverty. Welfare reform became a national political mandate throughout the United States. At the center of welfare reform were new time limits on eligibility for welfare and new requirements for work. The Damiano Center joined a collaboration of antipoverty organizations that focused on creating new employment opportunities. Out of that collaboration, Damiano converted its soup kitchen into a training program for restaurant cooks, a program they called Opportunities Cooking. This new initiative, begun formally at Damiano in 1998, was an adaptation of a widely disseminated national Community Kitchens model. What we're going to track here is what happened to that national model as it was adapted by Gornick and her staff in Duluth.

The Community Kitchens model originated in Washington, DC, where it was highly successful in combining food service to the hungry (running a "soup kitchen") with training low-income people for jobs as cooks. In support of taking the model to scale, the National Community Kitchens network was created with some 50 participating programs across the United States. The website has a "Best Practices" menu, but what it offers is not a recipe of required implementation steps and criteria but advice and street wisdom (principles) from the network of those operating kitchens in their own communities (National Community Kitchens, 2009).

The story of Opportunities Cooking in Duluth is one of bottom-up emergence, nonlinear dynamics, and adaptation based on effective principles of community engagement. A small initial action reverberated into ripples of ever wider reaction and response. Here's how it happened. Gornick got an "out-of-the-blue" call from a Western Lake Superior Sanitary District staff member inviting her to a national conference being held in Minneapolis and sponsored by an organization called Food Chain, a food rescue organization working to get food out of the waste stream. "During the introductions," she recalls, "a man named Robert Eggert introduced himself and said 'I run the coolest program in the whole United States.'" He was referring to his Community Kitchens program. He invited interested participants to a workshop he was offering, which Gornick attended. That, she says, is how the idea for what be-

came Opportunities Cooking in Duluth got planted.

Stimulated by her encounter with Robert Eggert and keenly aware that welfare reform was creating heightened anxiety among welfare recipients about finding work, Gornick started looking into transforming the Damiano soup kitchen into a teaching kitchen. She stayed in touch with Eggert for advice, conducted a needs assessment, contacted restaurants that were potential employers, examined potential training program materials, and worked with the Damiano board to make a decision about whether to enter this arena. She learned that Lake Superior College used to have a training program for chefs, but it had closed. After more than a year of documenting the need, laying the groundwork, and finding philanthropic funding, Damiano started Opportunities Cooking.

From the beginning, the national Community Kitchens model had to be tweaked to fit the smaller size and specific needs of Duluth. Damiano used the manual from Community Kitchens to develop its training curriculum for Opportunities Cooking, but Gornick had to pick and choose from the manual about what food preparations to teach because the variety of restaurants where chefs could be employed in the nation's capitol was far greater than in Duluth. The District of Columbia (DC) Community Kitchen program made extensive use of guest chefs for teaching. Eggert himself was a chef with strong connections to chefs at the best DC restaurants and so had great success recruiting them to do volunteer teaching. Damiano experimented with using guest chefs, but the pool was much smaller and guest chefs were not available during the intense summer tourist season. Gornick had the Opportunities Cooking program coordinator keep track of attempts to recruit guest chefs. Could they get someone to teach cooking fish? Someone for chicken? Someone for sauces? Someone for breakfast items? Someone for desserts? Reviewing systematically their recruiting efforts and getting feedback from chefs about why they would or would not participate as volunteers in the program, Damiano decided that they would have to change the program to have most of the cooking taught by a paid staff using occasional guest chefs to supplement the curriculum. Indeed, the use of guest chefs came to vary seasonally in accordance with the ebb and flow of seasonal business at Duluth restaurants. Here was an early example of program adaptation based on what amounts to internal developmental evaluation.

This constituted a change in the national model. Harking back to the distinction between improvements versus developments that was the centerpiece of Chapter 2, which is the defining difference between formative and developmental evaluation, this was not just a small program improvement. This was a significant change in the model itself, one with staffing, budget, and curriculum implications. Helping guest chefs do a better job of teaching at the level of participants would be (and was) an improvement in the program; changing the role and use of guest chefs from the centerpiece of the model to occasional and supplementary teachers constituted a change in the model, one that Gornick was conscious of, documented, and reported to her board and funders.

Let's turn to developments related to outcomes.

Damiano began Opportunities Cooking with the goal of training 20 hard-to-employ adults and assist them with finding employment in the food industry. The first year the program graduated 14 people, 60% of whom were still employed a year later, an average result for programs of this kind. The second year they began efforts to move people beyond entry-level positions and introduced the concept of career development. The outcomes they achieved changed very little for 3 years. Gornick reflected on those modest results:

"In hindsight, Damiano's early efforts at training people for employment were incredibly naive. So much so that today I am surprised we experienced even the limited degree of success we did. We were making program decisions based on assumptions rather than facts, and so we did some evaluation and used the findings to make several changes that greatly improved outcomes for our students."

It was during this time that Gornick participated in a series of workshop sessions on evaluation I was offering in Duluth with support from the Bremer Foundation, headquartered in Saint Paul, which was interested in supporting increased organizational effectiveness throughout Minnesota. It was immediately clear to me from her workshop questions and the evaluation project she undertook that Gornick *got it* about useful evaluation. She resonated with evaluative thinking, and was open to having her program's assumptions made explicit and tested. Evaluators tell lots of stories to each other at conferences about the frustrating resistance to evaluation they encounter, much of it a result of top-down mandates to comply with standardized procedures and reporting. Gornick took on evaluation because she saw it as a way to more effectively adapt what they were doing to increase outcomes for participants. That's the mindset that makes evaluation useful.

The evaluation findings about Opportunities Cooking led Gornick to recognize that they needed to think beyond the goal of a higher graduation rate and refocus on getting students employed and helping them stay employed. This posed challenges on both the supply and the demand side because the supply of potential participants and the demand for chefs was significantly different in Duluth compared to Washington, DC. First, the demand side: The employment market for chefs in Duluth is much, much smaller than that in Washington, DC, and Duluth chefs are paid poorly compared to the greater economic prosperity and diversity of the DC restaurant market. Indeed, Damiano found that they had to switch from the original model's goal of training and placing chefs to the more modest goal of training and placing kitchen workers. This shift was also driven by supply. The Washington, DC, program could choose participants from a large application pool and enforce rigorous discipline and rules (boot-camp style) because those who didn't make it in the program could be readily replaced. In Duluth, the program aimed to serve long-time welfare recipients and the chronically unemployed. This population came with multiple problems (histories of drug and alcohol use, family violence, culture-of-poverty issues, and mental health problems) that affected the services they needed, what level of training they could handle, and what kinds of jobs they could qualify for. However, the principle of the DC program that Damiano made the foundation of its own program, and maintained, was that participants practiced working while being trained. The program was set up and run as a working kitchen; participants learned to do kitchen work by doing it, which included demonstrating the expected behaviors of employees in real work settings: showing up on time, appropriate grooming, good hygiene practices, and appropriately respectful interactions.

Gornick formulated and tested a logic model of program processes related to outcomes. In creating the logic model of how the program functioned, she found that staff was spending more than a month a year celebrating graduation (planning, inviting, cooking, and decorating). She says they realized that they needed to shift emphasis:

"We retained the celebrations, recognizing their importance to people, but scaled them way back. The lead staff person began to spend more time bringing good employers to the table and instituting incentives for work retention. An example of this was a 3-month bonus for employment. Mentors and support groups, as well as staff support, were added for post-graduation support."

This is an example of grassroots program development that addressed emergent issues not found in the national model. These changes were not in conflict with the national model, but constituted a locally specific adaptation based on thoughtful reflective practice. The evaluative thinking manifested involved asking serious developmental questions: What are our priority outcomes? How does the way staff spends time align with those priorities? What could we try adding to the program in support of our priority outcomes? And once those changes are implemented (e.g., bring employers to the table, add incentives for work retention), how well do they work?

These kinds of developments are common at the grassroots level as thoughtful and creative local leaders adapt national models to local circumstances and experiences. But such changes are often done on an ad hoc basis without explicitly documenting and examining the database of observations and outcomes that lead to such adaptations and without following up those changes to monitor their implementation and effects on outcomes. Both formative evaluation (improving implementation of the national model) and developmental evaluation (adapting and changing the national model) can go on simultaneously, and did at Damiano. But it's important to know the difference. When are you improving a model? When are you developing and adapting it? When are you unsure (which can also be the case)? Making these distinctions helps those involved understand what they're doing, why they're doing it, and the consequences for desired outcomes.

Moreover, thinking about the differences between improvement and development (the focus of Chapter 2) goes to the heart of the question of what is meant by a "model." Gornick and the Damiano staff showed intentionality about making changes, documented changes and why they were making them, and tracked the consequences of those changes for original outcomes (getting low-income people trained as chefs and into jobs that they kept) and emergent intermediate outcomes—building long-term relationships with employers to better meet employers' needs, which meant further adapting the program to emergent employer needs and realistic participant capacities.

I know I'm belaboring the point of this story but I find that it's easily lost. Implementing a national model locally with high fidelity is fundamentally different from adapting a national model to local circumstances. Faithfully following a national recipe is fundamentally different from adapting principles identified by a national network of engaged reflective practitioners. Both methods have merit, but they involve fundamentally different approaches to bringing about change. And they involve fundamentally different evaluation questions, as shown in Exhibit 6.3.

EXHIBIT 6.3 Fidelity Evaluation Questions versus Developmental Evaluation

Note. These comparative evaluation questions are meant to illustrate different evaluation mindsets: evaluation of high-fidelity replication (or going to scale) of a validated best practices model (top-down dissemination) versus local implementation based on identified best principles that require adaptation to the local setting and therefore developmental evaluation. These questions are neither prescriptive nor exhaustive; they are illustrative. Thus, they are not required best practice evaluation questions but rather illustrative questions of different ways of framing an evaluation's purpose and focus.

Evaluation focus	Fidelity evaluation questions	Developmental evaluation questions
Implementation and process evaluation	Summative fidelity implementation question: Has the validated (*best practices*) model been fully and faithfully implemented (as it has been replicated in a new setting and/or taken to scale)? Formative implementation questions: What problems were encountered in implementing the model? How were those problems solved in a way that is faithful to the model? Have resources been adequate and appropriate to support full and faithful implementation?	How are the model's principles and practices being implemented? Which practices are being followed and which adapted? Why? What principles are being followed and which, if any, not followed? What adaptations have been made? How were decisions about adaptations made? What factors and considerations shaped and informed what was done, both following a model's practices and principles, and departing from or adapting those practices and principles? Based on what evidence and analysis? Periodic pause to ask: To what extent are we still really engaging with and being guided by someone else's model? What core elements remain? What's been left behind? What's been added? What's been developed? What's been learned?
Outcomes evaluation	To what extent have the model's specified outcomes been achieved? Is the level of achievement within the range of what was predicted by the model and does it constitute further validation of the model? If not, why not?	To what extent have the original model's specified outcomes proven appropriate? If so, how and why? If not, how have they been changed? What are the consequences of these changes for ongoing model development?

(cont.)

Evaluation focus	Fidelity evaluation questions	Developmental evaluation questions
Unanticipated consequences	What has occurred in replicating the model (or taking it to scale) that was not anticipated or predicted in the best practice model? What are the implications of those consequences for adherence to high-fidelity replication?	What has emerged during implementation and adaptation? How, if at all, has the context changed in ways that affect what is being done? How have staff's and participant's reactions, and responses to those reactions, affected what's been done?
Learnings	What has been learned about how to fully and faithfully replicate the model (or take it to scale)?	What has been learned about being guided by the model's principles and implementing them in this particular setting? What factors have proven important to monitor as a basis for adaptation? What's been learned about documenting the development process? What's been learned about development?

Watching for Unintended Outcomes and Consequences

Evaluative thinking and questioning also attend to unanticipated outcomes. Opportunities Cooking had the unanticipated consequence of creating a positive relationship with the business community, thereby changing how Damiano was viewed. The business community had been leery of Damiano as a hub for undesirables and a magnet for poor people near the city's business center. However, when Damiano began working with employers through Opportunities Cooking, a more positive view developed. Gornick created a steering committee for the program that included restaurant and businesspeople, as well as people knowledgeable about human services and poverty in the community.

Damiano also took an assertive and proactive stance in the face of increased demands for accountability. Rather than lodging accountability in adherence to a fixed model with fixed outcomes, they lodged it in learning and adaptability, showing funders how they were applying what they were learning from evaluation and the effects of those learnings on progress to achieve desired outcomes. They also framed these changes as *developments* not just improvements, a key

difference in perspective. Gornick said, as reported earlier in Chapter 2:

"At each stage we did the best we could with what we knew and the resources we had. Now we're at a different place in our development—doing and thinking different things. That's development. That's change. That's more than just making a few improvements."

The Challenge of Sustainability

Opportunities Cooking operated for 8 years conducting training programs four times a year. The program struggled with getting and keeping good staff. It was hard to find and retain staff who could teach kitchen work skills and also deal with sometimes difficult participants who resisted discipline and participant accountability. Funding cutbacks eventually ended the program. The program could no longer afford both a full-time chef trainer and a placement person, though both were critical for program success. Trying to run the program with part-time staff proved insufficient: it was not possible to run a quality program with part-time people. Gornick found herself spending more and more time supervising the program, which interfered with her other work. She had to take a hard look at the demands of the program and decided, "We couldn't let the program bring down the organization." An effort to transition into a collaboration with other employment programs proved to be a lot of work with little success and was abandoned. Applying the framework of the *adaptive cycle* (the focus of the next chapter), the Damiano story ends with creative destruction, terminating the program and releasing its resources for new exploration and other purposes. Damiano's development as an organization included creating Opportunities Cooking, adapting the national model to Duluth, and eventually terminating the program as the nonprofit funding crisis escalated so that Damiano itself could survive. Developmental issues and evaluation eventually yielded to summative judgment.

Kids Cafe

Damiano offers a second example of adaptive change, this time of a program that continues to this day. At the same time that Damiano began Opportunities Cooking, in the mid-1990s, the soup kitchen underwent other changes. Remember, the soup kitchen was originally meant to be a temporary response to the economic crisis of 1982. From the beginning, Jean Gornick says:

"There were always issues with kids. Kids couldn't come to the soup kitchen unless accompanied by an adult because of safety concerns. That meant that sometimes we had to turn kids away, hungry kids, and it was heart-wrenching. A volunteer might try to quickly make them a peanut butter and jelly sandwich, but we didn't have the capacity to supervise unaccompanied kids in the dining room."

Questions had also risen about the appropriateness of the soup kitchen food for young children. And having kids in the building was sometimes disruptive: kids are noisy, ac-

tive, and like to wander about. Volunteers and staff were increasingly complaining about the need to do something about and for the kids.

The situation came to a head for Gornick one night when she was working late in her office on the first floor, just above street level. She heard kids playing outside, then suddenly heard a crash. She went into the secretarial area adjoining her office and found a young Native American boy on the floor where he had fallen after being hoisted through the window by his cousin. He was 7 years old, a year younger than his cousin. They were hungry and trying to get to a small jar of candy they had spotted on the secretary's desk. He was crying, not from the fall but because the large heavy window had slammed shut on his fingers. She comforted him, cleaned him up, brought his cousin in, and made sandwiches for them when she learned they hadn't had any dinner and couldn't get into their house because no one was home and the door was locked.

Something had to be done for kids. Gornick convened all the people working with kids in the neighborhood: Head Start, the YWCA, school people, church volunteers, and human services agencies. "How are we going to get kids fed?" she asked the group. No one would touch it. So Damiano took it on and created a Duluth version of a national program called Kids Cafe®.

Kids Cafe had come to Gornick's attention as a national model that supported out-of-school meals for young people. Kids Cafe was created and sponsored by America's Second Harvest (now called Feeding America) and run in partnership with local food banks. The Northern Lakes Food Bank in Duluth served the northeast Minnesota region but wasn't interested in and didn't have the capacity to run a neighborhood-based café to feed kids. So right from the start, Damiano's program was organized differently than the national model. In exploring a formal connection with Kids Cafe, Damiano learned that it was eligible for a $25,000 start-up grant from ConAgra but would have to agree that all food would come from Con-Agra. Gornick's assessment was that Con-Agra's food was not the best available locally and would be insufficient for the number of children needing food in Duluth's Central Hillside. She thus refused the grant. These early negotiations and developments meant adapting the national program to fit the local situation. Kids Cafe runs year-round, serving dinner four nights a week. Children learn about nutrition and help prepare the food. Gornick says that staffing was initially a challenge: "It took a while to find good kid-friendly, kid-competent people." They've since developed their own curriculum attuned to their own population, which includes some pretty challenging situations, like kids suffering from the effects of fetal alcohol syndrome. In 2008, Kids Cafe served 4,935 meals to 470 children—an almost 30% increase over 2007. But, of course, 2008 saw the emergence of a new economic crisis, one even deeper and more far-reaching than the 1982 economic downturn that led to Damiano's supposedly temporary founding.

Another dynamic challenge was volunteer management for Kids Cafe. Damiano's soup kitchen began as an entirely volunteer-run operation and gradually added professional staff, but volunteers remain critical. Effective coordination and use of volunteers requires a lot of organization and management. Nor, once in place, is volunteer management static. The original volunteer force came from local churches and a vibrant elder community in the Central Hillside area. That generation and its commitment to volunteering has died off and, says Gornick, has been hard to replace. Kids Cafe now relies heavily on college students. College students present different challenges in recruiting, coordinating, and engaging than does working with senior citizens as volunteers. The dynamic nature of volunteer involvement is affected by the emergence and termination of programs. When Damiano introduced the Opportunities Cooking program to train cooks, the need for volunteers decreased because that program was supported by more paid staff. When the Opportunities Cooking program ended, it was initially hard to get volunteers back to the kitchen.

This is no more than a quick overview of Damiano's response to the needs of kids and families in poverty. Damiano negotiated to use the Kids Cafe brand and followed the national model's principles, but adapted the program to fit the local situation. From a top-down perspective, the Damiano version would be judged low on the adoption criterion of fidelity. From a bottom-up perspective, it has high local relevance and ownership. Developmental evaluation can help sort out and make sense of the degree of adaptation taking place and its implications for both implementation and results.

Damiano's story provides a view of change from the trenches. Exhibit 6.4 presents a generic theory-of-change model for bottom-up adaptive innovation.

Alternative Approaches to Change

So let's review where we are. I opened this chapter with a dialectic about how change occurs: top-down, high-fidelity dissemination of best practices versus bottom-up grassroots adaptations attuned to local context. Top-down change requires a high degree of knowledge about the variables and factors that lead to change (a summatively validated model) and a high degree of control over those variables and factors (control-over-model implementation), including measurements of treatment fidelity across sites (Zvoch, 2009). As the Damiano examples illustrate, an alternative to high-fidelity, top-down change is people living and working at the grassroots bringing their own knowledge and experience to bear as they adapt principles-based models from elsewhere, making modifications to fit the local context, and doing what's doable within the constraints of local resources and values.

And where does that leave us? With the Damiano story as context, I'm basically setting up the case for the synthesis position

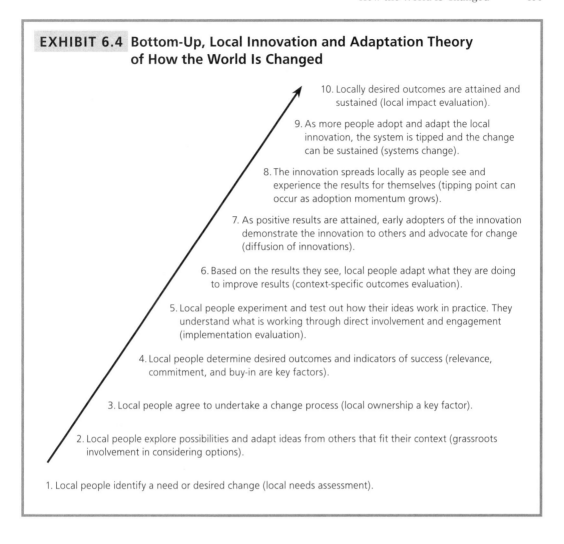

EXHIBIT 6.4 Bottom-Up, Local Innovation and Adaptation Theory of How the World Is Changed

10. Locally desired outcomes are attained and sustained (local impact evaluation).

9. As more people adopt and adapt the local innovation, the system is tipped and the change can be sustained (systems change).

8. The innovation spreads locally as people see and experience the results for themselves (tipping point can occur as adoption momentum grows).

7. As positive results are attained, early adopters of the innovation demonstrate the innovation to others and advocate for change (diffusion of innovations).

6. Based on the results they see, local people adapt what they are doing to improve results (context-specific outcomes evaluation).

5. Local people experiment and test out how their ideas work in practice. They understand what is working through direct involvement and engagement (implementation evaluation).

4. Local people determine desired outcomes and indicators of success (relevance, commitment, and buy-in are key factors).

3. Local people agree to undertake a change process (local ownership a key factor).

2. Local people explore possibilities and adapt ideas from others that fit their context (grassroots involvement in considering options).

1. Local people identify a need or desired change (local needs assessment).

posited at the beginning of this chapter: *In the global village, change often occurs in the middle where top-down and bottom-up forces collide, intersect, get entangled together, do battle, and otherwise encounter real-world complexities.* Thus, developmental evaluation aims to help innovators negotiate the complex nonlinear dynamics in the muddled middle where top-down forces and bottom-up approaches to change meet. This follows from the earlier discussion in this book about the nature and implications of complex nonlinear dynamics. Let's now look directly at action in the muddled middle and developmental evaluation's contributions.

Developmental Evaluation: The Action in the Muddled Middle

It is in middles that extremes clash.
—JOHN UPDIKE, Pulitzer Prize–winning author (quoted in Cohen, 2009)

By positioning developmental evaluation in the muddled middle, I work with social innovators to adapt and further develop their models to local conditions as they work to take them to scale for broader impact. I also work with local change leaders to inform local innovations through attention to larger system issues and knowledge-based

∼ Top-Down Evaluation Mandates and Bottom-Up Learning

On the whole, top-down mandates that require grassroots organizations to do evaluation leave neither the funder nor the program happy. Those in the trenches, forced to allocate scarce funds to comply with an evaluation mandate do so (what choice do they have?), but hate the mandate, mourn the waste of resources, and resent time spent on paperwork and what they perceive as irrelevant nonsense. But what is usual is not universal.

Experienced developmental evaluator Hallie Preskill, a former president of AEA, tells the story of working with a director of a statewide domestic abuse prevention organization who had always thought of evaluation as academic and costly, and as a result had put off meeting her funders' evaluation requirements. Then one of the organization's key funders told her that she could lose funding unless she got an evaluation done within the next 6 months. Searching quickly for an evaluator, she was referred to Preskill.

Preskill and her team began by inviting a cross-cultural group of women to attend a half-day meeting to help design the evaluation. The evaluators started the design meeting by having the women pair up with one another to tell a story about a time when they felt energized about making a difference for children and women throughout the state. The women told their stories with emotion. The evaluators facilitated identification of common themes from the stories, then turned to the question of priorities for evaluation. When the meeting was over, one of the Native American women approached the evaluators, and said:

"I really appreciated the opportunity to tell my story, and then to hear it told aloud by someone else. I would never have spoken up if we had started out having a large-group discussion. I felt my voice was honored. Thank you."

During the 4-month evaluation, the evaluators involved the director to make sure her priority issues were addressed and kept her informed of emerging findings. Staff participated in interpreting the findings and their implications, and used the results. The director became an evaluation enthusiast and advocate (Preskill, 2009).

This is an example of how top-down forces (program and evaluation mandates) and bottom-up forces (local participation and perspectives) can affect programs—and evaluation of programs. Developing a taste for useful evaluation can be the first step toward more ongoing engagement with developmental evaluation.

principles. General principles and knowledge from elsewhere can provide direction even when specific practices are locally embedded and home-grown to support change that is sustainable. Practices emerge from what makes sense to people based on their own experiences and experiments. In developmental evaluation, change is adaptive and context-sensitive whether its source is bottom-up or top-down. This perspective means that I respect and value local knowledge without romanticizing it; indeed, bringing evaluative thinking to bear locally means making local knowledge (or presumptions of knowledge) explicit so that it can be examined and tested. Likewise, I am skeptical that just because a model has worked elsewhere, even *many elsewheres*, and even when validated by summative evaluation, that it will work within a new context. That skepticism (important to distinguish from cynicism) is the source of ongoing evaluative inquiry. These dual and dueling skepticisms (skeptical that local knowledge is all-encompassing and sufficient while also skeptical that faraway experts understand local context and complexities) lead to developmental evaluation's focus on facilitating informed adaptive change in the face of complexity.

When the primary source of change is bottom-up, the developmental evaluator helps local innovators take a broader systems perspective, including understanding and attending to larger cross-scale forces that can affect the success of local action, helping them draw on knowledge and principles from elsewhere. When the primary source of change is top-down, the developmental evaluator helps conceptualize and test local adaptations, as appropriate. When the sources for change are simultaneously top-down (like Bob Dylan's "It's Blowin' in the Wind") *and bottom-up* (like legendary congressman Tip O'Neill's observation that "all politics is local"), *the developmental evaluator helps facilitate and navigate the interactive dynamics of the muddled middle.*

Research on Adaptive Innovation

Earlier in this chapter I reviewed and summarized Lisbeth Schorr's important findings about how successful innovations adapt. Let's now place the Damiano example in a larger context. By returning again to look at some classic but still relevant research on adaptive innovation and management we can see how widespread opportunities for developmental evaluation are likely to be. What's the scope and breadth of action in the muddled middle?

In a renowned large-scale study of innovation, the Rand Corporation, under contract to the U.S. Office of Education, studied 293 federal programs supporting educational change—one of the most comprehensive studies of educational innovation ever conducted. The Change Agent Study concluded that adaptive implementation "dominates the innovative process and its outcomes":

> In short, where implementation was successful, and where significant change in participant attitudes, skills, and behavior occurred, implementation was characterized by a process of mutual adaptation in which project goals and methods were modified to suit the needs and interests of the local staff and in which the staff changed to meet the requirements of the project. This finding was true even for highly

technological and initially well-specified projects; unless adaptations were made in the original plans or technologies, implementation tended to be superficial or symbolic, and significant change in participants did not occur. (McLaughlin, 1976, p. 169)

This is an old study (mid-1970s), but as I said in introducing it, it has become a classic and, more importantly, it remains relevant—and I haven't seen anything as comprehensive since. The Change Agent Study found that the usual emphasis on fidelity in dissemination of models was inappropriate. McLaughlin concluded:

> An important lesson that can be derived from the Change Agent Study is that unless the developmental needs of the users are addressed, and unless projects are modified to suit the needs of the user and the institutional setting, the promise of new technologies is likely to be unfulfilled. (1976, p. 180)

Evaluation of success ultimately requires stipulating criteria for success, even if those criteria are emergent. Top-down versus bottom-up approaches to change posit fundamentally opposite criteria for judging success. Throughout this chapter I've reiterated the idea that the primary criterion for judging top-down change is high-fidelity local replication of a best practice model. The primary criteria of success for bottom-up change are local effectiveness, relevance, meaningfulness, and ownership of the change model. Developmental evaluation negotiates these opposing criteria in a middle space that honors local context and ownership while attending to larger principles and broader system influences, and *making sure that the ultimate focus is the real impacts on people's lives*, both intended and unintended. It's a special niche and it's not easy to do.

Exhibit 6.5 presents an overview of developmental evaluation's middle niche graphically. Start with the top half of the graphic. At the top left are the forces and findings that inform and impel top-down initiatives: sum-

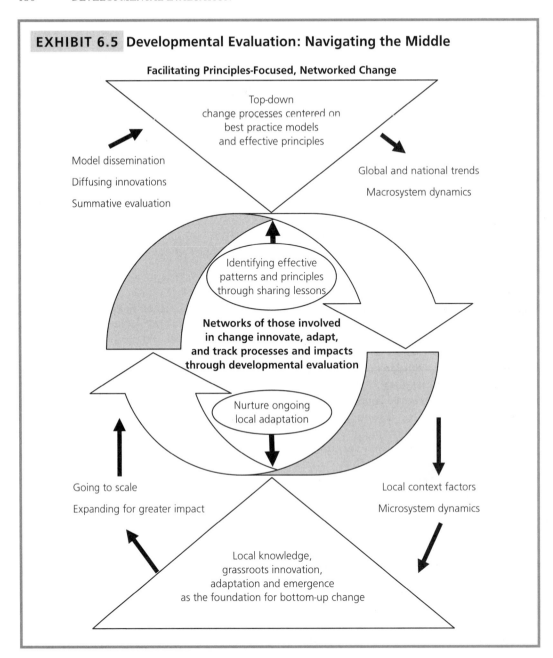

EXHIBIT 6.5 Developmental Evaluation: Navigating the Middle

Facilitating Principles-Focused, Networked Change

Top-down
change processes centered on
best practice models
and effective principles

Model dissemination

Diffusing innovations

Summative evaluation

Global and national trends

Macrosystem dynamics

Identifying effective
patterns and principles
through sharing lessons

**Networks of those involved
in change innovate, adapt,
and track processes and impacts
through developmental evaluation**

Nurture ongoing
local adaptation

Going to scale

Expanding for greater impact

Local context factors

Microsystem dynamics

Local knowledge,
grassroots innovation,
adaptation and emergence
as the foundation for bottom-up change

mative evaluation, diffusion of innovations, and model dissemination. These top-down forces get standardized into best practice models or, more generally, into statements of effective principles (the top triangle). In the top right corner top-down initiatives encounter and intersect with global and na-tional trends and macrosystem dynamics. Now turn to the bottom half of the graphic, beginning in the bottom right (the locus of bottom-up change). Local context factors and microsystem dynamics drive grassroots innovation. Grassroots innovation, adapta-tion, and emergence provide a foundation for bottom-up change. When grassroots initiatives are viewed as successful, the desire for sharing leads to expanding successful local initiatives for greater impact, which quickly becomes an initiative aimed at going to scale (bottom left part of the graphic).

In the middle are networks of people involved in change who are innovating, adapting, and tracking their innovative processes and impacts through developmental evaluation. Here is where the top-down forces of change and the bottom-up grassroots initiatives intersect. Developmental evaluation captures and guides the interactive developments that emerge in the middle. Those developments generate and reinforce effective principles (arrow leading from the middle upwards), thereby contributing to large-scale change even as they support and nurture ongoing local adaptation (arrow leading from the middle back down to the grassroots). This is an admittedly crude and inadequate graphic aimed at capturing a few of the broad dynamics of navigating the middle arena of action where top-down and bottom-up forces meet and take form in the actions and initiatives of change agents and social innovators.

Exhibit 6.6 provides examples of the questions that can inform and guide the developmental evaluator for different developmental circumstances. One set of questions frame a developmental evaluation when a model from elsewhere is being introduced into a new setting, as was the case with Kids Cafe and Opportunities Cooking in Damiano. A different set of questions frame a developmental evaluation for local innovators who are considering moving their model to scale in order to have a larger impact, as is the issue facing Steve Rothschild with Twin Cities Rise! in Chapter 2.

EXHIBIT 6.6 **Developmental Evaluation Questions for the Middle Space of Emergence and Adaptation**

Looking from the top down: Questions when a model from elsewhere is being introduced into a new setting where the primary issue is how the top-down principles and practices can be adapted locally during diffusion

Baseline questions when a model is being introduced to a new setting:
   What is the evidence of effectiveness for the model being offered? What is the model's underlying theory of change? In what settings under what conditions has the model been implemented and tested? Given what is known about the new setting, what aspects of the model appear to fit the new setting well? What aspects may need to be adapted? Why? In what ways? How will adaptation be tracked? How will you know if the adaptations are effective? What principles guide the adaptation? What is critical to be maintained and sustained as this model is adapted to the new setting?

Looking from the grassroots up: Questions for local innovators considering moving their model to scale in order to have a larger impact

Baseline questions when the model is being introduced:
   How has your approach emerged? What are the core elements, components, and/or dimensions of your model? How has the setting in which your approach emerged—the place and

(cont.)

space in which you developed and implemented your approach—affected, shaped, and defined your model? How do you know? What is the model's underlying theory of change? What are the general principles that undergird your specific practices? What is critical to be maintained and sustained as you offer your approach for adaptation elsewhere? What are your criteria and evidence for success that others should attend to? How, if at all, has this changed throughout the development process? How might implementing your approach on a broader scale affect implementation and outcomes? What issues of scale can you anticipate?

Questions from the middle looking both up and down

What are the sources of knowledge about effective principles? How does that knowledge get translated into action in local contexts? What are those involved in change (both top-down and bottom-up) learning about the dynamics of change and effective principles? What factors appear to drive successful innovations and initiatives? What are inhibiting factors and barriers? How are reinforcing versus inhibiting factors and forces identified and dealt with? What appear to be the consequences of adaptations made for intended outcomes? What's the evidence of those consequences? Have new intended outcomes been added during adaptation? To what extent has an innovation changed and developed as it is implemented elsewhere and/or taken to scale (implemented more broadly)? Have new unintended outcomes occurred?

What principles and practices of the innovation and change have been affirmed in new adaptations? What principles and practices of an original model have changed and developed? How significant are those changes and developments? What factors guided those changes? How has the overall theory of change developed as a result of diffusion and going to scale? What lessons can be drawn from these adaptations to guide future diffusion of the model? What patterns and principles of effectiveness emerge from cross-network sharing?

Networks of Change and Developmental Evaluation

Exhibit 6.5 identifies *networks of those involved in change* as one group of primary intended users for developmental evaluation. The World Wide Web age of rapid communications supports networked approaches to change that can simultaneously connect people in diverse communities with top-down models that are gaining cachet while sharing bottom-up lessons learned from local adaptations. Developmental evaluation can facilitate systematic inquiry in such networks, support rapid feedback, and bring rigor to the process of learning and sharing lessons. These kinds of sharing–learning–changing networks are springing up in every arena of innovation. Such networks are too fluid and dynamic to undertake their own formal evaluation as a network, though they can and do track and learn from evaluations

done by network participants as well as evaluations done by others outside the network. These networks can support developmental evaluation by using evaluative thinking and developmental evaluation questions as a stimulus for and source of the network's interactions and sharings. The sidebar on *Networked Going to Scale: Principles-Focused Learning and Evaluation across Communities and around the World* highlights two such networks.

Caught in the Middle

To illustrate the pressures that emerge in the middle between top-down fidelity to a model and bottom-up adaptation, let me share a serendipitous inquiry I received while writing this very chapter. The director of an organization with which I've had a long relationship e-mailed to ask me how to

⌒ *Networked Going to Scale: Principles-Focused Learning and Evaluation across Communities and around the World*

The World Wide Web age of rapid communications supports networked approaches to change that can simultaneously connect people in diverse communities with top-down models that are gaining cachet while sharing bottom-up lessons of local adaptation. Developmental evaluation can facilitate systematic inquiry in such networks, support rapid feedback, and bring rigor to the process of learning and sharing lessons. Here are two examples of networked going to scale.

VIBRANT COMMUNITIES ACROSS CANADA

Learning and evaluation is one of the key components of the Vibrant Communities initiative. Vibrant Communities, supported by the Tamarack Institute, networks communities working to reduce poverty in Canada to learn from and help each other. Engaged communities gain access to the latest research on poverty and models that are being advocated elsewhere (their website provides ready access to models and reports) while also learning from each other. One result is general tools that can be used and adapted locally, like identifying what makes a community vibrant; mapping the capacities and assets of individuals, citizens' associations, and local institutions; and generating and monitoring community building outcomes.

FUTURE GENERATIONS: ADAPTIVE GOING TO SCALE

Future Generations is an example of a principles-based, adaptive approach to "going to scale" internationally. Working in diverse settings like Afghanistan, China, India, and Peru, local communities share knowledge and learn lessons about patterns of success while building their own capacity to shape their own future by using locally available skills and resources applied to sustain solutions that fit local cultures, economies, and ecologies. They use a biological metaphor they call "SEED-SCALE" to describe their approach to "scaling up." They contrast their approach to the "Blueprint Model" (standardized top-down solutions). It is a networked approach consistent with the dynamics of ecosystem complex nonlinear dynamics.

Note. See *www.tamarackcommunity.ca/g2.php* for Vibrant Communities and *www.future.org/applied-research/process-change/going-scale* for Future Generations.

---

handle evaluation of a "proprietary" model. The organization was considering adapting this model to its own way of operating but had been told by those who provide national technical assistance on the model that *adaptation is not allowed*. They must implement as prescribed. Yet the director knew from colleagues in other states that people were adapting the model. She wanted to discuss these various adaptations on a professional listserv and at an upcoming national meeting of professionals. When she raised this possibility with her peers in other organizations, she received a number of responses that opened by asking that their e-mail be treated confidentially, then went on to say that they wished they could participate in the proposed discussion, but because they weren't following the model exactly (and it appeared that almost no one was), they didn't want to risk attracting attention to their departures from the model for fear of being sanctioned by the national organization promoting the model. National disseminators and trainers were adamant about adoption being all or nothing. They emphasized the importance of being policy-compliant and model-adherent. Shrewd and experienced directors feared finger pointing, so they quietly adapted while pretending to faithfully follow the prescribed model, hoping not to get found out. They justified this strategy by repeating the time-honored administrative wisdom that *it's better to ask forgiveness than permission.*

The stakes are high for those navigating the treacherous terrain where top-down mandates meet bottom-up needs and context sensitivities. One consequence is that savvy in-the-trenches adapters become liars, pretending to follow a model with high fidelity to keep getting funded, even as they adapt the model surreptitiously to meet local needs. And the model disseminators, and even evaluators, are forced into the role of fidelity police, sometimes even cultivating informers to squeal on and expose noncompliant adapters.

The problem has many manifestations. It's the problem of cheap knockoffs of designer products like Gucci fashions and Rolex watches. Businesses spend millions protecting their trademarks, patents, and brands. National programs likewise want to protect their models, in part because the reputation and future funding of the model is at stake if an adapted approach proves less effective and undermines the effort to diffuse a particular best practice. On the other hand, the people at the grassroots have a stake in effectively meeting the needs of the people they serve and their attitude of "do whatever it takes" places less emphasis on fidelity than on getting results.

Developmental evaluation is not appropriate for purists interested only in high-fidelity compliance with their model. But developmental evaluation can be used in top-down change processes to help those disseminating their model decide what kinds of modifications and how much adaptation, *if any*, is appropriate. For those working at the grassroots level to adapt models to fit local conditions, *a major use of developmental evaluation is to guide such adaptations.* The middle ground of developmental evaluation supports local adaptive innovators in documenting and testing their adaptations. The middle territory lies between the pure high-fidelity approach of top-down prescription that requires compliance monitoring and

the bottom-up grassroots purity of doing only what makes sense to the locals, embedded exclusively in local wisdom. What I hope is emerging is a sense of the kinds of situations for which developmental evaluation is especially appropriate. This requires situation recognition, which was the focus of Chapter 4.

Looking Back and Looking Forward

The first chapter provided an overview of developmental evaluation. The second chapter distinguished the purpose of developmental evaluation—innovative, program, or strategy *development*—as fundamentally and importantly different from improvement (formative evaluation) or judging a standardized model as ready for generalization and dissemination (summative evaluation). The third chapter used the Caribbean Agricultural Extension Project as an in-depth example of development challenges in a dynamic environment and how a developmental evaluation approach can help meet those challenges. The fourth and fifth chapters looked at developmental evaluation through the lens of complex nonlinear dynamics and key complexity concepts. This chapter has positioned developmental evaluation as informing and guiding model adaptation and development in the dynamic middle where top-down and bottom-up forces and imperatives collide and interact. This chapter concluded with developmental evaluation questions for different situations (Exhibit 6.6). Each of these situations involves classic evaluative thinking, so even as I position developmental evaluation as a distinct alternative, I want to continue to acknowledge its grounding in fundamental evaluative thinking: establishing baselines, identifying criteria, operationalizing criteria, making values explicit, rendering judgments about what is working (and what is not), and using findings to inform action and decisions.

Trade-Offs and Tough Choices

This chapter opened with the recognition that we live in a world that is hungry for "best practices" where "best" is what is fastest, cheapest, and highest quality to produce maximum impact. But in the real world, this combination is rare. Programs of the highest quality are typically expensive. Interventions that are fast and cheap rarely produce the greatest impact. The consultants oft-repeated adage is: You can have it fast, cheap, and effective—*pick any two.* In the real world, trade-offs rule. The trade-off featured in this chapter has been negotiating and navigating the middle space between high-fidelity implementation of a standardized model and bottom-up innovation driven entirely by local context. You may find yourself involved simultaneously in top-down diffusion and adoption and bottom-up emergence and adaptation. The result is meet-in-the-middle murkiness. Developmental evaluation is geared to support innovation in that uncertain, dynamic, and exciting space. It can also be a treacherous place, a point worth emphasizing by quoting again (wise insights deserve reiteration in case you breezed past the point the first time round) John Updike's observation that "it is in middles that extremes clash."

Many fields debate the relative merits of top-down versus bottom-up approaches. In financial management and the mutual fund industry, top-down approaches invest based on major market trends and dominant sector rotations while bottom-up money managers focus on individual businesses and specific companies. In economics, macro- and microapproaches compete for attention among policymakers. In sociology, theorists and methodologists from the beginning have argued about the relative merits of the general versus the particular, in general rewarding the former and disdaining the latter. More generally in science, deductive theory (top-down) contrasts with inductive field-based approaches (grounded theory). In religion, ecclesiastical debates rage about local adherence to denominational orthodoxies pronounced from "on high" (making the origins of the top-down flow of dogma quite explicit). In the military, there are regular battles between the headquarters-based generals and the in-the-trenches troop leaders. Management guru Peter Drucker once observed in this regard that one reason the Germans lost World War I was that not enough generals got killed, emphasizing his judgment that the headquarters people were so far removed from the action (and, therefore, reality) that they didn't really know what was really going on (Birinyi, 2009).

I acknowledge that positing a battle between top-down and bottom-up forces can evoke criticism that this is but another simplistic dualism like the competition between communism and capitalism that dominated the last half of the 20th century, or long-standing philosophical dualisms like mind versus body, materialism versus idealism, and religion versus science. But dualisms have their utility. They sharpen contrasts. They clarify end points on what, inevitably, will turn out to be a continuum. Dualities can be engaged as *complementary pairs* (Kelso & Engstrøm, 2008; see sidebar earlier in this chapter). That's how I think about the top-down versus bottom-up battle that has framed this chapter. That framing is useful, I think, in positioning developmental evaluation, even though that positioning is admittedly oversimplified and will, hopefully, gain nuance in practice.

In juxtaposing top-down and bottom-up approaches, the space that most interests and engages me is where they meet, not because I wish to be moderately in the middle, but because this in-between space is where ambiguity and paradox manifest in uncertainty and disagreement, the twin dimensions of complexity (see Exhibit 4.3 in Chapter 4). Advocates of top-down interventions purport to disseminate the best of modern knowledge, but in asserting claims of having discovered best practices, they inevitably overgeneralize and overreach, paying too little attention and being in-

⌒ *Dueling Skepticisms*

Developmental evaluators adopt a skeptical perspective about the extent to which faraway experts understand local context and complexities while at the same time being skeptical that local knowledge is all-encompassing and sufficient. The developmental evaluator invites innovators and funders to engage with these dueling skepticisms. Advocates of top-down interventions purport to disseminate the best of modern knowledge, but in asserting claims of having discovered best practices, they inevitably overgeneralize and overreach, paying too little attention and sensitivity to local particulars and context. On the other hand, I have long since shed any romantic notions that the locals know all that one needs to know about what is going on and that all one has to do is liberate and tap into local knowledge to solve local problems. I respect and want to hear local knowledge, but hear it as what it is, a perspective, one that contains a fair mix of wisdom and bias, insight and untested assumptions, practice-based and time-tested effective practices with old, ineffective patterns deeply ingrained in local belief systems. My value-added as an independent and external evaluator is not to coddle the locals and bow to their alleged inherent wisdom, but to engage with them in reality testing in which together we examine and test both top-down propositions and locally preferred solutions, understanding and evaluating each in context. That's my role as developmental evaluator.

time-tested effective practices with old, ineffective patterns deeply ingrained in local belief systems. My value-added as an independent and external evaluator is not to coddle the locals and bow to their alleged inherent wisdom, but to engage with them in reality testing in which together we examine and test both top-down propositions and locally preferred solutions, understanding and evaluating each in context. That's my role as developmental evaluator.

I've found myself in this middle space a lot, working with people who want to avoid being forced into an *either/or* choice, either adopt a model from elsewhere or develop their own unique approach locally. They want to engage in a *both/and* developmental process, drawing on well-established principles but doing so with sensitivity to local context and emerging challenges in a dynamic world. As a final addendum to this chapter (see Appendix 6.1), I'm including a discussion applying the bottom-up and top-down distinctions to the field of evaluation itself, positioning and contrasting developmental evaluation as a middle-navigating approach with bottom-up and top-down evaluation models. That postscript section is for those who, for reasons that probably defy explanation and would generate worried looks from those who might ask why you'd bother, care about sorting out and finding your way through the many-competing-models labyrinth that is the field of evaluation.

Final Reflections: Top-Down versus Bottom-Up and Good versus Evil Reprise

I said in opening this chapter that top-down versus bottom-up approaches is not a battle between good and evil, the world's oldest and most enduring dualism. This is a debate about competing "goods" between well-intentioned and deeply committed people on both sides who share the value of making the world a better place. Those of us who mediate in the middle also care about doing and supporting good. Or so I would

sensitive to local particulars and context. On the other hand, I have long since shed any romantic notions that the locals really know what is going on and that all one has to do is liberate and tap into local knowledge to solve local problems. I respect and want to hear local knowledge, but hear it as what it is, a perspective, one that contains a fair mix of wisdom and bias, insight and untested assumptions, practice-based and hope. But there is a contrary view, and in the interest of balance, I close with a contrary perspective.

Ayn Rand, novelist and founder of objectivist philosophy, has been experiencing a renaissance marked in part by two new biographies (Burns, 2009; Heller, 2009) and a huge upswing in sales of her novels *Atlas Shrugged* and *The Fountainhead*. She articulated an unambiguous preference for the wisdom and strength of elites at the top and disdain for what she perceived as weaklings at the bottom. But she reserved her greatest contempt for the middle, saying:

> There are two sides to every issue: one side is right and the other is wrong, but the middle is always evil.

Thus am I exposed. This chapter has been an invitation to join me on the shadow side of complexity.

APPENDIX 6.1

Positioning and Contrasting Developmental Evaluation with Other Evaluation Approaches

This chapter has positioned developmental evaluation as a middle approach navigating, sorting out, making sense of, and adapting top-down and bottom-up forces. How does this niche for developmental evaluation compare to other evaluation models and approaches? Throughout this book I've distinguished developmental evaluation from the traditionally dominant approaches of formative and summative evaluations, which are connected hand in glove: as formative evaluation has the primary purpose of preparing for summative evaluation, and summative evaluation is best when following high-quality formative evaluation. But the field of evaluation has generated many other models and approaches. Some support bottom-up evaluation, like participatory evaluation, which involves local people in formulating the evaluation (Baker & Sabo, 2004; Cousins & Whitmore, 2007; King, 2005). Empowerment evaluation aims to make the evaluation experience empowering by building local ownership and facilitating engagement while building evaluation capacity (Fetterman & Wandersman, 2005). Feminist evaluation emphasizes gender and contextual sensitivity to make knowledge a resource owned by and used for those affected by programs (Bam-berger & Podems, 2002; Seigart, 2005; Seigart & Brisolara, 2002). Transformative evaluation is an inclusive, bottom-up approach that makes change part of the evaluation process (Mertens, 2009). What these evaluation approaches share is using evaluation to promote capacity building, relevance, and use by engaging people actively and respectfully from the bottom up with special attention to adapting evaluation itself to local contexts to give it local meaning. Action research takes this bottom-up approach for organizational development (e.g., McGarvey, 2007; Wadsworth, 2008a, 2008b, 2009a, 2009b, 2010).

Evaluation also has prominent top-down approaches. Theory-driven evaluation (Chen, 2005) is top-down when it takes as its primary purpose testing social science theory as it is manifested and operationalized in various program settings, using a deductive approach to conceptualizing what is evaluated and measured. (Theory-based evaluation can also be done bottom-up when it focuses on generating and testing local program theory; see Chen, 2009.) Impact evaluations based on experimental designs and quasi-experimental methods explicitly seek top-down generalizable models (International Initiative for Impact

Evaluation, 2009; World Bank, 2009). Global monitoring and evaluation systems (e.g., Rugg, Peersman, & Carael, 2004) are driven by the need to standardize indicators in order to make cross-site comparisons and aggregate data to determine cumulative results. These are inherently top down approaches to evaluation, driven by the need to demonstrate major impact and accountability.

Realistic evaluation (Pawson & Tilley, 1997, 2005) has a more middle orientation with its emphasis on the importance of context and inquiry into what works for whom, in what ways, under what conditions, with what results. Developmental evaluation takes that inquiry and adds a dynamic dimension in recognition that the very notion of "what works" is subject to change under conditions of complexity.

Fidelity of Evaluation Approaches

Evaluation models, whether top-down or bottom-up, face the issue of fidelity versus adaptation. For example, calling an evaluation an experimental design evaluation does not make it a well-done experiment. In the vociferous methodological debate about whether randomized controlled trials (RCTs) constitute the top-of-the-heap "gold standard" for impact evaluation, those who defend the gold standard moniker have to separate themselves from the many examples where RCTs are badly designed and poorly implemented, producing weak results that cast aspersions on the method itself. Likewise, at the other end of the evaluation continuum, labeling an evaluation "participatory" doesn't make it participatory from the perspective of those supposedly involved. Nor does labeling an evaluation an *empowerment evaluation* make it empowering. Miller and Campbell (2006) studied 47 published studies labeled "empowerment evaluations." They found wide variation in what was done and which empowerment evaluation principles were followed, including a case of an evaluation that was designed and executed by an evaluator "with no input or involvement from stakeholders. . . . In this particular case, the evaluator indicated that the project was an empowerment evaluation because by allowing a disenfranchised population to respond to a survey, the population was afforded a voice" (p. 306). I've seen the same argument used to label as participatory evaluation the administration of surveys constructed solely by an evaluator with no participation by anyone, but because program participants were "allowed" to respond to the survey, it was labeled participatory.

I am regularly sent evaluations labeled "utilization-focused" that offer no evidence of focus on either intended users or intended uses, the defining criteria for utilization-focused evaluation (Patton, 2008c). And I'm already seeing a wide variety of evaluation approaches labeled "developmental evaluation" that, as near as I can tell, lack any developmental purpose or focus. Trying to clarify just what is—and what is not—developmental evaluation is a primary purpose of this book. Another labeling and fidelity issue that arises is whether developmental evaluation is different from action research, and if so, how. I take up that issue in Chapter 9 in discussing developmental evaluation methods.

7

The Adaptive Cycle
and Developmental Evaluation

The most stubborn habits which resist change with the greatest tenacity
are those which worked well for a space of time and led to the practitioner
being rewarded for those behaviors. If you suddenly tell such persons
that their recipe for success is no longer viable, their personal experience
belies your diagnosis. The road to convincing them is hard. It is the stuff
of classic tragedy.
—JAMSHID GHARAJEDAGHI, *Systems Thinking* (2006, p. 3)

Distinguished systems theorist and management consultant Jamshid Gharajedaghi opens his book *Systems Thinking* with this observation from an unpublished internal report about the experience of working with an important client who was resisting innovation. He goes on to observe that "it is well-known and even a tired secret that what underlies the fall of so many great enterprises is that somehow their recipe for success becomes ineffective" (2006, p. 4). He adds later that the temptation to expand beyond the boundaries of success contribute to many failures, especially "the fallacy that if X is good more X is even better. . . . A tendency to push one's strength to its limits transforms the strength into a destructive weakness" (p. 6). Thus do corporations, public policies, international development assistance, fashion fads, sports teams, nonprofit organizations, social programs, and much else rise and fall in a cycle of change. This chapter is about

the implications of such a recurring cycle for developmental evaluation. Such a cycle of rise and fall is not inevitable, but neither is it rare; when it occurs, as it does more often than may be appreciated, opportunities for developmental evaluation can support the reemergence of the legendary phoenix from the ashes of its own destruction.

This chapter is about a particular kind of cycle informed by complexity understandings, *the adaptive cycle.* I learned about the adaptive cycle from Frances Westley, now at the University of Waterloo, where she holds the prestigious J. W. McConnell Chair in Social Innovation and serves as director of the Social Innovation Generation initiative. She learned the adaptive cycle from ecologist C. S. (Buzz) Holling, who found its patterns first in forests and ecosystems, and then in myriad human and social systems. He studied how the health and resilience of forests involved regularly adapting to fires, disease, and periods of drought through four phases that make up a recurring adaptive cycle:

1. *Release* (forest fire or other form of destruction within a mature system).
2. *Reorganization and exploration* (new growth following the destruction).
3. *Exploitation* (accelerated growth of some varieties over others in the competition for resources).
4. *Conservation* (a mature forest dominated by one species).

And then the cycle repeats.

This cycling through phases (which we'll look at in depth in this chapter), with major transitions from one stage to another, can be observed, he posited, not only in healthy ecosystems, but also in resilient social systems, which includes communities, organizations, and programs. For example, in the last chapter Damiano's Opportunities Cooking program that trained unemployed people in poverty for jobs as chefs went through the full cycle. It began by generating resources to bring the national model to Duluth and exploring how to adapt it from Washington, DC, to northern Minnesota, which is the *reorganization and exploration* (new growth) phase. The program then added participants, staff, and supporters as the new initiative grew and attracted attention (the *exploitation* of resources phase). Next, it became a mature program that was a central part of Damiano programming (the *conservation* phase). Finally, after 8 years came the demise and eventual termination of the program as the environment changed and it was no longer able to attract resources (the *release* phase). In its place, new initiatives sprang up, and a new cycle began.

The adaptive cycle can be seen in economic booms and busts, and in the rise and fall of political movements and parties. Once you start looking, you'll find lots of examples in your own organization and perhaps even in your own life (courtship, then marriage, then rearing children, and then divorce is one such pattern for many in modern society). In the arena of social change, each phase of the adaptive cycle has implications for leadership, management, social innovation, adjusting to life's ups and downs, and, of course, evaluation. Transitions from one phase to the next can be especially treacherous—and fertile territory for developmental evaluation, for if adaptation doesn't occur from one phase to the next, the health of the system is threatened. We'll look at all this but focus on the implications for developmental evaluation, drawing on the insights and expertise of Frances Westley. So as I've done in each previous chapter, let me highlight once again the importance of the personal factor in evaluation and introduce you to one of the world's experts on social innovation, who from our first encounters contributed mightily to clarifying the nature and niche of developmental evaluation.

Some Context for Understanding the Adaptive Cycle: Poetry, Ecology, Sociology, Business, and Evaluation

In celebration of her 60th birthday, Frances Westley's daughters secretly invited family, friends, and colleagues to contribute verses to a poem following the structure of "The Walrus and the Carpenter" by Lewis Carroll, thereby creating an epic stream of memories and appreciation. Frances was well known for starting each day in the McGill–McConnell Fellows Program she directed, an intensive professional development initiative for national Canadian nonprofit leaders, with a centering poem, inviting participants to reflect on the previous day's work and become open to what the new day would offer. She brought that approach to our book, *Getting to Maybe* (Westley, Zimmerman, & Patton, 2006), in which each chapter opens with a poem. The poems both separate and connect the book's themes: Wallace Stevens's "Final Soliloquy of the Interior Paramour" that lights the first light of evening; David

Wagoner's invitation, indeed admonition, to "Stand Still"; Mary Oliver's "Wild Geese" calling to us, announcing our place in the family of things; Alison Hawthorne Deming's rush-hour redemption of the whole human race in "Urban Law"; Ellie Schoenfeld's universe of dandelions giving us extra chances despite *Difficult Valentines*; Seamus Heaney's hope for a great sea change when hope and history rhyme; and Adrienne Rich's world of possibilities in *The Fact of a Doorframe*, doors through which you either go, or don't.

As I got to know Frances it was not her love of poetry that connected us, but our common roots in sociology. We experienced the immediate bonding that comes from recognizing a fellow traveler who has mused at length on the Hobbesian question of order and suffered through Durkheimian positivism, Weberian rationalizations of institutional authority, Marxian materialism, Parsonsonian functional prerequisites, and Mertonian social stratification imperatives, not to mention social mobility equations, demographic imperatives, methodological paradigm debates, and that most insidious and debilitating of sociological afflictions, economics envy. Our postdoctoral paths of recovery had been different, but we shared having distilled from sociology some key notions that we found useful in our subsequent real-world work, *mutatis mutandis*.

Her father was a sociologist who, after building a renowned department of sociology at McGill University, turned to the more applied world of consulting and quality management. Her father, once Frances had gotten what she could from sociology, pointed her toward the business school at McGill University, and a colleague with whom he had connections there, Henry Mintzberg, the distinguished and influential management scholar and consultant. When she met the then dean of the business school, he told her about new Canadian government fellowships in management, which she applied for and received, taking a 2-year leave from the sociology department.

The transition from sociology to business was far from easy. Indeed, the adaptive cycle (patience, we will get to it shortly) emphasizes the dangers that lurk in transitions. Arriving at the business school, Frances sat in on management courses and found that she didn't know even the most basic jargon. Her grounding in the sociology of knowledge had somehow missed elucidating the meaning of *bottom line* and *CEO*. "You have to learn the new language of the people you're working with," she tells students, advice grounded in her own transition experience. The learning curve was steep and difficult, especially when she was pushed into teaching with the business case method, with which she had no prior experience. But she found that she liked it, and determined to perfect use of the Socratic method (having observed and experienced her facilitation skills in action, I can attest she has mastered the method). She gravitated toward courses on organizational analysis where she could use her social science knowledge. She became more deeply immersed in management scholarship as she realized that to stay in the business school she would have to publish in peer-reviewed management journals. This was made easier by the fact that Mintzberg had created an unorthodox group focused on putting theory into practice, not limited by narrow definitions of methodological rigor from looking at what was actually useful in practice. This work provided opportunities for publication and Frances got tenure.

What Am I Really Interested In?: A Personal Evaluation Inquiry Leads to a Major Transition

Frances began to find the focus on effective and efficient business management confining and asked herself, "What am I really interested in?" The answer: The environment. Not only because of the resonance and significance of the subject matter, but also because studying and working on environmental issues requires collaboration, her preferred style of engagement. She began by studying the challenges associated with the introduction of green products. This led to an interest in conservation more generally, including zoos that were trying to conserve endangered species, which led her to Ulysses S. (Ulie) Seal and his efforts to save endangered species. Working with Ulie Seal, Frances became chair of the Minneapolis-based Conservation Breeding Specialist Group under the auspices of the International Union for the Conservation of Nature and the innovative Population and Habitat Viability Assessments he created and ran. Seal's work became the basis of one of the case studies of high-impact social innovation we reported in *Getting to Maybe* (Westley et al., 2006, pp. 100–106, 123–124; for the full story, see Westley & Miller, 2003). Just before meeting Seal she had started a project with Henry Mintzberg and David Cooperrider on visionary leadership. Ulie Seal gave her an up-close and personal example of such leadership to observe and learn from.

Through her work with the network of scientists, wildlife managers, zoo directors, and environmentalists working to save endangered species, Frances connected with Buzz Holling and his work on ecosystem resilience, which is the framework for the adaptive cycle. She began working with Holling's resilience network of natural scientists; she was the only social scientist *and* the only woman involved in the group. Ulie Seal and Buzz Holling were towering figures, though modest and subtle in their leadership styles; they accomplished things by gently but persistently inspiring others. Frances was among those inspired as she observed their minds at work and how they put their commitments into practice working with others. She began teaching a course on sustainable development at McGill. By then she had come to understand her own niche, undergirded by a philosophy that she could contribute to change by focusing on how change occurs, on how effective social innovators have impact. Making a difference,

having an impact, requires social change, and Frances had come to understand that she knew about social change, and what she knew was valued by others. This knowledge established her niche and was the basis for her contributions to Holling's resilience alliance and Seal's network saving endangered species (cf. Westley & Miller, 2003). The opportunity to engage with these networks was, she reflects, a door that opened to her, and walking through that door gave new direction to her work and new purpose to her life. She says, looking back:

"I figured out what I was good at. Not sociology, at least not its academic form. I realized that I could see things taking shape in the group that others weren't noticing. I could see patterns emerging and make sense of them. I could crack codes embedded in interactions and exchanges. In any situation I could detect what the key issues were and where I could contribute.

"The challenge, then, was to align those skills and insights with things I really care about, the environment and global change. Doors open. When an opening comes and has potential, I've learned to walk through."

A Door Opens

One such door came in the form of a call from Tim Brodhead, president of the J. W. McConnell Family Foundation in Montreal. He wanted to fund a leadership development program for the voluntary sector in Canada and had solicited proposals, but was disappointed with the results. At the time, Frances knew nothing about philanthropic foundations. She was about to enter into a new organizational culture, just as she had done when she entered business school.

When Tim Brodhead called, she learned that his office was right across the street from her McGill office. She walked across Sherbrooke Street, listened to what he wanted, and designed a leadership development program aimed at major social change for national nonprofit leaders in diverse sectors across Canada. She had never taken on anything like this before, had never designed such a program, and had never worked on leadership development. But she resonated to the idea, appreciated its importance, and knew immediately that she could do it and that she wanted to do it. So she did it. She used a framework and curriculum architecture that Mintzberg had developed for business leadership development, adapting it to fit the nonprofit sector. As she immersed herself in the design, she says she experienced a strong sense that walking across the street and through the McConnell Foundation door had been the right thing to do.

Tim Brodhead liked what she proposed and they worked together to refine it. The result was the McGill–McConnell Fellows Program, which has provided in-depth leadership development for 120 national voluntary-sector leaders across Canada, the impacts of which have been significant and are still emerging. One impact has been that the McConnell Foundation has adopted the adaptive cycle as its theory of change for funding innovation initiatives across Canada (Pearson, 2007) and developmental evaluation as the approach most attuned to the adaptive cycle (Gamble, 2008).

The Complexity Doorframe Redux

Before turning to an in-depth look at the implications of the adaptive cycle for evaluation, let me call to your attention the elements of complexity that are embedded in this opening story. This will provide a quick review of Chapter 5 and the characteristics of complexity that are especially relevant for developmental evaluation.

• *Nonlinearity*, in which small initial actions can reverberate in unexpected and unpredictable ways to have huge impacts: I conducted a 1-day workshop on evaluation

for the McGill–McConnell Fellows Program, something I do many times a year and had been doing for years when I met Frances. But my encounter with her and her work on social innovation altered my intellectual journey and led to my focus on developmental evaluation over the last decade. I certainly did not have such a shift in mind nor foresee its impact when I went to do what I expected to be just another routine training gig.

• *Emergence*, in which patterns emerge from self-organization among interacting agents, in this case, interactions among Frances Westley, Brenda Zimmerman (featured in Chapter 4), and myself, and those with whom we engaged as we worked together. As described in Chapter 5, *emergence occurs as each agent or element pursues its own path but as that path intersects with other paths, and the agent interacts with other agents, also pursuing their own paths, patterns of interaction emerge and the whole of the interactions cohere, becoming greater than the separate parts. What emerges can be beyond, outside of, and oblivious to any notion of shared intentionality.* When we began interacting in the McGill–McConnell Fellows Program, we didn't expect that collaboration to turn into a 2-year think tank on social innovation out of which emerged *Getting to Maybe*, which led to this book. Nor did the conceptualization of the McGill–McConnell Fellows Program anticipate such spinoffs and impacts.

• *Adaptive. Uncertain. Dynamical. Coevolutionary.* All of these elements are present in the nonlinear story of how the ideas in this book, and the book itself, emerged over the last decade. Thus does personal experience intersect with and inform professional practice, in which biography undergirds social science (Chamberlayne, Bornat, & Wengraf, 2000), transforming what would be a matter of only minor individual serendipity into what the eminent sociologist C. Wright Mills called a critical public issue. Frances and I share admiration for Mills's contributions to an activist, real-world-grounded approach to sociology, so it seems appropriate to quote him in contextualizing and concluding this opening section.

> Issues have to do with matters that transcend the local environments of the individual and the range of his inner life. They have to do with the organization of many such milieux into the institutions of an historical society as a whole. . . . An issue, in fact, often involves a crisis in institutional arrangements. (Mills, 1959, pp. 8–9)

I resonate to complexity as a framework in part because it helps me make sense of my own personal and professional journey. What makes this an issue for the field of evaluation is that the relevance of systems thinking and complexity transcend personal experience and go to the heart of how evaluation is understood, organized, and conducted in many milieus and institutions throughout society at this historic time. The issue of how to adapt evaluation to conditions of complexity does involve a crisis in institutional arrangements. Engaging that crisis is what brought recovering sociologists Frances Westley and Michael Patton together to consider the implications of the adaptive cycle for evaluation.

Five Developmental Evaluation Purposes and Uses

We have reached the stage of the book where five situations and purposes particularly appropriate for developmental evaluation have emerged and taken shape. Let me summarize:

1. *Ongoing development* in adapting a program, strategy, policy, or innovation to new conditions in complex dynamic systems (the focus of Chapters 2, 3, 4, and 5);

2. *Adapting effective principles to a local context* as ideas and innovations are taken from elsewhere and developed in a new set-

ting, the work of developmental evaluation in the dynamic middle between top-down and bottom-up forces of change (the focus of Chapter 6);

3. *Developing a rapid response* in the face of a sudden major change (black swan event) or a crisis, such as a natural disaster or financial meltdown; exploring real-time solutions; and generating innovative and helpful interventions for those in need; high uncertainty because of lack of knowledge and stakeholder conflict, prime territory for social innovators and visionaries (also part of the positioning of developmental evaluation in Chapters 4 and 5);

4. *Preformative development of a potentially broad-impact, scalable innovation* to the point where it is ready for traditional formative and summative evaluation; and

5. *Major systems change and cross-scale developmental evaluation*, providing feedback about how an innovation may need to be changed and adapted as it is taken to scale to increase impact and contribute to major systems change.

Chapter 1 presents a more comprehensive and in-depth analysis of these five contributions of developmental evaluation as does the concluding chapter.

This chapter focuses on the fourth and fifth applications noted above. Preformative developmental evaluation involves working with social innovators during a period of creative exploration to take their emerging ideas and visionary hopes and shape them into a potential model that, once sufficiently conceptualized as a potentially scalable intervention, can be further evaluated through traditional formative and summative evaluation. Social innovators are often keenly interested in broad impact and hope that their successes, if they have any, will be taken to scale as effective principles and practices for use elsewhere. Developmental evaluation provides feedback about the extent to which a potentially scalable model is emerging (the fourth purpose in the list above).

When a model has emerged and shows promise for being taken to scale, not as a replication but in a process of cross-scale adaptation, developmental evaluation provides feedback about how an innovation may need to be changed and adapted as it is taken to scale in new, different, and larger contexts (the final purpose in the list of applications above). Let me emphasize these two new purposes for and uses of developmental evaluation by quickly reviewing the purposes and uses discussed in previous chapters (the first three items in the list above).

The first use of developmental evaluation is to assist and support social innovators with ongoing adaptation of their interventions in turbulent environments as they encounter the dynamics of complexity. For example, in Chapter 1 I described how trainers in a rural community leadership development program engaged in ongoing revision of their curriculum as target populations changed (adapting to a new generation of young people and immigrants from a new part of the world), new technologies emerged (how to use the Internet and cell phones for community development networking), and economic and political patterns shifted (recession or boom, conservatives or liberals in power). Developmental evaluation supports this kind of *ongoing* development and adaptation where no fixed model is expected— or even desirable, appropriate, or possible. The emphasis, you'll note, is on "ongoing." These innovators and program developers never expect to get to a steady-state or fixed model. They have a mindset open to ongoing development, ever adapting to an ever-changing world. They also are not particularly concerned about taking what they're doing to the wider world, though that can change if their local success attracts broader attention.

A second, quite different use of developmental evaluation can be to identify principles and patterns of effectiveness that have worked elsewhere, then to help bring them into a new setting and adapt them to the local context. In the last chapter I positioned developmental evaluation in the middle space between bottom-up adaptive management and top-down dissemination of best practices, facilitating innovation where top-down and bottom-up forces intersect. This may lead eventually either to a stable model appropriately adapted to the new setting or to ongoing adaptation as conditions change.

A third purpose and use of developmental evaluation is to support innovation in responding to crisis within a particular context without concern about scalability. During times of rapid change like natural disasters, outbreaks of violence, epidemic threats, and economic or political crisis (times of destruction when things seem to be falling apart in all directions), humanitarian agencies, crisis responders, and social innovators within the crisis context need and want to explore new possibilities for their own setting, without regard to scalability and without any notion of having broad impact. Once they experience success, that may change and their vision may expand, but developmental evaluation can support crisis response, exploration, and innovation before such a larger vision of impact emerges—and regardless of whether it ever emerges. This may include elements of adapting principles from elsewhere but the emphasis in this case is on local creativity and innovation.

This chapter looks at two additional innovation situations, both of which have to do with generating new innovations with the hope and expectation of broad impact. While in earlier chapters, especially Chapter 2, I labored mightily to distinguish developmental evaluation from formative and summative evaluation and identify its separate purpose and niche, my intention was not to devalue those classic approaches, nor to suggest that there are no connections among types and purposes. This chapter considers how and when developmental evaluation paves the way for formative and summative evaluation by developing a model that is ready for traditional evaluation. If summative conclusions are positive, developmental evaluation can support adapting an innovation as it is taken to scale and disseminated cross-scale where new complexities may be encountered. The adaptive cycle helps highlight these two purposes and uses of developmental evaluation (preformative development of models and cross-scale adaptation of models). We begin our discussion of the adaptive cycle with the idea of resilience.

Resilience and Developmental Evaluation

Based on work by ecologist C. S. Holling and applied to social systems by Frances Westley, the adaptive cycle is centered on ecosystem *resilience*, defined as "the magnitude of disturbance that can be absorbed before the system changes its structure by changing the variables and processes that control behavior" (Gunderson & Holling, 2002, p. 28).

> Resilience is the capacity to experience massive change and yet still maintain the integrity of the original. Resilience isn't about balancing change and stability. It isn't about reaching an equilibrium state. Rather it is about how massive change and stability paradoxically work together. (Westley et al., 2006, p. 65)

At the individual level, resilience is experienced during periods of major transition and challenge: graduation and leaving home; loss of a spouse or child; marriage or divorce; moving to a new community or even a new country; taking on a new job or suddenly losing a job; and other huge shifts in life. During these periods of massive change, nothing seems to be the same. And yet you are still you. A core "you" remains, resilient. There is an integrity to "you" that isn't altered in spite of all of the changes in your circumstances (Westley et al., 2006, p. 65).

Organizations also go through major transitions. Resources change with expansion or downsizing. New employees join, others leave. Locations change. New initiatives are added, old ones are phased out. Yet the organization's core remains recognizable as fundamentally the same. Key values and functions remain intact despite major reorientation. Core strategic perspectives and consistent patterns of behavior endure through periods of transition if the organization is resilient. Details change, but not strategic behavior. After studying many different organizations and businesses over time, Mintzberg (2007) concluded: "We make such a fuss about strategic change because there is not all that much of it" (p. 16).

Of course, individuals, organizations, communities, and ecosystems manifest different degrees of resilience. There is great interest in understanding and explaining these differences: why one individual bounces back from tragedy while another is crushed by it; why some organizations endure and others go under; and how healthy ecosystems can be made more resilient and sustainable. In addressing these important questions, competing definitions of resilience have emerged. No surprise there. That's what academics do: take a concept, define it in different ways, then argue about who's right. So let's join the fray. Why? Because how we think about and understand resilience is connected to how we think about major systems change in complex adaptive systems, which has implications for how we *evaluate* systems change, which brings us to developmental evaluation. Follow the yellow brick road.

System resilience, then, has implications for both innovation and evaluation. The perspective that informs developmental evaluation is based on cumulative empirical evidence about how complex adaptive systems and complex responsive processes function, informed first by studies of ecosystems and then validated in studying social systems. The premise of system resilience is that it is made manifest in an adaptive cycle. The very notion of a cycle connotes that change processes manifest repeating phases of growth, decline, reorganization, and new growth, repeating the cycle, what in economic terms are periods of boom and bust. Moreover, change is rarely if ever incremental and gradual. It is more often dynamical. It occurs in fits and starts, is episodic rather than continuous, with periods of increase or decrease interrupted by sudden changes in direction and transitions that alter fundamental processes and structures. In studying ecosystems Holling found that rare events like hurricanes, forest fires, extreme droughts, floods, or the invasion of alien species can alter ecosystems in fundamental ways, sometimes temporarily, sometimes permanently.

In economic systems, Taleb (2007) has documented how rare episodes like extreme financial bubbles or panics, what he calls "black swans" as a metaphor for their unexpected, unpredicted, and outlier characteristics, can shape economic and political systems for long periods. The global financial meltdown that began in late 2008 exemplifies the black swan phenomenon. The paradox is that such system-changing rare events are entirely predictable—"predictable" in the sense that we know that they will inevitably and certainly occur. We just can't know when, where, or with what magnitude they will occur. But they will occur at some time and some place with enough force to precipitate major systems change. Their occurrence may lead to irreversible changes or the effects may be slowly reversible. Innovations can accelerate change and be magnified by other forces when they ride a wave of system transformations.

The *Ceteris Paribus* Hoax: All Things Are Not Equal, Never Have Been, Never Will Be

Understanding and taking into account the adaptive cycle is important because it draws our attention to the realities of complex, dynamical systems. Both program models and evaluation of those models are typically framed within a *ceteris paribus* world—all things being equal, or holding all else constant, in which the environment is simply *assumed* to be stable, constant, and nonintrusive. That assumption makes for nice, neat, bounded, controlled, and fundamentally misleading evaluation studies if the object of study (the program, innovation, or intervention) happens, just happens, to be taking place in the real world. Excuse me. All things being equal? Holding all else constant? And in just what universe is that assumption viable? Certainly it's a seductive assumption. Alluring in its simplicity. Elegant in its Camelot-world way. It just happens to be nonsense. But why quibble over the nature of reality? Fairy tales can come true, it can happen to you, if you actually believe the formal methods write-ups in scholarly journals as opposed to the messy ways cutting-edge scientists actually do what they do, doings that lead to breakthrough findings (Waller, 2004). Indeed, like ecosystems and economies, science progresses through fits and starts, paradigms dominant and paradigms in decline, all of which is effected by what's going on around it (religious inquisitions, wars, a political regime hostile to science, outbreaks of disease, etc.).

The rise and fall of ecosystems, civilizations, marriages, sports dynasties, political regimes, scientific paradigms—pick your favorite cyclical poison—is everywhere about us and throughout history. It kind of makes one wonder how evaluation got to be so static, treating programs as if they are fixed entities that can be controlled and replicated. Boggles the mind, it does.

Yes, I'm ranting. Good of you to notice, kind reader. And now the rant is over. What, you were expecting a nice, clear, linear, and logical argument? But while we're on the topic, rants too manifest a cycle, abruptly emerging, then dying off as bored listeners turn their attention elsewhere. I'll try to limit the rants, but what's the use of going to all the trouble of writing a book if one can't vent a little now and again? Back to the issue at hand: resilience.

A Strategic Approach to Resilience: *Engineering Resilience* versus *Ecosystem Resilience*

In formulating the ecosystem adaptive cycle, Gunderson and Holling (2002) articulated *strategic criteria* compatible with both resilience and evolution. They then extended those criteria, and the adaptive cycle itself, to human systems and institutions. Here's where it gets interesting for our purposes, for they found that *resilience* had two quite different meanings in the ecological literature based on two different notions about what it means for a system to be "stable." This is at the heart of how one thinks about what it means for an intervention to become a *model* worthy of replication. The contrasting and, indeed, competing perspectives on stability and resilience point to the tension created between efficiency, on the one hand, and persistence, on the other, or between constancy and change, or between predictability and unpredictability:

> One definition focuses on efficiency, control, constancy, and predictability—all attributes at the core of desires for fail-safe design and optimal performance. Those desires are appropriate for systems where uncertainty is low, but they can be counterproductive for dynamic, evolving systems where variability and novelty result in high uncertainty. The other definition focuses on persistence, adaptiveness, variability, and unpredictability—all attributes embraced and celebrated by those with an evolutionary or developmental perspective. The latter attributes are at the heart of understanding and designing for sustainability. (Gunderson & Holling, 2002, p. 27)

These different perspectives and definitions led Gunderson and Holling to distinguish two fundamentally different ways of thinking about resilience: *engineering resilience* versus *ecosystem resilience*. Engineering resilience has traditionally focused on "stability near an equilibrium steady state, where resistance to disturbance and speed of return to the equilibrium are used to measure the property" (2002, p. 27). In contrast, ecosystem resilience "emphasizes conditions far from any equilibrium steady state, where instabilities can flip a system into another regime of behavior (i.e., to another stability domain). In this case resilience is measured by the magnitude of disturbance that can be absorbed before the system changes its structure by changing the variables and processes that control behavior" (pp. 27–28). Exhibit 7.1 summarizes the contrasts between engineering resilience and ecosystem resilience. Let's look at how this translates into actual patterns of organizational functioning.

A well-trained regular military unit formally organized in a strict command hierarchy and following a centralized plan based on standard rules of engagement exemplifies engineering resilience. A guerrilla unit using highly mobile tactics, employing horizontally networked communications, and adapting quickly to emergent conditions represents ecosystem resilience. In the arenas of large-scale education systems, human services agencies, and international development, engineering resilience is manifest in bureaucracies following detailed plans, hierarchical approval processes, and standardized procedures—basically trying to control what happens. Grassroots organizations working through networked collaborations and participatory decision-making processes exemplify ecosystem resilience. The widespread interest in and challenges facing leaders and managers trying to move from engineering resilience to ecosystem resilience is captured in a sample of books, both older and newer, about organizational resilience in the face of change:

When Giants Learn to Dance (Kanter, 1990)

Teaching the Elephant to Dance: The Manager's Guide to Empowering Change (Belasco, 1991)

Who Moved My Cheese?: An Amazing Way to Deal with Change in Your Work and in Your Life (Johnson, 1998)

EXHIBIT 7.1 **Alternative Resilience Perspectives: Engineering Resilience versus Ecosystem Resilience**

Engineering resilience

- Focuses on efficiency, control, constancy, and predictability in conditions of low uncertainty.

- Aims at optimal performance of systems by minimizing threats to performance and maintaining steady-state equilibrium.

- Concentrates on stability near an equilibrium steady state, where resistance to disturbance and speed of return to the equilibrium are used to measure sustainability.

- Management and policy emphasize micro-, command-and-control approaches.

- Evaluation focuses on stable and consistent elements of the system.

Ecosystem resilience

- Focuses on persistence, adaptiveness, variability, and unpredictability under conditions of high uncertainty.

- Aims to adapt by absorbing and adjusting to disturbances by evolving absorptive and adaptive structures and processes.

- Concentrates on the magnitude of disturbance that can be absorbed before the system changes its structure and processes, and the reality of more than one equilibrium.

- Management and policy emphasize the adaptive interplay between stabilizing and destabilizing properties for resilience.

- Evaluation focuses on adaptability of the system.

Note. Based on Gunderson and Holling (2002, pp. 27–29).

First, Break All the Rules: What the World's Greatest Managers Do Differently (Buckingham & Coffman, 1999)

Our Iceberg Is Melting: Changing and Succeeding under Any Conditions (Kotter & Rathgeber, 2006)

Organizations: Management without Control (Greenwald, 2007)

The themes of engineering resilience are control, stability, consistency, predictability, and equilibrium. The themes of ecosystem resilience are nimbleness, agility, adaptability, responsiveness, and responding to turbulence and uncertainties. Traditional evaluation practice has been dominated by an engineering resilience mindset. In part this flows from the fact that most programs operate from an engineering resilience mindset. Social innovators, in contrast, manifest an ecosystem resilience mindset, as does, then, the developmental evaluator supporting and facilitating social innovation.

Sustainability and Resilience

Sustainability as an evaluation criterion has generated worldwide interest and debate (EASY-ECO, 2009; Schröter, 2008, 2009). The two contrasting approaches to resilience constitute two fundamentally different understandings of what it means for a program or intervention to be "sustainable." Philanthropic foundations and international agencies, for example, typically make sustainability a priority criterion in their grant making and evaluation (see sidebar on the next page). Central to the leveraging strategy and accountability of philanthropic grant making is the belief that what they support should persist. This belief promotes evaluation criteria of sustainability defined in static terms as persistence, which is essentially an operationalization of the engineering resilience mindset. Sustainability from an engineering resilience mindset is inherent in these widespread criteria for evaluating sustainability:

- Persistence of the institution.
- Persistence of program activities, services, interventions (this includes transferability to other contexts or replication of programming).
- Persistence of resulting changes for individuals (humans), society (e.g., culture, institutions), the economy, and the environment (Schröter, 2009).

Philanthropic foundations and international development agencies typically eschew long-term funding of programs. They prefer to support pilot innovations and have them demonstrate effectiveness and stability, then turn them loose, like baby birds pushed out of the nest to fend for themselves. In the past, foundations hoped that some govern-

⌒ **Traditional, Static Definition of Sustainability: Sustainability Defined**

Since the 1990s the Development Evaluation Committee of the Organization of Economic Cooperation and Development (OECD-DAC) has included sustainability as one of its five evaluation criteria. The others are relevance, effectiveness, efficiency, and impact.

Sustainability is concerned with measuring whether the benefits of an activity are likely to continue after donor funding has been withdrawn. Projects need to be environmentally as well as financially sustainable. When evaluating the sustainability of a programme or a project, it is useful to consider the following questions:

"To what extent did the benefits of a programme or project continue after donor funding ceased?

"What were the major factors which influenced the achievement or non-achievement of sustainability of the programme or project?" (OECD-DAC, 2009)

ment agency would be impressed by what they had funded and pick up the demonstrations to make them ongoing and therefore sustainable. But given the recent fiscal crisis at all levels of government, legislators and bureaucrats are looking to shed programs, not add them. Nor do foundations like to pick up the leavings of other foundations. They each want to do their own thing. So nonprofit programs have developed expertise in reframing what they do just enough to repackage and propose it as innovation worthy of new funding, an adaptation to the realities of how philanthropy works. Large nonprofits and international agencies around the world employ full-time development staff who manage these gyrations and conceptual gymnastics; they have become adept at making the case that their proposals are both innovative and sustainable, that is, they will persist when the current foundation's funding ends, usually after 3–5 years, in some cases longer, and in others, shorter. What they don't say is that the way they will persist is by repackaging what they're doing as new and selling it to a new funder as innovative, fostering an insidious cycle of innovative illusion. Becoming skilled at creating illusions of innovation and sustainability/persistence is all part of the philanthropic and international development assistance funding game: *Those receiving grants pretend that they have a viable strategy for sustaining funding. Those making the grants pretend to believe them.*

The actual nonprofit strategy is to promise whatever it takes to get the money and worry about getting more funding later. The actual foundation strategy is to accept promises of sustainability as addressing the sustainability criterion while rigorously avoiding any follow-up evaluation that would actually assess whether sustainability has occurred. All of this feeds the shared delusion that a program meriting funding at some point in time should go on indefinitely—be "sustained"—as evidence of wise initial funding.

Ecosystem Resilience Criteria for Sustainability

The alternative criteria for sustainability (ecosystem resilience) focus on adaptability and responsiveness:

- Awareness of current and emergent needs.
- Ability to address emergent needs within the realm of the organization's mission and priorities.
- Capacity to adjust to changing contexts.
- Flexibility to adjust to unanticipated negative impacts and side effects (e.g., environmental degradation).
- Continuous adaptation of intervention to optimize benefits and minimize harm.
- Concern of potential harms of an intervention to future generations (intergenerational equity; inclusion of children and youth specifically) (Schröter, 2009).

This set of evaluation criteria fits the ecosystem resilience mindset.

Gunderson and Holling (2002) argue that sustainable relationships between people and nature require an emphasis on ecosystem resilience. This not only shifts the management and policy emphasis from micro-, command-and-control approaches to adaptive management ones, but it correspondingly *shifts the evaluation emphasis from fidelity and persistence to adaptability and responsiveness, the essence of ongoing developmental evaluation.* The stakes for which approach dominates the policy, programming, and evaluation world are high, indeed, and at the heart of discussions and debates about sustainable development.

> Exclusive emphasis on the first definition of resilience, engineering resilience, reinforces the dangerous myth that the variability of natural systems can be effectively controlled, that the consequences are predictable, and that sustained maximum production is an attainable and sustainable goal . . . [and] that leads to the pathology of resource management. . . . As ecosystem resilience is lost, the system becomes more vulnerable to external shocks that previously could be absorbed.
>
> These are two contrasting aspects of stability. One focuses on maintaining *efficiency* of function (engineering resilience); the other focuses on maintaining *existence* of function (ecosystem resilience). Those contrasts are so fundamental that they can become alternative paradigms whose devotees reflect traditions of a discipline or of an attitude more than of a reality of nature. (Gunderson & Holling, 2002, p. 28; original emphasis)

Alternative Paradigms

Gunderson and Holling trace at length the origins and assumptions of these alternative paradigms. Evaluators will find the paradigm distinctions familiar for they are at the heart of the enduring debate between advocates of the quantitative/experimental/deductive evaluation paradigm versus the qualitative/naturalistic/inductive paradigm. (For an in-depth discussion of these paradigm distinctions, their epistemological and methodological roots, and their evaluation implications, see Patton, 2008c, chap. 12.) Despite increasing attention to mixed methods and periodic calls for the end of the evaluation paradigm debates, the competing perspectives endure. Coming at the evaluation paradigm distinctions afresh through the lens of the contrasting resilience paradigms reinforces how fundamentally different these worldviews are, why it is hard to find common ground, and why the paradigm debates persist. Talk about sustainability!

But wait. All is not lost. Ironically, the adaptive cycle work of Holling and Westley offers another lens through which to view the paradigm distinctions and puts them in relationship with each other instead of in competition with each other. Each evaluation paradigm has a place in the adaptive cycle. The adaptive cycle highlights different system conditions at different phases of the cycle and suggests that the challenge is to match the evaluation approach to the phase of an innovation. Let's see how this works.

The Adaptive Cycle

As noted earlier, the adaptive cycle emerged from Holling's research on forests that had thrived for hundreds of years. He found that far from being stable or in a state of equilibrium, their health and resilience involved regularly adapting to crises such as fires, disease, and periods of drought. He identified four phases that make up a recurring adaptive cycle: release, reorganization, exploitation, and conservation. Not all parts of an ecosystem are involved in all phases at the same time, a phenomenon called "patch dynamics," where different parts are at different stages. This cycling through phases, with major transitions from one stage to another, was observable in all healthy ecosystems. However, making the transitions is far from guaranteed. If adaptation doesn't occur during transitions from one phase to another and a system is trapped in one

phase, the long-term resilience and health of the ecosystem is threatened. Exhibit 7.2 depicts the adaptive cycle.

It's worth working through and understanding the technical and scientific details of the adaptive cycle before we turn to its implications for evaluation generally and developmental evaluation specifically. The terminology and concepts can seem academic and dense upon first encounter, but the implications are sufficiently profound that it's worth struggling with them a bit. This brief overview is derived from the in-depth discussion in Gunderson and Holling (2002, chap. 2).

The adaptive cycle takes the form of an infinity figure constructed along two dimensions of a matrix. The horizontal dimension measures the diversity of the system along a "connectedness" continuum with great variety on one end, for example, high biodiversity in an ecosystem, and high sameness on the other end, for example, domination by a single species like pine trees in a forest. (The technical biological definition of *connectedness* is a bit daunting, having to do with the relationship among controlling variables in the system:

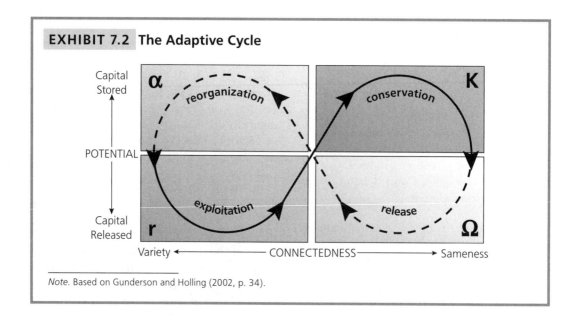

EXHIBIT 7.2 The Adaptive Cycle

Note. Based on Gunderson and Holling (2002, p. 34).

Low connectedness is associated with diffuse elements loosely connected to each other whose behavior is dominated by outward relations and affected by outward variability. High connectedness is associated with aggregated elements whose behavior is dominated by inward relations among elements of the aggregates, relations that control or mediate the influence of external variability. [Gunderson & Holling, 2002, p. 34]

What this means is that high internal "connectedness" resists larger external environmental influences by the very nature of the high degree of sameness [species domination].)

The vertical dimension of Exhibit 7.2 measures the extent to which the resources in a system are released or stored. When one species dominates, the ecosystem's resources are stored in that species. When the domination of a species is reversed (e.g., through fire), the ecosystem's resources are released for use by a greater variety of species. These two dimensions form a matrix of four quadrants. It's in understanding the quadrants, and the transitions from one quadrant to another, that the dynamics of the adaptive cycle are revealed.

The upper-right quadrant (*K*, for kappa) represents the *conservation phase* of a mature ecosystem, like a pine forest. Plant biodiversity is relatively low and the system's resources are devoted to (stored in) the dominating species, for example, the pines. The lower-left quadrant (r) is the *exploitation phase* when resources are being released in a variety of ways, the mirror image of conservation, like the varying kinds of new growth that emerge after a forest fire. The letters *K* and *r* to label the quadrants are taken from "the traditional designation of parameters of the logistic equation" in which *r* expresses a rate of growth of a population and *K* expresses its sustained plateau or maximum level (Gunderson & Holling, 2002, p. 33). In ecology, "r-types" grow rapidly with high competition among competing varieties,

like brush, while K-types grow more slowly but gradually capture more resources, like trees. Economic r-types would be entrepreneurs and small businesses, while K-types would be large bureaucracies and multinational corporations. In evaluation, r-types would be small-scale, short-time-line, local studies, while K-types would be large-scale, longer time-line, more controlled studies.

The lower-right quadrant (Ω, for omega), the *release phase*, is when resources that have been locked up in a dominant species are set loose, as occurs when a fire ravages a forest, or a large business fails, thereby opening up new opportunities for small businesses. What had been conserved as a dominant system ends (omega), opening the way for a new beginning (α, or alpha), the upper-left quadrant, designated the *reorganization phase*.

The real significance of the adaptive cycle, however, is not so much distinguishing the quadrants as depicting and understanding the relationships among them.

During this [adaptive] cycle, biological time flows unevenly. The progression in the ecosystem cycle proceeds from the exploitation phase (r phase) slowly to conservation (K phase), very rapidly to release (Ω phase), rapidly to reorganization (α phase), and rapidly back to exploitation. During the slow sequence from exploitation to conservation, connectedness and stability increase and a "capital" of nutrients and biomass is slowly accumulated and sequestered. Competitive processes lead to a few species becoming dominant, with diversity retained in residual pockets preserved in a patchy landscape. While the accumulated capital is sequestered for the growing, maturing ecosystem, it also represents a gradual increase in the potential for other kinds of ecosystems and futures. For an economic or social system, the accumulating potential could as well be from the skills, networks of human relationships, and mutual trust that are incrementally developed and tested during the progression from r to K. Those also represent a potential developed and used in one setting that could be available in transformed ones. (Gunderson & Holling, 2002, p. 35)

The Adaptive Cycle and Psychosocial Regimes

Frances Westley, having worked extensively with ecologists, notably on global initiatives to save endangered species (Westley & Miller, 2003), has creatively applied the adaptive cycle to innovation and organizational/societal change. In her framing, the four quadrants represent different "psychosocial regimes" (see Exhibit 7.3). During a *conservation* psychosocial regime, the controlling variables are bureaucratic rules that impose standardization; the emphasis is on accountability and increasing efficiency; technocrats and bureaucrats dominate. Dedicated commitment of capital (intellectual as well as financial) is essential for the efficiency necessary to optimize performance during the conservation phase. When things change, however, that commitment of capital becomes a liability rather than an advantage, and the rigidities of existing commitments and resource allocations become the basis for resistance to necessary change.

These regimes become increasingly rigid with inflexibility inhibiting adaptability until the regime topples into a phase of "creative destruction," the phrase coined by economist Alfred Schumpeter in the 1940s when he observed that healthy economies go through cycles of destruction that, painful and dislocating as such destruction tends to be, spur innovation and creativity.

CREATIVE DESTRUCTION

A senior developmental evaluation moment

"Damn! I had an emergent theory and I lost it."

Illustration by Mark M. Rogers.

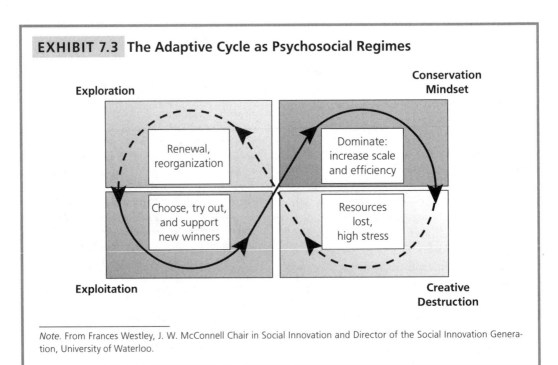

EXHIBIT 7.3 The Adaptive Cycle as Psychosocial Regimes

Exploration

Conservation Mindset

Renewal, reorganization

Dominate: increase scale and efficiency

Choose, try out, and support new winners

Resources lost, high stress

Exploitation

Creative Destruction

Note. From Frances Westley, J. W. McConnell Chair in Social Innovation and Director of the Social Innovation Generation, University of Waterloo.

During the psychosocial regime of *creative destruction*, resources become scarce, downsizing is widespread, fear increases, and trust breaks down, resulting in high stress, confusion, identity crisis, and depression among both individuals and groups. However, those who thrive on crisis, who've been on the outside looking in, and/or see the potential for new opportunities feel hopeful, even optimistic, as the old regime falls into disarray. They facilitate the transition to the psychosocial regime of *exploration*. This is a time of widespread, disparate experimentation; creative initiatives lead to lots of failures, but the few successes start to attract resources; there's a sense of openness, a desire, even demand for, innovation; but uncertainty is high, predictability is low, for things are in flux and it's not at all certain what will result. Creative people find each other, self-organizing networks emerge, entrepreneurs flourish with the buzz of big ideas and new opportunities, but those who need stability and control are flummoxed. As promising innovations emerge and attract resources, the transition from exploration to exploitation occurs.

The next phase, the psychosocial regime of *exploitation*, involves turning creative ideas and early prototypes into testable models and demonstration projects. A thousand flowers blooming (exploration) gives way to a few that attract favor, preference, and support. Team builders and engineers come into their own, showing how to take creative concepts and turn them into real projects and products. The divergence processes that characterize the exploration phase (looking everywhere and anywhere for ideas) converge into focusing on a few of the most promising possibilities, learning about them (steep learning curve in this phase), and concentrating resources. The competition among these projects and products leads to winners and losers, with the winners growing into dominance, and the cycle returns to where we began, the conservation regime of stability, locked-up resources, and the dominance of what are thought to be enduring "best practices."

Politics and the Adaptive Cycle

You can see the psychosocial regimes of the adaptive cycle in American politics as conservatives and liberals move through alternative phases of ascendance and decline. The conservative congressional victory led by Newt Gingrich in 1994 ushered in a period of exploitation of the specific proposals articulated in the "Contract with America." These proposals had emerged from a period of exploration after Republicans experienced the creative destruction of political loss of the White House to Democratic president Bill Clinton after 12 years of Republican presidential control (Ronald Reagan and George H. W. Bush). The subsequent election of George W. Bush and the crisis brought on by the September 11 terrorist attack allowed conservatives, led by Karl Rove and Dick Chaney, to consolidate power—creating a psychosocial regime of conservation, which those in power forecast would endure. Indeed, the primary political agenda of Republican leadership was to consolidate their power and create an all-dominant, controlling political regime that limited diversity and locked up resources in conservative policies and priorities for the foreseeable future—and beyond. After all, what's politics without a little hubris? But political control and domination led, as they inevitably do, to overreaching, rigidity, and isolation. The election of Barack Obama in 2008 was an omega event for Republicans and an alpha moment for Democrats, as the political wheel turned.

One can apply the adaptive cycle to map technological ups and downs, for example, small cars to large cars to SUV domination to Hummers to hybrids and demand for new approaches to smaller cars (e.g., electric, fuel cell), with the bankruptcy of General Motors along the way, its own example of the corporate adaptive cycle at work. Program officers of philanthropic foundations have been urged to track "the life cycle of ideas" in a pattern that corresponds to the adaptive cycle:

[A] single idea traverses a natural life cycle in four stages from latency to growth to peaking (or maturation) to decline (or institutionalization). Attending to the life cycle of an idea helps foundation program officers assess where, in the history of an idea, they are intervening—particularly to avoid investing in an idea in decline and to anticipate what might be needed to boost a latent idea to the growth stage. (Hirschhorn & Gilmore, 2004, p. 7)

Scientific paradigms can be mapped similarly. Consider the plight of Pluto. Discovered in 1930, then exploited as the final piece of our solar system, a perspective that dominated astronomy and, not incidentally, children's school books and science projects for 80 years. Then, creative destructive: Pluto reduced to merely one of many objects in the Kuiper belt, no longer a planet. In 2006, the General Assembly of the International Astronomical Union adopted a definition of planets that made Pluto a dwarf, at best. This has provoked continuing debate and, for long-time Pluto admirers and aficionados, heartache at its perceived demotion and loss, though Pluto itself is still out there, unchanged, and oblivious to its rollercoaster ride through the scientific adaptive cycle. Meanwhile, though diminished in status in astronomical circles, Pluto is ascendant in lexicology where the American Dialect Society chose "plutoed" as its 2006 Word of the Year, defining "*to pluto*" as "to demote or devalue someone or something." And politicians, sensing an opportunity to pander to confusion and ignorance, an opportunity never to be missed, rose to the defense of poor Pluto. As I write, politicians in at least two states (New Mexico and Illinois) have passed resolutions reaffirming Pluto's status as a planet. *The Pluto Files: The Rise and Fall of America's Favorite Planet* (Tyson, 2009) offers an intriguing example of an intellectual adaptive cycle, one preceded some 2,000 years ago by the rise and fall of Pluto as a Roman god. Pluto worshippers (god or planet) take heart. You're currently experiencing creative destruction (or in Holling's softer terminology, *release*), but be attentive to possibilities for exploration and reorganization, organize yourselves for a new phase of exploitation, and you too may once again dominate.

All kidding aside, the adaptive cycle is serious stuff. And the transitions from one phase (or regime) to the next can be quite problematic, offering perils, uncertainties, and traps. We'll look at those anon. First (and finally), let's look at the implications of the adaptive cycle for evaluation.

Evaluation and the Adaptive Cycle

Developmental evaluation is especially useful during the alpha phase of reorganization, exploration, and innovation. This is when social innovators try out new ideas, experiment, and learn by doing. Most of what's tried won't work; some will. Developmental evaluation helps innovators know the difference, moving on from dead ends and further exploring what looks promising. Identifying dead ends during exploration and innovation doesn't involve the rigorous evidence and high-stakes judgment of summative evaluation. For example, social innovators in a community may try to engage people around an issue like poverty alleviation and hold a meeting to present statistics on poverty and brainstorm solutions. Few attend. Key influentials and leaders are notably absent. Those who do attend are nonplused. Quick follow-up feedback from those who were absent as well as some who attended reveals that people have become skeptical about and impatient with community meetings. That's a dead end. A new strategy is needed to engage the community. Maybe those who held the meeting should have figured that out ahead of time. But they didn't. They held the meeting. It didn't work. The developmental evaluation feedback is pretty damn clear on that point. Don't try to improve the meeting (formative evaluation). A different approach is needed. Use what's been learned from the failed effort to develop a more innovative process of engagement.

In highly turbulent environments and complex situations, developmental evaluation may be ongoing in assisting and supporting social innovators who adapt their interventions as they encounter the nonlinear dynamics of complexity. But the adaptive cycle alerts us to the possibility, even the likelihood, that some ideas and innovations will emerge that hold the promise of becoming models for change that can be taken to scale to increase impact. Social innovators typically want to have big impacts. They are visionaries. They love to experiment and try things out, but as they discover something that works, they want to share it with others, expand the arena of impact, even make a global difference. When that happens, when aspirations turn from development and adaptation to model building and dissemination, developmental evaluation can yield to traditional formative and summative evaluation. Exhibit 7.4 shows this transition, mapping different purposes and uses of evaluation onto the adaptive cycle.

Summative evaluations judge the overall effectiveness, merit, worth, and significance of a program and are particularly important in making decisions about continuing or terminating an experimental program, demonstration project, policy, or other innovation. As such, summative evaluations are often requested by funders. *Formative evaluation*, in contrast, focuses on ways of improving and enhancing programs and innovations, getting them stabilized, standardized, and *ready for summative evaluation*. As noted in Chapter 1, Michael Scriven (1967, pp. 40–43) introduced the summative–formative distinction in discussing evaluation of educational curriculum, first improving a pilot curriculum (formative evaluation), then deciding if it should be judged effective and disseminated (summative evaluation). The distinction has since become a fundamental evaluation typology (Patton, 2008c). Chapter 2 discussed these distinctions and distinguished developmental evaluation from them.

The additional point here is that formative evaluation supports the exploitation phase of innovation by fine-tuning a model—improving and stabilizing it so that it is ready for and can be appropriately subjected to a summative test. A positive summative evaluation means that an interven-

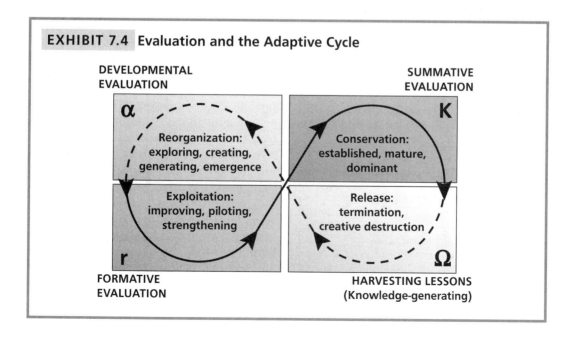

EXHIBIT 7.4 Evaluation and the Adaptive Cycle

DEVELOPMENTAL EVALUATION

SUMMATIVE EVALUATION

α

Reorganization: exploring, creating, generating, emergence

K

Conservation: established, mature, dominant

Exploitation: improving, piloting, strengthening

Release: termination, creative destruction

r

Ω

FORMATIVE EVALUATION

HARVESTING LESSONS (Knowledge-generating)

tion or innovation is ready for "prime time," meaning it is primed for taking to scale. It works. It is effective, and ideally cost-beneficial, at least within the context where it has been evaluated summatively. Going to scale means aspiring to dominance, which is the conservation quadrant of the adaptive cycle. Dominance is sustained (or attempts to be sustained) by adhering to the rules of engineering resilience discussed at the beginning of this chapter. The fore loop of the adaptive cycle, from exploitation to conservation, corresponds to the evaluation transition from formative to summative, in which summative evaluation validates the merit and worth of best practice domination.

Programs and innovations that attain summative confirmation because of demonstrated effectiveness are rightfully sought after, supported, and revered. Evaluation of the dissemination of such initiatives focuses on fidelity, assuring that the summatively validated model is appropriately and rigorously replicated. Resources get locked up in this most-favored, best practice model. Therein lies a potential rigidity trap, because context changes over space and time. Rigid adherence to a validated model in the conservation phase holds the seeds of its own destruction because things will inevitably change. The world won't stand still. The model will begin losing effectiveness and ad-

herents as new challenges emerge for which it is ill-suited. Resources controlled by the dominant model will be released and eventually lost. It will fall into disfavor and those dedicated to it will experience the woes and tumult of creative destruction.

Developmental evaluation can play a different role in taking an innovation to scale by adapting it to different conditions and cross-scale situations rather than insisting on replication and high fidelity. I discussed the issues involved around high-fidelity versus situational adaptability in the last chapter. We'll return to those issues shortly when we look at cross-scale interactions.

Knowledge-Generation and Harvesting Lessons Learned

Work eight hours and sleep eight hours, and make sure that they are not the same eight hours.
—T. BOONE PICKENS, oil tycoon, *The First Billion Is the Hardest* (2008, p. 247)

Decline, when it comes, ushers in an opportunity for knowledge generation and harvesting lessons learned (Patton, 2008c, pp. 131–137). Knowledge generation changes the unit of analysis as evaluators look across findings from different programs and innovations to identify *general patterns of effectiveness* to better understand how context affects and conditions effectiveness and efficiency. The lessons harvested during resource release and creative destruction can provide the foundation for new ideas and experiments in the exploration phase. The back loop in the adaptive cycle from release to reorganization is where lessons learned provide a framework for developmental evaluation inquiries, supporting exploration with principles and wisdom gleaned from past activities and initiatives. Developmental evaluation can also support back-loop activity as resources are reorganized and new explorations emerge by capturing the evolution of how innovators are thinking about and developing their ideas.

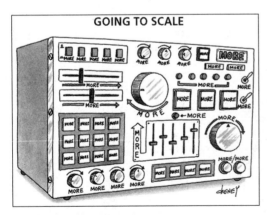

GOING TO SCALE

© Tom Cheney/Condé Nast Publications/
www.cartoonbank.com.

Let me be clear that I am not suggesting that the *only* time evaluation facilitates learning lessons is during creative destruction or, for that matter, when engaged in developmental evaluation. Identifying, capturing, and communicating learnings, especially under the popular moniker "lessons learned," has become a staple of evaluation, the meat and potatoes, rice and beans, or tofu and veggies that consumers of evaluation love to digest. Philanthropic funders, policymakers, nonprofit leaders, and the media are hungry for lessons learned. As the idea of "lessons" has become more and more valued as a form of bankable currency in the knowledge age, and the term manically popularized by the media in seriously reporting "lessons learned about life" as expounded by 18-year-old rock stars and television personalities, evaluation has had to raise the bar by differentiating *high-quality lessons* based on evidence and triangulation from just anybody's opinion-of-the-moment. There's "You know, like, I've learned that, you know, you have to, like, live life to the, you know, fullest, and like, seize the, I mean, *carp per diems*, and all that, in-the-minute kind of thing, and all that really matters, you know, is like love and stuff." Then there's "Evidence from multiple studies of stakeholder involvement in evaluations point to the importance of *skilled facilitation* to bring diverse stakeholders to agreement about priority evaluation questions and the appropriate design to answer those questions. Research from related fields, social science theory, expert analysis, and practitioner wisdom all confirm this finding" (see Patton, 2008c, chap. 3).

So, yes, evaluations of all kinds—formative, summative, theory-driven, participatory, and developmental—generate lessons. And developmental evaluation can and should generate lessons about social innovation and adaptability throughout the adaptive cycle. But harvesting lessons during creative destruction takes on added importance and urgency to the point of becoming the priority focus, supporting and facilitating the transition to new exploration.

Pacing, Time, and Speed

The transitions through the phases of the adaptive cycle do not all occur at the same rate. In the adaptive cycle graphic (Exhibits 7.2–7.4), the solid arrows within the infinity symbol depict slow change while the dashed arrows depict rapid change. When evaluation distinctions are added to the quadrants (Exhibit 7.4), the graphics show that the transition from formative to summative evaluation (the upward-sloping front loop) is relatively slow. For many programs and evaluation contracts, this transition takes 5–6 years with 2–3 years of formative evaluation followed by 2–3 years of summative evaluation. In contrast, the processes of creative destruction speed up the cycle, meaning that lessons have to be harvested quickly as things fall apart, resources are released, and a rapid transition to the exploration phase ensues (the downward-sloping back loop). In the case of the forest, it takes a long time for the trees to grow but a short time for fire to destroy them (somewhat longer with drought, disease, or insect invasions, but still considerably less time than the original growth into mature forest). Likewise, establishing a dominant, summatively evaluated best practice model and taking it to scale (domination) takes time. Severe budget cuts or major political transitions are the forest fires of the program world. Failure to adapt to changed conditions and emergent trends brings a slower but no less certain demise of long-established programs.

Exploration and Developmental Evaluation

Developmental evaluation has the most pronounced role in the upper-left quadrant of the adaptive cycle where exploration occurs. During this phase, things can change rapidly and everything is (or at least feels) in flux.

Exploration and reorganization are the white water rapids that developmental evaluation has to navigate in contrast to the long, slow, and controlled floating along a calm river that is summative evaluation. As creative destruction ushers in reorganization and exploration, as programming hits the rapids and staff becomes alert to the dangers of precipitous waterfalls, the importance of quick scanning, rapid feedback, and intense alertness replace the controlled action of summative evaluation. The formative-to-summative transition is steady, calculated, controlled, and relatively slow (front loop). The transitions from creative destruction to exploration (back loop), where new possibilities are generated, is frenetic, intense, turbulent, and beyond control—which may explain why evaluators have avoided that treacherous terrain and, when encountering it, have tried to impose the controlled pace of the formative–summative transition. Which, on the whole, doesn't work very well and tends not to be useful. Which is why innovators have resisted evaluation. Developmental evaluation has a different pace, one matched to the rapid rate of change on the left side of Exhibits 7.2–7.4.

Through the Looking Glass of the Adaptive Cycle: Examples of Organizational and Program Cycles

A new president is appointed at a philanthropic foundation with a mandate to dismantle some major long-term programs favored by her predecessor. Being sensitive to the havoc this will cause among program officers with expertise in these programs and existing grantees as they lose funding, the new president's language is gently bureaucratic; she refers to "pursuing new strategic opportunities," "revisiting priorities," and "aligning programs with a new vision and mission." In other words, it won't be called "creative destruction," but it is, and feels like it to those whose previous dominance is now

in decline. They're likely to miss the creative part. Evaluation-wise, a savvy new president will initiate a process of harvesting lessons: What worked well in the programs and initiatives being eliminated? What can be learned about how the foundation has done business in the past? What kinds of relationships with grantees had been established, with what benefits and what difficulties?

At the same time, the new president wants to begin innovative programming in an emergent arena, perhaps initiatives with *transnationals* (people who live in two or more countries, like Mexico and the United States, and move back and forth), integrated environmental and health economic approaches, or microfinance for indigenous and aboriginal peoples. The president or other innovative leader may use a network to create exploratory relationships with people knowledgeable about and involved in emergent arenas of action and begin making innovative, open-ended grants, giving grantees lots of room to try things out, build relationships, and see what emerges. Developmental evaluation supports the grantees' explorations and captures what is emerging so that those involved can learn from each other, strengthen their networks, and facilitate the foundation's decisions about where to put more resources. Such interactions, of course, require a high trust relationship between foundation, innovator, and evaluator. As these interactions unfold and results take shape, a few of the exploratory projects begin to look like models that are worthy of attracting national and international interest. New and higher levels of funding for these select models require proposals with clear, specific, and measurable outcomes—and a period of formative evaluation. Within 2 or 3 years, some of the models are expected to be sufficiently well formed and stabilized to be ready for rigorous summative evaluation. Those that demonstrate success will be supported to disseminate the model and expand the people and places engaged with the model.

Patch Dynamics and Ecosystem Resilience: A Diversified Portfolio Based on the Adaptive Cycle Quadrants and Transitions

Let's continue with the philanthropic foundation example. Suppose the foundation continues to fund social innovators and networks exploring new possibilities. Within a 5- to 10-year time span, the foundation's portfolio could have grants and corresponding evaluation activities *in each of the quadrants of the adaptive cycle*: exploratory and innovative endeavors supported by developmental evaluation; pilot models that have emerged from exploration that are being fine-tuned and formalized through formative evaluation (exploitation); promising models being validated through summative evaluation and, when successful taken to scale (conservation); and older initiatives being phased out (creative destruction). An organization's ecosystem resilience can be increased by having initiatives in each of the quadrants at any one time—a diversified portfolio, spread throughout the quadrants of the adaptive cycle that manifests what is called patch dynamics (a system with subsystems in different phases of the adaptive cycle at the same time).

An Exercise in Applying the Adaptive Cycle

When conducting training on the adaptive cycle, we have participants undertake an exercise in which they assess which projects and initiatives in their organization are in which quadrants. Anyone in an organization of any size can usually identify some areas of mature programming (dominance); some areas of actual, impending, or suspected decline; some areas of exploration and hoped-for innovation; and some areas where pilot models are being worked on and getting tested before being expanded or taken to scale (aspiring to become "best practice"). Participants find the exercise initially chal-

lenging, but ultimately useful and enlightening. They come to see that the adaptive cycle is not necessarily monolithic in an organization. One large program or organization can have activities and initiatives in each quadrant at the same time, as well as some in transition along the fore loop or back loop. And for our purposes here, they come to see that the evaluation issues and methods are different in each quadrant, and different on the fore loop (formative to summative) than on the back loop (harvesting lessons to support exploration and innovation). The importance of matching the evaluation to an initiative's stage of development becomes understood.

Other Applications and Examples

The adaptive cycle scenario can be applied to the ascent and decline of government initiatives. When the party in power changes, or when a new president or prime minister is elected, changes will occur. Some favorite initiatives of predecessors will fall by the wayside, while those of the new incumbent will emerge and take hold. Under the Bush administration (2000–2008), organizations that offered or supported abortion were not eligible for federal funds, domestically or internationally, a reversal of Clinton's policy. The conservative Bush policy became dominant. As soon as President Obama was elected, he reversed the Bush policy, not only allowing funding for organizations linked with abortion services or counseling, but promoting new initiatives aimed at exploring innovative approaches to family planning. The same policy reversal occurred with regard to stem cell research.

Cycles in university offerings can be illuminated and depicted similarly. Some university departments go through periods of centralization (carefully prescribed required courses in a discipline) followed by periods of decentralization (greater flexibility and more freedom in selecting courses for a major). When requirements are heavily prescribed, specifying core knowledge, mandated courses become dominant. Over time, students and faculty bristle at the narrowness of the restrictions and begin demanding more openness and increased options. A cycle of decentralization ensues, creatively destroying the previously dominant definition of what the discipline entailed and opening a period of innovation and exploration. New courses are developed, piloted, and adopted. Requirements and mandates are relaxed. Interdisciplinarity flourishes. Amid all this ferment, concerns arise about the lack of focus and the absence of agreed-on core disciplinary knowledge, and a period of centralization ensues. But the newly established core is not identical to the previously agreed-on core. What is dominant changes, sometime in major ways, sometimes more subtly, but rarely does the centralization–decentralization cycle end up in the same place. In sociology, I've lived through this cycle several times in my lifetime.

More generally, Kuhn's (1970) structure of scientific revolutions fits the adaptive cycle. Certain ideas become dominant in a discipline (e.g., Newtonian physics) until that framework fails to answer new questions. The dominance of the primary paradigm begins to wither under close examination and a period of innovation and competing ideas ensues, with new ideas (quantum physics) gathering force, being tested, and eventually becoming the new, dominant paradigm.

I came to the University of Minnesota in the 1970s and became part of the Minnesota Extension Service (historically known as agricultural extension or cooperative extension). The dominant model was an extension office and agents in every county. Minnesota has 87 counties, thus 87 county extension offices. This model was sacrosanct. It had been around for a century and had survived the Great Depression. The university's commitment to extension was absolute. Extension had enormous influence in the state legislature, where rural legislators, many of whom had come through extension's 4-H programs or had benefited from extension advice on their family farms, held controlling power. Then in the 1990s, it all unraveled, not only in Minnesota, but throughout the country. In the face of the decline of family farms, the increasing size of the much smaller number of remaining farms, the emergent dominance of corporate farming, the globalization of agriculture, communication changes with new technologies and the Internet that made information widely available, state and federal budget crises, refocusing in universities, the extension-agent-in-every-county model vanished. Regional offices have since emerged. Extension is seeking new roles and partners. New extension models and programs are being tested. Extension has had to adapt to a changing world—painfully, with both resistance and renewed vision, reactively and creatively, with longing looks backward and hopeful looks forward, but deeply enmeshed in uncertainty and turbulence. Extension's county agent model once ruled. Now it is gone. I was futures editor for the *Journal of Extension* in the 1980s. For 3 years I wrote columns about the new directions in extension and the need for adapting to emergent conditions. The only constant I foresaw, the one mainstay I was sure would endure, was the county-based agent, up-close and personal in a bottom-up, grassroots structure. The demise of the county agent was unimaginable to me. Had I understood the adaptive cycle in those days of futuring, I might have been more prescient. Or perhaps not.

Transitions and Traps

Cycling is not certain. Transitions from one quadrant to another are particularly hazardous, which provides opportunities for evaluation—and evaluators—to be especially useful. Exhibit 7.5 shows four transition traps where the adaptive cycle may be interrupted.

EXHIBIT 7.5 Transition Traps

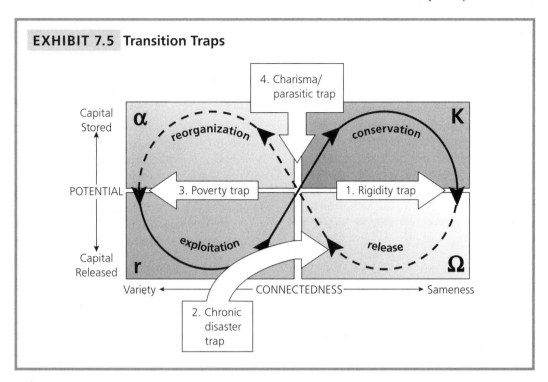

1. Rigidity Trap

Maladaption leads to system collapse when, says Holling, a system's potential, diversity, and resilience have been eradicated (Gunderson & Holling, 2002, p. 95). In the conservation stage this occurs when the dominant system resists change in the face of changed conditions and clamps down to maintain the status quo. National Park policies in the western United States aimed to stop all forest fires. Rocky Mountain National Park, with no forest fires in 100 years, became a rigid ecosystem of pine forest sameness. When the pine beetle hit in the mid-2000s, the forest was especially vulnerable and has since been decimated. Management practices interfered with diversity and a more natural adaptive cycle of resilience.

When something is called a "third rail" in politics, we know we're facing a rigidity trap. The third rail is the exposed electrical conductor in a subway track system that carries high-voltage power, resulting in electrocu-tion if touched. It has become a metaphor in politics for an issue so charged and un-touchable that anyone dealing with it risks political suicide. Social security reform is a political third rail, so the United States is locked into a rigid system that is financially unsustainable but seemingly impossible to change.

The French philosopher Emile Chartier might have been describing the rigidity trap when he mused: "Nothing is more danger-ous than an idea when it is the only one you have." Programs get locked into doing things one way. Advocates of "best practices" applaud doing things only one way. Social innovators can become fixated on one idea and, ironically, become resistant to new ideas. More irony: Achieving excellence in performance may make us more vulnerable to rigidity traps. In a classic study, Danny Miller (1992) examined companies that had attained a deserved reputation for ex-cellence. He found that these companies pursued what he called an "architecture of simplicity." They focused all their resources on the "one best way": they reduced slack to be lean and mean, and they reduced redundancy to ensure that everyone and everything was focused on their strategic priorities. As a result, they lost peripheral vision and perspective. He subtitled his book *How Exceptional Companies Bring About Their Own Demise*, and called the rigidity pattern he discovered the *Icarus paradox*. Like the fabled Icarus, in flying too close to the sun, they forgot that waxen wings melt. At the moment of greatest success they found themselves knocked off course by rivals they didn't even see coming. Miller's finding about rigid business strategies triangulates with Holling's analysis of rigid ecosystems. Hanging on to what we do best, when it is no longer working, is a trap. The trap makes the eventual fall longer and harder (Westley et al., 2006, pp. 68–69).

The implications of the adaptive cycle are that even in dominance (conservation), even at the moment of greatest success, it is important to diversify some resources into new ideas to avoid the rigidity trap and keep the system resilient. In the film *Patton*, there's a scene in which General George Patton recalls the Roman tradition that when a great military hero was celebrated with a triumphal parade through the city, a slave stood behind the victorious general whispering in his ear, "All glory is fleeting." Such a sense of inevitable change is what pushes prescient leaders to begin diversifying and innovating in anticipation of creative destruction. They understand that in order to manage risk you have to take some risk by being open to change. Understanding the complexities and dynamics of change, those at the height of success can paradoxically anticipate and plan for the next phase in the cycle, like a squirrel putting up nuts in anticipation of winter. Seasons flow from one to the other with great certainty. The phases of the adaptive cycle flow from one to the other with much less certainty and predictability, but change will come. Anticipating possibilities for change and being open to diverse alternatives helps avoid the rigidity trap. One of General Patton's most widely cited quotes is: "If everyone is thinking alike, then somebody isn't thinking." The rigidity trap is the organizational demand that everyone think—and act—alike.

An evaluation mindset can facilitate anticipation of and preparation for adapting to a new phase of innovation. Evaluation invites reflection on what has happened and why, harvesting lessons, and making sense of patterns. "You can't build to the next strategic phase if you don't understand where you've been and where you are," observes Frances Westley.

Knowing the dangers of rigidity, developmental evaluators are prepared to encourage questioning. Begin with the premise that even summatively validated and high-fidelity-implemented "best practices" are context-dependent. Thoughtful environmental scanning and rigorous questioning—Of what? Of everything!—can keep open the possibility for change. A developmental evaluator can help facilitate regular, systematic, and data-based reflective practice about how a program's context may be changing as well as internal reflections on internal challenges that cry out for adaptation: different participant characteristics (more immigrants, younger or older clients, more mental health problems), staff turnover, funding changes, new technological opportunities, and changing space needs. I often introduce such reflective practice sessions with a centering quotation about rigidity from the great societal observer Alexis de Tocqueville:

I cannot help fearing that men may reach a point where they look on every new theory as a danger, every innovation as a toilsome trouble, every social advance as a first step toward revolution, and that they may absolutely refuse to move at all.

2. Chronic Disaster Trap

Neither ecosystems nor organizations come with manufacturers' guarantees that in the event of creative destruction, a smooth and assured transition to reorganization and exploration will occur. Once things start falling apart in a system, it becomes vulnerable to a downward spiral of chronic disasters. (See Exhibit 7.5, trap 2.) This can be seen in overpopulated, low-lying areas subject to major flooding or monsoons, especially those inhabited by people in poverty who have nowhere else to go. That the area is not suitable for dense human habitation is well established. That another flood will hit is certain. Such a mix has the makings of a chronic ecosystem and human disaster. Such chronic disasters and their consequences have been especially well documented by Yale sociologist Kai Erikson (1995).

In programs and organizations this takes the form of a permanent state of crisis management leading to high staff burnout, perpetual staff turnover, and increasingly ineffective stopgap measures aimed at crisis alleviation. News media throughout the United States regularly carry headlines about the "Foster Care Crisis for Children." The crisis only hits the top of the news when a child dies in foster care, but the chronic disaster ebbs and flows unabated. Foster care children are bounced from home to home and institution to institution in chaotic conditions. Placements are barely adequate. Forget about effective services. Foster children are buffeted by instability, regular rejections, and severe stress. As efforts to identify child abuse and neglect have increased, including better identification in emergency rooms and school truancy tracking efforts, more children get taken from their parents for abuse or neglect. Meth and crack epidemics contribute to the problem, as does teenage pregnancy. Indeed, some teenagers in foster care have children who are then placed in foster care. The children are victims of a system that has become overloaded, overwhelmed, and subject to chronic disaster. With too few foster homes, children get sent back to inadequate and even abusive parents. Occasionally the crisis spills into public view and generates headlines and outrage—for a day, or maybe a week.

- A young, pregnant teenager is reported sleeping for weeks on a couch in a recreation room at a group home where 25 children live in space meant for 18.

- Disturbed teens languish for months in inadequately staffed observation centers where physical abuse of children by other children is chronic.

- Homeless children end up sleeping in city welfare offices because shelter beds and foster placements are insufficient.

- Budget cuts and mandates to "do more with less" exacerbate the crisis.

Such stories are the headlines of a chronic disaster trap in the midst of welfare reform, privatization of foster care services, and increasing numbers of children in poverty. Welfare agencies have difficulty adapting quickly to changes in the number of children needing foster care. When numbers increase rapidly, usually due to efforts at better reporting and detection in some other part of the system, the severity of the crisis deepens and reaches public attention. Short-term, emergency measures alleviate the severity for the moment, but the problem doesn't get solved. It just retreats into the bureaucratic shadows, out of public view and consciousness, until the next death of a child in foster care again makes headlines.

The chronic disaster trap evokes Albert Einstein's observation that insanity is "doing the same thing over and over again and expecting different results." Recognizing this offers an opening for evaluation. Part of harvesting lessons during creative destruction ought to include generating scenarios for what happens next. One possibility is moving into exploration and reorganization. But another possibility is falling into the chronic disaster trap. What indicators and benchmarks need to be tracked by funders, advocates, and social innovators to know which path is emerging? What are the system parameters, behaviors, and outcomes that point to chronic disaster? Labeling can be, in and of itself, an engine for change. When evaluators observe a system in chronic disaster mode, we need to call it what it is.

Moreover, and I want to emphasize this point, *one can't do developmental evaluation well in a chronic disaster situation.* All the thinking and action gets locked up in crisis management. When a program is overwhelmed, understaffed, and badly managed, evaluation isn't of much help; indeed, it can contribute to the crisis because it's one more thing to deal with, one more thing to manage. Some minimally effective management and open space for change has to be created with resources for exploration to move into serious reorganization where developmental evaluation can contribute to moving forward in the adaptive cycle.

3. Poverty or Scarcity Trap

The poverty or scarcity trap can undermine the transition from reorganization and exploration to exploitation and supporting promising new possibilities. (See Exhibit 7.5, trap 3.) The scarcity trap occurs when the resources released are insufficient to support vibrant exploration. Having experienced the trauma of creative destruction and the ambiguities and uncertainties of exploitation, funders can be understandably reluctant to commit new resources. The ferocious policy debate worldwide in early 2009 was about what level of government stimulus, if any, was needed to avoid worldwide recession and get the economy reenergized. In the United States, liberal economists like Nobel Prize–recipient Paul Krugman argued that the stimulus package would fail from being too small, too risk-averse, and too unimaginative (poverty of ideas). Conservative economists and politicians in opposition to the government stimulus feared huge waste and future inflation, and wanted to let creative destruction run its survival-of-the-fittest, free-market course.

Exploitation, following creative destruction, is the phase when new opportunities are sought and new connections made. In ecosystems, there is intense competition for available space and resources. After a forest fire, new growth appears quickly. Seedlings from different plants cover the ground with a blanket of reemergent life. In programs and organizations, the reorganization phase involves brainstorming, exploration, innovation, and experimentation. To move from everything-is-a-possibility exploration to focus-on-most-promising-ideas exploitation, the poverty trap must be avoided. If new ideas don't root and grow, if they fail to be nurtured and sufficiently resourced, the transition is short-circuited. In resilient adaptation, some selection is required. Competing species growing one inch apart cannot all grow to maturity. Holling and his colleagues found in studying ecosystems that some species must wither while others thrive, securing enough of the available resources to grow to maturity. Likewise, in resilient and innovative organizations, separate teams may compete to create promising prototypes, but only a few of the proposed programs and services that are imagined can be launched. So, some of the richness and variety of a thousand flowers blooming must be let go to properly nourish a few flowers to their full, healthy maturity.

Both philanthropic foundations and government funders push innovative initiatives into the poverty trap when they fund innovations for some short period like 3 years (yes, 3 years is a short time for an innovation to take root), then withdraw funding supposedly to avoid having the program become dependent. In 40 years of working with nonprofits, perhaps the most common complaint I've heard is the lament that funders have short and unrealistic time lines for success and withdraw their support too soon for innovations to be fully developed. This is where the rigidity trap intersects with the poverty trap. A rigid policy of "we only fund for 3 years" can result in inadequate time and resources to demonstrate the effectiveness (or even the ineffectiveness) of a significant innovation.

Here again is an opportunity for rigorous and flexible developmental evaluation. In the evaluation design negotiations between funders and innovators, two of the key developmental questions to anticipate and address are:

1. What's a realistic time line to demonstrate an idea's potential?
2. What resources will be needed to assess that potential?

Note that at this stage, the transition from reorganization/exploration to exploitation is different from the formative/summative transition (which we address next). This is a transition from open-ended possibility to worth-betting-on probability. This is the process of selecting which innovations to back for further development, moving from the thousand seedlings to those that will be nourished after weeding out the less promising.

Such selection is inherently an evaluative process. Criteria will be needed, perhaps more than one set of criteria to maintain some creativity and innovation. These are not the ultimate summative criteria for judging overall success. Those operational success criteria will come later when the innovations are better developed. At this stage, the evaluation question concerns which promising possibilities merit further development. Venture capitalists regularly make such assessments in deciding what new ideas to back. Some look for the best ideas, then they help turn those ideas into a development plan and find good people to try out the idea. Other venture capitalists begin with selection of innovative people— those with a track record of innovative and creative thinking. They trust these people to come up with new ideas and support them to do so. Still others begin by requiring a detailed business plan: "Show me the numbers, the potential market, the competition,

the potential profitability." If the numbers are convincing, they support prototype development. These are three different venture capitalist strategies for selecting what promising innovations to fund into fuller development.

Whatever the selection strategy, from an evaluation perspective the criteria should clarify and assess what it will take to move from promising idea to testable model. A developmental evaluation carried out during the reorganization phase will involve working with social innovators to decide whether a model has emerged with sufficient potential that it should be exploited (which means moving into formative evaluation connected to summative evaluation). Rushing too quickly from developmental evaluation to summative evaluation without either sufficient development or formative evaluation will generate a poverty trap of insufficient data to make an informed judgment.

Consider evaluation of a program aimed at helping African American men coming out of prison get jobs. The program developers had lots of good ideas and street smarts (some had themselves gone through this transition from prison to work). The need was clear. Lots of ineffective efforts filled the graveyard of once-high hopes. Innovation was clearly needed, but the uncertainties were mammoth. Would prisons cooperate? Who were good candidates for this kind of project? Would inmates respond to the opportunity? How could needs other than employment be met during the transition? What kind of staff–participant ratios would be needed? Where should the project be located for both access and security? Lots and lots of questions. A combination of philanthropic and government funding supported a pilot effort but with only a 2-year time line. The program got pushed into a demonstration model requiring summative evaluation before it had even had a chance to develop. The funders, in a rushed search for exemplars, rejected the idea of a developmental period with developmental evaluation. To get funding, the program accepted the requirement for summative evaluation, preordaining a negative judgment, which was, indeed, forthcoming. After a mere 2 years, the evaluation rendered a summative judgment of failure. In fact, it was the funders and the evaluators who failed. The funders failed by inappropriately requiring a premature and ill-advised summative evaluation. The evaluators failed by agreeing to render such a judgment. The poverty trap closed tight on the innovative program, killing it.

4. Charisma/Parasitic Trap

Businesses moving from early success as a venture capital innovation into national and international markets often need different management expertise and leadership to make this transition. Nonprofits can face a similar challenge, especially when the original organization was founded by a charismatic leader. A sustainable, maturing, and resilient nonprofit can have expansion and going-to-scale derailed by founders who can't give up control or staff who hang onto and become dependent on the founder's charisma. Studies of nonprofit life cycles have identified *founder's syndrome* as a common form of charisma trap (Gross, 2009; Simon, 2001; Stevens, 2002). After Frances Westley identified and labeled the charisma trap as a potential impediment in the transition from exploitation (pilot testing) to conservation (going to scale), Brenda Zimmerman added the parasitic label. Both designations connote strong attachment. The parasitic framing suggests that the parasite (e.g., the organization, the program) cannot survive without the host, often the founder or original major funder. Moreover, Brenda was concerned that charisma carried a potentially positive connotation not quite in keeping with the other adaptive cycle traps (rigidity, chronic disaster, and poverty). She said that she struggled with using the term *charisma* without also talking about parasites. (See Exhibit 7.5, trap 4.)

Mark Cabaj of Vibrant Communities in Canada has examined "The Cycles of Collab-

orative Efforts to Reduce Poverty" (2009a). Collaborations typically get started when a particular set of leaders come together and commit to work together. Cabaj observes: many collaborations stumble when the original founders, usually executive directors, leave the table and are replaced by middle-level managers without the same authority or expertise. He asks: How does a collaboration stay vibrant and moving forward as participants change? And new pilot projects, he notes, may initially evolve in symbiosis with other related interventions as all experience the initial glow of innovation, but how is that glow maintained as things shift, attention wanes, and parasitic traps (dependence on original leaders) come into play?

Taking an Innovation to Scale: Challenges and Traps in Cross-Scale Change

The charisma/parasitic trap calls attention to the particular challenges that innovative initiatives and social movements face in moving from local success to larger impacts through *going to scale*. Social innovators typically seek broad impact, as do their supporters and funders. But over and over again we find that the successes of small-scale programs are difficult to replicate over time and space. A program's first-generation successes are often a function of the high energy and commitment that creative and determined social innovators bring to new initiatives. Evaluators are trained to focus on identifying and assessing a formal model that distills out these personal and interpersonal characteristics in search of a best practices recipe that can be replicated in other places. But over and over it turns out that the model's original effectiveness was heavily dependent on the charisma, entrepreneurial spirit, and commitment of the original innovators, including their astute openness to adaptive management and use of ongoing formative feedback, *people factors* that appear quite difficult if not impossible to replicate.

In addition, summative evaluations aimed at judging whether a program is ready for prime time, that is, ready for replication and going to scale, often ignore contextual factors that are critical to success within the time and place where the program has operated. The strong focus on conceptualizing the elements of a replicable model narrows the evaluator's measures to internal validity—Can the outcomes observed be attributed to the program?—and give short shrift to generalizability and replicability (external validity). This is especially the weaknesses of randomized control trial designs for sum-

---

～ *Advice from an Experienced Developmental Evaluator*

Jamie Gamble is principal, Imprint Consulting, New Brunswick, Canada. He authored A Developmental Evaluation Primer *(2008), published by the J. W. McConnell Family Foundation in Montreal. The* Primer *came out of a series of developmental evaluation workshops we did together in 2005–2006. Here's Jamie's latest thinking.*

1. *Stay focused on what is being developed.* For many practitioners, developmental evaluation seems to resonate. Perhaps this is because people who are good at program design and delivery are very naturally developing things. There is a match between their intuitive mindset and an approach to evaluation that supports this. I think the other part that practitioners seem to like is that developmental evaluation can effectively support them in things that they are wrestling with: strategy, process, and group dynamics. The challenge in this is that the core focus of supporting that which is being developed can get buried. Developmental evaluators and social innovators need to check in with themselves as the process unfolds to make sure that fundamental questions of what is being developed do not get lost.

2. *Match evaluation to the stage of the innovation.* I have found that a useful function for someone who is playing a developmental evaluation role is to remind people about the stage they are in. As developmental processes unfold there can be pressure (from within or from external sources) to move to a more summative mode of confirmation. There can also be pressure to hang onto a developmental mode when perhaps it is time to move to another stage. It is helpful for developmental evaluators to remind people of the stage they are in, ask questions with respect to the timeliness of moving into a different stage, and point out when their actions or behaviors don't line up with the stage they are in.

3. *Understand and attend to collaboration dynamics.* I have found that in the process of supporting social innovations with developmental evaluation there is almost always some form of collaboration attached to the initiative. Perhaps this is because innovation is fundamentally about combining existing things in new and unique ways and so people are naturally drawn into new patterns of working together. It has been very helpful for me to learn about the theory and practice of collaboration, and to include some observation and analysis about the particular collaborative dynamics in the initiative as a support to the developmental process.

4. *Match evaluation to the pace of development.* When I first started working with developmental evaluation I assumed that it would, in all cases, be a high-intensity exercise requiring a high frequency of interaction. This has certainly proven true in situations where there is a very accelerated development process under way. However, I have since had several experiences where the pace and scale of change is slower, and it was more suitable for the application of developmental evaluation to match this pace.

5. *Be explicit about the developmental evaluation role.* Naming the developmental evaluator as an explicit role—especially when this is being fulfilled by someone who is internal to the organization—creates a permission for critical thinking and feedback in a way that seems to enhance how feedback is received.

mative evaluation that, in my review of such designs, almost completely ignore identifying and evaluating contextual factors that would be critical for going to scale.

In the previous chapter I discussed at some length competing views concerning how major change occurs: top-down dissemination of proven best practices (intervention recipes) or bottom-up adaptive management, which involves using guiding principles to build change in an empowering and context-specific way from the grassroots. I have positioned developmental evaluation as facilitating integration and synthesis in the dynamical middle where local knowledge intersects with larger macroforces and trends in the process of taking an innovation to scale. *The middle ground is developmental.* The adaptive cycle offers additional insights into the issues of going to scale and the role developmental evaluation can play in providing feedback to social innovators as they learn about and adapt to cross-scale interactions.

Panarchy: Cross-Scale Interactions

The adaptive cycle offers a way to conceptualize phases of innovation that climax in *going to scale*, a preoccupation, even an obsession, for those who aspire to make major social change. Attention to *scale* is a key component of resilience in Holling's work on the adaptive cycle in ecological systems. From the microscopic level of bacteria to the life and death of whole forests, systems existing at separate scales do not cycle together. "From the small scale of pine needles, to the larger scale of trees, to the life and death of whole forests, systems existing at different scales do not evolve and cycle in the same time frame" (Westley et al., 2006, p. 206). The same may be said of social systems. Individuals, groups, organizations, and institutions go through cycles at different rhythms, as do political issues, economies, cultural systems, and legal systems.

Many innovations and major system changes, therefore, are stimulated and affected by *cross-scale* interactions, which Holling called *panarchy* after the Greek god Pan, god of chaos and play. He explains:

> Our purpose is to develop an integrative theory to help us understand the changes occurring globally. We seek to understand the source and role of change in systems—particularly the kinds of changes that are transforming, in systems that are adaptive. Such changes are economic, ecological, social, and evolutionary. They concern rapidly unfolding processes and slowly changing ones—gradual change and episodic change, local and global changes.
>
> The theory that we develop must of necessity transcend boundaries of scale and discipline. It must be capable of organizing our understanding of economic, ecological, and institutional systems. And it must explain situations where all three types of systems interact. The cross-scale, interdisciplinary, and dynamic nature of the theory has led us to coin the term *panarchy* for it. Its essential focus is to rationalize the interplay between change and persistence, between the predictable and unpredictable. Thus, we drew upon the Greek god Pan to capture an image of unpredictable change and upon notions of hierarchies across scales to represent structures that sustain experiments, test results, and allow adaptive evolution. (Gunderson & Holling, 2002, p. 5)

The notion of taking an innovation to scale, then, inherently involves cross-scale interactions and is unlikely to be either linear or controllable. In part this is because different conditions are encountered at different scales, especially variations in the dynamics of complexity.

> Spatial attributes are neither uniform nor scale invariant over all scales. Rather, productivity and textures are patchy and discontinuous at all scales, from the leaf to the landscape to the planet. There are several different ranges of scales, each with different attributes of architectural patchiness and texture and each controlled by a specific set of abiotic and biotic processes. They make attributes of the natural

world lumpy, rather than continuous, thereby concentrating resources and opportunities at particular scales. (Gunderson & Holling, 2002, p. 26)

The adaptive cycle highlights the message that things change. Stuff happens. Some of it nasty, some of it good. Some of it small, and some of it big. Some of it fast, some of it slow. Gunderson and Holling (2002) emphasize that "episodic behavior is caused by interactions between fast and slow variables" (p. 26). In ecosystems, critical processes function at significantly different rates, some faster and some slower. Climate change is slower while invasion of news species can be quite rapid, with lots of varying rates in between. A snapshot of a system at a moment in time can make it appear relatively stable, but attention to cumulative interactions over time will show significant transitions. Elizabeth Kolbert (2009) has reported on the sudden threat of extinction of frogs, bats, and bees in our time due to the cross-ecosystem transmission of diseases, global climate changes, habitat destruction, and the increased rate of global human migration, an acceleration of processes that in the past would have taken hundreds or even thousands of years to play out, but can now happen in mere decades, with worldwide implications.

Taking cross-scale interactions into account, it becomes clear that *scaling up from small to large cannot be a process of simple aggregation: nonlinear processes organize the shift from one range of scales to another.* Innovations at lower levels can create unpredictable reactions at higher levels, pushing the broader system from the conservative phase into release. Cross-scale interactions can operate in an opposite fashion as well, reducing the scope of systems change, even stifling it altogether if the rigidity trap swallows the innovation by a process called "remembrance," in which the way things have been are preserved, at least for a time. Exhibit 7.6 depicts the dynamics of panarchic cross-scale inter-

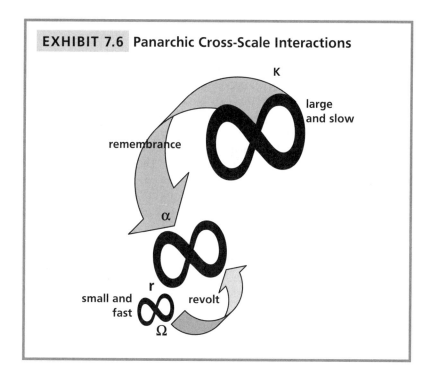

EXHIBIT 7.6 Panarchic Cross-Scale Interactions

actions. Developmental evaluation can support adaptive going-to-scale by gathering data and providing feedback about how an innovation is changed as it moves across the time and space of greater scale.

When Frances Westley began working with Buzz Holling, she immediately understood the implications of the adaptive cycle for social innovation, the importance of cross-scale interactions, and, subsequently in our discussions, the implications of both adaptation and cross-scale interactions for evaluation. It made sense to her that different kinds of evaluation would be needed at different stages and phases of innovation and experience. "When people try to map their initiatives, they see patterns in streams of decisions," she told me. "When they see something working, they naturally think about taking it to scale." But going to scale is difficult, and fails more often than it succeeds, in part because of the traps encountered along the way, and in part because cross-scale interactions are underappreciated or altogether ignored.

Going to scale in a highly controlled and formulaic manner can increase large-system rigidity. Holling found that ecosystem policies and management approaches that apply fixed rules create conservative-phase rigidities that reduce resilience. For example, large-scale agricultural practices aimed at achieving constant yields, fixing the carrying capacity of cattle or wildlife in an ecosystem, or fixing the sustainable yield of fish or wood, *independent of scale*, can lead to significant loss of resilience. The consequence is that these systems suddenly break down in the face of disturbances that previously could have been absorbed.

On the other hand, encouraging flexibility and diversity when going to scale and working on cross-scale interactions can increase resilience. In *Getting to Maybe* (Westley et al., 2006), Frances Westley described how Ulie Seal, in his network devoted to saving endangered species, deliberately tried to stimulate innovation by organizing

in different ways at different levels in order to induce change in a system. He paid particular attention to the complex adaptive processes of moving from local to regional to international action as well as to organizing simultaneously across different geographies.

The implications for evaluation of cross-scale interactions and panarchy challenge past ways of conceptualizing and evaluating what it means to take an innovation to scale. The recommendation to disseminate or scale an innovation has traditionally been a summative evaluation recommendation following formative evaluation to get the pilot project ready for summative evaluation. As noted, the primary purpose of summative evaluation has been to determine if a pilot effort is ready to be disseminated and replicated at scale. Such summative recommendations have typically ignored context and cross-scale interactions. The assumption has been that a pilot proven at small scale can simply be expanded in the same form at large scale, and therein accumulates an expanding graveyard of failed initiatives that worked at small scale but were disastrous when taken to larger scale. The rigid federal mandates of No Child Left Behind during the Bush administration years serve as an example. Indeed, it was the rigidity of the No Child Left Behind standards that created the most vocal opposition and demands for change.

This suggests that developmental evaluation can play an ongoing role in initiatives that involve taking innovations to scale, the role of watching for and assessing the effects of cross-scale interactions and helping social innovators adjust and adapt to the ways in which large scale affects an innovation's effectiveness. This is quite different from the fidelity-focused evaluation approach currently dominant in model replication and dissemination campaigns. Exhibit 7.7 at the end of the chapter provides an in-depth example of an evaluation framework for examining cross-scale systems change.

Panarchy-Informed Evaluation: The Fact of a Doorframe

Poet Adrienne Rich called her collection of poems *The Fact of a Doorframe* (2002). Fortunately (or not), few suffer from the evaluator's disease, as I do, in which everything evokes some aspect of evaluation. *The Fact of a Doorframe. The* fact. The *fact*. The fact? Reality. The way things are. *Doorframes.* Openings, and boundaries that define openings, and the framing of things. Like context, perspectives, relationships, and frameworks—the themes of systems thinking.

The adaptive cycle is a doorframe. Panarchy is a doorframe. As Rich ruminates in her poem, we can go through a door and take on the dual risks of entering new territory and leaving old territory behind, or we can choose not to go through the door. In appreciation of and inspired by Rich's insights about the fact of doorframes, and with apologies for any poetic license herein abused, I offer an adaptation of her musings for evaluators and those considering developmental evaluation.

Either you will adapt evaluation to the reality
    of cycles,
or you will not.
Release, reorganization, exploitation,
    conservation:
Where are you? Where have you been? Where
    are you going?
If you do enter the cycling doorframe, there
    is always the risk of traps,
for programs and for evaluations of
    programs:
rigidity traps, chronic disasters, poverty traps,
    and parasitic charisma.
If you do not enter into and use the adaptive
    cycle doorframe,
it is possible to evaluate worthily and with
    merit,
maintain evaluation standards,
hold onto established practices,
and complete work ably,
but, the poet warns,
much may blind you,
much evade you,
at some cost to yourself and others.
The adaptive cycle itself
makes no promises.
It is only a fact, the way the world is.

EXHIBIT 7.7 **Cross-Scale Patterns of Change: Tracking Principles (Simple Rules) across Different Complex Systems, Strengthening Families Example**

PRINCIPLES AND SIMPLE RULES TO STRENGTHEN FAMILIES AND PREVENT CHILD MALTREATMENT

Based on an extensive review of research, the Center for the Study of Social Policy (CSSP) developed an approach known as "Strengthening Families" to prevent child maltreatment (Strengthening Families, 2009). The approach is based on families developing five protective factors:

- Parental resilience
- Social connections
- Concrete support in time of need
- Knowledge of parenting and child development
- Social and emotional competence of children

(cont.)

These protective factors are *evidence-based principles* rather than best practices (i.e., an intervention recipe that prescribes precisely what to do) and can be thought of in complexity terms as "simple rules" that fundamentally shape the actions of agents in a complex adaptive system. These simple rules for strong families contrast to those that implicitly or explicitly guide the behavior of families in which child maltreatment occurs. The baseline assessment of the policy context concluded that these principles have not been sufficiently recognized by policymakers or social service agencies as important in preventing maltreatment. Moreover, the principles and the simple rules that have implicitly or explicitly guided program service providers and policymaker actions have focused heavily on reducing risk factors rather than building protective factors.

Being principles-driven, implementing the Strengthening Families approach is not about using a particular model or starting a new program. Rather it is about engaging existing programs, services, and other entities as partners around the use and promotion of the protective factors as their rules for action. It includes changes at multiple interrelated subsystems of a complex system including policy (governmental and organizational); formal and informal organizational connections; professional development for practitioners, programs, and activities; and changes in families' understanding of and use of protective factors. These subsystems can be thought of as primary points of influence that affect the whole complex system. Bringing about change in each of these subsystems involves cross-scale innovation and systems change.

Designing an evaluation of Strengthening Families involved developing a framework for tracking change toward use of protective factors. The framework presents the change process in terms of a shift in the simple rules that guide the actions/behaviors of the actors within all parts of the complex system. Taken together, these cross-scale system changes constitute a shift in paradigm. Meadows (2008) identifies shifting paradigms as one of the most powerful leverage points for changing a system.

MAPPING PATTERNS OF CHANGE IN A COMPLEX SYSTEM

The cross-scale summary table at the end of this exhibit on page 226 presents a framework of how attention to simple rules (principles), multiple system dynamics, and a tipping point can aid in understanding, evaluating, and influencing the embedding of protective factors in a state or region to reduce child maltreatment. Each part of the framework can be zoomed in on and elaborated to guide both action and inquiry. Using the Strengthening Families framework, the cross-scale graphic presents an example of how an evaluator might frame a way to look at the evolution of patterns within relevant subsystems that in turn help leaders of the initiative track and leverage multiple system dynamics. The statements within the framework provide the focus for evaluation activities.

The development of the framework begins by identifying subsystems within the overall complex system that have coherence of their own, interact with other subsystems, are likely to change in different ways and/or rates, and have been shown by past research to affect the whole complex system that interacts with child maltreatment. Thus they are important leverage points for systemic change. The idea is to work simultaneously in these multiple parts of the system with recognition that different patterns of change are likely for each subsystem because they have different system dynamics, especially differences in the extent and nature of organized and adaptive dynamics.

The second step in developing the framework is to identify aspects of change over time for each subsystem. In the cross-scale graphic each subsystem is observed first in regard to a baseline analysis of the subsystems when the investigation begins. Then (moving to the right in the diagram) attention is paid to the nature and extent of how people test ways to change each subsystem, build enough change to reach a tipping point, and then sustain a new balance

(cont.)

around the protective factors. Although the subsystems are displayed separately, recognize that the boundaries between the progression of change over time and the boundaries between the subsystems are fuzzy and permeable. Also, although all subsystems need to progress, it is not expected that they will change at the same rate or in the same time frame. Here is more detail about the progression from left to right in the diagram.

- **Baseline Analysis of Fundamentals and System Dynamics:** As an evaluation begins, the evaluator analyzes the current situation from the perspective of the five subsystems. The intent here is to develop an understanding of what current "simple rules" implicitly underlie how people behave in regard to these subsystems. Additionally, the evaluator is assessing the extent to which the protective factors might already be part of some of the underlying simple rules. The analysis also looks at the system dynamics to understand the balance and nature of the organized and adaptive dynamics. (See the questions in the column representing the first aspect of change.) Thus the evaluation is looking at the fundamentals (simple rules) and dynamics of the system.

- **Testing Applications of New Fundamentals and System Dynamics:** The next aspect of change is designing and implementing small-scale, carefully selected changes to understand how to embed protective factors in people's actions and leveraging both organized and adaptive dynamics. Some pilot tests might be done in a coordinated fashion across subsystems or within a subsystem with attention to the other subsystems. See Kellogg Foundation (2007) for a discussion of pilot test designs.

- **Tipping Point to New Fundamentals and System Dynamics Balance:** As changes are tested, people involved across subsystems attend to the developing depth of understanding and watch for movement to the next phase of change—the tipping point where momentum begins to shift to the protective factors as the predominant underlying way in which people are working within and across subsystems.

- **Sustainable Adaptive Balance of New Fundamentals and System Dynamics in Shifting Context:** The right side of the framework in the cross-scale graphic shows a sustainable dynamic balance grounded in the protective factors. The desired outcome of having the protective factors as the main driver of people's behavior would be embedded in that dynamic balance with recognition that there is continual adjustment of the system as the context changes with a likely oscillation over time of child maltreatment rates. Continual vigilance includes feedback about outcome levels *and* key system dynamics and elements. The "long-term outcome" is a situation where multiple agents across subsystems of the overall complex system are interacting and maintaining a dynamic balance that is continually adjusted in light of changing conditions to keep the child maltreatment rates low.

This framework allows an evaluation to follow and map the pattern and rate of change within and among the subsystems and engage in dialogue using an understanding of the features of complex systems to identify possible small changes that can have large impact in moving the system as a whole to the tipping point. See Parsons (1998, 2002) for more details on use of a similar tool in other settings. When looking across these subsystems and their interconnections, attention is directed to changes in boundaries, relationships, and differences in levels of energy to give clues as to how one might shift patterns within the complex systems (considering both organized and adaptive dynamics) toward greater use of protective factors as foundational to whichever aspect of the system is being addressed. As the tipping point is reached within each subsystem, the boundaries among the subsystems are likely to be even more permeable with the new knowledge about protective factors moving across boundaries and moving to a deeper level of understanding and integration.

Note. From Parsons (2009e).

Patterns of Change in Complex Systems: Strengthening Families Example

Points of Influence	Baseline Analysis of Fundamentals & System Dynamics — To what extent:	Testing Applications of New Fundamentals and System Dynamics	Tipping Point to New Fundamentals and System Dynamics Balance	Sustainable Adaptive Balance of New Fundamentals and System Dynamics in Shifting Context
Policy Context (state, organizational)	Are policies based on encouraging protective factors? Are policies attentive to both organized and adaptive dynamics?	Policies adjusted with engagement of multiple voices, perspectives, valuing of protective factors.	Policies overall predominately encourage building of protective factors. Policies leverage both organized and adaptive dynamics.	Policymakers balance attention to risk and protective factors tailored to micro-contexts. They adjust policy features that affect system fundamentals and dynamics over time based on data systems to maintain grounding in protective factors and related new knowledge.
Organizational Connections	Are connections built to encourage protective factors? Do connections support adaptive dynamics? Organized dynamics?	Entities, including ones not formerly involved, explore formal and informal connections to build attention to protective factors.	Key organizations have multiple inter-connections that encourage attention to protective factors on a micro and macro level. Attention to protective factors is fundamental to connections.	Organizations use data feedback to strategically shift connections to respond to contextual changes to ensure primary attention to protective factors. Shifts are based on attention to boundaries, relationships, and perspectives.
Professional Development (practitioners)	Do professional development activities address protective factors? Are professional development activities designed to model adaptive dynamics? Organized dynamics?	Professional development redesigned and tested with greater attention to protective factors and use of more interactive, peer-to-peer learning and learning from families.	Communities of practice grounded in peer-to-peer learning and application are common; include reflective practices for critical analysis of balance of protective and risk factor attention in different contexts.	Learning and teaching becomes woven into all aspects of practice with structured professional development sessions and communities of practice strategically used to shore up challenging areas. Practitioner knowledge and practice regularly assessed.
Families	Are families aware of and practicing protective factors? Are parents engaged with their child in supportive ways? Do parents use both organized and adaptive dynamics?	Families test use of protective factors and determine changes in relationships and boundaries in daily life. Families learn to self-assess use of protective factors.	Enough families are habitually using and self-assessing protective factors that community norms are shifting in support of protective factors.	Families are connected with other families who are skilled at using and building protective factors. Community norms support protective factors. Evidence of well being of families and levels of child maltreatment are regularly monitored in communities
Programs	Are programs designed around building protective factors? Do programs encourage adaptive dynamics between workers and families that support protective factors?	Programs pilot new ways of operating that are grounded in protective factors. They determine cost implications.	Programs commit to redesigned programs that incorporate protective factors. Programs leverage organized and adaptive dynamics	Programs use outcome and other data to adjust to social conditions in community with emphasis on supporting protective factors. Programs put high priority on leveraging both adaptive and organized dynamics.

8

Developmental Evaluation Inquiry Frameworks

Learn from yesterday, live for today, hope for tomorrow.
The important thing is not to stop questioning.
—ALBERT EINSTEIN (1879–1955), winner
of the 1921 Nobel Prize in Physics

The important thing is not to stop questioning. But which questions? Now there's the rub.

Developmental evaluation focuses on developmental questions: What's being developed? How is what's being developed and what's emerging to be judged? Given what's been developed so far and what has emerged, what's next? The developmental evaluator inquires into *developments*, tracks *developments*, facilitates interpretation of *developments* and their significance, and engages with innovators, change agents, program staff, participants in the process, and funders around making judgments about what is being developed, how it is being developed, the consequences and impacts of what has been developed, and the next stages of development.

That's the "big picture" view. But within that overarching framework, specific questions relevant to specific developmental process and impacts still have to be generated.

And there are lots and lots and lots of frameworks for generating questions. So we have to face the challenge of choosing.

As I was writing this chapter, Gene Shackman, an applied sociologist with the Global Social Change Research Project, initiated a discussion on *EvalTalk*, the AEA listserv, in which he asked professional evaluators what they experienced as the major challenges in doing evaluation. A quick consensus emerged around the challenge of engaging clients in determining *priority evaluation questions* the answers to which would be useful and actually used (Shackman, 2009). This chapter takes up the challenge of formulating and co-creating developmental evaluation questions. Asking "questions that matter" can be thought of as "a tool for working in complex situations" (Parsons & Jessup, 2009). I will identify 10 complexity situations and offer an inquiry framework for each. Matching evaluation questions to particular situations is the central challenge in developmental evaluation's situational responsiveness and adaptability, as in all utilization-focused evaluations.

Frameworks for Developmental Evaluation Inquiry

The foundation of fashion is wearing the right clothes for the occasion and having your wardrobe match: black (not brown) shoes with black trousers. And therein ends my fashion knowledge. But I have developed some expertise in matching questions to situations. Since I emphasize situational matching so much, as I have throughout this book, how, I'm regularly asked, do I decide which questions to use to frame a developmental evaluation inquiry. In this chapter I'm going to share what I've learned, offering my own heuristics insofar as I am aware of them. Like all self-reports, this one should be greeted with suspicion. But what follows is how I make sense of what I've done as a consultant and evaluator over a span of more than 30 years. There's no recipe, but there are some simple rules.

Simple Rules for Generating Framing Questions

1. Offer questions that connect with the ideas, language, and framework of the innovators with whom you're working. Listen

---

⌣ *Simple Rules and Min Specs: The Boids Simulation*

In 1986, computer programmer Craig Reynolds simulated the flocking behavior of birds. The simulation became famous for illustrating how complex adaptive systems can be based on a few simple rules or min specs (minimum specifications). It came to be called *Boids*, mimicking a stereotypical New York City accent saying "birds." The rules applied in the simplest flocks of boids are as follows:

- **Separation**: steer to avoid crowding local flockmates
- **Alignment**: steer toward the average heading of local flockmates
- **Cohesion**: steer to move toward the average position of local flockmates

For an illustration of the Boids simulation and discussion of its implications, see Reynolds (2001).

One potential focus of inquiry in developmental evaluation is looking for and making explicit the simple rules that inform innovation and decision making in an emergent initiative.

Glenda Eoyang (2009), founder and director of the Human Systems Dynamics Institute, has specified the six simple rules that inform her work:

1. Teach and learn in every interaction.
2. Reinforce strengths of self and other.
3. Search for the true and the useful.
4. Give and get value for value.
5. Attend to the part, the whole, and the greater whole.
6. Engage in joyful practice.

One of the tasks of developmental evaluation can be to identify, document, make explicit, and examine the applications of simple rules. For more on what are called "simple rules" or *min specs* by complexity theorists and researchers, see Eoyang (2009), Morgan (1997), Stacey (2007), Wheatley (1999), and Zimmerman and colleagues (1998).

to how they talk about what they're doing. Watch how they respond to optional inquiry frameworks you offer. Which ones resonate?

2. Less is more. Limit the number of questions within the inquiry framework you use. There is no right number but, in general, three is focusing, 10 is a laundry list; you may well end up in between. Developmental evaluation can easily spin out of control, trying to do much too much, worrying about capturing everything or missing something. Let me assure you of this: You won't capture everything. You will miss some things. *C'est la vie.* But you'll capture the big and important stuff if you stay grounded and focused. Better to do a really excellent, in-depth, and useful job on a few focused questions than a lousy job on a lot of questions where you only scratch the surface.

3. Keep the evaluation grounded in whatever basic developmental inquiry framework you and those you're working with choose to guide your work together. (As noted, I'll be reviewing 10 such inquiry frameworks below.) When you're struggling and feeling overwhelmed in the face of complexity, uncertainty, turbulence, and the sheer number and variety of things that can be observed and evaluated, return again to the basic inquiry framework you're using.

4. Distinguish overarching inquiry questions (those that are central to the developmental evaluation inquiry framework you're using) from detailed implementation, what-do-we-do-next, and why-are-we-doing-this questions. Questions of all kinds come up all the time. Sort the ones that are subquestions within the inquiry framework from those that are figuring things out about day-to-day, week-to-week procedures. For example, if appreciative inquiry is the framework you're using, all questions about strengths, assets, excellence, distinction, and positive achievements fall within the larger question of *What do we do well?* A question about how far back to go in identifying strengths is an operational, detailed question, distinct from the overall focusing inquiry questions. Know the difference.

5. *There are stupid questions.* You've probably heard that there are no stupid questions. It's a lie, even in the classroom. People in my workshops ask stupid questions all the time, usually because they haven't been paying attention (which is absolutely never my fault). I hear a stupid question and I think to myself, "That's a really stupid, annoying question." But to the student or client, I say, "Good question. Gives me a chance to go back over the basics." Even seemingly dumb questions are informative. They tell you what people are getting and not getting, what's sticking and not sticking, and what people need to hear again. Questions from those you're working with are data. Listen to what they tell you.

6. Always in developmental evaluation, regardless of what specific questioning framework may be guiding a particular inquiry, the fundamental focus is: *What is being developed?* The niche of developmental evalua-

---

∽ **The Anatomy of Inquiry**

Interestingly we don't start with talking about methods or techniques. Or even by going and reading the literature about what others have done or thought. We start in the middle of everyday life by noticing something, stopping, and "experiencing" a question (one that might not yet even be consciously articulated). A kind of question mark appears over the discrepancy like a genie coming out of the friction of rubbing a lamp. And away around the cycle of questioning we go.

Our questions lead to new questions, and it is this sequence that leads us through an inquiry, all the way from how things are to what they could be, and from what they could be to how they now are.

Note. From Wadsworth (2010), *Building It In: Research and Evaluation for (Truly) Living Human Systems.*

tion is those situations in which something, usually an innovation, is being developed. Not improved. Not summatively judged. Not accountability-driven. Not researched. But developed. *What is being developed?*

So, with these guidelines (simple rules) in mind, let me offer a sample of 10 *frameworks for developmental evaluation inquiry*. To keep it simple, I'm going to describe a situation and offer a matching questioning framework. I'll begin with two basic and classic frameworks, move to some specialized inquiry frameworks, and close with a final basic developmental evaluation framework. These 10 inquiry frameworks do not exhaust possibilities. Rather, they offer illustrations of how to match the inquiry to the nature of the situation.

Basic Descriptive Questions

1. Complex Situation: Crisis-Laden Environment

A major not-for-profit organization supported by United Way, philanthropic foundations, government contracts, and community fundraising hits the end of its fiscal year just as the depth of the global financial crisis becomes obvious. All funders warn them to be prepared for significantly reduced resources in the coming year. At the same moment a long-time senior staff person falls ill and needs to take leave. The chair of the board resigns, unprepared to deal with the added stress of the impending crisis. And on top of all this, demand for much-needed services from people in poverty is increasing. More demand for services, fewer resources, staff turnover, and uncertainty about how long the crisis will last. Lots going on. Many people involved. Multiple directions being pursued at once. Turbulent. Hyperactive. Manic. Confusing. Hard to track and sort out what's happening. A sense of crisis pervades the atmosphere, though there is some comfort taken in the oft-cited observation by economist

Milton Friedman: "Only a crisis, real or perceived, produces real change."

How does an evaluator get grounded in a turbulent, crisis-soaked, chaotic environment? This is a job that cries out for that great developmental evaluation pioneer Rudyard Kipling and his questioning toolkit for all occasions, especially chaotic and crisis-laden ones. Stay grounded in the basics.

I keep six honest serving-men
(They taught me all I knew);
Their names are What and Why and When
And How and Where and Who.
— RUDYARD KIPLING (1865–1936),
The Elephant's Child

Inquiry Framework:
Basic Descriptive Questions

For professionals as diverse as journalists, police detectives, and researchers, Kipling's *Five W's and One H* is the formula for full understanding and a complete report. These are descriptive, factual, and open-ended questions. None can be answered "yes" or "no." You have to find out what happened. When first entering a complex situation with action-oriented, attention-deficit social innovators, it's wise to begin with some basic facts to get the lay of the land. Keep it simple:

Who's doing what? Where? When? How? Why?

These questions, memorialized in Kipling's children's poem, have an ancient and distinguished lineage. In ancient Greece and Rome, rhetoric and reasoning were greatly valued and assiduously studied. Great forensic orators like Socrates, Aristotle, Demosthenes, and Cicero were persuasive not only in philosophy and politics but also in judicial inquiries. They systematically and skillfully addressed what came to be understood as the seven universal dimensions or "circumstances" of an issue, including religious confessions (Copeland, 1995; Robertson, 1946): *Quis, quid, cur, quomodo, ubi, quando, quibus auxiliis* (Who, what, when, where, why, in what way (how), by what means)? This list, the observant reader will have astutely noted, adds one more question to Kipling's *Five W's and One H*, the seventh being *by what means*? Immediately, we see that more than one framework exists for what questions have priority.

Who, what, where, when, why, and how. These are *descriptive questions.* Colonel Mustard murdered the maid Saturday night in the library in a jealous rage by shooting her with a revolver. Or in the more relevant example of the agency in crisis that opened this section, get grounded in a description of the crisis situation: What has changed? Why? Who is affected? In what ways? With what consequences? Where has the organization come from? Where is it now? What are the options going forward? The developmental evaluator can contribute to the next stage of adaptation and development by getting the key players on the same page about the nature of the crisis (good, solid description of what's happened). That description will then have to be interpreted through evaluative thinking, teasing out consequences and implications. This also, it turns out, was an essential element in ancient forensic rhetoric.

> As the ancient Athenian orator Demosthenes implied, "laws" do not interpret themselves—one of the most remarkable achievements of the Graeco-Roman world, then, was to develop an entire system of practical rhetoric to aid in that *interpretive process.* (Humfress, 2007, p. 4; emphasis added)

To see the influence of this interpretive process, we fast-forward a couple of millennia to the 1880s in the United States where Professor William Cleaver Wilkinson popularized the "Three W's"—What? Why? What of it?—as a method of universal study and speech. "It is, in fact," he wrote, "an almost immemorial orator's analysis. First the facts, next the proof of the facts, then the consequences of the facts" (quoted in Trumbull, 1888, p. 120). It's a short leap from there to

one of the most basic, simple, and elegant evaluation inquiry frameworks: *What? So what? Now what?*

2. Complex Situation: Getting Started with People New to Evaluation

A new environmental initiative is created as a result of changed local government policy and philanthropic funding. The initiative leads to a new organization made up of people with strong substantive knowledge of the environment but no evaluation experience. Working with people who are new to formal evaluation poses the challenge of keeping it simple even in the face of complexity. Evaluation novices can be subject-matter specialists and social innovators, but also program staff, board members, policymakers, or funders—pick your stakeholder poison of choice. They don't know much about evaluation, need to get started with some simple evaluative thinking, are worried about evaluation taking too much of their time, being too complicated, even complex, and may, as a group, give off signals that it won't be easy to get them to agree on priority issues. How they will respond to evaluation is uncertain. So keep it simple. Be attentive to how they react. Probe, sense, respond. Sometimes you may use the basic descriptive inquiry framework I offered as the first option above. Here, however, is another option.

Inquiry Framework: What? So What? Now What?

Glenda H. Eoyang, executive director of the Human Systems Dynamics Institute in Minnesota, has described how she uses this evaluative framework in her complexity-focused organizational development institute to "shape our work together toward adaptive action" (quoted in Patton, 2008c, p. 6).

> WHAT? What do we see? What does data tell us? What are the indicators of change or stability? What cues can we capture to see changing patterns as they emerge?

SO WHAT? So, what sense can we make of emerging data? What does it mean to us in this moment and in the future? What effect are current changes likely to have on us, our clients, our extended network, and our field of inquiry and action?

NOW WHAT? What are our options? What are our resources? When and how can we act—individually or collectively—to optimize opportunities in this moment and the next? (Eoyang, 2006, p. 1)

While Eoyang finds this simple inquiry framework especially helpful in working with those relatively new to evaluation, she also has found it useful in getting more experienced clients moving together through an evaluation. She offers these examples:

A social service agency faced radical changes in public policy that would have a direct effect on their clients and the resources they had available to meet clients' needs. What? So what? Now what?

A medical technology company focused on getting processes under control and ensuring lean, high quality product development and deployment procedures. What? So what? Now what?

An organization in the midst of internal transformation faced backlash from disgruntled workers. What? So what? Now what?

In each of these cases, the three questions helped leadership focus on critical options and effective actions. What emerged was not a sophisticated and complicated plan for an unknowable future. No. What did emerge was a shared understanding of emerging challenges and clear focus on actions that could shift emergencies into emergent possibilities. (Eoyang, 2006, p. 1)

This is the most basic kind of evaluative thinking. Developmental evaluation brings that basic evaluative thinking to inquiries about social innovations: *What* is the innovation? What do the results of innovative efforts mean? (*So what?*) What do the findings reveal about next steps? (*Now what?*) The developmental evaluator works with those for whom the evaluation is being done to select methods, data collection approaches, indicators, samples, evidence, and feedback time lines that put flesh on the bones of these questions. But don't collect too much data too quickly. Honor the learning curve of people new to evaluation. Keep it manageable and add more specific questions and data as their capacity to deal with, interpret, and use data develops.

Every professional sports team begins a new season with a training camp for both newcomers and returning veterans where they go over the basics and immerse themselves in fundamentals. Opera singers and concert pianists prepare for performances by practicing scales. Evaluators dealing with complexity need to be grounded in the basics. When complexity seems overwhelming, as it often does; when situational uncertainty generates evaluation uncertainty; when nonlinear dynamics feel like chaos—and may well be chaos; when the action is unfolding fast and furious, it can help to find grounding in a basic framework.

Throughout this book I've emphasized the particular niche and contribution of developmental evaluation. And it does occupy a special niche and make a special contribution. But it's still evaluation. It's still grounded in the basic logic of evaluative thinking. The difference is that in developmental evaluation the turnaround between question asking, question answering, question interpretation, and use-for-action often happens in short, iterative, and ongoing cycles with a *focus on development*. I recently worked with an organization whose mission is major systems change. Every staff person I met with described an organizational culture dominated by *a sense of urgency*. Developmental evaluation had to incorporate that sense of urgency in asking questions:

What is being developed *now*?

What do the results of what has been developed mean *now*?

What are the next steps *now*? What is the next phase of development *now*?

3. Complex Situation:
Steep Learning Curve

An inner-city organization whose mission is developing housing for low-income families is faced with a sudden influx of Somali immigrants due to civil conflict in that country. Most speak no English or, at best, English as a second language. The organization receives new funding to work with this new immigrant population, helping them find suitable housing and get settled. They will have to collaborate closely with other organizations working with refugee resettlement. The organization has evaluation experience, some good, some not so good (aka *bad*), most of it focused on external accountability and compliance reporting. They understand that they have a lot to learn to serve this new population and to deal with an expanded mission outside their past experience and comfort zone. They've decided that they must dedicate themselves to learning; they have heard about learning organizations; one of them has read *The Fifth Discipline* on the art and craft of learning (Senge, 2006); they think of themselves as open, learning-oriented, and innovative; but, in fact, they have no systematic approach to learning, aren't sure what it means to learn high-quality lessons that inform future action, and need a starting place. The thing that stands out, that really characterizes the situation, is the language of and commitment to *learning*. Oh, and they recognize that things are complex. Whatever that means.

I often run into this situation with organizations that exude rhetoric about *learning, learning, learning*—but don't actually do much of it. The good news is they genuinely want to learn. And they are open to an inquiry framework that will help them do so.

Inquiry Framework:
Beliefs, Knowledge, Action

This framework begins by distinguishing beliefs from knowledge. Action (e.g., running a program, intervening in the world,

promoting innovation) flows from a combination of what we believe (including our theory of change) and what we know. The problem comes from confusing these two. We treat our beliefs as knowledge. We have typically held fundamental beliefs for a long time. They are part of who we are. We come to believe that our beliefs are, in fact, knowledge. The way to test this premise is to make explicit the knowledge base for action. Here's how it works.

I ask a social innovator, or a program group with whom I'm working, to give me an example of some action they're taking. Let's say the response (the action) is working to engage people in poverty in planning a community-based antipoverty program. "Okay," I ask, "what's your knowledge base for that approach?" Response: "We believe that low-income people have the right to full participation in things that affect them." Good answer, but notice the verb. *Believe.* This is a values statement, say I. An important value. A meaningful value. An appropriate value. That value leads you to believe that something you care about is possible. But on what, if any, knowledge is it based? What research do you draw on that has examined the effects of low-income community participation? How up to date is that evidence? To what extent does the evidence fit this context? What evaluations of such interventions have you examined? What systematic inquiry have you undertaken to examine your own processes and outcomes?

The answers usually reveal that the basis of action is primarily beliefs (often informed by some set of values), not much evidence or knowledge. One inquiry framework we'll review later (number 7) in this chapter is values-based, and that can be an appropriate framework to use in a situation where the action is heavily values-driven. But where the emphasis is more on learning than on being true to basic values, a learning framework is appropriate. A *learning organization*, I suggest, is one that, over time, is moving more and more of the support for its actions from beliefs to knowledge. In fact, that is my basic definition of a learning organization. Developmental evaluation uses this framework to capture lessons about what is being learned over time and then uses those cumulative learnings to support and inform ongoing development. Exhibit 8.1 offers a graphic of this framework, summarizes the framework's basic premises, and presents a triangulated way of thinking about what constitute high-quality lessons, namely, lessons supported by multiple and diverse knowledge sources (evaluations, research, experts, beneficiary and community wisdom, practitioner experience, and social science theory). Exhibit 8.1 also offers questions for inquiring into just what a *high-quality lesson* is (see page 236).

Action learning (McNamara, 2002a, 2002b; Pedler, 2008; Revans, 1980; Zuber-Skerritt, 2009) is another framework that is relevant for developmental evaluation. For thoughtful reflections on the hand-in-glove relationship between evaluation and learning, see King (2008) and Preskill (2008). In the next chapter we'll look in depth at reflective practice as a learning process that can be used in developmental evaluation inquiries (Schön, 1983).

The situational matching guidance is this: When the people you're about to engage with come to developmental evaluation with a focus on learning, use the language of learning, and are genuinely excited about learning, make learning the focus of the evaluation. *Duh!* The triangulated learning framework is one way to do that.

4. Complex Situation: Positive Thinking

Now we encounter a program group or social innovation design team that is all about the art of thinking positively. They're "not into negativity." They may have had some bad experiences with highly judgmental people in their lives: authoritarian elementary school teachers, dogmatic clergy, and demanding and impossible-to-satisfy parents, perhaps. And negative evaluators. They've likely had bad experiences with judgmental, *look-at-all-*

the-problems-you've-got evaluators. In contrast to such negativity-exuding evaluators, these are people who, by inclination, personality, and philosophy see the glass half-full rather than half-empty. (Evaluators, in general, are the 8-oz-glass-has-4-oz-of-liquid kind of folks.) These social innovators are visionary, can-do, will-do, and why-not, let's-get-on-with-it people. Which is just fine, perhaps even necessary, because social change is tough work, often discouraging and debilitating. Working on homelessness, HIV/AIDS, family violence, and child abuse can drain hope quickly. International challenges include basic health care, food insecurity, labor repression, ethnic or gender discrimination, environmental degradation, and even slavery (see Free the Slaves, 2009). Evaluation can be just another stick that people feel beaten up with. Which is why hopeful, caring, and determined visionaries and social innovators often eschew evaluation. Here's an example of what a hopeful visionary would say. Listen carefully and think about what evaluation approach this person might resonate to.

> Change doesn't happen because of how we invest our money. Change happens because of how we invest our human energy, and it always has since we came down from the trees. Everyone's got a margin of discretionary energy—ten percent, twenty percent—that isn't used up making your way in the world. That's the energy that's available for social change. If you can get a whole community to start focusing their energy together, building on success just as a business builds on successful products, then you get social change. (Daniel Taylor, Future Generations, an international nonprofit organization; quoted in McKibben, 2007, p. 211)

Appreciative inquiry offers a framework for engaging in developmental evaluation from a positive, hopeful place while still asking hard questions and engaging in serious inquiry. I'll also note some other positive-thinking inquiry frameworks in the next section.

EXHIBIT 8.1 Triangulated Learning Framework

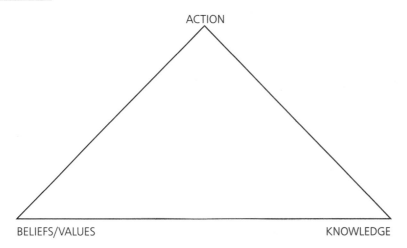

PREMISES

1. Action flows from some combination of beliefs (informed by values) and knowledge.

2. Informed action has a strong knowledge base. *Becoming a learning organization involves moving more of the basis for action from beliefs to knowledge.*

3. By testing and evaluating beliefs, we learn and build knowledge, thereby making our actions more informed and empirically based.

4. People have varying predilections that lean more toward one of these dimensions than others(e.g., more action-oriented, more values-driven, or more knowledge-oriented). All three styles are valuable and needed for sustainable program, organizational, and/or community development.

In short, ACTIONS flow from some combination of BELIEFS (theory–vision–values) and KNOWLEDGE (evidence).

**Image of Alignment
between
Actions, Beliefs, and Knowledge**

Nonaligned	*Alligned*
Inconsistencies between actions, beliefs, and knowledge	Consistency between actions, beliefs, and knowledge

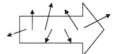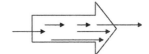

(cont.)

HIGH-QUALITY LESSONS LEARNED (KNOWLEDGE FOR ACTION)

Knowledge that can be applied to future action supported by diverse, triangulated sources:

1. Evaluation findings—patterns across programs;
2. Basic and applied research;
3. Practice wisdom and experience of practitioners;
4. Experiences reported by program participants/clients/intended beneficiaries;
5. Expert opinion;
6. Cross-disciplinary connections and patterns;
7. Assessment of the importance of the lesson learned; and
8. Strength of the connection to outcomes attainment.

The idea is that the greater the number of supporting sources for a "lesson learned," the more rigorous the supporting evidence, and the greater the *triangulation of supporting sources*, the more confidence one has in the significance and meaningfulness of a lesson learned. Lessons learned with only one type of supporting evidence would be considered a "lessons learned hypothesis." Nested within and cross-referenced to lessons learned should be the actual cases from which practice wisdom and evaluation findings have been drawn. A critical principle here is to maintain the contextual frame for lessons learned, that is, to keep lessons grounded in their context. For ongoing learning, the trick is to follow up future intended uses of lessons learned to test their wisdom and relevance over time in action in new settings.

QUESTIONS FOR GENERATING HIGH-QUALITY LESSONS LEARNED

1. What is meant by a "*lesson*"?
2. What is meant by "*learned*"?
3. By whom was the lesson learned?
4. What's the evidence supporting each lesson?
5. What's the evidence the lesson was learned?
6. What are the contextual boundaries around the lesson (i.e., under what conditions does it apply)?
7. Is the lesson specific, substantive, and meaningful enough to guide practice in some concrete way?
8. Who else is likely to care about this lesson?
9. What evidence will they want to see?
10. How does this lesson connect with other "lessons" and knowledge.

Inquiry Framework: Focusing on Strengths and Assets

Appreciative inquiry (AI) has emerged as a popular organizational development approach that emphasizes building on an organization's or community's assets and strengths rather than focusing on problems, or even problem solving. Conceived and described in the work of David Cooperrider and his colleagues at Case Western Reserve's School of Organization Behavior (Watkins & Cooperrider, 2000), AI offers "a worldview, a paradigm of thought and understanding that holds organizations to be affirmative systems created by humankind as solutions to problems. It is a theory, a mindset, and an approach to analysis that leads to organizational learning and creativity" (p. 6).

AI has found its way into evaluation as evidenced by a volume of *New Directions for Evaluation, Using Appreciative Inquiry in Evaluation* (Preskill & Coghlan, 2003). However, some still find the combination of the words *appreciative* and *evaluation* to be oxymoronic. AI remains controversial in evaluation (Patton, 2003), has been criticized for discouraging constructive criticism (Golembiewski, 2000), and is especially disparaged by and anathema to those who hold onto their objectivity like a crack addict to a dime bag. Thus, AI may have to be "reframed" for evaluative inquiry (Preskill, 2005; Preskill & Catsambas, 2006).

What interests us here is that AI can be adapted to developmental evaluation and may be especially useful to support trust building "because it acknowledges individual contribution and supports the overall cffcctiveness of the change effort" (Gamble, 2008, p. 51). AI often uses a form of reflective practice that includes a dialogue process among participants based on their interviewing each other. They ask each other questions that "elicit the creative and life-giving events experienced in the workplace" (Watkins & Cooperrider, 2000, p. 9). In developmental evaluation, those engaged

in social change interview each other to elicit the creative processes and identify the outcomes of innovation and development. Exhibit 8.2 shows how to convert classic AI questions into questions for developmental evaluation inquiry. These questions aim at generating specific examples, stories, and metaphors about successes and positive aspects of organizational life. These specific examples are the data about what success looks like, are the evidence for success that makes the process evaluative. Participants in the process analyze the results in groups looking for the themes and topics that can become the foundation for and inform positive development going forward.

> For example, if the original data suggests that COMMITMENT is an important factor in many of the stories about the best of times in the organization, then the workgroup might choose to ask more questions from others in the workplace about their experiences with commitment. This second round of interviews produces information about four to six topics that become the basis for building "Possibility Propositions" that describe how the organization will be in the future. Each topic or theme can be fashioned into a future statement. And these statements become an integral part of the vision for the organization. Often, this process is completed with a future search conference that uses the Appreciative Inquiry data as a basis for imaging a positive and creative future for the organization. (Watkins & Cooperrider, 2000, p. 10)

AI practitioners have generated easily accessible support resources (Appreciative Inquiry Commons, 2009) that can be adapted to developmental evaluation purposes. Charles Elliott (1999) and Sarah Michael (2005) have provided examples of effective use of AI in developing countries with in-depth analysis of when and how to usc AI to support development.

Other positive and affirming approaches that emphasize building on strengths and learning from successes are listed here as suggestive possibilities. I have heard from

---

EXHIBIT 8.2 Appreciative Inquiry Questions for Developmental Evaluation Inquiry

Classic appreciative inquiry questions (Watkins & Cooperrider, 2000, p. 9)	Developmental evaluation adaptations focused on innovation
1. Looking at your entire experience with the organization, remember a time when you felt most alive, most fulfilled, or most excited about your involvement in the organization. . . .	1. Looking at your entire experience with efforts at *social innovation and change* in the past, remember a time when you felt most alive, most fulfilled, or most excited about your involvement in innovation.
2. Let's talk for a moment about some things you value deeply; specifically, the things you value about yourself, about the nature of your work, and about this organization. . . .	2. Let's talk for a moment about some things you value deeply; specifically, the things you value about yourself, about the nature of your work, and especially about being engaged in *social innovation*. . . .
3. What do you experience as the core factors that give life to this organization? Give some examples of how you experience those factors.	3. What do you experience as the core factors of *successful social innovation*? Give some examples of how you have experienced or seen those factors in social change initiatives.
4. What three wishes would you make to heighten the vitality and health of this organization?	4. What three wishes would you make to heighten the vitality and health of this social innovation design team and change initiative?

---

developmental evaluators who have used these approaches and frameworks successfully.

• *Asset-based community development* (ABCD) was pioneered by John Kretzmann and John McKnight (1993) of the Northwestern University Asset-Based Community Development Institute. ABCD identifies and mobilizes local assets as the primary building blocks for "sustainable community development."

> Building on the skills of local residents, the power of local associations, and the supportive functions of local institutions, asset-based community development draws upon existing community strengths to build stronger, more sustainable communities for the future. (ABCD Institute, 2009)

(See also Wilke, 2006, for more on asset-based community development.)

• *Positive deviance*, pioneered by social innovators Jerry and Monique Sternin, is an approach based on the premise that "in every community there are certain individuals or groups whose uncommon behaviors and strategies enable them to find better solutions to problems than their peers, while having access to the same resources and facing similar or worse challenges. The Positive Deviance approach is an asset-based, problem-solving, and community-driven approach that enables the community to discover these successful behaviors and strategies and develop a plan of action to promote their adoption by all concerned" (Positive Deviance Initiative, 2009). This approach gained international attention when cited by the *New York Times* as one of the best and most influential ideas of 2008 (Gertner, 2008).

• *Success case method*, the focus of a book by Robert Brinkerhoff (2003), combines analysis of successful outliers with qualitative case study methods and storytelling. Successful and unsuccessful cases are compared. The approach, when used in developmental evaluation, would pay particular attention to the contextual factors that differentiate successful from unsuccessful innovations, innovators, and adopters of innovations. The approach

> intentionally seeks the very best that a program is producing, to help determine whether the value a program is producing is worthwhile and whether it may be possible to leverage this to a greater number of participants. A "success story" is not a testimonial or a critical review. It is a factual and verifiable account—citing evidence that would "stand up in court"—that demonstrates how and how valuably a person used some new method or tool or capability. (Brinkerhoff, 2005, p. 402)

An example of this approach is a study called *What It Takes to Change Government* (Booz Allen Hamilton, 2009; Kelman & Myers, 2009).

• *Most significant changes.* This approach to capturing positive changes and outcomes was developed by the Institute of Land and Food Resources at the University of Melbourne in Australia (Dart, Drysdale, Cole, & Saddington, 2000; Davies & Dart, 2005). It involves several steps. (1) Key program stakeholders and participants (e.g., farmers in an extension program) come to an agreement on which "domains of change" to monitor with stories. (2) Monthly stories of change written by participants in the innovation (e.g., farmers and field staff) are collected. (3) Volunteer reviewers and evaluators use agreed-on criteria to select the "most significant stories" during regional and statewide committee meetings. (4) At the end of some period of inquiry (e.g., a year) a document is produced containing all the "winning" stories. (5) This document forms the basis for a roundtable discussion with "key influentials" and funders of the project who then also select the most significant stories according to their views.

FINDINGS FROM AN APPRECIATIVE INQUIRY

"It's not just that he walks upright and uses complex tools. He also makes me laugh."

© Mick Stevens/Condé Nast Publications/*www.cartoonbank.com.*

This approach goes beyond merely capturing and documenting client stories; each story is accompanied by the storyteller's interpretation and, after review, the stories are also accompanied by the reviewer's interpretation. One of the ideas behind the process is that it promotes a slow but extensive dialog up and down the project hierarchy each month. (Jessica Dart, quoted in Patton, 2002, p. 196)

• When adapted for developmental evaluation inquiry, the "winning stories" would focus on the innovation being tracked and interpretations of what the innovation meant and yielded from the various points of view of those involved.

5. Complex Situation:
Focus on Systems Change

In studying the cases of major social change by social innovators we reported in *Getting to Maybe* (Westley et al., 2006), we found that their vision was aimed at disrupting existing systems, which they found unacceptable, and making a lasting difference by *changing systems*. They didn't always use the language of systems change, but their vision was never piecemeal and modest. They wanted to change the world and that meant changing the status-quo systems that constitute the world.

Visions of systems change can be found in the strategies of philanthropic foundations (e.g., Kellogg Foundation, 2009; MacArthur Foundation, 2009), advocacy groups, social movements, nonprofit programs, international agencies, and government reformers that have come to realize that to really help people in poverty, to make a difference on homelessness, to combat community violence, or to make lasting differences on any of a host of problems, it's not enough to provide needed services, even effective needed services. The systems that have given rise to those problems must be changed. Many of these systems-change-oriented innovators will quote Albert Einstein in their organizational vision statements, project proposals,

and even in their e-mail signatures: "You can never solve a problem on the level on which it was created" or "No problem can be solved from the same level of consciousness that created it." In fact, there seem to be a number of versions of this widely cited Einstein quotation, which is the nature of widely disseminated quotations, but the same meaning shines through the various versions: to solve problems look at the larger systems of which they are a part. This means *disrupting* existing systems as part of the change process (Christensen, Baumann, Ruggles, & Sadtler, 2006). Disruption will lead to pushback and resistance, which not every program and funder that talks about systems change is willing to face. Not really. So it's important to note that not everyone who talks about systems change is actually prepared to engage at a systems level, or has the capacity to do so. As the popularity of the language of systems change has increased geometrically and more and more people engaged in change make changing systems their mantra, the evidence about how hard it is to actually change systems has likewise increased exponentially. This is not, it turns out, work for the faint-hearted.

Frances Westley, whose work on the adaptive cycle was featured in Chapter 7, has been both studying and facilitating social innovation generation as the J. W. McConnell Chair in Social Innovation at the University of Waterloo. She has found that when a social innovation has a broad or durable impact, it will be *disruptive and catalytic*, meaning it will challenge the social system and social institutions that support the established order by affecting the fundamental distribution of power and resources and/or the basic beliefs that define the system, including the laws, policies, and funding flows that govern it. This kind of change goes beyond the many smaller innovations that are continually introduced at various levels. To disrupt and change the broader system, there must eventually be a disruptive encounter with power, routine, and beliefs. To do so, Westley has found, a social innovation must cross multiple social boundaries to reach more people and different people, more organizations and different organizations, organizations nested across scales from local to regional to national to global (Westley & Antadze, 2009, p. 6). Exhibit 7.7 in the last chapter presents a diagram of one example of cross-scale change.

So when a developmental evaluator engages with social innovators using the language of and sharing a vision of systems change, what questions can frame the evaluation?

Inquiry Framework:
Systems Change *Questions*

What do those involved mean by "systems change"? What system or systems are they targeting for change? How is the system that is the primary focus of change related to other systems?

These three questions are derived from the patterns identified by Bob Williams and Iraj Iman (2007) in their excellent and important volume *Systems Concepts in Evaluation.* They identified three concepts that are especially relevant for evaluators working with a systems framing: perspectives, boundaries, and entangled systems/interrelationships (p. 6). Finding out the perspectives being used by those talking about systems change is critical because, as noted in Chapter 5, in which I discussed how a complex systems framework can inform evaluation, there are as many as a thousand separate frameworks and methods that "fall under the systems banner"—because there is no single agreed-upon definition of a "system" (Williams, 2008). So we begin the developmental evaluation dialogue by asking: What do those involved mean by systems change? The initial answer (or answers if there are multiple stakeholders, as is likely) constitutes a baseline. It's what those involved bring to the table at the beginning. One task of developmental evaluation will be to track and document how the meaning of *systems change* itself changes and develops over time.

The second question follows from the first by asking about boundaries. What system or systems are those involved targeting for change? Systems are social constructions. Boundaries around "systems" are arbitrary, driven by our need to make sense of things. System boundaries are not real in any absolute sense, but rather are more or less useful. Here, too, changes in understandings will likely occur over the course of a systems change initiative, so the developmental evaluator will need to capture how boundaries expand, contract, and otherwise morph along the way, using systems mapping as one technique, that is, literally drawing pictures of the targeted system over time. See Chapter 5, Exhibit 5.3, for an example of a systems map (see also Patton, 2008c, pp. 360–369).

> Boundaries drive how we "see" systems. Boundaries define who or what lies inside and what lies outside of a particular inquiry. Boundaries delineate or identify important differences (i.e., what is "in" and what is "out"). Boundaries determine who or what will benefit from a particular inquiry and who or what might suffer. Boundaries are fundamentally about values—they are judgements about worth. Defining boundaries is an essential part of systems work/inquiry/thinking. (Williams & Iman, 2007, p. 6)

The third question is about interrelationships (entangled systems). Relationships and interrelationships are the heart of systems inquiry. Relationships define interactions within systems and across systems.

> One can observe and perceive systems within systems, systems overlapping other systems, and systems tangled up in other systems. Thus it is unwise to focus on one view or definition of a system without examining its relationship with another system. Where does one system begin and the other end? Is there overlap? Who is best situated to experience or be affected by that overlap? What systems exist within systems and where do they lead? A systems thinker always looks inside, outside, beside, and between the readily identified systems boundary. He or she then critiques and if nec-

essary changes that initial choice of boundary. (Williams & Iman, 2007, p. 6)

A systems approach to developmental evaluation illustrates the value of having a simple and generic inquiry framework as a place to begin. Systems inquiry is inherently complex and easily overwhelming. Endless layers of questions are possible. As one un-peels the onion-like layers of systems within systems, more questions emerge and new op-portunities for inquiry appear. It is helpful then to have some way of staying grounded. Bob Williams does as much evaluation using a systems framework as anyone in the pro-fession. He is one of the pioneering thought leaders in bringing systems thinking into evaluation. He teaches systems approaches to evaluation. He consults around the world on systems evaluation. And how does Bob Williams stay grounded in the face of end-less complexity and borderline (or actual) chaos? He returns over and over to these three basic issues: Perspectives. Boundaries. Interrelationships (entangled systems).

At the same time, Williams uses these three categories of questions to open up more specific inquiries:

Perspectives

- What are the different ways in which this situation can be understood?

- How are these different understandings going to affect the way in which people judge the success of an endeavor?

- How will it affect their behavior, and thus the behavior of the system, espe-cially when things go wrong from their perspective? With what result and signifi-cance?

Boundaries

- What differences make a difference to the way in which a situation is under-stood or behaves?

- Who or what is being excluded, margin-alized, or made a victim by the way in which this situation is being viewed or is operating?

- What does this say about what is "valued," by whom, in this situation?

- What are the consequences of boundary-setting decisions?

Interrelationships

- What is the nature of the interrelation-ships within a situation?

- What is the structure of these interrela-tionships?

- What are the processes between them?

- What are the patterns that emerge from those processes, with what consequenc-es for whom? Why does this matter? To whom? In what context?

While these three dimensions (perspec-tives, boundaries, interrelationships) get at the systems framing of innovation, the eval-uative lens must also be applied. So, then, one can ask about each of these dimensions: What? So what? Now what? In doing so, the developmental evaluator is staying focused on what is being developed. And the ulti-mate questions: What is the evidence that systems change has occurred? To what ex-tent? In what ways? With what consequenc-es, intended and unintended? Through this series of entangled and interrelated inqui-ries, systems thinking and evaluative think-ing are integrated.

I used a systems framework to evaluate a campaign to influence a U.S. Supreme Court decision aimed at overturning the juvenile death penalty. The campaign tar-geted the following systems: the federal ju-dicial system; six state legislatures that had pending legislation to overturn the juvenile death penalty at the state level; national, in-ternational, and local advocacy groups long involved in overturning the death penalty; three philanthropic foundations support-ing human rights reform; national and local media covering the Court case; social sci-ence researchers with relevant new knowledge about the development and functioning of the human brain during adolescence; police, prosecutors, and victims advocacy associations that opposed overturning the existing law; and professional associations of lawyers and legal advocates knowledgeable about the case and its implications. The primary system being targeted was the federal judiciary, more specifically the nine justices on the Supreme Court. But all of these other systems came into play, both in developing the arguments to be presented to the Court and in monitoring public and expert opinion that constituted the context for the case and that, given what is known about how justices actually make their decisions, were of possible great importance in affecting the justices' views.

The core advocacy team operated with an explicit systems change perspective. They had a shared understanding of both system boundaries and interrelationships, and those understandings were the foundation of their campaign. The developmental evaluation formally documented the perspectives within the various systems, the interactions across systems and perspectives, and the way in which the campaign shifted its emphasis based on systems dynamics during the campaign. To see examples of the systems maps used to describe and evaluate the campaign, available online, see Patton (2008a). (Also, see Exhibit 7.7, near the end of Chapter 7, for an extended example of a developmental evaluation of cross-scale systems change. For a range of systems thinking and modeling examples and methods, see Sterman, 2000.)

6. Complex Situation: Collaboration for Innovation

When social innovation is framed around collaborating for change, the basic theory of action is: *Bring good people together and good things will happen.* Bring creative people together and creative things will happen. Bring innovative people together and innovations will emerge. Bring good, creative, committed, and innovative people together—and find a way to keep them together—and you can change the world. The favorite quote of this group is from Margaret Mead: "Never doubt that a small group of thoughtful, committed people can change the world. Indeed, it is the only thing that ever has."

This is the people-focused approach to innovation. Some venture capitalists focus on funding good ideas. Other venture capitalists only fund proposals that present a detailed business plan and return on investment numbers, dreaming big dreams with dollar signs. The third approach to venture capital focuses on people. Good people will generate good ideas and generate big-impact numbers. Start with the people. To the extent that the people brought together agree on what is to be done and how to do it, and are working on problems that are fairly well understood, their collaborative effort may just be complicated. But to the extent that participants disagree on key parameters and are working on problems without known solutions, the collaboration will be operating in complex territory and be subject to complex nonlinear dynamics and complex human responses.

Collaborations created by shotgun marriages forced by funders, of which there are many, are especially prone to dynamical (unpredictable, turbulent, up-and-down) patterns. But social innovators interested in major change also have a way of finding each other, sometimes self-organizing as strange attractors. As one experienced developmental evaluator said to me: "The more time I spend around innovation the more I am convinced that collaboration is going to always accompany the innovation process at some level. I think this is because innovation is most often a creative and unique combination by innovators of things already existing in some form. Coming together they can take those things, in combination, to a new level and broaden the impact."

I've experienced collaboration-focused innovation often enough to believe it constitutes a specific innovation niche and therefore merits a specific developmental evaluation inquiry framework.

Inquiry Framework: Degree and Nature of Collaboration Questions

What can we do together that we can't do separately? What will each of us contribute to the whole? How will we work together? What differences will we make together?

Funders push collaborations both because they believe that people working together can accomplish more than those same people working apart, but also because it makes funding administratively easy: fund one entity (the collaboration) rather than many. But collaborations are not inherently good. They can be quite hard to manage and huge time-wasters for all involved. At a youth conference once I heard a presenter compare working collaboratively to teenage sex: *Everyone talks about it all the time. Everyone thinks everyone else is doing it. Those who are doing it aren't doing it very well. Despite that, everybody talks about how good it feels.*

One experienced social innovator, a veteran of many collaborations, told me:

"A common myth I run into is that collaboration will save resources when in fact it often demands more resources, at least in the beginning, because of all the transaction costs (meetings, negotiations, time building trust, etc.). But, if it works, the payoff is the creation of something innovative. The greater the differences among those who come together, the more difficult it is to make it work, but the greater the degree of innovation if successful."

Evaluators enter the fray by asking the hard reality-testing questions about what the collaboration is actually doing and achieving. Since collaborations are inherently unstable and potentially dynamical entities, developmental evaluators contribute by providing those working in collaboration with feedback about how the interactions are actually unfolding (which is unlikely to

be either simple or linear) and what the collaboration is actually accomplishing (which is unlikely to be obvious, simple to measure, or straightforward to attribute). Asking questions about how those working together see themselves and their shared effort can be informed by classic distinctions between different degrees of engagement, as shown in Exhibit 8.3. The exhibit presents a continuum of engagement from networking (low mutual engagement) through partnering (shared goals, decisions, and resources), with cooperating, coordinating, and collaborating as increasingly engaged ways of working together along the continuum.

Obviously, ordinary language is much less precise than this continuum and its definitional distinctions suggest. The developmental evaluator, with this framework or some other in mind, can help those working together inquire into their shared (or diverse) understandings of how they hope to and actually do engage each other. The developmental evaluator documents the behavioral interactions that actually develop (compared to rhetoric about and hopes for those interactions) as well as providing feedback that helps those collaborating (and those funding the collaboration) assess what they are accomplishing.

Outcome mapping (International Development Research Centre, 2007) is a tool for mapping the contributions of people and agencies working together on large, complicated/complex, multidimensional, and even multisectoral initiatives; it provides a conceptual framework for mapping the contributions of collaborating partners in uncertain and dynamical environments where simple notions of linear attribution are neither meaningful nor accurate. Issues of how to divide up credit for successes (or blame for failures) can be dealt with through *contribution analysis* rather than the traditional attribution analysis of simple linear causation (Mayne, 2007; Patton, 2008c, pp. 494–496).

Many frameworks are available for conceptualizing collaborations and their es-

EXHIBIT 8.3 Degrees of Working Together Continuum

Low-level working together as distinct entities

Networking: Sharing information and ideas.

Cooperating: Helping distinct members accomplish their separate individual goals.

Coordinating: Working separately on shared goals.

Collaborating: Working together toward a common goal but maintaining separate resources and responsibilities.

Partnering: Shared goals, shared decisions, shared resources within a single entity.

High-level, fully integrated working together

Developmental evaluation note: These are context-specific and dynamic distinctions. Networking to share information can lead to partnering for the specific purpose of undertaking an advocacy campaign or change initiative, then move into coordinating or cooperating after the campaign or intense initiative (partnering), and may eventually return to networking. Thus, one group of people over a period of time (months, years) may exhibit any of these patterns and distinctions at various times. The developmental evaluation would capture and report those developments, how the transitions occurred, and what the implications were for both the group and its accomplishments.

sential elements. For example, a *transformational collaboration* framework originated in Australia and derived from complexity theory is specifically designed for communities engaged in major change (Earles, Lynn, & Jakel, n.d.). A collaborating group involved in developmental evaluation may want to become a *community of practice*, a way for groups working together to also inquire together for sharing learning, constructing meaning, and facilitating identity (Wenger, 1999; Wenger, McDermott, & Snyder, 2002). Because collaboration is inherently difficult, and often there can be clashes of values or beliefs between collaborators that only get surfaced in the process of trying to collaborate, evaluation can bring evidence to bear on the extent and effects of these conflicts as a means to help untangle them.

Thus, whatever the overarching collaborative framework, the developmental evaluator helps those working together engage in reality testing about what is being developed— and what difference is being made. This is a critical role because collaborations can bring together enthusiastic and committed social innovators whose very commitment and enthusiasm can be a barrier to thoughtful inquiry into how the group is actually functioning and what it is accomplishing. Collaboration is not just a variety of people sitting in a room together. When collaboration works, the process creates whole new ways for those people to interact with each other. When individuals and systems interact effectively, they can optimize use of their resources and find solutions to seemingly intractable problems. Collaborative processes have the potential for creating revolutionary changes in our communities and in our world. At least that is the hope—and often the promise. Developmental evaluation inquires into whether those hoped-for and promised revolutionary changes actually emerge.

Collaboration expert Tom Wolff (2004) has identified six key components of effective collaborations.

1. Engage a broad spectrum of the community.

2. Encourage true collaboration as the form of exchange.

3. Practice democracy, and promote active citizenship and empowerment.

4. Employ an ecological approach that builds on community strengths.

5. Take action by addressing issues of social change and power.

6. Align the goals with the process.

Such a framework for collaboration, whether this one or another, offers criteria that developmental evaluation can monitor to provide feedback on how the collaboration is functioning and what it is accomplishing.

7. Complex Situation: Values-Driven Social Innovation

Many social innovators are driven more by values than by specifiable outcomes. They aren't necessarily sure what SMART (specific, measurable, attainable, realistic, timely) goals are, nor do they particularly care, and they aren't very explicit in advance about what outcomes can be attained, but *they are sure about what values will drive their efforts.* In the outcomes mania of our accountability-focused and results-driven culture, how things get done—processes, values, principles—have been relegated to secondary importance, if given any attention at all. But for values-driven social change activists and innovators *how* outcomes are attained is at least as, if not more, important than the outcomes themselves. Process matters. The means to ends matter, not just the ends. Indeed, given the uncertainties of complex interventions and interactions, where the ends (outcomes, impacts, results) are uncontrollable, unpredictable, and emergent, values can become the anchor, the *only* knowable in an otherwise uncertain, unpredictable, uncontrollable, and complex world.

In *Getting to Maybe* (Westley et al., 2006), our inquiry into the motivations of social innovators revealed that those involved expressed *a sense of calling.* They saw things through their own personal and community lenses of strong values. When they looked they saw things that were unacceptable, problems that were outrageous, and they felt compelled to act. They were driven by a vision of how the world should and could be a better place. These were not management-by-objectives folks, these were value-driven visionaries. If they were to engage with evaluators, those evaluators would need to be able to engage with them around their values. An inspiring quotation oft-cited by values-driven social innovators is:

> All that is necessary for the triumph of evil is that good men do nothing.
> —EDMUND BURKE (1729–1797), Irish philosopher and political leader

Dov Seidman (2007) is CEO of LRN, a company that helps businesses build ethical corporate cultures. His book *How* focuses on the importance of how things are done and is appropriately subtitled: "Why How We Do Anything Means Everything in Business (and in Life)." In an interview with *New York Times* columnist Thomas Friedman, Seidman said:

> In a connected world, countries, governments and companies also have character, and their character—*how* they do what they do, *how* they keep promises, *how* they make decisions, *how* things really happen inside, *how* they connect and collaborate, *how* they engender trust, *how* they relate to their customers, to the environment and to the communities in which they operate—is now their fate. (quoted in Friedman, 2008)

Evaluation trainers, among whom I include myself, like to point out that in the middle of the word *evaluation* is the word *valu[e].* The standards adopted by the evaluation profession mandate values identification and articulation so that the basis for value judgments can be known and assessed (Joint Committee on Standards, 1994, standard U4). But I find that most evaluators, well trained in social science methods, are much more comfortable with technical discussions than with values discussions. The primacy of outcomes-driven programming and evaluation (a mutually reinforcing, symbiotic relationship where each sings the praises of and benefits from staying focused on results) assures that discussions will turn quickly to specifying clear, specific, and measurable outcomes and then on to laying out the logic model that will presumably accomplish those outcomes. Values are more often left implicit and assumed rather than made explicit and examined.

This was brought home to me recently in a discussion with an evaluator about *the qualities* of values like social justice, compassion, mutual respect, and reciprocity. His instantaneous reflex was to counter: "Look, if something exists, it exists in some quantity. If it exists in some quantity, it can be measured. Let's get on with the measuring."

Such an attitude, I would suggest, with its underlying values about what is meaningful and worthwhile (namely, what can be quantified and *only* what can be quantified), is not well suited for the often ambiguous and qualitative nature of values-clarification exercises. But for social innovators driven by values, such exercises are crucial—and much valued.

Inquiry Framework: Values-Driven Questions

What are the priority values that will guide how we engage the world? How we will track and judge whether we are true to those values, whether we are "walking our talk"? How do we get feedback from those with whom we engage about how they experience our values and the consequences of those values? Where does living out our values take us, to what actions and results, to what differences in the world?

When I first encountered social entrepreneur Steve Rothschild, whom I introduced in Chapter 2, he was motivated first and foremost by his commitment to combat racism, social injustice, and inequality. Before articulating intended outcomes (e.g., living-wage jobs with benefits), which he could do and valued the importance of, he talked about the principles and values that would be the foundation of the program. He wanted to be sure that any evaluator he worked with shared those values, otherwise how could they trust each other? So, the first exercise I facilitated when Steve had assembled his program design team was clarifying the values and principles on which the innovative program would be based. That was the very first document produced in the design process. To this day, though revisited periodically, it remains the program's fundamental guidance document and action framework. The five major principles are: being purpose-driven, being market-driven, being learning-driven, valuing mutual accountability, and supporting personal empowerment (Rothschild, 2010). Listed in the abstract like this, these principles may

---

∿ **Cultural Sensitivity and Competence: Silence, Being Present, Observing, and Listening as Inquiry**

David Carline (2005) an indigenous *Kooma* man from Queensland, Australia, drawing on a cultural tradition that has sustained itself for more than 40,000 years, offers insight into an approach to inquiry that is appropriate to his people's ways of interacting. It is considered "rude to ask questions," he explains. Learning is about waiting, saying "I don't understand that," being shown, and keeping the peace of the group (p. 9).

Whatever the developmental evaluation inquiry framework, matching it to the people with whom one is working and their situation includes cultural sensitivity and deep respect for their ways of engaging and learning.

not appear to provide much guidance. But through ongoing discussion, reflective practice, and reaffirmation, they have vitality and specific meaning within the organization, and have provided important direction at major forks in the road. The early years of developmental evaluation focused on what they meant in practice.

I worked with a family foundation that faced the challenge of transitioning to the next generation when the founding parents both died within a short time interval. Their deaths led to a substantial infusion of new assets into the endowment, a much larger philanthropic operation, more formal processes, increased staff, and greatly expanded grant making. I was asked to facilitate a board retreat (adult children and grandchildren of the founders and a couple of trusted, long-time family friends) to begin a strategic planning process that would focus the foundation's mission going forward. After interviewing board members individually and hearing over and over again about the values that the founders lived by, I suggested that we devote the retreat to articulation of those values and offered a "theory of philanthropy" that was values-driven rather than outcomes-driven. Over the course of a 2-day retreat, board members told stories about the founders that made explicit how they lived their values. Those values became the foundation's guiding strategic document, one that they returned to year after year in subsequent retreats, always asking the values-driven evaluation question: *Are we walking the talk?* Are we operating in a way that the founders would recognize as upholding their values? Are the things we're accomplishing with the endowment they created true to what they cared about? One of the things the founders cared about was courageously taking risks and supporting innovation. So we evaluated the grants portfolio using criteria of risk taking and innovation.

Values matter to value-driven social innovators because a deep sense of values undergirds their initiatives as their vision gets implemented through day-to-day operations and interactions. Strategies and tactics must be values-based. Outcomes are thought of as manifestations of values. Innovation is what you promote, but *values are who you are.* Values inform decisions about which way to go at inevitable forks in the road. When a problem arises that challenges the innovator in ways not foreseen by strategy, then values provide guidance for reconciling tensions. For example, assessing how short-term outcomes lead toward (or away from) the long-term, broader vision is as much a calculation of how to be true to basic values as how to accomplish hoped-for impacts. The role of the developmental evaluator is to track these choices and decisions, provide feedback to those acting about how their actions are perceived, and facilitate reflective practice around the question: *Do our actions reflect our values?* Developmental evaluation also helps values-driven social innovators generate a range of strategic options for moving forward, and then supports the learning process about which of those options have the greatest effectiveness and remain true to their values.

Environmental activist and author Wendell Berry emphasizes the fundamental importance of values, especially in the face of uncertainty, because, he posits, *there will never be enough certain knowledge to guide action.* Values, then, are a way to deal with the *unknowability*—the inherent ignorance—of the human condition. His manifesto about how to act in the world epitomizes a values-driven perspective:

> Some scientists and their gullible followers think that human ignorance is merely an agenda for research. Eventually, they think, we humans will have in hand "the secret of life" or "the secret of the universe," and then all our problems will be solved and all our troubles and sorrows ended.
>
> There are kinds and degrees of ignorance that are remediable, of course, and we have no excuse for not learning all we can. Within limits, we can learn and think; we can read, hear, and see; we can remember. . . .

But . . . our ignorance ultimately is irremediable. . . . Some problems are unsolvable and some questions unanswerable. . . . Do what we will, we are never going to be free of mortality, partiality, fallibility, and error. The extent of our knowledge will always be, at the same time, the measure of the extent of our ignorance.

Because ignorance is thus a part of our creaturely definition, we need an appropriate way: a way of ignorance, which is the way of neighborly love, kindness, caution, care, appropriate scale, thrift, good work, right livelihood. Creatures who have armed themselves with the power of limitless destruction should not be following any way laid out by their limited knowledge and their unseemly pride in it. (Berry, 2006, p. ix)

Some philanthropic foundations have been founded in this heavily values-oriented tradition while others are explicitly outcomes- or problem-focused. Mission statements of organizations reflect the differences between results-focused missions and values-focused missions. Exhibit 8.4 contrasts these different approaches to mission statements with a look at the implications for evaluation.

Lack of values clarification or values conflict can affect intervention effectiveness at any moment. An experienced developmental evaluator told me about working with a long-time facilitator of community collaboratives who was seeking guidance on some process problems that had arisen in several communities. As they discussed the evidence about what was happening, they came to see a recurring theme of a lack of explicit and shared values—part of the glue in effective collaborations. They decided to introduce a developmental evaluation inquiry in which

---

⌒ Values and Evaluators: Neutrality or Advocacy?

Distinguished evaluation theorist and methodologist Bob Stake (2004) has written eloquently about evaluators' values and advocacy in an article provocatively entitled: "How Far Dare an Evaluator Go toward Saving the World?" He began by noting that evaluators often care about the thing being evaluated—*and should care*. Evaluators don't have to pretend neutrality about the problems that programs are attacking in order to do fair, balanced, and neutral evaluations of those programs. Stake identified six things evaluators do and should care about:

1. We often care about the thing being evaluated.
2. We, as evaluation professionals, care about evaluation.
3. We advocate rationality.
4. We care to be heard. We are troubled if our studies are not used.
5. We are distressed by underprivilege. We see gaps among privileged patrons and managers and staff and underprivileged participants and communities.
6. We are advocates of a democratic society.

So, evaluators do not have to pretend neutrality about the problems innovators are attacking in order to do fair, balanced, and neutral evaluations of those programs. Who wants an uncaring evaluator who professes neutrality about homelessness, hunger, child abuse, community violence, or HIV/AIDS? My younger brother died of AIDS early in the epidemic. My entire family has since been involved actively in AIDS walks and other activities. When I am engaged with HIV/AIDS monitoring and evaluation systems, I do not pretend neutrality. I want to see prevention programs work. That means I am motivated to hold staff's feet to the fire of evaluation to assure that the program works—because I know from personal experience that lives are at risk.

EXHIBIT 8.4 Outcomes-Focused versus Values-Driven Missions: Contrasting Approaches and Their Implications for Evaluation

	Problem-focused mission aimed at specific outcome	Values-focused mission that states how the work is to be done
Mission statement	A *problem-focused mission* aims at solving a problem, e.g., reducing poverty, increasing educational attainment, or enhancing the development of youth.	A *values-driven mission* describes how the work will be done, e.g., helping people help themselves, informing public policy, or building sustainable capacity.
Mission example	*Promote immigration reform and improve the quality of life of immigrants.*	*Work collaboratively with community partners to develop new approaches based on shared values.*
Theory of action	A problem-focused mission should be undergirded by a *theory of change* that states how the desired results will be accomplished, e.g., how the quality of life for immigrants will be improved; how poverty will be reduced; how educational attainment will be enhanced; or how youth will be developed.	A values-driven mission should be undergirded by a *theory of action* that articulates how the work will be done, e.g., helping people help themselves. Such a theory of action can then be applied to any problem—helping immigrants, poverty reduction, youth development, disease prevention—but the mission focus is on how the work will be done.
General evaluation implications	A problem-focused mission is evaluated by its impact on the problem of concern, e.g., whether poverty is reduced.	A values-based mission is evaluated by how the organization engages in its work. Does it live up to its values? Does it walk the talk of its values?
Developmental evaluation implications	Track, monitor, and provide feedback on progress and developments related to problem reduction and attainment of desired outcomes.	Track, monitor, and provide feedback on how the work is carried out, how values inform developments, and the connection between values and developments. Process (how the work is done) is as important, if not more important, than the solution of the problem (because the means matter as much as the ends).

---

they asked community leaders to identify the top 10 decisions made by the group in the last year—explicit or implicit—and then reflect on and surface what values were in operation around those decisions. The leaders found important patterns in the decisions that clarified their values. Those insights helped get the community development processes back on a values-driven track that reenergized the work.

The overall developmental evaluation question for a values-focused inquiry is nicely captured by a message discovered in the elevator of a Shanghai hotel, an example of what is referred to as "Chinglish," the inaccurate translation of English. The sign read: "Please leave your values at the front desk."

Developmental evaluators help value-driven social innovators make sure that doesn't happen.

8. *Complex Situation:* Complexity *Framing of Innovation*

The language, concepts, ideas, thinking, and theory of complexity have spread like, well, a complex nonlinear dynamic—not unlike the H1N1 virus, which began as swine flu and led, among many other things, to the unnecessary slaughter of all pigs in places like Cairo, just one of many cascade effects in the face of panic and fear, which are premier modalities for rapid diffusion of whatever. So nowadays funders, bureaucrats, activists, practitioners, and even intended beneficiaries can be heard proclaiming the "complexities" of the situation they find themselves in. Since I am adding to the chorus with this book, this rant is not a complaint but a recognition of a situation evaluators are likely to encounter with increasing frequency, at least until the predictable (I predict) disillusionment sets in as those mouthing complexity mantras learn that saying the words themselves are about as useful as ritualized muttering of prayers. Still, the words are repeated endlessly: nonlinearity, tipping points, black swans, power curves, patch dynamics, strange attractors, min specs, emergence, self-organizing slime mold, butterfly effects, boids, chaos theory, coevolution, fitness landscapes, instability models, swarmware, and let's certainly not leave out the physics metaphors of a quantum world and the Heisenberg uncertainty principle. Hearing this language spoken by aspiring social innovators may or may not mean that those using it have acquired some sophistication about the implications of complexity for either innovation or evaluation. But finding that out is a good place to begin. Let me hasten to add that these are serious ideas with important implications. If I didn't think so I wouldn't have written this book. But there is also the phenomenon of taking oneself and one's ideas too seriously. Thinking in terms of complexity is, on the whole, a good thing, but there can be too much of a good thing. And those aren't even innovative observations. They're as old as the first observers of and commentators about the human condition, back then called prophets, now called pundits.

Inquiry Framework: Distinguishing Simple, Complicated, and Complex

This inquiry framework addresses how to begin with people who've discovered that, at bottom and looked at in a certain way, *everything is complex*, which is true enough, but not necessarily useful. So, a good place to start is by introducing and working with the basic distinctions presented in Chapter 4 between simple, complicated, complex, and chaotic. Let's do a quick review.

The simple is the mindscape of recipes, best practices, and linear logic models ending in clear, specific, measurable, controllable, known outcomes attained through known, predictable, and controllable cause–effect relationships.

The complicated mindscape faces the challenge of coordinating and integrating lots and lots of parts and elements, like sending a rocket to the Moon or mobilizing a community collaborative of diverse people. Taking action involves elements of uncertainty, but within a particular context and problem definition what to do is knowable and doable, like finding a flu vaccine and vaccinating enough of the world to prevent a pandemic.

Complexity, in contrast, presents a mindscape of high uncertainty, high conflict, and low control where cause and effect are unknown and unknowable until after the effect has emerged and been observed. Action, reaction, and interactions are dynamical, emergent, unpredictable, and sometimes iterative. Operating under complex conditions requires ongoing adaptation, as we see in parenting or becoming involved in a new romantic relationship, both of which unfold in unpredictable ways and are largely immune to recipes and formulas, though there are principles to guide practice. These principles suggest that some things to be tried are likely to be better than others (but there are no money-back guarantees).

And chaos? Maybe its function is to make complexity look manageable and a better place to be, even a hopeful place to inhabit.

All of these—simple, complicated, complex, and chaotic—are *mindscapes* in the sense that they are distinctions of the mind that affect how we see things. And how we see things matters because, as the Thomas theorem so eloquently posits, *What is perceived as real is real in its consequences.*

What does this suggest for the developmental evaluator entering the fray in a complexity-rich environment? Perhaps this: It is no more useful to see everything as complex than it is useful to see everything as simple. Being situationally responsive requires being able to make meaningful and *useful* distinctions. Within interventions, environments, programs, and innovations of all kinds, there are likely to be simple, complicated, and complex elements. Atul Gawande (2007b) has documented how a simple intervention like employing checklists can be effective in a complex environment like a hospital intensive care unit. In *Getting to Maybe*, we found in the cases of social innovation we examined that "successful social innovation combines all three problems—simple, complicated and complex" (Westley et al., 2006, p. 10). Exhibit 4.8 near the end of Chapter 4 identifies and distinguishes the simple, complicated, and complex elements of an international agricultural extension program.

These examples suggest that an inquiry framework that a developmental evaluator can use to disentangle a complex situation is to ask: What here is simple? What here is complicated? What here is complex? And what are the implications of those distinctions? Let me reiterate the evaluation implications. In simple situations the relationships of cause and effect are known and agreed on, so logic models and outcomes measurement take center stage. In complicated situations, the relationships of cause and effect are initially unknown but can become knowable and generally agreed on with systematic testing and evaluation; systems maps and systems change case studies are particularly useful. In complex situations, the relationships of cause and effect are disputed and unknowable until after the effect emerges; this means the evaluation has to be designed to track what emerges and provide rapid feedback to inform choices under conditions of high uncertainty. Working through these distinctions with social innovators or a program staff provides an inquiry framework guided by complexity concepts. See Chapter 4, especially Exhibits 4.8. 4.9, and 4.10, for guidance on making these distinctions, and working with others to make them.

9. Complex Situation: Sophisticated Innovators Wanting to Take On Really Tough Issues

Here's another situation. The program or organization has a solid foundation. It's not in crisis. The straightforward problems have been solved. Things are functioning at a pretty good level; indeed, many perceive effectiveness and efficiency as excellent. Staff is professional and sophisticated—high performers committed to excellence. They believe in ongoing development and getting better and better, and they are willing to work at it. They want to go to "the next level," but aren't sure what that is. There is no consensus on what the problems are that deserve priority attention, nor how to address the complex issues they realize await them at *the next level.* They are prepared to face the naysayers and doubters who they know will tell them *it can't be done,* where "IT" is whatever greater achievement they want to accomplish. They know that:

> When you innovate, you've got to be prepared for everyone telling you you're nuts.
> —LARRY ELLISON, founder and CEO of Oracle Corporation

Inquiry Framework: Asking Wicked Questions

Wicked questions provide one pathway to take on wicked problems. There are a set of problems that cannot be resolved with traditional analytical approaches. In an influential article on "Dilemmas in a General Theory of Planning," Horst Rittel and Melvin Webber (1973) labeled such problems "wicked." This is not *Wizard of Oz* wicked, but complexity wicked as defined by the outer reaches of the degree of uncertainty/degree of conflict matrix (Chapter 5): low certainty about how to take on problems at "the next level," low-to-no agreement about where to focus, and cause–effect relationships unknowable until after effects have emerged and been observed. Among the characteristics of wicked problems identified by Rittel and Webber were these:

- *No definitive formulation of the problem.* The problem and any potential solution are so intertwined that any identified solution changes the understanding of the problem.

- *No clear solutions or end points.* Not being able to clearly formulate the problem means that it is impossible to clearly formulate the solution. There is no clear, specific, and measurable end point—which drives evaluators crazy. Imposing clear outcomes will not solve the problem and may well make it worse.

- *No immediate or ultimate test of a solution to a wicked problem.* Attempted solutions generate cascades of consequences, some intended, many unintended, and it is impossible to predict or control how things will unfold once attempted solutions are put in motion.

- *Problems are intertwined such that any given problem, and its interactions with others, will open doors and windows to still other problems.* Looked at through a complexity lens, a wicked problem is a set of interlocking issues that defy pinning down or holding still

because they are embedded in a dynamic system within a larger dynamic context. Moreover, multiple stakeholders with diverse perspectives present varied and conflicting ideas about what they perceive the problem to be, what is causing it, and how to resolve it.

Public policy examples include climate change, health care reform, achieving both environmental protection and economic growth, population control, school reform, and virtually any aspect of major urban development anywhere in the world. Organizational and program examples of wicked problems include how to pursue emergent opportunities while staying true to a focused mission; how to change and resolve weaknesses without undermining past strengths; how to congratulate staff on current successes while motivating them to work in new ways; and how to find the time to update technology and train staff when everyone is already overworked meeting current demands.

> Wicked problems arise when an organization must deal with something new, with change, and when multiple stakeholders have different ideas about how the change should take place.
>
> How might you identify a wicked problem? The thing to look for is divergence. If requirements are volatile, constraints keep changing, stakeholders can't agree and the target is constantly moving, in all likelihood, you are dealing with a wicked problem. If considerable time and effort has been spent, but there isn't much to show for it, there is probably a wicked problem lurking somewhere. (Poppendieck, 2009, p. 2)

Wicked questions provide a pathway to take on wicked problems by exposing the assumptions that underlie the issue or situation. Articulating assumptions makes explicit patterns of thought that frame the problem and bring to the surface the defining differences in a group. Through inquiry into assumptions, patterns, and possibilities, those involved can find common ground and generate creative alternatives for dealing with wicked problems. Zimmerman and colleagues (1998) identified several uses for *wicked question inquiries* that are relevant to developmental evaluation:

- to change the role of leadership from having *the* answers to having *the* questions
- when there are polarized positions in a group and there seem to be only either-or answers
- to bring in new information to a problem or issue by exposing differences in how it is understood
- when the context seems overwhelming and confusing, and the group needs an approach to make sense of the patterns
- to make the "undiscussable" discussable— to articulate the assumptions held by members in a group. (p. 150)

Wicked questions often express an embedded paradox or tension. Recognizing and articulating a wicked question to explore a wicked problem (a first step in the developmental evaluation process in this situation) can create an opportunity for creativity and innovation, sometimes at the very edge of chaos.

> A wicked question is not a trick question. With a trick question, someone knows the answer. Wicked questions do not have obvious answers. Their value lies in their capacity to open up options, inquiry and bring to the surface the fundamental issues that need to be addressed. (Zimmerman et al., 1998, p. 151)

So let's move from the abstract to the concrete with some actual examples of wicked questions for developmental evaluation. I was working with an international organization on building an evaluative perspective into its strategic planning. The strategy called for becoming more collaborative and creating new partnerships while also becoming more flexible, responsive, and nimble in

---

⌒ *Examples of Wicked Questions*

A Children's Mental Health Centre in Canada argued that their purpose was about preventing mental health problems in children. They also believed in being customer focused. They asked themselves this wicked question: "How does focusing on our clients limit the impact of what we do?"

Four doctors and two nurses run a practice for families in a city in Canada. They believe in paying attention to research findings on the determinants of health. They asked this wicked question: "Are the determinants of health sufficiently reflected in our medical practice?"

A large metals distributor had a stated goal of mobilizing and empowering front-line people. At a strategy planning retreat, the senior management team asked each other the wicked question: "Are we ready to put responsibility for work on the shoulders of the people who do it?"

Note. From Zimmerman (2000).

---

the face of rapid change. But collaborations typically take time and slow things down. *Wicked developmental evaluation question: How does partnering increase flexibility and nimbleness?* Note: This isn't a question aimed at improving the effectiveness of the current way of operating. It's a question aimed at developing a new way of operating while recognizing the tension inherent in their rhetoric.

In a keynote speech at a major evaluation conference I was presenting developmental evaluation ideas about resilience and adaptability as evaluation criteria for organizations that go beyond the traditional dominant and largely static evaluation criteria of effectiveness and efficiency. The first question was: How can we be more effective and efficient while also being more resilient and adaptive? Good question. In fact, a good developmental evaluation question. Effectiveness and efficiency are static

> ### ⌇ Creative Staff Engagement in Pondering and Elaborating Wicked Questions
>
> In one organization, an initial list of wicked questions from a staff retreat was posted on a wall near the office coffee station. Sheets of paper and markers were left by the wall and people were invited to add to the questions, move them around in new configurations, and create their own. The question sheets stayed posted for about 6 weeks after the original session. People in the organization talked about the issues and shared ideas for further inquiry and action. There was no stated agenda or specific meetings allocated to this activity. The organizations' inquiry emerged from the group, the questions on the wall, and the connections created.
>
> ---
>
> *Note.* Adapted from Zimmerman et al. (1998, p. 152).

criteria based on clear, fixed, and targeted outcomes. Resilience and adaptability are about emergent responses in the face of dynamical uncertainty. Put these together and you have a wicked developmental evaluation question: How can we be more effective and efficient while also being more resilient and adaptive?

You may have noted that a complexity inquiry framework and a wicked questions inquiry framework overlap a great deal. How do you decide whether to choose a complexity framework versus a wicked questions framework? Indeed, how does one decide among any of these frameworks, including whether to combine some, which is also possible. It's largely a matter of what resonates in the group. For groups new to complexity inquiries, I'd start with distinguishing simple, complicated, and complex. For more sophisticated groups that already have some experience using a complexity framework and want to get more deeply engaged with wicked issues of paradox, for example, how

inquiry itself becomes an intervention that affects both the inquiry and the intervention, then taking on wicked questions is likely to resonate.

The inquiry framework of wicked questions is one of many ways for developmental evaluators to help innovators inquire more deeply into complex issues and processes. Asking wicked questions can lead into using other concepts and techniques for depicting and studying complexity like fitness landscapes, strange attractors, inquiries into paradoxes, clockware and swarmware, minimum specifications, complementary pairs, network dynamics, flow dynamics, and panarchic cross-scale analyses (Gunderson & Holling, 2002; Kelso & Engstrøm, 2008; Westley et al., 2006; Zimmerman et al., 1998).

Wicked questions, then, take you deeper into complexity. What do you do after you've gotten comfortable with wicked questions? Take on wicked, wicked questions. Then wicked, wicked, wicked questions. Complexity offers no end to the levels of wickedness you can ascend (or descend) and inquire into. In this way we join the poet in that "We shall not cease from exploration/And the end of all our exploring/Will be to arrive where we started/And know the place for the first time" (T. S. Eliot, "Little Gidding"). Know the place for the first time. *Wicked knowing.*

10. Complex Situation: Interest in Monitoring and Comparing Progress against Ideals

Idealistic visionaries are often better at articulating their ideals than at operationalizing goals. A world where every child is valued, loved, and cared for is an ideal—an audacious ideal. How does one assess progress toward such an ideal? And what's the baseline against which progress is to be compared? Often there's a lot of space and distance between the starting point for a group of visionary social innovators and where they hope to get to. They understand that some form of accountability is necessary and that they'll need some benchmarks along the way. But they don't feel that simple outcome indicators and linear logic models can capture and do justice to their ideals or vision.

Comparing actual progress to ideals involves the most basic kind of evaluative thinking. Sometimes the creative process of generating evaluation questions with enthusiastic inquirers and deeply curious innovators can fill a room with pages of newsprint. Brainstorming, cogitating, imagining, diverging, and converging will generate no shortage of fertilizer, enough to let a thousand questions bloom. At such times, it can help to return to simple basics. Where are we now (current baseline)? Where are we going? What should we look for along the way? But ask these questions with an understanding that the answers will be complex. Let's look, then, at how complexity thinking can inform and adapt some evaluation fundamentals.

All sports begin a new season by practicing fundamentals, including basic drills for both rookies and long-time veterans. In preparation for a performance, dancers practice basic moves and singers run through scales. In the midst of evaluation plenty (having garnered overwhelming riches of questions and more questions and still more questions), a little back-to-basics can provide clarity and grounding for everyone. Nothing is more fundamental in evaluation than the idea of the baseline. Evaluative thinking fundamentally and ultimately involves comparative analysis, comparing some starting point (baseline) with some subsequent points along the way (progress benchmarks), and finally, an ending point (at least at some moment in time, even if only temporarily). So evaluations typically begin by establishing a baseline. Straightforward, right? Yes and no. Straightforward in simple situations, not so much in complex ones.

Inquiry Framework: Actual–Ideal Comparative Framework with Emergent and Retrospective Baselines

Some social innovators engage in change with a comparative mindset deeply interested in and attentive to monitoring progress. They may resonate to an explicitly comparative sequence of questions: Where did we begin? Where did we want to get to? Where are we now? How does where we wanted to be compare to where we ended up? What do we do next? These questions are an elaboration of the earlier framework—What? So what? Now what?—but with the emphasis on comparing baselines with benchmarks and outcomes. These questions lead to the most basic kind of actual–ideal comparison shown in Exhibit 8.5. Traditionally, such actual–ideal comparisons are fixed and static because the ideals (mission, vision, and goals) are assumed to be constant and the baseline is assumed to be fixed at some starting point. The pathway from baseline to ideals is traditionally constructed as a linear logic model. However, given the complexities of innovation, emergence, and learning, both baselines and ideals can be emergent, revised, and updated as engaging in change brings to light new data and understandings of the situation. Retrospectively revised and emergent (updated) baselines are a function of the learning that occurs during the change process. Goals and ideals may be emergent and updated under conditions of complexity because the pathways to progress are uncertain and what constitutes "progress" may change. Let's look more closely at this heretical notion of revising and updating baselines and targets.

Staff in human services programs of all kinds—employment training, chemical dependency, help for the homeless, mental health, parenting, community development—know that at the time of intake into such programs, those seeking help are wary, suspicious, careful about what they disclose, and disinclined to tell the whole truth and nothing but the truth for fear of being de-

EXHIBIT 8.5 Dynamical Actual–Ideal Comparative Evaluation Framework

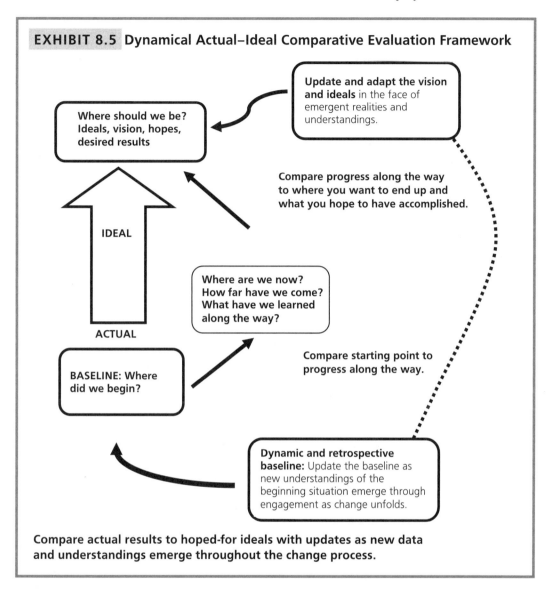

Update and adapt the vision and ideals in the face of emergent realities and understandings.

Where should we be? Ideals, vision, hopes, desired results

Compare progress along the way to where you want to end up and what you hope to have accomplished.

IDEAL

Where are we now? How far have we come? What have we learned along the way?

ACTUAL

BASELINE: Where did we begin?

Compare starting point to progress along the way.

Dynamic and retrospective baseline: Update the baseline as new understandings of the beginning situation emerge through engagement as change unfolds.

Compare actual results to hoped-for ideals with updates as new data and understandings emerge throughout the change process.

nied services. They have good reason for such fear: the wrong response can make them ineligible.

Example: An unemployment program is targeted to people who haven't held a job in the last year. "Have you had a job in the last year?" asks the intake staff person.

"I temped for 2 days last winter cutting Christmas trees from a farm. Then I hurt my back."

"Sorry. You're not eligible for this program."

"Why?"

"Because this program is for people who haven't had a job in the last year."

"But it wasn't really a job. I only worked 2 days. I only made $60."

"It counts as a job under our eligibility guidelines. Sorry. Next."

And that's hardly even self-disclosing. The intake interview may also ask whether you've used illegal drugs in the last year; whether you have a history of family violence; whether you've been homeless; whether you have mental health problems. No. No. No. No. Regardless of the facts.

So this person gets into the program and, over the next few months, as the participant and the staff come to know each other, trust each other, even feel some mutual respect and develop shared understandings, it comes out that, yes, the participant uses marijuana now and again; has a history of family violence; has been in and out of stable housing, periodically living on the streets; and suffers from bipolar disorder. The intake baseline as formally recorded is not accurate. Indeed, the intake data are fundamentally invalid and unreliable. But, in most management and evaluation information systems, what was recorded at intake is the baseline. It is fixed for all time in the data entry and management information system, which is the basis for determining the starting point in evaluating progress and subsequent outcomes. Does this make sense? Of course not. It makes sense to treat participants' baseline as emergent and retrospectively add to it as new information comes to light. But that opens a whole new can of worms about the potential for data manipulation. And when does it ever end? Establishing a baseline seems simple.

Unpeel the onion and inside it gets quite complex (uncertain and controversial about how to do it).

Developmental evaluation, expecting complexity, treats baselines as emergent and subject to revision as new information becomes known. Retrospective baselines (looking back to add to what was known at the time) make sense in a world where reality is socially constructed as shared meanings are created through interactions over time, interactions that lead to trust and risk taking (willingness to risk telling the truth). I've worked with some programs serving people in chronic poverty where the likelihood of mental health problems, alcohol and drug abuse history, family violence experiences, and a record of criminal activities are so high that they don't even bother with baseline data at intake. They know that it will be months before sufficient trust is established to get the real story. Others gather intake data but treat it as a baseline of deception and consider the first benchmark of progress the moment when the original story can be revised to capture more accurately that person's real challenges and background. The developmental story is not linear, for innovations or for people's lives.

⌢ *A Penetrating Glimpse of the Obvious*

Developmental evaluation inquiry questions can change over time. What was once of great interest and huge import may fade as answers emerge and new issues arise. When this happens the inquiry may yield *PGO*—a penetrating glimpse of the obvious.

Not all the questions and answers in developmental evaluation yield new insights. Sometimes it is helpful and important to confirm what is already known—just to make sure it's not one of those things people think they know that turns out not to be so, because "It ain't what you don't know that gets you into trouble. It's what you know for sure that just ain't so." This witty observation has been attributed to many, including Mark Twain, but the original source appears not to be verifiable, so I'm not sure whether the attribution is true or not (Kalsey, 2008), though its veracity is quite verifiable through experience.

The risk of evaluating what people think is already known is that the results may be derided as a PGO, but it wasn't so obvious before it was made obvious through inquiry into whether what might appear to be obvious is in fact a fact.

(cont.)

A RETROSPECTIVE PGO EXAMPLE

Some years ago I undertook a developmental evaluation of a rural grants program of the McKnight Foundation that had created six new "Initiative Funds" in upstate Minnesota ("Lake Woebegon" country, euphemistically called "Greater Minnesota"). These Initiative Funds were to become minifoundations distributing philanthropic funds to ease the deteriorating conditions associated with the farm crisis of that time. In framing evaluation issues with a group of intended evaluation users, including the McKnight Foundation trustees and staff, rural leaders, grassroots organizations, and farm family participants, a major concern at the outset was whether the proposed minifoundations that were to distribute funds (essentially a regranting mechanism for McKnight Foundation funds) would be able to rise above parochial interests, conflicts of interests, and local relationships to base grant decisions on a rigorous process of applying criteria. Millions of dollars were involved. Could rural people without prior philanthropic experience form selection panels, distribute funds, and adhere to universalistic criteria, thereby rising above particularistic, local connections?

Well, truth be told, that was the academic phrasing of the inquiry. What the funders and expert advisers involved were asking was: Will the funds be distributed fairly? Will grant decisions be credible? Can local people be trusted to make trustworthy decisions? The astute will, perhaps, suspect a certain urban arrogance in these questions about how rural folks would behave, but they were real questions, the answers to which were evaluatable and genuinely in doubt at the beginning, with important implications for the future of the innovative initiative.

Partly because the early evaluation work with intended users surfaced, refined, and focused this concern, those charged with implementing the rural funds gave careful attention to establishing credible, criteria-based decision-making processes. Within a few months, the Initiative Funds were operating effectively and, under the scrutiny of external evaluators and the visibility that accompanied establishing the Initiative Funds in rural communities, the staff and volunteers of the new minifoundations were working hard to be fair and rigorous in their grant-making decisions.

When, after 2 years, the interim oral evaluation feedback report discussed these developments at some length, many of the people involved at the beginning were saying: "Of course the rural communities did a good job of managing the money. We never doubted. Tell us something we don't already know. Why is the evaluation making such a big deal of this?"—and other PGO reactions, at which point I produced the actual baseline quotations from those same people, quotations that identified the original concerns as both primary and major, and the rankings of potential evaluation questions that placed concern about how grant decisions would be made near the top of potential foci. I then facilitated a discussion of what had changed. They came to recognize that they had learned a great deal in the interim months, that those lessons were worth capturing and substantiating, and that what they had learned had major implications for attracting additional resources as well as informing the larger field of philanthropy about effective regranting efforts.

The point is that the willingness to really delve into the findings and consider in some depth the implications of the findings was due to some extent to the fact that we had their original concerns and state of knowledge. They couldn't recognize as a group what they had learned without clear evidence of where they had begun. Having once had this experience, they became eager to periodically reexamine their state of knowledge in order to systematically track their own learnings, capture lessons learned, and ask ever more sophisticated questions.

In effect, this involved applying the simplest logic of evaluation: Where did we begin? Where are we now? How have things developed along the way? How close are we to where we want to be? What have we learned? Where do we go now?

In short: What? So what? Now what?

Retrospective Developmental Program Baselines. The same approach to emergent and revised baselines and ideals can be taken at the program level. Sometimes the developmental evaluator is invited to join a new venture and gets in at the beginning of an innovation. That was the case in my experience with Twin Cities Rise!, the innovative employment program I described in Chapter 2 targeted at chronically unemployed men of color. I became part of the design team when the idea for the program was still germinating. In contrast, Damiano, the antipoverty program described in Chapter 6, presented quite a different scenario.

When I began working with the Damiano staff, the program's 20-year history in the Central Hillside area of Duluth kept coming up. Any new developments would clearly be an outgrowth of and affected by their history—a history that included important developments and forks in the road. So, to honor that history and illuminate the context for future developments, we created a retrospective history of key developments in the past. In effect, we did a *retrospective developmental evaluation.* I have included the results of that inquiry in the next chapter as an in-depth example of one of the forms developmental evaluation can take.

Finally, as long as I'm being heretical and suggesting retrospective, revised, and emergent baselines, let me acknowledge the further heresy of skipping the baseline exercise altogether. Shocked? Aghast? In fear for your evaluation soul? Take a deep breath and consider this: An experienced international developmental evaluator told me that he sometimes finds that it's not worth going through the work of getting agreement about the baseline if, for example, a program sets out to influence changes in the behavior, relationships, activities, policies, or practices of the protagonists of a social change initiative and the starting point, the baseline, is simply the nonexistence of that desired change. Since, he continued, in complex environments you cannot predefine what changes you will actually influence, or perhaps even those you want to influence, the most that can be said at the beginning—and sometimes not even that—is who has to change in order to fulfill your vision, values, and mission. He continued:

"To tell the truth, in the evaluations I do—summative, formative, as well as developmental—rarely is there a baseline. When we try to reconstruct it, people who would be needed to do the reconstructing have changed so much that we decide the reconstruction would be artificial and a waste of time. Other times, the idea of reconstructing a baseline is seen as unnecessary—they just want to focus on what differences will result from their efforts."

In response to this observation, one can make the case that there's an implicit baseline (the status quo) even if it is not systematically and rigorously defined for comparison purposes. But I take the larger point to be, consistent with the theme of this chapter and, indeed, of this whole book, that what we do as evaluators is situationally variable—if we are, as urged, situationally responsive. There are situations where people express a sense of urgency about changing things and don't have much tolerance for looking back or generating a solid baseline. At other times, coming together around a baseline, even one subject to future revision, is energizing and connecting for those involved. So you pick your battles. You listen to the people you're working with and attend to what resonates—and what doesn't. There are many inquiry frameworks. Find the one that works for the situation you're in. Don't worry about committing evaluation heresies. Worry about doing what's sensible and useful—and what will support development. That can mean, among other things, a retrospective and/or emergent baseline, or no baseline at all.

Developmental Evaluation Inquiry Frameworks: Ten and Counting . . .

This chapter has presented 10 complex situations with matching inquiry frameworks. I began with some basics: (1) Kipling's six descriptive questions and (2) basic evaluative questions: *What? So what? Now what?* I then offered some specialized situations and developmental inquiry frameworks: (3) learning-focused inquiry; (4) building on strengths, for example, appreciative inquiry; (5) systems change questions; (6) collaborative inquiry into and by collaborations; and (7) values-driven innovation matched by values-focused evaluation, to wit, *Are we walking the talk of our values in what we do and how we work?* I turned next to specific complexity frameworks (8) distinguishing the simple, complicated, and complex as an inquiry framework and (9) wicked questions. Finally, to round out this top-10 list, I ended with (10) an emergent and revisable actual–ideal comparative evaluation framework featuring changeable baselines, changeable ideals, and changeable progress markers along the path from beginning to wherever the journey ends, if it does. Many situations will require developmental evaluations that draw upon several or a combination of these frameworks, and the framework or combinations used may change over time as the situation changes and new questions and issues emerge. Exhibit 8.6 summarizes these inquiry frameworks highlighting the kinds of situations that are particularly well matched to each framework.

EXHIBIT 8.6 Developmental Evaluation Inquiry Frameworks: Examples, Options, and Situationally Dependent Guidance

Inquiry frameworks	Complex situational matching guidance
1. Basic descriptive questions. Kipling's *Five W's and One H:* What? Why? When? How? Where? Who?	Crisis-laden environment where the challenge is to bring some focus by getting grounded in a basic understanding of the situation, getting everyone on the same page. Basic descriptive questions are often a good place to begin when entering a complex situation.
2. Fundamental evaluative thinking: What? So what? Now what?	Introduces people new to evaluation to fundamental evaluation thinking; also highlights the connection between analysis (What?), interpretation (So what?), and action for the next stage of development (Now what?).
3. Triangulated learning framework: beliefs, knowledge, action.	If the innovators come to developmental evaluation with a focus on *learning*, use the language of *learning*, and are genuinely excited about *learning*, then make learning the focus of the evaluation. Premise: A learning organization is one that, over time, has an increasing proportion of its action informed by knowledge (evidence) rather than just beliefs.
4. Focus on strengths and assets: appreciative inquiry and related approaches.	Engaging in developmental evaluation from a positive, hopeful place while still asking hard questions and undertaking serious inquiry. This can be especially appropriate where people have had negative past experiences with evaluation and are leery of being unfairly judged. Options include asset-based community development, positive deviance, success case method, and the most significant changes framework, any one of which can be matched to the particulars of the developmental evaluation situation.

(cont.)

Inquiry frameworks	Complex situational matching guidance
5. Systems change: perspectives, boundaries, interrelationships.	Social innovators articulate a vision of disrupting existing systems, which they find unacceptable, and making a lasting difference by *changing systems*. They think in systems terms and envision results expressed as systems changes. Use a systems change framework.
6. Collaboration: What's the nature and degree of working together? Networking? Cooperating? Coordinating? Collaborating? Partnering?	When social innovation is framed around collaborating for change, the basic theory of action is: bring good, creative, committed, and innovative people together—and find a way to keep them together—and you can make a real difference in the world. This emphasis invites inquiry into the nature and consequences of collaboration.
7. Values-driven inquiry.	The process (how the work is done) is as important to the innovators as what is accomplished. Means are as important as ends. A strong sense of values guides change efforts and sustains the work in the face of difficulties and setbacks. The evaluation focuses on the extent to which innovators are true to their values, that is, whether they are *walking their talk*.
8. Complexity framework: distinguishing simple, complicated, and complex.	When the language, concepts, ideas, thinking, and theory of complexity frame social innovation, distinguishing degrees of complexity can guide the evaluation. It is no more useful to see everything as complex than it is useful to see everything as simple. Being situationally responsive requires being able to make meaningful and *useful* distinctions between the simple (cause and effect are known and agreed on), the complicated (cause and effect are initially unknown but knowable with systematic inquiry), and the complex (cause and effect is a source of intense conflict and unknowable until after the effect emerges). Use these distinctions to guide inquiry and select methods.
9. Wicked questions.	Somewhat sophisticated innovators want to take on really tough issues and are willing to deal with paradoxes, intrinsic ambiguities, and inherent tensions in how change unfolds in complex adaptive systems.
10. Actual–ideal *comparative framework* with retrospectively updated and emergent baselines, and revised benchmarks and targets.	Some social innovators engage in change with a comparative mindset deeply interested in and attentive to monitoring progress. They may resonate to an explicitly comparative sequence of questions: Where did we begin? Where did we want to get to? Where are we now? How does where we wanted to be compare to where we ended up? What do we do next? Given the complexities of innovation and emergence, this can also include retrospective and dynamic approaches to both baselines and ideals, updating each as new data and understandings emerge during the change process.
11. Combinations of any of the above.	Over time a developmental evaluation may incorporate more than one inquiry framework and sometimes more than one at the same time.

The final framework, the 11th, is also really the first. It is where I began, with an overarching developmental evaluation framework emphasizing that *developmental evaluation focuses on developmental questions:* What is being developed? How is what's being developed (what's emerging) to be judged? Given what's been developed so far (what has emerged), what's next? The developmental evaluator inquires into *developments*, tracks *developments*, facilitates interpretation of *developments* and their significance, and engages with innovators, change agents, program staff, participants in the process, and funders around making judgments about what is being developed, what has been developed, and the next stages of development. It's within this overarching developmental evaluation framework that the 10 other inquiry frameworks presented in this chapter are undertaken, as specific ways of focusing the developmental inquiry in a way that is matched to and congruent with the characteristics and dynamics of a particular situation and the perspectives and priorities of specific social innovators.

Never Stop Questioning

The chapter began with a nod to Rudyard Kipling's "six honest serving-men" as a basic framework asking descriptive questions. But in the opening, I quoted only the first stanza in which the six questions are listed. The full poem, from his *The Elephant's Child*, moves from the simple to the complex by evoking, dare I suggest it, a quintessential developmental evaluator who has taken to

heart Einstein's admonition, cited at the beginning of this chapter, to *never stop questioning.* Each developmental evaluation inquiry I've suggested throughout this chapter begins with a short set of framing questions. Those are points of entry. More and deeper questions will emerge along the way, ever repeating a cycle of ongoing iterative inquiry: Where were we? What have we developed? Where are we now? What do we develop next? And again at a later point: Where were we? What have we developed? Where are we now? What do we develop next? Details to emerge by collaborating and co-creating with Kipling's six honest serving-men as ever new questions emerge. Never stop questioning.

> I keep six honest serving-men
> (They taught me all I knew);
> Their names are What and Why and When
> And How and Where and Who.
> I send them over land and sea,
> I send them east and west;
> But after they have worked for me,
> I give them all a rest.
>
> I let them rest from nine till five,
> For I am busy then,
> As well as breakfast, lunch, and tea,
> For they are hungry men.
> But different folk have different views;
> I know a person small—
> She keeps ten million serving-men,
> Who get no rest at all!
>
> She sends 'em abroad on her own affairs,
> From the second she opens her eyes—
> One million Hows, two million Wheres,
> And seven million Whys!

9

Developmental Evaluation *Bricolage*

Reflective Practice, Sensitizing Concepts,
Action Research, Abduction, Systems Change,
and Retrospective Developmental Evaluation

We think in generalities but we live in details.
—ALFRED NORTH WHITEHEAD (1861–1947),
English philosopher

The creative, practical, and adaptive developmental evaluator draws on varied inquiry traditions and uses diverse techniques to fit the complexities of a particular social innovation and situation. It is in this sense that *we think in generalities but we live in details.* And it is in this regard that we may be thought of as *bricoleurs.* The term comes from anthropologist Claude Lévi-Strauss (1966) who defined a *bricoleur* as a "jack of all trades or a kind of professional do-it-yourself person" (p. 17). He brought into the world of research the tradition of the French *bricoleur* who traveled the countryside using odds and ends, whatever materials were at hand, to perform fix-it work. The inquirer "as bricoleur or maker of quilts uses the aesthetic and material tools of his or her craft, deploying whatever

strategies, methods, or empirical materials are at hand. If new tools or techniques have to be invented, or pieced together, then the researcher will do this" (Denzin & Lincoln, 2000, p. 4). Drawing on creativity and pragmatism opens up new possibilities, the *bricolage* of combining old things in new ways, including alternative and emergent forms of data collection and transformed evaluator–innovator relationships.

The last chapter explored alternative inquiry frameworks to guide developmental evaluation. This chapter looks in depth at some specific *bricolage*-like applications that I hope will illuminate how developmental evaluation intersects with other approaches to engage with and understand social innovation and change. We look at some detailed applications of these general approaches by way of further opening up possibilities for cross-fertilization and creative practice. And I may throw in a rant now and then at no extra change.

As we draw on varied traditions and explore their applications in this chapter, we need to keep in mind that *no definitive list of developmental evaluation inquiry approaches can or should be constructed.* Developmental evaluation creatively adapts whatever approaches and methods fit the complexities of the situation and are responsive, appropriate, and credible to social innovators in opening up new understandings and guiding further development. In being creative, the developmental evaluator is also practical and pragmatic, doing the best job possible within available resources and other constraints. Constraints always exist and do what constraints do: constrain. Our ability to think of alternatives is limited. Resources are always limited. Time is of the essence. We do what we can. Part of what we can do is adapt other inquiry traditions to the purposes of developmental evaluation.

Reflective Practice for Developmental Evaluation Inquiry and Engagement

One fruitful focus for developmental evaluation can be inquiring into the meanings and applications that emerge around and in response to the key concepts that guide a social innovation. For example, the Planned Lifetime Advocacy Network (PLAN) in Canada has been working on reframing how communities engage with people with disabilities. Early in their work, one of PLAN's guiding principles was *a home is a sanctuary, not a warehouse.* Inquiring together into what this principle meant for engagement with people with disabilities led PLAN to questions about related concepts: quality of life and relationships. As the work unfolded and they reflected systematically on what they were hearing, experiencing, and

doing—sharing stories, reflecting on what they heard people saying—PLAN came to the fundamental principle that has guided their work ever since: *Relationships do not lead to quality of life; they are quality of life.*

Al Etmanski, PLAN's founding director and current codirector, has described the work they did on their guiding concepts:

> We had to fight for these concepts. They didn't just slip into your hand and you'd say, "Oh, I think I'll follow that one for a while." We would go over an issue five meetings in a row, agree on something, and then at the sixth meeting decide to go in a completely different direction. We were civil, but there was tension there to figure out what the values meant. . . . There was a lot of comfort in ambiguity. . . . I had just come from a job in which I made 20 decisions a day—probably all of them were bad decisions, but I was able to make them—to a job in which I was expected to make no decisions for months. We persevered, walked around the issue, had a look at it, said, "Okay, this is it; we might as well go in this direction." And then we'd change our minds. And we still do that. We were a learning group. Everyone was curious. (quoted in Westley et al., 2006, p. 75)

This kind of dynamic, uncertain, unpredictable, nonlinear, and emergent process drives traditional evaluators crazy. Traditionalists force innovators into using linear logic models and operationalized concepts to get clear, specific, and measurable goals. But that can interfere with, short-circuit, and constrain the exploratory and innovative processes. The role of the developmental evaluation in this kind of situation is to help the group keep track of the various meanings they explore, be systematic in capturing the stories and experiences they share, and facilitate deeper understanding of and engagement with the key guiding concepts and emergent principles—without ever expecting them to necessarily be operationalized as research measures. PLAN has been working for two decades and is still inquiring into and learning about the meanings, dimensions, variations, and implications of *relationships.* This inquiry is the cutting edge of ongoing innovation and initiatives aimed at taking their work to scale driven by a vision of "embedding it into the water supply" across Canada and the world.

Such engagement, formally facilitated by or with a developmental evaluator, can use the methods and techniques of reflective practice. The formal reflective practice process involves sharing stories as data about the idea or concept under inquiry. It's not a discussion of the concept. It's data-based, story-based, and experienced-based engagement with the concept. After stories and experiences are shared at a particular reflective practice session, the developmental evaluator facilitates identifying patterns and themes in the stories, and that leads to both possible actions based on those insights and patterns and to further questions for focused inquiry and reflective practice. Exhibit 9.1 summarizes the reflective practice process. Exhibit 9.2 graphically depicts the reflective practice cycle.

EXHIBIT 9.1 **Reflective Practice Process for Developmental Evaluation**

1. Group identifies a focus for inquiry and learning. A sensitizing concept, basic premise, or fundamental value often offers a useful focus: an idea that provides direction and vision to the desired change but the meaning of which is still emergent.

   a. Example from PLAN Canada in working to create nurturing communities for people with disabilities (see text for details): *Relationships do not lead to quality of life; they are quality of life.*

   b. Example from a group designing a professional development course on social innovation: *Definitional premise:* Social innovation is a complex process of introducing products, processes, or programs that profoundly change the basic routines, resource, and authority flows or beliefs of the social system in which they arise. Such successful social innovations have durability and broad impact (Westley & Antadze, 2009). *Sensitizing concepts:* "successful social innovations," "profound change," "durability," and "broad change."

2. Turn the concept, idea, value, or vision into an experiential inquiry question. The question is not an abstract question for intellectual discussion. It is a question that evokes experience.

   a. Example: *What relationship have you had with someone different from you, different in some significant way, that made a difference to your quality of life?*

   b. Example: *What experience have you had in what you consider a successful social innovation?*

3. Participants in the reflective practice (RP) group share a personal experience (a real-life anecdote, a lived experience story) that responds to the question.

   Helpful facilitation guidelines:

   a. It has to be that person's own experience, not sharing an experience he or she knows about from someone else, heard about secondhand, or read about. It's his or her *own* experience.

   b. It's not their life story. They have to be able to tell the story in 3–5 minutes.

(cont.)

c. They just tell the story. Don't explain it. Don't analyze it. Tell the story: beginning, middle, and end (or where it is now if there is no ending).

d. For larger RP groups, break into smaller groups (four to six people) for the sharing and interacting. Then the small groups report back to the full group (step 6).

4. Group members can ask short clarifying questions. This is not a time for discussion or analysis. The focus is on understanding the story, on what happened and why. Example: If it's not clear what made this a *relationship that made a difference to quality of life*, ask the person to describe that connection. "Please say a little more about the difference the relationship made to your quality of life. I think I understand, but just say a bit more so that I don't misinterpret."

Facilitation guidelines:

a. Establish norms of confidentiality; what is shared stays in the group.

b. Be prepared for emotions; alert the group to expect that some stories may evoke strong feelings. That's okay. That's part of the process. Be sensitive. But it's also not a therapy group. *It's a reflective practice group.*

c. Enforce time lines gently and sensitively. Don't be obnoxious and anal–compulsive about time. These are people's stories, their lives they are sharing. But time is short and precious. Nudge people along as needed.

d. The developmental evaluator can be, and usually should be, a full participant in the RF experience *if* he or she has relevant experience to share. For example, on a generic question like experience with a successful social innovation reflected on by a planning group, I participated fully. If the story-sharing focuses on staff members' experiences in promoting and implementing a *specific social innovation*, I would facilitate rather than participate because I'm not a staff member and don't have that experience.

5. After all stories have been told, participants are asked to identify patterns and themes in the stories.

Facilitation guidelines:

a. You may or may not distinguish patterns from themes, depending on the sophistication of the group. The first time I'm working with a group, I don't emphasize the distinction. Over time, part of capacity building with the group can be learning to make the distinction. Oh, and what is the distinction? I'm glad you asked.

Actually, there's no hard-and-fast distinction. The term "pattern" usually refers to common, specific observable behaviors and reports. For example, I facilitated reflective practice with a group of university administrators who participated in a wilderness program. One descriptive *pattern* was: "Almost all participants reported feeling fear when they rappelled down the cliff." A theme takes a more categorical, general, or topical form: FEAR. So, putting the two together, the reflective practice analysis revealed a *pattern* of participants reporting being afraid when rappelling down cliffs, running river rapids, and hiking along ledges; many also initially experienced the group process of sharing personal feelings as evoking some fear. Those patterns make DEALING WITH FEAR a major *theme* of the wilderness education program experience (Patton, 2002, p. 453). Patterns are common, concrete observations grounded in the data. Themes cut across patterns and involve moving to an interpretation of meaning.

(cont.)

    b. Not every story has to have a theme or pattern. In a group of six, commonalities among three people's stories is a pattern. This isn't research. The purpose is not generalization. The purpose is deepening understanding, generating shared insights, and learning, often for further ongoing inquiry.

    c. Someone in the group needs to keep track of the stories. Either that person, or someone else, needs to be identified to report out the themes and patterns to the larger group (if more than one group is engaged in the RP exercise).

    d. The developmental evaluator needs to be sure to get the notes from each group, so alert them in advance that their summary notes will be collected; when collected, make sure the summary notes are legible, understandable, and interpretable.

6. If there is more than one small group engaged in the RP exercise, each group reports their themes and patterns to the full group. The facilitator (sometimes but not always the developmental evaluator) records the themes and patterns, and combines those that appear to be similar or duplicative.

7. Implications discussion and analysis. The group picks one or two themes that have important implications for the work at hand. They discuss those implications. This often involves identifying important lessons.

    a. Example. A pattern in the PLAN relationship stories was that the person who was not disabled got as much or more out of the relationship as the disabled person. The initial focus had been on helping the disabled. The implication was that building community involves mutuality. Lesson: Focus on the relationship, not just on what is happening to the disabled person in the relationship. Both are affected.

    b. Example: The social innovations group had about 30 participants who did RP in five small groups. A dominant theme across the five groups was *intense feelings and emotions* throughout the innovative initiative.

8. Generate action agreements and next steps for reflective practice.

    a. Example: An RP group that has generated the lesson of staying focused on the relationship and discovered the importance of mutuality may decide to immediately incorporate that learning into the training they do for new staff and community organizers. Then, the next phase of RP involves a new set of further RP inquiry questions: What is mutuality? How does it happen? What are its variations? How is mutuality facilitated? What nurtures mutuality? What are barriers? These become questions for further, and deeper, reflective practice the next time the RP group comes back together.

    b. Example: The social innovations group decides that any professional development curriculum on social innovation and any staff involved in the program will need to be comfortable with and prepared to deal with strong emotions. This runs counter to the usual university mantra: "Stay in your head, don't get emotional." Question for future reflective practice: How have you personally dealt with the emotional rollercoaster ride of being involved in social innovation? This becomes the focusing question for further, and deeper, reflective practice the next time the RP group comes back together.

(cont.)

VARIATIONS AND ADDITIONAL GUIDANCE

- People come prepared with their stories written in advance. This can increase thoughtfulness and anticipation, and makes it far easier for the developmental evaluator to capture the stories (data) from the RP participants. Potential downside: Less spontaneity.

- Tape the stories as a group record and transcribe them so the developmental evaluator—*and the group*—has a record of the "data" from the stories. This is only for the group's use, keeping in mind the agreement about confidentiality.

- If the RP stories (as opposed to just the patterns and themes) are to be used for formal, external evaluation reporting, how the stories are reported (e.g., whether identities are disguised) has to be negotiated with the RF group and informed consent procedures followed.

- Instead of simply listing themes, arrange them into a generic story or a systems map showing how themes are interrelated and interconnected (spider web of themes rather than a linear list).

- A variation on the sharing process with large groups is to do a second round of thematic analysis after the first round. So, let's say we have a group of 25. Five small groups of five people each engage in the initial RP process. Then, instead of reporting their themes to the full group, each group numbers off from 1 to 5. Everyone has the list of themes from their group. The 1's assemble as a new cross-cutting group; likewise the 2's, etc. Now we have five new groups that can synthesize the patterns and themes they bring from their first-round-of-analysis groups. These groups then report to the whole group, which as a whole synthesizes the final set of patterns and theme.

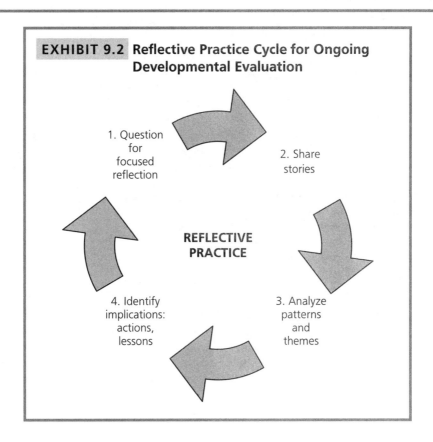

EXHIBIT 9.2 **Reflective Practice Cycle for Ongoing Developmental Evaluation**

1. Question for focused reflection

2. Share stories

REFLECTIVE PRACTICE

4. Identify implications: actions, lessons

3. Analyze patterns and themes

Reflection-in-Action
and Reflection-on-Action

An optimist is someone who thinks the future
is uncertain.
                    —Graffiti in the toilet of a bar

Reflective practice as a formal method of
inquiry for learning originated with Donald
Schön (1983, 1987), but informally it is as old
as Aristotle and Plato. Schön distinguished
reflection-in-action (thinking on our feet)
from reflection-on-action (looking back and
figuring out what happened, why, and what it
means). When we engage the world as reflective practitioners, he posited, we are committed to testing our assumptions, theories, and
ideas against how the world actually works in
the company of others similarly committed.
When the focus of reflective practice is evaluative in nature (What's working? What's not
working? How do we tell the difference?), it
can be useful to have a developmental evaluator facilitate, record, and feed back to the
group its reflections, patterns, conclusions,
and subsequent questions.

Schön emphasized the idea that participants in reflective practice often experience
surprise, puzzlement, or confusion. Those
involved examine past experiences but also
formulate new actions and behaviors that
become experiments (innovations) for generating new understandings and fomenting
change. Over time, the group produces a
portfolio or repertoire of learnings that document their inquiry journey. A developmental evaluator can be (but does not have to
be) the keeper of the portfolio, both keeping it before the group and keeping it (and
adding to it) as the history of the group's
work and progress. This process supports
ongoing adaptation.

> When a practitioner makes sense of a situation
> he perceives to be unique, he *sees* it *as* some-
> thing already present in his repertoire. To see
> *this* site as *that* one is not to subsume the first
> under a familiar category or rule. It is, rather,
> to see the unfamiliar, unique situation as both

similar to and different from the familiar one,
without at first being able to say similar or different with respect to what. The familiar situation functions as a precedent, or a metaphor,
or . . . an exemplar for the unfamiliar one.
(Schön, 1983, p. 138)

In this way, Schön posited, we engage with
new situations both individually and collectively, and continue to learn, adding to the
innovators' understanding and expanding
their repertoire of possibilities.

Sensitizing Concepts as a Focus
for Reflective Practice and
Developmental Evaluation

Linguistic pundit William Safire devoted
a *New York Times* column to defining the
"preautumn of life." What, he pondered, is
"middle age"? He considered several operational definitions, judging each inadequate.
Ironically, the more precise the definition
(e.g., age 45 to 60), the more problematic
its general utility. He concluded that the inherent ambiguity of the term "middle life"
and the resulting implication that each of
us must define it *in context*, made it not a eu-
phemism, but rather a "usefulism" (Safire,
2007). Safire's playful term is what qualitative inquirers call a *sensitizing concept*. The
sensitizing concepts that guide innovations
provide a powerful focus for reflective practice and developmental evaluation.

Qualitative sociologist Herbert Blumer
(1954) is credited with originating the idea
of the "sensitizing concept" to orient fieldwork. Sensitizing concepts in the social sciences include loosely operationalized notions like victim, stress, stigma, and learning
organization that can provide some initial
direction to a study as one inquires into how
the concept is given meaning in a particular
place or set of circumstances (Patton, 2002,
2007). The observer moves between the sensitizing concept and the real world of social
experience, giving shape and substance to

the concept and elaborating the conceptual framework with varied documented manifestations of the concept. Such an approach recognizes that while the specific manifestations of social phenomena vary by time, space, and circumstance, the sensitizing concept is a container for capturing, holding, and examining these manifestations to better understand patterns and implications.

Evaluators commonly use sensitizing concepts to inform their understanding of situations. Consider the notion of "context," the theme of the 2009 annual AEA conference. Any particular evaluation is designed within some *context*. We are constantly admonished, a chorus to which I have contributed throughout this book, to take *context* into account, to be sensitive to *context*, and to watch out for changes in *context*. But what is *context*? The AEA conference produced no definition, a source of frustration to some, a source of intellectual stimulation for others.

Not long ago an animated discussion on *EvalTalk*, the AEA listserv, explored this issue. Systems thinkers posited that system boundaries are inherently arbitrary, so defining what is within the immediate scope of an evaluation versus what is within its surrounding context will inevitably be arbitrary, but the distinction is still useful. (I discussed systems concepts as an inquiry framework in the last chapter.) Indeed, deciding what is in the immediate realm of action of an evaluation and what is in the enveloping context can be an illuminating exercise— and different stakeholders might well provide different perspectives. In that sense, the idea of *context* is another "usefulism," or a sensitizing concept. Those on *EvalTalk* seeking an operational definition of context ranted in some frustration about the ambiguity, vagueness, and diverse meanings of what they, ultimately, decided was a useless and vacuous concept. Why? Because it had not been (and could not be) operationally defined—and they displayed a low tolerance

for the ambiguity and diversity that is inherent in such sensitizing concepts. They would not, in my judgment, make good developmental evaluators. But I could be wrong.

A sensitizing concept raises consciousness about something and alerts us to watch out for it within a specific context. This can be especially important where social innovators are, at least initially, more driven by a vision than by a concrete, operational plan. They are following the counsel of Antoine de Saint Exupéry who advised:

> If you want to build a ship, don't drum up the men to gather the wood or divide the work and give orders. Instead, teach them to yearn for the vast and endless sea.

Now, then, suppose you were de Saint Exupéry's developmental evaluator and you propose to facilitate a reflective practice inquiry derived from this vision and counsel. You gather the workers together and, before they begin building, you proceed thusly:

> "Think of a time when you experienced *yearning*. Share the story of that experience. What was the focus and nature of your *yearning*? How did it emerge and unfold? What barriers, if any, did you experience in opening yourself to *yearning*? What resulted from your *yearning*? What were its consequences, intended and unintended? Based on your experience of *yearning*, what lessons or principles emerge?"

Then you help them apply those lessons and principles to the work they are about to undertake. Get the idea? Does this example make you *yearn* to facilitate reflective practice around some sensitizing concept that intrigues you? Give it a try. A good *bricoleur* can turn most any idea or issue into a sensitizing concept for reflective practice. Once you get the hang of it and start paying attention, you'll find sensitizing concepts popping up all over the place like spring flowers after a warm rain.

> ### ~ Unnovation: A Sensitizing Concept for Evaluation Inquiry
>
> Developmental evaluation supports social innovation in complex adaptive systems. Innovation thrives on creativity, experimentation, trying things out, and adapting to what emerges as things are tried out. When traditional up-front evaluation requirements like clear, specific, and measurable outcomes and fully formulated logic models are imposed too early in the innovative process, evaluation can be experienced by social innovators as *unnovation*: the opposite of innovation (Business Strategy Innovation, 2009; Zimmer, 2009). Indeed, traditional forms of evaluation can be a barrier to innovation. Evaluation is sometimes accused of only evaluating innovative efforts, usually critically, while ignoring the status quo, making evaluation an inadvertent conservative force.
>
> But unnovation can also emerge as an issue in programs that want to be, and may even fancy themselves as being, innovative. The evaluation questions one might pursue include: How can one track and evaluate *unnovation*? How does *unnovation* relate to innovation from a systems perspective? What can be learned by thinking about *unnovation*–innovation interactions and dynamics?
>
> Australian evaluation theorist and practitioner Patricia Rogers has commented that *unnovation* can be thought of as *innovation that fails to create authentic, meaningful value*. She added:
>
> > Corporate history is full of *unnovation*. There seems to be a strong incentive system for executives to restructure an organization—it seems to look good on a resume. I know many organizations that have been beset by repeated restructures, which have taken staff away from doing the real work, and which have been redone by the new person coming in to replace the restructure architect who has gone on to bigger things, leaving a trail of disillusioned staff behind. (Rogers, 2009a)
>
> Rogers nominated as a specific case of *unnovation* a well-documented case of a university's unfortunate experience with an academic management system information technology implementation project, which failed to achieve its targets, vastly exceeded its budget, corrupted existing student data, and led to an auditor-general enquiry.
>
> ---
>
> *Note.* From *archive.audit.vic.gov.au/reports_mp_psa/PSA_Feb03_Part5b.pdf*.

Process Use as a Sensitizing Concept

Consider process use as a sensitizing concept (Patton, 2007). Process use, as I've explained in earlier chapters, is distinct from findings use. Process use calls attention to how people involved in an evaluation are affected by the evaluation process quite apart from their use of its findings. For example, focusing on the meaning of a key program concept like PLAN's *relationships* can affect how people engage with each other before any data about that engagement are even gathered. In evaluation, the idea of *process use* says, things are happening to people and changes are taking place in programs and organizations while evaluation takes place, especially when stakeholders are involved in the process. Watch out for those things.

Pay attention. Something important may be happening. The process may be producing outcomes quite apart from findings. Think about what's going on. Help the people in the situation pay attention to what's going on, if that seems appropriate and useful. Perhaps even make process use a matter of intention and reflection. But don't judge the maturity and utility of the concept by whether it has "achieved" a standardized and universally accepted operational definition. Judge it instead by its utility in sensitizing us to the variety of outcomes that an evaluation may produce beyond findings.

So with all that as context, let's gather together our *bricoleur*'s swag and take a voyage to New Zealand to visit two Kiwi evaluators who have been facilitating reflective practice and inquiry into an innovative sen-

⌒ Sensitizing Concept: Holy Prostitutes

Sensitizing concepts offer an opportunity to inquire into the various context-dependent meanings of terms. The following old story provides insight into what it means to engage in prostitution. I have used this story in workshops to stimulate discussion about context-dependent sensitizing concepts and terms. Even when some find it offensive—and it is not meant to but can give offense—what it is that makes it offensive becomes part of the discussion.

A man is driving down a deserted stretch of highway when he notices a sign out of the corner of his eye. . . . It reads:

> SISTERS OF ST. FRANCIS
> HOUSE OF PROSTITUTION
> 10 MILES

He thinks this is a figment of his imagination and drives on without a second thought. Soon he sees another sign, which reads:

> SISTERS OF ST. FRANCIS
> HOUSE OF PROSTITUTION
> 5 MILES

Suddenly he begins to realize that these signs are for real and comes upon a third sign saying:

> SISTERS OF ST. FRANCIS
> HOUSE OF PROSTITUTION
> NEXT RIGHT

His curiosity gets the best of him and he pulls into the drive. On the far side of the parking lot is a stone building with a small sign next to the door reading:

> SISTERS OF ST. FRANCIS

He climbs the steps and rings the bell. The door is answered by a nun in a long black habit who asks, "What may we do for you, my son?"

He answers, "I saw your signs along the highway and was interested in possibly doing, hmmm, some business."

"Very well, my son. Please follow me." He is led through many winding passages and is soon quite disoriented. The nun stops at a closed door and tells the man, "Please knock on this door."

He does so and another nun in a long habit, holding a tin cup, answers the door. This nun instructs, "Please place $100 in the cup then go through the large wooden door at the end of the hallway." He puts $100 in the cup, eagerly trots down the hall, and slips through the door, pulling it shut behind him. The door locks, and he finds himself back in the parking lot facing another sign:

> GO IN PEACE.
> YOU HAVE JUST BEEN SCREWED BY THE
> SISTERS OF ST. FRANCIS
> SERVES YOU RIGHT, YOU SINNER.

sitizing concept for initiatives that involve the Māori people. I hope this example, and meeting Kate McKegg and Nan Wehipeihana, who are using developmental evaluation as the framework for this initiative, will give you a deeper sense of the power and utility of inquiring deeply into a core idea around which everything else revolves. As in previous chapters, hearing from Kate and Nan is a reminder and reaffirmation of the importance of *the personal factor in evaluation* (also a sensitizing concept, but you'd already figured that out, right?). We'll start, as they did when I met them, with their own context. Watch for the sensitizing concepts in their story.[1]

Kia ora

Kate McKegg is a sixth-generation *Pakeha* (non-Māori New Zealander of European settlers lineage) descended from Irish, Scottish, and English immigrants who came to New Zealand in the 1800s. She lives in Te Awamutu, in the north island of New Zealand. Kate says:

"I kind of 'fell into' evaluation in the early 1990s. Much of the early evaluation work in New Zealand was happening in the employment/labour market area. We had high unemployment, and particularly high Māori unemployment. I went to work for an employment agency and my very earliest evaluation experience was on job programmes for Māori. Although I was *Pakeha*, my boss seemed to think that I could work well with Māori and in Māori contexts. This is when I first met Nan; I was doing some qualitative training at the research company she worked for. I remember being introduced to her briefly by one of her colleagues."

---

[1] In the sections that follow, I have retained the British English and Māori spellings within quotations to retain the authenticity of the language and people talking.

Nan Wehipeihana is Māori. She explains: "On my mum's side my tribal links are to *Ngati Porou* and *Te Whanau-a-Apanui*, on the east coast of the north island of New Zealand and on my dad's side, my tribal links are to *Ngati Tukorehe* just North of Wellington." Nan says that, ironically, despite being Māori, most of her early evaluation work did not have a specific focus on Māori. But then that changed.

"Over time my evaluation work began to have more of a focus in part, or exclusively, on Māori programmes targeted at Māori or services provided by *iwi* (tribe) and Māori organisations. Much of this work did not take account of Māori cultural values in its approach or in the rendering of evaluative conclusions.

"So my own work began to have an increased focus on evaluation with and by Māori and I began to explore the place of *tikanga* Māori (Māori cultural values and practices) and what being Māori meant in evaluation. It was during this time that I first began to engage with *Kaupapa* Māori theory (Smith, 1999), which takes for granted the validity and legitimacy of Māori language, knowledge, and culture. There was an increasing call for evaluation with and in Māori communities to be led by or involve Māori, so I established my own evaluation consultancy in the late 1990s in response to this market need and my own desire to develop evaluation approaches and ways of working that better met the need and aspirations of Māori."

Kate says that despite being a *Pakeha*, most of her early evaluation work was on Māori programs and in Māori contexts. She had an opportunity early in her evaluation career to work with a Māori organization where she managed a small evaluation team charged with developing evaluation capacity inside the organization, as well as in local and regional contexts. In 2002, she established her own consulting practice. Her first job was for a large Māori higher education institution (a *Wananga*). She says: "I was immersed in an environment where Māori values were at the core, and where there was energy and passion for creating social change for Māori, by Māori, in Māori ways—with Māori in control." She learned a lot through this immersion.

"It was in this role that I began to more deeply understand historical injustices and how I might play more of a role in supporting the wider political aspirations of Māori in New Zealand, and I also came to appreciate that what is good for Māori is good for all New Zealanders."

Kate and Nan crossed paths over the course of a decade, increasingly and intentionally engaging together around their shared interests in developing Māori evaluation capacity. The evaluation community is quite small in New Zealand, they note, so they met at conferences, professional development workshops, and through evaluation project work. They explain:

"We were both profoundly aware that so much evaluation work had a focus on Māori, but did not adequately, or at all, take account of Māori values, perspectives, and principles. Just engaging with Māori was problematic, and there was such a critical need to create some space for Māori to be Māori, and to be valued in evaluation at the time."

Their first shared project around this *kaupapa* (purpose) was to write a proposal with Lois-Ellin Datta, one of evaluation's distinguished pioneers (Datta & Miller, 2004), to secure funding from the W. K. Kellogg Foundation, the Hawaii County Department of Research and Development, and the Kohala Center for Māori and Hawaiian evaluators to come together to share evaluation stories, approaches, and practices. They explain:

"The broader social, political, and economic backdrop to our own journeys was one where Māori aspirations for self-determination were increasingly being played out in many new contexts, including evaluation. The Treaty [of *Waitangi*] settlement process (begun in 1975) was really gearing up, and this provided a platform for Māori sovereignty aspirations to begin flourishing. Alongside, government policy and agencies were beginning to also reflect these aspirations in their own visions, strategies, and programmes. An example is the Māori Potential Framework, *Te Puni Kōkiri* (Ministry of Māori Development), and *Ka Hikitia* (Ministry of Education)."

Deepening Engagement Together

The Māori evaluation focus deepened in 2008 when they began working together with Sport and Recreation New Zealand (SPARC), helping them build internal evaluation capacity. They began working with "a wonderful Māori woman (Ronnie), who had this big bold vision to reclaim and build a space for Māori in sport and recreation, to participate *as Māori*. And in our sports-mad country (passionate rugby and netball followers), her vision for achieving this through revitalising traditional Māori sport and recreational activities was both exciting and courageous." Nan says:

"I met with Ronnie, pored over relevant programme documentation as well as a range of Māori development literature, and began a series of iterative and reflective conversations. It was evident very early on in our conversations that Ronnie had a theory of change that drew threads together from 20 years of Māori development.

"She was keen, hungry, and open for help. Of course she wanted some help around evaluation, but she also wanted help explaining to the non-Māori leadership in the organisation what this programme was about."

Kate adds:

"Up until this moment, increasing participation *by Māori* in programmes and services such as education, health, et cetera, had been the focus of most government policy, programming, and evaluation we had been involved in. Participation *as Māori* is a groundbreaking conceptual shift that in very recent years has come to the fore through the work of a prominent Māori academic, Mason Durie (2005, 2007), but very few people or policies, or programmes had yet to articulate what this meant, especially in practice.

"Ronnie's conception of *as Māori* acknowledges and recognises the marked changes that have occurred in *Te Ao Māori* (the Māori world) and in wider New Zealand society. The past 15 years have been characterised by stronger assertion by Māori of cultural identity, improved capability in management areas, and growing capacity and intent for self-determination.

"The concept of *as Māori* also recognises the desire of Māori to have control over their future direction as well as the strong motivation for Māori to determine the solutions that work for them. Furthermore, it affirms the validity and legitimacy of Māori knowledge and ways of doing things, of the need for space for Māori to live and participate in New Zealand as Māori.

"Her conception of Māori participating in sport and recreation *as Māori* really broke new ground."[2]

As they engaged with Ronnie, Nan and Kate say they came to recognize that their roles were not going to be those of traditional evaluators, so they gravitated to developmental evaluation that allowed them to join the process of inquiry even as they facilitated evaluating what was developing.

"Although we knew that we would still have to develop a more formal evaluation framework, and this was how we shaped our contractual relationship with the organisation, the journey required us all to find a way to move from a conceptual vision to something concrete and tangible that the organisation could understand, such as program specifications, guidelines, and outcomes.

"We knew that we needed to produce enough of an articulation of a 'model' of a programme to provide assurance to the organisation, but without stifling the opportunities for Māori communities to experiment, innovate, and learn, and to come to know, in a truly grounded sense, what it means to participate *as Māori* in sport and recreation."

Focusing on the Sensitizing Concept *as Māori*

Nan and Kate facilitated many cycles of reflection, questioning, and discussion, and multiple written iterations of the program documentation.

---

[2] *Te Puni Kōkiri* (Ministry of Māori Development) established *He Oranga Poutama* (HOP) in 1995 to promote healthy lifestyles for Māori through sport and physical activity. Funding became a SPARC responsibility in 2001 and SPARC is now the sole funder and manager of HOP.

In 2009, a new program strategic goal has been defined to align HOP with a Māori Potential approach and SPARC's sport and recreation outcomes. The strategic goal of the HOP program is to "increase participation and leadership *as Māori* in sport and traditional physical activity at community level."

The HOP goal signals SPARC's intention to in-

vest in and enable a stronger platform for Māori to participate *as Māori*. The HOP goal further recognizes that a strong and secure cultural identity helps facilitate access to wider society, as well as being vital to overall well-being, and affirms the validity and legitimacy of Māori knowledge and ways of doing things. It acknowledges that Māori will maximize their potential when they are able to participate and succeed in New Zealand and the world *as Māori*; and this underpins SPARC's support for *as Māori/Māori-led initiatives*.

The HOP differentiates the program from many of SPARC's other programs where participation by Māori is the focus. The "*as Māori*" element enables SPARC to recognize cultural distinctiveness.

"The circles got smaller, the closer we got to something that authentically represented the vision, and also could be understood by the organisation.

"We tried out our ideas with some Māori programme providers who, through storytelling and reflection, assessed, questioned, and analysed what we had done. These providers found it really valuable to participate in a process that genuinely helped them to think hard about what the programme was going to be about, and how they might achieve the vision.

"When we had finalised the programme guidelines, a senior manager in the organisation expressed amazement at what we had done, moving from a concept, a vision, to something grounded and tangible. He saw the programme guidelines as something that breathed life into the vision in a way that *Pakeha* could understand."

Nan elaborates:

"The process to date has been a series of conversations and storytelling. This type of approach fits the sense-making and reflection practices that are naturally part of Māori cultural practices. Māori are very in tune with metaphors for learning. Historically, a lot of research and evaluation has taken a deficit approach and hasn't served us well. The focus in this work has been on learning, innovation, values, vision; there's something about developmental evaluation that accepts the taken-for-grantedness of being Māori."

The Relevance of Developmental Evaluation

Calling what they're doing *developmental evaluation* has worked well for engaging in this process in a culturally appropriate way. Nan explains:

"There's been a gradual realisation that we've been engaged in a developmental

(evaluation) journey. Developmental evaluation, it seems to me, starts from a space of positive potential, that being Māori and what we do is valid, it's just a given, we don't have to explain it, and this is the basis for starting our enquiry. It allows the development of visions and programmes to emerge and develop within the control of those implementing and innovating. It sits alongside, doesn't control or dampen the core values of innovation. I don't see developmental evaluation as an easy option. It's tough. But it's more culturally attuned to our way of doing things."

Kate and Nan worry that developmental evaluation in New Zealand has a flavor of "the latest fad." They comment:

"Developmental evaluation is not really well understood, and to many in government it doesn't seem 'solid' or robust enough. So, practicing developmental evaluation in a government context was a constant balancing act for us. On the one hand, we needed to acknowledge the organisation's sense of uncertainty about developmental evaluation and, on the other hand, we had to take a leadership role in promoting developmental evaluation as the most appropriate approach for *He Oranga Poutama* (Steps to Health and Wellness).

"In order to provide reassurance about using a developmental evaluation approach, as an appropriate and valid form of evaluation, even at this early stage, we realised that we had to regularly provide them with tangible reporting outputs.

"It was also really useful having Michael Quinn Patton come to New Zealand and do a workshop on developmental evaluation. The personal factor was very real for us in this instance."

Acceptance of developmental evaluation, they observe, was the culmination of working hard on trusting relationships and building on the credibility they had established previously in their evaluation work. Other reflections and lessons from their experiences with developmental evaluation are summarized in Exhibit 9.3. They concluded:

"Without building trust and credibility, we're not sure they [SPARC] would really have gone for the approach. It's still quite a radical approach for them, and still appears somewhat risky, but they can see that it offers them the most value in this context, and they trust us, and they trust that it is going to be more than just a series of conversations.

"Although we have already journeyed many months, we recognise that we are all at the very early stages of an ongoing development process. What it means to participate *as Māori* is still to emerge. The *He Oranga Poutama* programme 'on the ground,' in communities, is poised now to begin in earnest—with ongoing development."

EXHIBIT 9.3 From Theory to Practice: Reflections on Developmental Evaluation from New Zealand

At the 2009 annual conference of the AEA, Nan Wehipeihana and Kate McKegg reported what they had learned about using developmental evaluation for the *He Oranga Poutama* initiative in New Zealand aimed at revisioning and changing the orientation of sports and recreation from increasing participation *by Māori* to focus on participation *as Māori*. *Tino rangatiratanga* (self-determination) was the foundational principle of the innovation.

FOCUS OF THE EVALUATION

What does *as Māori* participation look like as it emerges and develops in the initiative?

WHY DEVELOPMENTAL EVALUATION?

- Uncertainty around the program; not sure what participation *as Māori* would involve
- New, innovative program
- Vision-driven rather than based on predetermined goals that were clear, specific, and measurable
- No formal evaluation evidence from other efforts about what to expect (which increases uncertainty)
- Complexity of the environment, including a contracting economy, dynamic political environment around Māori development, and a changing, developing organization

ORGANIZATIONAL CONTEXT

- Strong leadership: visionary and innovative
- Organizational buy-in to the idea that developmental evaluation was appropriate
- Program's openness and willingness to try developmental evaluation

(cont.)

EVALUATORS

- Able to be ourselves
- Share visionary values of the leadership
- Mutual trust and respect
- Experience with multiple methods
- Knowledgeable about the context
- Teaming together and supporting each other to deal with uncertainties and any emergent areas of discomfort

REFLECTIONS TO DATE: IMPORTANT FACTORS IN DEVELOPMENTAL EVALUATION SUCCESS

- Relevancy and credibility of developmental evaluation lies in relationships of trust built up over time
- Developmental evaluation requires evaluators to be highly responsive—sometimes soft and probing, other times edgy and assertive
- Ability to thoughtfully process on the run and facilitate reflective moments
- Alignment of developmental evaluation with Māori development aspirations and world-view

SOME TRAPS TO WATCH OUT FOR

- Developmental evaluation can be perceived as just "the latest fad"
- Making sure the approach and methods are appropriate
- Making it more than "just a series of conversations," but instead involving real, meaningful data-driven reflection and feedback
- Requires evaluators to have a deep methodological toolkit (multiple and mixed methods) and excellent communication and facilitation skills, so that tailoring of method to context can happen responsively
- Deal with anxieties about no clear, hard, predetermined evaluation outputs through regular data-based reporting on progress, learnings, and developments
- Thinking it will be easy when it can actually be quite hard and challenging

---

Note. Based on Wehipeihana and McKegg (2009).

Action Research and Developmental Evaluation

Reflective practice and sensitizing concepts are inquiry traditions that can be adapted creatively to serve developmental evaluation purposes. We can also *bricole* (from the French verb *bricoler*, meaning "to tinker" or "to fiddle with") *action research* for use in developmental evaluations. How are developmental evaluation and action research alike and different? When used as part of organizational development, action research is often oriented toward solving specific problems. But action researcher John Elliott asserts that "good action research is developmental" (2005, p. 8).

Participatory action research (McGarvey, 2007) is a tradition from organizational and community development that has broad applicability. But for our purposes here, the focus must be on *development*, not just problem solving, as some action research is. Australian scholar and practitioner Bob Dick is one of the world's premier action research theorists and consultants, and his website is unmatched as an action research resource (Dick, 2009a). The way Bob Dick (2009b) describes action research clearly makes it an option for use in undertaking developmental evaluations:

> Action research can be described as a family of research methodologies which pursue action (or change) and research (or understanding) at the same time. In most of its forms it does this by
>
> - using a cyclic or spiral process which alternates between action and critical reflection and
> - in the later cycles, continuously refining methods, data and interpretation in the light of the understanding developed in the earlier cycles.
>
> It is thus an *emergent* process which takes shape as understanding increases; it is an *iterative* process which converges towards a better understanding of what happens. In most of its

forms it is also participative (among other reasons, change is usually easier to achieve when those affected by the change are involved) and qualitative.

Action research and reflective practice have much in common. Which tradition to *bricole* and adapt for developmental evaluation purposes will depend on how those with whom you are working resonate to the different terms and how much they know about these approaches, if anything. Let's consider, then, how developmental evaluation and action research intersect.

Intersections of Developmental Evaluation and Action Research: A Distinguished Evaluation Pioneer Reflects

Elliot Stern is particularly well positioned to provide insights on this issue because of his strong background in both organizational development and evaluation. Stern was the founding president of the United Kingdom Evaluation Society, has served as president of the European Evaluation Society, and helped establish the International Organization for Cooperation in Evaluation. He founded and has served for 15 years as editor of *Evaluation: The International Journal of Theory, Research and Practice*. He is professor of evaluation research at Lancaster University and previously headed up a dedicated evaluation unit at the Tavistock Institute in London.

When Elliot and I have discussed our intellectual and evaluation practice journeys, we found many parallels as well as points of divergence. We first met at the international evaluation conference in Vancouver in 1995 sponsored jointly by the Canadian Evaluation Society and the AEA. Since that time, as our paths have crossed, we have shared thoughts on evaluation in general and developmental approaches in particular.

Stern has engaged in and worked with development and evaluation through community development, technology development, pedagogic development, organizational development, and eventually, international development. He has always brought a *developmental perspective* to these endeavors. He has also engaged in action research and worked with action researchers. Moreover, he has incorporated complexity ideas in his developmental evaluation and action research work.

In 1987 Stern wrote a paper for the European Union entitled "Evaluation Strategies for Local Economic Development" in which he focused on local development projects in which (1) it may be impossible to specify in advance the expected form of program outcomes, or (2) it was very difficult to separate out the evaluation role from that of local animation and program coordination. These are both important themes of what I'm calling developmental evaluation in this book. Also in the late 1980s Stern and colleagues worked on what they titled a "Development Review" of a major national vocational training program in the United Kingdom. They argued that this title for their work was a legitimate relabeling of an "objective evaluation" (what they were initially asked to deliver) because it was important that learning from the program would be available as the program developed. In 1989 Stern wrote a discussion paper for the Evaluation Centre he headed up at the Tavistock Institute on "Developmental Evaluation: Learning from Social and Organisational Innovation." At that time he was fully committed to a definition of evaluation that centered around learning, both organizational and individual. In a 1990 keynote speech delivered to a European Union policy conference on "economic and social integration," he linked programs for the marginalized (countering poverty, tackling long-term unemployment, working to integrate persons with disability, etc.) with a high level of complexity and uncertainty as they usually deal with intractable and enduring social and economic problems, and projects and even programs may fail or

cease to exist while being evaluated. Therefore, he concluded, "To get the full yield from these programs requires learning what they tell us about both problems and their contexts."

Recalling his engagement with these issues and his emergent approach to evaluation, Stern reflects on how his thinking was shaped by working in European policy arenas. Much of his work at that time, as well as that of his colleagues, was grounded in the perspective that learning in the *policy community* was a legitimate outcome of evaluation in innovative and developmental settings. They concluded, for example:

- We not only need to learn about success and failure, but also to understand some of the complex dynamics that make programs for the marginalized groups and communities themselves vulnerable.

- When organizations that innovate are as often as not temporary, then it is especially important that learning networks achieve some greater degree of permanence.

His clients were often national U.K. government agencies or European institutions and they initiated programs, pilots, or experiments in order to develop policy. In many cases the commitment was less to the pilots themselves than to learning from them. In a 1994 essay about the development of learning technology programs of the European Union, Stern and his colleagues elaborated on the individual and organizational aspects of the evaluation as a learning model. They argued that their *individual* learning perspective derived from understandings about how actors involved in complex sociocultural processes learn through action and that the *organizational* perspective was shaped by the domain of action (in this case pedagogics):

Learning has to be seen in context, embedded in settings and institutions both personal and economic; learning is an essentially embedded and social activity and cannot be decontextualized.

In the presentation that Stern gave with Elizabeth Sommerlad at the 1995 Vancouver International Evaluation Conference (*Evaluation for a New Century*), they reviewed a set of evaluations they had undertaken and observed that some were mostly delivery-oriented and some were more experimental or exploratory; and some had predetermined goals while others were evolving throughout a program's life:

- Most of the programs referred to had evolving goals. From the outset a very general "target" or "task" was specified and only when the program was underway did more particular objectives emerge.
- The evaluation cannot therefore take specific aims and objectives for granted; their evolution has to be tracked.

As evaluators they tracked change that was continuous and offered evidence, critical reflection, and feedback to support an innovative process. In identifying their institutional, intellectual, and practice roots at the Vancouver conference, they included:

- An action research perspective oriented to setting up social and organizational experiments and with the processes likely to ensure their success.
- An interest in organizational theory, how organizations change, and how to design implementation and delivery systems including networks and multiple organizations.
- Systems frameworks, descriptive of complex interdependent systems, and therefore making it natural to locate projects and programs within a wider explanatory context.
- A broad background in the social sciences with a theoretical rather than a methodsled bias and a willingness to experiment with qualitative, quantitative, normative, and critical methods and techniques.
- Expertise in industrial and community-based action research projects where differences in objectives, values, and interests were to be expected and worked with rather than ignored.
- A strong commitment to making the outputs of research and experiments useful and usable, and an inherited toolkit of implementation devices intended to ensure the diffusion of innovation.
- A well-established institutional identity that encouraged professional independence and a broad understanding of the ethical responsibilities and role of researchers and consultants in any social milieu.

Elliot Stern has been especially pioneering in linking action research explicitly with evaluation. He has framed the linkage thusly:

- Judgment and explanation require analysis, on the one hand, and
- Development and empowerment require action, on the other.

Action research integrates evaluation types:

- Judgment with development
- Explanation with empowerment

and thereby combines

- Analysis with action
- Theory with practice

Stern traces the intellectual roots of his views to Kurt Lewin (1948):

> It is important to understand clearly that social research concerns itself with two rather different types of questions, namely the study of general laws of group life and the diagnosis of a specific situation. (p. 204)

Drawing on Lewin's observation, Stern has consistently argued that laws do *not* tell *what* conditions exist locally, at a given place at a given time. In other words, the laws don't do the job of diagnosis *that has to be done locally*. Neither do laws prescribe the strategy for change. Quoting Lewin, again he argues that what is needed is

> a circle of planning, executing, and reconnaissance or fact-finding for the purpose of evaluating the results of the second step, for preparing the rational basis for planning the third step, and for perhaps modifying again the overall plan. Rational social management, therefore, proceeds in a spiral of steps each of which is composed of a circle of planning, action, and fact-finding about the result of the action. (p. 206)

Stern has generated four dimensions that in his view characterize an action research perspective in evaluation:

- Purpose: Research and evaluation are for action and not only for understanding.
- Epistemology: Relevant and valid knowledge is produced through action—through learning by doing.
- Contextualization: There is a need to embed understandings in local settings.
- Relationships: Greater equality between evaluator/researcher and "actors" (who have "agency" and are *not* merely subjects/objects/targets).

Building on this framework, in a presentation to the Scottish Evaluation Network in 2004, Stern suggested that in addition to analytic skills an action research approach to evaluation also requires:

- Facilitation
- Negotiation
- Consensus building
- Partnering
- Innovation management

This requires the deployment of skills and knowledge that includes:

- Feedback and dialogue
- Grounded theory
- Reframing and iterative theory building
- Process understandings
- Collaborative experiments
- Community development

He further argues that *all* evaluators need a similar skill set nowadays because of the nature of contemporary policymaking in the decentralized, multistakeholder, often socially fragmented, and consensus-reliant governmental state.

As much as anyone engaged in evaluation, Elliot Stern's intellectual journey and significant contributions show the integration of action research and developmental evaluation. These two inquiry approaches are both compatible and mutually reinforcing. As I commented at the beginning of this section, how one labels a particular inquiry depends on how those for whom it is being done understand and value one approach (or designation) over the other, the preferences of those engaged in the inquiry, and the tradition within which the inquiry is framed (organizational development or program evaluation).

Reasoning and Developmental Evaluation

There is an art and craft to *bricolage*. *Bricoleurs* are creative thinkers. And critical thinkers. So come, let us reason together as we *bricole*.

Tom Schwandt's 2007 plenary address to the 2007 annual conference of the AEA was a tour de force on reasoning, both how to and why it is important. It was also a lamentation on the dearth of complexity-informed reasoning. He titled it "Educating for Intelligent Belief in Evaluation." It has been published in the *American Journal of Evaluation* and I heartily recommend it to thoughtful evaluators everywhere (Schwandt, 2008). Here is a taste of what he had to say:

- Intelligent belief in evaluation is a matter of both embracing and explaining to aspiring evaluators and the public the complexity of social systems and the limitations on our ability to predict, plan, and control their behavior. It may indeed mean that in the face of such complexity, we need an experimenting society committed to innovation, social reality testing, learning, self-criticism, and the avoidance of self-deception. . . .

- An experimenting society is an evaluating society, not a scientific society or an audit society.

- In such a society, we are modest in our expectations to solve social problems through policy supported by evaluation efforts. We recognize that the processes involved in the formulation, implementation, and evaluation of policies and programs are not exercises in scientific thinking. Rather . . . , they are essentially communicative acts, involving dialogue and argument shaped by rules, conventions, and power structures. Moreover, in such a society . . . , we are fully aware that the policy maker and the service provider do not simply seek to deal with uncertainty on a technical basis using evidence but rather seek to cope with ambiguity on a practical basis, making wise judgments about the appropriateness of their actions in relation to a range of technical, political, moral, and ethical concerns.

- To successfully manage complexity and exercise practical reason requires a set of traits or dispositions—dispositions that should be most obvious among those who call themselves evaluators, but also dispositions that evaluators aim to cultivate in others. For an evaluating society to flourish, it needs citizens and professionals who are marked by their capacity to be inquisitive, systematic in their inquiry, judicious in their claims, truth seeking, analytical, intellectually humble, sympathetic to opposing points of view, self-critical, and open-minded—not simply open-minded in the sense of being tolerant of other points of view, but open-minded in the sense of recognizing the challenges to one's own way of seeing things that arise from others'

ways of making distinctions of worth. These are the dispositions of a critical thinker. . . . (Schwandt, 2008, pp. 148–149)

Abductive Reasoning

Tom Schwandt has eloquently made the case that evaluation is ultimately more about reasoning than about data and methods. We use methods to generate data, but the data have to be interpreted and given meaning, and that involves reasoning. In Chapter 6 I discussed the reasoning processes involved in extrapolating findings and implications from one setting to another. With Schwandt's thoughtful and provocative exhortations as context, I want to focus for a bit on what I consider an underappreciated form of reasoning that can be especially useful to developmental evaluation *bricoleurs*.

Abductive inference, also called "inference to the best explanation" (Harman, 1965; Lipton, 1991), is reasoning that begins with an observation that something has occurred, what evaluators would call an "outcome," and works backwards to track the pathway that led to that observed outcome. Abductive inference is common in interpreting forensic evidence and has been made popular by crime scene investigation television shows. For example, if pieces of a knife blade are found in the skull of a victim, the best explanation may be that a knife wound contributed to the death. Abductive inference has been recognized as centrally important in artificial intelligence because it captures how experts in all fields reason to solve problems (Walton, 2004, pp. 17–22). Abduction is especially relevant to and appropriate for drawing inferences about social innovations in a developmental evaluation.

Charles S. Peirce, the American pragmatic philosopher and scientist who coined the term "abduction," emphasized its scientific importance especially at the discovery stage of scientific hypothesis formation (Peirce, 1965). Peirce illustrated what he meant by abductive inference with examples of common, everyday reasoning.

I once landed at a seaport in a Turkish province; and, as I was walking up to the house which I was to visit, I met a man upon horseback, surrounded by four horsemen holding a canopy over his head. As the governor of the province was the only personage I could think of who would be so greatly honored, I inferred that this was he. This was an hypothesis. (quoted in Walton, 2004, p. 5)

Rather than the highfalutin' word *abduction*, my father called this kind of reasoning "common sense" (which he pointed out I was often lacking despite all my "book learning"). Peirce was interested in making explicit the logic embedded in both common sense and scientific discoveries. The relevance of abduction to developmental evaluation is the underlying reasoning process involved in discoveries and innovations.

Deduction, Induction, and Abduction

Peirce divided reasoning into three mutually exclusive categories: deductive reasoning, inductive reasoning, and abductive reasoning. Each type of reasoning has a different modality. Deduction involves reasoning from the general to the specific. Induction involves reasoning from the specific to the general. Abduction works back and forth between general and specific to solve a particular problem. In this manner it supports developmental evaluation's niche in helping social innovators navigate the muddled middle between theory-driven, general principles, and top-down general knowledge versus bottom-up, particular, and local knowledge. Where these oft-conflicting bases of knowledge intersect is where the dynamics of innovation adaptation occur, our focus in Chapter 6. Peirce positioned abduction as "the process of forming an explanatory hypothesis. . . ." He wrote: "Every single item of scientific theory which stands established today has been due to Abduction" (quoted in Walton, 2004, p. 8).

Abduction, then, is how a scientist forms the hypothesis that is later tested using deductive or inductive reasoning. Several characteristics of abduction have been extracted by Walton from Peirce's writings:

> First, it is a technique used to narrow down the number of alternatives by picking out one or a few hypotheses from a much larger number of them that are available. Second, it is a process of guessing, or picking the right guess, and thus it is clear that it is a fallible process that can lead to wrong hypotheses as well as to right ones. Third, it comes into play when a new phenomenon is observed, in other words, a phenomenon that has not yet been explained, or explained well enough, in science. (Walton, 2004, p. 9)

Peirce ultimately tied abduction to pragmatism, which together constitute what I consider to be the epistemological foundation of developmental evaluation for those who are interested in such matters. Walton concludes that

> one has to go beyond the narrow framework of deductive and inductive reasoning to understand abduction. . . . Peirce's view of abductive inference can be seen as genuinely innovative and pioneering. It was on the frontiers of logic when he wrote, and it still is more than a century later. (2004, p. 14)

An Example of Abductive Reasoning

Famous fictional detective Sherlock Holmes relied on abduction more than on deduction or induction, at least according to William Sanders's (1976) review of Holmes's analytical thinking in *The Sociologist as Detective*. In the evaluation of the rural community leadership program I described in Chapter 1, we did follow-up interviews with participants to find out how they were using their training. We found ourselves with a case not unlike the "Silver Blaze" story in which Sherlock Holmes made much of the fact that the dog at the scene of a crime had not barked during the night while the crime was being committed. In our case, we discovered that graduates of the leadership program were not leading. In fact, they weren't doing much of anything. Were their skills inadequate after only a week of intense training? Did they lack confidence? Were they discouraged? Disinterested? Intimidated? Incompetent? Unmotivated?

So, we had a finding. We had an outcome, or more precisely, the lack of an outcome. We worked backward from the experience of the training, examined what happened during the training right up to the final session, and tried to connect the dots between what had happened and this unexpected result. We also returned to the participants for further reflections that might explain this general lack of follow-up action.

The participants expressed great interest in and commitment to exercising community leadership and engaging in community development. They expressed confidence in their abilities and felt competent to use the skills they had learned. But at perhaps the most teachable moment of all, in the final session of training as participants enthusiastically prepared to return to their communities and begin to use their learnings, the director of the program had offered a closing word of caution.

"Take your time when you return. Don't go back like a cadre of activists invading your community. You've had an intense experience together. Let things settle. It can be pretty overwhelming to the people back home when they get a sense that you've been through what for many of you has been a transformative experience. So go easy. Take your time. Resettle."

And so they did. More than he imagined. What he had neglected to provide was any guidance about how to know when it was time to begin engaging after the reentry period of resettling. So they waited. And waited. And waited. Not wanting to get it wrong.

Of all the explanations we considered, that one fit the evidence the best. Its accuracy was further borne out when the director changed his departing advice at the end of the program and we found a different result in communities. A developmental evaluator is a detective, using both data and reasoning to solve the mystery of how an innovation has unfolded and assess its consequences.

Abduction, Discovery, and Innovation

Philosopher Atocha Aliseda (2006) calls abduction "the logic of discovery" and distinguishes it from the logic of confirmation or proof (pp. 12–18). This follows from distinguishing well-structured from ill-structured problems, with the logic of proof applied to well-structured problems (simple problems in the framework presented in Chapter 4) while the logic of discovery is appropriate for ill-structured problems, which is the realm of complexity in this book.

Walton (2004) presents a method for evaluating abductive arguments built around a dialogue process of discovery. The dialogue is back and forth between possibilities (hypotheses) and explanations, with observations (data) mediating the dialogue.

> Explanations are elicited from facts as these facts are pieced together and marshaled in sets of statements called accounts, filled out by inserting implicit assumptions as new data are collected in an investigation. The best explanation is selected out of this process. Abductive reasoning provides evidence to confirm a hypothesis through a discovery process of questioning and answering in which competing accounts are examined by probing into the weaknesses in them. (p. 4)

Archeology provides excellent examples of abductive reasoning. Leakey and Lewin (1992, pp. 28–29) have described how a fossil hunter recognized a partially exposed bone fragment as part of a hominid skull. The fragment was fairly flat with just a slight curvature, indicating that it was part of a skull of a large-brained animal. The impression of the brain on the inner surface was very faint. The inference to the best explanation of these observations was that the fragment was part of a hominid skull. This plausible possibility, which amounted to a working hypothesis, was a reason for carrying the investigation forward and doing some more excavations, which led to the discovery of a nearly complete *Homo erectus* skeleton. This interaction between evidence and reasoning illustrates abductive reasoning in archeology: the conclusion that the bone fragment was hominid derived from close inspection of the fragments and the site. From these observations a plausible hypothesis was formed that could then be tested by further investigations, providing more data that could support or refute the hypothesis.

This interaction and dialogue between reasoning and evidence, with attention to context and relationships, is how an ongoing developmental evaluation inquiry unfolds. Make observations. Interpret the findings to test hypotheses about how the innovation is unfolding compared to how it was expected or hoped to unfold. Act on the conclusion, thus generating more data to further test hypotheses (expectations about what will happen) as well as watching for the emergence of unanticipated consequences that are at odds with or a variation of what was predicted.

In Tom Schwandt's (2008) discourse on evaluation reasoning, he argued that evaluation is, well, *an argument*. He explained:

My concern here is that in the press to master methods of generating data we ignore the idea of developing a warranted argument—a clear chain of reasoning that connects the grounds, reasons, or evidence to an evaluative conclusion. . . . Developing a warrant means asking the question "What else might this mean?" and then convincingly ruling out plausible rival explanations of value to come to the conclusion that this is [the] best explanation of apparent value we have at present. . . .

The word *argument* here signifies that an evaluative judgment is not a matter of logical demonstration but a matter of persuading a particular audience (using reason and evidence) that something is the case. The characteristics of such an argument are that it is

1. Practical and presumptive. The term practical signifies that we are dealing with decisions incapable of being made in an algorithmic way. Presumptive means that that argument is about what is considered most likely and reasonable in the circumstances—rather than a matter of proof.

2. Contextual. An evaluation argument is contextualized in two senses. First, the context determines, in part, what comprises reasonable evidence, criteria, and data. In other words, for example, the value of a program is studied in a particular context of debate, conflict of opinion, value preferences, criticism, and questioning about the relative merits of those opinions, values, preferences, and criticisms. Second, it is with reference to a context composed of some particular client(s) and stakeholders that the evaluator aims to make a persuasive case for her or his judgment. Evaluation arguments are always indexed in this way to some particular context of contentious ideas.

3. Dialectical. The argument that the evaluator constructs is dialectical because it is designed to respond to particular doubts that clients might raise about the credibility, plausibility, and probability of the evaluator's conclusion. In addition, evaluators also have an imagined or real metaevaluator or peer group in mind in constructing their arguments. They develop their judgments while thinking "Would this stand up to the scrutiny of my peers?"

4. Persuasive and based on inquiry. The evaluator aims to persuade clients of her or his conclusion or point of view on the value of the evaluand. Thus, the rhetoric of the written or oral argument—its clarity, thoroughness, organization, and so on—matter, for the evaluator always asks, "How can I put my case so that others will not misunderstand?" At the same time the argument is based on inquiry; it is a knowledge-based or evidentiary argument. (pp. 146–147)

In developmental evaluation, those peers who scrutinize the evidence and arguments include the social innovators with whom we co-create interpretations and arguments, examine the evidence, and reason together.

In Praise of Methodological Diversity and Appropriateness: A Methods and Tools Rant

I promised a rant. Here it is. It follows from our exploration of reasoning above. It places methods and tools within a reasoning framework. As *bricoleurs* developmental evaluators can use any methods or tools deemed appropriate for the inquiry at hand. But there are no developmental evaluation methods per se.

Yet, the most common question I get is, "What are the methods and tools of developmental evaluation?" Participants in my workshops tell me by the first morning break that they buy the idea of developmental evaluation. They *get it* that development is different from improvement; that complex situations require evaluator agility and flexibility; that attending to emergence requires openness and responsiveness; that conditions of uncertainty call for special alertness and sensitivity to the unintended, expecting the unexpected; that working with social innovators in dynamic environments means speed and real-time feedback; and that being part of a team and engaging in co-creation requires a close working relationship based on mutual trust and respect. They get all this, they tell me. "So when do we get to methods and tools?" they ask with a sense of urgency.

And I see the look of initial confusion in their eyes, then disappointment on their faces, and ultimately disbelief in their overall body language when I say, "It's all about persistently asking questions and pursuing credible answers in time to be used. Questioning is the ultimate method. Questions are the quintessential tools." That's why the last chapter presented different inquiry frameworks for different situations.

But the methods question persists—and with good reason. Once questions are framed, they have to be answered, at least insofar as something resembling "answers"

is possible in complex and dynamic systems and environments. So how ought we to approach selection of methods and tools? Pick methods and tools that are appropriate to the situation and context, that will provide meaningful, credible, practical, and useful answers for the primary intended users given the primary intended purpose of the evaluation. The next chapter provides examples of how to do this within a utilization-focused framework for developmental evaluation design decisions.

Let me once again bring in Tom Schwandt (2008) to elaborate the point that conclusions include reasoning, critical thinking, judgment, and argument—and cannot be reduced to methods and data:

> Instead of providing a warrant for our claims, we often rehearse the research methods used or state something like "conclusions are justified because they were based on the use of" (you fill in the blank): "multi-faceted and richly detailed data," "multiple methods," "standard experimental procedures," and so on. However, those are not warrants for the credibility and validity of an argument.... [A] warranted argument is not reducible to any particular method of data collection. (p. 147)

Developmental evaluation is purpose-and-relationship-driven not methods-driven. Making methods decisions is one part of this process, but the methods are useless unless they are embedded in a coevolutionary process of ongoing reality testing, inquiry, learning, and action—action informed by both data and values. In short, methods don't stand alone. No matter how sophisticated and rigorous the methods, if the relationship of shared inquiry and co-creation does not work, the potential of developmental evaluation to contribute to innovation development will not be fully realized.

On Methods and Tools

Perhaps I'm a bit hard on the tool seekers. I may have become jaded by the incessant requests for tools on the *EvalTalk* listserv. Scarcely a day goes by but that someone posts, "I've just been assigned to do an evaluation of *x*-type program. Does anybody have a tool they can recommend? Please. With sugar. I'd really appreciate help here. Help!"

On good days, some patient, experienced, and good-hearted soul will respond by asking for some context: "What's the purpose of the evaluation? Who are the participants? What are the intended outcomes? How's the evaluation going to be used?" The original questioner will provide pithy replies to these annoying inquiries and then quickly reiterate: "Hmmmm, about those tools I was asking for? Someone? Any one? I need a tool."

Again, I find that I share the views of Tom Schwandt (2008) about tools.

> The last time I checked Google I found more than 200,000 hits for the phrase evaluation toolkits. Tools and procedures for evaluative inquiry are wonderful things, but manualizing and proceduralizing evaluation in society are not. As an association and as university educators, we need to develop more evaluation-thinking kits. That is what educating for intelligent belief in evaluation demands. That is what our society needs. (p. 149)

Premature Experimentation

Of course, in addition to tool seekers, we also have those evaluators with deep expertise who do not need to inquire into contextual factors or purpose distinctions. Only one kind of evaluation is worth doing, the so-called "gold standard" kind, to wit, impact evaluations with randomized controlled trials (RCTs). The 2009 conference of the Australasian Evaluation Society in Canberra featured a presentation by a rabid RCT fundamentalist who opened his presentation by asserting unequivocally: "The purpose of evaluation is to estimate the effect of a program relative to a counterfactual and the RCT is the gold standard method

for doing so." Former AEA president and distinguished evaluation methodologist William Trochim, who shared the stage for the session, responded that the gentleman appeared to be suffering from a severe case of "premature experimentation."

I resonate to this diagnosis, which I find widespread. In Chapter 2 I described the innovative Twin Cities Rise! program aimed at chronically unemployed people in poverty. At the very first design team meeting, when the idea of an initial pilot program was being considered to begin the process of innovation and development, the university professor in the group insisted that the program being evaluated use an RCT right from the beginning. He reiterated this point vociferously and often at that and subsequent meetings, despite the agreement among others that the program should be piloted first to figure out basic implementation issues. He suffered from a virulent case of *premature experimentation*. And he became so disruptive that he had to be diplomatically eased off the design team.

It's a widespread affliction that begins with early signs of hardening of the categories: an RCT is the evaluation gold standard and, well, there really is nothing else worth doing. My dissent from this *methodological fundamentalism* (House, 2005) has popped up here and there throughout this book, so finding it again in this chapter ought not surprise the reader. Elsewhere I have reviewed at length the fallacies, indeed dangers, of the view that RCTs constitute a gold standard (Patton, 2008c, chap. 12), a variety of the *abstract empiricism* that the great sociologist C. Wright Mills (1959) denounced a half-century ago in making the case for less mechanical measuring and more *sociological imagination*. But, alas, *abstract empiricism* in the form of *methodological fundamentalism* flourishes today like a weed resistant to all efforts to contain its spread.

Those who find in developmental evaluation an approach that makes sense for evaluating innovations in complex environments should be prepared to make the case that *the real gold standard is methodological appropriateness*, namely, matching methods to the nature of the question and the purpose of the evaluation, rather than blind adherence to one particular design. In that spirit, one of the design examples featured later in the next chapter is an RCT to compare and assess the effects of alternative messages during an advocacy campaign. I am not hostile to RCTs. I am hostile to their being treated as the gold standard, which connotes, among other distortions, that every other design is inferior.

To understand my agitation at how narrow gold standard fundamentalism afflicts developmental evaluation, let me offer as a case in point a proposal to use multiple and diverse methods to evaluate an innovative systems change initiative. In the context of this chapter, systems change can be thought of as another sensitizing concept; the proposed design that follows also included a reflective practice component. In the last chapter I offered systems thinking as one inquiry framework for developmental evaluation. This proposal illustrates how systems thinking can inform both an innovation and an evaluation design, and how a lack of systems thinking by others can impede both the innovation and the evaluation, the two being intricately linked.

Systems Change and Developmental Evaluation

A Systems Change Proposal

A major human services department at the county level wanted to change the system for working with highly dysfunctional, high-needs families. (In the United States counties are the primary governmental unit that administers welfare, health, and mental health programs.) A cross-department county team had identified a particular subset of families with young children that were simultaneously involved in the welfare system (because of poverty), the child pro-

〜 **A View from Wales**

Bill Fear engages in evaluation from Penarth, Wales, where his shingle reads *William James Consulting*, which tells you a lot about his perspective. Bill is a frequent contributor to the AEA listserv, *EvalTalk*. I asked Bill, who is always provocative, always thoughtful in his postings, if I could include his rant on evaluation methods in this chapter. He kindly consented, so here's the view from his perch in Wales.

I remember the AEA conference where **METHODOLOGY** was put forward as the new Deity for Evaluation. I have seen this track into the UK. It is one of, perhaps the only, disenchantment I have had with Evaluation. I speak as someone who is a natural evaluator—according to my personality profile as measured by the OPQ32 and the 16PF.

I'd rather have method in the madness than be mad for the method or mad about the method or driven mad by the method.

Don't get me wrong. I'm all for rigour and discipline—but the results will still need to be interpreted and the data will always be dirty. The assumption that *The Methodology* will result in *The Evidence* popping out of the other end is like. . . . I'll leave that to your imaginations.

Personally, I blame it all on RCTs and the false notion that they are the only way to properly establish causation.

Could I dedicate my life to this? Now that is a big question!!

—*EvalTalk*, September 8, 2008
Dr. William J. Fear
William James Consulting
Penarth, Wales

It sounds like Bill will be engaged in a long-term developmental evaluation inquiry to answer his big question. And we won't have an answer for a long, long time, I hope—wishing Bill long life and many more postings to *EvalTalk* as he keeps us apprised of the progress of his inquiry. I invite readers to monitor *EvalTalk* for Bill's developmental updates.

tection system (because of child abuse and neglect), the substance abuse service system (because of drug addiction, especially methamphetamine use and alcoholism), the criminal justice system (because one or more adults had been convicted of crimes), the health care system (because of frequent health emergencies that, without health insurance, meant heavy emergency room use), the mental health system (because of chronic mental illness), the employment training system (because of requirements by the welfare system to get employment and get off welfare), the school truancy system (because kids were missing lots of school and failing to achieve minimal school achievement standards), and aging services (because grandparents were sometimes involved).

The team estimated that as much as 80% of the county's intervention services were spent on the 20% of families that were in a cycle of perpetual crisis and dysfunction. These families, typically with 4–10 school-age children, experienced crises frequently and usually had some children in out-of-home placement (county-mandated foster care) or at risk of such placement. Moreover, it was clear that these families were not benefiting from traditional treatment strategies. The county planned to create cross-professional/cross-agency/cross-department intervention teams working with a small number of crisis families to break the cycle of system dependence for children that, it was hoped, would support the healthy development of children and, it was hypothesized, result in significant, long-term financial savings for the county by reducing the huge drain on county resources from serving these chronically-in-crisis families. One systems change strategy regularly joked about was buying bus tickets and sending these families a long way away. Besides the fact that courts in other areas had found such an approach to be illegal, the group recognized that bus tickets wouldn't help the children and families mired in dysfunction and poverty.

A Systems Change Approach: Intensive Team-Based Interventions with High-Needs Families

The county team proposed adapting an intensive team-based intervention program originally developed for adults in crisis. The targeted high-needs families (highly dysfunctional family systems) were expected to need intensive, long-term intervention and support to improve their functioning.

Contributing to the complexity of the problem was the fact that these targeted child–family systems were unstable in that adult members came and went (e.g., changes in stepparents and paramours, parental absenteeism due to incarceration) and the children were sent to live with relatives and friends for periods of time. For example, a "child–family system" might include a mother, her two children from two previous marriages, a new paramour, with the occasional presence of his child from a previous marriage. The fathers of the mother's two children and the mother of the new paramour's child might sometimes be present in the family environment. As a result many complex and challenging relationships could exist. Further, because of substance abuse, parents might be limited in their ability to attend to and actively parent their children. In addition to involvement with the child welfare and substance abuse systems, these families generally had a high rate of co-occurring health and social problems, such as mental illness and domestic violence. The families had very low incomes and lived in poverty. Children in these families generally had poor developmental outcomes (physical, intellectual, social, and emotional) and might be abusing drugs or be at high risk for doing so. Teenage pregnancy was also a major problem and ongoing risk.

Because of the presence of so many serious and interrelated problems, treatment programs provided by the child welfare system, the substance abuse system, the mental health and other categorically funded systems alone had not been successful in producing positive outcomes and healthy family environments that could provide for safety, permanency, and child well-being. As a result, an intervention that addressed the totality of the families' long-term needs and issues was proposed.

Connecting with Families

The proposal called for a multiskilled intervention team to approach a family to offer services (the program was to be voluntary, not mandated). The team would get to know the family, monitor the family's well-being and issues, and provide quick help in any dimension of need like food or shelter. Part of the notion was that problems would be fixed while they were smaller and manageable to get out of the perpetual crisis spiral of family dysfunction and, by getting family members more safe and stable, longer term interventions on fundamental problems could be provided.

Developmental Evaluation of Systems Change

Much of this description comes directly from a 30-page funding proposal with much more detail, including a well-articulated theory of systems change. I assisted with a developmental evaluation proposal after all those involved went through 2 full days of evaluation training with me to be sure that they were prepared to include meaningful evaluation as part of the systems change initiative. The evaluation would document how the teams functioned with families as well as include in-depth, longitudinal case studies of families using both data in the team's files and data independently collected by the evaluator through family visits and interviews. The precise nature of the team interventions were expected to be highly individualized and the overall approach was expected to be adjusted as the initiative unfolded.

The many uncertainties and complex systems interdependencies made a develop-mental evaluation particularly appropriate. The case studies would include the families' perspectives on the intervention, what they have experienced within the family, how they viewed changes (or lack of changes) in their family's dynamics, and critical incidents and responses. Because the approach would be highly individualized for and responsive to the particular needs of each participating family, in-depth, longitudinal case studies were deemed especially appropriate for documenting variations in treatment, outcomes, and impacts over time. The teams would also engage in regular reflective practice sessions with the evaluator.

Small, Targeted Pilot Intervention to Support Development and Learning

The systems change design team anticipated beginning with 15–20 families. Because of the priority given to longitudinal data, some expected attrition, and the addition of families over time, the sample for case studies was designed to be partly emergent as the program itself emerged and family participation patterns became clear. The evaluation would have to adapt to how the program unfolded. To the extent possible, families that exited the intervention but stayed in the area, and for whom initial interviews had been conducted, would be maintained in the longitudinal design. Dropout families would be provided with noncash incentives (e.g., gift certificates) to seek their continued participation in the case studies. The emergent sample would be selected to maximize variation along such dimensions as family composition, methamphetamine use and other drug-use history, family diagnoses and assessments, and variations in baseline scores on quantitative evaluation instruments that the team would administer as part of the intervention diagnosis and intake baseline. The baseline would be updated as new information emerged once trust was established with the families.

Evaluating Systems Changes

The full evaluation design proposal (14 pages) went into great detail about process and outcomes evaluation, case study methods, attribution issues in a systems change evaluation, triangulation of data and methods, the theory-based nature of the intervention, and the developmental uses of the evaluation as the pilot unfolded. The design proposed to evaluate systems change at two levels: the changes in family systems and the changes in the county's human services systems. The evaluation was developed collaboratively with the systems change design team, which spent a lot of time on evaluation issues and developed a solid commitment to build developmental evaluation into the innovation from the beginning, and track how the intervention developed and what was achieved (and not achieved).

Evaluation Approach Mismatch

Unfortunately, from my perspective, this story does not have a happy ending. The federal and state government funding program that had solicited proposals for innovative approaches to families in crisis, with special attention on drug and alcohol addiction, re-

jected the proposal as nonresponsive, in part because the funding agencies insisted on evaluations that were conducted as randomized controlled trials based on the pharmaceutical paradigm of experimentation. The lengthy section in the proposal about why a randomized control trial for this innovation at this stage in its development was neither feasible, useful, nor ethical was, apparently, unpersuasive. The county did not have sufficient funds of their own to implement the innovation.

Final score. Traditional rigid evaluation paradigm: 1. Developmental evaluation: 0.

Be forewarned: Developmental evaluation is not an easy sell to funding committees deeply schooled in traditional evaluation research designs and a simple, recipe-based (as opposed to complex) way of looking at interventions and innovations.

Am I bitter? Let's just say that stories like these fueled my motivation to write this book. And if you've gotten this far in the book, you may be part of tipping the evaluation system from simple linear models and rigid, standardized designs to developmental evaluation based in complexity understandings. You just might be that one additional person who tips the system.

"Dear Mr. Gandhi, We regret we cannot fund your proposal because the link between spinning cloth and the fall of the British Empire was not clear to us."

Written by Mark M. Rogers and illustrated by Ariv R. Faizal, Wahyu S., and Ary W. S., creative team, Search for Common Ground in Indonesia.

∽ *"System" as a Sensitizing Concept: An Integrated and Multifaceted Evaluation Design Using Both Traditional Evaluation Methods and an Adaptive, Emergent Design to Evaluate Efforts to Prevent Child Maltreatment in a Complex Dynamic Systems Environment*

DEVELOPMENTAL EVALUATION QUESTIONS

- How do 17 grantees working to implement, spread, and sustain high-quality home visiting programs aimed at preventing child maltreatment adapt within their complex system in response to their changing situations and environments?

- What do these grantees mean by "system"? Who and what is in their system? What does systems change involve and look like for them?

MULTIFACETED EVALUATION FRAMEWORKS

1. Traditional logic-model and outcomes-focused evaluation that tracks implementation and results of the home visiting model, including fidelity to the model, outcomes, and costs.
2. System change evaluation design focusing on the adaptive dynamics of the initiative.

METHODS

1. Capture and track how the grantees change and adapt their initiatives by working with each grantee to create grantee-specific evaluation plans in which each grantee defines what they mean by "system," who and what is in their system, what system change would look like for them, their strategies for achieving those changes, and indicators of those system changes.
2. Create grantee-specific baseline program system models and evaluation plans that the grantees update every 6 months in response to critical events and any other changes in their plans and environments.
3. Three waves of partner social network analysis among partners based on surveys with each grantee to track how their partner networks change within and across system levels over time.

INITIAL FINDINGS

In the first year of the evaluation, major adjustments were made in grantees' strategies and plans in response to the 2008–2009 recession, changes in federal administration, and local changes in context.

Note. From Hargreaves and Paulsell (2009).

And so as not to end this discussion of systems change evaluation with an example of a failed proposal, I'm including two examples of systems change evaluations that are currently and successfully under way. One describes evaluation of changing systems for HIV services (see the next page). The other describes high-quality home visiting programs aimed at adapting interventions to prevent child maltreatment in a complex dynamic systems environment (see above).

Retrospective Developmental Evaluation

This bricolage chapter exploring various approaches to and perspectives on develop-

⌢ *Exploratory, Developmental Policy Evaluation Focused on Systems of Care for HIV Services*

DEVELOPMENTAL EVALUATION QUESTIONS

- What are HIV service providers doing to meet the growing demand for HIV care within increasing workforce constraints?
- What adaptations, if any, are occurring in response to constraints?

METHODS

Case studies and interviews with experts.

FINDINGS

HIV providers were engaged in self-organizing of formal and informal HIV "systems of care" at multiple levels (organizational teams, community-level partnerships, regional collaboration) to extend the reach of their HIV expertise.

ORIGINAL FRAMING OF THE ISSUE

Individual-level economic model focused on supply and demand: gap between the supply of individual clinicians with HIV expertise compared to the demand of individual patients needing HIV care.

EMERGENT SYSTEMS REFRAMING OF THE ISSUE

Understanding HIV care capacity and cross-scale systems of care at the organizational, community, and regional levels.

SYSTEMS CHANGE RECOMMENDATIONS

1. Develop exchanges/relationships between those with and without HIV expertise, to expand the boundaries and scope of who should receive HIV clinical training.
2. Recognize the importance of "differences that make a difference"—exposing more students to HIV patients and building multidisciplinary teams to provide HIV specialty and primary care.

Note. Based on Gilman, Hargreaves, Au, and Kim (2009).

mental evaluation ends with an in-depth example of a retrospective developmental evaluation. When working with innovators who have a history together or an organization or program that has been around awhile, a retrospective developmental evaluation can be a great place to start. It not only captures and honors that history, and sets the context going forward, but it's an important opportunity for the developmental evaluator to establish trust and build rapport. People with

a history of engagement in social change and innovation want that *backstory* understood. The developmental evaluator needs to know that story of the past to know some of the places to look and things to expect going forward. Here's an example.

In 2008–2009 the AEA began a transition from a traditional nonprofit board to a policy-focused board inspired by the governance approach, ideas, and prescriptions for board effectiveness articulated by John

Carver (2006). This transition became a developmental process because some of Carver's ideas had to be adapted to AEA, which was a membership-based professional service organization rather than a nonprofit board. The developments and adaptations would grow out of and flow from AEA's history. I have worked with policy governance boards over the years, in part because policy governance emphasizes a strong mission-oriented monitoring and evaluation function for boards, so the AEA board invited me to work with them on the transition. In our first session together, we created a retrospective baseline for the transition. As a former AEA president, I knew some of the developmental history. Others had other pieces. But, in fact, AEA's history had never been pulled together, especially a history of AEA's strategic *developments*. There had been major forks in the road: the merger of the Evaluation Network and the Evaluation Research Society to form the AEA in 1984–1985; the decision to convert the informal-tone, practice-oriented journal *Evaluation Practice* into a peer-reviewed scholarly journal, the *American Journal of Evaluation*; the decision to make the thematic journal *New Directions for Evaluation* a membership benefit included in member dues; the decision to move from an entirely volunteer-run organization to one managed by paid, professional staff as AEA increased dramatically in size and services over the years; and decisions about the annual conference, state affiliates, and subject-specialized Topical Interest Groups. These developments, and others we identified, were all significant milestones in AEA's history. The transition to a policy-focused governance approach was one more in a long line of developments. The AEA board was committed to monitoring and evaluating the functioning of the new approach to governance going forward, and adapting the governance system based on feedback, data about effectiveness, and emergent but as yet unknown events and trends. But the first critical step was to conduct a retrospec-

tive developmental evaluation to establish a baseline for developments going forward. Nor was this historical baseline fixed. New historical developments of importance will be added to the baseline as they become known over time through dialogue with founders, pioneers, and old-timers, kind of a focused oral history project centered around major strategic developments over time.

Prospective evaluation looks ahead, as when a developmental evaluator works with an innovative design team to anticipate evaluation questions and data. Retrospective evaluation, in contrast, looks back at what has already occurred. Such a backward glance can be especially appropriate

~ **Retrospective Developmental Evaluation**

The story is told that after Saddam Hussein was ousted in 2003, an old man determined to present his grievances and sufferings to the government to seek compensation. Being illiterate, he sought out a young educated man who wrote letters for hire. He told the letter-writer his litany of woes and they were substantial. "In the '50s, they destroyed my house. In the '60s, they killed two of my sons. In the '70s, they confiscated my properties."

The man continued telling of one affliction after another right up to the present day. The letter-writer recorded every word just as it was told to him. When he was done, the man asked the letter-writer to read it back to him before he handed it to the governor. So the letter-writer read it aloud.

When he got done, the man hit himself on the head and said, "What a story. That is so beautifully told. I had no idea all this happened to me."

Note. Iraq Deputy Provincial Council Chairman Rebwar Talabani (reported by Friedman, 2009).

and useful when developmental evaluation is introduced into an ongoing program or organization that has a lot of history to build on. When I begin working with an established program or organization that is looking ahead to new innovations and developments, I like to begin, in classic evaluation fashion, by establishing the baseline—in this case a retrospective developmental baseline, one that can be added to over time as new information about the past is remembered or resurfaces. Guiding questions include: Out of what past developments has the current program emerged? What have been the forks in the road, or the critical incidents, that have shaped the program? What values, principles (simple rules), dialogues, and debates can we identify looking back, things that provide an important historical context for the present and future? What local, regional, state, national, and international trends influenced where you are today? Who have you collaborated with over the years and how have those collaborations affected where you are today?

Answers to these questions help contextualize evaluation issues and prove especially valuable for supporting smooth staff, board, and leadership transitions as new people, including evaluators, come into an organization without knowledge of its history. When new developments and social innovations are undertaken, not only does the retrospective developmental evaluation capture the past context, but guiding values are illuminated and lessons learned are made explicit to inform future developmental evaluation inquiries. Meanwhile, the retrospective exercise helps assure program staff that the developmental evaluator *understands.* Credibility and mutual trust are important to effective developmental evaluation. When working with an ongoing program or organization, taking the time to get grounded in the program's or organization's history is part of the process of establishing mutual understanding out of which flows mutual trust.

Damiano Revisited

In Chapter 6, I used the story of Damiano's adaptations of two national programs, the Community Kitchens model for training low-income people for jobs as chefs and Kids Cafe®, which provides meals to children in poor families, to illustrate the intersection of top-down change (dissemination of models) and bottoms-up adaptation (fitting those models to the local situation). When I started working with Jean Gornick and the Damiano program, we began constructing a history of Damiano's past developments as a baseline for future developments. The process began informally and later became more systematic. Essentially, over time, this amounted to pulling together a *retrospective developmental evaluation.*

As context, we discussed how few organizations have a sense of their own history. Gornick's 20-year tenure with Damiano is rare. During that time, many other staff had come and gone. We had each had a recent experience working with an organization undertaking a new strategic planning process with a new director, Gornick as a collaborator and me as a consultant. In both cases key staff members were also new. In neither case could the director locate a copy of the last strategic plan. No one seemed to know anything about how the last strategic plan had been formulated. Staff and board lacked a sense of their own history. How can people in an organization look forward with any perspective when they haven't looked backwards, don't know the organization's roots, and have scarcely any sense of past battles, both victories and defeats? How can staff engage in future development when, essentially, they have no sense of past development?

It's not that it can't be done—it's done all the time. But the baseline for forward-looking developmental evaluation includes knowing what past forks in the road were faced and why one direction was chosen over another. These things are almost never written down. They are part of institutional memories soon lost, though the effects of the developmental journey are there to behold, if one only knows how to look. *Retrospective developmental evaluation is an invitation to look.*

Philosopher George Santayana famously observed that "those who cannot remember the past are condemned to repeat it" (1905, p. 284). The evaluation version of this wisdom is: Those who cannot learn from program and organizational history are doomed to repeat past mistakes and past excuses, proclaiming when things go badly, "We had no way of knowing." But there was a way of knowing. It's called *retrospective developmental evaluation.*

Damiano's Retrospective Developmental Evaluation

Let me move from the abstract idea of *retrospective developmental evaluation* to the concrete example of Damiano's developmental history and how it set the stage for future strategic developments and *prospective* developmental evaluation. Here are some turning points in Damiano's history, some of which I'm bringing forward from the earlier discussion in Chapter 6, but most of which are new here.

Basic Needs: From Food to Clothing

In 1983, Damiano created a volunteer-run clothing exchange as volunteers in the soup kitchen observed the need for basic clothing and thought about how they could mobilize the churches supporting the soup kitchen to provide used clothing to those who came for meals. That program, which began quite small and was staffed entirely by volunteers, grew to have a full-time staff person and in 2008 distributed over 422,000 articles of clothing and household goods.

One thing often leads to another (emergence). The Opportunities Cooking program led to another Damiano program, Clothes That Work, providing clothing to people going for job interviews or those who landed a job that required better clothes than they owned. In 2008 Clothes That Work helped 1,945 people with over 12,000 articles of appropriate work clothing.

From Soup to Social Services

In 1987 Damiano added a social worker on staff and began formally providing some social services. This innovation again emerged in response to the needs expressed by people coming for meals at the soup kitchen. These people needed not only food and clothing but also housing, protection from domestic violence, basic health care, mental health services, help with caring for young children, and transportation. But among these many needs, after food and clothes, housing was always the number one need. Always. Food, housing, safety. The bottom rung of Maslow's hierarchy. That's where the Damiano Center operated, on that bottom rung. Gornick recalled:

"When the economic crisis that gave rise to Damiano had eased, the surprise was that the demand for meals did not subside. The population served by Damiano, people on the margin, a transient population, and people unable to work, did not participate in the economic upturn. So Damiano continued because the need continued, though there was no thought that we'd still be operating 20 years later."

Documenting an Organization's Niche within Larger Systems

Damiano's history makes explicit its niche. Damiano's history was tied to the history of its setting. In 1994, Duluth, Minnesota, gained unwanted national prominence as a community with a large population in poverty when it was featured in a cover story in *U.S. News and World Report* on "The White Underclass" as a "social catastrophe" (Whitman, Friedman, Linn, Doremus, & Hetter,

1994). Gornick winced as she remembered the community's reaction to being labeled nationally as a "white ghetto and slum." She recalled that "it wasn't a pretty image. It hurt a lot of feelings. It hurt Duluth's pride. But the numbers were true. Duluth had a large number of families living in poverty—and still does."

In 2008, Damiano Social Services helped over 1,600 individuals and families needing crisis services. The Housing Access Program helped over 500 people keep their housing or find new housing through eviction prevention and homelessness services. These are small numbers nationally (viewed from the top down), but large numbers locally (viewed from the bottom up). Past community perceptions of poverty are part of a baseline that affects how new initiatives will be received and perceived.

Organizational Developments

As Damiano began addressing needs beyond food, organizational issues had to be resolved. By 1990, it had become clear that Damiano was not just a temporary organization operating a soup kitchen in response to a temporary crisis, so the board began thinking about more professional staffing.

Jean Gornick had been hired as manager of the soup kitchen. There being no executive director, a management team emerged to coordinate the soup kitchen, operation of the building, and the social services. None of these staff was full time. In response to the need for more coordination, the position of executive director was created and Gornick was asked to take on that new position.

The building out of which Damiano operated became the home to other tenants serving the poor including a homeless organizing project and advocates for low-income renters. The new building tenants increased the management and maintenance challenges of sharing the building.

The building itself, a 100-year-old dark-red brick building on a steep hill above the Lake Superior harbor, was a challenge. The soup kitchen had opened in the former cafeteria of an empty school owned by the Catholic diocese. The bishop hoped to sell the building as a warehouse, but pending finding a buyer had agreed to its temporary use for the soup kitchen. Because it had been vacant for a number of years, it was in a poor state of maintenance. Building renovation would be costly, so the Damiano staff and board members began to look for an alternative site. Several possibilities in the downtown business area were considered, but the business leaders wanted to keep Damiano in its existing Central Hillside location away from the city center. From the perspective of the downtown chamber of commerce, the people who came to Damiano for meals and services were not likely to be good for business and might keep regular customers away. After considerable discussion and negotiation, the Catholic diocese sold the building to the Damiano Center for $1.

Challenges of Modernizing

In taking ownership of the building, Damiano had taken another step toward becoming an ongoing institution. It became organized legally as a not-for-profit, had to establish personnel policies, and had to begin engaging in fundraising, including a capital campaign to remodel the building. It was especially urgent to upgrade and modernize the kitchen. When it was functioning as a temporary soup kitchen, Damiano was not required to adhere closely to all code requirements by the public health authorities. As a permanent institution, however, meeting code became a necessity. This, it turned out, would require major renovation of the entire building, for not only was the kitchen subpar, but the building had major water seepage and drainage problems that sometimes led to flooding in the kitchen.

More problems: The old live steam heating system posed safety problems. The building was inadequately insulated against the severe northern Minnesota winter. The roof leaked, not just on the top floor of the building: in heavy rains puddles appeared on floors throughout the building. Bathrooms were inadequate. Electrical wiring was old and below code. Damiano, begun as a charitable impulse to feed the hungry in time of crisis, now faced finding the expertise and funds to carry out a major building renovation. And Gornick had to develop expertise in managing building contractors and inspectors.

Notice in this story the recurring complexity themes of this book: emergence, uncertainty, small initial actions having big impacts (nonlinearity), turbulence, and adaptation. Social change visionaries and innovators like to focus on people problems and big-picture issues. But more than once those visions and innovations have floundered because nobody was dealing with emergent basic challenges, like operating in a building that meets city code and making the setting safe.

Simple Rules and Basic Principles

While deeply attuned to local needs and the local context, Damiano's development decisions were also shaped by national trends. The 1980s and 1990s were a time of great ferment nationally about dealing with alcoholics and drug addicts. The issue came to the Damiano Center in the form of a challenge about whether to serve meals to drunks. Many who came to the soup kitchen were chronic alcoholics. Because alcoholism is such a problem and at the root of many other problems, the human services community in Duluth, influenced by national political trends, proposed a united zero tolerance policy: *People who had been drinking cannot receive services. No exceptions.*

This policy conflicted with Damiano's commitment to create a "welcoming environment." The soup kitchen adopted the principle that alcoholics and drug addicts could be served as long as their behavior was appropriate in the dining room and build-

ing. Gornick said, "Food is a human rights issue. It is not charity. It is not an intervention. We were not trying to change alcoholics and drug addicts. We were offering them food."

This policy set Damiano at odds with the rest of the Duluth human services community, which wanted to use the leverage of services to get people into treatment. They wanted to set a community-wide standard requiring sobriety to receive services. Damiano hosted a meeting of community service providers to resolve the issue. Based on the premise that "you can't train drunks," the human services community wanted a united front. Gornick recalls spending a sleepless night after that meeting. It was a tough issue with significant implications for Damiano's future. She decided that, personally, she wanted to adhere to the principle that *food is a right*, not a treatment or an intervention lever. She knew from long experience that chronic alcoholics will drink. Damiano was a soup kitchen, not a chemical dependency intervention program. But it wasn't her decision to make alone. She took the issue to her board with the caveat that she could not support the zero tolerance policy and would resign if the board decided to go in that direction. After discussion, the board reaffirmed Damiano's mission and niche, and supported Gornick in focusing on food as a right and appropriate behavior as the standard rather than sobriety.

This incident reveals a lot about Damiano's standing in the community and the kinds of issues that can arise in new initiatives and collaborations. It is also a good example of *a fork in the road.* Are we going this way, or that way? What is negotiable, and what is not? Why do we go one way and not another? What values inform decisions? What are the larger implications of what may appear, on the surface, to be bounded policy questions? What ripple effects emerge from such decisions? These are fundamental developmental evaluation questions, both retrospectively and prospectively.

Simple Rules Undergirding Complex Dynamics

An action leads to consequences that lead to new developmental quandaries. Damiano came to be known as a welcoming place, a place that treated people with respect. But that didn't mean that it was a place with no boundaries. Gornick had to work with police to establish ways of handling people who came into the building inebriated or high on drugs. Those who were drunk but not disruptive were given a sandwich and sent on their way. If someone became disruptive, police were called for help, usually as a last resort.

For Gornick, creating an environment that was welcoming included posting no rules on the wall. It is typical at shelters and soup kitchens to post rules in large print. Damiano had no such wall "decorations"—no rules posted at the entry to the building, anywhere on walls, or in the main dining hall. The only "rules" posted were on a small sign near the serving window for food:

- Everyone is welcome.
- Meals must be eaten in the dining room.
- Diners may return for additional trays of food as long as there is food.
- Disruptive behavior will not be tolerated.
- Incidents will be dealt with as they arise.

These are examples of what complexity theorists called "simple rules" or *min specs* (minimum specifications), discussed in Chapter 8. One of the tasks of developmental evaluation can be to identify, document, make explicit, and examine the existence, applications, and consequences of simple rules.

Situational Adapting to What Emerges

I asked Gornick for examples of situations that had to be dealt with as they arose. She described a full continuum of such situations from potentially dangerous to outrageously humorous. On the one end of the continuum was an incident with a Vietnam veteran who brought a machete into the dining hall and began waving it around. Gornick heard the commotion from her office upstairs, ran down to the kitchen, began talking calmly, and kept things under control until the police arrived. "No rule would've prevented that situation," she observed. "Posttraumatic stress disorder does not obey rules. We dealt with such things one incident at a time. Such incidents come with the territory of working with a marginalized population that can and does include people with severe mental health problems." She continued:

"Of course, people need to feel safe. In the early days, in the 1980s and early '90s, the people involved in Damiano were activists, organizers, and advocates. They were grounded in low-income neighborhoods and comfortable dealing with people of all kinds, from all backgrounds, with all kinds of problems. Over time, as Damiano became a permanent organization, staff with technical skills was needed and hired—cooks, teachers, social workers, and managers. These new staff had less experience with and were therefore less comfortable with some of the people who showed up at Damiano from time to time. And they were not comfortable with the ambiguity of one incident at a time. They wanted rules.

"But rules have to be enforced. So when staff would say, *We need a rule!*, I'd ask: Who's going to enforce the rules? I didn't want to become a rule enforcer. That's not what I signed on for."

On the other end of the continuum of situations to be dealt with as they arose was the birthday cake incident. Damiano received leftover food from bakeries. Volunteers and staff separated the food into items that would be served in the soup kitchen as part of regular meals and items that were put out on a table that people could take away with them. Cakes were kept in the storeroom and served with meals. Only staff and volunteers were allowed in the storeroom. One evening Gornick came upon an incident where a father was pleading for a birthday cake to take home for his young daughter. The staff person in charge that evening explained that the cakes were kept in the storeroom until they were served as a part of regular meals, that cakes were not part of the food that could be taken away, and that no one was allowed in the storeroom except staff, so he couldn't just go pick one out himself.

Gornick listened for a moment to this exchange, went into the store room, brought out a cake, and gave it to the much-relieved and appreciative father. That was dealing with the situation as it arose. The incident wasn't dangerous. It was more tragic-comic, drawing a line in the sand over a birthday cake. But where does one draw lines?

It turns out there was another simple rule at play here, a rule embedded in Gornick's perspective developed from years working in the trenches. She talked about how hard it was to see parents with children on birthdays with no presents to give. Scarcely a day went by but that she witnessed firsthand the dispiriting and ravaging effects of poverty. As she finished telling the story of retrieving the birthday cake from the storeroom, and laughing about the absurdity of it all, she turned serious and reflected:

"We did what we could. It never got easy to see people in hunger and anguish. I came to realize that we sure weren't going to make a dent in world poverty, not even a dent in poverty in Duluth, but we could make a difference in individual lives. *One person at a time.* I felt completely overwhelmed by the need around me. We did what we could, what needed to be done, one person at a time, one meal at a time, one birthday cake at a time."

These, then, were the simple rules operating from the bottom up:

- One person at a time.
- One meal at a time.
- One incident at a time.
- Do what you can.

Ongoing Development

I've given only a brief overview of what emerged in Damiano's retrospective developmental evaluation. Let me add just a few more of the challenges that shaped Damiano's development to further illustrate the kinds of things that can affect a program's future and therefore become important to capture and understand in a retrospective developmental evaluation.

- Damiano was affected by changes in recycling of food. By the late 1990s increased emphasis on diverting food from garbage made it possible to salvage more food. Authorities wanted to get food out of the waste stream. Damiano began recycling its waste to pig farmers. Special bins were provided for this recycling at no cost during the first 2 years of the waste diversion initiative, but then government subsidies were withdrawn, making the program too expensive for Damiano to maintain (an illustration of the full adaptive cycle from innovation to stability to termination, discussed in Chapter 7).

- The building was listed on the National Register of Historic Places. That "honor" added significant challenges to renovation. Any proposed change got carefully appraised down to the smallest details. For example, the grout used in replacement windows had to match historic sand.

- Making the building no smoking in 1992, before prohibiting smoking became a national movement, created challenges of enforcement both for program clients and staff.

• The fact that most participants in Opportunities Cooking were African American created challenges in the Duluth environment. Duluth, as a predominantly white community, was often experienced by African Americans as racist. An issue for the program became how much to push participants to adapt to Duluth versus trying to get the community to adapt to participants. For example, participants with dreadlocks were told that continuing to wear dreadlocks would limit their employability in the Duluth marketplace. Nor is jewelry allowed among chefs—things like nose rings and lip studs. Thus, Opportunities Cooking had to develop a training approach that created chefs who could find employment in the local market, and this meant both cooking skills and work on developing the habits and attitudes that would lead to success in Duluth restaurants given the local community. This approach, however, opened the program itself to charges of racism, since it involved encouraging African Americans to adjust to white employment preferences.

• Damiano became the target of a unionizing effort aimed at nonprofit organizations. The 6-month unionization campaign, aimed at the 16 full-time and seven part-time staff, and subsequent contract negotiation increased stress for all involved, affected interpersonal relationships, and introduced new personnel and workplace rules that reduced Damiano's flexibility.

Looking Back, Looking Forward: Staying Focused on the Developmental Story

Prospective developmental evaluation looks forward and accompanies social innovators on the journey of innovation, documenting what emerges, facilitating ongoing inquiry into what's working and not working, helping those involved make sense of and decisions about what is unfolding in the face of dynamic complexities and changing context. But for programs and social innovators with history, part of what emerges will be grounded in that history. Retrospective developmental evaluation captures and honors that history, making it available to inform interpretations of what happens going forward.

Developmental Evaluation *Bricolage*

This chapter has offered a hodgepodge of ideas, approaches, examples, and rants to stimulate your thinking about the possibilities for engaging in developmental evaluation. I won't pretend that the chapter is particularly coherent or well integrated. It is messy, like complexity, and real-world evaluation practice. That's why I chose the metaphor of *bricolage*. I have scoured my developmental evaluation experiences and encounters picking out and sharing odds and ends that can be used to illustrate possibilities and pitfalls. Reflective practice, sensitizing concepts, action research, abductive reasoning, systems change, and retrospective developmental evaluation: *bricolage* components, elements, and ingredients that each in their own way, and sometimes in combination, open the world to us and provide guidance for inquiry into the emergent and uncertain dynamics of complex systems, and innovations within those systems.

In "Organizational Redesign as Improvisation," distinguished organizational development scholar and consultant Karl Weick (2001) identified four requisites for successful *bricolage*:

• an intimate knowledge of resources, so that you know what you have to work with in creatively engaging as a *bricoleur*;

• careful observation and listening so that you know the context and conditions under which you will be engaging in *bricolage*;

• trust in your own ideas and creativity as a *bricoleur*; and

- self-correcting structures, with feedback, so that you can adapt your creation to what is needed as the process unfolds. (pp. 62–64)

This last point deserves emphasis. The developmental evaluator both gives feedback and receives it. A lot of the emphasis in evaluation is on the skilled giving of feedback, providing accurate feedback, meaningful feedback, relevant feedback, and giving feedback in a way that can be heard. All of that is important. But we must also be adept at receiving feedback. As Weick makes clear, the *bricolage* process depends on quality feedback.

In his widely shared "*The Last Lecture: Really Achieving Your Childhood Dreams*," delivered on September 18, 2007, terminally ill professor Randy Pausch said that the best gift you can give someone is "genuine feedback." He went on to observe that "when people aren't giving you feedback any more, they've given up on you."

Have you received any good feedback today?

10

Utilization-Focused Developmental Evaluation

Engagement Practices, Diverse Designs, and Adaptive Methods

The scientific method, so far as it is a method, is nothing more than doing one's damnedest with one's mind, no holds barred.
—PERCY W. BRIDGMAN, Harvard physicist who won the 1946 Nobel Prize for discoveries in the field of high-pressure physics (quoted in Waller, 2004, p. 106)

The distinguishing characteristic of developmental evaluation is contributing to something that's being developed. That's the purpose: *development.* Data collected during the evaluation provides quick, credible feedback for adaptive and responsive development. But the developmental evaluator is not just gathering data, analyzing it, and writing a report. Developmental evaluation is a process of engagement. The developmental evaluator is co-creating an innovation with social innovators through inquiry into the nature and consequences of that innovation. The developmental evaluator and social innovators ponder together (*everyone doing their damnedest with their minds, no holds barred*). The co-creation process involves conceptualizing the social innovation together (not once, but throughout its development and trials), generating inquiry questions, establishing priorities for what to observe and track, figuring out what data to collect and how to collect it, interpreting findings together, and drawing conclusions together about the implications for next steps, especially adaptations in the face of changing conditions, new learnings, and whatever is emerging.

Different Kinds of Developmental Evaluation

Beginning with the first chapter, and as the book has unfolded, I've been making the case that developmental evaluation is particularly appropriate for but needs to be matched to five different complex situational challenges and developmental purposes.

1. *Ongoing development* in adapting a project, program, strategy, policy, or other innovative initiative to new conditions in complex dynamic systems (the focus of Chapters 2, 3, 4, and 5).

2. *Adapting effective general principles to a new context* as ideas and innovations are taken from elsewhere and developed within a new setting, the work of developmental evaluation in the dynamic middle between top-down and bottom-up forces of change (the focus of Chapter 6).

3. *Developing a rapid response* in the face of a sudden major change (black swan event) or a crisis, like a natural disaster or financial meltdown; exploring real-time solutions; and generating innovative and helpful interventions for those in need.

4. *Preformative development of a potentially scalable innovation* to the point where it is ready for traditional formative and summative evaluation; preformative developmental evaluation works with emerging ideas and visionary hopes in a period of exploration to shape them into a potential model that is a more fully conceptualized, potentially scalable intervention within the framework of the adaptive cycle (the focus of Chapter 7). As models emerge out of exploratory and innovative initiatives, some may move into more traditional formative and summative evaluation to determine scalability and generalizability, while others may remain in developmental mode, undergoing either further development or continuous experimentation in the search for new models.

5. *Major systems change and cross-scale developmental evaluation,* providing feedback about how major systems change is unfolding, evidence of emergent tipping points, and/or data about how an innovation is or may need to be changed and adapted as it is taken to scale, that is, as its principles are shared and disseminated in an effort to have broader impact (discussed in Chapter 7). Horizontal scaling across systems or vertical scaling to broader systems may involve more than adaptation; these dissemination and scaling processes can evolve an essentially new development, the emergence of which can be documented and analyzed as part of a developmental evaluation.

Exhibit 10.1 (on pages 308–313) summarizes these five purposes, including identifying particular complex systems challenges that give rise to each; primary specific developmental evaluation uses appropriate for each type; real-world examples of each with specific primary intended users for each type; and the implications of the different types for evaluation and social innovation. The focus in utilization-focused evaluation on intended use by intended users provides the organizing template for this summary exhibit. There's a lot of information densely packed into the summary table.

These five different uses of developmental evaluation provide different lenses through which to understand and engage in evaluating social innovations under conditions of systems change and complexity. Taken together they constitute a specific niche in the large and diverse field of evaluation.

At the end of Exhibit 10.1 (final row) I note that combinations are possible and *patch dynamics* are such that a single organization might be engaged in more than one of these purposes at the same time. (*Patch dynamics* refers to the notion that different dynamics can be occurring at different scales at the same time within the same or interdependent/adjoining organizations or systems.) Moreover, these are heuristic distinctions that can become blurred in the complexities of the real world just as different complex systems challenges can be overlapping and simultaneous. Thus specific and distinct developmental evaluation uses may overlap as challenges and purposes intersect and overlap. Uses and processes that are common across all five types include creating a documentary record of developments, identifying forks in the road, generating feedback for adaptation, and extrapolating principles to inform future developments and innovations. One distinct purpose may also morph or transition into another. Doing developmental evaluation for the purpose of ongoing development may suddenly change to exploring responses to crisis approaches when a crisis erupts. The nature of complex systems is such that the purposes and uses of developmental evaluation may change when system dynamics are influenced by extenuating circumstances, as often occurs. Given that change is constant and its direction uncertain in a complex dynamic system, developmental evaluation supports programs and innovators to adapt as they face these different challenges, whether one at a time, more than one at a time, or in some sequence or cycle. The purpose of making the distinctions is to better match the developmental evaluation design to the nature of the complex situational challenges that pertain at any given time within a particular context. It is to that challenge that the rest of this chapter, and this book, turns once again.

Diversity of Design and Methods Options

Developmental evaluation does not rely on any particular evaluation method, design,

or tool. A developmental evaluation can include any kind of data (quantitative, qualitative, mixed), any kind of design (e.g., naturalistic, experimental, quasi-experimental, rapid appraisal), a variety of measures (indicators, surveys, tests), and any kind of focus (processes, outcomes, impacts, costs, and cost–benefit, among many possibilities). Design, methods, measures, and analysis depend on the priority questions that will support development of and decision making about an innovation based on the nature and stage of the innovation and the situation in which the evaluation takes place. This can include randomized controlled trials, surveys, focus groups, interviews, observations, performance data, community indicators, network analysis—whatever sheds light on key questions.

The remainder of this chapter presents examples of developmental evaluation processes and designs based on a utilization-focused evaluation template for determining what is situationally appropriate. These examples are meant to be generative and suggestive of the great variety of designs and methods that can be used, not by any means prescriptive or exhaustive of design and methods possibilities. As a foreshadowing of the methodological diversity you'll find in this chapter, and hoping to whet your appetite for a feast of possibilities, here's a starting list of options for developmental evaluation we'll examine:

- Rapid feedback interviews with program participants.
- Bellwether surveys of influential policy-makers.
- Participatory action research.
- Social network analysis.
- Randomized comparison trials of advocacy campaign messages.
- Reflective practice sessions with innovative program staff.

EXHIBIT 10.1 Five Purposes and Uses for Developmental Evaluation

Primary developmental evaluation purpose	Complex systems challenges	Primary specific developmental evaluation uses	Examples with specific primary intended users	Implications
1. Ongoing development.	A project, program, policy, or other innovative intervention is being implemented in a complex dynamic environment.	▪ Adapt to changing social, political, economic, environmental, technological, and demographic patterns. ▪ Adapt to emergent developments in populations and groups being worked with. ▪ Identify key forks in the road and basis for decisions about which direction is taken. ▪ Create a documentary record of changes made. ▪ Generate feedback and learnings for ongoing development. ▪ Contingency planning for the future.	Rural community leadership program design team adapts its curriculum and training process to economic ups and downs, changes in public policies affecting rural communities, emerging regional patterns of commerce, foreign immigrants moving to rural communities, and the emergence of the Internet and mobile phones for communication.	The program doesn't intend to become a fixed, standardized model. It does, however, identify effective principles that inform its ongoing development.

| 2. Adapt effective principles from elsewhere to a new context (which can be local, regional, national, or cross-national).

An innovative project, program, policy, intervention, or idea is being disseminated by social innovators; people in a new area are interested in developing their own version based on adaption of effective principles and knowledge from elsewhere.

The specific dynamics of the new system and situation are such that adaptation (rather than replication) is most appropriate. | ■ Identify relevant principles, knowledge, and ideas to be adapted.
■ Help keep the adapters attentive to larger and broader guiding principles, knowledge, and ideas.
■ Document the consequences of adaptations of and departures from what has been done elsewhere. | a. The Damiano antipoverty agency director and staff in Duluth, Minnesota, adapted the national Kids Café® model to its own adult-oriented soup kitchen for the poor, changing the food provided and how the national program was implemented to fit its local population, facility, and resources.

b. The Global Water Partnership decided to adapt outcome mapping (OM) methodology for its 70-plus national water partnerships in 13 regions around the world. This complex, 2,000-member network is challenged to develop a customized planning, monitoring, and evaluation system across many cultural, social, political, and economic divides, maintaining the OM principles while meeting a diversity of needs. | ■ Developmental evaluation operates in the middle between top-down and bottom-up forces for change, facilitating synthesis of top-down forces (general principles and knowledge being disseminated) and bottom-up sensitivity to context, experiences, capabilities, and priorities.
■ Effective, validated principles are adapted (developmental evaluation) rather than best practices being adopted (high-fidelity evaluation monitoring to assure replication of a validated model). |

(cont.)

Primary developmental evaluation purpose	Complex systems challenges	Primary specific developmental evaluation uses	Examples with specific primary intended users	Implications
3. In the face of a sudden major change (a black swan event) or a crisis, exploring real-time solutions and generating innovative responses.	Existing programs and initiatives are no longer effective as conditions suddenly change (e.g., a dramatic shift in resources, major policy change, or an emergent new problem like homeless people living with HIV/AIDS). In the midst of crisis, there is no time for formal model development. Action is needed now, but what to do is uncertain and contentious. Rapid feedback is needed about efforts to intervene to mitigate the crisis or disaster. This is the situation ushered in by destruction of previously dominant patterns as new initiatives are explored and resources are reorganized to adapt to radically altered conditions, the kind of real-time developmental response that occurs in major natural disasters, outbreaks of violence, suddenly emergent social problems (e.g., meth drug use epidemic), and new disease threats.	■ Support development of new initiatives to meet emergent needs and crisis conditions. ■ Facilitate creative collaboration of local, national, and/or international response teams and innovators by bringing evaluative thinking into rapid response initiatives and crisis management. ■ Provide timely feedback on reactions to and results of early efforts at intervening as those efforts are tried out. ■ Help crisis responders prioritize their efforts and adapt as effects of interventions emerge under conditions of high uncertainty and rapid change.	a. Children in preschool programs need to get the H1N1 vaccine quickly; a vaccination campaign aimed at reaching this population quickly and comprehensively has never been done in many communities before. Parents are afraid of both the virus and the vaccination and need information. The public health team needs rapid feedback about how the campaign is unfolding, emergent problems, and unanticipated issues that require quick action. b. The national advocacy campaign leadership trying to pass immigration legislation in the U.S. Congress has to completely reorganize in the middle of the presidential campaign when the politics of immigration suddenly shift, the planned campaign falls into disarray, and a rapid reorganization is required.	Planning, execution, and evaluation occur simultaneously. Everything must happen at once. The stakes can be quite high. Errors and miscalculations need to be corrected quickly. Decision makers need the best information and analysis available even as they have to make decisions with incomplete data. Time is of the essence. Credible, relevant, and real-time data can save lives.

| 4. Preformative development of a potentially broad-impact, scalable innovation. | Changing and dynamic systems require innovative solutions and creative new approaches to worsening conditions. Social innovators aspire to major change with broad impact, expecting to engage in disruptive systems change with a new model. But *that new model does not exist and needs to be developed*, reorganizing and exploring new possibilities as old systems show signs of collapse and dysfunction (and may have already fallen apart). | ▪ Help the innovators track their evolving understanding of the problem and their response, creating manageable and testable boundaries around the innovation.
▪ Support getting a potential new model sufficiently well developed and formulated that it can be further developed through formative and then summative evaluation, to identify whether it is ready to be taken to scale (broadly disseminated) for major impact.
▪ Identify key issues that will need to be addressed going forward as the developmental evaluation findings are used to formalize which model is most promising among a number of innovative possibilities, and the transition is made from exploratory and generative developmental evaluation to more traditional formative and summative evaluation. | Innovators adapting mobile phone technology need feedback about innovative applications as mobile phone technology has been globalized. New uses of mobile phones are being explored by innovators to deal with a broad range of issues, for example, getting peasant farmers real-time information about market prices for their crops so they can't be manipulated by unscrupulous middlemen; helping people living with HIV/AIDS stay current with their medications; helping pregnant women get timely prenatal care when problems emerge; and mobilizing young people for environmental action in local communities. After a period of innovative development and developmental evaluation, any of these and similar real-time communication models can be formalized and subjected to formative and summative evaluation as part of innovators' and disseminating funders' interests in taking these new applications to scale globally. | As models emerge out of exploratory and innovative initiatives, some may move into more traditional formative and summative evaluation to determine scalability and generalizability, while others remain in developmental mode, undergoing either further development or continuous experimentation in the search for new models. At this preformative stage developmental evaluation can help innovators think about different potential scaling options and inform which scaling strategy (if any) to pursue. |

(cont.)

Primary developmental evaluation purpose	Complex systems challenges	Primary specific developmental evaluation uses	Examples with specific primary intended users	Implications
5. Major systems change and cross-scale developmental evaluation.	▪ Disrupting the existing system and tipping it in the new, desired direction. ▪ Taking an innovation to scale. An innovative intervention has been developed, then formatively evaluated, and successfully summatively evaluated. The success is sufficient enough that social innovators and funders now want to take the innovation to scale, expanding to new systems horizontally (more of the same units elsewhere, e.g., new cities) as well as vertically (from cities to regions and entire countries). ▪ Major systems change and changing scale will add levels of complexity, new uncertainties, new disagreements, and unexpected consequences.	▪ Look out for system change indicators and any emergent tipping point. ▪ Gather feedback on how a model is and needs to be adapted as it is taken to scale, including the possibility that either horizontal or vertical scaling will constitute not just an adaptation but essentially an evolution of a new development. ▪ Identify critical cross-scale factors that affect dissemination. ▪ Track developments in the model itself as it adapts to cross-scale challenges. ▪ Help social innovators taking a model to scale, determining appropriate and inappropriate adaptations along the way and deciding what adaptations to support and which to resist.	a. The Planned Lifetime Advocacy Network (PLAN), starting in Vancouver, developed a different approach to creating supportive communities for and with people with disabilities. They developed and built relationship networks, demonstrated positive results, and began disseminating the PLAN model across Canadian provinces, learning and adapting to new conditions as they went. They also decided to change scale and target national government policy, a cross-scale intervention. b. The Grameen Bank, started by Nobel Prize–recipient Mohammed Yunus, has adapted as it has expanded its microfinance model from Asia	Models change as they are taken across time and space, and broadened to change larger systems. One approach to dissemination across scales is to focus on replication and maintaining fidelity. In contrast, adaptive cross-scale innovations assume that the complex nonlinear dynamics and adaptive cycles of scale will require agility, responsiveness, and adjustments. Developmental evaluation provides the data to be agile, responsive, and adaptive in the face of cross-scale dynamics. Horizontal scaling across systems or vertical scaling to broader systems may involve more than adaptation; these scaling processes can evolve an essentially new development, the emergence of which can

• Track and learn from cross-scale innovations and adaptations to inform future efforts.

Clarifying note: Combinations are possible and patch dynamics are such that a single organization might be engaged in more than one of these purposes at the same time. These are heuristic distinctions that can become blurred in the complexities of the real world.

Clarifying note: Challenges can be overlapping and simultaneous.

. to communities and countries around the world, ranging from people in poverty in Africa to urban industrialized communities of low-income people in North America where new policies and procedures had to be adapted in new financial, economic, and social contexts.

Clarifying note: Uses may overlap as challenges and purposes intersect and overlap. Uses that are common across all five types include:
• Create a documentary record of changes made.
• Generate feedback and learnings for ongoing development.
• Contingency planning for the future.

Clarifying note: Doing developmental evaluation for the purpose of ongoing development may suddenly change to exploring innovative approaches when a crisis erupts. Given that change is constant and its direction uncertain in a complex system, developmental evaluation supports programs and innovators to adapt as they face these different challenges at the same time or in some sequence or cycle.

be documented and analyzed as part of a developmental evaluation.

Clarifying note: The nature of complex systems is such that the purposes and uses of developmental evaluation may change when system dynamics are influenced by extenuating circumstances, as often occurs.

⌢ Co-Creating by Challenging: Being Active–Reactive–Interactive–Adaptive

One of the misunderstandings I run into about utilization-focused developmental evaluation is that the evaluator on the team is just a technician or methodologist who does whatever the innovators want but never challenges or disagrees with them. I've emphasized that developmental evaluation involves a process of co-creation (Chapter 5) and have described utilization-focused evaluators as being *active–reactive–interactive–adaptive* (Patton, 2008c). This explicitly recognizes the importance of the individual evaluator's experience, orientation, and contribution by placing the mandate to be active first in this quadratic role description. Situational responsiveness does not mean rolling over and playing dead (or passive) in the face of innovators' interests or perceived needs. Just as the evaluator in utilization-focused evaluation does not unilaterally impose a focus and set of methods on a program, so too the innovators with whom we are working are not set up to impose their initial predilections unilaterally or dogmatically. Arriving at the final evaluation design is a negotiated process that allows the values and capabilities of the evaluator to intermingle with those of intended users.

The utilization-focused evaluator, in being active–reactive–interactive–adaptive, is one among many at the design negotiating table. At times there may be discord in the negotiating process; at other times harmony. Evaluators need to be deliberative and intentional in representing their own professional interests in design negotiations. The *active* part of being active–reactive–interactive–adaptive is bringing your own concerns, issues, and values to the table. The evaluator is also a stakeholder—not the primary stakeholder—but, *in every evaluation, an evaluator's reputation, credibility, integrity, and beliefs are on the line*. A utilization-focused evaluator is not passive in simply accepting and buying into whatever an intended user initially desires. The active–reactive–interactive–adaptive process includes an obligation on the part of the evaluator to represent the standards and principles of the profession as well as his or her own sense of morality and integrity, while also attending to and respecting the beliefs and concerns of other primary users.

Thus, there may well be instances in which the developmental evaluator challenges the innovators' own sense-making process and results, for example, their conclusions about what the data mean. An experienced developmental evaluator told me about an instance of deciding to purposefully irritate a group that seemed determined to avoid arriving at any conclusions (and therefore any decisions about moving forward). At a lull in the seemingly endless process of interpreting the data, the evaluator proclaimed that, given the pace and scale of their progress, it appeared clear that they had "met and in fact dramatically exceeded their targets" (which they technically had, but new things had emerged that they were not grappling with). Therefore, continued the evaluator, they should feel comfortable telling themselves and others that they could stamp SUCCESS-FUL on the project and end both their deliberations and the project.

The evaluator confessed to being quite nervous about what their reaction would be. But the evaluator's assertion led to a more focused and serious conversation about what could be concluded from their work and they decided that, although they had met their operational targets, they now knew much more about the problems that needed to be addressed and were interested in continuing in new directions. The evaluator's timely intervention in the discussion moved the group forward in a way that appeared unlikely had the evaluator been passive.

Active–reactive–interactive–adaptive evaluators are genuinely immersed in the challenges of each new setting and authentically responsive to the intended users of each new evaluation.

It is the paradox of decision making that effective action is born of reaction. Only when organizations and people take in information from those around them and the environment and react to changing conditions can they act to reduce uncertainty and increase discretionary flexibility. The same is true for the individual decision maker or for a problem-solving group.

Action emerges through reaction and interaction and leads to adaptation.

Utilization-Focused Developmental Evaluation

In the first chapter I positioned developmental evaluation within the larger context of *utilization-focused evaluation* (Patton, 2008c). By way of review, *utilization-focused evaluation* is evaluation done for and with specific primary intended users for specific, intended uses. Utilization-focused evaluation begins with the premise that evaluations should be judged by their utility and actual use; therefore, evaluators should facilitate the evaluation process and design any evaluation with careful consideration for how everything that is done, from beginning to end, will affect use. Use concerns how real people in the real world apply evaluation findings and experience the evaluation process. Therefore, the focus in utilization-focused evaluation is on achieving *intended use by intended users*. In developmental evaluation, the intended use is development, which I have argued throughout this book is a distinct and important evaluation purpose. More specifically, it is one of the five uses illustrated in Exhibit 10.1. The primary intended users are specific social innovators, program staff, community members, leaders, and others working to bring about major change including funders of social innovations and the expected beneficiaries of whatever is developed.

Ten Utilization-Focused Developmental Evaluation Design Examples

To conclude this book I want to offer an overview of 10 developmental evaluation designs that highlight matching engagement and methods to particular complex systems challenges. In Chapter 8 I offered 10 different inquiry frameworks matched to different complexity situations. The focus there was on highlighting various *inquiry frameworks* like the triangulated learning framework (beliefs, knowledge, and action), appreciative inquiry, systems thinking (boundaries, perspectives, and interrelationships), degrees of complexity distinctions (simple, complicated, complex), and actual–ideal comparisons with revisable and emergent baselines and targets. This chapter brings additional utilization-focused evaluation criteria more explicitly into play, especially specific developmental evaluation uses by specific intended users. The format for presenting these designs takes pains to place design and methods decisions in context (a specific complex systems challenge and a particular developmental purpose) and focuses on appropriate designs and methods to answer specific developmental evaluation questions. Exhibit 10.2 summarizes this generic utilization-focused evaluation format.

EXHIBIT 10.2   Utilization-Focused Evaluation Template for Developmental Evaluation Designs

OVERVIEW OF COMPLEX SYSTEMS INNOVATION AND DEVELOPMENT CHALLENGES

What is the nature of the innovation? What makes the situation and system complex? Contextual factors to consider include turbulence in the environment (e.g., economic, political, and/or social changes unfolding rapidly); dealing with controversial, contentious, and emotional issues; trying out new things and/or targeting new groups with uncertainty about what effects will result; likelihood that unpredictable and uncontrollable interactions will lead to emergent and unanticipated responses; many actors engaged simultaneously doing both different and sometimes overlapping interventions; and dynamical interactions such that small actions could ripple quickly to create large-scale (nonlinear) reactions and consequences.

(cont.)

1. *Developmental evaluation purpose and intended evaluation use*: Which of the five types of developmental purposes is primary? (See Exhibit 10.1 for the five types.) What is being developed? What are developmental priorities? What forks in the road (decisions about alternative directions) are being considered that evaluative data can inform?

2. *Primary intended users and developmental evaluation partners*: Who is co-creating the design and participating in design, process, data collection, and methods decisions?

3. *Key developmental evaluation questions*: What needs to be answered? What framework will be used to generate questions, for example, systems change, reflective practice on sensitizing constructs, participatory action research, appreciative inquiry, social networks, learning organization framework; see Exhibit 8.2 for elaboration of inquiry framework options.

4. *Time line for feedback*: What's the pace of data gathering and feedback needed to influence developments? What are target dates for evaluative feedback to influence developmental decisions?

5. *Appropriate developmental evaluation engagement, design, and methods options*: The nature and extent of the developmental evaluator's engagement with the primary intended users (social innovators) is part of the evaluation design. What inquiry framework, if any, will guide the evaluation? (See Exhibit 8.6 in Chapter 8 for illustrative inquiry framework options.) In the co-creation process of active–reactive–interactive–adaptive engagement, data collection priorities are established together: what data will be collected (quantitative, qualitative, mixed) with what design features (surveys, individual interviews, focus groups, observations, experiments, staff reflections, random samples, purposeful samples, routine monitoring data, community statistics, etc.)?

6. *Example and commentary*: Caveats; strengths and weaknesses; things to watch out for; particular constraints and issues.

These are standard evaluation utilization-focused evaluation design questions with a developmental emphasis, twist, and focus.

Template Applications and Examples

Complex Systems Development Challenge 1:

Developing a new, innovative program; uncertainties about how participants will react and what issues will emerge; ongoing development as the program unfolds and implementation proceeds (Type 1 in Exhibit 10.1)

- *Developmental evaluation purpose and intended evaluation use*: Rapid feedback for ongoing development. Staff needs rapid feedback about how program participants react to the program; staff reflections and learning will be used to make changes.

- *Primary intended users and developmental evaluation partners*: Program staff.

- *Key developmental evaluation questions*: How are participants reacting to the innovative program? What are staff observing and learning that leads them to make changes as the innovation unfolds?

- *Time line for feedback*: Periodic staff meetings devoted to interpreting evaluation data. Early in the innovation, evaluation feedback may be generated often (say monthly); over time, reflective practice sessions with staff may occur quarterly, or as special issues emerge.

- *Appropriate developmental evaluation engagement, design, and methods options*: Reflective practice sessions with staff and/or participants that track program developments, document changes, and facilitate staff reflection on feedback from participants.

• *Example and commentary*: The program Twin Cities Rise!, used as an example in Chapter 2, was created as an innovative approach to employment training. The pilot involved an extensive selection and initial assessment process aimed at individualizing the coaching model and providing coaches with lots of information about participants from the beginning. However, more than half of those selected and screened didn't show up for the actual program. Rapid follow-up discovered that they were so intimidated and put off by the selection and assessment program that they dropped out before the program began. The intensive selection and assessment was intended to communicate caring, individualization, and comprehensiveness. Instead it created anxiety, evoked bad school experiences, and generated lots of intimidating paperwork. The entire selection and assessment process had to be completely redesigned. The fact that the evaluation was set up for immediate feedback was critical. Dropouts are legendarily hard to find. They had to be tracked and contacted immediately, within a couple of days of not showing up, to find them and get their feedback about what had happened.

• *Other applications*: Reflective practice, discussed at length in Chapter 9, can be used for any innovative initiative that is developing and adapting over time. See Exhibit 9.1 for steps in facilitating reflective practice and Exhibit 9. 2 for a summary graphic depiction of the reflective practice cycle, both presented earlier in the previous chapter.

Complex Systems Development Challenge 2:

Ongoing adaptation and development of a program in response to changing conditions, like new kinds of participants, new technology, new public policies, or fluctuations in the economy (Type 1 in Exhibit 10.1)

• *Developmental evaluation purpose and intended evaluation use*: Evaluator participates in program design change discussions to document rationales and identify expected results of those changes, gathering follow-up data to find out what actually happens.

• *Primary intended users and developmental evaluation partners*: Program design team.

• *Key developmental evaluation questions*: What changes are occurring in the environment that indicate a need for program adaptation? What are the rationales for program adaptations? What are the effects of design changes on participants and staff?

• *Time line for feedback*: Time evaluation findings to guide program design team meetings and discussions.

• *Appropriate developmental evaluation engagement, design, and methods options*: Direct observation of program changes as they are implemented. Follow-up with participants to find out their views of the changes and see how it affects desired outcomes.

• *Example and commentary*: I introduced the Blandin Community Leadership Program in Chapter 1. The program trained cohorts of rural leaders selected by their own communities. I participated in annual design team meetings to facilitate discussions of larger trends that could affect the program, like new immigrants moving into rural Minnesota in search of jobs, the effects of changing technology (like the Internet and mobile phones), the increasing regionalization of the economy, and new public policies and initiatives that had community development implications. As program changes were made, I worked with the design team to create evaluation follow-up processes to assess those changes. This included my direct observation of the changes, observing staff meetings as implementation details were worked out, interviews with a sample of participants after each cohort's training, and interviews with community leaders to find out what program participants contributed to their communities after training as well as what they saw as emergent trends and issues. These findings were used by the design team to redesign, adapt, and further develop the program each summer.

• *Other applications*: Any program or intervention committed to ongoing development and adaptation will benefit from having a developmental evaluator help them scan the environment for trends affecting the program, observe implementation of changes made, and get timely feedback from participants to inform future program adaptations and innovations.

Complex Systems Development Challenge 3:

Building on the successes of a completed program to extrapolate general principles that can inform development of and support for new initiatives in new settings elsewhere (Type 5 in Exhibit 10.1)

• *Developmental evaluation purpose and intended evaluation use*: Explore new possibilities for cross-scale innovation based on evaluation of a program's success and lessons learned.

• *Primary intended users and developmental evaluation partners*: Funders and innovators interested in disseminating effective principles to support innovation in new settings.

• *Key developmental evaluation questions*: What new opportunities are emerging as a result of past program successes where principles of effectiveness can be disseminated for others to adapt? What cross-scale initiatives hold promise and are worth further exploring with new funding?

• *Time line for feedback*: Funders' decision process and proposal consideration process.

• *Appropriate developmental evaluation engagement, design, and methods options*: First, ongoing tracking results of a successful program to substantiate longer-term results; this can be done with periodic follow-ups to gather outcomes and impact data. Second, tracking efforts at disseminating the results and promoting adaptation of the innovation

elsewhere; documenting and evaluating adaptations in new settings.

• *Example and commentary*: The McGill–McConnell Leadership Program was designed to provide professional development to three cohorts of 40 national leaders in the Canadian nonprofit sector—then end. There was no formal summative evaluation of the program model, though it was deemed highly successful by those involved, including the funder. The program was designed as a one-time, major intervention to infuse 120 highly skilled and innovation-minded leaders into the voluntary sector across Canada. The foundation tracked collaborations, partnerships, innovative ideas, emergent networks, and new proposals and injected new funding into ideas that built on the leadership program's successes and ongoing relationships with graduates of the program. As noted in the acknowledgments, the support of the J. W. McConnell Family Foundation for developmental evaluation was one of the unanticipated and emergent outcomes of the McGill–McConnell Leadership Program. The developmental evaluation identified effective principles of the program and discrete elements that contributed to success. Those were shared with policymakers, other funders, and nonprofit leaders interested in adapting the model under different conditions.

A common criticism of philanthropic funders is that they have short attention spans and fail to follow up successes, moving on instead to new interests and priorities. Doing developmental evaluation follow-up of prior successes and building on relationships established during previous funding can keep new opportunities in front of funders, especially if they set up accelerated decision-making mechanisms to move new funds quickly when innovative ideas are ripe for launching.

Many reports are published and disseminated offering models for adoption by others, but it is rare for those who put out such reports to systematically follow up and evaluate how those ideas are used and what kind of cross-scale impacts occur, if any.

Complex Systems Development Challenge 4:

Many different agencies and project teams working collaboratively on the same problem with complicated interactions, impossible-to-attribute outcomes, diverse responses to unexpected events and crises, and uncertainties about cumulative and aggregate impacts; the challenge is ongoing development of the collaborative effort and providing feedback about its effectiveness (Type 1 in Exhibit 10.1)

• *Developmental evaluation purpose and intended evaluation use*: Support ongoing development of an effective collaborative response to a complex problem, like HIV/AIDS, which involves complex health, family, economic, political, social, community, and religious interactions; provide feedback to the collaboration about the effects of intervention initiatives and emergent opportunities.

• *Primary intended users and developmental evaluation partners*: Collaboration leadership and coordination team.

• *Key developmental evaluation questions*: What's working and not working well in the collaboration? How is the way collaborative relationships are unfolding affecting the collaboration process and shared outcomes? How do inevitable tensions and conflicts get handled? How do emergent issues affect the collaboration, its division of labor, and its shared engagement?

• *Time line for feedback*: Meetings of the collaboration leadership, both face-to-face and virtual.

• *Appropriate developmental evaluation engagement, design, and methods options*: Shared outcome mapping (International Development Research Centre, 2007) and contribution analysis (Mayne, 2007) could be undertaken as collaboration activities. In addition, the evaluator can build relationships with individual members of the collaboration to monitor activities, types and levels of engagement, communication and decision-making patterns, and perceptions of the collaboration. This monitoring can include e-mail exchanges, telephone interviews, and interactions at meetings, including direct observations (participant observation by the evaluator) and conversations at informal, opportune times. Patterns across the collaboration are synthesized and reported to the group, possibly as a reflective practice exercise.

• *Example and commentary*: A major philanthropic foundation pushed five environmental organizations to collaborate in an effort to stimulate innovative thinking and new approaches to protecting the environment. The developmental evaluator attended monthly collaboration meetings and interviewed participating leaders between meetings. The evaluator was copied on all documents generated by collaboration members and shared among them, including plans of work and meeting minutes, as well as ongoing e-mail exchanges. Within the first 3 months, it became clear that the collaboration was a shotgun marriage (created by the interested funder through the magnet of funds), but each member was more interested in pursuing its own agenda; a genuinely shared commitment and plan of work was not emerging. Various efforts were made to enhance communications, create a shared vision, and build trust, none of which worked. At the end of a year of struggle, after myriad failed attempts at team building, much paperwork on what the collaborative structure and process might look like, and increasing tension, including the funders' expectations that something get done and that results be shown, the developmental evaluator participated in a year-end summit, reported these findings to all concerned, especially speaking truth to power (the funder), and facilitated a discussion of alternative strategies going forward, including moving to an informal cooperative relationship, which is what the group agreed to do rather than continue to struggle with creating a more intensely engaged collaboration. The developmental evaluator, knowing the perspective of each leader and the funder but playing an independent role of monitoring, documentation, and feedback, having carefully and credibly tracked and documented what had been tried and the effects of those efforts, and being able to skillfully report the findings in a way that could be heard and acted on, was able to help the group find and develop a new path.

Collaborations are highly valued by funders. On the surface, it often seems like a no-brainer to bring people together who are working on similar problems. Collaborations also make it easier for funders to administer funds, making one grant to a collaboration rather than many separate grants and merely hoping for or urging collaboration. But collaborations are hard work, can take lots of time, and add layers of complication to interventions. Developmental evaluation can be used to strengthen a collaboration, identify emergent problems before they become a crisis, and help all involved better understand each other's perspectives and capacities. When the collaboration is floundering, the neutral evaluator is sometimes, indeed often, the only person who can say so with credibility and integrity, and without conflict of interest. Collaboration as an inquiry framework was discussed in Chapter 8, as example 6. Exhibit 8.3 in Chapter 8 provides a collaboration continuum that could be used as a basis for reflective practice with a group working together. (For more on evaluating collaborations, see Mattessich, Monsey, & Murray-Close, 2001; Ray, 2002; Taylor-Powell & Rossing, n.d.)

⌒ Advice from an Experienced Developmental Evaluator

Dr. Keiko Kuji-Shikatani works to infuse evaluative thinking into education initiatives as an education officer for the Student Success Learning to 18 Implementation, Training and Evaluation Branch, Student Achievement Division of the Ontario Ministry of Education in Canada. She is especially attentive to issues of evaluation use and evaluation capacity building. Prior to joining the ministry, she provided services as a program evaluation and learning consultant for organizations with training, skills development, and behavioral and attitudinal change programs in increasingly sensitive and complex situations both in Canada and internationally. Developmental evaluation, she says, has become part of her repertoire of utilization-focused evaluation approaches as she learns about and works increasingly with "complex programs addressing complex problems in complex situations." Keiko is passionate about the role of evaluation in supporting programs for the betterment of society and is active in the community of evaluators as the first vice president of professional designation programs for the Canadian Evaluation Society.

Here is her sage advice to an evaluator new to developmental evaluation about things to do and pay attention to.

BEING PART OF A TEAM IS REWARDING

If the situation truly calls for developmental evaluation, it is very rewarding to use your evaluation knowledge as a team member in the process of *getting there*. Here are some suggestions.

- **Be certain that you have the full support of your primary intended users** (whether this is your client or your boss) **and a shared understanding of the primary intended use.** The preliminary steps in engaging in developmental evaluation are the same as in any utilization-focused evaluation.

(cont.)

- **Begin by doing a thorough situational analysis**. Listen and observe, use various data collection techniques, let the program stakeholders tell you their story. You may miss something if you jump to conclusions—so be open-minded. Pay attention to all the stakeholders involved at multiple levels. Learn the complexity of the system in detail—speak with people, learn their roles, pressures, responsibilities, tasks, information needs, language used, modes of engagement, interests, dispositions, and learning and communication preferences and styles.

- **Once you start getting the picture, begin asking questions to clarify your understanding**. Be respectful, sincere, and collaborative—demonstrate that you truly value their input in a constructive manner. Whenever it is appropriate, I make my own position clear by explaining that in all the years of working with organizations, I have found that everyone has good intentions for those they are serving and that my passion is to provide support to the success of programs through evaluation practice. Earning trust and establishing credibility in a nonthreatening manner is critical to working with the stakeholders and in understanding the complexity of the system that you are trying to support.

- **Use diagrams and other communication instruments to illustrate what is understood so far**. This may be a theory of change logic model or simple flow charts or tables. The tools used depend on what the stakeholder is comfortable with. Since this is all about communicating your understanding of the complexity of the program, the tools may be differentiated for stakeholders depending on their perspectives. The stakeholders' response will further your understanding as well as allow you to know their preferred mode of communication. You want to know where they are trying to get to, why, what they value, what challenges there are, what their assets are, and so on.

- **Ask questions to figure out what their information needs are**. The information needs may be process-related or outcome-related or may be part of their accountability needs. What are the likely forks in the road? Who needs this information? Who needs to use this information? What are the decision points? What is the program cycle? Etc., etc., you get the picture!

- **Once you have a thorough understanding of what level of information is useful for the various stakeholders, then provide support in developing program instruments and mechanisms that fit their complex system**. This may vary and could include client-intake forms; learning plans for students or staff; communication logs for multilevel systems; reporting requirements or meetings scheduled at key points of the program; and program logic models. At this point, the stakeholders will start seeing that you are very systematic in collecting useful data and that you understand the nature of their program well. You become part of their team. You've earned their trust. As an evaluator, this allows you to clearly understand the information needs of the program and where the critical decision points are at multiple levels and how they intersect: the Map of the Possible Forks in the Road!

- **Now that you have the map to start with, be sure to support the system in real time, receiving, analyzing, collaboratively interpreting the information that comes in and planning the next steps**. Being user-friendly is the key. Be responsive during the journey. Nothing is written in stone. Maps, models, and systems will change since emergence is the norm for developmental evaluation.

Complex Systems Development Challenge 5:

Community generating and developing its own community-based response to a problem, like poverty (could have elements of Types 1 and 4 in Exhibit 10.1)

• *Developmental evaluation purpose and intended evaluation use*: Support the community's efforts at community development not only by providing timely and credible feedback on initiatives undertaken and helping them extract lessons from their experiences, but also by building the community's capacity to engage in evaluation and think evaluatively.

• *Primary intended users and developmental evaluation partners*: Community leaders and members engaged in the community development initiative.

• *Key developmental evaluation questions*: What is the nature of the community development initiative and what are its effects and consequences as it unfolds? What emerges as the development process unfolds? What is being learned to inform ongoing engagement? What model for community engagement on this issue, if any, is being developed? What evidence of effectiveness is credible and useful to ongoing development and adaptation, and potentially to others outside the community?

• *Time line for feedback*: Work with community members to identify the expected pace of community development activities and time the evaluation to fit that pace. Given the capacity-building purpose included in the evaluation process, create short feedback cycles (e.g., quarterly) on focused questions early in the initiative so that those involved learn to value and use evaluation. Early, meaningful, understandable, and useful feedback whets the appetite of community members for more evaluation.

• *Appropriate developmental evaluation engagement, design, and methods options*: Participatory evaluation approach in which community members undertake data collection, gather and analyze data on primary community indicators, participate in designing surveys that they administer as part of the initiative, conduct interviews, and do descriptive reports on community events and important meetings (e.g., who is there, who is not there, what happens, why, and what are the consequences and impacts).

• *Example and commentary*: Vibrant Communities is a Canadian initiative that supports and links over a dozen urban centers experimenting with comprehensive and collaborative approaches to reduce poverty across Canada. It was launched in 2002 by the Caledon Institute of Social Policy and the Tamarack Institute for Community Engagement. Evaluation and reflective practice have been built in from the beginning, aimed at encouraging community groups to be more rigorous in flushing out, fleshing out, and testing their emerging "frameworks" for change. They are committed to surfacing the broad range of effects emerging from their work, figuring out what is working and what is not, and scanning the environment and extracting lessons to guide ongoing development of their local efforts. The national group collaborates together to mine their diverse experiences, surface common patterns and themes, and share experiences across communities. Periodically Vibrant Communities produces summary documents that capture and communicate lessons and emergent frameworks that communities find useful. These documents include stories and data from the communities. One example is *A Comprehensive Approach to Poverty Using Strategic Drivers: An Aide for Action* by Garry Loewen (2009). Mark Cabaj and Eric Leviten-Reid of Tamarack have introduced developmental evaluation as a resource and framework for these communities, and periodically pull together and publish summaries of what is being learned about poverty reduction across initiatives (Cabaj, 2009a, 2009b). Cabaj reports that community leaders and members are more willing—and at times enthusiastically so—to engage with developmental evaluation because they understand what they are doing as innovative, principles-based, and developmental rather than implementation of a recipe-like model. The website maintained by Tamarack (2009) provides a number of evaluation ideas, resources, and summary findings on lessons.

And now a cautionary tale about a different community-based poverty initiative that included lots of rhetoric about meaningful evaluation, but botched the job to the point that the lack of evaluation at the community level, and a poor-quality external evaluation when they finally got around to it, contributed to the eventual demise of the whole effort. The short version of the story, from my jaded perspective, is that a philanthropic foundation made a major commitment to work with a targeted set of communities by providing substantial resources in a multiyear, long-term poverty reduction effort. The initiative rhetoric treated poverty reduction as inherently and fundamentally complex and committed to a process of learning-by-doing based on a genuine foundation–community partnership. The work was decidedly developmental, with the expectation of rapid responses to whatever emerged.

But creating a genuine partnership between a foundation with lots of resources and communities eager to do whatever it took to get those resources proved problematic from the get-go. Thus, disingenuousness set in as an interactive pattern at the outset. This spilled over to evaluation. Lots of rhetoric, verbiage, expressions of commitment and enthusiasm, token plans, and genuflection to the evaluation gods on all sides— but little capacity building at the community level and staff who themselves got busy doing other things and never quite grasped the significance of evaluation for the kind of community development process they were funding. Nor did they know how to generate lessons or use evaluation feedback to support developmental choices. They fell back

on old reporting procedures and eventually turned to an external evaluation conducted by a large, national firm.

Senior people from the firm designed the evaluation but sent junior, inexperienced staff into the field who had no idea what they were looking for and defaulted to a traditional, linear logic model with specific goals and performance indicators selected by the evaluators, and an academic reporting format. The messiness of the whole process and lack of either documented outcomes or meaningful developments led the board to turn to classic accountability mutterings. The whole thing came to a bad end for all involved. At the heart of the mess, I am convinced, was insufficient attention to, support for, and engagement with an appropriate evaluation approach, one matched to the developmental process of community engagement. It's not just a matter of getting it right. Getting it wrong has consequences. And, by the way, community-based developmental evaluation is hard to do and do well. Tamarack's work with Vibrant Communities is the best I've seen.

• *Other applications*: Participatory approaches to evaluation take many forms and have become established as an important option in how evaluations are conducted. The issue here is *focusing any such participatory approach on innovation development*. Participatory evaluation (Baker & Sabo, 2004; Cousins & Whitmore, 2007; Daigneault & Jacob, 2009), empowerment evaluation (Fetterman & Wandersman, 2005), transformative evaluation (Mertens, 2009), participatory beneficiary assessments in international development (Salmen & Kane, 2006), and feminist evaluation (Bamberger & Podems, 2002), to name but a few of the more prominent examples, articulate the importance of and processes for including program participants and intended beneficiaries in evaluation in serious and meaningful ways that include building capacity and enhancing evaluative thinking. But those approaches are not inherently and necessarily used to develop innovations. They can be. But that must be the primary and focused purpose to use these approaches for developmental evaluation.

Brad Cousins, long-time distinguished editor of the *Canadian Journal of Program Evaluation* and recipient of the AEA's prestigious Lazarsfeld Award for Contributions to Evaluation Theory, has summarized the generic benefits of participatory and collaborative approaches:

> In our approach to collaborative evaluation (called practical participatory evaluation) primary users of evaluation data participate directly in the evaluation process from start to finish, including many of the technical activities such as instrument development, data collection, processing, and interpretation and reporting. We suggest that engagement in such activities engenders deep levels of understanding, by evaluators and program practitioners alike. . . . Collaborative evaluation of this sort is consistent with a utilization-oriented, problem-solving approach. (2001, pp. 115–116)

• Developmental evaluation, then, would be a particular application of more generic participatory and collaborative approaches where the focus is on innovation development and adaption to complexity. But, alas, I repeat myself. I do so because again and again I hear that developmental evaluation is just one more participatory approach. It is inherently collaborative (the evaluator is part of the program innovation team), but it is not inherently participatory in the sense of involving program participants and community members in all aspects of the evaluation. When people say that developmental evaluation is just one more participatory approach, they are placing the emphasis on its collaborative nature. But what they are often missing is the developmental focus. That must be primary. That is developmental evaluation's fundamental and distinct purpose and niche.

Complex Systems Development Challenge 6:

Humanitarian crisis: earthquake, tsunami, flooding, civil war; chaos and catastrophe reign; many people are homeless and hungry, lack basic services; relief agencies and emergency teams appear and need to be coordinated; aid and assistance requires management (Type 3 in Exhibit 10.1, and potentially Type 2)

• *Developmental evaluation purpose and intended evaluation use*: Direct resources where they are most needed; identify gaps; identify and direct support to self-organizing efforts; identify and communicate emergent issues that relief agencies can respond to quickly before they reach new crisis proportions; stem misinformation that feeds panic and deepens the crisis. Provide a credible source of trusted information to reduce uncertainty and contribute to stability.

• *Primary intended users and developmental evaluation partners*: Leaders in relief agencies coordinating the humanitarian response; local leaders involved with relief agencies; workers and those in need who hunger for credible information as well as food and shelter.

• *Key developmental evaluation questions*: What are the primary needs? What bottlenecks are arising that interfere with the delivery of assistance? How are local, national, and international responses being coordinated? What rumors are circulating with what effects? What processes are emerging that are especially effective in mitigating the crisis? What's actually going on? To what extent are lessons learned from other crises and principles of effective humanitarian relief being adapted to the situation at hand? What are those adaptations? What informs them?

• *Time line for feedback*: Initially, feedback may be hourly, at least every few hours, then daily or whenever there is something to report—real time, immediate, and ongoing.

• *Appropriate developmental evaluation engagement, design, and methods options*: Direct independent observation. Listening and tracking posts. Rapid reconnaissance. Networked reporting.

- *Example and commentary*: Setting up coordinated communications is a priority in disaster responses. Erikson (1995) has documented and examined "*the human experience of modern disasters*" and shown the critical importance of credible and timely information in mitigating disasters and saving lives, as well as the downward spiral that deepens humanitarian crises when political, administrative, and market dynamics are insufficient to mount an appropriate response.

Trust is a key issue. Developmental evaluation can monitor the quality of information being generated and shared, identify misinformation and its consequences, and help map what's happening across the territory of people and relief in the affected area. "Listening posts" are field staff in humanitarian agencies who have training in reporting what they are seeing as part of their rescue and relief responsibilities. As part of the team of people receiving field reports, mapping responses, identifying patterns, and tracking decisions, a developmental evaluator contributes to more effective real-time interventions as well as longer-term lessons about what works. Ramalingam, Jones, Reba, and Young (2008) have been doing pioneering work exploring how complexity insights can enhance humanitarian efforts around the world, including systematic, real-time monitoring and evaluation.

Complex Systems Development Challenge 7:

Supporting a network to take an innovation to scale (dissemination) through adaptation (Type 5 in Exhibit 10.1, plus some of Types 1 and 2)

- *Developmental evaluation purpose and intended evaluation use*: Track and share innovation about adaptations across the network for learning and ongoing development.
- *Primary intended users and developmental*

evaluation partners: Those supporting and facilitating the diffusion and dissemination process and members of the diffusion and dissemination network.

- *Key developmental evaluation questions*: How are local adopters of the innovation adapting it to fit local circumstances? What are the consequences of those adaptations, both intended (achieving desired results) and unintended? What is being learned about adapting and further developing the innovation? How is the innovation and its impacts changed as it goes to scale?
- *Time line for feedback*: Periodic feedback depending on the speed and scope of diffusion and the intensity of network interactions; the network members and participants should establish feedback time lines. Stay open to unscheduled, emergent feedback as significant findings come in from the evaluation.
- *Appropriate developmental evaluation engagement, design, and methods options*: Cross-site and cross-scale syntheses of local-level evaluations of adoption and adaptation experiences; social network analysis tracking interactions around the going-to-scale and diffusion processes.
- *Example and commentary*: Chapter 6 described and discussed Damiano's adaptation of the national Community Kitchens model that combines training chefs with operating a soup kitchen to feed the poor. In support of taking the model to scale, the National Community Kitchens network was created with some 50 participating programs across the United States. The diffusion and dissemination process included "best practice" ideas based on experiences from those adapting the national model and street wisdom (principles) from the network of those operating kitchens in their own communities (Community Kitchens, 2009). What might a developmental evaluator bring to this network?

First, those in the network would need to agree to do developmental evaluations at the local level where they are implementing and adapting the principles of the Community Kitchens approach (Type 2 in Exhibit 10.1). This doesn't mean having an external developmental evaluator at each site, but someone would need to have formal responsibility for systematically documenting what is implemented, what adaptations are made, and what results are achieved. The national network developmental evaluator would be a technical and methodological resource for local evaluations, would synthesize findings from network members, and would facilitate network discussion of the findings and their implications for ongoing model development and further diffusion.

Additionally, social network analysis and mapping could be used to track and document network traffic, knowledge sharing, and network growth and development. Networks are often primarily self-organizing and manifest complex nonlinear dynamics. Thus, social network analysis can be a powerful technique for tracking and documenting network development for evaluation purposes, including feeding back to the network information about its own emergent patterns and development. Social network analysis has become a cutting-edge new direction in evaluation (Benjamin & Greene, 2009; Cross, Dickmann, Newman-Gonchar, & Fagan, 2009; Durland & Fredericks, 2005), as well as widely used in social science more generally (Breiger, 2004; Dick & Mason, 2008; Freeman, 2006; Hesse-Biber & Leavy, 2008; Hine, 2008; Sarkisian, 2008; Scott, 2000; Tilly, 2005; Valente, 1995). There is, naturally, an International Network for Social Network Analysis (*www.insna.org*).

There are a number of proprietary software packages for network analysis. These allow ongoing tracking of dynamics such as who are the go-to people on various subjects and issues. Who's at the center of the network? Who are key connectors to subnetwork modules? How close and intense (in traffic and information flows) are network connections? Where are individuals and subgroups located in the network? How dense and large is the network (tracked over time)? Who are the peripheral players? Who are boundary spanners? How is this particular network connected to (networked with) other networks? What is the ebb and flow of network interactions? What inputs generate greater intensity of interactions? What creates positive network "energy" (as defined by members)? What creates negative energy?

Mark Cabaj (2007, 2009a, 2009b) and Eric Leviten-Reid have played the role of developmental evaluators with the Vibrant Communities antipoverty initiative discussed earlier, where one of the developmental evaluator tasks is trying to understand the *essence of community-based efforts to reduce poverty*—not a particular approach, unique practice, or detailed manifestation of that essence, but some more core essence that is both manifest in and transcends all the communities. (*Essence* in this context is a sensitizing concept, as discussed in Chapter 9). Cabaj and Leviten-Reid, as developmental evaluators, facilitate this inquiry into transcendent *essence* as well as generating and sharing lessons among network members.

Complex Systems Development Challenge 8:

Major systems change initiative where the intervention initiative aims to "tip" a system in a major new direction, not just achieve narrow program outcomes; system dynamics come into play including nonlinear and interactive effects (e.g., momentum, achieving critical mass), emergent responses, rapid ripples through the system, and interdependencies between the system (however defined) and its environment (however understood) (Type 5 in Exhibit 10.1)

• *Developmental evaluation purpose and intended evaluation use*: Feedback about observed systems dynamics and emergent interactions that can support development of the systems change process, both deepening understanding of the system and helping those involved respond to what happens at the systems level.

- *Primary intended users and developmental evaluation partners*: Those directing the systems change, which would typically be a team of people, often from different organizations partnering together.

- *Key developmental evaluation questions*: How is the system being defined? What is the baseline system, its boundaries, parts, and interrelationships? What is the vision of a healthier system? What leverage points are being tried to enter and tip the existing system? What systems interrelationships are expected to be affected by the change effort? What are different perspectives about how the system functions and the effects of those different perspectives as the change process unfolds? What are early benchmarks that things are moving in the desired direction? Where is pushback, resistance to the systems change, emerging? What are the implications of resistance for system change tactics? What might a tipping point indicating successful systems change look like?

- *Time line for feedback*: The developmental evaluator will be part of the systems change team and time feedback to fit the pace of activities and ongoing decision making.

- *Appropriate developmental evaluation engagement, design, and methods options*: Systems mapping (visual displays of the baseline system from different perspectives and showing the perceived relationships among the elements that make up the system). Indicators of system functioning over time; indicators of systems change in activities levels and interaction intensity. Feedback from (regular interviews with) key knowledgeables, well placed to observe the system and any changes in it.

- *Example and commentary*: In 1986 the Robert Wood Johnson Foundation began discussing making grants to improve end-of-life care in the United States. This would mean changing the medical and nursing education systems, as well as the health care system generally. Such a massive systems change initiative was complex because con-flict about what to do was high, including those who didn't think anything needed to be done, and it was far from clear how to proceed to bring about the needed changes. Systems change in this case involved changing overlapping subsystems: hospital care systems, medical and nursing education systems, accreditation policies and practices, public health priorities, physicians' practice, senior citizen advocacy systems, and general public understanding, to name but a few. Thus, success would involve both major systems change within particular end-of-life care systems and cross-scale innovations from institutional to professional, national, and international levels.

From 1988 through 1994, the Robert Wood Johnson Foundation funded a landmark study of how Americans die entitled SUPPORT—Study to Understand Prognoses and Preferences for Outcomes and Risks of Treatments. SUPPORT findings documented the inadequacies of care at the end of life (Lynn, 1997). For example, elderly, fatally ill persons were often heroically treated in intensive care units even if their families objected, prolonging suffering and driving up costs. The foundation's investment in SUPPORT was considerable, $31 million over nearly 10 years. The strategic point of entry for systems change was producing and disseminating high-quality research findings about the problems and uncertainties of end-of-life care. The first phase of the research was a descriptive, observational study of 4,301 patients hospitalized with life-threatening medical conditions who were expected to die within 6 months. The findings showed that physicians did not know what patients wanted with regard to resuscitation, even those at high risk of cardiac arrest, and that orders against resuscitation, if written at all, were written in the last few days of life. Most patients who died in the hospital spent their last days on ventilators in intensive care, often with high levels of pain (Lynn, 1997, 2004).

These findings led the research team to develop a comprehensive intervention that included (1) validated prognostic models so that physicians could better assess the likelihood of severe disability or death, (2) specially trained nurses to help patients and their families clarify and assert their wishes, and (3) detailed written instructions about those wishes given to physicians. After 3 years of implementation accompanied by a rigorous evaluation, the results unequivocally showed *no effects*. The evaluation findings showed that those involved had underestimated the depth and complexity of the problem (Lynn, 1997, 2004; Lynn et al., 2000; Patrizi Associates, 2007).

Expecting the evaluation findings to be positive, the foundation was prepared to take the SUPPORT interventions to scale with a national best practices dissemination and diffusion initiative. The unexpected failure of the SUPPORT interventions led to a dramatic and fundamental reconceptualization of what needed to be done, acknowledging the need for a comprehensive systems change approach that targeted organizational, institutional, educational, and economic systems (cross-scale systems change). This included building a new field of medical knowledge, education, and practice—a field focused on *end of life*. Moreover, such a major systems change initiative, they determined, had to be communicated in a way that would capture public and professional emotion and attention.

This is a story of a developmental fork in the road: what was expected to be an initiative taking a proven intervention to scale turned into a more complex, longer-term, and uncertain effort at field building and comprehensive systems change. The evaluation findings stimulated and supported this developmental change of strategy.

The subsequent systems change strategy unfolded in both planned and unplanned ways over a decade. Between 1996 and 2005, the foundation invested $150 million in end-of-life grants (Robert Wood Johnson Foundation, 2009). The retrospective evaluation of that strategy conducted by Patrizi Associates (2007) concluded that in formulating and implementing such a multifaceted and comprehensive systems change:

> There is no one right way to construct a strategy. The most productive approaches seem to land somewhere in between the extremes of uncertainty and certainty, between those program officers who throw up their hands and say the world is too uncertain a place for planning to succeed and those who act as if change can fairly easily be planned via tightly locked "if/then" statements and logic models. The truth is that the level of planning certainty depends on the nature of the problem and its circumstances. But the bigger point is that foundation management has an important role in pushing for clarity in strategy even as it acknowledges uncertainty, identifies where learning is needed, and explicitly makes calculated guesses as new patterns emerge. (p. 2)

The retrospective strategic evaluation concluded that the Robert Wood Johnson Foundation had a major impact in shaping and building the field of *end of life*, including influencing medical and nursing education and preparing the field to deliver better and more appropriate care in hospitals. The combined effects of various initiatives and grants moved the issue "from the fringe to the center of the health care debate" (p. 13). The evaluation documented the following systems change impacts, among others:

1. Created demand for enhanced knowledge and skills in end-of-life care by engaging and convincing the National Board of Medical Examiners and the National Council of State Boards of Nursing to include questions on palliative care in their licensing exams for physicians and nurses; this created incentives to align the rest of the system with the changed standards, generating ripple effects throughout medical education systems.

2. Supported some of the core infrastructure of the emerging field by developing standards of care and the capacity to assess and monitor those standards across institutional settings, including adoption of a new

standard for assessment and treatment of pain.

3. Built a knowledge base for the new field through support for research, publishing, curricula development, and approaches to training faculty, including in areas of clinical care and organization and delivery of services.

4. Created an institutional model, the Center to Advance Palliative Care at Mount Sinai School of Medicine in New York, to meet increased demand for knowledge of palliative care within the hospital setting, which garnered the attention of hospital administrators through the country.

5. Fostered, in partnership with the Project on Death in America, the advancement of careers and emerging leadership in a relatively undeveloped field (Patrizi Associates, 2007; Robert Wood Johnson Foundation, 2009).

The Robert Wood Johnson case example illustrates that systems change benefits from a developmental perspective precisely because such a multifaceted and comprehensive change strategy is complex, requiring ongoing monitoring of and adaptation to emergent issues and evaluation findings, adapting to the dynamics of ripple effects as change in one subsystem (like medical education) affects other subsystems (like hospital procedures), and confronting political, economic, and sociocultural developments in the larger societal context, which is both a target of change and a factor in how systems change unfolds. Multiple evaluation methods and cumulating learning from discrete, project-specific evaluations need to be aggregated and synthesized over time to support learning, adaptation, and interpretation of impacts as the developmental journey unfolds and to inform decision making about where to focus attention to keep momentum moving toward sustainable and lasting change.

This example also illustrates that strategy is an evaluable unit of analysis (*evaluand*) distinctly different from traditional evaluation units of analysis like projects, programs, grants, policies, or even organizations. *Evaluating Strategy* (Patrizi & Patton, in press) invites a developmental evaluation approach (or strategy) precisely because strategy unfolds in both planned and unplanned ways as initial uncertainties (at the moment of planning) turn into complex and emergent realities that require strategic adaptation (Mintzberg, 2007; also see the discussion on strategy in Chapter 1).

Illustration by Mark M. Rogers.

Complex Systems Development Challenge 9:

Advocacy initiative to influence public policy and/ or legislation (Type 1 in Exhibit 10.1; could include some of Type 2; if successful, could move into Type 5)

- *Developmental evaluation purpose and intended evaluation use*: Track how influential policymakers view the issue being advocated to inform development of advocacy tactics, messages, and contacts; adapt as events unfold and new issues arise; and respond to emergent controversies and correct misinformation from initiative opponents.

- *Primary intended users and developmental evaluation partners*: Advocacy leadership team and communications staff in charge of messaging.

- *Key developmental evaluation questions*: How do key policy influentials view the issue of concern in relation to other issues? What are their priorities? What affects their priorities? How are their priorities changing as new information is provided and political events unfold?

- *Time line for feedback*: Periodic feedback based on the nature and timing of the advocacy campaign; during slow periods of laying groundwork, less frequent data collection and feedback; as an issue comes to a critical decision point (e.g., legislation to be voted on), more frequent data collection and feedback. The evaluator works with the advocacy leadership to connect the timing of data collection and feedback to advocacy campaign decision making.

- *Appropriate engagement, design, and methods options*:

1. *Bellwether surveys of knowledgeable, innovative, and influential thought leaders whose views on important policy issues carry substantial weight and predictive value.* Periodic bellwethers data can track the dynamics of an issue in relation to other policy priorities. Bellwether survey results aim to help advocates develop and focus their organizing, contacts, and messaging to increase an issue's understandability, target significant nuances about why the issue matters, increase visibility, and rev up the sense of urgency. The Harvard Family Research Project (HFRP) developed the bellwether methodology to track whether advocacy efforts were gaining traction toward the goal of getting universal preschool onto the state-level policy agenda in California (Blair, 2007). Advocacy campaigns are particularly fertile ground for developmental evaluation, for, as Julia Coffman (2007), one of the pioneers of and leaders in advocacy evaluation has explained, "Advocacy strategy typically evolves over time, and activities and desired outcomes can shift quickly" (p. 1). Bellwether surveys can be used to develop tactics and messages in any legislative initiative. How key policy influentials are perceiving an issue, and the advocacy campaign itself, helps advocates adapt to changing perspectives and emergent conditions.

2. *Tracking media and trends.* While we're on advocacy evaluation and campaigns, developmental evaluation can include systematically tracking how media handle an issue, especially watching for unexpected and emergent coverage that requires a quick response. The campaign to overturn the juvenile death penalty in the United States included a media tracking group that monitored all editorials and news items about the issue as the case made its way to the Supreme Court in the autumn of 2004. Related stories about juvenile crime, especially violent crime, were also monitored. For example, the sniper attacks involving John Lee Malvo, age 17 at the time of his arrest, took place during 3 weeks in October 2002 in the Washington, DC, metropolitan area. Ten people were killed and three others critically injured. The prosecution and trial negotiations in 2004 made headlines as the Supreme Court date to hear arguments about the juvenile death penalty approached; media coverage and public opinion about the Malvo case were part of the dynamical context that the campaign monitored, even though the Supreme Court hearing was on

⌒ An Advocacy Campaign Using Developmental Evaluation

Since 2005, Innovation Network, Inc.—a nonprofit evaluation firm based in Washington, DC—has used a developmental approach in its evaluation of a broad coalition working to enact immigration reform at the federal level. The coalition's strategy involves linking a national-level legislative campaign with grassroots advocacy and a collaboration between diverse organizations representing many sectors, including immigrant rights advocates, labor unions, and faith-based organizations, as well as those on the political left and right. The evaluation, requested by the Atlantic Philanthropies, has had a goal from the outset to provide analysis that would help guide and develop the coalition's programmatic and organizational strategies.

With a directive to focus the evaluation on development and learning, developmental evaluation surfaced as a sensible and appropriate option. The ultimate decision to proceed developmentally came in recognition of the often fast-paced, dynamic, and ever-shifting nature of advocacy and policy change efforts. We at Innovation Network can confirm that programs that tend to benefit from a developmental evaluation never expect to arrive at a steady state of programming because they're constantly tinkering as participants, conditions, learnings, and context change. Moreover, in the complex world of advocacy and policy change, it becomes difficult—if not impossible—to parse out one advocate's impact from the myriad factors that contribute to desired policy and systems changes. Recognizing this, we focused the developmental evaluation on fostering continuous learning so that coalition leadership could make real-time adjustments to their strategies and tactics.

Entering the fifth year of the evaluation, we can highlight three specific characteristics of developmental evaluation that have proven particularly critical to success.

EMBEDDED EVALUATORS

We began, as is usual in our work, by forming an evaluation work group to guide and inform the evaluation design, select and implement the data collection instruments, and analyze and interpret evaluation findings. Evaluation work groups help ensure buy-in to the evaluation and effective use of the results. In a developmental evaluation, evaluation work groups are essential. The immigration coalition evaluation work group is made up of representatives of several organizations participating in the coalition as well as members of the group's central leadership. The evaluators meet regularly with the work group to stay abreast of the coalition's information needs and to present and discuss the implications of new findings. During particularly eventful periods, the work group has met as frequently as every other week. However, even when activity has slowed down, the work group has always met on at least a quarterly basis.

Over time, as evaluators we have effectively become members of a larger team that contributes input into the development of both external and internal strategy. The evaluators are not there to judge the merits of the program, as is sometimes the case with traditional evaluation. The evaluators were "embedded" in order to monitor the coalition's strategies and provide an evaluative perspective.

As embedded evaluators, Innovation Network is regularly present at the coalition's strategy meetings and telephone conference calls. As a result, coalition members came to develop a sense of trust for the developmental evaluators that is atypical of many traditional external evaluations. In turn, as evaluators we gained both an intimate knowledge of the coalition and a level of access to key stakeholders that enabled us to elicit more specific and richer information through corresponding interviews and other data collection activities.

(cont.)

DIVERSE AND INNOVATIVE DATA COLLECTION METHODS

The context of advocacy and policy work presented new methodological challenges requiring innovation. Meaningful data needed to be shared with coalition members in a timely manner (sometimes referred to as "real time" or "right time") so that results could be used effectively. Because the intensity of the immigration reform debate has fluctuated and evolved over time, the evaluation has experimented with different approaches to ensure the evaluation remains both useful and minimally burdensome for the coalition.

One innovative method—the *intense period debrief* (Stuart, 2007)—was developed when it became clear that the narrative behind the coalition's advocacy efforts, particularly on the legislative side, was not being fully documented. Advocacy often involves simultaneous interactions on the part of a number of players, often behind closed doors. As evaluators we were often forced to wait until after periods of heavy activity were over to find out how a particular legislative fight had played out. Using a debrief interview protocol, the evaluators interviewed key players shortly after a policy window or intense period had occurred to capture (1) the public mood and political context of the opportunity window; (2) what happened and how the campaign members responded to events; (3) what strategies they followed; (4) their perspective on the outcomes of the period; and (5) how they would change their strategies going forward based on what they learned during that period.

The evaluators also gathered quantitative data on the coalition's three core strategies, tracking and analyzing: (1) coalition members' contacts with members of Congress, for example, which members of Congress were contacted, what specific messages conveyed, which coalition members were most active, and how many contacts of various kinds occurred; (2) field activities aimed at mobilizing communities around the nation, for example, the overall number held, which cities/ states were most active, and uniformity of messaging; and (3) media content of articles relevant to the campaign, for example, stance on immigration reform, mentions of coalition members, mentions of coalition principles or key messages, and statements made by members of Congress.

Other methods included regular interviews with coalition members about outcomes, benchmarks, and setbacks on the legislative, field, media, and organizational fronts, and a survey of coalition members involved in grassroots advocacy and organizing to get a perspective outside of central leadership on the performance and capacity of the coalition as well as strategies and activities of the campaign. Our observations of meetings and listening in on conference calls provided additional tracking data about campaign developments.

COLLABORATION BETWEEN EVALUATOR, FUNDER, AND GRANTEE

This type of evaluation, in which the coalition's needs are the driving force, requires a close collaboration and engagement between the coalition, its philanthropic funder, and the evaluators, based on trust and transparency. The evaluation work group has served as an important venue for gradually building trust. At these meetings, we have shared honest evaluation feedback that showed that we were there as allies in supporting learning and development, rather than judges.

However, to a large degree, this developmental evaluation approach was only possible through explicit support of the coalition's funder, the Atlantic Philanthropies. Atlantic is outspoken in its views that evaluation should be used to inform strategy development and support continuous learning. Atlantic's evaluation unit—aptly named Strategic Learning and Evaluation—originated the goal that the evaluation should help guide and develop the coalition's strategies. This language—and the corresponding actions of Atlantic's staff—were essential in building the coalition's comfort with this approach.

Note. Contributed by Ehren Reed, Senior Associate with Innovation Network.

a different case from Missouri. Campaign organizers prepared a variety of rapid responses, including getting favorable expert opinion into the discussion quickly, in an effort to affect the public political climate within which the case was heard.

• *Example and commentary*: In the heat and turmoil of public policy debates, things can change quickly. Efforts at immigration reform in the United States in 2008 were affected by the ups and downs of the presidential election campaigning also occurring that summer. At one point it looked as if a bill would pass, but suddenly there was a huge backlash and the legislation died. A large team of immigration reform advocates held daily teleconferences to monitor the ebb and flow of support. It was important to have solid data about how different national legislators viewed immigration reform in relation to other issues. For more on evaluation of the immigration reform campaign, see the sidebar that describes *An Advocacy Campaign Using Developmental Evaluation*.

Complex Systems Development Challenge 10:

Political campaign messaging (Type 1 in Exhibit 10.1)

• *Developmental evaluation purpose and intended evaluation use*: Adapt and fine-tune political messages to target audiences as events unfold and new issues arise.

• *Primary intended users and developmental evaluation partners*: Campaign decision makers and communications staff in charge of messaging.

• *Key developmental evaluation questions*: How do target audiences respond to different messages? Which messages (in content, format, and delivery mode) generate effective responses?

• *Time line for feedback*: Early in the campaign, new messages every month; in the middle of the campaign, new messages every 2 weeks; near the end of the campaign, new

messages weekly or as critical events occur that require immediate response. Evaluation of and feedback about message effectiveness is needed within days after each set of messages are sent out.

• *Appropriate developmental evaluation engagement, design, and methods option*: Randomized assignment and comparison of messages and modes of message delivery (e-mail, text, Twitter, etc.).

• *Example and commentary*: In the heat and turmoil of election campaigns, things can change lightning fast. Candidates for major national offices have communications staff who are constantly updating supporters, mobilizing for major events, and raising funds. They have e-mail and snail-mail lists of thousands, even hundreds of thousands for national campaigns. It's simple, fast, and illuminative to have two, three, or four versions of a communication, send the different versions randomly, and quickly analyze responses, for example, donations, reactions to new policy statements, or feedback on campaign slogans and materials. Or you can send the message randomly using different delivery technologies (e-mail, text messages, Twitter, etc.).

• *Other applications*: This same rapid-development, random-testing, rapid-response approach can be used to get feedback from large networks, associations, and programs with multiple sites. Subsequent communications are fine-tuned based on what is learned about effective messaging and what generates responses, both positive and negative. This is real-time feedback for decision making.

Developmental Evaluation Engagement, Design, and Methods Summary

This chapter has reviewed 10 complex systems innovation and development challenges and suggested appropriate utilization-focused developmental evaluations matched to those challenges. Exhibit 10.3 summarizes

EXHIBIT 10.3 Overview and Summary of Development Challenges and Matching Developmental Evaluation Engagement and Design Options

Complex systems development challenges	Appropriate developmental evaluation engagement, design, and methods options
1. Developing a new, innovative program; uncertainties about how participants will react and what issues will emerge.	Reflective practice sessions with staff and/or participants that track program developments, document changes, and facilitate staff reflection on feedback from participants.
2. Ongoing adaptation and development of a program in response to changing conditions, like new kinds of participants, new technology, new public policies, or fluctuations in the economy.	Direct observation of the program changes as they are implemented. Follow up with participants to find out their views of the changes and see how it affects desired outcomes.
3. Building on the successes of a completed program to extrapolate general principles that can inform development of and support for new initiatives in new settings elsewhere.	First, ongoing tracking results of a successful program to substantiate longer-term results; this can be done with periodic follow-ups gathering outcomes and impact data. Second, tracking efforts at disseminating the results and promoting adaptation of the innovation elsewhere; documenting and evaluating adaptations in new settings.
4. Many different agencies and project teams working collaboratively on the same problem with complicated interactions, impossible-to-attribute outcomes, diverse responses to unexpected events and crises, and uncertainties about cumulative and aggregate impacts.	Outcome mapping, contribution analysis, and evaluator monitoring, documenting, and synthesizing planned and emergent patterns in the collaboration, and reflective practice of group members around those patterns and their implications.
5. Community generating and developing its own community-based response to a problem, like poverty.	Participatory evaluation methods in which community members undertake data collection, gather and analyze data on primary community indicators, participate in designing surveys that they administer as part of the initiative, conduct interviews, and do descriptive reports on community events and important meetings (e.g., who is there, who is not there, what happens, why, and what are the consequences and impacts).
6. Humanitarian crisis: earthquake, tsunami, flooding, civil war; chaos and catastrophe reign; many people are homeless and hungry, lack basic services; relief agencies and emergency teams appear needing to be coordinated; aid and assistance requires management.	Direct independent observation. Listening and tracking posts. Rapid reconnaissance. Networked reporting.
7. Supporting a network to take an innovation to scale (dissemination) through adaptation.	Social network analysis tracking interactions around the going-to-scale and diffusion processes. Cross-site and cross-scale synthesis of local-level evaluations of adoption and adaptation experiences.

(cont.)

Complex systems development challenges	Appropriate developmental evaluation engagement, design, and methods options
8. Major systems change initiative where the intervention initiative aims to "tip" a system in a major new direction, not just achieve narrow program outcomes; system dynamics come into play including nonlinear and interactive effects (e.g., momentum, attaining critical mass), emergent responses, rapid ripples through the system, and interdependencies between the system (however defined) and its environment (however understood).	Systems mapping (visual displays of the baseline system from different perspectives, showing the perceived relationships among the elements that make up the system). Indicators of system functioning over time; indicators of systems change activities levels. Feedback provided from regular interviews, observations, revised mapping, and new systems understandings.
9. Advocacy initiative to influence public policy and/or legislation.	*Bellwether surveys* of knowledgeable, innovative, and influential thought leaders whose views on important policy issues carry substantial weight and predictive value. *Tracking media and trends.*
10. Political campaign messaging.	Randomized assignment and comparison of messages and modes of message delivery (e-mail, text, Twitter, etc.).

these challenges and matching engagement and design approaches. We can conclude several things about design and methods from this chapter and the rest of the book.

1. *The process of engagement between the primary intended users (social innovators) and the developmental evaluator is as much the method of developmental evaluation as any particular design, methods, and data-collection tools.* Chapter 9 provided an in-depth example of reflective practice on a sensitizing concept (participation *as Māori* vs. participation *by Māori*) in which the relationship between the evaluators and the innovation team, and their inquiry together into what was being developed, was the heart of developmental evaluation.

2. *Developmental evaluation does not rely on or advocate any particular evaluation method, design, or tool.* A developmental evaluation can include any kind of data (quantitative, qualitative, mixed), any kind of design (e.g., naturalistic, experimental), and any kind of focus (processes, outcomes, impacts, costs, and cost–benefit, among many possibili-

ties), depending on the nature and stage of an innovation and the priority questions that will support development of and decision making about the innovation. This can include randomized controlled trials, surveys, focus groups, interviews, observations, performance data, community indicators, and network analysis—whatever sheds light on key questions.

3. *Whatever methods are used or data are collected, rapid feedback is essential. Speed matters.* Dynamic complexities don't slow down or wait for evaluators to write their reports, get them carefully edited, and then approved by higher authorities. Any method can be used but will have to be adapted to the necessities of speed, real-time reporting, and just-in-time, in-the-moment decision making. That's a major reason the developmental evaluator is part of the innovation team, to be present in real time as issues arise and decisions have to be made.

4. *Methods can be emergent and flexible; designs can be dynamic.* Contrary to the usual practice in evaluation of fixed designs that are implemented as planned, developmen-

tal evaluation designs can change as the innovation unfolds and changes. If surveys and interviews are used, the questions may change from one administration to the next, discarding items that have revealed little or are no longer relevant, and adding items that address new issues. The sample can be emergent (Patton, 2002, chap. 5) as new participants, partners, and sites emerge, and others are abandoned. Both baselines and benchmarks can be revised and updated as new information emerges. (One of the inquiry frameworks in Chapter 8 was an actual–ideal comparative framework with emergent and retrospective baselines.)

5. *Developmental evaluators need to be agile, open, interactive, flexible, observant, and have a high tolerance for ambiguity.* The developmental evaluator is, in part, the instrument. Because the evaluation is co-created and the developmental evaluator is part of the innovation team, bringing an evaluation perspective and evaluative thinking to the team, the evaluator's capacities to be part of the team and facilitate the evaluation elements of the innovative process both involves essential people skills and is part of the method for developmental evaluation. The advice from experienced developmental evaluators offered throughout this book has affirmed and reinforced this point.

6. *Reasoning is at the heart of developmental evaluation analysis, synthesis, interpretation, and shared meaning making with the innovation team members.* Reasoning: "The only method is to be very intelligent." Poet T. S. Eliot made this observation about writing poetry (quoted in Gross, 2009, p. 21), but it could also be said of developmental evaluation. Being intelligent, however, is not just (or even primarily) about book learning. It includes street smarts, organizational smarts, emotional intelligence (Goleman, 2006), and "doing one's damnedest with one's mind, no holds barred," as asserted by Nobel Prize–winning physicist Percy W. Bridgman when asked to describe the scientific method (quoted at the opening of the chapter). Abduction, or

∿ Dynamic Research Designs

In a ground-breaking study, McTavish, Brent, Cleary, and Knudsen (1975) studied implementation of 126 research projects funded across seven federal agencies. All 126 projects were rated by independent judges along seven descriptive methodological scales. Both original proposals and final reports were rated; the results showed substantial instability between the two. The researchers concluded that designs are highly dynamic.

Our primary conclusion from the Predictability Study is that the quality of final report methodology is essentially not predictable from proposal or interim report documentation. This appears to be due to a number of factors. First, research is characterized by significant change as it develops over time. Second, unanticipated events force shifts in direction. Third, the character and quality of information available early in a piece of research makes assessment of some features of methodology difficult or impossible. (pp. 62–63)

Earlier in the report, they had pointed out that

among the more salient reasons for the low predictability from early to late documentation is the basic change which occurs during the course of most research. It is, after all, a risky pursuit rather than a pre-programmed product. Initial plans usually have to be altered once the realities of data or opportunities and limitations become known. Typically, detailed plans for analysis and reporting are postponed and revised. External events also seem to have taken an expected toll in the studies we examined. . . . Both the context of research and the phenomena being researched are typically subject to great change. (p. 56) thinking like a detective, can be a particularly important and useful form of reasoning (see the discussion on abductive reasoning in Chapter 9).

Developmental Evaluation's Niche within Evaluation

As I end this long journey exploring the niche of developmental evaluation, let me refer the reader back to Chapter 1 and Exhibit 1.2 (pp. 23–26), which provides an overview of the niche of developmental evaluation. If you've read this book sequentially, I would think that in returning to that overview and summary table, you might return to where we began and know that place anew with deeper understandings of the niche distinctions I offered there. In that summary I contrasted developmental evaluation with some broad-brush traditional approaches to evaluation to help, as I wrote in introducing that exhibit, *position developmental evaluation in the many-starred evaluation universe.* Those comparisons and contrasts are meant to be suggestive and illuminative, not definitive. Any one contrast, I noted, is arguable, possibly overgeneralized, and oversimplified. Viewed as a whole, however, I hope the integration of those many elements provides a sense of what developmental evaluation offers.

And as the completion of this journey takes us back to the beginning, let me end by taking us all the way back to the beginning.

The First Developmental Evaluation: A Creation Story

Because I value evaluative thinking and want to bring others to value it, I look for ways to connect people to evaluative thinking through things they're already familiar with. That's how I got into telling creation stories and interpreting them through an evaluation lens. For many years I've done

this for evaluation thinking in general. To close this book, I want to do it for developmental evaluation.

One of the few universals in the world is that every culture has a creation story, an explanation for how a particular group of people in a particular place, came to be. I've found that taking a familiar creation story, and looking at it from an evaluation perspective, connects with people and opens up a dialogue about the nature of evaluation. Since the first edition of *Utilization-Focused Evaluation* in 1978, where this story first appeared, I have opened workshops with an evaluation version of the traditional biblical creation story and, as many readers of this book have experienced, I often use this to open speeches and training sessions. It goes like this:

> *In the beginning God created the heaven and the earth.*
> *Then God stood back, viewed everything made, and proclaimed "Behold, it is very good." And the evening and the morning were the sixth day.*
> *And on the seventh day God rested from all work.*
> *God's archangel came then, asking, "God, how do you know that what you have created is 'very good'? What are your criteria? On what data do you base your judgment? Just what results were you expecting to attain? And aren't you a little close to the situation to make a fair and unbiased evaluation?"*
> *God thought about these questions all that day and God's rest was greatly disturbed. On the eighth day God said, "Lucifer, go to hell."*
> *Thus was evaluation born in a blaze of glory.*
> (Patton, 2008c, p. 1)

This is essentially a summative evaluation. God looks at creation and renders an overall judgment of merit and worth: "It is good." A great many creation stories around the world have this form in which a god, or gods, create the world, stand back, and congratulate themselves on a job well done. Summative self-evaluation! I like to ask program practitioners how credible they find God's summative self-evaluation. Most find it to be a bit on the self-serving, self-congratulatory side. Then I ask them about the credibility of their own judgments about their effectiveness. Hmmmmm. Let there be light.

On my first trip to New Zealand for an Australasian Evaluation Society meeting held in Aukland, when I first met Kate McKegg whose work with Nan Wehipeihana and Māori programs I featured in Chapter 9, I learned about and was quite taken with the Māori creation story, in part because it is not summative. Indeed, it is a developmental evaluation story—and thus tells of the world's first developmental evaluation. Let me hasten to add that one of the characteristics of creation stories is that there tend to be multiple versions and that different storytellers emphasize, add, or delete different elements depending on the occasion and the point the storyteller wants to make. I've heard versions of this story with different emphases from both Māori and *Pakeha* colleagues, and have read somewhat different accounts in books and on websites about Māori culture and history. With that caveat in mind, let me share my favorite version and the one I use to illustrate developmental evaluation.

> In the beginning *Ranginui* (Rangi), Sky Father, and *Papatuanuku* (Papa), Earth Mother, were intertwined in a fierce embrace. They bore their children between them in a tight, closed space that shut out all light. Confined in darkness, the children became disgruntled and began to plot to separate their parents to create more room and light. After considerable sibling conflict and failed efforts by some of the weaker children, *Tāne Mahuta* (Tane) tried. He had carefully observed the failures of his siblings, who tried pushing the parents apart with their arms. Instead, he placed his shoulders against the earth and his feet against the sky and pushed slowly with both his upper and lower body. He strained with all his might. Seeing what he was doing, his siblings joined their strength to the effort. Soon, and yet not soon, for the time was vast, the Sky and Earth began to yield. Eventually, the separation was complete, and a clearly defined sky and earth emerged.

As the light poured in, Tane saw Rangi, the Sky Father, weeping at the separation from his beloved, and his tears became the rain. Tane also saw that he had exposed the nakedness of Papa, Earth Mother. Ashamed and embarrassed, Tane set about to clothe his mother by planting trees in the earth to adorn her. But because he was inexperienced and ignorant of how plants grow, he planted the trees upside down. He put the leaves in the earth, instead of the roots. When he had done this, he stood back and looked at his handiwork. Even as he gazed at what he had done, he could see that the trees were dying.

Tane reflected on what he saw, took new trees, tried again, and laid them flat on the earth. The trees began to shrivel.

So he tried yet again, this time planting the roots in the ground, with the leaves in the air. Immediately birds flew into the branches and animals came to graze in the shade. He smiled, satisfied. He instantly understood that the trees were a part of and connected to other living systems, so planting trees was also to develop a forest with many interdependent plants and animals living together. With this understanding, and continuing to learn about how to sustain healthy forests for his Mother Earth, *Tāne Mahuta* became the god of forests.

This Māori creation story is quite different from the summative evaluation of Genesis. *Tāne Mahuta* is creating a new world. He is an innovator. He watches and learns from what his siblings try that doesn't work. Once he sets out to clothe his Mother Earth, he tries one thing, and when that doesn't work, he tries something else. He's not even sure what he's trying to create. The outcomes are uncertain. But he knows it when he sees it, when it emerges.

And so we have a creation story of developmental evaluation, of trying something out, watching what emerges, seeing whether or not it works, and then, if finding it did not work, changing the practice to something that does work. In this way new developments are created and social innovation moves forward. Developmental evaluation is itself emergent, still being developed. This book is by no means the last word. As I engage with innovators and other evaluators around developmental evaluation, clarifying its niche, expanding and contracting its boundaries, adapting methods and tools to developmental purposes, figuring out what it is and is not, my overwhelming sense is of forward-propelled development. And I am reminded, in this regard, of Woody Allen's observation near the end of the 1977 Academy Award–winning film *Annie Hall*: "Relationships are like sharks; they have to keep moving forward or they die."

Developmental evaluation is a relationship between social innovators and evaluators, a co-created, dynamic, and ever-emergent relationship. And this developmental evaluation relationship, like sharks, has to keep moving forward or it dies.

This book has been an invitation to join in and contribute to that ongoing development and forward movement.

References

ABCD Institute. (2009). *Asset-based community development. www.abcdinstitute.org.*

Ackoff, R. L. (1999). *Ackoff's best: His classic writings on management.* New York: Wiley.

Akerlof, G. A., & Shiller, R. J. (2009). *Animal spirits: How human psychology drives the economy, and why it matters for global capitalism.* Princeton, NJ: Princeton University Press.

Aliseda, A. (2006). *Abductive reasoning: Logical investigations into discovery and explanation.* Dordrecht, The Netherlands: Springer.

Alkin, M. C. (1985). *A guide for evaluation decision makers.* Beverly Hills, CA: Sage.

Alkin, M. C. (Ed.). (1990). *Debates on evaluation.* Newbury Park, CA: Sage.

Alkin, M. C. (2004). *Evaluation roots: Tracing theorists' views and influences.* Thousand Oaks, CA: Sage.

Alkin, M. C., Daillak, R., & White, P. (1979). *Using evaluations: Does evaluation make a difference?* Beverly Hills, CA: Sage.

Alkin, M. C., & Patton, M. Q. (1987). Working both sides of the street: The client perspective on evaluation. In J. Nowakowski (Ed.), *New Directions for Evaluation,* no. 36, 19–32.

American Evaluation Association (AEA). (1995). Guiding principles for evaluators. Task Force on Guiding Principles for Evaluators. *New Directions for Evaluation,* no. 66, 19–34. *www.eval. org/Publications/GuidingPrinciples.asp.*

American Evaluation Association (AEA). (2009). AEA awards honor contributions to the field of evaluation. *www.eval.org/awards.09winners. asp.*

Appreciative Inquiry Commons. (2009). Discipline of positive change. *appreciativeinquiry. case.edu.*

Argyris, C., & Schön, D. (1978). *Organizational learning: A theory of action perspective.* Reading, MA: Addison-Wesley.

Baker, A., & Sabo, K. (2004). *Participatory evaluation essentials: A guide for nonprofit organizations and their evaluation partners.* Cambridge, MA: Bruner Foundation.

Bamberger, M., & Podems, D. (2002). Feminist evaluation in the international development context. *New Directions for Evaluation, 96*, 83–96.

Belasco, J. A. (1991). *Teaching the elephant to dance: The manager's guide to empowering change*. New York: Plume (Penguin Books).

Benjamin, L. M., & Greene, J. C. (2009). From program to network: The evaluator's role in today's public problem-solving environment. *American Journal of Evaluation, 30*(3), 296–309.

Berry, W. (2006). *The way of ignorance—and other essays*. Berkeley, CA: Counterpoint Books.

Best Practices. (2009). *www.best-in-class.com*.

Bialik, C. (2009, May 20). Top-ten lists abound, but following the herd can make you wonder about the wisdom of crowds. *Wall Street Journal. online.wsj.com/article/SB124277816017037275. html?mod=djemnumbers*.

Birinyi, L. (2009, January 5). Interview with Laszlo Birinyi. *Barron's, 89*(1), 32–33.

Blackburn, S. (2005). *Truth: A guide*. New York: Oxford University Press.

Blair, E. (2007). Evaluating an issue's position on the policy agenda: The bellwether methodology. *Evaluation Exchange, 13*(1–2), 29.

Blumer, H. (1954). What is wrong with social theory? *American Sociological Review, 19*, 3–10.

Boisot, M. H. (1998). *Knowledge assets: Securing competitive advantage in the information economy*. New York: Oxford University Press.

Boisot, M. H., MacMillan, I. C., & Han, K. S. (2008). *Explorations in information space: Knowledge, actor, and firms*. New York: Oxford University Press.

Booz Allen Hamilton. (2009). *What it takes to change government*. McLean, VA: Author. *www.boozallen.com/publications/what-it-takes-to-change-government*.

Bornstein, D. (2007). *How to change the world: Social entrepreneurs and the power of new ideas*. New York: Oxford University Press.

Breiger, R. L. (2004). The analysis of social networks. In M. Hardy & A. Bryman (Eds.), *Handbook of data analysis* (pp. 505–526). London: Sage.

Brinkerhoff, R. (2003). *The success case method*. San Francisco: Berrett Koehler.

Brinkerhoff, R. (2005). Success case method. In S. Mathison (Ed.), *Encyclopedia of evaluation* (pp. 401–402). Thousand Oaks, CA: Sage.

Brooks, D. (2008, December 16). Lost in the crowd. *New York Times*, p. A37. *www.nytimes. com/2008/12/16/opinion/16brooks.html?_r=1*.

Buckingham, M., & Coffman, C. (1999). *First,* break all the rules: What the world's greatest managers do differently. New York: Simon & Schuster.

Burke, D. D. (2007). System dynamics-based computer simulations and evaluation. In B. Williams & I. Iman (Eds.), *Systems concepts in evaluation: An expert anthology* (pp. 47–59). Point Reyes, CA: EdgePress of Inverness.

Burns, J. (2009). *Goddess of the market: Ayn Rand and the American right*. New York: Oxford University Press.

Burton, R. A. (2008). *On being certain: Believing you are right even when you're not*. New York: St. Martin's Griffin.

Business Strategy Innovation. (2009). *Unnovation award. www.business-strategy-innovation. com/2007/08/unnovation-award-inaugural.html*.

Butler, E., & Myers, T. (2007). *Grand obsession: Harvey Butchart and the exploration of the Grand Canyon*. Flagstaff, AZ: Puma Press.

Cabaj, M. (2007). *The land of big ideas*. Waterloo, Ontario, Canada: Tamarack Vital Communities. *www.tamarackcommunity.ca/downloads/ index/MC_Big_Ideas.pdf*.

Cabaj, M. (2009a). Framing poverty as a complex issue. *Engage!, 6*(9), 1–2. *www.tamarackcommunity.ca/index.php*.

Cabaj, M. (2009b). *Understanding poverty as a complex issue and why that matters*. Ottawa, Ontario, Canada: Caledon Institute for Social Policy.

Canadian Evaluation Society (CES). (2010). *Competencies for Canadian evaluation practice*. Ottawa, Ontario: Author. *www.evaluationcanada. ca/txt/20090531_competencies_companion.pdf*.

Carline, D. (2005). Know one another. *The Australian Friend: Journal of the Religious Society of Friends in Australia*, pp. 9–10.

Carlsson, J., Eriksson-Baaz, M., Fallenius, A. M., & Lövgren, E. (1999). *Are evaluations useful?: Cases from Swedish development co-operation*. Stockholm: SIDA Department for Evaluation and Internal Audit.

Carver, J. (2006). *Boards that make a difference* (3rd ed.). San Francisco: Jossey-Bass.

Chamberlayne, P., Bornat, J., & Wengraf, T. (2000). *The turn to biographical methods in social science*. London: Routledge.

Chen, H. (2005). Theory-driven evaluation. In S. Mathison (Ed.), *Encyclopedia of evaluation* (pp. 415–419). Thousand Oaks, CA: Sage.

Chen, H. (2009, November 12). *Using context, evidence, and program theory to build external validity*. Discussion at the American Evaluation Association annual conference, Orlando, FL.

Christensen, C. M., Baumann, H., Ruggles, R., & Sadtler, T. M. (2006, December). Disruptive innovation for social change. *Harvard Business Review, 84*, 94–101.

Christensen, C. M., Grossman, J. H., & Hwang, J. (2008). *The innovator's prescription: A disruptive solution for health.* New York: McGraw-Hill.

Coffman, J. (2007). What's different about evaluating advocacy and policy change? *Evaluation Exchange, 13*, 2–4.

Cohen, R. (2009, June 7). Ask not for a great line. *New York Times. www.nytimes.com/2009/06/08/opinion/08iht-edcohen.html?_r=1.*

Collins, J. (2001). *Good to great: Why some companies make the leap . . . and others don't.* New York: HarperBusiness.

Columbia Accident Investigation Board. (2003). *Final report* (Vols. I–VI). Washington, DC: U.S. Government Printing Office. (See also *caib. nasa.gov.*)

Community Kitchens. (2009). *Training manual.* Washington, DC: DC Central Kitchen. *www. dccentralkitchen.org/dcck/kinc/Left_Navigation/Training_Manual/General_Information/General-Information.shtml.*

Conger, S. (2009). Social inventions. *Innovation Journal, 14*(2). *www.innovation.cc/books/conger_social_inventions1_09232009min.pdf.*

Copeland, R. (1995). *Rhetoric, hermeneutics, and translation in the Middle Ages: Academic traditions and vernacular texts.* Cambridge, UK: Cambridge University Press.

Cousins, J. B. (2001). Do evaluator and program practitioner perspectives converge in collaborative evaluation? *Canadian Journal of Evaluation, 16*(2), 113–133.

Cousins, J. B. (Ed.). (2007). *Process use. New Directions for Evaluation,* no. 116.

Cousins, J. B., & Whitmore, E. (2007). Framing participatory evaluation. *New Directions for Evaluation, 114,* 87–105.

Covey, S. R. (2004). *The seven habits of highly effective people.* New York: Free Press.

Cronbach, L. J. (1975). Beyond the two disciplines of scientific psychology. *American Psychologist, 30,* 116–127.

Cronbach, L. J. (1982). *Designing evaluations of educational and social programs.* San Francisco: Jossey-Bass.

Cronbach, L. J. (1988, August–September). Playing with chaos. *Educational Researcher, 17*(6), 46–49.

Cronbach, L. J., & Associates. (1980). *Toward reform of program evaluation.* San Francisco: Jossey-Bass.

Cross, J. E., Dickmann, E., Newman-Gonchar, R., & Fagan, J. M. (2009). Using mixed-method and network analysis on measure development of interagency collaboration. *American Journal of Evaluation, 30*(3), 310–329.

Czeisler, C. A. (2006). Sleep deficit: The performance killer. *Harvard Business Review, 84*(10), 53–59.

Czeisler, C. A. (2009, January 4). Asleep at the wheel. *New York Times,* p. B4. (See also *drowsydriving.org/about/facts-and-stats.*)

Daigneault, P., & Jacob, S. (2009). Toward accurate measurement of participation: Rethinking the conceptualization and operationalization of participatory evaluation. *American Journal of Evaluation, 30*(3), 330–348.

Dallaire, R. A., & Beardsley, B. (2004). *Shake hands with the devil: The failure of humanity in Rwanda,* Toronto: Random House Canada.

Dart, J. J., Drysdale, G., Cole, D., & Saddington, M. (2000). The most significant change approach for monitoring an Australian extension project. *PLA Notes, 38,* 47–53. London: International Institute for Environment and Development.

Datta, L., with Miller, R. (2004). The professional development of Lois-Ellin Datta: The oral history project. *American Journal of Evaluation, 25,* 243–253.

Davies, R., & Dart, J. (2005). *The "most significant change" (MSC) technique: A guide to its use. mande.co.uk/docs/MSCGuide.htm.*

De Coninck, J., Chaturvedi, K., Haagsma, B., Griffioen, H., & van der Glas, M. (2008). *Planning, monitoring and evaluation in development organisations.* London: Sage.

Denzin, N. K., & Lincoln, Y. S. (2000). Introduction: The discipline and practice of qualitative research. In N. K. Denzin & Y. S. Lincoln (Eds.), *Handbook of qualitative research* (2nd ed., pp. 1–28). Thousand Oaks, CA: Sage.

Dick, B. (2009a). *Action research resources. www.scu.edu.au/schools/gcm/ar/arhome.html.*

Dick, B. (2009b). *What is action research? www.scu.edu.au/schools/gcm/ar/whatisar.html.*

Dick, B., & Mason, B. (2008). Hypermedia methods for qualitative research. In S. N. Hesse-Biber & P. Leavy (Eds.), *Handbook of emergent methods* (pp. 571–600). New York: Guilford Press.

Dominique, J. (n.d.). The World Trade Organization (WTO) and Caribbean bananas. News-

Dominica.com. *www.newsdominica.com/articles/articles.cfm?Id=1884.*

Drucker, P. (1998). *Lessons in leadership.* San Francisco: Jossey-Bass.

Drucker, P. (2008). *The five most important questions you will ever ask about your organization.* San Francisco: Jossey-Bass.

Durie, M. (2005). Te Tai Tini: Transformation. Paper presented at Hui Taumata, Wellington, NZ. *www.temata.massey.ac.nz/massey/research/research-centres/te-mata-o-te-tau/publications/publications_home.cfm*

Durie, M. (2007). *Nga Kahui Pou: Launching Maori futures.* Wellington, NZ: Huia.

Durland, M., & Fredericks, K. (Eds.). (2005). *Social network analysis in program evaluation. New Directions for Evaluation,* no. 107.

Earles, W., Lynn, R., & Jakel, J. (n. d.). *Transformational collaboration. www.engagingcommunities2005.org/abstracts/Earles-Wendy-final.pdf.*

EASY-ECO. (2009). Evaluation of sustainability. European Conferences and Training Courses. *www.sustainability.eu/easy.*

Elliott, C. (1999). *Locating the energy for change: An introduction to appreciative inquiry.* Winnipeg, Manitoba, Canada: International Institute for Sustainable Development. *www.iisd.org/pdf/appreciativeinquiry.pdf.*

Elliott, J. (2005). Action research. In S. Mathison (Ed.), *Encyclopedia of evaluation* (pp. 8–10). Thousand Oaks, CA: Sage.

Eoyang, G. H. (2003). *Voices from the field: An introduction to human systems dynamics.* Circle Pines, MN: Human Systems Dynamics Institute Press.

Eoyang, G. H. (2006, January). What?: So what?: Now what? *Attractors,* Info-letter of the Human Systems Dynamics Institute, *3*(1). *www.hsdinstitute.org/learn-more/read-the-latest/attractors/archive/18-ATTRACTORS-Jan-2006.pdf.*

Eoyang, G. H. (2007). Human systems dynamics: Complexity-based approach to a complex evaluation. In B. Williams & I. Iman (Eds.), *Systems concepts in evaluation: An expert anthology* (pp. 123–139). Point Reyes, CA: EdgePress of Inverness.

Eoyang, G. H. (2008a, October). Dynamical change. *Attractors,* Info-letter of the Human Systems Dynamics Institute, *5*(10). *www.hsdinstitute.org/learn-more/read-the-latest/attractors/archive/51_-_ATTRACTORS_v2-_Oct_2008.pdf.*

Eoyang, G. H. (2008b, November 6). *What difference does it make?: Systems approaches to evaluation.* Think tank at the American Evaluation Association annual conference, Denver, CO.

Eoyang, G. H. (2009, August). *Simple rules for complex times. Attractors,* Info-letter of the Human Systems Dynamics Institute, *6*(8).

Eoyang, G. H., & Berkas, T. (1998). Evaluation in a complex adaptive system. Circle Pines, MN: Chaos Limited. *www.chaos-limited.com/EvalinCAS.pdf.*

Erikson, K. (1995). *A new species of trouble: The human experience of modern disasters.* New York: Norton.

Fetterman, D. M., & Wandersman, A. (Eds.). (2005). *Empowerment evaluation principles in practice.* New York: Guilford Press.

Free the Slaves. (2009). Ending slavery. *www.freetheslaves.net/Page.aspx?pid=292.*

Freeman, L. (2006). *The development of social network analysis.* Vancouver, BC, Canada: Empirical Press.

Friedman, T. L. (2008, October 14). Why how matters. *New York Times. www.nytimes.com/2008/10/15/opinion/15friedman.html.*

Friedman, T. L. (2009, July 15). Goodbye Iraq, and good luck. *New York Times,* p. A25.

Funnell, S., & Rogers, P. (2010). *Purposeful program theory: Effective use of logic models and theories of change.* San Francisco: Jossey-Bass.

Gamble, J. A. (2008). *A developmental evaluation primer.* Montreal: J. W. McConnell Family Foundation.

Gandhi, M. (2009, October 9). Quoted by Michael Kesterton. *The Toronto Globe and Mail. www.theglobeandmail.com/life/facts-and-arguments/no-news-is-bad-news-a-genuine-flake-and-pms-retirement-job/article1325143/.*

Garnsey, E., & McGlade, J. (Eds.). (2006). *Complexity and co-evolution: Continuity and change in socio-economic systems.* Cheltenham, UK: Edward Elgar.

Gawande, A. (2004, January 12). Medical dispatch: The mop-up. *New Yorker,* pp. 34–40.

Gawande, A. (2007a, May 1). The power of negative thinking. *New York Times,* p. A23.

Gawande, A. (2007b, December 10). The checklist. *New Yorker. www.newyorker.com/reporting/2007/12/10/071210fa_fact_gawande.*

Gertner, J. (2008, December 14). Positive deviance. *New York Times Magazine,* p. 68. *www.nytimes.com/2008/12/14/magazine/14ideas-section3-t-005.html?scp=2&sq=Positive%20deviance&st=cse.*

Gharajedaghi, J. (2006). *Systems thinking: Managing chaos and complexity* (2nd ed.). Boston: Butterworth-Heinemann.

Ghere, G., King, J. A., Stevahn, L., & Minnema, J. (2006). A professional development unit for reflecting on program evaluation competencies. *American Journal of Evaluation, 27*(1), 108–123.

Gigerenzer, G., Todd, P., & ABC Research Group. (1999). *Simple heuristics that make us smart.* New York: Oxford University Press.

Gilbert, D. (2009, May 20). What you don't know makes you nervous. *New York Times. happydays. blogs.nytimes.com/2009/05/20/what-you-dont-know-makes-you-nervous/.*

Gilman, G., Hargreaves, M., Au, M., & Kim, J. (2009). *Assessment of clinician workforce capacity issues in Ryan White HIV/AIDS program care settings.* Cambridge, MA: Mathematica Policy Research, Inc.

Gladwell, M. (2002). *The tipping point: How little things can make a big difference.* Boston: Little, Brown.

Gleick, J. (1987). *Chaos: Making a new science.* New York: Penguin Books.

Goleman, D. (2006). *Emotional intelligence: Why It can matter more than IQ* (10th Anniversary ed.). New York: Bantam.

Golembiewski, B. (2000). Three perspectives on appreciative inquiry. *OD Practitioner, 32*(1), 53–58.

Government Accountability Office (GAO). (2009). *Program evaluation: A variety of rigorous methods can help identify effective interventions* (GAO-10-30). Washington, DC: Author. *www.gao.gov/Products/GAO-10-30.*

Greenspan, A. (2007). *The age of turbulence: Adventures in a new world.* New York: Penguin Press.

Greenwald, H. P. (2007). *Organizations: Management without control.* Thousand Oaks, CA: Sage.

Groopman, J. (2007, January 29). What's the trouble?: How doctors think. *New Yorker,* pp. 36–41.

Gross, S. (2009). *Seven turning points: Leading through pivotal transitions in organizational life.* Saint Paul, MN: Fieldstone Alliance.

Guba, E. G. (1978). *Toward a methodology of naturalistic inquiry in educational evaluation.* (CSE Monograph Series in Evaluation No. 8). Los Angeles: Center for the Study of Evaluation, University of California.

Guba, E. G., & Lincoln, Y. S. (1981). *Effective evaluation: Improving the usefulness of evaluation results through responsive and naturalistic approaches.* San Francisco: Jossey-Bass.

Gunderson, L., & Holling, C. S. (Eds.). (2002). *Panarchy: Understanding transformations in human and natural systems.* Washington, DC: Island Press.

Hage, J., & Aiken, M. (1970). *Social change in complex organizations.* New York: Random House.

Hanna, N., & Picciotto, R. (Eds.). (2002). *Making development work.* London: Transaction.

Hargreaves, M., & Parsons, B. (2009, November 11). *Evaluating complex system interventions.* American Evaluation Association annual conference workshop, Orlando, FL.

Hargreaves, M., & Paulsell, D. (2009). *Evaluating systems change efforts to support evidence-based home visiting: Concepts and methods.* Cambridge, MA: Mathematica Policy Research, Inc.

Harman, G. (1965). The inference to the best explanation. *Philosophical Review, 74,* 88–95.

Heller, A. C. (2009). *Ayn Rand and the world she made.* New York: Nan A. Talese.

Henderson, T. H., & Patton, M. Q. (1985). Agricultural extension for rural transformation: The CAEP model. In P. I. Gomes (Ed.), *Rural development in the Caribbean* (pp. 194–221). New York: St. Martin's Press.

Hesse-Biber, S. N., & Leavy, P. (Eds.). (2008). *Handbook of emergent methods.* New York: Guilford Press.

Hine, C. (2008). Internet research as emergent practice. In S. N. Hesse-Biber & P. Leavy (Eds.), *Handbook of emergent methods* (pp. 525–542). New York: Guilford Press.

Hirschhorn, L., & Gilmore, T. N. (2004). Ideas in philanthropic field building: Where they come from and how they are translated into actions. In P. Patrizi, K. Sherwood, & A. Spector (Eds.), *Practice matters: The Improving Philanthropy Project.* New York: Foundation Center. *foundationcenter.org/gainknowledge/research/pdf/practicematters_06_execsum.pdf.*

Hofstetter, C. H., & Alkin, M. (2003). Evaluation use revisited. In T. Kellaghan, D. L. Stufflebeam, & L. Wingate (Eds.), *International handbook of education evaluation* (pp. 189–196). Boston: Kluwer.

Holling, C. S. (Ed.). (1978). *Adaptive environmental assessment and management.* New York: Wiley.

Homer-Dixon, T. (2006). *The upside of down: Catastrophe, creativity, and the renewal of civilization.* Toronto: Knopf.

Hopson, R. (Ed.). (2000). *How and why language matters in evaluation. New Directions for Evaluation,* no. 86.

House, E. R. (2005). Qualitative evaluation and changing social policy. In N. Denzin & Y. S. Lincoln (Eds.), *Handbook of qualitative research* (3rd ed., pp. 1069–1081). Thousand Oaks, CA: Sage.

House, E. R., & Howe, K. (1999). *Values in evaluation and social research.* Thousand Oaks, CA: Sage.

House, E. R., & Howe, K. (2000). Deliberative democratic evaluation: Evaluation as a democratic process. *New Directions for Evaluation,* no. 85, 3–12.

Humfress, C. (2007). *Orthodoxy and the courts in late antiquity.* New York: Oxford University Press.

Imas, L. G. M., & Rist, R. (2009). *The road to results: Designing and conducting development evaluations.* Washington, DC: World Bank.

Inbar, M. (1979). *Routine decision-making.* Beverly Hills, CA: Sage.

Independent Evaluation Group (IEG). (2009). *Annual review of development effectiveness.* Washington, DC: World Bank.

Infinite Innovations. (2009). *Brainstorming: Think outside the box. www.brainstorming.co.uk/puzzles/ninedotsnj.html.*

International Development Evaluation Association (IDEAS). (2009). *A brief history of the International Development Evaluation Association (IDEAS). www.ideas-int.org/content/index.cfm?navID=2&itemID=21&CFID=338165&CFTOKEN=30387255.*

International Development Research Centre (IDRC). (2007). *Outcome mapping.* Ottawa, Ontario, Canada: Author. *www.idrc.ca/en/ev-26586-201-1-DO_TOPIC.html.*

International Initiative for Impact Evaluation. (2009). *Better studies. Bigger impact. www.3ieimpact.org.*

Jirsa, V. K., & Kelso, J. A. (Eds.). (2004). *Coordination dynamics: Issues and trends.* Heidelberg, Germany: Springer Verlag.

Johnson, S. (1998). *Who moved my cheese?: An amazing way to deal with change in your work and in your life.* New York: Putnam.

Johnson, S. (2001). *Emergence: The connected lives of ants, brains, cities, and software.* New York: Scribner.

Joint Committee on Standards. (1994). *The program evaluation standards.* Thousand Oaks, CA: Sage. *www.wmich.edu/evalctr/jc/.*

Kahneman, D., & Tversky, A. (Eds.). (2000). *Choices, values, and frames.* New York: Cambridge University Press.

Kakutani, M. (2009, April 28). The age of adapting quickly. *New York Times,* p. C1.

Kalsey, B. (2008). It ain't what you don't know. *wellnowbob.blogspot.com/2008/07/it-aint-what-you-dont-know.html.*

Kanter, R. M. (1990). *When giants learn to dance.* New York: Free Press.

Kellogg Foundation. (2007). *Designing initiative evaluation: A systems-oriented framework for evaluating social change efforts.* Battle Creek, MI: Author. *www.wkkf.org/DesktopModules/WKF.00_DmaSupport/ViewDoc.aspx?LanguageID=0&CID=6&ListID=28&ItemID=5000521&fld=PDFFile.*

Kellogg Foundation. (2009). *Systems change.* Battle Creek, MI: Author *www.wkkf.org/Default.aspx?tabid=90&CID=3&ItemID=5000005&NID=5010005&LanguageID=0.*

Kelman, S., & Myers, J. (2009). *Successfully executing ambitious strategies in government: An empirical analysis* (Harvard Kennedy School Faculty Research Working Papers RWP09-009). *web.hks.harvard.edu/Publications/Workingpapers/Citation.aspx?PubId=6563.*

Kelso, J. A., & Engstrøm, D. A. (2008). *The complementary nature.* Cambridge, MA: Bradford.

Kidder, T. (2009). *Strength in what remains: A journey of remembrance and forgiveness.* New York: Random House. *www.thecomplementarynature.com/wordpress/?p=1854.*

King, J. A. (2005). Participatory evaluation. In S. Mathison (Ed.), *Encyclopedia of evaluation* (pp. 291–294). Thousand Oaks, CA: Sage.

King, J. A. (2008). Bringing evaluative learning to life. *American Journal of Evaluation, 29*(2), 151–155.

King, J., Stevahn, L., Ghere, G., & Minnema, J. (2001). Toward a taxonomy of essential program evaluator competencies. *American Journal of Evaluation, 22*(2), 229–247.

Knight, F. H. (1921). *Risk, uncertainty, and profit.* Boston: Hart, Schaffner & Marx/Houghton Mifflin.

Kolbert, E. (2009, May 25). The sixth extinction? *New Yorker,* pp. 52–63.

Kotter, J., & Rathgeber, H. (2006). *Our iceberg is melting: Changing and succeeding under any conditions.* New York: St. Martin's Press.

Kretzmann, J., & McKnight, J. P. (1993). *Building communities from the inside out: A path towards finding and mobilizing a community's assets.* Northwestern University, Center for Urban Affairs and Policy Research, Evanston, IL.

Kuhn, T. (1970). *The structure of scientific revolutions.* Chicago: University of Chicago Press.

Kurtz, C. F., & Snowden, D. J. (2003). The new dynamics of strategy: Sense-making in a complex and complicated world. *IBM Systems Journal, 48*(3), 462–483.

Kushner, S. (2000). *Personalizing evaluation*. London: Sage.

Kuzmin, A. (2009). Development of evaluation capacity in the Siberian Center for Civic Initiatives Support. In A. Kuzmin, R. O'Sullivan, & N. Kosheleva (Eds.), *Program evaluation: Methodology and practice* (pp. 305–325). Moscow: Presto-RK.

Kuzmin, A., O'Sullivan, R., & Kosheleva, N. (Eds.). (2009). *Program evaluation: Methodology and practice*. Moscow: Presto-RK.

Lacayo, V., Obregon, R., & Singhal, A. (2008). Approaching social change as a complex problem in a world that treats it as a complicated one: The case of *Puntos de Encuentró*, Nicaragua. *Investigación y Desarrollo, 16*(2), 138.

Lane, A. (2009, September 14). Road show: The journey of Robert Frank's "The Americans." *New Yorker*, pp. 84–91.

Leakey, R. E., & Lewin, R. (1992). *Origins reconsidered: In search of what makes us human*. New York: Bantam.

Lévi-Strauss, C. (1966). *The savage mind* (2nd ed.). Chicago: University of Chicago Press.

Lewin, K. (1948). Action research and minority problems. In *Resolving social conflicts: Selected papers on group dynamics*. New York: Harper & Row.

Lincoln, Y., & Guba, E. (1985). *Naturalistic inquiry*. Thousand Oaks, CA: Sage.

Linden, R. M. (2002). *Working across boundaries: Making collaboration work in government and nonprofit organizations*. San Francisco: Jossey-Bass.

Lipton, P. (1991). *Inference to the best explanation* (2nd ed.). London: Routledge.

Lockley, S. W., Landrigan, C. P., Barger, L. K., & Czeisler, C. A. (2006). When policy meets physiology: The challenge of reducing resident work hours. *Clinical Orthopaedics and Related Research, 449*, 116–127.

Loewen, G. (2009). *A comprehensive approach to poverty using strategic drivers: An aide for action*. Waterloo, Ontario, Canada: Tamarack Vital Communities. *tamarackcommunity.ca/downloads/vc/Strategic_Drivers_GL_052609.pdf.*

Lynn, J. (1997). Unexpected returns, insights from SUPPORT. In S. L. Isaacs & J. R. Knickman (Eds.), *To improve health and health care* (Vol. 1). Princeton, NJ: Robert Wood Johnson Foundation. *www.rwjf.org/files/research/anthology97chapter8.pdf.*

Lynn, J. (2004). *Sick to death and not going to take it anymore! Reforming health care for the last years of life.* Berkeley and Los Angeles: University of California Press.

Lynn, J., Arkes, H. R., Stevens, M., Cohn, F., Koenig, B., Fox, E., et al. (2000). Rethinking fundamental assumptions: SUPPORT's implications for future reform. *Journal of the American Geriatrics Society, 28*(5), S214–S221.

MacArthur Foundation. (2009). *Models for change: Systems change in juvenile justice.* Chicago: Author. *www.modelsforchange.net/index.html.*

Mackay, H. (2008, December 13–14). *Annual oration, Australian Psychological Society.* Summarized in the weekend edition of the *Sydney Morning Herald.*

Martin, J. (2005). *Miss Manners guide to excruciatingly correct behavior.* New York: Norton.

Mathison, S. (Ed.). (2005). *Encyclopedia of evaluation.* Thousand Oaks, CA: Sage.

Mattessich, P., Monsey, B., & Murray-Close, M. (2001). *Collaboration: What makes it work. A review of research literature on factors influencing successful collaborations.* Saint Paul, MN: Fieldstone Alliance.

Mayne, J. (2007). Contribution analysis: An approach to exploring cause–effect. ILAC (Institutional Learning and Change) Brief. *www.outcomemapping.ca/download.php?file=/resource/files/csette_en_ILAC_Brief16_Contribution_Analysis.pdf.*

McGarvey, C. (2007). *Participatory action research.* New York: GrantCraft/Ford Foundation.

McKibben, B. (2007). *Deep economy: The wealth of communities and the durable future.* New York: Times Books/Holt.

McLaughlin, M. (1976). Implementation as mutual adaption. In W. Williams & R. F. Elmore (Eds.), *Social program implementation* (pp. 167–180). New York: Academic Press.

McNamara, C. (2002a). *Field guide to leadership and supervision for nonprofit staff.* Minneapolis, MN: Authenticity Consulting. *www.authenticityconsulting.com/pubs.htm.*

McNamara, C. (2002b). *Nuts and bolts guide to leadership and supervision in business.* Minneapolis, MN: Authenticity Consulting. *www.authenticityconsulting.com/pubs/Mgmnt/MS_pubs.htm.*

McTavish, D., Brent, E., Cleary, J., & Knudsen, K. R. (1975). *The systematic assessment and prediction of research methodology: Vol. 1. Advisory report* (Final report, Grant No. OEO 005-P-20-2-74). Minneapolis: University of Minnesota, Minnesota Continuing Program for the Assessment and Improvement of Research.

Meadows, D. (2008). *Thinking in systems*. White River Junction, VT: Chelsea Green.

Mertens, D. M. (2009). *Transformative research and evaluation*. New York: Guilford Press.

Michael, S. (2005). The promise of appreciative inquiry as an interview tool for field research. *Development in Practice, 15*(2), 222–230.

Midgley, G. (Ed.). (2003). *Systems thinking*. London: Sage.

Miller, D. (1981). *The book of jargon*. New York: Macmillan.

Miller, D. (1992). *The Icarus paradox: How exceptional companies bring about their own demise*. New York: HarperCollins.

Miller, R. L., & Campbell, R. (2006). Taking stock of empowerment evaluation: An empirical review. *American Journal of Evaluation, 27*(3), 296–319.

Mills, C. W. (1959). *The sociological imagination*. New York: Oxford University Press.

Mintzberg, H. (2000). *The rise and fall of strategic planning*. Toronto: Financial Times/Prentice Hall.

Mintzberg, H. (2007). *Tracking strategies*. New York: Oxford University Press.

Mitchell, M. (2009). *Complexity: A guided tour*. New York: Oxford University Press.

Morell, J. A. (2010). *Evaluation in the face of uncertainty: Anticipating surprise and responding to the inevitable*. New York: Guilford Press.

Morgan, G. (1997). *Images of organizations* (2nd ed.). Thousand Oaks, CA: Sage.

Morris, M. (2008). *Evaluation ethics for best practice: Cases and commentaries*. New York: Guilford Press.

National Community Kitchens. (2009). *www.dccentralkitchen.org/dcck/kinc/Left_Navigation/Kitchens_Folder/CommunityKitchens.shtml*.

National Sleep Foundation. (2009). *How sleep works*. Washington, DC: Author. *www.sleepfoundation.org/site/c.huIXKjM0IxF/b.2419253/k.7989/Sleep_Facts_and_Stats.htm*.

National Stroke Association. (2009). *Act F.A.S.T.* Centennial, CO: Author. *www.stroke.org/site/PageServer?pagename=SYMP*.

New Yorker. (2008, November 3). Caption contest. *www.newyorker.com/CaptionContest.aspx?id=167*.

Nunn, R. J. (2007). Complexity theory applied to itself. *E:CO, 9*(1–2), 93–106.

Organization of Economic Cooperation and Development, Development Assistance Committee (OECD-DAC). (2009). *DAC criteria for evaluating development assistance*. Originally adopted in 1991. *www.oecd.org/document/22/0,2340,en_2649_34435_2086550_1_1_1_1,00.html*.

Pagels, H. R. (1988). *The dreams of reason: The computer and the rise of the sciences of complexity*. New York: Simon & Schuster.

Paley, J. (2007). Complex adaptive systems and nursing. *Nursing Inquiry, 14*(3), 233–242.

Pandolfini, B. (1998). *The winning way: The how what and why of opening strategems*. New York: Fireside Books.

Panos London. (2009). How can complexity theory contribute to more effective development and aid evaluation? *www.panos.org.uk/?lid=29888*.

Parsons, B. (1998). Using a systems change approach to building communities. In *The policymakers' program, The first five years: Implementation tools, Vol. 2*. St. Louis, MO: Danforth Foundation.

Parsons, B. (2002). *Evaluative inquiry: Using evaluation to promote student success*. Thousand Oaks, CA: Corwin Press.

Parsons, B. (2009a). *Concepts from complexity science*. Fort Collins, CO: InSites. *www.insites.org/pub_tools.html*.

Parsons, B. (2009b). *Data collection questions to understand self-organizing dynamics and evaluative questions addressed and features within each type of evaluation design*. Fort Collins, CO: InSites. *www.insites.org/pub_AEA2008.html*.

Parsons, B. (2009c, November 11). *Evaluating complex system interventions*. 2009 professional development workshop, American Evaluation Association, Orlando, FL. *www.insites.org/pub_AEA2009.html*.

Parsons, B. (2009d). Evaluative inquiry for complex times. *OD Practitioner, 41*(1), 44–49.

Parsons, B. (2009e, November 10). *Evaluating patterns of change in complex systems: Strengthening families example*. Fort Collins, CO: InSites. Developed for 2009 Professional Development Workshop on Evaluating Complex System Interventions, American Evaluation Association, Orlando, FL.

Parsons, B., & Hargreaves, M. (2008). *Human systems dynamics theory applied to evaluation practice*. American Evaluation Association annual conference workshop, Denver. *www.insites.org/pub_AEA2008.html*.

Parsons, B., & Jessup, P. (2009). *Questions that matter: A tool for working in complex situations*. Fort Collins, CO: InSites. *www.insites.org/pub_tools.html*.

Patrizi Associates. (2007). *Death is certain. Strat-*

egy isn't. Assessing RWJF's end-of-life grantmaking. Fieldbuilding in end of life. Final evaluation report. Princeton, NJ: Robert Wood Johnson Foundation.

Patrizi, P., & Patton, M. (in press). Evaluating strategy. *New Directions for Evaluation.*

Patton, M. Q. (1983). Similarities of extension and evaluation. *Journal of Extension, 21,* 14–21.

Patton, M. Q. (1984). Sampling the best. *Extension Review, 55*(1), 20–21.

Patton, M. Q. (1987). *Creative evaluation.* Newbury Park, CA: Sage.

Patton, M. Q. (1994). Developmental evaluation. *Evaluation Practice, 15*(3), 311–320.

Patton, M. Q. (1999). *Grand Canyon celebration.* Amherst, NY: Prometheus Books.

Patton, M. Q. (2000). Language matters: How and why language matters in evaluation. *New Directions for Evaluation,* no. 86, 5–16.

Patton, M. Q. (2002). *Qualitative research and evaluation methods* (3rd ed.). Thousand Oaks, CA: Sage.

Patton, M. Q. (2003). Inquiry into appreciative inquiry. In H. Preskill & A. T. Coghlan (Eds.), *Using appreciative inquiry in evaluation. New Directions for Evaluation,* no. 100, 85–98.

Patton, M. Q. (2004). Utilization-focused evaluation: Theoretical underpinnings and origins. In M. Alkin & C. Christie (Eds.), *Roots of evaluation theory* (pp. 276–292). Thousand Oaks, CA: Sage.

Patton, M. Q. (2006). Evaluation for the way we work. *Nonprofit Quarterly, 13*(1), 28–33.

Patton, M. Q. (2007). Process use as a usefulism. *New Directions for Evaluation,* no. 116, 99–112.

Patton, M. Q. (2008a). Advocacy impact evaluation. *Journal of Multidisciplinary Evaluation, 5*(9), 1–10. *www.survey.ate.wmich.edu/jmde/index.php/jmde_1/issue/view/25.*

Patton, M. Q. (2008b). sup with eval ext? *New Directions for Evaluation, 120,* 101–115.

Patton, M. Q. (2008c). *Utilization-focused evaluation* (4th ed.). Thousand Oaks, CA: Sage.

Patton, M. Q. (2009, November 13). *Evaluation for dynamically complex contexts.* American Evaluation Association Presidential Strand presentation, Orlando, FL.

Pawson, R., & Tilley, N. (1997). *Realistic evaluation.* Thousand Oaks, CA: Sage.

Pawson, R., & Tilley, N. (2005). Realistic evaluation. In S. Mathison (Ed.), *Encyclopedia of evaluation* (pp. 362–367). Thousand Oaks, CA: Sage.

Pearson, K. (2007). *Accelerating our impact: Philan-thropy, innovation, and social change.* Montreal: J. W. McConnell Family Foundation. *www.mcconnellfoundation.ca/utilisateur/documents/EN/Initiatives/Sustaining%20Social%20Innovation/Accelerating%20Our%20Impact.pdf.*

Pedler, M. (2008). *Action learning for managers.* Burlington, VT: Glower.

Peirce, C. (1965). *Collected papers of Charles Sanders Peirce.* Cambridge, MA: Harvard University Press.

Peters, T. (1996). *Liberation management.* New York: Ballantine Books.

Peters, T., & Waterman, R. (1982). *In search of excellence.* New York: Harper & Row.

Picciotto, R. (2002). The logic of mainstreaming: A development evaluation perspective. *Evaluation, 8*(3), 322–339.

Pickens, T. B. (2008). *First billion is the hardest: Reflections on a life of comebacks and America's energy future.* New York: Three Rivers Press.

Podems, D. (2007). Process use: A case narrative from southern Africa. *New Directions for Evaluation,* no. *116,* 87–98.

Pollan, M. (2009). *In defense of food: An eater's manifesto.* New York: Penguin Books.

Poppendieck, LLC. (2009). *Wicked problems.* Eden Prairie, MN: Author. *www.poppendieck.com/wicked.htm.*

Positive Deviance Initiative. (2009). *www.positivedeviance.org/.*

Preskill, H. (2005). Appreciative inquiry. In S. Mathison (Ed.), *Encyclopedia of evaluation* (pp. 18–19). Thousand Oaks, CA: Sage.

Preskill, H. (2008, November 8). *Evaluation's second act: A spotlight on learning.* Plenary speech at the annual meeting of the American Evaluation Association, Baltimore. *American Journal of Evaluation, 29*(2), 127–138.

Preskill, H. (2009). The value of evaluation: A true story. *FGS Social Impact Advisors Perspectives,* 20. *www.fsg-impact.org/nl/Issue20/#value_evaluation.*

Preskill, H., & Catsambas, T. T. (2006). *Reframing evaluation through appreciative inquiry.* Thousand Oaks, CA: Sage.

Preskill, H., & Coghlan, A. T. (Eds.). (2003). *Using appreciative inquiry in evaluation. New Directions for Evaluation,* no. 100.

Ramalingam, B., & Jones, H., with Reba, T., & Young, J. (2008). *Exploring the science of complexity: Ideas and implications for development and humanitarian efforts* (Working Paper No. 285). London: Overseas Development Institute.

Ray, K. (2002). *Nimble collaboration: Fine-tuning*

your collaboration for lasting success. Saint Paul, MN: Fieldstone Alliance.

Revans, R. W. (1980). *Action learning: New techniques for management.* London: Blond & Briggs.

Reynolds, C. (2001). *Boids: Background and update. www.red3d.com/cwr/boids/.*

Rheingold, H. (1988). *They have a word for it.* Los Angeles: Tarcher.

Rich, A. (2002). Prospective immigrants please note. In *The fact of a doorframe* (pp. 24–25). New York: Norton.

Rittel, H., & Webber, M. (1973). Dilemmas in a general theory of planning. *Policy Sciences, 4,* 155–169.

Robert Wood Johnson Foundation. (2009). *Evaluation of the Robert Wood Johnson Foundation's body of work in end-of-life care.* Princeton, NJ: Author. *www.rwjf.org/pr/product.jsp?id=40848.*

Robertson, D. W., Jr. (1946). A note on the classical origin of "circumstances" in the medieval confessional. *Studies in Philology, 43*(1), 6–14.

Rogers, P. (2008). Using programme theory to evaluate complicated and complex aspects of interventions. *Evaluation, 14*(1), 29–48.

Rogers, P. (2009a). Matching impact evaluation design to the nature of the intervention and the purpose of the evaluation. *Journal of Development Effectiveness, 1*(3), 217–226.

Rogers, P. (2009b, September 23). *Unnovation.* Thought Leaders Forum, American Evaluation Association. *www.eval.org/thought_leaders.asp.*

Rogers, P. (2010). *Because: Evidence for what works and why.* Manuscript in preparation.

Rothschild, S. (2010). *How five proven business principles can reduce poverty and strengthen America.* Manuscript in preparation.

Rugg, D., Peersman, G., & Carael, M. (Eds.). (2004). *Global advances in HIV/AIDS monitoring and evaluation. New Directions for Evaluation,* no. 103.

Safire, W. (2007, May 6). Halfway humanity. On Language. *New York Times Sunday Magazine. www.nytimes.com/2007/05/06/magazine/06wwln-safire-t.html.*

Salmen, L., & Kane, E. (2006). *Bridging diversity: Participatory learning for responsive development.* Washington, DC: World Bank.

Sanders, W. (1976). *The sociologist as detective* (2nd ed.). New York: Praeger.

Santayana, G. (1905). *Life of reason, reason in common sense.* New York: Scribner's.

Sarkisian, N. (2008). Neural networks as an emergent method in quantitative research: An example of self-organizing maps. In S. N. Hesse-Biber & P. Leavy (Eds.), *Handbook of emergent methods* (pp. 625–654). New York: Guilford Press.

Schön, D. A. (1983). *The reflective practitioner.* New York: Basic Books.

Schön, D. A. (1987). *Educating the reflective practitioner.* San Francisco: Jossey-Bass.

Schorr, L. B. (1989). *Within our reach: Breaking the cycle of disadvantage.* New York: Anchor Books.

Schorr, L. B. (1997). *Common purpose: Strengthening families and neighborhoods to rebuild America.* New York: Anchor Books.

Schorr, L. B. (2009, August 20). Charities work demands flexible evaluation. *Chronicle of Philanthropy,* pp. 33, 37.

Schröter, D. C. (2008). *Sustainability evaluation: Development and validation of an evaluation checklist.* Doctoral dissertation, Western Michigan University, Kalamazoo. *www.evaluation.wmich.edu/phd/documents/SustainabilityEvaluation.pdf.*

Schröter, D. C. (2009). *Sustainability evaluation website. www.sustainabilityeval.net/.*

Schwandt, T. (2001). *Dictionary of qualitative inquiry* (2nd rev. ed.). Thousand Oaks, CA: Sage.

Schwandt, T. (2008). *Educating for intelligent belief in evaluation* (Plenary speech at the annual meeting of the American Evaluation Association, Baltimore, November 9, 2007). *American Journal of Evaluation, 29*(2), 139–150.

Scott, J. (2000). *Social network analysis: A handbook* (2nd ed.). Newbury Park, CA: Sage.

Scriven, M. (1967). The methodology of evaluation. In R. W. Tyler et al. (Eds.), *Perspectives of curriculum evaluation* (AERA Monograph Series on Curriculum Evaluation, 1, pp. 39–83). Chicago: Rand McNally.

Scriven, M. (1991). *Evaluation thesaurus* (4th ed.). Newbury Park, CA: Sage.

Scriven, M. (Ed.). (1993). *Hard-won lessons in program evaluation* [Special issue]. *New Directions for Evaluation, 58,* 1–103.

Seidman, D. (2007). *How: Why how we do anything means everything in business (and in life).* New York: Wiley.

Seigart, D. (2005). Feminist evaluation. In S. Mathison (Ed.), *Encyclopedia of evaluation* (pp. 154–157(. Thousand Oaks, CA: Sage.

Seigart, D., & Brisolara, S. (Eds.). (2002). *Feminist evaluation: Explorations and experiences. New Directions for Evaluation,* no. 96.

Senge, P. M. (2006). *The fifth disciple: The art and practice of the learning organization.* New York: Doubleday.

Seuss, Dr. (1953). *The sneetches and other stories.* New York: Random House.

Shackman, G. (2009). Introduction to evaluation: Evaluation questions and methods. *Research Methods Knowledge Base. www.socialresearchmethods.net/kb/intreval.htm.*

Shirky, C. (2007). In defense of ready, fire, aim. *Harvard Business Review, 85*(2), 20–56.

Simon, H. (1957). *Administrative behavior.* New York: Macmillan.

Simon, H. (1978). On how we decide what to do. *Bell Journal of Economics, 9,* 494–507.

Simon, J. K. (2001). *Five life stages of nonprofit organizations: Where you are, where you're going, and what to expect when you get there.* Saint Paul, MN: Fieldstone Alliance.

Smith, L. (2007). *Chaos: A very short introduction.* New York: Oxford University Press.

Smith, L. T. (1999). *Decolonizing methodologies: Research and indigenous peoples.* London: Zed Books.

Smith, M. F. (1994a). Evaluation: Review of the past, preview of the future. *Evaluation Practice, 15*(3), 215–227.

Smith, M. F. (1994b). From the editor. *Evaluation Practice, 15*(3), 213.

Snowden, D. J., & Boone, M. E. (2007). A leader's framework for decision making. *Harvard Business Review, 85*(11), 68–77.

Stacey, R. D. (1992). *Managing the unknowable: Strategic boundaries between order and chaos in organizations.* San Francisco: Jossey-Bass.

Stacey, R. D. (1996). *Complexity and creativity in organizations.* San Francisco: Berrett-Koehler.

Stacey, R. D. (2001). *Complex responsive processes in organizations: Learning and knowledge creation.* New York: Routledge.

Stacey, R. D. (2007). *Strategic management and organisational dynamics: The challenge of complexity to ways of thinking about organizations.* New York: Prentice Hall/Financial Times.

Stake, R. E. (1978). The case study method in a social inquiry. *Educational Researcher, 7,* 5–8.

Stake, R. E. (1995). *The art of case study research.* Thousand Oaks, CA: Sage.

Stake, R. E. (2000). Case studies. In K. Denzin & Y. S. Lincoln (Eds.), *Handbook of qualitative research* (2nd ed., pp. 435–454). Thousand Oaks, CA: Sage.

Stake, R. E. (2004). How far dare an evaluator go toward saving the world? *American Journal of Evaluation, 25*(1), 103–107.

Stake, R. E. (2010). *Qualitative research.* New York: Guilford Press.

Sterman, J. D. (2000). *Business dynamics: Systems thinking and modeling for a complex world.* Boston: Irwin McGraw-Hill.

Stevens, S. (2002). *Nonprofit lifecycles: Stage-based wisdom for nonprofit capacity.* Wayzata, MN: Stagewise Enterprises.

Stewart, J. B. (2009, September 21). Eight days: The battle to save the American financial system. *New Yorker,* pp. 58–81.

Strengthening Families. (2009). *Strengthening families. www.strengtheningfamilies.net.*

Stuart, J. B. (2007). Necessity leads to innovative evaluation approach and practice. *Evaluation Exchange, 13*(1), 10–11.

Summerville, G., with Raley, B. (2009). *Laying a solid foundation: Strategies for effective program replication.* Philadelphia: Public/Private Ventures.

Sutcliffe, K., & Weber, K. (2003). The high cost of accuracy. *Harvard Business Review, 81,* 74–82.

Szulanski, G., & Winter, S. (2002, March). Getting it right the second time. *Harvard Business Review, 80,* 62–69.

Taleb, N. N. (2005). *Fooled by randomness: The hidden role of chance in life and in the markets.* New York: Random House.

Taleb, N. N. (2007). *The black swan: The impact of the highly improbable.* New York: Random House.

Tamarack Institute for Community Engagement. (2009). *www.tamarackcommunity.ca/.*

Taylor-Powell, E., & Rossing, B. (n.d.). *Evaluating collaborations: Challenges and methods.* American Evaluation Association Topical Interest Group on Extension Education Evaluation. *www.danr.ucop.edu/eee-aea/rossing.html.*

Thaler, R. H., & Sunstein, C. R. (2009). *Nudge: Improving decisions about health, wealth, and happiness.* New York: Penguin.

Tilly, C. (2005). *Identities, boundaries, and social ties.* Boulder, CO: Paradigm Press.

Triana, P., & Taleb, N. N. (2009). *Lecturing birds on flying: Can mathematical theories destroy the financial markets?* New York: Wiley.

Trumbull, H. C. (1888). *Teaching and teachers.* Philadelphia: John D. Wattles. *www.books.google.com/books?id=VAYCAAAAYAAJ&pg=PA1*

20&vq=w's&dq=teaching+and+teachers&num=100&source=gbs_search_r&cad=1_1#v=onepage&q=w's&f=false.

Tversky, A., & Fox, C. (2000). Weighing risk and uncertainty. In D. Kahneman & A. Tversky (Eds.), *Choices, values, and frames* (pp. 93–117). New York: Cambridge University Press.

Tversky, A., & Kahneman, D. (2000). Advances in prospect theory: Cumulative representation of uncertainty. In D. Kahneman & A. Tversky (Eds.), *Choices, values, and frames* (pp. 44–65). New York: Cambridge University Press.

Tyson, N. (2009). *The Pluto files: The rise and fall of America's favorite planet.* New York: Norton.

Valente, T. W. (1995). *Network models of the diffusion of innovations.* Cresskill, NJ: Hampton Press.

Viadero, D. (2009, November 10). Research advisory board wants a higher bar for innovation grants. *Education Week. www.blogs.edweek.org/edweek/inside-school-research/2009/11/the-national-board-that-advise.html.*

Wadsworth, Y. (2008a). Is it safe to talk about systems again yet?: Self-organising processes for complex living systems and the dynamics of human inquiry. *Systematic Practice and Action Research, 21*(2), 153–170. *www.springerlink.com/content/d423tx5p6q07660h/?p=45f8809029a34fc6953db3297620f5a6&pi=3.*

Wadsworth, Y. (2008b). Systemic human relations in dynamic equilibrium. *Systematic Practice and Action Research, 21*(1), 15–34. *www.springerlink.com/content/5654w6105588451q/?p=ea694c906f674becbaff7639ee64645c&pi=1.*

Wadsworth, Y. (2009a). *Do it yourself social research.* Sydney, Australia: Allen & Unwin.

Wadsworth, Y. (2009b). *Everyday evaluation on the run* (3rd ed.). Sydney, Australia: Allen & Unwin.

Wadsworth, Y. (2010). *Building it in: Research and evaluation for (truly) living human systems.* Sydney, Australia: Allen & Unwin.

Waller, J. (2004). *Fabulous science: Fact and fiction in the history of scientific discovery.* New York: Oxford University Press.

Walters, C. (1986). *Adaptive management of renewable resources.* New York: Macmillan.

Walton, D. (2004). *Abductive reasoning.* Tuscaloosa: University of Alabama Press.

Watkins, J. M., & Cooperrider, D. (2000). Appreciative inquiry: A transformative paradigm. *OD Practitioner, 32*(1), 6–12.

Wehipeihana, N., & McKegg, K. (2009, November 14). *Developmental evaluation in an indigenous context: Reflections on the journey to date.*

Paper presented at the American Evaluation Association Conference, Orlando, FL.

Weick, K. E. (2001). Organizational redesign as improvisation. In *Making sense of the organization* (pp. 57–90). Malden, MA: Blackwell.

Weick, K. E., & Sutcliffe, K. (2001). *Managing the unexpected: Assuring high performance in an age of complexity.* San Francisco: Jossey-Bass.

Wenger, E. (1999). *Communities of practice: Learning, meaning and identity.* Cambridge, UK: Cambridge University Press.

Wenger, E., McDermott, R., & Snyder, W. M. (2002). *Cultivating communities of practice.* Cambridge, MA: Harvard Business School Press.

Westley, F., & Antadze, N. (2009). *Making a difference: Strategies for scaling social innovation for greater impact.* Framing paper, Social Innovation Generation, University of Waterloo, Canada.

Westley, F., & Miller, P. S. (Eds.). (2003). *Experiments in consilience: Integrating social and scientific responses to save endangered species.* Washington, DC: Island Press.

Westley, F., Zimmerman, B., & Patton, M. Q. (2006). *Getting to maybe: How the world is changed.* Toronto: Random House Canada.

What Works Clearinghouse. (2007). *Intervention: Literacy express. www.ies.ed.gov/ncee/wwc/reports/early_ed/lit_express/.*

Wheatley, M. (1992). *Leadership and the new science: Discovering order in a chaotic world.* San Francisco: Berrett-Koehler.

Wheatley, M. (1999). *Leadership and the new science: Discovering order in a chaotic world* (rev. ed.). San Francisco: Berrett-Koehler.

Whitman, D., Friedman, D., Linn, A., Doremus, C., & Hetter, K. (1994). The white underclass: Does the rise in out-of-wedlock babies and white slums foretell a social catastrophe? *U.S. News and World Report. www.usnews.com/usnews/news/articles/941017/archive_012096_4.htm.*

Wilke, J. (2006). *Understanding the asset-based approach to community development. www.neighboraustin.com/PDF/Understanding%20the%20Asset-based%20Approach%20to%20Community%20%20Development.pdf.*

Williams, B. (2008, December). Bucking the system: Systems concepts and development. *The Broker,* pp. 16–19. *www.thebrokeronline.eu/en/articles/Bucking-the-system.*

Williams, B., & Iman, I. (Eds.). (2007). *Systems concepts in evaluation: An expert anthology.* Point Reyes, CA: EdgePress of Inverness.

Williams, B. K., Szaro, R. C., & Shapiro, C. D. (2007). *Adaptive management: The U.S. Department of the Interior technical guide.* Washington, DC: U.S. Department of the Interior.

Wolff, T. (2004). *Collaborative solutions—six key components.* Amherst, MA: Tom Wolff & Associates. *www.tomwolff.com/collaborative-solutions-fall04.html.*

World Bank. (2009). *Impact evaluation: Overview.* Washington, DC: World Bank. *web.worldbank. org/WBSITE/EXTERNAL/TOPICS/EXTPOVER-TY/EXTISPMA/0,,menuPK:384339~pagePK:1621 00~piPK:159310~theSitePK:384329,00.html.*

Zimmer, B. (2009, September 20). The age of undoing. *New York Times Sunday Magazine,* p. 18. *www.nytimes.com/2009/09/20/ magazine/20FOB-onlanguage-t.html?_ r=1&ref=magazine.*

Zimmerman, B. (2000). *Examples of wicked questions.* Bordentown, NJ: Plexus Institute. *www.*

plexusinstitute.org/edgeware/archive/think/main_ aides5.html

Zimmerman, B., & Glouberman, S. (2004). Complicated and complex systems: What would successful reform of Medicare look like? In P.-G. Forest, T. McIntosh, & G. Marchildon (Eds.), *Health care services and the process of change* (pp. 21–53). Toronto: University of Toronto Press. (Originally published as *Discussion Paper No. 8.* (2002). Ottawa: Commission on the Future of Health Care in Canada.)

Zimmerman, B., Lindberg, C., & Plsek, P. (1998). *edgeware: insights from complexity ideas for health care leaders.* Irving, TX: VHA.

Zuber-Skerritt, O. (Ed.). (2009). *Action learning and action research.* Rotterdam, The Netherlands: Sense Publishers.

Zvoch, K. (2009). Treatment fidelity in multisite evaluation. *American Journal of Evaluation, 30*(1), 44–61.

Author Index

Subject Index

Page numbers followed by *e* indicate exhibit, *n* indicate note

D

Damiano Center
  adaptive cycle and, 190
  adaptive innovation and, 179–181, 180e,
    181e–182e
  overview, 169–176, 173e–174e, 177e, 309e
  retrospective developmental evaluation and,
    297–303
  utilization-focused evaluation and, 325–326
Data collection, 332
Debriefing a project activity, 61–62
Deductive reasoning, 285. *See also* Reasoning
  processes
Deductive theory, 185. *See also* Top-down
  processes
Degree of uncertainty/degree of conflict
  matrix, 86, 87e
Deliberate strategy, 49, 49e. *See also* Strategic
  development process
Descriptive questions, 230–231, 261e. *See also*
  Questions
Development
  compared to growth, 37
  compared to improvement, 36–40, 40e
  comparing the types of evaluations and,
    44e–47e
  overview, 21, 41–42
  See also Ongoing development; Program
    development
Development evaluation, compared to
  developmental evaluation, 20–21
Developmental evaluation overview, 1–7, 30–34,
  46e–47e, 75–79, 75e, 306–307, 333–337,
  334e–335e
  complexity theory and, 7–11, 8e
  creation stories and, 337–339
  development evaluation and, 20–21
  purposes and uses for developmental
    evaluation, 21–27, 23e–26e, 308e–313e
  situational responsiveness and, 108
  See also Adaptation; Ongoing development;
    Preformative use of developmental
    evaluation; Response needs; Systems
    thinking
Disappearance, complexity and, 128
Discovery, abduction and, 286–287
Dispositions, reasoning processes and, 284
Dissemination of knowledge, 155–157. *See also*
  Bottom-up processes; Top-down processes
Distinctions
  example of, 100–104, 104e–105e
  importance of, 4

overview, 2–4, 49–51
situation recognition heuristics and, 91–93,
  92e, 95–97
Diversity
  going-to-scale and, 222
  methodological, 288–290
  overview, 307
Double-loop learning, 11–12
Dualities, 185–186
Dynamic change, 139, 139e–140e
Dynamic contextual cohort analysis, 139e–140e
Dynamic interactions, 148–149, 148e
Dynamical contextual cohort analysis,
  139e–140e
Dynamical systems, 7, 8e, 17, 136–142,
  139e–140e, 151e, 193–194

E

Eating, complexity and, 129–130
Ecology, adaptive cycle and, 190–193
Ecosystem adaptive cycle, 198–202, 199e
Ecosystem resilience
  adaptive cycle and, 191–192, 197
  example of, 211
  overview, 18–19, 198–202, 199e
  sustainability and, 201
  See also Resilience
Effective principles
  vs. best practices, 167, 168e
  overview, 194, 195
Effectiveness, 255
Efficiency, 255
Eggert, Robert, 170
Emergence
  complexity-sensitizing concepts, 148–149,
    148e
  overview, 7, 8e, 150e, 193
  systems thinking and, 126–131
Emergent baseline, 255–260, 257e
Emergent strategy
  action research as, 280
  overview, 49, 49e, 75e
  reflective practice and, 60–63
  systems change and, 295
  See also Strategic development process
Empirical medicine, 93
Empowerment evaluation, 187
Engagement
  adaptation and, 132
  evaluation questions and, 30
  overview, 333–337, 334e–335e

Exploitation phase
  overview, 18–19, 190, 202–203, 202*e*, 207*e*
  poverty trap and, 217
  psychosocial regimes and, 204*e*
  transitions and, 213*e*
Exploration evaluation
  adaptive cycle and, 209–210
  overview, 310*e*
  systems change and, 295
Extension work
  case example of, 74
  creative evaluation and, 54–59
  external evaluators and, 64–75, 72*e*

situation recognition and, 104*e*–105*e*
  See also Caribbean Agricultural Extension Project (CAEP)
External evaluation, 64–75, 72*e*, 75*e*, 76
External validity, 156–157, 161–162
Extrapolation, 165–166, 168

F

Factual questions, 230–231. *See also* Questions
Family systems, 290–294
Feedback, evaluation, 132–133
Feedback loops, 137–138
Feminist evaluation, 187
Fidelity
  best practices and, 156, 158–159
  example of, 173, 173*e*–174*e*, 177*e*
  going-to-scale and, 222
  overview, 188
Financial meltdown in late 2008 through 2009, 141
Fittingness, 165. *See also* Generalizability
Flexibility
  complexity theory and, 10–11
  going-to-scale and, 222
  high-fidelity and, 158–159
  methods and, 335–336
  poverty trap and, 217
  uncertainty and, 133–134
Focus of evaluation, 23*e*–24*e*
Food, complexity and, 129–130
Formative evaluation
  adaptive cycle and, 207, 207*e*, 209–210
  distinctions and, 50
  duration of, 37–38
  overview, 2–4, 45*e*, 51
  poverty trap and, 217
  social innovation and, 36–37
Funding, ongoing development and, 41

G

Gamble, Jamie, 219
Gawande, Atul, 84, 252
Generalizability, 156–157, 161–163, 163–165
Gladwell, Malcolm, 120, 124
Global bifurcations, 141–142
Global complexity, 10, 141–142. *See also* Complexity
Global Social Change Research Project, 227–228

About the Author

Michael Quinn Patton is an independent organizational development and program evaluation consultant whose company, Utilization-Focused Evaluation, is based in St. Paul, Minnesota. A former President of the American Evaluation Association (AEA), he teaches regularly in AEA's professional development workshops, The Evaluators' Institute, and The World Bank's International Program in Development Evaluation Training. Dr. Patton is a recipient of both the Myrdal Award for Outstanding Contributions to Useful and Practical Evaluation Practice from the Evaluation Research Society and the Lazarsfeld Award for Lifelong Contributions to Evaluation Theory from the AEA. He is the author of *Utilization-Focused Evaluation* (4th ed., 2008) and *Qualitative Research and Evaluation Methods* (3rd ed., 2002) and coauthor, with Frances Westley and Brenda Zimmerman, of *Getting to Maybe: How the World Is Changed* (2006), which applies complexity theory and systems thinking to innovation and developmental evaluation.